ASHGATE
RESEARCH
COMPANION

THE ASHGATE RESEARCH COMPANION TO THE SIDNEYS, 1500–1700

VOLUME 1

ASHGATE
RESEARCH
COMPANION

The *Ashgate Research Companions* are designed to offer scholars and graduate students a comprehensive and authoritative state-of-the-art review of current research in a particular area. The companions' editors bring together a team of respected and experienced experts to write chapters on the key issues in their speciality, providing a comprehensive reference to the field.

The Ashgate Research Companion to The Sidneys, 1500–1700

Volume 1: Lives

Edited by

MARGARET P. HANNAY
Siena College, USA

MICHAEL G. BRENNAN
University of Leeds, UK

MARY ELLEN LAMB
Southern Illinois University, USA

ASHGATE

Published by
Ashgate Publishing Limited
Wey Court East
Union Road
Farnham
Surrey, GU9 7PT
England

Ashgate Publishing Company
110 Cherry Street
Suite 3-1
Burlington, VT 05401-3818
USA

www.ashgate.com

British Library Cataloguing in Publication Data
A catalogue record for this book is available from the British Library.

Library of Congress Cataloging-in-Publication Data
The Ashgate research companion to the Sidneys, 1500–1700 / edited by Margaret P. Hannay, Michael G. Brennan, and Mary Ellen Lamb.
     2 volumes cm
  Includes bibliographical references and index.
  Contents: Volume 1: Lives – Volume 2: Literature.
  ISBN 978-1-4094-5038-2 (v. 1 : hardcover) – ISBN 978-1-4094-5040-5 (v. 2 : hardcover)
1. Sidney family. 2. Politics and literature–Great Britain–History–16th century. 3. Politics and literature–Great Britain–History–17th century. 4. Authors, English–Early modern, 1500–1700–Biography. 5. Upper class families–England–History. 6. Literature and society–Great Britain–History–16th century. 7. Literature and society–Great Britain–History–17th century.
I. Hannay, Margaret P., editor. II. Brennan, Michael G., editor. III. Lamb, Mary Ellen, editor.
  DA306.S6A84 2015
  929.20942--dc23

                                                                2014042349

ISBN: 9781409450382 (hbk)

Printed in the United Kingdom by Henry Ling Limited,
at the Dorset Press, Dorchester, DT1 1HD

Contents

List of Illustrations	*vii*
Notes on Contributors	*xi*
Preface: Volume 1	*xvii*
Acknowledgments	*xxi*
List of Abbreviations	*xxiii*
Chronology	*xxvii*
The Sidney Family Tree	*xlv*

PART I   **OVERVIEW**

1   Family Networks: The Sidneys, Dudleys, and Herberts   3
     Michael G. Brennan

PART II   **BIOGRAPHIES**

2   Sir Henry Sidney (1529–1586)   23
     Valerie McGowan-Doyle

3   Lady Mary Dudley Sidney (c. 1531–1586) and Her Siblings   31
     Carole Levin and Catherine Medici

4   Philip Sidney (1554–1586)   41
     Alan Stewart

5   Mary Sidney Herbert (1561–1621), Countess of Pembroke   59
     Margaret P. Hannay

6   Those Essex Girls: The Lives and Letters of Lettice Knollys,
     Penelope Rich, Dorothy Perrott Percy, and Frances Walsingham   77
     Grace Ioppolo

7   The Life of Robert Sidney (1563–1626), First Earl of Leicester   93
     Robert Shephard

8   Barbara Gamage Sidney (c. 1562–1621), Countess of Leicester,
     Elizabeth Sidney Manners (1585–1612), Countess of Rutland, and
     Lady Mary Sidney Wroth (1587–1651)   103
     Margaret P. Hannay

9   Robert Sidney (1595–1677), Second Earl of Leicester   123
     Germaine Warkentin

10   A Triptych of Dorothy Percy Sidney (1598–1659), Countess of Leicester,
     Lucy Percy Hay (1599–1660), Countess of Carlisle, and Dorothy Sidney
     Spencer (1617–1684), Countess of Sunderland   133
     Nadine Akkerman

11   Algernon Sidney's Life and Works (1623–1683)   151
     Jonathan Scott

12   Henry Sidney (1641–1704), Earl of Romney, and Robert Spencer
     (1641–1702), Second Earl of Sunderland   169
     Michael G. Brennan

PART III   THE SIDNEYS IN IRELAND AND WALES

13   The Sidneys in Ireland   179
     Thomas Herron

14   The Sidneys and Wales   191
     Willy Maley and Philip Schwyzer

PART IV   THE SIDNEYS AND THE CONTINENT

15   The Sidneys and the Continent: The Tudor Period   203
     Roger Kuin

16   The Sidneys and the Continent: The Stuart Period   223
     Michael G. Brennan

PART V   THE SIDNEYS AND THE ARTS

17   The Sidneys and Public Entertainments   241
     Arthur F. Kinney

18   The Sidneys and Literary Patronage   261
     Lisa Celovsky

19   Penshurst Place and Leicester House   281
     Susie West

20   The Sidneys and the Visual Arts   297
     Elizabeth Goldring

21   The Sidneys and Music   317
     Katherine R. Larson

Index   329

List of Illustrations

The illustrations are located between pages 200 and 201.

1   View of Baynard's Castle, copper engraved print by John G. Wooding for *The New, Complete, and Universal History, Description, and Survey of the Cities of London and Westminster* (London, 1784) and *Picturesque Views of the Antiquities of England & Wales* (London, 1786). Private collection.

2   View of London, 1616 (cartographic material), by Nicholas John (Claes Jansz) Visscher, showing the position of Baynard's Castle on the River Thames. Map L85c no. 28. By permission of the Folger Shakespeare Library.

3   Penshurst Place in 1757, by George Vertue. From Edward Hasted, *The History and Topographical Survey of the County of Kent* (Canterbury, 1778–99). Private collection.

4   Penshurst Place, copperplate engraving by Johannes Kip from a drawing by Thomas Badeslade. From John Harris, *The History of Kent* (London, 1719). Private collection.

5   Sir Henry Sidney, English School. By kind permission of Viscount De L'Isle from his private collection at Penshurst Place, Kent.

6   Lady Mary Sidney (*née* Dudley), by Henry Bone, after unknown artist, pencil drawing squared in ink for transfer. NPG D17112. © National Portrait Gallery, London.

7   Sir Philip Sidney, by unknown artist, oil on panel, *c.* 1577. NPG 5732. © National Portrait Gallery, London.

8   Portrait of Hubert Languet, tutor to Sir Philip Sidney, with identifying inscription and date "ANNᵒ DOMINI 1564, ÆTATIS SVÆ 51," English School, oil on panel. By kind permission of Viscount De L'Isle from his private collection at Penshurst Place, Kent.

9   Mary Sidney Herbert, Countess of Pembroke, by Nicholas Hilliard, watercolor on vellum, *c.* 1590. NPG 5994. © National Portrait Gallery, London.

10   Mary Herbert, Countess of Pembroke, engraving by Simon de Passe, 1618, sold by John Sudbury, sold by George Humble. NPG D19186. © National Portrait Gallery, London.

11   Letter from Penelope Rich to Robert Cecil, CP101/25. Hatfield House, Hatfield. Reproduced by permission of Hatfield House.

12   Letter from Frances Essex to Robert Cecil, CP86/123. Hatfield House, Hatfield. Reproduced by permission of Hatfield House.

13   Sir Robert Sidney, unknown artist, oil on canvas, *c.* 1588. NPG 1862. © National Portrait Gallery, London.

14   Sir Robert Sidney in mourning for Sir Philip Sidney, unknown artist, oil on canvas, *c.* 1587–88. Private collection, courtesy of The Weiss Gallery.

15   *Robert Sidney, first Earl of Leicester, depicted (as described in a Penshurst inventory of c. 1623) "at length in his vicounte Robes,"* attributed to Robert Peake, oil on canvas, *c.* 1605. By kind permission of Viscount De L'Isle from his private collection at Penshurst Place, Kent.

16   An example of Arthur Collins's intervention in the text of a letter from Rowland Whyte, to Robert Sidney. Kent History and Library Centre (formerly Centre for Kentish Studies), Maidstone, Kent. KHLC U1475 C12/147. By kind permission of Viscount De L'Isle from his private collection.

17   *Portrait group of Barbara, Countess of Leicester (née Gamage) with six of her children: Elizabeth, Robert, Philippa, William, Mary, Katherine,* by Marcus Gheeraerts II, oil on canvas, *c.* 1596. Barbara has her hands on Robert and William. By kind permission of Viscount De L'Isle from his private collection at Penshurst Place, Kent.

18   *Double portrait of two ladies (probably) Lady Mary Wroth and Lady Barbara Sidney, the landscape with haymakers. With inscription Lady Wroth and Lady Gamage dated 1612,* by Marcus Gheeraerts II, oil on panel. By kind permission of Viscount De L'Isle from his private collection at Penshurst Place, Kent.

19   *Portrait of Lady Mary Sidney (1587–1651), daughter of Sir Robert Sidney 1st Earl of Leicester and wife of Sir Robert Wroth,* full-length, holding an archlute, attributed to John de Critz, oil on canvas. By kind permission of Viscount De L'Isle from his private collection at Penshurst Place, Kent.

20   Miniature by Isaac Oliver, traditionally described as William Herbert, third Earl of Pembroke, but possibly Philip Herbert, fourth Earl of Pembroke. Folger FPm10. By permission of the Folger Shakespeare Library.

21   William Herbert, third Earl of Pembroke, after Daniel Mytens, oil on canvas, *c.* 1625. NPG 5560. © National Portrait Gallery, London.

22   Philip Herbert, fourth Earl of Pembroke, attributed to Alexander Cooper, watercolor on vellum. NPG 4614. © National Portrait Gallery, London.

23   Robert Sidney, second Earl of Leicester, by Cornelius Janssens (Jonson). By kind permission of Viscount De L'Isle from his private collection at Penshurst Place, Kent.

24   Fols. 348v–349r from a commonplace book of Robert Sidney, second Earl of Leicester, dating from *c.* 1638–45, with additions in 1652 and 1662. KHLC U1475 Z1/9. By kind permission of Viscount De L'Isle from his private collection.

25   Algernon Sidney, after Justus van Egmont, oil on canvas. NPG 568. © National Portrait Gallery, London.

26   Double portrait of Lucy Percy Hay, Countess of Carlisle, and Dorothy Percy Sidney, Countess of Leicester, after Sir Anthony Van Dyck. By kind permission of Viscount De L'Isle from his private collection at Penshurst Place, Kent.

27   Lady Dorothy (Sidney) Spencer, Countess of Sunderland, by Anthony Van Dyck and studio. Private collection, by courtesy of Hoogsteder & Hoogsteder, The Hague.

28   Philip Sidney, third Earl of Leicester, attributed to Gerard Honthorst. By kind permission of Viscount De L'Isle from his private collection at Penshurst Place, Kent.

29   Penshurst Place, Kent, *c.* 1600, centered on the Great Hall, after *The Architectural Development of Penshurst Place* (IPC Business Press Ltd., 1975).

30   Penshurst Place, reconstructed ground-floor plan *c.* 1600. © Susie West.

31   Leicester House, London, artist unknown, watercolor on paper, *c.* 1720. Private collection. © Bridgeman Education.

32   Musical setting of Mary Sidney's Psalm 130. British Library Add. MS 15117 fol. 5. © The British Library Board.

Notes on Contributors

Nadine Akkerman is a postdoctoral researcher and lecturer in Early Modern English Literature at Leiden University, the Netherlands, and an Associate of the Centre of Editing Lives and Letters (CELL, UCL) in London. She has published extensively on women's history, diplomacy, and masques, and curated several exhibitions. In 2014 she was Distinguished Visiting Fellow at the Institute of Advanced Studies at Birmingham University. She has co-edited a volume on ladies-in-waiting, *The Politics of Female Households* (2013), and is currently completing a monograph on seventeenth-century British female spies or so-called "she-intelligencers." She is the editor of *The Correspondence of Elizabeth Stuart, Queen of Bohemia* (3 vols., two published to date, 2011–), for which her prize-winning PhD (2008) serves as the groundwork. She is also under contract to write a biography of Elizabeth Stuart.

Michael G. Brennan is Professor of Renaissance Studies at the University of Leeds. He has worked on the Sidneys of Penshurst for almost forty years, and for over twenty years in close collaboration with Margaret Hannay and the late Noel Kinnamon, leading to eight jointly authored volumes and numerous articles, essays, and lectures. He has also published other books on the Sidneys, such as *Lady Mary Wroth's Love's Victory: The Penshurst Manuscript* (1988) and *The Sidneys of Penshurst and the Monarchy: 1500–1700* (2010). His early modern researches encompass Western European travel writing, including editions of travel diaries, *The Origins of the Grand Tour* (2004), a study of Continental travel during the English Civil War, and (forthcoming) Richard Hakluyt's accounts of the Spanish Armada (1588) and Cadiz Expedition (1596). His books on twentieth-century literature include *Graham Greene: Fictions, Faith and Authorship* (2010), *Evelyn Waugh: Fictions, Faith and Family* (2013), and *Graham Greene: The Political Writer* (forthcoming).

Lisa Celovsky is Associate Dean of the College of Arts and Sciences and Associate Professor of English at Suffolk University. She has published on generational connections among the Sidneys and on networks involving the seventeenth-century Sidneys in *Studies in Philology* and the *Sidney Journal*. Her current work investigates how Mary Wroth negotiates her relationship to familial investments in chivalric forms and traditions.

Elizabeth Goldring is an Associate Fellow at the Centre for the Study of the Renaissance, University of Warwick. She is the author of *Robert Dudley, Earl of Leicester, and the World of Elizabethan Art: Painting and Patronage at the Court of Elizabeth I* (2014), general editor of *John Nichols's The Progresses and Public Processions of Queen Elizabeth I* (5 vols., 2014), and co-editor of *The Intellectual and Cultural World of the Early Modern Inns of Court* (2011, rpt. 2013) and *The Progresses, Pageants, and Entertainments of Queen Elizabeth I* (2007, rpt. 2014), among other publications.

Margaret P. Hannay, Professor of English Literature Emerita, Siena College, is the author of the biographies *Philip's Phoenix: Mary Sidney, Countess of Pembroke* (1990) and *Mary Sidney, Lady Wroth* (2010), the latter of which won the Book of the Year Award from the Society for the Study of Early Modern Women. She edited the Countess of Pembroke's works with Noel Kinnamon and Michael Brennan as *Collected Works of Mary Sidney Herbert, Countess of Pembroke* (2 vols., 1998); *Selected Works of Mary Sidney Herbert, Countess of Pembroke* (2005), and (with Hannibal Hamlin) *The Sidney Psalter* (2009). Hannay, Brennan and Kinnamon have also edited family correspondence of Robert Sidney, first Earl of Leicester (2005), of Dorothy Percy Sidney, Countess of Leicester (2010), and the *Letters (1595–1608) of Rowland Whyte* (2013). In 2013 she received the Jean Robertson Lifetime Achievement Award from the International Sidney Society, and in 2014 a Lifetime Achievement Award from the Society for the Study of Early Modern Women.

Thomas Herron is Associate Professor of English at East Carolina University. He is author of *Spenser's Irish Work: Poetry, Plantation and Colonial Reformation* (2007) and co-editor with Michael Potterton of two essay collections, *Ireland in the Renaissance, c. 1540–1660* (2007) and *Dublin and the Pale in the Renaissance, c. 1540–1660* (2011). In 2013 he co-curated with Brendan Kane an exhibit at the Folger Shakespeare Library, *Nobility and Newcomers in Renaissance Ireland*, with an accompanying catalogue. In 2011 he was co-editor with Willy Maley of a special double issue of the *Sidney Journal, Sir Henry Sidney in Ireland and Wales* (29.1–2).

Grace Ioppolo is Professor of Shakespearean and Early Modern Drama at the University of Reading. She has also taught at UCLA, UC Berkeley, and the Shakespeare Institute at the University of Birmingham. She is the author of *Revising Shakespeare* (1991) and *Dramatists and their Manuscripts in the Age of Shakespeare, Jonson, Middleton and Heywood: Authorship, Authority and the Playhouse* (2006). She was the co-editor of *Elizabeth I and the Culture of Writing* (2007). She is the Founder and Director of the *Henslowe-Alleyn Digitisation Project*[1] and the general editor of *The Collected Works of Thomas Heywood* (forthcoming). She has published extensively on literary manuscripts and letters, and is preparing a critical biography of the four women of the Essex family: Lettice Knollys, her daughters Penelope and Frances, and her daughter-in-law Frances Walsingham.

Arthur F. Kinney, Thomas W. Copeland Professor of Literary History, University of Massachusetts Amherst, has research interests that include Renaissance prose, poetry, and drama and twentieth-century American literature, with specialties in William Faulkner, Flannery O'Connor, and Dorothy Parker. He has published widely in both areas, including the books on *Humanist Poetics: Thought, Rhetoric, and Fiction in Sixteenth-century England* (1986); John Skelton, *Priest as Poet: Seasons of Discovery* (1987); and *"Lies Like Truth": Shakespeare, Macbeth, and the Cultural Moment* (2001); four books on Faulkner's families, and studies of Flannery O'Connor and Dorothy Parker. He has also edited a volume of Renaissance Drama and Entertainments, *The Witch of Edmonton* (1998); *The Cambridge Companion to English Literature 1500–1600* (1999); and *The Oxford Handbook to Shakespeare* (2012). His current project is *Shakespeare and the Mind's Eye*, based on Renaissance and current cognitive studies, revising *Titled Elizabethans*, and publishing a volume of *Selected Essays*. He is the only recipient of both the Paul Oskar Kristeller Lifetime Achievement Award from the Renaissance Society of America and the Jean Robertson Lifetime Achievement Award from the International Sidney Society.

---

1   http://www.henslowe-alleyn.org.uk.

Roger Kuin is Professor Emeritus of English Literature at York University. With degrees from Amsterdam and Oxford, he has published an edition of Robert Langham's *Letter (1575)* (1983), *Chamber Music: Elizabethan Sonnet-sequences and the Pleasure of Criticism* (1998), and a two-volume edition of *The Correspondence of Sir Philip Sidney* (2012), which won the MLA's Morton Cohen Award and the Sixteenth Century Society's Bainton Award. He has published numerous articles on Sidney and Anglo-Continental relations, and is a founder member of the International Sidney Society. He lives in the South of France.

Katherine R. Larson is Associate Professor of English at the University of Toronto. She is the author of *Early Modern Women in Conversation* (2011) and the co-editor of *Re-Reading Mary Wroth* with Naomi J. Miller and Andrew Strycharski (2015) and of *Gender and Song in Early Modern England*, with Leslie C. Dunn (2014). Her articles have appeared in journals including *English Literary Renaissance*, *Milton Studies*, the *Sidney Journal*, and *Early Modern Women: An Interdisciplinary Journal*. Her current book project integrates her training as a singer in its exploration of the affective function of women's song performance and of the singing body in early modern literature and culture.

Carole Levin is Willa Cather Professor of History and Director of the Medieval and Renaissance Studies Program at the University of Nebraska, where she specializes in English Renaissance cultural and women's history. Her books include *The Heart and Stomach of a King: Elizabeth I and the Politics of Sex and Power* (1994; 2nd ed. 2013), *The Reign of Elizabeth I* (2002), *Dreaming the English Renaissance: Politics and Desire in Court and Culture* (2008), and (with John Watkins), *Shakespeare's Foreign Worlds* (2009). She was awarded a 2015 Fulbright Scholarship to the University of York to work on a book on representations of queens in Elizabethan and Stuart England.

Willy Maley is Professor of Renaissance Studies at the University of Glasgow. His recent work includes *Shakespeare and Wales: From the Marches to the Assembly*, co-edited with Philip Schwyzer (2010), *This England, That Shakespeare: New Angles on Englishness and the Bard*, co-edited with Margaret Tudeau-Clayton (2010), and *Celtic Shakespeare: The Bard and the Borderers*, co-edited with Rory Loughnane (2013). In 2011 he also co-edited with Thomas Herron a special double issue of the *Sidney Journal*, *Sir Henry Sidney in Ireland and Wales* (29.1–2).

Valerie McGowan-Doyle teaches Irish history at John Carroll University and is Associate Professor of History at Lorain County Community College. She is the author of *The Book of Howth: Elizabethan Conquest and the Old English* (2011) as well as essays on early modern Ireland, and was co-editor with Brendan Kane of *Elizabeth I and Ireland* (2014). Her current research addresses violence against women in early modern Ireland.

Catherine Medici is a PhD student and Graduate Assistant in the Women's and Gender Studies Program at the University of Nebraska, and is currently writing her dissertation on Jane Dudley, Duchess of Northumberland, and her daughters Lady Mary Dudley Sidney and Lady Katherine Dudley Hastings, Countess of Huntington, and their political involvement. She received the 2014 NACBS Huntington Library Graduate Fellowship to support this dissertation research.

Philip Schwyzer is Professor of Renaissance Literature at the University of Exeter. His interests include literary and cultural relations between England and Wales in the early modern period. He is the author of *Shakespeare and the Remains of Richard III* (2013), *Archaeologies of English Renaissance Literature* (2007), and *Literature, Nationalism, and Memory* *in Early Modern England and Wales* (2004). He was co-editor with Willy Maley of *Shakespeare and Wales: From the Marches to the Assembly* (2010), and with Simon Mealor of *Archipelagic Identities: Literature and Identity in the Atlantic Archipelago, 1550–1800* (2004).

Jonathan Scott is Professor and Head of History at the University of Auckland, New Zealand. He was born in Auckland, but grew up in Wellington and received his initial education at Victoria University of Wellington. He was a Commonwealth Scholar at Trinity College, Cambridge, where he received his doctorate in 1986. Subsequently he was Fellow and Director of Studies in History at Downing College, Cambridge, and then Carroll Amundson Professor of British History at the University of Pittsburgh, before returning to Auckland in 2009. He has written a number of books and many articles on early modern intellectual, cultural and political history, most recently *When the Waves Ruled Britannia: Geography and Political Identities, 1500–1800* (2011). He has also published poetry and a memoir of his father, *Harry's Absence: Looking for my Father on the Mountain* (1997).

Robert Shephard is Professor of History at Elmira College in Elmira, New York, and has held a Regional Visiting Fellowship at the Institute for European Studies at Cornell University. Essays he has written on early modern European politics and culture have appeared in the *Sixteenth Century Journal*, the *Journal of Modern History*, the *Sidney Journal*, and the anthology *Sex and Sexuality in the Premodern West* (1996). His published works on the Sidney family include the biography of Robert Sidney, first Earl of Leicester, in the *Oxford Dictionary of National Biography* and articles on the political commonplace books of Robert Sidney (for which he received the Gerald R. Rubio Prize), on the Sidney family correspondence, and on Sir Henry Sidney's *Memoir*.

Alan Stewart is Professor of English and Comparative Literature at Columbia University, and International Director of the Centre for Editing Lives and Letters in London. His publications include *Close Readers: Humanism and Sodomy in Early Modern England* (1997), *Hostage to Fortune: The Troubled Life of Francis Bacon* with Lisa Jardine (1998), *Philip Sidney: A Double Life* (2000), *The Cradle King: A Life of James VI and I* (2003), *Letterwriting in Renaissance England* with Heather Wolfe (2004), and *Shakespeare's Letters* (2008). Most recently he edited volume 1 of the *Oxford Francis Bacon*, Bacon's *Early Writings, 1584–1596* (2012), and with Garrett Sullivan was co-general editor of the three-volume Wiley-Blackwell *Encyclopedia of English Renaissance Literature* (2012). In 2011–12 he was the recipient of a John Simon Guggenheim Fellowship.

Germaine Warkentin is Professor Emeritus of English at the University of Toronto and a Fellow of the Royal Society of Canada. She taught, does research, and publishes across several disciplines: English (Renaissance, especially the Sidneys), Italian (the vernacular writings of Petrarch), history (Canadian exploration), and book history. She edited *The Educated Imagination and Other Writings on Critical Theory 1933–1963* (vol. 21 of the *Collected Works of Northrop Frye*, 1996), and *The Writings of Pierre-Esprit Radisson* (2 vols., 2012, 2014), and co-edited *The Library of the Sidneys of Penshurst Place, Circa 1665* (with Joseph L. Black and William R. Bowen, 2013). She is currently working on a study of the materiality of the book and its relation to the structures and development of the brain and textual communication.

Susie West is an architectural historian of the English country house. She researches UK heritage practices and the English country house, with particular attention to the history and heritage of the private library, and is based in the Department of Art History at The Open University. Interdisciplinary research characterizes her interests. Her PhD research at the University of East Anglia was an interdisciplinary project on private libraries in country houses of the long eighteenth century. It united the interdisciplinary field of book history with architectural history to produce a new chronology for the emergence of the formal library room in country houses. She then researched the Sidney family of Penshurst Place and their early modern rooms for books. After working for English Heritage as a Senior Properties Historian, she joined The Open University in 2007, where she pursues her interests in visual and material culture.

Preface: Volume 1

The Sidneys of Penshurst Place, near Tonbridge in Kent, were justifiably proud of their distinguished historical and cultural heritage and sustained personal service to the English monarchy for over two hundred years between 1500 and 1700. Through their remarkable range of literary works and their impact on national and international affairs they remain today of paramount importance to literary scholars and historians. The imaginative creativity of Sir Philip Sidney, along with his acclaimed political identity as a hero of Continental Protestant militancy, tended to dominate literary discussions until the mid-twentieth century, but other members of the family are now widely recognized as having made a major contribution to the development of English literature. Sir Philip's sister, Mary Sidney Herbert, Countess of Pembroke, became the first widely celebrated non-royal woman writer and patron in England; and her brother, Robert Sidney, first Earl of Leicester, was also a poet and patron of letters and music. His daughter, Lady Mary Wroth, is now acknowledged not only as the most important imitator of Sir Philip Sidney's writings in prose, verse, and drama, but also as a major literary figure in her own right.

From a political perspective and from the latter half of the seventeenth century, the constitutional significance of Algernon Sidney's republican writings has long been recognized, but other earlier family members also played a major role in English politics. Sir William Sidney, the founder of the family's fortunes at the early Tudor court and a close associate of King Henry VIII, was appointed as governor to the household of the infant Prince Edward. His son, Sir Henry Sidney, served Queen Elizabeth in the taxing roles of Lord President of Wales and Lord Deputy in Ireland. Various other seventeenth-century Sidneys, most notably William and Philip Herbert, third and fourth Earls of Pembroke (the sons of Mary Sidney Herbert, Countess of Pembroke, and the "incomparable pair of brethren" of the Shakespeare First Folio), and Robert Sidney, second Earl of Leicester, held important court and diplomatic positions. The constitutional significance of the Sidneys culminated in the leading role played by Henry Sidney, Earl of Romney (the youngest brother of Algernon), in ensuring the succession of the Dutch House of Orange to the English throne in 1689.

The Sidneys' sustained personal interaction with members of the royal court at this period can only be rivaled by a few other influential English families, such as the Dudleys (Earls of Warwick and Leicester and Duke of Northumberland), the Herberts (Earls of Pembroke and Montgomery), Percys (Earls of Northumberland), Cecils (Lord Burghley and Earls of Salisbury and Exeter), Talbots (Earls of Shrewsbury), and Howards (Earls of Arundel, Northampton, Nottingham, Suffolk, and Surrey, and Earls and Dukes of Norfolk). Significantly, many members of these distinguished families enjoyed close personal and official dealings with the Sidneys themselves.

In common with other dynastic families of the period, the Sidneys regularly commissioned family portraits from the leading artists of the day, many of which still remain in the major private art collection at Penshurst Place, with a selection from these paintings included by kind permission of their owner, Viscount De L'Isle, as illustrations to this first volume of *The Ashgate Research Companion to the Sidneys (1500–1700)*. These portraits eloquently testify to the Sidneys' determination to preserve a lasting historical sense of the importance of their family name and dynasty. Architectural historians have also long focused attention on Penshurst Place, granted to Sir William Sidney by the young King Edward VI and still today in the ownership of the Sidney family, as one of the most important late medieval and Tudor private homes in England. This striking and idyllic country residence provided not only a personal and intellectual focus for their literary, political, and cultural engagements, but also a psychologically reassuring and often idealized family home for successive generations of the Sidneys. More recently, architectural and cultural research has also focused on the Herbert family's vast London mansion, Baynard's Castle, where the Sidneys often stayed between 1550 and 1650, and their own now lost seventeenth-century London mansion, Leicester House, built by Robert Sidney, second Earl of Leicester, and (significantly, since he was often away from London on court and diplomatic duties) his wife Dorothy.

The Ashgate Research Companion to the Sidneys (1500–1700) offers forty-two specially commissioned and previously unpublished essays by both senior and more junior academics on this remarkable family's central historical and cultural importance to the Tudor and Stuart periods. All of the contributors bring considerable expertise and fresh insights to their chosen fields of research. This first volume of the collection, comprising twenty-one chapters, seeks to establish the current state of scholarship in a diverse range of historical, biographical, geographical, and cultural areas of Sidneian studies, and no less importantly, to map out possible new areas and avenues of future research for the next generation of Sidney scholars. These chapters therefore place a distinct emphasis not only upon how these multifaceted and interdisciplinary fields of study are currently understood, but also how they might be explored in new and challenging ways.

The Sidneys, originally a Kentish gentry family, owed their rise to public prominence at the Tudor royal court to Sir William Sidney, who served Henry VIII with distinction both as a naval commander and at the Battle of Flodden against the Scots in 1513. Sir William was chosen to supervise the early guardianship and education of Henry VIII's only son and heir, Prince Edward, who as King Edward VI, died in the arms of Sir William's son, Sir Henry Sidney. Sir Henry, who served Queen Elizabeth for long periods as both President of her Council in Wales and her Lord Deputy in Ireland, bonded the Sidneys with the powerful and intensely ambitious Dudley family through his marriage to Mary Dudley, sister of Robert, Earl of Leicester. The careers and accomplishments of three of Sir Henry's children, Sir Philip Sidney, Robert Sidney, first Earl of Leicester, and Mary Sidney Herbert, Countess of Pembroke, have dominated Sidneian literary studies for many decades. But, as the chapters in this volume demonstrate, they made major contributions to the historical and cultural developments of the late Elizabethan and early Stuart courts, enjoying a significant presence in English public life and on the Continent. Later generations of the Sidneys, including Robert, second Earl of Leicester, his son, the republican Algernon Sidney, Algernon's youngest brother Henry Sidney, Earl of Romney, and their nephew Robert Spencer, second Earl of Sunderland, all played major roles in public and political life. Their experiences, as traced in this collection of historical and culturally focused essays, provide a richly informative insight into the lives of a closely knit and highly politicized English family from the Civil War, through the Interregnum and Commonwealth, to the Restoration and Exclusion Crisis and accession of William III in 1689.

In recent years it has been increasingly appreciated that a distinctive characteristic of the Sidneys at this period lies in their highly educated women often being as politically and culturally influential as male members of the family. The essays in this first volume therefore focus specifically and extensively upon the importance of Mary Dudley Sidney (Sir Henry's wife) and her influential family network, and the prominence at court and in literary matters of Mary Sidney Herbert, Countess of Pembroke, whose marriage to Henry

Herbert, second Earl of Pembroke, provided the Sidneys with, arguably, their most important and long-lasting family connection with the Herberts of Wilton. Other chapters explore the family significance to the Sidneys of Lettice, Penelope, and Dorothy Devereux and Frances Walsingham Sidney (the wife of Sir Philip Sidney); Barbara Gamage Sidney, Countess of Leicester; Elizabeth Sidney Manners, Countess of Rutland (Sir Philip Sidney's daughter), and Lady Mary Wroth, whose imaginatively diverse writings are now recognized as having played a key role in sustaining the Sidney family's unparalleled literary productivity at this period. During the seventeenth century the family's court and political fortunes rested heavily upon the intelligence, court connections, and diplomatic skills of Dorothy Percy Sidney, Countess of Leicester, and Dorothy Sidney Spencer, Countess of Sunderland. This collection of essays conclusively demonstrates that, without taking into account the achievements of the Sidney women, only a partial understanding of the importance and influence of this prominent family can be appreciated.

This first volume also focuses research upon the Sidneys' dominant role in both Ireland and Wales during the sixteenth and seventeenth centuries, alongside their wide-ranging political and cultural interests, both as observers and interventionists, in Continental affairs during the Tudor and Stuart periods. Their interests in the visual arts and music are also explored in detail since both merit further investigation, as do their major architectural endeavors at Penshurst Place and their London residence, Leicester House. The Sidneys' reputation for literary patronage has already proved a long-standing area of literary investigation, but there is still important work to be done on their patronage of not only literature, but also other arts during the Tudor period, and especially the entire seventeenth century.

As proposed in "Future Sidney Studies," the concluding chapter to the second volume of this collection, there still remains much work to be done on the Sidneys by other scholars. These areas incorporate the already familiar topics of literary criticism, historical analysis, book history, material studies, and a continuing expansion of both academic and popular interest in diverse members of the Sidney family other than its still most renowned figure, Sir Philip Sidney. Fresh ideas and approaches will surely be brought to these areas by new generations of researchers, along with a broader and still developing awareness of the major significance of the Sidneys during this period to the manuscript and print circulation of their original works, their book collecting, their religious and theological perspectives, and their substantial and sometimes crucial contribution to English political debate and constitutional affairs.

In conclusion, this collection demonstrates that several key areas of Sidney studies definitely merit further and sustained examination by other scholars. The last twenty-five years have seen a timely and influential growth in interest in the activities and achievements of the female members of the Sidney family, but more work remains to be done in exploring and defining the contribution to both private and court life of the Sidney family's remarkable mothers, daughters, wives, and other female relatives and friends. It is also apparent from essays included in this collection that further examination of the Sidneys' involvements in Continental affairs and international exploration may prove a fruitful area of investigation. Likewise, the art collections (especially portraiture) and voluminous personal papers of the Sidneys have more recently become major new areas of historical and critical study, but much further work still remains to be done, as is also the case with their voluminous personal and public correspondence with an impressively wide network of relatives, friends, and political associates, both within the British Isles and abroad. In this respect, the Sidney family's published works and private archive of personal and estate papers (now at the Kent History and Library Centre) remain among the most important surviving collections of manuscript and printed documents from the early modern period. They offer an unrivaled opportunity to understand the public and private affairs, as well as the psychological and intellectual workings, of these prominent, creative, and memorable members of the Tudor and Stuart aristocracy and county gentry.

Margaret P. Hannay, Michael G. Brennan, and Mary Ellen Lamb

Acknowledgments

Our greatest debt in compiling this collection of essays on the Sidneys of Penshurst is to the present Viscount De L'Isle, MBE, Lord Lieutenant of Kent, and to his father, the late Viscount de L'Isle, VC, KG, for their long-term generosity and support in allowing us access to their unique collection of family papers and art collections. We are also especially grateful for the expert guidance and advice of the staff at the Kent History and Library Centre (formerly the Centre for Kentish Studies) at Maidstone, Kent, where the Sidney family papers are now housed.

This collection of essays was originally planned by Margaret Hannay, Michael Brennan, and our close friend and long-term collaborator, Noel J. Kinnamon. Sadly, however, ill health prevented the late Professor Kinnamon from carrying out this editorial role, but we are immensely grateful to him for contributing to this collection, as his final academic publication, an erudite and richly informative essay on the Sidney Psalter. Equally, Margaret Hannay and Michael Brennan would wish to acknowledge the great generosity of Mary Ellen Lamb in so readily taking over this demanding editorial role and providing the collection with the benefit of her long-standing expertise as the editor of the *Sidney Journal*.

David Hannay, through his great computing expertise and invaluable assistance in both assembling the illustrations and assisting with other editorial matters, has also become a key member of the editorial team as we put together this large collection of essays. His advice and support, so generously given, has been much appreciated by all three of this collection's editors.

We are also very grateful to all those many individuals who have guided our research into the Sidney family for over thirty years and responded so helpfully to queries, especially for this collection, to Georgianna Ziegler and Heather Wolfe, both at the Folger Shakespeare Library. We would also wish to acknowledge the helpful collaborative spirit of many of the contributors to this collection of essays who have so generously responded both to our queries as editors and to others raised by their fellow contributors.

We are grateful for the professional assistance of the staff of the following libraries and institutions: Bridgeman Education, London; the British Library, London; the Brotherton Library, University of Leeds; Essex Record Office, Chelmsford; the Folger Shakespeare Library, Washington DC; Hatfield House, Hertfordshire; the Huntington Library, California; Inner Temple Library, London; Lambeth Palace Library, London; The National Archives, Kew; the National Library of Wales, Aberystwyth; the National Portrait Gallery, London; the Newberry Library, Chicago; the Standish Library, Siena College, New York; Trinity College Library, Cambridge; Warwickshire Record Office, Warwick; the Weiss Gallery, London; and the Swindon History Centre, Chippenham, Wiltshire.

Finally, as we planned and steadily assembled this collection of essays, we have been greatly indebted to our ever-helpful Commissioning Editor at Ashgate, Erika Gaffney, for her regular and always wise guidance and advice, and Barbara Pretty, Senior Editor, whose technical expertise, excellent advice and unwavering patience have been greatly appreciated by the editors. We would also like to thank at Ashgate for their professional skills, Huw Jones, copy-editor, Mary Murphy, proofreader, and Tom Norton, indexer.

List of Abbreviations

Cross-references to chapters within this collection are cited in the format: author second name *ARC* volume number:chapter number (for example, Brennan *ARC* 1:1; Black *ARC* 2:1).

APC	*Acts of the Privy Council of England*. Ed. J. R. Dasent. London: HMSO, 1906.
BL	British Library
Bodl.	Bodleian Library, Oxford
CKS	Centre for Kentish Studies, Maidstone, Kent (now Kent History and Library Centre)
Collins	*Letters and Memorials of State*. Ed. Arthur Collins. 2 vols. London: T. Osborne, 1746.
Correspondence DPS	*The Correspondence (c. 1626–1659) of Dorothy Percy Sidney, Countess of Leicester*. Ed. Michael G. Brennan, Noel J. Kinnamon, and Margaret P. Hannay. Farnham: Ashgate, 2010.
Correspondence SPS	*The Correspondence of Sir Philip Sidney*. Ed. Roger Kuin. 2 vols. Oxford: Oxford UP, 2012.
CSP	*Calendar of State Papers*
CSPD	*Calendar of State Papers Domestic*
CSPF	*Calendar of State Papers French*
CSPS	*Calendar of State Papers Spain*
CSPV	*Calendar of State Papers Venetian*
DPFA	*Domestic Politics and Family Absence: The Correspondence (1588–1621) of Robert Sidney, First Earl of Leicester, and Barbara Gamage Sidney, Countess of Leicester*. Ed. Margaret P. Hannay, Noel J. Kinnamon, and Michael G. Brennan. Aldershot: Ashgate, 2005.
ELH	*English Literary History*
ELR	*English Literary Renaissance*
Gender and Authorship	Mary Ellen Lamb, *Gender and Authorship in the Sidney Circle*. Madison, WI: U of Wisconsin P, 1990.
HLQ	*Huntington Library Quarterly*
HMC	Historical Manuscripts Commission

HMC *De L'Isle and Dudley*	HMC *Report on the Manuscripts of Lord De L'Isle and Dudley Preserved at Penshurst Place, 1925–66*. 6 vols. London: HMSO, 1925–66.
HMC *Salisbury*	HMC *Calendar of the Manuscripts of the Most Hon. The Marquis of Salisbury, K.G. … Preserved at Hatfield House, Hertfordshire*. 24 vols. London: HMSO, 1883–1976.
HMSO	Her Majesty's Stationery Office
Holinshed, *Chronicles* 1587	Raphael Holinshed, *Chronicles of England, Scotlande, and Irelande*. 3 vols. London: Henry Denham et al., 1587.
KHLC	Kent History and Library Centre (formerly Centre for Kentish Studies), Maidstone, Kent
MSH, *Collected Works*	*The Collected Works of Mary Sidney Herbert, Countess of Pembroke*. Ed. Margaret P. Hannay, Noel J. Kinnamon, and Michael G. Brennan. 2 vols. Oxford: Oxford UP, 1998.
MSLW	Margaret P. Hannay, *Mary Sidney, Lady Wroth*. Farnham: Ashgate, 2010.
ODNB	*Oxford Dictionary of National Biography*. Ed. H. C. G. Matthew and Brian Harrison. Oxford: Oxford UP, 2004–14. Web. http://www.oxforddnb.com/
Philip's Phoenix	Margaret P. Hannay, *Philip's Phoenix: Mary Sidney, Countess of Pembroke*. Oxford: Oxford UP, 1990.
RQ	*Renaissance Quarterly*
Scott, *Algernon/Republic*	Jonathan Scott, *Algernon Sidney and the English Republic, 1623–1677*. Cambridge: Cambridge UP, 1988 and 2004.
Scott, *Algernon/Restoration*	Jonathan Scott, *Algernon Sidney and the Restoration Crisis, 1677–1683*. Cambridge: Cambridge UP, 1991 and 2002.
SEL	*Studies in English Literature, 1500–1900*
Sidney Chronology	Michael G. Brennan and Noel J. Kinnamon, *A Sidney Chronology: 1554–1654*. London: Palgrave Macmillan, 2003.
Sidney, *New Arcadia*	*The Countess of Pembroke's Arcadia (The New Arcadia)*. Ed. Victor Skretkowicz. Oxford: Clarendon P, 1987.
Sidney, *Old Arcadia*	*The Countess of Pembroke's Arcadia (The Old Arcadia)*. Ed. Jean Robertson. Oxford: Clarendon P, 1973.
Sidney, *Poems*	*The Poems of Sir Philip Sidney*. Ed. William A. Ringler, Jr. Oxford: Clarendon P, 1962.
Sidney, *Psalter*	*The Sidney Psalter: The Psalms of Sir Philip and Mary Sidney*. Ed. Hannibal Hamlin, Michael G. Brennan, Margaret P. Hannay, and Noel J. Kinnamon. Oxford: Oxford UP, 2009.
Sidneys of Penshurst	Michael G. Brennan, *The Sidneys of Penshurst and the Monarchy, 1500–1700*. Aldershot: Ashgate, 2006.
SJ	*Sidney Journal*
SP	State Papers at TNA
STC	*A Short-title Catalogue of Books Printed in England, Scotland, & Ireland and of English Books Printed Abroad, 1475–1640*. 1st ed.

compiled by A. W. Pollard and G. R. Redgrave; 2nd revised and enlarged ed. begun by W. A. Jackson and F. S. Ferguson, completed by K. F. Pantzer. London: Bibliographical Society, 1976–91.

TNA   The National Archives, Kew

Whyte   *The Letters (1595–1608) of Rowland Whyte*. Ed. Michael G. Brennan, Noel J. Kinnamon, and Margaret P. Hannay. Philadelphia, PA: American Philosophical Society, 2013.

Wroth, *Love's Victory*   *Lady Mary Wroth's Love's Victory: The Penshurst Manuscript*. Ed. Michael G. Brennan. London: The Roxburghe Club, 1988.

Wroth, *Poems*   *The Poems of Lady Mary Wroth*. Ed. Josephine A. Roberts. 2nd ed. Baton Rouge, LA: Louisiana State U, 1992.

Wroth, *Urania 1*   *The First Part of the Countess of Montgomery's Urania*. Ed. Josephine A. Roberts. Tempe, AZ: Arizona Center for Medieval and Renaissance Texts and Studies, 1995.

Wroth, *Urania 2*   *The Second Part of the Countess of Montgomery's Urania*. Ed. Josephine A. Roberts, completed by Suzanne Gossett and Janel Mueller. Tempe, AZ: Arizona Center for Medieval and Renaissance Texts and Studies, 1999.

Chronology

Sidney family affairs are in roman; general historical information is in italics.

1503 (8 Aug.)	*King James IV (1488–1513) of Scotland marries Princess Margaret, sister of Henry VIII*
1509 (21 Apr.)	*death of King Henry VII and accession of King Henry VIII*
1510	execution of Edmund Dudley (b. *c.* 1462), great-grandfather of Sir Philip Sidney (1554–86)
1511	William Sidney (*c.* 1482–1554) serves in the English expedition to Spain to assist Ferdinand, King of Aragon and Castile, against the Moors
1512	death of Nicholas Sidney (b. *c.* 1451), father of William Sidney who is then serving in the English navy during the war with France
1513 (18 Apr.) (9 Sept.)	William Sidney knighted after a naval engagement off Brest (Mar.) *King James IV of Scotland killed at the Battle of Flodden*; William Sidney fights there with distinction
1514 (1 Feb.) (Jul.)	Charles Brandon, friend and patron of Sir William Sidney, created Duke of Suffolk; Thomas Howard, Sir William's commander at Flodden, restored to the dukedom of Norfolk Sir William Sidney awarded a life annuity of 50 marks by Henry VIII
1515 (1 Jan.)	death of King Louis XII of France; in Feb. Charles Brandon secretly marries his widow, Mary, sister of Henry VIII; their union publicly celebrated at Greenwich (May); at this period or later, the Sidneys appropriate the French king's personal emblem of the porcupine
1517 (?)	Sir William Sidney marries Anne Pagenham (d. 1543)
1520 (Jun.)	*"Field of the Cloth of Gold" meeting in the Plain of Ardres between Henry VIII and François I of France*; Sir William Sidney prominent among the English jousters
1523/24	Sir William Sidney joins Suffolk's military campaign in France
1529 (20 Jul.)	birth of Henry Sidney (d. 1586) with Henry VIII as a godparent

1531 (?)	birth of Mary Dudley Sidney (d. 1586), wife of Henry Sidney
1532 (15 May)	*English Church supports King Henry VIII against the Papacy*
1532/33?	birth of Robert Dudley (d. 1588), later Earl of Leicester, uncle of Sir Philip Sidney
1533 (25 Jan.)	*King Henry VIII marries Anne Boleyn after divorcing Catherine of Aragon*
1536 (19 May)	*Anne Boleyn executed*
(30 May)	*King Henry VIII marries Jane Seymour*
(autumn)	*Pilgrimage of Grace uprising against Henry VIII's break with the Roman Catholic Church*
1537 (12 Oct.)	*Prince Edward born to King Henry VIII and Jane Seymour*
(24 Oct.)	*Jane Seymour dies*
1538	Sir William Sidney appointed Chamberlain (until 1544) to Prince Edward, and his son Henry becomes one of Prince Edward's closest childhood companions
1543	death of Anne Pagenham Sidney, wife of Sir William Sidney
1546 (?)	William Herbert (*c.* 1501–70), later first Earl of Pembroke, appointed Keeper of Baynard's Castle on the banks of the River Thames
1547 (28 Jan.)	*death of King Henry VIII and accession of King Edward VI*
1549 (20 Jun.)	*Norfolk Rebellion begins*
1550 (18 Apr.)	Henry Sidney appointed a Gentleman of the Privy Chamber
1550–53	William Herbert, later first Earl of Pembroke, Lord President of the Council of Wales
1551 (29 Mar.)	Henry Sidney marries at Asser Mary, daughter of John Dudley, Earl of Warwick and sister of Robert and Ambrose Dudley (later Earls of Leicester and Warwick)
(Jul.)	Henry Sidney accompanies the Marquis of Northampton's embassy to France
(11 Oct.)	Henry Sidney knighted, and John Dudley (d. 1553), Earl of Warwick, created Duke of Northumberland; William Herbert created first Earl of Pembroke
1552 (25 Apr.)	King Edward VI grants the estate and manor of Penshurst Place, Kent, to Sir William Sidney
1553 (21 May)	marriage of Lady Jane Grey and Lord Guildford Dudley, son of John Dudley, Earl of Warwick and Duke of Northumberland
(21 Jun.)	Sir Henry Sidney witnesses King Edward VI's will

(6 Jul.)	*death of King Edward VI, reputedly cradled in the arms of Sir Henry Sidney; accession (9 Jul.) of Lady Jane Grey (executed 12 Feb. 1554), who reputedly was first told of her accession by Mary Dudley Sidney, wife of Sir Henry Sidney*
(19 Jul.)	*accession of Queen Mary*
(22 Aug.)	execution on Tower Hill of John Dudley (b. 1504), Earl of Warwick and Duke of Northumberland, grandfather of Sir Philip Sidney
1554 (7 Feb.)	*rebellion against the Spanish marriage proposed for Queen Mary led by Sir Thomas Wyatt*
(7 or 10 Feb.)	death of Sir William Sidney at Penshurst
(13 Mar.)	Sir Henry Sidney accompanies Earl of Bedford's embassy to Spain to accompany Philip of Spain back to England for his marriage (25 Jul.) with Queen Mary
(2–5 May)	*Queen Mary's Second Parliament accepts terms for the Spanish marriage*
(13 Jul.)	Sir Henry Sidney sails from La Coruña for England with Philip of Spain; *royal marriage celebrated (25 Jul.)*
(Nov.)	*Queen Mary's Third Parliament restores Papal Supremacy to England*
(30 Nov.)	birth of Philip Sidney (d. 1586), named in honor of his godfather, Philip of Spain, the husband of Queen Mary
1555 (25 Oct.)	*Emperor Charles V resigns the Netherlands in favor of Philip of Spain*
1555–58	William Herbert, first Earl of Pembroke, Lord President of the Council of Wales
1556 (Jan.)	*Queen Mary's husband formally becomes Philip II of Spain following his father's abdication*
(May)	Sir Henry Sidney leaves for Dublin to become Vice-Treasurer and General Governor of Revenues
1557 (Apr.)	Sir Henry Sidney now informally serving as Lord Justice in Ireland
(10 Aug.)	*English-Spanish victory over the French at St. Quentin;* serving in the English forces are the brothers of Mary Dudley Sidney, Ambrose, Robert, and Henry, and Henry Herbert, later second Earl of Pembroke and husband of Mary Sidney Herbert, Countess of Pembroke
1558 (7 Jan.)	*loss of Calais, England's last French possession*
(24 Apr.)	*marriage of Mary Queen of Scots to the French Dauphin, later François II*
(17 Nov.)	*death of Queen Mary and accession of Queen Elizabeth I*
(20 Nov.)	*Sir William Cecil appointed Secretary of State and Queen Elizabeth's principal adviser*
(12 Dec.)	Sir Henry Sidney promoted to Lord Justice in Ireland
1559 (Feb.)	*Philip II of Spain makes a tentative offer of marriage to Queen Elizabeth I; Treaty of Câteau-Cambrésis (3 Apr.) marks end of hostilities between France and Spain; accession (24 Apr.) of François II of France, husband of Mary Queen of Scots*
1560 (5 Dec.)	*death of François II of France and accession of Charles IX*
1560–86	Sir Henry Sidney, Lord President of the Council of Wales

1561 (27 Oct.)	birth of Mary Sidney (d. 1621), later Countess of Pembroke, at Tickenhall (Ticknell) near Bewdley, Worcestershire
(26 Dec.)	Ambrose Dudley, uncle of Philip Sidney, created Earl of Warwick

1562 (Jul.)	Sir Henry Sidney's mission to Scotland to meet with Mary Queen of Scots; meets John Knox while he is at Edinburgh
(Oct.)	Queen Elizabeth, Mary Dudley Sidney and Philip Sidney catch smallpox; fears for the royal succession as the queen insists on Robert Dudley being named as Protector of the Realm; Mary Sidney is left with severe facial scars, as reflected in the tale of Argulus and Parthenia in the *New Arcadia*
(?)	birth of Barbara Gamage (*c.* 1559–1621), later wife of Robert Sidney, first Earl of Leicester

1563 (19 Nov.)	birth of Robert Sidney (d. 1626), later first Earl of Leicester, named in honor of his maternal uncle and godfather, Robert Dudley (d. 1588)

1564 (26 Apr.)	*William Shakespeare baptized at Stratford-upon-Avon*
(14 May)	Sir Henry Sidney installed as a Knight of the Garter, alongside King Charles IX of France
(29 Sept.)	Robert Dudley (d. 1588) created Baron Denbigh and Earl of Leicester
(17 Oct.)	Philip Sidney enters Shrewsbury School with his lifelong friend, Fulke Greville

1565 (22 Jun.)	Sir Henry Sidney appointed as Lord Deputy of Ireland (serves until 1571)
(29 Jul.)	*marriage of Mary Queen of Scots and Lord Darnley*

1566 (13 Jan.)	Sir Henry and Lady Mary Sidney arrive in Dublin after losing much of their household possessions and jewels when one of their ships is wrecked
(Apr.)	Sir Henry Sidney formulates a plan for each of the four provinces of Ireland to have a president and council
(19 Jun.)	birth of James Stewart, later King James VI of Scotland and I of England
(Aug.)	Philip Sidney visits Kenilworth, the residence of his uncle Robert Dudley, Earl of Leicester; he then travels to Oxford for Queen Elizabeth's visit
(8 Sept.)	Philip Sidney leaves Oxford

1567 (10 Feb.)	*murder of Lord Darnley*
(15 May)	*Mary Queen of Scots marries Earl of Bothwell*
(2 Jun.)	Shane O'Neill is assassinated, and Sir Henry Sidney has his head placed on Dublin Castle
(24 Jul.)	*abdication of Mary Queen of Scots and accession of King James VI (aged one year)*

1568 (Feb.)	Philip Sidney begins his university studies at Christ Church, Oxford
(May)	*Mary Queen of Scots escapes from captivity and flees to England*

1569 (Jan.)	*English colonization of Ulster begins*
(Feb.)	proposal for marriage (until Feb. 1570) between Philip Sidney and Anne, daughter of Sir William Cecil
(25 Mar.)	birth of Thomas (d. 1595), son of Sir Henry and Mary Dudley Sidney
(summer)	Sir Henry Sidney suppresses opposition in Munster, Connaught and Ulster and approves the Munster plantation (Jun.)

(Nov.)	*Rebellion of the northern earls in support of Mary Queen of Scots*
1570 (25 Feb.)	*Queen Elizabeth excommunicated by Pope Pius V's Papal Bull*
(17 Mar.)	death of William Herbert, first Earl of Pembroke, succeeded by his son Henry Herbert (d. 1601) as second earl
	negotiations between England and France for a marriage between Queen Elizabeth I and the Duc d'Alençon
1571 (Jan.–Sept.)	*Ridolfi Plot to depose Queen Elizabeth in favor of Mary Queen of Scots*
(25 Feb.)	Sir William Cecil created Lord Burghley
(Mar.)	Sir Henry Sidney's second term of office in Ireland concludes
(Apr.)	Philip Sidney leaves Oxford because of an outbreak of plague
1572 (19 Apr.)	*Treaty of Blois, providing a defensive alliance between England and France, agreed in draft*
(25 May)	Philip Sidney granted a license to travel on the Continent for two years to study languages; joins entourage of Edward Fiennes de Clinton, who led the English delegation for the signing of the Treaty of Blois
(2 May)	Sir Henry Sidney declines a barony in his wife's letter to William Cecil, due to its related expenses
(15 Jun.)	*ratification of the Treaty of Blois*
(8 Jul.)	*the Protestant Henri de Navarre arrives at Paris; marries Marguerite de Valois (18 Aug.)*
(9 Aug.)	Philip Sidney created Baron de Sidenay at the French court
(24/25 Aug.)	*St. Bartholomew's Day Massacre at Paris,* leading to Philip Sidney's departure for Germany (mid-Sept.)
(winter)	Philip Sidney stays at Frankfurt under guidance of Hubert Languet
1573 (Mar.)	Philip Sidney attends the Frankfurt book fair
(late May)	Philip Sidney leaves Strasbourg to visit the court of the Holy Roman Emperor Maximilian at Vienna
(early Sept.)	Philip Sidney visits Bratislava in Hungary and then returns to Vienna (late Oct.)
(Nov.)	Philip Sidney visits Italy and is based at Venice and Padua until Aug. 1574, and has his portrait painted by Veronese
1574 (Aug.)	Philip Sidney leaves Venice and travels to Innsbruck and then the Imperial court of Emperor Maximilian II at Vienna
(Oct.)	Philip Sidney visits Cracow, Poland and then returns to Vienna (Nov.)
1575 (7 Feb.)	Philip Sidney leaves Vienna for Prague; heads homewards via Dresden, Leipzig and Frankfurt (Mar.)
(late Feb.)	death of Ambrosia Sidney (b. c. 1564) leads to invitation to royal court of her elder sister Mary
(early May)	Philip Sidney at Antwerp; sails (31 May) from there to England
(Jun.)	Robert Sidney matriculates from Christ Church, Oxford; Philip Sidney in London and at court
(9–27 Jul.)	Kenilworth royal entertainment, attended by Sir Henry and Lady Mary Sidney and their daughter, Mary; Philip, Mary, Robert, Thomas, and their mother also attend the queen at Woodstock (Sept.)

1575–78	Sir Henry Sidney, Lord Deputy of Ireland

1576 (Jul.)	Philip Sidney visits Ireland; back in England by early Nov.
(12 Oct.)	*death of Holy Roman Emperor Maximilian II; succeeded by his Catholic son Rudolf*
(1–7 Nov.)	*Antwerp falls to Spanish mercenaries*
(?)	birth of Robert Wroth (d. 1614), later husband of Mary Sidney (d. 1651)

1577 (16 Jan.)	Philip Sidney meets John Dee, probably at Mortlake
(Feb.)	preparations for Philip Sidney's embassy to Emperor Rudolf to offer condolences on the death of his father
(Mar.–Jun.)	Philip Sidney at Ostend, Brussels, Louvain, Heidelberg, Nuremberg, Prague, Frankfurt, Antwerp, Middelberg, and Bruges
(21 Apr.)	Mary Sidney (d. 1621) marries Henry Herbert (d. 1601), second Earl of Pembroke; wedding attended by her brother Robert, and henceforth the Sidneys are regular guests at the Herbert residences at Wilton and Baynard's Castle, London
(17 Nov.)	Philip Sidney participates in Accession Day tilts as "Philisides," and then stays at Wilton House (Dec.)

1578 (21 Sept.)	Robert Dudley, Earl of Leicester, secretly marries Lettice Knollys Devereux (d. 1634) with Sir Henry Sidney attending

1579 (Apr.)	Robert Sidney sets out on his Continental travels
(17–27 Aug.)	The French Duc d'Anjou visits England to pursue marriage negotiations with Queen Elizabeth; Philip Sidney's tennis court quarrel with the Earl of Oxford (late Aug.)

1580 (8 Apr.)	birth of William Herbert (d. 1630), later third Earl of Pembroke; at his christening (28 Apr.) the godparents are Queen Elizabeth and the Earls of Leicester and Warwick; Philip Sidney is probably based at Wilton House Apr.–Aug.

1581 (15 Jan.)	Philip Sidney takes part in the "Callophisus Challenge"
(15/16 May)	Philip Sidney takes part in *The Four Foster Children of Desire*
(Nov.)	Duc d'Anjou again in England for marriage negotiations; leaves in early Feb. 1582 and dies in Jun. 1584

1582 (spring)	Robert Sidney returns to England

1583 (13(?) Jan.)	Philip Sidney knighted to enable him to stand proxy for Count Casimir at his installation as a Knight of the Garter
(spring)	plans for Sir Philip Sidney to marry Frances, daughter of Sir Francis Walsingham; marriage celebrated 21 Sept.

1584 (29 Jun.)	*assassination of the Prince of Orange, leading to England's involvement in the Dutch wars*
(23 Sept.)	marriage of Robert Sidney and Barbara Gamage (d. 1621), promoted by Henry Herbert, second Earl of Pembroke

(16 Oct.)	birth of Philip Herbert (d. 1650), later fourth Earl of Pembroke and Montgomery, with Mary Dudley Sidney, Sir Philip and Robert Sidney as godparents
(autumn)	circulation of the libelous *Leicester's Commonwealth*

1585 (26 Aug.)   England to send forces to Low Countries, led by the Earl of Leicester with Sir Philip Sidney as Deputy and Governor of Flushing
  (early Nov.?)birth of Elizabeth (d. 1612), daughter of Sir Philip and Frances Sidney
  (18 Nov.)   Sir Philip and Robert Sidney sail for Flushing

1586 (1 or 5 May) death of Sir Henry Sidney at Worcester
  (9 Aug.)   death of Lady Mary Dudley Sidney at London
  (23 Sept.)   Sir Philip Sidney wounded during a skirmish at Zutphen
  (7 Oct.)   Robert Sidney is knighted by his uncle, Robert Dudley, Earl of Leicester, for valor at Zutphen
  (17 Oct.)   death of Sir Philip Sidney

1586–1601   Henry Herbert, second Earl of Pembroke and husband of Mary Sidney Herbert, President of Wales

1587 (8 Feb.)   *execution of Mary Stuart*
  (16 Feb.)   funeral of Sir Philip Sidney at St. Paul's Cathedral, London
  (18 Oct.)   birth of Robert Sidney's daughter, Mary (d. 1651), later Lady Mary Wroth; her christening is probably held in the Great Hall at Baynard's Castle

1588 (16 Jul.)   Sir Robert Sidney appointed Governor of Flushing
  (Aug.)   *Spanish Armada crisis*; Robert Sidney joins the English forces at Tilbury, led by his uncle, Robert Dudley, Earl of Leicester, and is then dispatched on a mission to King James VI of Scotland to ensure Scotland's support for England against Spain
  (23 Aug.)   the stationer William Ponsonby is granted publication rights for the *Arcadia* and Sidney's translation of Du Bartas
  (4 Sept.)   death of Robert Dudley, Earl of Leicester

1589 (1 Aug.)   *assassination of King Henri III of France*

1589–1616   Robert Sidney serves as Governor of Flushing

1590 (21 Feb.)   death of Ambrose Dudley, Earl of Warwick
  (10/11 Nov.) birth of William (d. 1612), eldest son of Sir Robert and Barbara Sidney
  (?)   publication of *The Countess of Pembroke's Arcadia*; probable year of marriage of Frances Walsingham Sidney, widow of Sir Philip Sidney, to Robert Devereux (1565–1601), second Earl of Essex

1591 (autumn)   publication and "taking in" of *Astrophil and Stella*
  (22 Dec.)   marriage of Thomas Sidney to Margaret Dakins Devereux

1592 (?)   publication of the Countess of Pembroke's translations of Duplessis-Mornay's *A Discourse of Life and Death* and Garnier's *Antonius*

1593 (9 Mar.)	William and Philip Herbert matriculate from New College, Oxford
(?)	publication of *The Countess of Pembroke's Arcadia*, with Books I–III from 1590 edition and IV–V from manuscript
1594 (Jan.–Apr.)	Sir Robert Sidney sent on an embassy to King Henri IV of France
(?)	probable date of completion of the Sidney Psalter
1595 (26 Jul.)	death of Thomas Sidney
(17 Sept.)	beginning of the surviving correspondence of Rowland Whyte (whose grandfather had been in the service of William Herbert, first Earl of Pembroke) to Sir Robert Sidney (until 28 Dec. 1602)
(1 Dec.)	birth of Robert Sidney (1677), later second Earl of Leicester, at Baynard's Castle
1596 (Apr.)	Sir Robert Sidney meets with King Henri IV at Boulogne to discuss the retaking of Calais from the Spanish
(19 Aug.)	*birth of Princess Elizabeth, daughter of James VI of Scotland and later Queen of Bohemia*
(?)	Marcus Gheeraerts II paints portrait of Barbara Gamage Sidney and six of her children
1597 (23/24 Jan.)	Sir Robert Sidney serves with distinction at Siege of Turnhout; he then unsuccessfully seeks the Wardenship of the Cinque Ports (Mar.), and later a peerage and the post of Vice-Chamberlain (Oct.)
1598 (5 Mar.)	Sir Philip Sidney's daughter Elizabeth marries Roger Manners, Earl of Rutland
(?)	birth of Dorothy Percy Sidney (d. 1659), later wife of Robert Sidney, second Earl of Leicester; publication of a "collected works" of Philip Sidney, including *The Countess of Pembroke's Arcadia, Defence of Poetry*, and *Astrophil and Stella*
(5 Aug.)	*death of William Cecil, Lord Burghley*
1599 (Jul.)	a proposed royal visit to Wilton House is cancelled; William Herbert welcomed to court (2 Jul.) by Queen Elizabeth
(c. 29 Sept.)	birth of Lucy Percy (d. 1660), later Countess of Carlisle
(?)	pirated edition of *Arcadia* is printed in Scotland for Robert Waldegrave
1600 (19 Nov.)	*birth of Prince Charles, later King Charles I*
(?)	transcription of the Countess of Pembroke's translation of Petrarch's *Triumph of Death*
1601 (19 Jan.)	death of Henry Herbert, second Earl of Pembroke
(Feb.)	William Herbert, now third Earl of Pembroke, refuses to marry Mary Fitton, who bears him a stillborn child (Mar.)
(7/8 Feb.)	*rebellion led by Robert Devereux, Earl of Essex (executed 25 Feb.)*
1602 (?)	Publication of the Dowager Countess of Pembroke's "A Dialogue" in Francis Davison's *Poetical Rhapsody*

1603 (24 Mar.)	*death of Queen Elizabeth and accession of King James VI of Scotland and I of England*
(13 May)	Sir Robert Sidney created Baron Sidney of Penshurst; appointed Queen Anne's Chamberlain and Surveyor of Revenues (Nov.); sent to Canterbury to welcome the French ambassador (early Jun.)
(29/30 Aug.–Dec.)	King James visits Wilton House on several occasions
(?)	marriage of Frances Walsingham Sidney, widow of Sir Philip Sidney and Robert Devereux, Earl of Essex, to Richard Burke (1572–1635), fourth Earl of Clanricarde
1604 (Jan.)	William and Philip Herbert and Sir Robert Sidney prominent in court entertainments
(27 Sept.)	Mary Sidney marries Sir Robert Wroth at Penshurst
(4 Nov.)	William Herbert, third Earl of Pembroke, marries Mary Talbot, daughter of the Earl of Shrewsbury, at Wilton House
(27 Dec.)	Philip Herbert marries Susan de Vere, daughter of the Earl of Oxford, at London
1605 (4 May)	Robert Sidney (d. 1626) created Viscount Lisle; Philip Herbert created Earl of Montgomery; Star Chamber rejects the claim on the estate of Robert Dudley, Earl of Leicester, made by his illegitimate son, Robert(o) Dudley
(Aug.)	Robert Sidney's vessel to Flushing blown off course and forced to moor at Gravelines (then under Spanish control)
(5 Nov.)	*discovery of the Gunpowder Plot*
1606 (Jun.–Jul.)	*visit to England of Queen Anne's brother, King Christian IV of Denmark*
1607 (27 Feb.)	Robert Sidney (d. 1677) matriculates with his brother William (d. 1612) from Christ Church, Oxford
1608 (Jan.)	Rowland Whyte describes the harsh winter conditions at Baynard's Castle, London
1609	*plantation of Ulster by English Protestants*
1610 (Jan.)	Prince Henry's Barriers, involving William and Philip Herbert
(14 May)	*assassination of King Henri IV of France and accession of King Louis XIII*
(2–5 Jun.)	*investiture of Prince Henry as Prince of Wales*; Robert Sidney (d. 1677) created a Knight of the Bath
1611 (?)	*publication of King James Bible*
(?)	Ben Jonson resident at Penshurst
1612 (24 May)	*death of Robert Cecil, Earl of Salisbury*
(6 Nov.)	*death of Prince Henry*; Sidney family deaths in 1612 include Roger Manners, Earl of Rutland (26 Jun.); Elizabeth Sidney Manners, Countess of Rutland (*c.* 1 Sept.); Sir Henry Sidney of Walsingham (2 Nov.), and William Sidney (3 Dec.), eldest son of Robert Sidney, Viscount Lisle

1613 (14 Feb.)   *marriage of Princess Elizabeth to Frederick V, Elector Palatine*
  (Apr.–Aug.) Robert Sidney, Viscount Lisle, escorts Princess Elizabeth to Germany; travels home with his son Robert (d. 1677), who is then commanding a military company at Flushing

1614 (Feb.)   birth of Lady Mary Wroth's only legitimate son, James (d. 1616)
  (14 Mar.)   death of Sir Robert Wroth
  (25 Jun.)   Mary Sidney Herbert, Dowager Countess of Pembroke, arrives at Flushing, and probably remains abroad until Dec. 1616

1615 (17 Oct.)   arrest of Robert Carr, Earl of Somerset, and his wife, Frances Howard, on suspicion of the murder of Sir Thomas Overbury
  (23 Dec.)   William Herbert, third Earl of Pembroke, appointed Lord Chamberlain

1616 (early)   Robert Sidney (d. 1677) marries Dorothy Percy (1598–1659), daughter of the Earl of Northumberland; the Sidneys' neighbor, Lady Anne Clifford, notes in her diary (Feb. 1616) that their union is "openly known" to their family circle; it does not become public knowledge until Mar. 1617
  (23 Apr.)   *death of William Shakespeare*
  (6/7 May)   Robert Sidney, Viscount Lisle, created a Knight of the Garter
  (30 May)   Robert Sidney, Viscount Lisle, accompanied by his son Robert, formally hands over Flushing to the Dutch
  (5 Jul.)   death of James Wroth, son of Mary Sidney Wroth
  (late?)   Mary Sidney Herbert, Dowager Countess of Pembroke, arrives back in England and receives by royal grant a life interest in Houghton Park, Bedfordshire, where she builds herself a new mansion

1617 (5 Jan.)   *George Villiers created Earl of Buckingham*
  (5 Oct.)   baptism of Dorothy Sidney (d. 1684), later Countess of Sunderland, the first child of Robert and Barbara Sidney
  (6 Nov.)   marriage of Lucy Percy (d. 1660) and James Hay (d. 1636), later Earl of Carlisle

1618 (1 Jan.)   *George Villiers created Marquis of Buckingham*
  (13 May)   *Defenestration of Prague, leading to initiation of the Thirty Years' War*
  (2 Aug.)   in a public ceremony, Robert Sidney (d. 1626) created first Earl of Leicester (after a private ceremony on 22 Jul.); Robert Sidney (d. 1677) succeeds his father as Viscount Lisle

1619 (10 Jan.)   birth of Philip Sidney (d. 1698), son of Robert and Dorothy Sidney, later third Earl of Leicester
  (3 Apr.)   marriage of Barbara Sidney (1599–1644) and Thomas Smythe (c.1599–1635), later Viscount Strangford
  (13 May)   Robert Sidney, Earl of Leicester, Mary Sidney Herbert, Dowager Countess of Pembroke, Dorothy Percy Sidney, Mary Sidney Wroth, and Philippa Sidney Hobart attend the funeral of Queen Anne (d. 2 Mar.), as do most of their male relatives
  (4 Nov.)   *Frederick Elector Palatine and Princess Elizabeth crowned King and Queen of Bohemia*

1619/20(?)   probable date of Lady Mary Wroth's *Love's Victory*

1620 (Aug.)   *Pilgrim Fathers sail in* Mayflower *for America*
   (8 Nov.)   *Battle of the White Mountain; Frederick and Elizabeth lose Bohemia*

1621 (21 Feb.)   christening of Philip Herbert (d. 1669), later fifth Earl of Pembroke
   (24(?) May)   death of Barbara Gamage Sidney, Countess of Leicester; buried at Penshurst (26 May)
   (25 Sept.)   Mary Sidney Herbert, Dowager Countess of Pembroke, dies from smallpox at her house in Aldergate Street, London; funeral at St. Paul's and burial at Salisbury Cathedral
   (?)   publication of Lady Mary Wroth's *The Countess of Montgomery's Urania* and poems *Pamphilia to Amphilanthus*; denounced by Edward Denny

1623 (14/15 Jan.)   birth of Algernon Sidney (executed 1683), son of Robert and Dorothy Sidney
   (18 May)   George Villiers created Duke of Buckingham
   (May)   Robert Sidney, first Earl of Leicester, transfers the Penshurst estate to his eldest son, Robert, later second Earl of Leicester
   (?)   First Folio of Shakespeare's plays dedicated to William Herbert, third Earl of Pembroke, and Philip Herbert, Earl of Montgomery

1624? (spring)   birth of William and Katherine, illegitimate children of William Herbert, third Earl of Pembroke, and Lady Mary Wroth
   (Nov.)   *marriage agreed between Prince Charles and the French Princess Henrietta Maria*

1625 (27 Mar.)   *death of King James I and accession of King Charles I; plague begins to spread across London and southern England*
   (1 May)   *King Charles I marries (by proxy) Henrietta Maria, daughter of King Henri IV of France*
   (18 June)   *King Charles I's First Parliament (18 Jun.–11 Jul., 1–12 Aug.); beginnings of war with Spain and disastrous English expedition to Cadiz (Oct.)*
   (Oct.)   King Charles I and Queen Henrietta Maria visit Wilton House
   (30 Nov.)   *Treaty of The Hague, under which England, the Palatinate, and the United Provinces form an alliance with King Christian IV of Denmark*

1626 (2 Feb.)   *coronation of King Charles I (delayed from Jan. due to plague)*
   (23 Feb.)   *impeachment of George Villiers, Duke of Buckingham, begins*
   (25 Apr.)   Robert Sidney, first Earl of Leicester, marries Sarah Blount Smythe (d. 1655), widow of Sir Thomas Smythe
   (15 Jun.)   *King Charles I dissolves Parliament and refuses to dismiss Buckingham*
   (13 Jul.)   death of Robert Sidney, first Earl of Leicester; buried at Penshurst on 16 Jul.; succeeded by his son, Robert Sidney, second Earl of Leicester
   (Aug.)   William Herbert, third Earl of Pembroke, appointed Lord Steward; his brother Philip, Earl of Montgomery, appointed Lord Chamberlain
   (19 Sept.)   christening of Robert Sidney (d. 1668), son of Robert and Barbara Sidney
   (Oct.)   King Charles I visits Wilton House

1627 (Jul.)   *expedition to La Rochelle and the isle of Rhé under Duke of Buckingham; the remnants of his defeated forces return to England (Oct.)*

1628 (7 Jun.)	*King Charles I accepts the Petition of Right, denying him the option of making forced loans and imprisonment at his personal command*
(23 Aug.)	*assassination of Duke of Buckingham*
(18 Oct.)	*fall of La Rochelle to King Louis XIII of France*
1628–29	*King Charles I's Third Parliament (17 Mar.–26 Jun. 1628, 20 Jan.–10 Mar. 1629)*
1629 (Jan.)	death of Susan Vere, the first wife of Philip Herbert, Earl of Montgomery
(10 Mar.)	*King Charles I dissolves Parliament and begins eleven years of personal rule*
(Apr.)	*peace with France through the Treaty of Susa*
1630 (10 Apr.)	death of William Herbert, third Earl of Pembroke
(29 May)	*birth of Prince Charles, later King Charles II (d. 1685)*
(3 Jun.)	Philip Herbert, fourth Earl of Pembroke, marries Lady Anne Clifford, widow of Richard Sackville, Earl of Dorset, and daughter of George Clifford, Earl of Cumberland; this union effectively breaks down in 1634
(5 Nov.)	*peace with Spain through the Treaty of Madrid*
1631 (17 Feb.)	funeral of Frances Walsingham/Sidney/Devereux/Burke, Countess of Essex and Clanricarde, widow of Sir Philip Sidney and Robert Devereux, Earl of Essex
1632 (Jan.)	*Viscount Wentworth appointed Lord Deputy of Ireland*
(Sept.–Nov.)	embassy of Robert Sidney, second Earl of Leicester, to Denmark, accompanied by his sons, Philip and Algernon
(late?)	Van Dyck commissioned to paint a series of Sidney and related family portraits
1633 (6 Aug.)	*William Laud appointed Archbishop of Canterbury*
(14 Oct.)	*birth of Prince James, later King James II (d. 1701)*
1635 (15 Mar.)	*Archbishop Laud appointed as First Lord of the Treasury*
(9 May)	*France declares war on Spain*
1636 (Apr.)	Robert Sidney, second Earl of Leicester, appointed ambassador extraordinary to France; leaves England on 7 May, accompanied by his sons, Philip and Algernon; arrives in Jun. and serves there until May 1641; his wife, Dorothy Percy Sidney, manages the Penshurst estate and the building of their London residence during his absences abroad
1637 (5 Feb.)	*Ferdinand III succeeds as Holy Roman Emperor after death of Ferdinand II*
1638 (1 Mar.)	*Scottish National Covenant signed at Edinburgh*
1639 (Feb.)	Robert Sidney, second Earl of Leicester, temporarily recalled from France (returned in Aug.) and sworn a Privy Councillor on 5 May. He is accompanied in France by his wife Dorothy Percy Sidney, Countess of Leicester, between Sept. 1639 and Oct. 1641
(11 Jul.)	Dorothy Sidney (1617–84) marries Henry Spencer (1620–43), later Earl of Sunderland, at Penshurst

1640	*King Charles I's "Short Parliament" (13 Apr.–5 May)*
	King Charles I's "Long Parliament" begins (30 Nov. 1640–20 Apr. 1653)
1641 (May)	Robert Sidney, second Earl of Leicester, and his sons, Philip and Algernon, recalled to England
(spring?)	birth of Henry Sidney (d. 1704), son of Robert and Dorothy Sidney, later Earl of Romney
(14 Jun.)	Robert Sidney, second Earl of Leicester, appointed Lord Lieutenant of Ireland (but he never travels there)
(Jul.)	Philip Herbert, fourth Earl of Pembroke and Montgomery, resigns as Lord Chamberlain
(Aug.)	Robert Sidney, second Earl of Leicester, briefly returns to France until early Oct.
(5 Sept.)	birth of Robert Spencer (d. 1702), son of Dorothy Sidney Spencer (d. 1684), later second Earl of Sunderland
(Oct.)	*rebellion in Ireland*
1642 (4 Jan.)	*King Charles I attempts to arrest the "five members" of Parliament and leaves London*; Robert Sidney, second Earl of Leicester, attempts to cross to Ireland, but is recalled by the king
(Apr.)	Philip and Algernon Sidney arrive in Ireland
(May–Jun.)	Robert Sidney, second Earl of Leicester, serves as temporary Speaker of the House of Lords and is appointed Lord Lieutenant for Kent (replaced in Aug.)
(Jun.–Jul.)	*King Charles I issues Commissions of Array, and the navy declares for Parliament*
(Oct.)	*Battle of Edgehill (indecisive)*
(Nov.)	*royalist forces advance to Turnham Green (parliamentarian victory)*
(Dec.)	*formation of the Eastern Association, a parliamentarian army drawn from forces in the east of England; commanded by Edward Montagu, second Earl of Manchester, and including an elite cavalry troop led by Oliver Cromwell (disbanded in early 1645 and incorporated into the New Model Army)*
1643 (Jan.)	Philip Herbert, fourth Earl of Pembroke and Montgomery, is one of the parliamentary commissioners sent to Oxford to offer peace propositions to King Charles I
(14 May)	*death of King Louis XIII and accession of King Louis XIV of France*
(22 Jun.)	Philip and Algernon Sidney leave Ireland
(15 Sept.)	*English royalists agree to a ceasefire in Ireland*
(20 Sept.)	death of Henry Spencer (b. 1620), first Earl of Sunderland, at the Battle of Newbury (indecisive)
(26 Sept.)	Penshurst sequestered by the Kent County Committee
(Nov.)	Robert Sidney, second Earl of Leicester, replaced as Lord Lieutenant of Ireland by Earl of Ormond; *the Scots agree to send an army to assist Parliament*
1644 (Jan.)	*royalist Parliament summoned at Oxford; Scottish army crosses into England to assist the Long Parliament*
(15 Apr.)	Algernon Sidney appointed colonel of a parliamentarian regiment of horse
(Jun.)	Robert Sidney, second Earl of Leicester, leaves royalist Oxford and retires to Penshurst

(2 Jul.)	Algernon Sidney serves as a parliamentarian cavalry officer at the Battle of Marston Moor (*parliamentarian victory*)
(Aug.)	*Battle of Lostwithiel (royalist victory)*
(Oct.)	*second Battle of Newbury (indecisive)*

1645 (Jan.–Feb.)	*Uxbridge peace negotiations between king and Parliament fail; Archbishop Laud executed (10 Jan.)*
(15 Feb.)	*creation by Parliament of New Model Army*
(18 Mar.)	Algernon Sidney appointed colonel in cavalry regiment of the New Model Army and Governor of Chichester (10 May)
(19 May)	marriage of Philip Sidney (1619–98), later third Earl of Leicester, and Catherine Cecil (d. 1652)
(Jun.)	*Battle of Naseby (parliamentarian victory)*

1646 (21 Jan.)	Algernon Sidney elected MP for Cardiff
(May)	*surrender of King Charles I to Scots*
(Jun.)	*Oxford surrenders to Parliament; end of the First Civil War*
(18 Nov.)	Philip Sidney, Viscount Lisle, appointed Lieutenant Governor of Ireland; Algernon Sidney appointed Governor of Dublin Castle

1647 (Jan.)	*Scots hand King Charles I over to Parliament*
(1 Feb.)	Philip and Algernon Sidney return to Ireland, but both soon lose their posts there
(Jun.)	*King Charles I seized by the army*
(Nov.)	*King Charles I escapes and flees to the Isle of Wight*; Algernon Sidney is involved in the negotiations with the king
(Dec.)	*King Charles I's "engagement" with the Scots is agreed, restoring Presbyterianism and abolishing episcopacy in Scotland; in return, the Scots agree to support the king's restoration*

1648 (Apr.–Aug.)	*Second Civil War*
(Jun.)	Algernon Sidney appointed Governor of Dover Castle (until May 1651)
(Jul.)	*Scottish invasion of England on behalf of King Charles I*
(Aug.)	*Battle of Preston; defeat of the Scots; end of Second Civil War*
(Sept.)	*Treaty of Newport; negotiations between the king and Parliament continue*
(Dec.)	*Colonel Pride's Purge of Parliament*
	Peace of Westphalia (a series of treaties signed during 1648) brings the end of the Thirty Years' War

1649 (30 Jan.)	*execution of King Charles I*; described by Algernon Sidney as "the justest and bravest act … that ever was done in England or anywhere" (BL Add. MS 32680/9–10); watched from a nearby window by Philip Herbert, fourth Earl of Pembroke and Montgomery
(14 Feb.)	*Council of State set up (dissolved 20 Apr. 1653)*, with Philip Herbert, fourth Earl of Pembroke and Montgomery, as one of its five peers; *Charles II declared king in Edinburgh*
(14 Mar.)	death at Leicester House of Harry Spencer (b. 1643), son of Dorothy Sidney Spencer, Countess of Sunderland

(15 Mar.)	Lucy Percy Hay, Countess of Carlisle and sister of Dorothy Percy Sidney, Countess of Leicester, imprisoned in the Tower of London (released 1 Oct. 1650)
(16 Mar.)	*kingship abolished*
(9 Apr.)	*birth of Prince James (illegitimate), later Duke of Monmouth*
(May)	*England declared a free commonwealth*
(14 Jun.)	two of the royal children, Prince Henry, Duke of Gloucester, and Princess Elizabeth, are lodged at Penshurst (until 9 Aug. 1650) having previously been in the charge of Algernon Percy, tenth Earl of Northumberland
(Dec.)	Robert Sidney, second Earl of Leicester, accepts wardship of his nephew, Philip Smythe, Viscount Strangford
(?)	birth of Robert Sidney (d. 1702), later Viscount Lisle and fourth Earl of Leicester

1650 (23 Jan.)	death of Philip Herbert, fourth Earl of Pembroke and Montgomery
(22 Aug.)	marriage at Penshurst of Isabella Sidney (b. 1634), daughter of Robert and Dorothy Sidney, to her cousin Philip Smythe, Viscount Strangford

1651 (Jan.)	*Charles II crowned King of Scots at Scone*
(Mar.?)	death of Lady Mary Wroth
(Aug.)	*Oliver Cromwell captures Perth, and Stirling Castle surrenders to the English; Scottish army crosses into England*
(3 Sept.)	*Battle of Worcester; defeat of Charles II, leading to his flight to France (Oct.)*
(1 Dec.)	Philip Herbert, fifth Earl of Pembroke, elected to the Council of State

1652 (Jan.)	the "Countess of Leicester's Case," concerning Princess Elizabeth's jewels
(May)	*war breaks out between England and the United Provinces over trade disputes; Battle of the Downs*
(8 Jul.)	Dorothy Sidney Spencer, Countess of Sunderland, marries Robert Smythe at Penshurst
(18 Aug.)	death of Catherine Cecil Sidney, wife of Philip Sidney (1619–98), later third Earl of Leicester, triggers a bitter and long-running quarrel with his father over his allowances; in December he strikes his father during an argument
(Nov.)	Algernon Sidney elected to Council of State

1653 (20 Apr.)	*Long Parliament dissolved*
(29 Apr.)	*another Council of State set up;* Philip Sidney, later third Earl of Leicester, serves as its president
(4 Jul.)	*Little (or "Barebones") Parliament (dissolved 12 Dec.)*
(28 Sept.)	Philip Smythe, Viscount Strangford, revokes Robert Sidney's title to his guardianship and institutes legal proceedings against him
(16 Dec.)	*Oliver Cromwell invested as Lord Protector*

1654–59	*the Parliaments of the Protectorate (3 Sept. 1654–22 Jan. 1655, 17 Sept. 1656–26 Jun. 1657, 27 Jan.–22 Apr. 1659)*

1654 (Apr.)	*Union of Scotland and England formally proclaimed; peace agreed with the United Provinces*

1655 (Mar.)	*royalist uprising in Wiltshire suppressed*
(May)	*rebellion in Scotland ended; Cromwell's expedition to the West Indies and the capture of Jamaica*
1656 (Jun.)	Philip Sidney, later third Earl of Leicester, prominent in the ceremony marking the second installation of Oliver Cromwell as Protector
1657 (Mar.)	*offensive alliance between England and France against Spain*
1658 (Feb.)	Robert Sidney, second Earl of Leicester, planning to live apart from his wife Dorothy, but she falls terminally ill
(Jun.)	*English forces defeat Spanish army, and Dunkirk is handed over to England*
(3 Sept.)	*death of Oliver Cromwell; succeeded by his son, Richard Cromwell*
1658–64	Henry Sidney, later Earl of Romney, and his nephew, Robert Spencer, later Earl of Sunderland, travel on the Continent, with only brief visits back to England
1659	*"Rump" Parliament begins (7 May–13 Oct., 26 Dec. 1659–16 Mar. 1660)*
(24 May)	*Richard Cromwell abdicates as Lord Protector*
(10 Jul.)	Dorothy Percy Sidney, Countess of Leicester, makes her will
(20 Jul.)	Algernon Sidney arrives in Elsinore, Denmark, on official embassy
(20 Aug.)	death of Dorothy Percy Sidney, Countess of Leicester; buried 23 Aug. at Penshurst
1660 (29 May)	*accession of King Charles II*; Algernon Sidney remains abroad, living at Hamburg and then in Italy (until *c.* 1663), then Geneva, Brussels, the United Provinces, Rotterdam, and Montpellier; he also travels widely in France during the 1670s, and finally retires to Nérac in Gascony *Convention Parliament (25 Apr.–13 Sept., 6 Nov.–29 Dec. 1660)*
(31 May)	Robert Sidney, second Earl of Leicester, named as a Privy Councillor
(Oct.)	Robert Sidney, second Earl of Leicester, retires to Penshurst because of ill health; his son, Philip, formerly a prominent supporter of Cromwell, is granted a pardon under the Great Seal (30 Oct.)
(5 Nov.)	death of Lucy Percy Hay, Countess of Carlisle
1661 (23 Apr.)	*Coronation of King Charles II*; Philip Herbert, fifth Earl of Pembroke, carries the spurs (as his father had done at coronation of King Charles I)
(31 May)	Robert Sidney, second Earl of Leicester, named as a Privy Councillor; but soon claims ill health and withdraws to Penshurst
1662 (21 May)	*King Charles II marries Catherine of Braganza*
1665 (?)	Robert Spencer, second Earl of Sunderland, marries Anne, daughter of George Digby, Earl of Bristol, and takes up residence at his family seat, Althorp
1666 (2 Sept.)	*Great Fire of London, which largely destroys Baynard's Castle*
1669 (11 Dec.)	death of Philip Herbert, fifth Earl of Pembroke

1674 (1 Aug.)	death of William Herbert (b. 1640), sixth Earl of Pembroke
1675 (Jul.)	Henry Sidney purchases the position at court of Master of the Robes
1676 (?)	birth of Philip Sidney (d. 1705), later Viscount Lisle and fifth Earl of Leicester
1677 (early Sept.)	Algernon Sidney returns to England to visit his ailing father
(2 Nov.)	death of Robert Sidney, second Earl of Leicester, succeeded by his son, Philip (d. 1698), as third Earl
(4 Nov.)	*Mary Stuart marries William of Orange (grandson of King Charles I)*
1678 (May)	Henry Sidney, later Earl of Romney, leads as colonel an infantry regiment to Flanders and begins long friendship with William, Prince of Orange
(Sept.)	*discovery of the "Popish Plot" to murder King Charles II*
1679–81	*Exclusion Crisis, seeking to exclude Charles II's Catholic brother James, Duke of York, from the English throne*
1680 (18 Aug.)	William Herbert, seventh Earl of Pembroke, kills an officer of the watch; found guilty of murder (21 Jun. 1681), but granted a royal pardon
(?)	birth of John Sidney (d. 1737), later Viscount Lisle and sixth Earl of Leicester
1682	birth of Jocelyn Sidney (d. 1743), later Viscount Lisle and seventh Earl of Leicester
1683 (29 Aug.)	death of Philip Herbert (b. 1653), seventh Earl of Pembroke; buried at Salisbury Cathedral (10 Sept.); succeeded by his younger brother, Thomas Herbert (1656/57–1733), as eighth Earl of Pembroke, who later enjoys an illustrious political career serving King William III as First Lord of the Admiralty, Lord Privy Seal, and Lord President of the Council
(7 Dec.)	execution of Algernon Sidney for complicity in Rye House Conspiracy; his brother Henry Sidney is allowed to arrange for his funeral at Penshurst and to claim his estate
1685 (6 Feb.)	*death of King Charles II and accession of King James II (d. 1701)*
(15 Jul.)	*execution of James, Duke of Monmouth;* Robert Spencer, second Earl of Sunderland, presides over the brutal legal suppression of this rebellion
(Nov.)	Henry Sidney leaves for the Continent and travels abroad during the next two years, remaining close to William, Prince of Orange, as he decides to take the English throne
1688 (10 Jun.)	birth of Prince James (d. 1766), the "Old Pretender," son of King James II and Queen Mary of Modena
(30 Jun.)	a letter, perhaps drafted by Henry Sidney and signed by him and six others, invites William, Prince of Orange, to take the English throne; Henry Sidney meets the Prince at Aix-la-Chapelle (Aug.)
(5 Nov.)	William of Orange lands at Torbay, accompanied by Henry Sidney; Robert Spencer, second Earl of Sunderland, flees first to France and then Rotterdam
(11 Dec.)	*King James II flees from England*

1689 (13 Feb.)   *accession of King William III and Queen Mary II supported by Henry Sidney, later Earl of Romney*

    (9 Apr.)   *coronation of King William III*; Henry Sidney created Baron Milton and Viscount Sidney of Sheppey; then appointed a Privy Councillor, First Gentleman of the Bedchamber, Lord Lieutenant of Kent, Warden of the Cinque Ports, and Constable of Dover Castle

1690 (Apr.)   Robert Spencer, second Earl of Sunderland, and his wife return to England and retire to their Althorp estate

    (1 Jul.)   *King William III defeats James II at the Battle of the Boyne*; Henry Sidney serves with distinction in this conflict and during the Siege of Limerick (Aug.–Sept.)

1691 (May)   Henry Sidney named as overall commander of all foot regiments during the king's absence in Flanders

1692 (Mar.)   Henry Sidney appointed Lord Lieutenant of Ireland; arrives in Aug. and is recalled in late spring 1693

1693 (28 Jul.)   Henry Sidney appointed Master-General of the Ordnance

1694 (14 May)   Henry Sidney (1641–1704) promoted to Lieutenant-General and created Earl of Romney

    (28 Dec.)   *death of Queen Mary II*

1697 (19 Apr.)   Robert Spencer, second Earl of Sunderland, appointed as Lord Chamberlain

    (22 Apr.)   Henry Sidney and Robert Spencer both named among the justices to govern the country during the king's absences abroad

1701 (12 Jun.)   *Act of Settlement establishes right of the House of Hanover to the English throne*

    (6 Sept.)   *death of King James II*

1702 (8 Mar.)   *death of King William III and accession of Queen Anne (d. 1714)*

    (28 Sept.)   death of Robert Spencer, second Earl of Sunderland

1704 (8 Apr.)   death of Henry Sidney, Earl of Romney, son of Robert and Dorothy Sidney

The Sidney Family Tree

Sir William Sidney (1482–1554) = Anne Pagenham (d. 1543)

Sir Henry Sidney (1529–86) = Mary Dudley (1531–86)

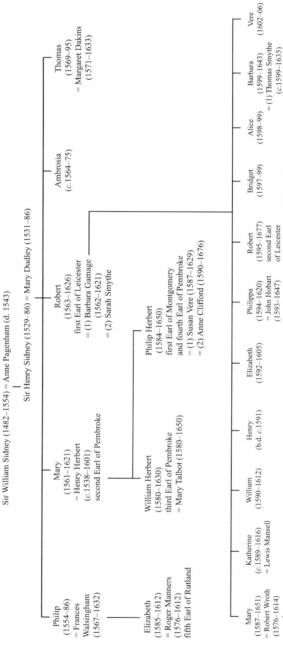

Philip (1554–86)
= Frances Walsingham (1567–1632)

Mary (1561–1621)
= Henry Herbert (c.1538–1601) second Earl of Pembroke

Robert (1563–1626) first Earl of Leicester
= (1) Barbara Gamage (1562–1621)
= (2) Sarah Smythe

Ambrosia (c.1564–75)

Thomas (1569–95)
= Margaret Dakins (1571–1633)

Elizabeth (1585–1612)
= Roger Manners (1576–1612) fifth Earl of Rutland

William Herbert (1580–1630) third Earl of Pembroke
= Mary Talbot (1580–1650)

Philip Herbert (1584–1650) first Earl of Montgomery and fourth Earl of Pembroke
= (1) Susan Vere (1587–1629)
= (2) Anne Clifford (1590–1676)

Mary (1587–1651)
= Robert Wroth (1576–1614)
(1) James (1614–16)
(2) William and Katherine (b. c.1624) by William Herbert, third Earl of Pembroke

Katherine (c.1589–1616)
= Lewis Mansell

William (1590–1612)

Henry (b.d. c.1591)

Elizabeth (1592–1605)

Philippa (1594–1620)
= John Hobart (1593–1647)

Robert (1595–1677) second Earl of Leicester
= Dorothy Percy (1598–1659)

Bridget (1597–99)

Alice (1598–99)

Barbara (1599–1643)
= (1) Thomas Smythe (c.1599–1635)
= (2) Thomas Colepeper (1598–1643)

Vere (1602–06)

Barbara

Dorothy

Philip

Thomas

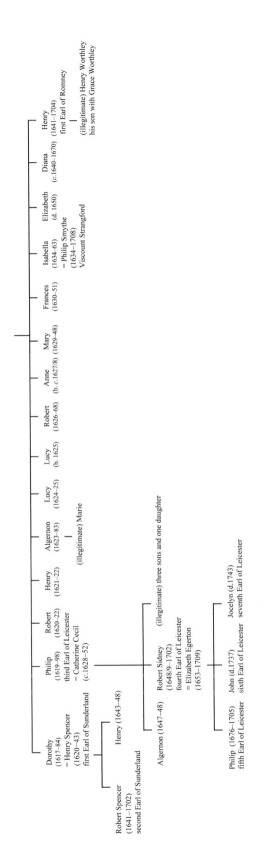

The Sidney Family Tree

PART I
Overview

Family Networks:
The Sidneys, Dudleys, and Herberts

Michael G. Brennan

Pre-1580

Between 1500 and 1700 the Sidneys cultivated contacts with numerous influential English families, including the Brandons, Dudleys, Cecils, Herberts, Walsinghams, and Percys. Frequently, it was these close familial links, confirmed through marital unions, which supported the Sidneys' rise into important court and county positions. For example, the early court prominence of Sir William Sidney (c. 1482–1554), owed much to his family connections with the influential Brandons through his mother, Anne Brandon, the aunt of Charles Brandon (c. 1484–1545). Sidney and Brandon often jousted together in royal tournaments, and the latter's friendship with the king led to his creation in 1514 as Duke of Suffolk. In the following year he became the king's brother-in-law when he married Henry's sister Mary, the widow of King Louis XII of France (from whom the Sidneys derived their porcupine family crest). Sir William Sidney continued to prosper at the Henrician court, in 1538 becoming chamberlain to the household of the king's infant son and heir, Prince Edward, with his wife, Anne, serving as the prince's governess and his sister-in-law, Sybil Penne, as dry-nurse (Brennan, *Sidneys of Penshurst* 13–20).

From the mid-sixteenth century onwards no family was more important to the Sidneys, apart perhaps from the Dudleys, than the Welsh Herberts, Earls of Pembroke; their London mansion, Baynard's Castle, a late medieval castellated mansion on the north bank of the Thames near Blackfriars and St. Paul's, came to play a central role in the history of the Tudor and Stuart Sidneys (Illustrations 1 and 2). In 1546 William Herbert, the brother-in-law of Queen Catherine Parr, and from October 1551 first Earl of Pembroke, was appointed as its keeper. After Henry VIII's death, Baynard's Castle came permanently into his possession, and he built a large extension to the property during the 1550s. From then until the 1640s it served as the Herberts' main London residence. After the marriage on 21 April 1577 of his son Henry, second Earl of Pembroke, to Sir Henry Sidney's daughter Mary (Illustrations 5 and 9), the Sidneys also frequently used Baynard's Castle as their family base in London until the completion of their own mansion, Leicester House (Illustration 31), in the 1630s (Collins 1:82; TNA PROB 11/36).

On 29 March 1551 Henry Sidney married Mary Dudley, the daughter of John Dudley, Earl of Warwick, and sister of Robert and Ambrose Dudley (later Earls of Leicester and Warwick). On 11 October 1552 Sidney was knighted, and this day also saw the creations of his father-in-law, John Dudley, as Duke of Northumberland and William Herbert as Earl of Pembroke (*CSPD 1547–80* 35). Through his family connection with Henry VIII's final marriage, William Herbert now outranked both Sir William Sidney and his son, Henry. But the personal connections between the Sidneys and the Earl of Pembroke remained strong and friendly enough to ensure that a decade later the Earl of Pembroke was named as godfather to Sir Henry's and Lady Mary's eldest surviving daughter, Mary (Illustrations 9 and 10), after her birth on 27 October 1561 (Hannay, *Philip's Phoenix* 15). The consecutive presidencies of the Council of Wales held by the Herberts and Sidneys also contributed to the sustained bonding between these two families during Queen Elizabeth's reign since the first Earl of Pembroke served two terms as president (1550–53, 1555–58), followed by Sir Henry Sidney (1560–86) and then the second Earl of Pembroke (1586–1601). The marriage on 21 April 1577 of the fifteen-year-old Mary Sidney to the almost forty-year-old Henry Herbert, second Earl of Pembroke, provided public confirmation of the now well-established links between the two families which were to last until the 1650s and often revolved around convivial or political meetings at the Herbert residences, Baynard's Castle and Wilton House near Salisbury, and the Sidneys' at Penshurst (Illustrations 3, 4, 29, and 30).

In August 1577 Sir Henry Sidney's secretary, Edmund Waterhouse, visited Wilton and found Philip and Robert Sidney staying with their sister and her new husband (Collins 1:209). The Sidneys' closest family associates, Robert and Ambrose Dudley, Earls of Leicester and Warwick, were also regular guests at Wilton. In the previous June they had both stayed there with the Earl and Countess of Pembroke, prior to Leicester and Pembroke's heading off together to the spa at Buxton (Collins 1:191; HMC, *Salisbury* 2:154). In late 1578 various members of the Herbert, Sidney, and Dudley families again assembled at Wilton House for a protracted celebration of Mary's seventeenth birthday (Wright 2:95). During the same period Sir Henry Sidney stayed at Baynard's Castle and then visited Wilton in January 1579 after his wife Lady Mary and son Philip had accompanied the Earl and Countess of Pembroke to the court at Richmond to exchange New Year gifts with the queen (Nichols 2:265, 268–71). In the following February and March Sir Henry Sidney was back at Baynard's Castle, where his son Robert (Illustrations 13, 14, and 15) also came to stay on vacation from Oxford (HMC, *De L'Isle and Dudley* 1:267). In April the Earl and Countess of Pembroke traveled with Philip Sidney to Penshurst, and in June Philip went to stay at Wilton (*Philip's Phoenix* 42). Finally, as anxieties grew within Leicester's Protestant faction over the proposed marriage between Queen Elizabeth and the Duke of Anjou, on 25 August 1579 the Spanish ambassador reported that Leicester, Sir Henry Sidney, and other associates had secretly assembled at the Earl of Pembroke's "London house" (that is, Baynard's Castle), when the genesis of Philip Sidney's "A Letter to Queen Elizabeth" may have been first discussed (*CSPS* 2:695). Court suspicions over Sir Henry Sidney's recurrent visits to the Herberts' residences were such that by June 1580 Sir Francis Walsingham was obliged to advise him that the queen "hath commanded me to recommend unto your Lordship the more earnestly, for that she is given to understand, that your Lordship doth sometime resort to Wilton; which … she somewhat misliketh" (Collins 2:274).

1580–1603

Family christenings and marriages during the 1580s provided less controversial opportunities for the Sidneys, Herberts, and Dudleys to enjoy one another's company. The Pembrokes' first son, William (Illustrations 20 and 21), was born on 8 April 1580, and so named after his grandfather, William Herbert, and great–grandfather, Sir William Sidney. At the christening, held at Wilton on 28 April, Queen Elizabeth and the Earls of Leicester and Warwick were named as godparents, with the Countess of Warwick standing as proxy for the queen and Philip Sidney (Illustration 7) for his uncle Leicester. When some eighteen months later the Countess of Pembroke gave birth to a daughter, Katherine, Sir Henry Sidney stood as godparent, and after the birth of her second daughter, Anne, in spring 1583 the Countesses of Warwick and Talbot (Henry Herbert's widowed sister) were named as godparents (*Philip's Phoenix* 50–52). Similarly, the marriage of Robert Sidney (Illustrations 13, 14 and 15) to Barbara Gamage (Illustrations 17 and 18), a rich Welsh heiress, on 23 September 1584 was actively promoted not only by his father, but also by Henry Herbert, second Earl of Pembroke, who attended the wedding at St. Donat's. Without Pembroke's influence, this highly advantageous union would probably not have taken place. It proved a crucial factor in the fortunes of the Sidneys, since not only was Barbara a loving and supportive wife, but also her fortune provided "approximately half of the Sidneys' income throughout their lives" (CKS U1475 T327/8; *DPFA* 1–2; Hannay, *MSLW* 9–11). Soon after his marriage the twenty-one-year-old Robert Sidney was elected as a Member of Parliament (MP) for Glamorganshire, another clear indication of the influence of both his father, who was then Lord President of Wales, and his brother-in-law, the Earl of Pembroke (Hay 42–3). The Countess of Pembroke had not attended this wedding because she was then eight months pregnant. On 16 October 1584 she gave birth to her second son, Philip, later Earl of Montgomery and fourth Earl of Pembroke (Illustrations 20 and 22), whose godparents were his grandmother Lady Sidney and his uncles, Sir Philip and Robert Sidney. On the same day the Herberts and Sidneys would also have been united in their grief for the death of her little daughter Katherine (*Philip's Phoenix* 55).

The successive deaths in 1586 of Sir Henry Sidney (5 May), Lady Mary Sidney (9 August) and Sir Philip (17 October) drew the Countess of Pembroke, her husband, and her brother Robert even closer together. Pembroke succeeded Sir Henry Sidney as Lord President of Wales, and Robert soon came to regard his much older brother-in-law as a surrogate father-figure—a sentiment bolstered by the deaths of his Dudley uncles, Leicester and Warwick, in 1588 and 1590. The Herberts allowed Robert and Barbara Sidney to use Baynard's Castle as their regular London base, and from the late 1580s they and their growing family were often in residence there, especially during the autumn, winter, and early spring seasons. Their first child, Mary (so named after her aunt and godmother, the Countess of Pembroke. Illustration 17), was probably born there on 18 October 1587 and christened in the Great Hall of Baynard's Castle, as were Alice (b. 1598) and Barbara (b. 1599). The midwifery support at Baynard's Castle was clearly superior to anything available at Penshurst since Robert's most trusted family servant and friend, Rowland Whyte, noted in a letter of 13 October 1599 that he had just left the heavily pregnant Barbara at Penshurst, but that she was "now resolved to be brought to bed in Baynard's Castle" (352; *MSLW* 20). The very first surviving letter in a series of over three hundred from Robert to Barbara, dated 26 April 1588, was also sent from Baynard's Castle; and their son, Robert (later second Earl of Leicester), was born there *c.* 1 December 1595, when his mother Barbara was resident there with their three eldest children, Mary, William, and Katherine (102; *DPFA* 23, 79). In late May 1588 Barbara was staying with the Countess of Pembroke and her brother, Thomas Sidney, at her rural retreat of Ivychurch, Wiltshire, and as the Armada crisis escalated in the following July, Barbara and her household were evacuated from Penshurst to Wilton, where they stayed until mid-September, since it was assumed that a successful Spanish invasion would rapidly overrun most of Kent (*DPFA* 23–8).

During the 1590s Rowland Whyte (whose grandfather had been in the service of William Herbert, first Earl of Pembroke) was also often at Baynard's Castle, and provided another valuable link with the Herberts (Illustration 16). On 25 November 1595 Whyte reported to Robert that his wife Barbara had been staying with the Earl of Pembroke at Baynard's Castle and had been at court lobbying for her husband to be allowed some home leave from Flushing (94–5). On 19 March 1597 Whyte recorded how he had taken a boat from court directly to Baynard's Castle (177), and his letters contain various references to the Countess of Pembroke's ordering rooms to be made available for Robert (274, 305–8). The huge size of Baynard's Castle meant that Robert could have his whole family staying with him there, as Whyte's comment of 10 March 1598 makes clear: "I do prepare Baynard's Castle for you, where you shall have all the rooms upon the waterside for my Lady and the children" (310).

Whyte also kept Robert Sidney fully briefed on the various marriage plans for the Countess of Pembroke's eldest son, William Herbert (Illustrations 20 and 21). On 15 October 1595 he reported plans to marry William to Elizabeth Carey, the daughter of Lord and Lady Hunsdon. There had apparently been some secret meetings at Wilton House, although by 22 November Whyte noted that these match-making plans had come to nothing, as did later plans for a match with Bridget de Vere and Elizabeth Cecil Hatton (Whyte 60–63, 87–9). In the same November letter he also advised Robert Sidney that William's father, Henry, second Earl of Pembroke, had reputedly fallen out with the Earl of Essex—a worrying state of affairs since both men were influential court allies for Sidney. By 1597 the Earl of Pembroke's health was steadily declining, and Robert Sidney began to hope for his (and his late father's) post as Lord President of Wales, not least as a means of extricating himself from his hated Flushing governorship.

Robert's relationship with his nephew, William Herbert, grew steadily more important as Pembroke's health continued to deteriorate. In April 1599 Sidney unsuccessfully requested permission from Robert Cecil to return from Flushing to be with his brother-in-law (HMC, *Salisbury* 9:141–2). Pembroke's eldest son and heir, William, was also beginning to prepare for his future role as his father's heir, following a formal invitation from the queen in July to attend her court, to which his mother, the Countess of Pembroke, sent a profusely grateful reply (*Philip's Phoenix* 163; MSH, *Collected Works* 1:290–92). At first, he focused on obtaining some military experience, and on 4 August 1599 Whyte reported that he has been asked by young William to see if Robert could loan him any armor or pistols, since he was resolved to "follow the camp." On 11 August he passed on another such request, this time for any spare armor or weapons which Robert had stored at Baynard's Castle (312–13, 315–17). Whyte was closely monitoring William's progress at court since it was now clear that he would soon inherit his father's title and could eventually prove a valuable personal ally for the Sidneys. Writing from Baynard's Castle on 8 September 1599, Whyte advised Robert that the Earl of Pembroke's health was still failing, and "My Lord Herbert is a continual courtier, but doth not follow his business with that care as is fit. He is too cold in a matter of such greatness." On 12 September Whyte gloomily commented: "he is much blamed for his cold and weak manner of pursuing her Majesty's favour, having had so good steps, to lead him unto it. There is want of spirit and courage laid to his charge, that he is a melancholy young man" (327–33). Happily, by 24 November 1599 Whyte was able to report to Sidney that William Herbert was now "exceedingly beloved at court of all men" (379–80). Despite these public vicissitudes, a friendly intimacy between Robert Sidney and William continued to develop, and on 30 October 1600 Whyte advised Robert that his nephew "means to be exceeding merry with you this winter in Baynard's Castle, where you must take physic" (550–52).

Henry Herbert, second Earl of Pembroke, died on 19 January 1601, when Robert Sidney had already left Baynard's Castle to stay with his sister at Wilton. He wrote to Robert Cecil about his grief for the man "to whom of all men (my father and mine elder brother excepted) I have been most bound unto" (HMC, *Salisbury* 9:13). Family problems mounted when in February William Herbert, now third Earl of Pembroke, admitted that he had made pregnant a court lady, Mary Fitton, whom he had met in June 1600 at the wedding of his cousin Henry Somerset, Lord Herbert. Her father, Sir Edward Fitton, was a former Vice-Treasurer in Ireland under the command of Sir Henry Sidney, who had knighted him in 1566. William flatly refused to marry her, and in late March the outraged queen ordered his incarceration in the Fleet Prison, where he lingered until his release on 26 April, followed by his banishment from the court, first to Baynard's Castle and then to Wilton House (*Philip's Phoenix* 160–61; *MSLW* 79–83).

The new Earl of Pembroke's personal disgrace with the queen did not seem to inhibit his ongoing intimacy with his Sidney relatives. From the late 1590s the Sidney family was ever more frequently based at Baynard's Castle, especially when Robert was away at Flushing (August 1599–October 1600; August–September 1601, and August–October 1602). From at least 1599 Rowland Whyte also had accommodation there, from where his letters to Robert were often sent at this period. Even when he was away attending court, as on 1 March 1599, Whyte took care to reassure his master: "My Lady and all your sweet creatures are in good health at Baynard's Castle" (433–5). While still barred from court in December 1602, Pembroke joined Robert Sidney for Christmas revels on the estate of Sir John Harington at Exton (552–3). Robert Sidney's last known letter to his wife during Queen Elizabeth's reign, dated 12 January 1603, refers to him traveling back with William Herbert to Baynard's Castle so that they can meet up again with her and the children (*DPFA* 114). The queen's death on 24 March 1603 effectively marked the end of William Herbert's banishment from the royal court. At the state funeral, also attended by his mother, the dowager countess, his brother Philip carried the standard of the Greyhound and, with Thomas Lord Howard, William carried the great banner of England (Nichols 3:620–26; *Philip's Phoenix* 171–2).

1603–1625

Both the Sidneys and the Herberts, now firmly associated through close bonds of personal friendship and shared political interest, assiduously cultivated the personal favor of King James and Queen Anne during the early years of the new regime. Robert had personally known King James VI since 1588, and both the Earl of Pembroke (now aged twenty-three) and his brother Philip (aged nineteen), as well as their sister Anne, joined the huge entourage of courtiers heading northwards to escort the new king and queen to London (*Philip's Phoenix* 180). The Sidneys and the Herberts were rapidly rewarded with personal honors. In May 1603 Robert Sidney was appointed as Queen Anne's Lord Chamberlain (and in November, Surveyor of the Queen's Revenues), while the Earl of Pembroke and his brother Philip became Gentlemen of the Privy Chamber. In July Philip was created a Knight of the Bath and William Herbert was invested, along with Prince Henry as a Knight of the Garter. This last honor, also attended by the dowager countess and her daughter Anne, marked a signal favor from the new Stuart monarchy for the Earl of Pembroke, and it would be another thirteen years before his uncle, Robert Sidney, achieved the same court status (Nichols 1:193–5). London was hit by an outbreak of the plague in late summer 1603, and a western progress was hastily arranged for the royal family, taking in the Herberts' Wiltshire residence at Wilton House. The royal entourage stayed there on 29–30 August, 6 and 20–24 October, and again in early December, when the King's Men (formerly Shakespeare's company, the Lord Chamberlain's) reputedly traveled from Surrey to Wiltshire to perform before the court for a fee of £50 (*Philip's Phoenix* 187; *Sidneys of Penshurst* 114–15). By the Christmas and New Year season of 1603–04 both the Sidneys and the Herberts had secured for themselves a genuinely friendly and trusting intimacy with King James and Queen Anne.

Participation in court entertainments provided the Sidneys and Herberts with a congenial (if expensive) means of consolidating their personal contacts with the royal family. A masque "brought in by a magician of China" was staged at court on 1 January 1604, with the Earl of Pembroke as a masquer. He also played a prominent role in the ceremonial presentation to

James of a jewel reputedly worth £40,000 as an expression of England's loyal allegiance to the new king. His handsome younger brother Philip (Illustration 22) made an even stronger impression on James, bearing the device of "a fair colt in a fair green field" like Bucephalus, who could be mounted only by "one as great" as Alexander. The Sidneys' eldest daughter, Mary (Illustrations 18 and 19), had pleased the aged Queen Elizabeth with her dancing in December 1602, and it was now the turn of both Robert (Queen Anne's Lord Chamberlain) and his nephew Pembroke to perform as invited dancers in Samuel Daniel's *Vision of the Twelve Goddesses*.

In the latter part of 1604 the first of three key marriages was celebrated, which also served to draw the Sidneys and Herberts ever more closely into the royal circle. From July until October the dowager countess and her daughter Anne were frequently at Penshurst with Barbara Sidney while her husband Robert and his nephew Pembroke were on progress with the court (CKS C81/108, 115). On 27 September Robert's daughter Mary married Sir Robert Wroth, one of the king's favored hunting companions, who had been knighted following the accession. On 4 November 1604, at Wilton, the Earl of Pembroke married Mary (d. 1650), daughter of Gilbert Talbot, Earl of Shrewsbury. In subsequent years she enjoyed autumn visits to Penshurst to stay with Barbara Sidney and her children, and was recorded there in September 1606 and 1607 (Lambeth Palace MS 3202/101 and 3205/110; *Philip's Phoenix* 271; *MSLW* 96–7). Pembroke's younger brother, Philip, completed the family's marital unions by his marriage on 27 December to Susan, daughter of Edward de Vere, Earl of Oxford, and his wife Anne Cecil (Burghley's daughter, who had once been considered as a spouse for Philip Sidney). The Sidneys, including Lady Wroth, stayed at Baynard's Castle for the wedding, and James I gave the bride £500 in land and the bridegroom £1,000. Susan de Vere had danced in the *Vision of the Twelve Goddesses*, and the wedding celebrations, including a three-hour masque in which the Earl of Pembroke took the role of principal masquer, culminated with the arrival on the following morning of the king himself in the marital bedroom to offer his congratulations to the couple. He was now so informally at ease with the Herbert brothers that Dudley Carleton reported James's wry comment that if he had not already been married he would have kept the bride for himself. It also seems (with Robert Sidney's active connivance) that just as Philip Herbert had rapidly caught the eye of King James I, so his elder brother Pembroke had successfully endeared himself in Queen Anne's affections (Carleton 66–9; *Sidneys of Penshurst* 116; *MSLW* 103).

The still rising pre-eminence of the Sidneys and Herberts at the Jacobean court was confirmed when on the same day, 4 May 1605, Robert Sidney was raised to the title of Viscount Lisle (Illustration 15) and Philip Herbert was created Baron of Shurland and Earl of Montgomery. Their good fortune during the next decade continued to be given public expression through the medium of court entertainments. The cast-list of the *Masque of Blackness* by Ben Jonson and Inigo Jones, staged at the Whitehall Banqueting House on 6 January 1605, illustrates the Sidneys' and Herberts' diligent participation in these lavish events in which the queen took such delight. Staying again at Baynard's Castle and with her father in the audience as Lord Chamberlain, Mary Sidney Wroth danced the role of Baryte, along with Susan, the wife of Philip Herbert, her cousin Lady Anne Herbert (William's and Philip's sister), and Lucy Harington Russell, Countess of Bedford, who was to become a close friend of Philip's elder brother, the Earl of Pembroke. Similarly, 1606 began with the Earl of Montgomery dancing in Jonson's *Hymenaei*, staged to celebrate the marriage of Robert Devereux (now restored to his Essex earldom) to Lady Frances Howard, the daughter of the Earl of Suffolk. In late June Queen Anne's brother, Christian IV of Denmark, visited England and was entertained by a wide array of often riotous festivities, most of which Robert Sidney was obliged to attend in an official capacity. In early July military tilts were held in Christian's honor at Greenwich Park, with the Earls of Pembroke and Montgomery taking two of the four lead roles in an elaborate chivalric event, "Four Knights Errant Dominated by the Fortunate Islands" (*Sidneys of Penshurst* 118–19; *MSLW* 124–9).

In stark contrast to the joyful festivities of court entertainments, King James and Queen Anne were also drawn closer to Robert and Barbara Sidney at this period by their shared bereavements over the deaths of their respective children. By 1607 the Sidneys had lost as infants Henry, Elizabeth, Bridget, Alice and Vere and the royal couple had lost Margaret, Robert, Mary and Sophia. James and Anne found these losses so traumatic that they could not bring themselves to attend their children's funerals—a duty shouldered instead by the queen's Lord Chamberlain, Robert Sidney. In 1607 he was obliged to attend the autopsy of Princess Mary and to supervise her funeral arrangements, and Robert described these mournful duties to his wife Barbara in a letter of 19 September written from Baynard's Castle (*DPFA* 126–7). Several of his other letters at this period confirm just how closely the Sidneys and Herberts were still continuing to interact. In the same letter Robert mentioned that his sister, the Dowager Countess of Pembroke, was hoping to come and stay with Barbara at Penshurst, and on 27 September, this time from Hampton Court, he let Barbara know that she should expect some additional guests, including the Countess of Montgomery and the Earl of Pembroke. On the following day he sent another letter to Barbara, suggesting that she should arrange for their eldest daughter, Mary Wroth, to join this planned Penshurst party. On 5 October Robert notified Barbara that he was about to visit Loughton Hall to see Lady Wroth and he was also expecting to meet there his nephew the Earl of Pembroke. On 20 October he provided Barbara with yet another update on his meetings with Lady Wroth and the Countess of Montgomery. As their fortunes continued to rise at the Jacobean court, the Sidneys and Herberts remained assiduous courtiers (except for Pembroke's wife, Mary, who, as Rowland Whyte pointedly commented, was "a most worthy lady but no good courtier") and depended heavily upon one another's personal support in both their public and private lives (*DPFA* 127–30; Lambeth Palace Library MS 3202/15; *Sidneys of Penshurst* 119–20). The powerful familial bonds that existed between the Sidneys and the Dudleys during the Tudor period had now been constructively replaced by those between the Sidneys and the Herberts.

In January 1608 the Sidneys and Herberts were once more prominent in court festivities. On 6 January Robert Sidney, Mary Wroth, and the Earls of Pembroke and Montgomery were among the elite audience which attended Jonson's *The Masque of Beauty* staged at the newly rebuilt Whitehall Banqueting House (*MSLW* 129–30). On 9 February Philip Herbert danced in Jonson's *The Haddington Masque*, staged to celebrate the wedding of Viscount Haddington and Lady Elizabeth Radcliffe, the daughter of the Earl of Sussex. On the following 23 April he was elevated, as his brother William had been in 1603, to the rank of a Knight of the Garter. On 18 September Robert Sidney wrote to his wife Barbara from Baynard's Castle, where he was staying with his nephew, the Earl of Pembroke. Another letter to Barbara of 3 October vividly illustrates the happy intimacy that then existed between the Sidneys and the Herberts. That day he was planning with the Countess of Montgomery a visit to Durham House where they hoped to meet up with the Earls of Pembroke and Montgomery. As usual, the Sidneys and Herberts, drawn together by long-established bonds of genuine friendship and loyalty, seem to have been operating as a unified family and political grouping, both at court and in London metropolitan life.

Rowland Whyte, although in 1598 appointed to the time-consuming role of postmaster to the royal court, still provided a key link between the Sidneys and Herberts. This position (which Whyte held until 1615) required him to supervise the distribution of all official Privy Council letters and documents. As a direct appointee of the council, he was allowed lodgings at court and a daily allowance. He was also required, along with Robert Sidney and the Herbert brothers, to accompany the royal family on their various provincial progresses.

Whyte frequently liaised on Robert's behalf with William Herbert (for whose marriage negotiations he had been actively involved in 1604), and with the Earl's rich and powerful in-laws, the Earl and Countess of Shrewsbury. In return, Whyte continued to stay with Sidneys and Herberts at Baynard's Castle, from where he sent to the Earl of Shrewsbury in January 1608 a vivid account of that year's especially harsh winter, describing how the "frost continues here in a very strange manner, the Thames so hardly frozen, that it is made a beaten highway to all places of the city, but all bridges are in great danger upon a thaw" (Lambeth Palace Library MS 3202/131).

Although Robert Sidney's nephews, the Earls of Pembroke and Montgomery, now outranked him in terms of aristocratic precedent, he was still was regarded as the head of the Sidney–Herbert grouping at court. This family status was very much in evidence during 1609 and 1610, with Robert always heavily preoccupied by his court duties and liaising whenever possible with William and Philip Herbert, the latter's wife, Susan, and his eldest daughter, Mary Wroth. Courtly entertainments continued to provide recurrent elements of their most intimate interaction with the royal family. On 2 February 1609 the Countess of Montgomery performed in Jonson's *The Masque of Queens*, which was dedicated to a now major presence at the English court, Prince Henry (who was fifteen on 19 February). In the following year Prince Henry's barriers—echoing the old chivalric tenets of the Tudor tiltyards on which Sir William (c. 1482–1554), Sir Henry (1529–86) and Sir Philip Sidney (1554–86) had all once excelled—were held on 6 January, with Jonson penning the speeches and Jones designing the sets. The prince issued a ceremonial challenge and, with his own supporters, held the barriers against fifty-eight challengers, including the Earls of Pembroke and Montgomery, both of whom were awarded prizes for their performances (*Sidneys of Penshurst* 122).

The most important court event of 1610 was the creation in early June at the Parliament House of Henry as Prince of Wales, following his coming of age. Robert Sidney and the Earls of Pembroke and Montgomery were in prominent attendance, with Pembroke acting as the Prince's server at the feast held in the Great Hall. Tilts were staged, with Pembroke again chosen to offer a gift to the prince, and the Countess of Montgomery performed in Samuel Daniel's queen's masque *Tethys' Festival*, presented at Whitehall in collaboration with Inigo Jones. In January 1611 the Earl of Pembroke was involved in Jonson's *Oberon, the Faery Prince*, in which Henry himself took the role of Oberon. On 29 September Robert reported to Barbara that his nephew, the Earl of Pembroke, had just been sworn in as a member of the Privy Council. The importance of this appointment to the Sidneys was eloquently conveyed in Robert's final remark to Barbara: "so as now I have one friend more among them, who will be both willing and able to do me good" (*DPFA* 169; *Sidneys of Penshurst* 122–3).

The links of amity between the Sidneys and Herberts continued to develop down the generations. In about 1612 Philip Herbert was appointed Keeper of Elsings, a former royal palace, situated close to the Wroth's home at Durrance in Enfield. The Earl and Countess of Montgomery therefore became Lady Mary Wroth's near neighbors, and both families regularly attended the local parish church of St. Andrew's, Enfield. Hence, as Margaret Hannay observes: "When Wroth named her prose romance *The Countess of Montgomery's Urania*, it was not the usual effort to enlist patronage, but rather an acknowledgement that the two friends had spent many happy hours talking about that fictional world" (*MSLW* 138). The Sidneys and Herberts were also closely bonded from spring 1613 onwards in their support for James I's daughter, Princess Elizabeth, who married Frederick V, Elector Palatine, on 14 February at Whitehall Palace. This marriage was intended as part of a wider alliance between England and the German Protestant union, and on 26 April Robert Sidney set out for the Continent as one of the four royal commissioners accompanying her to Germany. Although their marriage was a happy one, the couple's political problems escalated after Frederick's acceptance of the crown of Bohemia at Prague on 4 November 1619. The Sidneys and Herberts keenly sought news of their vicissitudes when in autumn 1620 the Spanish occupied large areas of the Lower Palatinate, culminating in the devastating defeat on 8 November of Frederick's troops at the Battle of the White Mountain. Elizabeth and Frederick were forced to flee their territories, and in 1621 established an exiled palatine court at The Hague (*DPFA* 230). On 9 May 1621, Robert Sidney advised his wife Barbara: "The King and Queen of Bohemia are still at The Hague, in very good health and much respected: and the war is like to grow on there very hotly" (*DPFA* 232). Poignantly, this was the last item of political news which Robert was to pass on to his wife, since Barbara unexpectedly died later in the same month.

In November 1613 Robert Sidney was at court for the creation of King James's now most influential favorite, Robert Carr, as Earl of Somerset. As usual, the Sidneys and Herberts were prominent in such an important ceremonial event, with the Earl of Pembroke carrying the sword of honor. On 26 December Carr married Frances Howard, formerly the wife of Robert Devereux, second Earl of Essex, the son of Philip Sidney's widow, Frances. This first marriage had been annulled, supposedly on the grounds of its non-consummation, a circumstance which must have been difficult for the Sidneys, who knew the Devereuxs so well. Nevertheless, the Earls of Pembroke and Montgomery dutifully performed in Campion's *Squire's Masque* at the Banqueting House, Whitehall, and also joined the tilts in celebration of this royally approved wedding (*Sidneys of Penshurst* 126).

In February 1614 Mary Wroth gave birth to her only legitimate offspring, James. At the christening, attended by both Sidney grandparents, her cousin, the Earl of Pembroke, stood proxy for King James (*MSLW* 169). The indifferent health of Sir Robert Wroth had been a source of concern for some years, and on 2 March 1614, the day before the christening of his son, he drew up his will with Robert Sidney and Pembroke as its overseers, dying only twelve days later, on 14 March. According to John Chamberlain, he left his widow in severe financial difficulties, with some £23,000 of debts charged to his estate. Mary Wroth soon slipped out of the inner circle of the royal family, but she retained her home, Loughton Hall, and continued to stay with her parents at Penshurst and at Baynard's Castle and frequently drew upon their financial support, as well as that of her cousin, the Earl of Pembroke (*Sidneys of Penshurst* 126–7; *MSLW* 170–71). Wroth's aunt, Mary Sidney Herbert, Dowager Countess of Pembroke, however, was absent from these various family gatherings from summer 1614 until late autumn 1616 since she was traveling on the Continent.

On 14 June 1614 the pro-Spanish and pro-Catholic Henry Howard, Earl of Northampton, died. Since the early 1600s he and Robert Sidney had been diametrically opposed in almost all of their political perspectives and, in a calculated act of personal disservice, Northampton had vigorously sought to block the transfer of the Kenilworth estates to the Sidneys. In a deathbed letter to the Earl of Somerset he described Robert Sidney and the Earl of Pembroke as his worst enemies and begged that none of his court offices should be transferred to them. Northampton's passing does seem to have had a beneficial effect on the Sidney–Herbert families' fortunes, most notably with the appointment of their long-term friend and ally, Fulke Greville, as Chancellor of the Exchequer in the following October (*Sidneys of Penshurst* 127). Additional honors also continued to come the way of Robert's two nephews, with the Earl of Montgomery appointed as High Steward of Oxford University on 10 June 1615 and the Earl of Pembroke as Lord Chamberlain on 23 December 1615. This latter post gave William Herbert authority over the above-stairs royal household and the arrangement of court entertainments, including masques, plays, and musical performances, as well as the office of works and licensed theatres.

Robert Sidney was preoccupied in late August 1616 with arrangements for the christening at Wilton of the Earl of Montgomery's son, planned for 18 September. King James and the Earl of Pembroke were to act as godfathers, and the Dowager Countess of Pembroke was hoping to return to England to stand as godmother. Ultimately, Pembroke's close friend, the Countess of Bedford, proved a willing reserve since his mother did not arrive back in time (*Sidneys of Penshurst* 128). At the end of August 1616 Robert Sidney also attended the creation of King James's new favorite, George Villiers, as Baron Whaddon and Viscount Villiers. His rise into royal favor hints at yet more strategic court links between the Sidneys and the Herberts. In July 1614 Somerset had been appointed as Lord Chamberlain, a post to which Robert's nephew, the Earl of Pembroke, had also aspired. In response, in April 1615 Pembroke hosted a meeting at Baynard's Castle where he and several of Somerset's opponents, including Archbishop George Abbot, agreed to sponsor the career of George Villiers, whose looks and personality had recently attracted King James. Pembroke lent Villiers clothing and worked with Abbot to gain the queen's approval for the young man. On 23 April 1615 Villiers was knighted in the queen's chamber and, given that Robert Sidney was her Lord Chamberlain, it seems very probable that he was fully complicit with this promotion of Villiers as a means of displacing the Earl of Somerset in King James's affections.

Both Robert and his nephew the Earl of Pembroke remained meticulous in their cultivation of the goodwill of the still ever-rising George Villiers, who was created Earl (5 January 1617) and Marquis (1 January 1618) of Buckingham by his infatuated monarch. The Earl of Pembroke was also honored on 29 January/February 1617 by being appointed in a lavish ceremony at Baynard's Castle as Chancellor of Oxford University, a position of considerable pride to both Pembroke and Robert Sidney (and once held by the latter's uncle, the Earl of Leicester). William Herbert contributed £100 towards the construction of the Bodleian Library, and in 1629 donated 250 Greek manuscripts which he had purchased for £700. The rest of Pembroke's Greek manuscripts arrived at the Bodleian in 1654.

Early in 1617 Robert and Barbara Sidney gained a new daughter-in-law when their son Robert (Illustration 23) secretly married Dorothy (Illustration 26), the daughter of Henry Percy, ninth Earl of Northumberland. This new family link, which became public knowledge in March (*CSPD 1611–18* 425) would prove to be a crucially powerful one from the 1620s onwards, with Dorothy's sister, Lucy Percy Hay, Countess of Carlisle (Illustration 26), and her increasingly influential brother, Algernon (Illustration 25), often willing to offer their personal support in a variety of important ways to the Sidneys. The Sidney–Herbert network also continued to meet up amicably outside the court, with the Earl of Montgomery visiting his mother at her new residence at Houghton House before moving on to stay at Penshurst in late July (CKS C81/278; *Philip's Phoenix* 203). Robert Sidney was himself often obliged to be in London or at Oatlands Palace or Windsor Castle as the Queen's Chamberlain, but with his nephew Pembroke now also in place as the King's Chamberlain, he could take pleasure in the fact that the Sidneys and Herberts were at the zenith of their power and influence at court.

During summer 1617 the Sidneys, including Lady Mary Wroth and her new sister-in-law, Dorothy Percy Sidney, assembled at Penshurst for a family gathering, and Philip Herbert, Earl of Montgomery, joined them in late July after visiting his mother, the dowager countess (*DPFA* 202). On 4 August 1617, probably while Montgomery was still there, Barbara Sidney also welcomed to Penshurst Richard Sackville, Earl of Dorset, whose then wife, Anne Clifford Sackville (later to become Montgomery's second wife), joined the Penshurst party on 19 August and recorded their visit in her famous diary (*Sidneys of Penshurst* 129; *MSLW* 198). At the end of August the Montgomerys' infant son, James, died and Robert Sidney went immediately to visit them to offer his personal condolences (*DPFA* 210).

On 22 July 1618 Robert Sidney wrote from London to Barbara with the joyful news that he had just been created Earl of Leicester by the king in a private ceremony (*DPFA* 216). The public ceremony was held on 2 August in the hall of the Bishop's Palace at Salisbury just before King James was due to take up residence at Wilton House with the Earl of Pembroke.

Robert was also invited to stay there afterwards so that he could attend the king. Clearly, the Sidneys and Herberts now stood proudly together in their joint intimacy with the king and queen, just as the Sidneys and Dudleys had once occupied a similar position during the reigns of Edward VI, Mary, and Elizabeth. Robert Sidney's earldom, coupled with his nephew Pembroke's potency at court, had triumphantly reasserted their influence with the monarchs of England (*Sidneys of Penshurst* 129).

The Sidneys and Herberts continued to regard themselves as an extended family and political unit, and this was very much in evidence at the next grand state occasion which they attended. The granting of the Leicester earldom to Sidney had owed much to Queen Anne's personal support for him and this honor came just in time, since she died on 2 March 1619. Sidney, as her long-serving Lord Chamberlain, was in charge of the arrangements for her funeral, held on 13 May at Westminster Abbey, and he and Prince Charles walked before the coffin as it was processed into Henry VII's chapel. The Earl of Pembroke, as Lord Chamberlain to James's court, was one of the six lords who processed alongside the coffin, and his brother Montgomery carried the Great Banner. The Countess of Arundel (the sister of Pembroke's wife, Mary Talbot Herbert) was Principal Mourner, and her assistants included Barbara Gamage Sidney, Countess of Leicester, and the Dowager Countess of Pembroke. Twenty-one other court ladies also processed, including Lady Mary Wroth, her sister Philippa Hobart, and Dorothy Percy Sidney, Lady Lisle (*MSLW* 203).

In March 1620 the Sidneys shared the delight occasioned by the safe birth, with the Dowager Countess of Pembroke assisting at the delivery, of the Earl of Pembroke's only legitimate son, Henry—so named in honor of both his father Henry Herbert and Sir Henry Sidney, and born after sixteen years of marriage. The dowager countess and her son Montgomery stood as godparents, and inevitably, they also shared the sadness of the Earl and Countess of Pembroke when the infant Henry died some three months later at Baynard's Castle (*Philip's Phoenix* 204; *MSLW* 222–3). In 1620 King James I paid another summer visit to Wilton House, and when in November Robert Sidney was preoccupied with official duties at the royal palace of Theobalds, his main consolation seemed to lie in brief but friendly meetings with the Countess of Montgomery, who, as usual, enquired solicitously about the welfare of Barbara Sidney (*Sidneys of Penshurst* 130).

The death on 25 September 1621 of the Dowager Countess of Pembroke from smallpox at her London house in Aldergate Street came as a great loss to the Earl of Leicester, who wrote to his son Robert: "My sister is to be buried privately by her husband at Salisbury, and a funeral made according to her quality in Paul's," where in 1587 her brother, Sir Philip, had been interred (CKS U1475 Z53/81; *Philip's Phoenix* 205). The service at St. Paul's, next to Baynard's Castle, would have been one of the last duties of its Dean, Valentine Cary, who had just been confirmed at Bishop of Exeter. But he may have been assisted by his appointed successor, John Donne, who formally took over the Dean's duties in November and knew well several members of the Herbert family. He had personally presented the Countess of Montgomery with one of his sermons delivered on 18 April 1619, commemorated (probably posthumously) the dowager countess's versification of the Psalms of David in his "Upon the Translation of the Psalms by Sir Philip Sidney, and the Countess of Pembroke His Sister," and was intimate with his son, the Earl of Pembroke, who ended a letter of 20 May 1619 by lamenting the death of the actor Richard Burbage, with the postscript: "commend my best love to Mr. Doctor Donne" (BL Egerton MS 2592 fol. 81).

For the remainder of King James I's reign, the Earl of Leicester played a less prominent role at court. In 1621 *The Countess of Montgomery's Urania* by his daughter, Lady Mary Wroth (Illustrations 18 and 19), was published, although his personal response to it is unknown. It was so titled in honor of Wroth's erstwhile masquing partner, Susan Vere Herbert, Countess of Montgomery. A central problem with this romance lay in the fact that, although Wroth was an impressively skilled imitator of her uncle's literary forms, her prose style seemed to informed readers far more directly allusive to contemporary events. Her first cousin, the Earl of Pembroke, was clearly the model for Amphilanthus. Wroth had long enjoyed a close personal relationship with her cousin, probably pre-dating her marriage to Robert Wroth, and *c.* 1624 she gave birth to illegitimate twins, William and Katherine, by the Earl of Pembroke. It is unknown for how long their sexual relationship lasted after these births, but William (and then, after his death in 1630, his brother Philip) assisted Wroth in protecting her from creditors when burdened with debts. The Herbert family, including Philip and their cousin Sir Henry Herbert, later assisted young Will with royal bestowment of Irish property and then military placement during the civil wars; Philip probably also assisted with Katherine's excellent marriage to John Lovet (*MSLW* 250–52, 282–97). Again, Robert Sidney's personal response to these births is unknown.

Nor is there any evidence to suggest how he responded to his nephew's increasingly anti-Spanish stance at court. Pembroke consistently sought ways of challenging Spanish interests at home and abroad. He sponsored the Virginia and Guiana Companies and other colonial ventures which threatened the potency of Spain in the New World, and he also opposed a Spanish match for Prince Charles which was vigorously supported by Buckingham. But whether Robert Sidney was ever personally committed to anti-Spanish policies or, with failing health, he simply sought to keep out of factional court struggles cannot be ascertained. Similarly, little is known about how he viewed the personal lives of the Herbert brothers. Both had a reputation as philanderers, in contrast to Sidney himself, whose correspondence reveals him to have enjoyed a loving and mutually supportive relationship with his wife Barbara. Edward Clarendon sternly remarked that William Herbert was "immoderately given up to women," and during the second decade of King James I's reign Philip Herbert openly formed a relationship with his wife's niece, Elizabeth Norris, who had been living in their London home for several years, until she secretly married another man in March 1622 (*MSLW* 200).

1625–1650

Following the death of King James on 27 March 1625, Pembroke as Lord Chamberlain held ultimate responsibility for the funeral and processed immediately before the coffin. Prince Charles's assistants included both Leicester and Montgomery, and the former's son, Robert Sidney, was also a member of the cortege. Pembroke is likely to have sought out his uncle Leicester's advice on the administrative arrangements, since he had been in charge of Queen Anne's funeral in 1619 (*MSLW* 257). Both men were also involved in the May marriage by proxy at Notre Dame of the new king to Henrietta Maria, and Philip Herbert, Earl of Montgomery, joined the embassy which escorted Charles I's queen from France to England. However, as plague hit London in early July 1625, Parliament was forced to adjourn to Oxford from Westminster and Leicester withdrew to his Penshurst estates. Partly to avoid the unhealthy metropolitan environment, in October 1625 Charles and Henrietta Maria honored the Herberts with a visit to Wilton House, a source of much satisfaction to Leicester, who remained close to his nephew Pembroke. But plague conditions still prevailed at London, and even the coronation procession scheduled for mid-January had to be cancelled. Finally, Charles I was crowned at Westminster Abbey on 2 February 1626, with Leicester (as one of his parents' most trusted and long-serving courtiers) in expected attendance, the Earl of Pembroke carrying the crown, and the Earl of Montgomery carrying the spurs (*Sidneys of Penshurst* 138; *MSLW* 257).

Leicester's wife Barbara had died in the latter half of May 1621, and in May 1623 he transferred the entire Penshurst estate to his son Robert, presumably because of his own declining health and to avoid any inheritance complications if he remarried (*Sidneys of Penshurst* 138; *MSLW* 258). To the surprise of most observers, and perhaps even his own children, on 25 April 1626 Leicester married Sarah Blount Smythe, the widow of Sir Thomas Smythe, former Ambassador to Russia and Governor of the East India Company. Little is known of this late second marriage, although some of Leicester's outgoing correspondence written from Baynard's Castle, coupled with a warm letter of 13 June 1626 from the Earl of Pembroke to his eldest son Robert (Illustration 23), indicate that his long-standing friendship with the Herberts continued unabated until the end of his life (Collins 2:369). On 13 July 1626 Robert Sidney, Earl of Leicester, died at the age of sixty-two after returning by water from court to his lodgings at Baynard's Castle. He was buried three days later at Penshurst, with the Earl of Montgomery in attendance and Rowland Whyte supervising the embalming of the body and other funeral arrangements. On 27 July Whyte wrote his last known letter from Baynard's Castle to the younger Robert Sidney, now second Earl of Leicester, communicating news about the activities of the Earls of Pembroke and Montgomery (Collins 2:369–70).

In August 1626 Pembroke was appointed Lord Steward (below stairs) of the royal household, and his brother Montgomery assumed his former role as Lord Chamberlain. King Charles I made another visit to Wilton in October 1626 and was keen to see amicable relations established between the Herberts and his now most influential courtier, the Duke of Buckingham. A marriage alliance was duly brokered between Buckingham's four-year-old daughter, Mary, and Montgomery's eldest son and heir, Charles (aged seven), who was also Buckingham's godson. The wedding did eventually take place in January 1635, but Charles died in the following year while touring the Continent (*MSLW* 259). Philip Herbert's first wife, Susan, died in January 1629 of smallpox, and in June 1630 he married Anne Clifford, widow of Richard Sackville, Earl of Dorset, and daughter of George Clifford, Earl of Cumberland. On 9 April 1630 the Earl of Pembroke dined with the Countess Devonshire, and he died the following morning at Baynard's Castle. The response of Robert Sidney, second Earl of Leicester, to his cousin's death is unknown, although he maintained contact with his younger brother, Philip Herbert, now Earl of Montgomery and the fourth Earl of Pembroke (Illustrations 20 and 22).

Little evidence has survived relating to the personal and court involvements of the Sidneys and Herberts during the 1630s and early 1640s, probably due to the second Earl of Leicester being largely away from England on his French embassy (1636–41) and Lord Deputyship of Ireland (1641–43). Although Philip Herbert was appointed in 1641 at Baynard's Castle as Chancellor of Oxford University, after his second marriage in 1630 to Anne Clifford (a union which effectively broke down in 1634), he tended not to live at either Wilton or Baynard's Castle (where his brother's widow, Mary Talbot Herbert, stayed), and instead resided mainly at London in rooms at the Cockpit near the court. Later, during the Civil War, he sent his wife Anne to live with his brother's widow at Baynard's Castle to protect the family's property there (*MSLW* 262). After the Restoration, Baynard's Castle (Illustrations 1 and 2) was occupied by Francis Talbot (1623–68), eleventh Earl of Shrewsbury, and was largely destroyed in 1666 during the Great Fire of London. There is no reason to suspect, however, that Leicester did not maintain some form of contact with his cousin Philip Herbert whenever their respective commitments allowed. The fourth Earl of Pembroke's sons, Charles and Philip, traveled on the Continent during 1635–37, and the latter may have stayed briefly at his uncle's embassy at Paris.

It also seems likely that Philip Herbert assisted the early military career of Lady Mary Wroth's illegitimate son, William, by his late brother, the third Earl of Pembroke. Young William may even have been resident at some point in Philip Herbert's house at Elsings (near Wroth's own home), and if so, would have gotten to know well there his cousin, Philip Herbert, later fifth Earl of Pembroke. After William's first military command during the First Bishop's War (1639), Philip Herbert lobbied the king on his behalf in late 1640 for a Munster estate in Ireland. Sadly, the Munster Rising (1641–42) swept away this property, and instead William enlisted under Prince Maurice's elite regiment in the royalist army. The fourth Earl of Pembroke may also have supported at the same period the marriage of William's twin sister, Katherine, first to a wealthy John Lovet (d. 1643) of Oxfordshire, and then to a Welshman, James Parry, whose family lived near the Pembroke estates in Wales (*MSLW* 284–9, 294–5).

When Philip Herbert was forced to resign his Lord Chamberlain's post in July 1641—a major breach with the king, and the beginning of his allegiance to Parliament—it is unlikely that he would have remained in regular court or political communication with Leicester. Also, Queen Henrietta Maria, with whom Leicester's wife, Dorothy Percy Sidney, and her sister, Lucy Percy Hay, Countess of Carlisle, maintained a long intimacy (Illustration 26), actively disliked Philip Herbert for his brusque and often choleric behavior and had personally lobbied for his dismissal as Lord Chamberlain. Nevertheless, it is possible that the Sidney and Herbert families, at least on a private level, remained on amicable terms. Pembroke worked closely during the early 1640s with the royalist Earl of Holland (who later became the lover of Lucy Percy Hay and well known to the Sidney family at Penshurst), and he always sought to retain a moderate reputation as a parliamentarian, often acting as an intermediary with the king and his supporters. On 9 March 1642 he and Holland met Charles I at Royston, where they presented him with a declaration from both the Commons and Lords alleging his misgovernment; and in January 1643 Pembroke was one of the commissioners sent to Charles at Oxford to offer peace propositions. It may be suspected that Pembroke's affiliation to Parliament was largely motivated by his desire to retain Wilton and to be on the winning side, just as the Earl of Leicester's studied neutrality and his withdrawal to his Penshurst estates in 1644 implicitly confirmed the primacy of his commitment to the preservation of his ancestral home.

During the mid-1640s Pembroke loosely allied himself in the House of Lords with the associates of the Earl of Northumberland, who was the Earl of Leicester's brother-in-law and one of his most reliable and trusted supporters. In 1645 Pembroke supported Northumberland in advocating the Self-denying Ordinance and the creation of the New Model Army. In March 1645 Leicester's son, Algernon, was appointed as colonel of one of the eleven cavalry regiments of the New Model Army, commanded by Sir Thomas Fairfax and answerable directly to Cromwell as its Lieutenant-General. A Colonel William Herbert, then also serving under Fairfax, may have been the illegitimate son of Mary Wroth and the third Earl of Pembroke (*MSLW* 284–9). After August 1646 Pembroke began to distance himself from Northumberland and became an outspoken critic of the army, although after it entered London in August 1647 he immediately renounced such views and once again attempted to identify himself with Northumberland and his supporters. Always a self-interested moderate, in December 1648 he joined Northumberland in a delegation which sought an eleventh-hour compromise with the king. When this mission failed, the Commons appointed Pembroke as Constable of Windsor Castle, thereby making him in effect the king's gaoler. On 14 February 1649, two weeks after Charles I's execution, he was one of only five peers appointed to the newly established Council of State, and was also elected in the following April as MP for Berkshire.

The private diary of Robert Sidney, second Earl of Leicester (Illustration 24), sheds fascinating light on the behavior of Philip Herbert, fourth Earl of Pembroke, during the king's trial and execution. Probably based on conversations with his son Algernon (Illustration 25) and Pembroke, Leicester notes on 1 January 1649 the selection of judges from the Upper and Lower Houses for Charles I's trial. A court of 136 commissioners was established, including Leicester's sons Algernon and Philip (Illustration 28), which met on 15 and 19 January to consider the charges. At the opening of the trial on 19/20 January, Leicester noted that the "King was brought from Windsor to St James's, where he lay that night strongly guarded [and then] from St James' in the Earl of Pembroke's chair … into Westminster Hall." On 25 January Leicester pointedly emphasized in his diary that his two sons, Philip and Algernon, were at Penshurst during 22–29 January, "so as neither of them was at the condemnation of the King." The defensive tone of these words underlines Leicester's determination to ensure that his two sons were not implicated in the actual judgment process over the king's fate.

The execution of the king on 30 January 1649 was watched incognito from a nearby window by Philip Herbert, Earl of Pembroke, and it seems likely that soon afterwards he provided Leicester with his diary's first-hand account. Both Algernon and Philip were probably at the House of Commons at the moment when the axe fell, attending the sitting at which a resolution was passed to abolish both the monarchy and the House of Lords. The "Rump" of the Commons then assumed supreme power over the nation by parliamentary resolution (*Sidneys of Penshurst* 153–4). The Earl of Leicester's privately held views over the execution of Charles I are brought into sharp focus by his diary's record of the death of Philip Herbert, Earl of Pembroke, on 23 January 1650 at his lodgings at the Cockpit "of a fever and gangrene." On 30 January Sidney wrote that on this very day "the late King was beheaded at Whitehall gate," and observed that Pembroke had not lived for even one year beyond this event. He deplored how Pembroke had told him that he watched from "his chamber window" the king's progress to the "place of his death," sharply noting that he "should not have done," and instead should have "retired himself to pray for him, and to lament his misfortune, to whom he had so great obligations" (*Sydney Papers* 54, 96; *Sidneys of Penshurst* 156).

1651–1702

Philip Herbert's heir, his son Philip, now second Earl of Montgomery and fifth Earl of Pembroke, was elected on 1 December 1651 as a member of the Council of State, and served briefly in summer 1652 as its president. His amenable personality ensured that he made a smooth transition into the court of King Charles II after the Restoration. He was appointed as a councillor for trade and navigation on 7 November 1660, and at the coronation on 23 April 1661 he carried the spurs (symbolically reasserting the Herberts' allegiance to the monarchy, since his father had performed the same role at Charles I's coronation). Although Robert Sidney, second Earl of Leicester, was able to resume his seat in the House of Lords in April 1660 and was named as a Privy Councillor on 31 May, as soon as Charles II's first Parliament adjourned in October he took the opportunity to plead ill health and withdrew permanently to Penshurst. He did not attend the coronation, and there is no evidence to suggest that he sustained any significant level of personal contact with the fifth Earl of Pembroke. During the 1650s his parliamentarian son, Philip (later the third Earl of Leicester), had loyally served the Commonwealth, and in 1653 was President of the Council of State (Illustration 28). He remained close to Cromwell, and played a prominent role in June 1656 at the ceremonials marking Cromwell's second installation as Protector. In 1658 he had readily signed the proclamation asserting the succession of Richard Cromwell to his father's political roles, but was granted a pardon under the Great Seal on 30 October 1660. From then until his death in 1698 he took little part in public affairs. After his father's death in 1677 he was largely preoccupied with his Penshurst estate and his London mansion, Leicester House, and acrimonious inheritance squabbles with his surviving brothers, Algernon and Henry.

Philip Herbert, fifth Earl of Pembroke, died in December 1669 and was succeeded by his only son by his first wife, William Herbert (1640–74), sixth Earl of Pembroke. He died unmarried, and was succeeded by his half-brother and eldest son of his father's second marriage, Philip Herbert (1653–83), seventh Earl of Pembroke, a violent and ill-disciplined individual who was imprisoned in the Tower for blasphemy and who killed at least two men. He died, largely unlamented by either the Herberts or the Sidneys, on 29 August 1683. His dissolute life afforded a stark contrast to that of his high-principled republican cousin Algernon Sidney (Illustration 25), who was beheaded on Tower Hill on 7 December 1683 following the ill-fated Rye House Plot to assassinate Charles II and his brother, James, Duke of York. The seventh earl's younger brother, Thomas (1656/57–1733), who had probably been born at Baynard's Castle, succeeded him as the eighth Earl of Pembroke. He later enjoyed the trust of King William III, whose accession to the English throne had been actively supported by Henry Sidney, later Earl of Romney (the youngest brother of Philip Sidney, third Earl of Leicester, who held this title until 1698), who had personally known William as Prince of Orange since the late 1670s. The eighth Earl of Pembroke enjoyed an illustrious administrative and diplomatic career under William III, serving as an ambassador to the Dutch states, a Privy Councillor, first Lord of the Admiralty, Lord Privy Seal, and Lord President of the Council. Similarly, Henry Sidney remained a key military and strategic figure following William III's accession. Once again, from 1688 until the king's death in 1702, the Sidneys and Herberts were drawn together through their respective royal and court service.

Bibliography

Manuscript Sources

British Library
Egerton MS 2592
Centre for Kentish Studies
C81/108, 115, 278
CKS 1475 C12/108, 218
CKS U1475 T327/8
CKS U1475 Z53/81
Lambeth Palace
MS 3202/15, 101, 131
MS 3205/110
The National Archives, Kew (TNA)
TNA PROB 11/36

Primary and Secondary Sources

Brennan, Michael G. *The Sidneys of Penshurst and the Monarchy, 1500–1700*. Aldershot: Ashgate, 2006.
Calendar of State Papers Domestic … 1547–80. Ed. Robert Lemon. London: Longman, Brown, Green, Longmans, and Roberts, 1856.

Calendar of State Papers Domestic ... 1611–18. Ed. Mary Anne Everett Green. London: HMSO, 1858.

Calendar of State Papers Spanish .... Ed. Martin A. S. Hume. London: HMSO, 1894.

Carleton, Sir Dudley. *Dudley Carleton to John Chamberlain 1603–1624: Jacobean Letters.* Ed. Maurice Lee, Jr. New Brunswick, NJ: Rutgers UP, 1972.

Collins, Arthur. *Letters and Memorials of State ....* 2 vols. London: T. Osborne, 1746.

Hannay, Margaret P. *Mary Sidney, Lady Wroth.* Farnham: Ashgate, 2010.

—. *Philip's Phoenix. Mary Sidney, Countess of Pembroke.* Oxford: Oxford UP, 1990.

Hay, Millicent. *The Life of Robert Sidney, Earl of Leicester (1563–1626).* Washington, DC: Folger Shakespeare Library, 1984.

Herbert, Mary Sidney. *Collected Works of Mary Sidney Herbert, Countess of Pembroke.* 2 vols. Ed. Margaret P. Hannay, Noel J. Kinnamon, and Michael G. Brennan. Oxford: Clarendon P, 1998.

HMC. *Calendar of the Manuscripts of the Most Hon. The Marquis of Salisbury, K.G. ... Preserved at Hatfield House, Hertfordshire.* 24 vols. London: HMSO, 1883–1976.

—. *Report on the Manuscripts of Lord de L'Isle and Dudley Preserved at Penshurst Place.* 6 vols. London: HMSO, 1925–66.

Nichols, J. *The Progresses and Public Processions of Queen Elizabeth.* 3 vols. London: John Nichols, 1823.

Page, William, ed. *The Victoria History of London: including London within the Bars, Westminster & Southwark.* London: Constable, 1909.

Sidney, Robert, first Earl of Leicester. *Domestic Politics and Family Absence: The Correspondence (1588–1621) of Robert Sidney, First Earl of Leicester, and Barbara Gamage Sidney, Countess of Leicester.* Ed. Margaret P. Hannay, Noel J. Kinnamon, and Michael G. Brennan. Aldershot: Ashgate, 2005.

Slater, Victor. "William Herbert, Third Earl of Pembroke (1580–1630)." *ODNB.*

Smith, David L. "Philip Herbert, First Earl of Montgomery and Fourth Earl of Pembroke (1584–1650)." *ODNB.*

Sydney Papers, Consisting of A Journal of the Earl of Leicester, and Original Letters of Algernon Sydney. Ed. R. W. Blencowe. London: John Murray, 1825.

Whyte, Rowland. *The Letters (1595–1608) of Rowland Whyte.* Ed. Michael G. Brennan, Noel J. Kinnamon, and Margaret P. Hannay. Philadelphia, PA: American Philosophical Society, 2013.

Williams, Penry. "Henry Herbert, Second Earl of Pembroke (b. in or after 1538, d. 1601)." *ODNB.*

Wright, T., ed. *Queen Elizabeth and Her Times.* 2 vols. London: Henry Colburn, 1838.

PART II
Biographies

Sir Henry Sidney (1529–1586)

Valerie McGowan-Doyle

At the age of nine Henry Sidney (Illustration 5) acquired a privilege available to few other children, that of companion to the young Prince Edward. When Edward became king in 1547, Sidney advanced to Gentleman of the Privy Chamber, maintaining such a close relationship with the new king that Edward would die in his arms (Sidney, *Memoir* 106). Sidney went on to fare remarkably well under the new monarchs, Mary and Philip, particularly for one of non-noble status, acquiring numerous accolades and posts. When Elizabeth became queen, Sidney advanced yet higher, becoming Lord President of the Council in the Marches of Wales in 1560, and in 1565 he received the first of his two appointments to the highest office in Ireland, Lord Deputy. This early and seemingly flourishing career, however, stalled before the decade was over, and Sidney thereafter found it increasingly difficult to maintain the support and confidence of Elizabeth. He died at the age of fifty-seven bitterly frustrated that Elizabeth refused to extend the recognition or compensation he believed were merited by his service to the Crown. Although he retained his post in Wales until his death in 1586, Sidney faced increasing criticism in that position from the early 1570s on. His two terms as Lord Deputy of Ireland (1565–71 and 1575–78) would prove even more tumultuous, for Sidney and for Ireland. Recalled from this post on both occasions, Sidney's time in Ireland marked a critically transitional phase in the intensification of English conquest in Ireland (see Herron *ARC* 1:13).

Early Life

Born in 1529 to Sir William Sidney and Anne Pagenham Fitzwilliam, it was William's position as chamberlain to Prince Edward that afforded Henry such an unusually close association with the prince. Although the Sidney family had long-established ties to prominent court families, notably the Brandons and Dudleys, it was more likely Sidney's association with King Edward VI that led John Dudley, Duke of Northumberland, to arrange a marriage between his daughter Mary and Henry Sidney in 1551, the same year in which Sidney received knighthood. Marriage and family ties would continue to play a substantial part in Sidney's career, particularly through a nexus of brothers-in-law, including Sir William Fitzwilliam, married to Sidney's sister Anne, but more critically Thomas Radcliffe, Earl of Sussex, husband to Sidney's sister Frances, and his wife Mary's brother, Robert Dudley, later titled Earl of Leicester. Though his relationship to Leicester, Elizabeth's long-time favorite, ultimately brought Sidney advancement, it also created difficulties, particularly as rivalry between Leicester and Sussex grew at court. It also presented a dire threat to Sidney's security early in his career when his father-in-law and another of his brothers-in-law, Guildford Dudley, were executed in the aftermath of their attempt to place Jane Grey on the throne following Edward's death in 1553.

Sidney successfully negotiated this crisis and resumed prominence under Mary and Philip. He had already become MP for Brackley in 1547 and MP for Kent in 1553, and went on to serve on numerous foreign missions, appointments for which his linguistic abilities in French and Spanish, as well as Italian, served him well. Significant among these diplomatic missions, Sidney traveled to Spain as one of the entourage negotiating Queen Mary's marriage to Philip II, thus restoring his royal associations after Edward's death and the Jane Grey debacle. At this point Sidney privileged his connection to Sussex, and when Sussex became Viceroy of Ireland in 1556, Sidney accompanied him as second-in-command in the position of vice-treasurer. This brought Sidney new administrative responsibilities and experience serving in Sussex's place during Sussex's periodic absences in England over the later 1550s.

Sidney continued to fare well in the early years of Elizabeth's reign, and certainly Elizabeth's well-known fondness for his brother-in-law Leicester seemed to herald yet greater opportunity for Sidney, as it did for his wife, who became lady-in-waiting to Elizabeth. Sidney now privileged his family attachment to Dudley over his attachment to Sussex, and thereafter it was Dudley who would serve as Sidney's principal patron. Following his appointment as vice-treasurer in Ireland, Sidney was next appointed President of the Council in the Marches of Wales in 1560, a post he would hold until his death in 1586 in spite of his lengthy absences during 1562–71 and 1575–78 (see Maley and Schwyzer ARC 1:14). During the early years of the Welsh presidency Sidney continued to travel on court business, notably to Scotland and France in 1562, and received the prestigious Knight of the Garter in 1564. In 1565 Sidney achieved yet greater appointment as a Member of the Privy Council and the first of his two appointments as Lord Deputy in Ireland. These positions, which gave him control of roughly one-quarter of Elizabeth's realms (Brennan 39), coupled with his close association with Leicester, would seem to have poised Sidney for ever greater influence at court. Such was not to be the case, however, and Sidney would never thereafter enjoy the intimacy or confidence of Elizabeth that he had under Edward or under Mary and Philip. From his 1565 appointment as Lord Deputy of Ireland to his death, Sidney would not again take up ambassadorial positions; the remainder of his life would be split between his posts in Ireland and Wales.

The naming practices employed for Sidney's children, no less than their marital arrangements, help to underscore the powerful circles in which he moved as well as his political needs (Brennan 43). Royal connections figure prominently in the naming of Sidney's eldest children. His eldest son Philip (1554–86) was named after King Philip, Mary Margaret (1556–58) after both her mother and Queen Mary, and Elizabeth (1560–67) after Queen Elizabeth; Mary (1561–1621) was named after her mother. Two of his younger children were named after Mary Dudley's brothers: Robert (1563–1626) after Robert Dudley, and Ambrosia (c. 1564–74) after Ambrose. (Notably, they chose not to use the names of Mary's executed father John or brother Guildford). Sidney endeavored to repair his relationship with Sussex by naming his youngest son, Thomas (1569–95), after him. Sussex also stood as Thomas's godfather along with William Cecil, Lord Burghley, Elizabeth's key adviser, with whom marital negotiations were underway between Burghley's daughter Anne and Philip Sidney (Brennan 43). Although this marriage did not take place, Philip later married Frances Walsingham, daughter of Francis Walsingham, Elizabeth's "spymaster" and another key adviser, thereby securing for Sidney another powerful ally at court, essential in the midst of factionalism and criticism. Sidney also expanded his alliances in Wales through the marriages of his daughter Mary to Henry Herbert, second Earl of Pembroke, from a powerful Welsh family (and who would later follow Sidney as Lord President of Wales in 1586–1601), and his son Robert to the Welsh heiress Barbara Gamage, both furthering the Pembroke faction in Wales and securing Robert's election as Knight of the Shire for Glamorgan. Sidney, however, did not employ family marriage as a political tool in Ireland, a significant reflection of the stark differences between his positions in Wales and Ireland as well as those with whom he sought favor and influence.

Lord President of Wales

The Council of the Marches in Wales was a relatively new institution when Sidney became its president in 1560. Created to facilitate formalization of English control under the Act of Union (1536–43), though a less formal council had existed since the 1470s, its function was to ensure centralization, royal control, coastal defense, and importantly, to resolve what was deemed to be rampant lawlessness and disorder in Wales. The council's judicial function therefore consumed much of its efforts. Following a rapid turnover of presidents in the first few years of Elizabeth's reign, the post had been left vacant for six months prior to Sidney's appointment (Williams 249–51). He seemed a likely candidate. He was well known at court, had served well on diplomatic missions, and had experience in Ireland. There is some debate, however, regarding the precise reason for his appointment. It may have been due to Leicester's influence with Elizabeth, for, as Penry Williams noted, the post had already become a "prize" of powerful factions (35–6, 252). Alternatively, the appointment may have been advanced by Cecil as a means to remove Sidney from court following his entanglement in problematic developments regarding Elizabeth's possible marriage to Robert Dudley (Brennan 35; Williams 252), a harbinger of what became a lifelong struggle for Elizabeth's favor. In either case, the post reflects an early stage of the impact that factionalism and Elizabeth's wavering confidence would have on Sidney's career. His tenure in Wales began on a platform of moderate reform of the council's procedures (Williams 254), and he worked cooperatively with the two other influential officers in Wales at the time, William Gerrard and John Throckmorton. Repeated absences would figure prominently in Sidney's tenure in Wales, in his first few years in France and then Scotland, and then during 1565–71 in Ireland as Lord Deputy. Although Gerrard and Throckmorton served efficiently in Sidney's absence, little was accomplished in this first decade of Sidney's presidency.

Opposition and criticism on the Welsh council emerged with Sidney's return from Ireland in 1571 and would dominate the remainder of his tenure as lord president. Concerns about the need for reform of abuses and inefficiencies led the Privy Council to dispatch Henry Townshend to make recommendations (Jones 103). Again little was accomplished, and when Sidney left to take up his second term as Lord Deputy of Ireland in 1575–78, criticism of him grew. Within months of Sidney' departure, David Lewis wrote to Walsingham complaining of Sidney's leniency in Wales and recommending harsher punishments against disorder and the continuance of Welsh customs (Williams 257–60). Sidney successfully maneuvered this difficulty, producing some procedural amendments to council, only to face renewed complaints, in particular from his old adversary on the Welsh council, Sir James Croft, and a new appointment to the council, Archbishop Whitgift, who complained of Sidney's leniency towards Catholics. This situation led to the renewal of unwelcome attention from the Privy Council as well as Elizabeth. Elizabeth seemed particularly receptive to complaints about Sidney, leading Walsingham to warn Sidney in 1580 to watch himself carefully (Williams 267). Although Sidney's position was weakened by the loss of his old advocates on the council, Throckmorton and Gerard, he retained the support of the Leicester faction, and compensated for the loss of old allies by aligning himself with the powerful Welsh Herbert family through the marriage of his daughter Mary to the Earl of Pembroke, and by Pembroke's placement on the Welsh council in 1576. This alliance assisted Sidney in overcoming opposition, but in the end little was accomplished over the entire tenure of his Welsh presidency beyond reforming some of council's procedural inadequacies and remediating judicial inefficiencies. Neither the abuses of court officials nor council finances had been adequately remedied. In fact, as Williams argued, the Welsh council lost much of its authority during Sidney's time as president (272). The situation in Ireland would be entirely different.

Lord Deputy in Ireland

Sidney's diplomatic service and his earlier time in Ireland, complemented now by his experience in Wales, might have recommended him for the position of Lord Deputy in Ireland, but Ireland was in a far different situation than Wales. Wales was already effectively under English control, its territory shired, organized, and administered by English institutions. Sidney's principal objective there was thus to further establish order through more rigorous implementation of the law. Conversely, although England had claimed control of the whole of Ireland in the 1541 Act for Kingly Title, England exercised effective control over very little of its territory. Sidney's task in Ireland therefore extended far beyond ensuring order: his task was to complete the failed and only partial medieval conquest. This task bred a far more comprehensive slate of policies than for Wales, on economic and military matters in particular, which in turn bred far greater destabilization and opposition than Sidney would ever face in Wales.

During Sidney's two periods as Lord Deputy of Ireland English control passed from earlier Tudor phases of vacillation between policies of conciliation and assimilation into a period of coercion and increasingly aggressive and violent conquest. Determining Sidney's role in this has generated far more study and debate of his tenure in Ireland than his tenure in Wales. Nicholas Canny's seminal 1976 publication *The Elizabethan Conquest of Ireland: A Pattern Established, 1565–76* set the stage for later studies in identifying Sidney's first term as critical to this transformational stage in the relationship between England and Ireland, one in which a platform of reform of English governance in Ireland was replaced by adherence to the position that conquest, followed by plantation, was necessary to secure English control. Ciarán Brady argued conversely in *The Chief Governors: The Rise and Fall of Reform Government in Tudor Ireland, 1536–1588* that Sidney privileged reform over conquest, though inconsistently (114), relying on a commitment to the extension of English law to secure completed conquest, and that the shift to conquest over reform was therefore a later Elizabethan development. Brady argued as well that Sidney's policies were predominantly continuations of those of his predecessor in office, Sussex, rather than novel or radically new directions (117–19). Certainly, developments such as provincial councils and plantation had been set in motion before Sidney's arrival. However, they developed rapidly under him (Collins 1:29), generating the costly opposition that characterizes much of his tenure. Resistance from the Gaelic Irish and Old English colonial communities alike, expressed in parliamentary opposition and rebellion, led Sidney into military action and spiraling violence of the sort that did not occur in Wales. Compounded by factionalism at court, Elizabeth's inconsistent support, contradictory directives, the notorious difficulty of ruling as proxy experienced by all of her viceroys (Morgan), and her insistence that Irish conquest be secured as inexpensively as possible, Sidney failed to produce the results he assured the queen he could deliver upon taking office (Brady 119), and he was recalled in 1571 and again in 1578.

Sidney encountered far more opposition from the traditional ruling class in Ireland, the Old English, than in Wales. When Sidney arrived, this community, descendants of the Anglo-Norman conquest who had served as arbiters of English control in Ireland over the medieval period, was in the early stages of displacement at the hands of newly arriving servitors, officers, and settlers, known as the New English. Old English displacement was thus another of the developments inherited by Sidney, but one that intensified under him. They initially welcomed Sidney after encountering difficulties under Sussex, but this phase passed quickly. Sidney's policies generated substantial resistance from many of the Old English, though he was able to garner some support, notably from Sir Lucas Dillon, who served as Chief Baron of the Exchequer and Member of the Irish Council.

Sidney played a direct hand in generating fears that they too would lose land for colonization when he blatantly intervened on behalf of the newcomer Peter Carew's claims to land held by the Butlers and other Old English families of the Pale (Lennon 185). He similarly contributed substantially to Old English displacement in the military (Brady 116), and repeatedly requested the replacement of Old English judges with New English appointments (Collins 1:216–17). An Old English explosion of resistance to many of Sidney's economic and military policies thwarted his plans for the 1569 Parliament, leading Nicholas White to report to London only two months after its opening that the relationship between a lord deputy and the Old English had never been worse (TNA SP 63/27/44). The situation was compounded by denigration of the Old English in parliamentary debate and in O'Neill's attainder, which blamed the Old English explicitly for the failed medieval conquest, thus justifying their displacement. The Old English were also denigrated for their Gaelicization, the adoption of Gaelic custom, an issue in which Sidney took a particular interest, compiling a list of Old English families and the degree to which they had "degenerated" (Campion 10–14). Their opposition took a devastating turn when the Butlers entered into rebellion the following summer, followed by the Desmonds. Suppression of these rebellions saw escalating violence in Munster and the widespread use of martial law. Sidney's second term saw Old English opposition to Sidney's economic policies spark again in the cess (land tax) controversy of 1577–78. Sidney's imprisonment of his opponents in Dublin Castle while their legal representatives were imprisoned in London spawned two years of defensive positioning from Sidney and from the cess opponents, who insisted that Sidney had overstepped his authority (McGowan-Doyle 22–8).

As with the Old English, Sidney cultivated very few collaborative relationships with leading figures in the Gaelic world. Here his attempts to extend the conquest often deteriorated into military action, contributing to rising administrative costs, and in turn generating yet more concern in London (and resistance from the Old English). In some cases destabilization was a function of the imposition of provincial councils as the framework for Anglicization through the dismantling of magnate power, restructuring of military resources, and the extension of English law (Lennon 243). Resistance from the Earls of Thomond and Clanricarde was compounded by the more extensive rebellion of the Mac an Iarlas (sons of the Earl of Clanricarde). Sidney later recorded his suppression of these figures in his memoirs in language reflective of the levels of instability and violence. Describing his suppression of the O'Briens, Sidney noted succinctly: "Of this wicked generation some I killed, some I hanged by order of law" (*Memoir* 87). Of the Mac an Iarlas taken into custody, Sidney wrote that he would rather have hanged them (87). In other regions, notably Ulster and Laois/Offaly, destabilization and violence were bred by the confiscation of land for colonization, a process augmented by Sidney's deep interest in producing maps of Ireland (Andrews). In one of the more notorious episodes during Sidney's second term, the massacre at Mullaghmast saw the decades-old attempt to establish plantations of soldiers in the midlands escalate into annihilation of the O'Mores (Carey 305–12).

Promoting and Defending Sidney

From the time Sidney took office in Ireland in 1565 to the final years of his life, he was persistently promoted in a variety of texts ranging from government correspondence to histories, and he engaged as well in self-promotion through writing, but even more monumentally in an exhaustive program of building, particularly in Ireland. Known as an ardent antiquarian and collector, Sidney sponsored histories that offered a vehicle for his praise and, when needed, defense of his contentious policies and actions. In Wales he patronized David Powel's 1584 *Historie of Cambria*, a revised and augmented version of Humphrey Llwyd's *Cronica Walliae*. This text stressed the peacefulness and orderliness of Wales and its people—a calculated rhetorical move, Philip Schwyzer argued, designed to defend Sidney against critics of his leniency such as Lewis and Whitgift (211–15). By this time, though, Sidney was already well versed in the use of history as a defensive tool in Ireland. Edmund Campion's 1571 *Two Bokes of the Histories of Irelande* had been composed, like Powel's, under Sidney's patronage, and both authors had been given access to Sidney's library and documents. Campion permitted Sidney to speak on behalf of his policies and against his opponents by incorporating into his history's closing passages Sidney's final speech before the Dublin Parliament in 1571, to which Campion appended a final and overwhelmingly laudatory portrait of Sidney (145–51). Sidney had been similarly praised lavishly in 1569 in a text of another sort, though one which relied heavily on history: the Act for the attainder of Shane O'Neill. Here Sidney was portrayed as Ireland's savior, bringing the long-failed medieval conquest to an end and ushering in a period of peace and security under English control (*Statutes at Large* 333–4). Like Powel's later text, O'Neill's attainder promoted Sidney's controversial policies as essential, in this case essential to completed English conquest. It is, however, justification of violent conquest, rather than peaceful control, that figures prominently in yet another text composed in Sidney's defense, John Derricke's 1581 *Image of Irelande* (Moroney 147–9). Placing Sidney within a grand historical overview of conquest, Derricke exaggerated the threat posed by Rory Óg O'More to justify Sidney's violent elimination of him and to defend of the larger pattern of violence perpetrated against the O'Mores and throughout the midlands (Carey 312–15).

Sidney's administrative correspondence offers a trove of self-promotional and defensive posturing, in particular his lengthy letter to Elizabeth of May 1577 defending himself against the cess opponents, whom he maligns as seditious, dishonest, and untrustworthy papists (TNA SP 63/58/29). In 1583 Sidney engaged in another form of self-promotional writing, composing a lengthy and elaborate memoir directed to Walsingham, perhaps with the help of Philip Sidney and/or advice from the Earl of Leicester. Ciarán Brady's 2002 edition of this memoir with an extended introduction sparked renewed interest in this unusual text. Most curious is the fact that Sidney's rendition of his successes and failures focuses almost exclusively on Ireland in spite of his much longer tenure in Wales. As Robert Shepard argued, this apparent oddity reveals Sidney's purpose, providing details to be used by Walsingham and Philip Sidney as they advocated at court on his behalf for another term as Lord Deputy of Ireland (Shepard 176–8). Sidney's memoir is therefore as highly rhetorically charged as texts written on his behalf, defending violent conquest in disturbingly casual language (Maley 104–5).

Sidney engaged even more extensively in self-promotion through construction and renovation. Although he patronized work at the family seat of Penshurst and at Ludlow Castle, his council seat in Wales (Kinsella 136), Ireland offered Sidney greater opportunity for expression of his profound "understanding of architecture's political and memorial power" (Siegfried 204). Construction and renovation thus became a literal manifestation of the claims in O'Neill's attainder that Sidney was responsible for building a new Ireland.

In fact, Sidney had already begun this work even before O'Neill's death, spending £1,352 on repairs and new construction at Dublin Castle in 1566 alone (Kinsella 131). Even at this early date, Sidney had already begun what would become a pattern of self-glorification in stone; two of the stones on the gates at Dublin Castle included plaques in Latin stating: "These stones do truly tell of Sidney's praise" and "Your worthy praise, O Sidney, cannot pass away" (Manning 10).

Sidney also took a particular interest in bridges, building or repairing bridges at Johnstown (Co. Kildare), Ballinasloe, Carlow, Islandbridge, and Blackwater (Ulster) (Manning 9–10; Kinsella 132–4), but most notably at the strategic site of Athlone. This bridge, a "raw statement of government power," as John Bradley described it (173), was decorated profusely with plaques memorializing Sidney. He also undertook extensive repair and building work elsewhere, including fortifications and castles as well as churches and mills in Carrickfergus, Kinsale, Drogheda, and Termonfeckin (Manning 9–10; Kinsella 136).

Churches provided Sidney with the opportunity for simultaneous self-promotion and advance of the Protestant Reformation, patronizing repairs at St. Peter's in Drogheda and at St. Nicholas in Dublin, though at St. Mary's, Dublin he had the chapel repurposed as a bakehouse rather than refurbishing it (Kinsella 132). Sidney's most substantial work, however, was at Christ Church Cathedral in Dublin. This site held both religious and administrative importance, where sessions of Parliament usually met, and was additionally a site of personal significance for Sidney as it housed the tomb of his daughter Elizabeth, who died in 1567 at the age of seven (Kinsella 117–18). Stuart Kinsella's study of Christ Church Cathedral reveals the extent to which Sidney used this site to create, in effect, a royal chapel (110), embellishing it with plaques that, as at Athlone bridge and Dublin Castle, simultaneously served self-promotion as much as "colonial propaganda" (127). Sidney's restoration of Strongbow's tomb at Christ Church Cathedral was a particularly poignant example of Sidney's simultaneous advancement of self and English control, a memorial to the Anglo-Norman conquest, and his claim to have completed that conquest (Kinsella 129).

Sidney died in May 1586, bitterly disappointed that he had devoted his life in service to the Crown, but never to receive the merits he believed were warranted. A request for a life patent of his post in Wales had been denied in 1565, his attempt to obtain payment and a barony in 1572 failed, and he was unsuccessful again in 1582 at obtaining title and land in compensation. If Sidney accomplished little constructive in Wales, and the council in fact lost authority as Williams argued, the case was quite otherwise in Ireland. The Tudor conquest of Ireland was already in progress when Sidney arrived, inheriting developments such as plantation and the establishment of provincial councils, but his zealous and rapid attempts at their aggressive extension destabilized an already tenuous process. He failed in securing England's desire for cost-effective control as he trod ever deeper into increasing military actions and their concomitant costs, exacerbating Elizabeth's disfavor and entrenching Ireland, no less than England, in a bitter future.

Bibliography

Manuscript Source

The National Archives, Kew
    SP 63. *State Papers, Ireland*

Primary and Secondary Sources

Andrews, J. H. "The Irish Surveys of Robert Lythe." *Imago Mundi* 19 (1965): 22–31.

Bradley, John. "Sir Henry Sidney's Bridge at Athlone, 1566–67." *Ireland in the Renaissance, c. 1540–1660.* Ed. Thomas Herron and Michael Potterton. Dublin: Four Courts Press, 2007. 173–94.

Brady, Ciarán. *The Chief Governors: The Rise and Fall of Reform Government in Tudor Ireland, 1536–1588.* Cambridge: Cambridge UP, 1994.

Brennan, Michael. *The Sidneys of Penshurst and the Monarchy, 1500–1700.* Aldershot: Ashgate, 2006.

Campion, Edmund. *Two Bokes of the Histories of Ireland (1571).* Ed. A. F. Vossen. Assen: Van Gorcum, 1963.

Canny, Nicholas. *The Elizabethan Conquest of Ireland: A Pattern Established, 1565–76.* New York: Harper and Row, 1976.

Carey, Vincent P. "John Derricke's *Image of Irelande*, Sir Henry Sidney, and the Massacre at Mullaghmast, 1578." *Irish Historical Studies* 31 (1999): 305–27.

Collins, Arthur, ed. *Letters and Memorials of State ….* 2 vols. London: T. Osborne, 1746.

HMC. *Report on the Manuscripts of Lord De L'Isle and Dudley Preserved at Penshurst Place.* 6 vols. London: HMSO, 1888–1905.

Jones, J. Gwynfor. *Early Modern Wales, c. 1525–1640.* New York: St. Martin's Press, 1994.

Kinsella, Stuart. "Colonial Commemoration in Tudor Ireland: The Case of Sir Henry Sidney." *SJ* 29 (2011): 105–45.

Lennon, Colm. *Sixteenth Century Ireland: The Incomplete Conquest.* 2nd ed. Dublin: Gill & Macmillan, 2005.

MacCaffrey, Wallace T. "Sir Henry Sidney." *ODNB.*

Maley, Willy. "Apology for Sidney: Making a Virtue of a Viceroy." *SJ* 20 (2002): 94–105.

Manning, Conleth. "Arms and the Man." *Archaeology Ireland* 24 (2010): 8–11.

McGowan-Doyle, Valerie. *The Book of Howth: Elizabethan Conquest and the Old English.* Cork: Cork UP, 2011.

Morgan, Hiram. "'Never any realm worse governed': Queen Elizabeth and Ireland." *Transactions of the Royal Historical Society* 14 (2004): 295–308.

Moroney, Maryclaire. "'The Sweetness of Due Subjection': John Derricke's *Image of Irelande* (1581) and the Sidneys." *SJ* 29 (2011): 147–71.

Schwyzer, Philip. "'A Happy Place of Government': Sir Henry Sidney, Wales, and *The Historie of Cambria* (1584)." *SJ* 29 (2011): 209–17.

Shephard, Robert. "The Motives of Sir Henry Sidney's *Memoir* (1583)." *SJ* 29 (2011): 173–86.

Sidney, Henry. *A Viceroy's Vindication? Sir Henry Sidney's Memoir of Service in Ireland, 1556–1578.* Ed. Ciarán Brady. Cork: Cork UP, 2002.

Sidney State Papers, 1565–70. Ed. Tomás Ó Laidhin. Dublin: Irish Manuscripts Commission, 1962.

Siegfried, Brandie. "Rivaling Caesar: The Roman Model in Sir Henry Sidney's *Memoir* (1583)." *SJ* 29 (2011): 187–208.

Statutes at Large, Passed in the Parliaments Held in Ireland, 1310–1800. 20 vols. Dublin, 1786–1801.

Williams, Penry. *The Council in the Marches of Wales under Elizabeth I.* Cardiff: U of Wales P, 1958.

Lady Mary Dudley Sidney (*c.* 1531–1586) and Her Siblings

Carole Levin and Catherine Medici

In 1562 Mary Dudley Sidney (Illustration 6) devotedly nursed Queen Elizabeth during her attack of smallpox. Catching the disease herself, she was severely scarred, leading to a perhaps erroneous image of her for future generations as a woman with a veil hiding her ruined face. Mary Dudley Sidney is for the most part best known because of her family: her son, Philip, her daughter, Mary, and to a lesser extent, her brother, Robert. But while Lady Sidney cared deeply about her family and worked for their advancement, there is much more to her than her familial relationships. She was a woman of intelligence and education who played a significant role in the early years of Elizabeth I's court and in her husband's career in Ireland. Lady Mary Sidney can be found in many important primary sources, including the State Papers and the Sidney family letters, but she usually appears only in scholarship devoted primarily to other family members like her son Philip (for example, Duncan-Jones; Stewart), or her daughter Mary, Countess of Pembroke (Brennan; Hannay), or to Queen Elizabeth (Cole; Levin; Whitelock).[1]

Mary, born *c.* 1531–35, was one of five daughters and eight sons of John Dudley (1504?–52) and his wife Jane (1508–55). Those who lived to adulthood were John (1527?–54), Ambrose (1530?–90), Henry (1531?–57), Robert (1532?–88), Guildford (1535?–54), and Katherine (1545–1620). The Dudley children were educated at home in the humanist tradition under a variety of tutors, including John Dee. This education also included the girls, who learned languages, composition, and natural philosophy under the supervision of their mother, Jane Dudley, who was widely noted for achieving a level of education uncommon for women (Collins 1:33). The Spanish ambassador Alvaro de Quadra later wrote of her valuable knowledge of foreign languages, such as Italian and French (*CSPS* 1:95).

The Dudley family's political fortunes greatly affected Mary and the other Dudley children. Because of their father's status under Henry VIII, the children were the chosen companions of young Prince Edward. When the royal children's households were combined under Catherine Parr, the children also became companions for Princess Elizabeth. The relationship formed between the Dudley children and the young Princess Elizabeth during their childhood has been emphasized in research focusing on the relationship between the queen and Robert Dudley, but was also important for Mary Dudley. John Dudley steadily rose in power and prestige during the reign of Henry VIII; however, his role in the reign of the young Edward VI brought the family to the heights of power, and ultimately to the

---

1   She also appears in fictionalized descriptions, such as Violet A. Wilson's *Society Women of Shakespeare's Time* (New York: E. P. Dutton, 1925), and Philippa Gregory's *The Virgin's Lover* (New York: Touchstone, 2004), and is a notable character in the BBC series *Elizabeth R*.

bottom of fortune's wheel. Dudley participated in a power struggle with Edward Seymour, Duke of Somerset, and won, becoming Lord President of the Privy Council and Duke of Northumberland; young Edward trusted him, and he was the most powerful man in the realm.

During the family's time of influence and power under Edward, the lives of the Dudleys became intertwined with the monarch. The Dudley sons were companions to the young king and held positions at the court. Young John held the position of Master of the Buckhounds and then Master of the Horse, while Robert was a member of the king's Privy Chamber and became Chief Carver and Master of the Hounds after his brother. The family's relationship with the king also allowed Mary to meet her future husband, Henry Sidney, who grew up alongside the young king and was one of the principal Gentlemen of his Privy Chamber (Collins 1:82, 83). Henry was a friend of her brother's, and apparently knew Mary well. Margaret Hannay suggests that the marriage appears to have been based on real affection between them (5). The pair married in 1551, and while Henry Sidney continued to serve the king, it appears that Mary was also present at court. The couple had seven children, three of whom died in childhood. The other four were Sir Philip Sidney (1554–86), Mary Sidney Herbert, Countess of Pembroke (1561–1621), Robert Sidney, Earl of Leicester (1563–1626), and Sir Thomas Sidney (1569–95). Two of Mary's brothers had married in 1550; Robert married Amy Robsart, and John married Anne Seymour. Soon after her marriage, her brother Ambrose married his second wife, Elizabeth Tailboys, in 1552 or early 1553, and Henry married his wife, Margaret Audley, in 1553.

The events at the end of Edward's reign in 1553 were significant for the Sidneys. In May of 1553 Northumberland married his son Guildford to Edward's cousin, Lady Jane Grey. In the same ceremony young Katherine Dudley married Henry Hastings, the son of the Earl of Huntingdon. In July, Edward died in Henry Sidney's arms, and apparently on her father's instruction, Mary informed Jane that Edward VI's will had bypassed his two sisters; Jane was the new queen. The plan failed, and Mary Tudor became queen without a battle. Northumberland's grasp for power nearly led to the downfall of the entire Dudley clan. Northumberland was beheaded, and six months later, in the aftermath of the Wyatt rebellion, so too were Jane and Guildford Dudley. The other Dudley brothers were imprisoned in the Tower and found guilty of treason in November 1553. Katherine's husband, Lord Hastings, and his father, the earl, were also imprisoned. Henry Sidney fled to Penshurst, the Sidney family estate in Kent (Illustrations 3 and 4), immediately following Edward's death, and somehow, in a way that is unclear, Lady Sidney escaped entanglement in the downfall of the rest of the family. Henry even managed to gain a position in Mary Tudor's government, perhaps due to the queen's fondness for his niece, Jane Dormer. Lord Hastings's mother, Katherine, was the granddaughter of Queen Mary's godmother, Margaret Pole, Countess of Salisbury, and Mary's affection for the Pole family led her to pardon Lord Hastings in November 1553.

Their ability to avoid the fate of much of the rest of the family made the Sidneys particularly useful at this time. Alongside Jane Dudley, Duchess of Northumberland, and Ambrose's wife Elizabeth, Mary and Henry worked tirelessly for the release of the Dudley men from the Tower, as well as for the restoration of their rights to inherit titles and remain peers (Collins 1:33, 84). During the negotiations for Mary I's marriage, Henry was part of the entourage that traveled to Spain, and he used the opportunity to develop a relationship with Philip of Spain. After the marriage of Philip and Mary in 1554, the Sidneys asked Philip to be godfather and namesake to their first son. The Sidneys' campaign for influence with the Spanish circle at court worked, as Philip convinced the queen to release John, Henry, and Robert from the Tower in October 1554 (Collins 1:36–7, 98). After their release, the Dudley men went to Penshurst, where John Dudley died the following day. The eldest surviving brother, Ambrose, was released by December 1554. Henry Sidney's power and prestige increased throughout Mary's reign. The surviving Dudley brothers, Ambrose, Robert, and Henry, attempted to win the favor of the queen. Robert and Ambrose participated in the royal tournament celebrating the marriage of Mary and Philip in late 1554. The Dudley brothers served the Crown in the wars in France, participating in the St. Quentin expedition in 1557, where Henry was killed.

While Mary Tudor's reign was a time of rising fortunes for the Sidneys and redemption for the Dudleys, the accession of Elizabeth in 1558 allowed their power and influence to expand. When Elizabeth became queen she immediately appointed Robert her Master of the Horse, and eventually Earl of Leicester (1564). After the mysterious death of his wife Amy in 1560, Robert attempted unsuccessfully for many years to convince Elizabeth to marry him. Until his death in 1588 Robert Dudley was one of the most important men at Elizabeth's court, a status he held due to her deep affection for him. Lady Sidney's other surviving brother also held significant positions during Elizabeth's reign. Ambrose was named Chief Pantler and Master of the Ordnance. In December 1561 he became Earl of Warwick. The following year he led an expeditionary force to Newhaven (Le Havre), which he held until July 1563, and he was highly regarded for his leadership. He did, however, receive a serious leg wound from which he never recovered, leading to ill health until his death in 1590 after his leg had turned gangrenous. After being widowed again, in 1565 he married Anne Russell, eldest daughter of Francis, Earl of Bedford, but this marriage too was childless.

Lady Sidney was the only member of Elizabeth's Privy Chamber at her coronation who was not a relation or had not been serving her for years before. Her position was unsalaried. Elizabeth's accounts of Robert Dudley as a childhood friend would suggest that Mary was as well, allowing her entry into Elizabeth's court from the beginning. Elizabeth surrounded herself with those she knew and could trust, those who had been with her for years or were related to her (Adams, *Leicester* 17, 30). Lady Sidney was an outlier or exception in the first iteration of Elizabeth's court. Her brother's closeness to the queen certainly played a role in the appointment; however, it seems that her political skills and a bond created in childhood could also have been significant. The success of Lady Sidney and her husband in getting her brothers released from the Tower and reinstated to their titles and lands demonstrated her political acumen (see Brennan *ARC* 1:1).

In 1559 Katherine had reached an age where she could participate in the family's political alliance. She and Huntingdon were by now living as a married couple, and Katherine requested assistance from her brother, Robert Dudley, at court to deal with money owed to Huntingdon. This was the beginning of Huntingdon's involvement with the Dudley family political machine. Katherine remained involved in using her family relationships and friendship with the queen to prevent financial disaster (Cross; Hannay).

Elizabeth put Lady Mary Sidney's political skills to use early in her reign, but in a way that left Mary feeling used and alienated. One evening in September 1559 Queen Elizabeth summoned Mary along with her brother Robert and instructed her to begin discussions with Spanish ambassador de Quadra about the potential marriage match with Archduke Charles, son and later brother to the Holy Roman Emperor and Hapsburg connection to the Spanish Crown. Lady Sidney acted on Elizabeth's instruction and approached the Spanish ambassador and Caspar von Brüner, the Ambassador for the Holy Roman Emperor, and advised them that "this was the best time to speak to the Queen about the Archduke." Mary took her mission seriously, answering de Quadra's doubts about Elizabeth's true intentions by assuring him that "it is the custom of ladies here not to give their consent in such matters until they are teased into it." Lady Sidney not only provided de Quadra with information about what Elizabeth had said were her intentions to marry Archduke Charles, but also inside information about foreign affairs and conflicts. This included an assassination threat from within the court, when some members of the Scottish fraction planned to poison the queen when she ate with the Earl of Arundel (*CSPS* 1:96).

In October de Quadra approached Elizabeth about the match with the archduke and found Elizabeth "surprised" and "not wishing to be approached on that side." De Quadra noted that her attitude and speech countered the information that he had from Mary, but this did not diminish the importance the ambassador placed on Mary's information. He wrote: "I do not believe Lady Sidney and Lord Robert could be mistaken" (*CSPS* 1:98–101). In the middle of November a fight between Mary and Robert over his feelings that "she was carrying the affair further than he desired" caused de Quadra to question the queen about her intentions towards the archduke and push her to be "more open to us than hitherto." Elizabeth was furious, and told the ambassador "that some one had done this with good intentions, but without any commission from her." Despite Elizabeth's effort to sacrifice Mary to her own diplomacy, de Quadra did not believe her, thinking that both he and Lady Sidney had been fooled in the matter. As Tracy Borman suggests, Lady Sidney, "humiliated and aggrieved," believed both Elizabeth and Robert had exploited her because of the respect the Spanish ambassador had for her (217). This incident caused a break between Mary Dudley Sidney and her most important alliances at court, the queen and her brother Robert. The alliances were eventually restored, though Elizabeth never used Mary in this way again.

In the fall of 1562 Lady Sidney's loyal service to Queen Elizabeth was put to the test. The queen fell ill with smallpox, and Mary stayed with her, helping to nurse her back to health. The queen had few scars, but Mary caught smallpox herself and emerged disfigured. Much later, Henry Sidney complained that twenty years before, when he left his wife she was "a full faire Ladye in myne eye at least the fayerest," but when he returned he "found her as fowle a ladie as the smale pox could make her" (*Memoir* 105) After her disfigurement, Mary Sidney continued to be a presence at court, but no longer spent most of her time there. She was in the country or sometimes moving the family to both Wales and Ireland as her husband took up positions as President of the Council of Wales and Lord Deputy of Ireland.

After having been briefly in Ireland with Sir Henry when he served there in Mary I's reign, Lady Sidney returned in January 1566 when Henry was Lord Deputy. She lost most of what they needed to set up a household in Dublin along with her all her clothing and jewelry in a shipwreck. She arrived with little more than the clothes she was wearing, and had to establish their household. Ireland was often difficult for her, but carefully using what she had learned at the Tudor courts, she also played an important public role. As Karen Holland points out, "Mary Sidney eventually went beyond the office customarily allotted to women and played a direct role ... in calling up troops" while Henry was away (58). Knowing that Sidney was in another part of Ireland, Shane O'Neill attacked Drogheda, planning to kidnap Mary to strengthen his negotiating position. To protect her family and the town, Lady Sidney convinced Patrick Sarsfield, Mayor of Dublin, to provide defense. While Edmund Campion was convinced that Lady Sidney's foresight saved Drogheda (128), Holland adds that Henry Sidney gave Mary no credit in his 1583 *Memoir*, and referred to her in that "belittling tone that had become the hallmark of his later relationship with his wife" (9).

Mary became ill and returned to England by the spring of 1567; Henry did not return until late that autumn. When he returned to Ireland in October 1568, Mary, pregnant with their last child, did not accompany him. Nor did she join him later, though he was there until 1571. By 1575, when he returned to Ireland yet again, the deterioration in Mary's health and of their relationship meant that Mary stayed in England. Despite her ill health, she continuously worked for her family's political goals through her correspondence with members of the court and occasional visits when requested by the queen or needed by her family. Mary's maintenance of her court connections appears in her letters to her husband's secretary, Edmund Molyneux. In 1574 she offered "to be at the Court, to stand my dear Lord in what steed, my duty and being there with her Majesty, and my Friends, might do" in an effort to have Henry named as the Lord Deputy of Ireland for a third time (Collins 1:67). In 1578, Mary instructed Molyneux to go to various members of the court, including her brothers, to gain support for Henry's policies in Ireland.

Mary Sidney's letters show the physical and emotional toll of this service. In an anxious missive to her husband's secretary Mary Sidney complained about the difficulty of her accommodations at court because she was "continually sick and not able to be much out of bed" and thought the room was she was given "very little." Mary did not think this room would be appropriate, as "the Queen will look to have my chamber always in a redines, for her majesties coming" (Collins 1:271). Despite the difficulties of attending the queen, Mary did so until 1580, when she made the decision to leave court for the last time in support of her family members' opposition to the marriage negotiations with the Duke of Anjou.

The fortunes of the Dudley family rose to spectacular heights during the reign of Elizabeth, taking the Sidneys with them. At one time during Elizabeth's reign, between their own lands and the lands they controlled through government offices, the Dudley-Sidney family controlled one-third of English lands (Brennan 32). This immense amount of control gave the family significant political importance; unfortunately, for the Sidneys it did not translate into financial gain. Lady Mary Sidney's political involvement during Elizabeth's reign included lobbying the queen directly for her husband while he was serving the queen far from court as Lord Deputy of Ireland and President of the Councils of the Welsh Marches. She consistently argued for the queen to repay him money spent in government service, echoing his many letters to Elizabeth, William Cecil, Lord Burghley, and the Privy Council. The disadvantages of the Sidneys' loyal service to the queen appear in Lady Sidney's 1572 note to Burghley. She asked him to hold back a motion to name Henry a baron because of the Sidneys' "ill ability to maintain a higher title than we now possess"; they could not afford to uphold the responsibilities that came with the position (TNA 63/36/30). Henry Sidney's loyalty to the queen and years of service had cost the Sidney family much of their fortune.

Lady Mary Sidney's Dudley family lineage was important to Henry Sidney and the way he represented himself. After their marriage Henry modified the Sidney family badge to include the Dudley bear and ragged staff alongside the Sidney porcupine. Sir Henry and Mary wrote to their son in April 1566, when he was eleven years old: "Remember my sonne the Noble bloud you are discended of by your mothers side, & thinke that only by virtuous life and good action, you may be an ornament to that ylustre family." Mary added in a postscript: "Your Noble and carefull Father hath taken paynes with his owne hand, to giue you in this his letter, so wise, so learned, and most requiste precepts for you to follow" (*Correspondence SPS* 1:4–5). The Dudley connections prove more important when looking at the way family ties affected the Sidney marriage. Lady Sidney highlighted the importance of the Dudley connection when she wrote to her husband's secretary in London while she was away and asked him to "go often in my name, to inquire how my deare Brothers do" (Collins 1:67). While serving in Ireland, Sidney's greatest ally at court was his brother-in-law, Robert Dudley. Henry frequently wrote to Robert to request his assistance in getting support from the queen for his Irish policies and commitments to fund them. Michael Brennan argues that the Dudleys' and Sidneys' public and political fortunes depended on strong family loyalty and connection, like many prominent families, but the Dudley-Sidney dependence on the women of the family's political involvement and instincts set them apart (Brennan 50). The interconnection between Lady Sidney and the Dudleys in the political realm was part of Mary's life in Elizabeth's court from beginning to end.

Though the marriage of Henry Sidney to Mary Dudley began with great affection, it grew more distant. Sir William Fitzwilliam wrote from Ireland in concern to Cecil that "Sir Henry Sydney to be openly cautioned against keeping company with Mrs. Issam," the wife of one of his captains (TNA 63/13/138). In 1583 Henry rather coldheartedly considered the possibility of a second family with a younger wife: "Nor yet am I so old, nor my wife so healthy, but that she may die, and I marry again and get children" (Memoir 43). But Henry died in May 1586, a few months before Mary's death, after a long illness, in August (Hannay 55).

After the death of Mary Sidney and Robert Dudley in 1586 and 1588 the Dudley family presence at court was retained by the increased involvement of the Countess of Huntingdon in court politics. Because Huntingdon was put forward as a possible heir during Elizabeth's illness in 1562, Elizabeth did what she could to distance Henry and Katherine from official power. Katherine was an important member of the group at court that centered on her brothers Robert Dudley, Earl of Leicester, and Ambrose Dudley, Earl of Warwick, and was dedicated to advancing Puritanism at court, promoting ties to other Protestant causes across Europe, and advocating for alliances with other Protestant countries. The dedications of religious works place Katherine as a strong Protestant and a member of the Sidney–Russell circle of literary patronage. By the 1590s, Katherine was an important presence at court. Katherine was also an important political patron for the members of the Dudley–Sidney alliance. Rowland Whyte, personal agent for Katherine's nephew Robert Sidney, noted in his letters that Katherine and the queen met in private meeting at least once a day, and at one time twice a day (Whyte 284–5). She continued to help her Sidney relatives through the rest of her life.

Rowland Whyte even argued that Katherine "governes the Queen" because of the "many Howres together very private" (Collins 2:206). In addition to being sought out by her Sidney relations, Katherine was sought out by other members of the family network. Katherine was repeatedly visited by Frances, Countess of Essex, when the earl was being held at York House for disobeying the queen's orders as her commander in Ireland and returning without her permission. Frances was part of the family network in two ways: she was the widow of Katherine's nephew, Philip Sidney, and then the wife of Robert Dudley's stepson, Robert Devereux, Earl of Essex (see Ioppolo ARC 1:6). After the death of Elizabeth, Katherine remained an important member of her family's political circle and a champion of Puritan Protestantism in England until her death in 1620.

The representations of Lady Mary Sidney made later during her lifetime and shortly after her death show how she was valued. Views of Lady Sidney survive in a variety of sources, mostly tied to the men in her life, particularly her husband and her son Philip. Surprisingly, despite the importance of their relationship, few accounts of her brother, Robert Dudley, Earl of Leicester, even mention Mary.

Fulke Greville, a close childhood friend of Mary's son Philip, wrote one of the most evocative descriptions of Lady Sidney in his biography of her son. Greville is the source of the image of Mary's covering her smallpox-ravaged face, one of the lasting and most commonly known impressions of Lady Sidney. The combination of two of his descriptions allows the impression, most probably erroneous, that Mary roamed the halls of the court covered in a veil. He wrote that she "chose rather to hide her self from the curious eyes of a delicate time" and "the mischance of sickness having cast such a kind of veile over her excellent beauty" (Greville 5, 6). In his conversations with William Drummond in Scotland in 1618 Ben Jonson demonstrated how much this was believed by early seventeenth century: "After she had the little pox never shew her self in Court thereafter bot Masked" (30).

Greville's further description of Lady Sidney posited her as an exemplar of a noble woman on the surface, but a deeper analysis reveals there was far more to her. He notes her "descent of great nobility" and credits it for her "large ingenuous spirit" (5). By doing so, Greville pointed out Mary's generosity and high-mindedness. He also referred to her "ingenious sensibleness." These few words create an image of a woman who was able to use her intellect to benefit herself, her family, and those connected to her. In his description of her response to disfigurement he noted that her modesty kept her from most public life, but he also remarked on her courage. Greville asserted that Mary had a "native strength" and a "heroic-call sprit." Throughout his brief description of Lady Sidney Fulke Greville produced an image of a woman who was intelligent and strong enough to withstand the stares of a society that was thoroughly intolerant of difference.

Molyneux, secretary to Sir Henry Sidney, was devoted to the family and knew Mary well. In 1586, after the deaths of the Sidneys, Molyneux provided material about them for the second edition of *Holinshed's Chronicles*. Molyneux presented Mary as a female ideal, asserting that she was "the most noble, worthie, beneficent, and bounteous ladie" (Holinshed, *Chronicles* 1587 2:1553). He also emphasized her Protestant piety, describing it in connection with her eloquence: "She used such godlie speeches, earnest and effectuall persuasions to al those about hir." He also praised her "good speech, apt and readie conceipt, excellencie of wit, and notable eloquent deliverie." Her eloquence was at its height when she was on her death-bed, leaving this world "most confidentlie, and to God (no doubt) most gloriouslie" (1553).

For many years most scholarship on the Dudley siblings has centered on Leicester. The most significant recent research on Leicester is by Simon Adams, in his collection of essays, *Leicester and the Court*. There has been little scholarship produced on the Earl of Warwick beyond the excellent entry by Adams in the *ODNB*, as unfortunately, after his widow's death his papers were destroyed. As Adams points out, this lack of evidence has reinforced the view that Ambrose existed very much in Robert's shadow.

Scholarship on Mary Sidney is almost exclusively found in accounts of her more famous relatives. A rich primary source is the 1746 edition of Sidney papers edited by Arthur Collins (who sometimes condenses or revises the family letters he presents; see the recent edition of Rowland Whyte's correspondence). To date, the most extensive information about her family role is found in Margaret Hannay's biography of Mary's daughter, *Philip's Phoenix: Mary Sidney, Countess of Pembroke*. Michael Brennan's study of the Sidney family, *The Sidneys of Penshurst and the Monarchy, 1500–1700*, also includes information about Mary's political role. Dennis Kay addresses Sir Philip Sidney's relationship with his mother and the queen in his essay "She was a Queen, and Therefore Beautiful." In her chapter on Mary Dudley Sidney in *Ten Remarkable Women of the Tudor Courts and Their Influence in Founding the New World, 1530–1630* Elizabeth Darracott Wheeler contends that she was important in the history of exploration and colonization because she was the wife and mother of men influential in these areas. Many of Wheeler's assertions are highly speculative, but her assertions about the importance of Lady Mary Sidney's role in her husband's colonial endeavors could be an avenue for further study. Karen Holland's fine essay "The Sidney Women in Ireland, *c.* 1556–1594" is one of the most developed pieces of scholarship on Mary Dudley Sidney, focusing particularly on her time in Ireland alongside her sisters-in-law Frances Sidney Radcliffe and Anne Sidney Fitzwilliam. Holland emphasizes Lady Sidney's public role in terms of patronage, religion, and military affairs. Catherine Medici's essay "To Persuade and Connect: Mary Sidney's Essential Role in Henry Sidney's Irish Rule" further examines Mary's contributions to Irish colonization in Ireland and from England through her cultivation of support for Henry's policies at court and her involvement with political negotiations in Ireland.

Lady Sidney is also found in studies of politics during Elizabeth's reign. Natalie Mears uses Lady Mary Sidney's role in the marriage negotiations with the Spanish ambassador to argue for the political significance of women in Elizabeth's reign in her essay "Politics in the Elizabethan Privy Chamber: Lady Mary Sidney and Kat Ashley." In addition, though Pam Wright doubts the political agency of the women of the Privy Chamber, she uses Lady

Sidney's actions to argue that Elizabeth used her Privy Chamber women as mediators to allow her the most freedom in political decisions in her essay "A Change in Direction: The Ramifications of a Female Household, 1558–1603." Catherine Howey-Stearn's article "Critique or Complaint? Lady Mary Sidney's 1573 New Year's Gift to Queen Elizabeth I" considers the relationship between the sisters Lady Sidney and the Countess of Huntingdon with the queen, and their political role at court as seen in the use of gift exchange to influence the queen's image and patronage.

As with her sister, accounts of Katherine Hastings can be mostly found in scholarship focused on her relatives. The most extensive coverage of Katherine's life is found in Clare Cross's 1967 biography of Katherine's husband, *The Puritan Earl: The Life of Henry Hastings, Third Earl of Huntingdon, 1536–1595*, and her entry on Katherine in the *ODNB*. Katherine can also be found in both Hannay's and Brennan's work.

There are various avenues for further exploration of Mary Dudley Sidney, such as analysis of her role in court politics and the family political alliance. In addition, her involvement in Ireland and in Wales alongside her husband and other early exploration ventures can offer an important window into the ways English women participated in early exploration and colonial rule, along with Sidney family female portraiture and, most importantly, her full biography. The study of both Mary and Katherine can illuminate women's roles in family networks and their political influence during Elizabeth's reign.

Bibliography

Manuscript Sources

British Library, London
  Cotton Titus B/II/304
The National Archives, Kew
  SP 63/13/136, 63/16/83, 63/36/30, 63/99/215

Primary and Secondary Sources

Adams, Simon. "Dudley, Ambrose, Earl of Warwick (*c.*1530–1590)." *ODNB*.
—. "Dudley, Robert, Earl of Leicester (1532/3–1588)." *ODNB*.
—. *Leicester and the Court: Essays on Elizabethan Politics*. Manchester: Manchester UP, 2002.
Borman, Tracy. *Elizabeth's Women: Friends, Rivals, and Foes Who Shaped the Virgin Queen*. New York: Bantam Books, 2009.
Brennan, Michael G. *The Sidneys of Penshurst and the Monarchy, 1500–1700*. Aldershot: Ashgate, 2006.
Calendar of Letters and State Papers Relating to English Affairs [of the Reign of Elizabeth] Preserved Principally in the Archives of Simancas. Transl. Martin Andrew Hume. London: HMSO, 1892.
Calendar of State Papers Spanish .... Ed. Martin A. S. Hume. 13 vols. London: HMSO, 1894.
Campion, Edward. "A History of Ireland Written in the Year 1571." *Two histories of Ireland. The one written by Edmund Campion, the other by Meredith Hanmer Dr of Divinity*. Ed. James Ware. 3 vols. Dublin: Society of Stationers, 1633.
Cole, Mary Hill. *The Portable Queen: Elizabeth I and the Politics of Ceremony*. Amherst, MA: U of Massachusetts P, 1999.

Collins, Arthur, ed. *Letters and Memorials of State ....* 2 vols. London: T. Osborne, 1746.

Cross, Claire. "Hastings, Katherine, Countess of Huntingdon (*c.*1538–1620)." *ODNB*.

—. *The Puritan Earl: The Life of Henry Hastings, Third Earl of Huntingdon, 1536–1595.* New York: Macmillan, 1967.

Drummond, William. *Ben Jonson's Conversations with William Drummond of Hawthornden.* Folcroft, PA: Folcroft, 1969.

Duncan-Jones, Katherine. *Sir Philip Sidney: Courtier Poet.* New Haven, CT: Yale UP, 1991.

Gregory, Philippa. *The Virgin's Lover.* New York: Simon & Schuster, 2004.

Greville, Fulke. *The Life of the Renowned Sir Philip Sidney.* London: Henry Seile, 1652.

Hannay, Margaret P. *Philip's Phoenix: Mary Sidney, Countess of Pembroke,* New York: Oxford UP, 1990.

Harris, Barbara. *English Aristocratic Women 1450–1550: Marriage and Family, Property and Careers.* New York: Oxford UP, 2002.

HMC. *Report on the Manuscripts of Lord de L'Isle and Dudley Preserved at Penshurst Place.* 6 vols. London: HMSO, 1925–66.

Holinshed, Raphael. *Chronicles of England, Scotlande, and Irelande.* 3 vols. London: Henry Denham, 1587.

Holland, Karen. "The Sidney Women in Ireland, *c.* 1556–1594." *SJ* 29.1–2 (2011): 45–69.

Howey-Stern, Catherine. "Critique or Complaint? Lady Mary Sidney's 1573 New Year's Gift to Queen Elizabeth I." *SJ* 30.2 (2012): 109–27.

Kay, Dennis. "'She Was a Queen, and Therefore Beautiful': Sidney, His Mother, and Queen Elizabeth." *Review of English Studies: A Quarterly Journal of English Literature and the English Language* 169.43 (1992): 18–39.

Levin, Carole. *The Heart and Stomach of a King: Elizabeth I and the Politics of Sex and Power.* 2nd ed. Philadelphia, PA: U of Pennsylvania P, 2013.

Loades, David. "Dudley, John, Duke of Northumberland (1504–1553)." *ODNB*.

Mears, Natalie. "Politics in the Elizabethan Privy Chamber: Lady Mary Sidney and Kat Ashley." *Women and Politics in Early Modern England, 1450–1700.* Ed. James Daybell. Aldershot: Ashgate, 2003. 67–82.

Medici, Catherine. "To Persuade and Connect: Mary Sidney's Essential Role in Henry Sidney's Irish Rule." *A Mirror for Medieval and Renaissance Studies: Selected Proceedings of the Newberry Center for Renaissance Studies 2012 Multidisciplinary Graduate Student Conference.* Ed. Laura Aydelotte. Chicago, IL: Newberry Library, 2012. 61–71.

Richardson, G. J. "Dudley, Lord Guildford (*c.*1535–1554)." *ODNB*.

Sidney, Henry. *A Viceroy's Vindication? Sir Henry Sidney's Memoir of Service in Ireland, 1556–1578.* Ed. Ciarán Brady. Cork: Cork UP, 2002.

Sidney, Philip. *The Correspondence of Sir Philip Sidney.* Ed. Roger Kuin. 2 vols. Oxford: Oxford UP, 2012.

Stewart, Alan. *Philip Sidney: A Double Life.* London: Random House, 2000.

Wheeler, Elizabeth Darracott. "Mary Sidney." *Ten Remarkable Women of the Tudor Courts and Their Influence in Founding of the New World, 1530–1630.* Lewiston, NY: Edwin Mellen, 2000. 57–65.

Whitelock, Anna. *Elizabeth's Bedfellows: An Intimate History of the Queen's Court.* London: Bloomsbury, 2013.

Whyte, Rowland. *The Letters (1595–1608) of Rowland Whyte.* Ed. Michael G. Brennan, Noel J. Kinnamon, and Margaret P. Hannay. Philadelphia, PA: American Philosophical Society, 2013.

Wilson, Violet. *Society Women of Shakespeare's Time.* New York: Dutton & Co., 1924.

Wright, Pam. "A Change in Direction: The Ramifications of a Female Household, 1558–1603." *The English Court: From the Wars of the Roses to the Civil War*. Ed. David Starkey. New York: Longman, 1987. 147–72.

Philip Sidney (1554–1586)

Alan Stewart

Philip Sidney (Illustration 7) was born at his family's Kent estate of Penshurst on 30 November 1554, the first of seven children of Sir Henry Sidney (1529–86) and his wife, Mary Dudley Sidney (1530–86) (Illustrations 5 and 6). He was named for Queen Mary's husband, Philip of Spain, who stood godfather at his baptism, alongside his maternal grandmother, Jane Dudley, Duchess of Northumberland, and John Russell, first Earl of Bedford. Through his mother, Sidney was a member of the powerful Dudley family, with whom he would be strongly identified: his uncles Ambrose Dudley, later Earl of Warwick, and Robert Dudley, later Earl of Leicester, were childless, and Sidney was their heir presumptive.

Raised at Penshurst, Sidney had as his first tutor the Frenchman Jean Tassel, who accompanied him in October 1564 to Shrewsbury School, where for four years he continued his education close to Ludlow, where his father served as Lord President of the Council in the Marches. In Shrewsbury Philip lodged with the family of the local MP, George Leigh; his headmaster was the St. John's College, Cambridge, fellow Thomas Ashton, and among his schoolfellows was his kinsman Fulke Greville. In 1565 his father was appointed Lord Deputy of Ireland, a post he would hold twice (1565–71, 1575–78) in addition to his Welsh appointment (see McGowan-Doyle *ARC* 1:2, Herron *ARC* 1:13, and Maley and Schwyzer *ARC* 1:14). August 1566 was marked by visits to Kenilworth, the Warwickshire seat of his uncle Leicester, and Oxford University, of which Leicester was chancellor, where Queen Elizabeth was received. The Gray's Inn registers record that Sidney was enrolled on 2 February 1567, but there is no evidence that he resided there.

In 1568 Sidney matriculated at Christ Church, Oxford, encountering a new set of intellectual influences: his tutors Thomas Cooper, Nathaniel Baxter, and Thomas Thornton, and peers, including Greville, Walter Ralegh, Richard Hakluyt, Thomas Bodley, Henry Savile, John Lyly, and William Camden. Sidney was praised by the mathematician Thomas Allen, who may have cast his horoscope; he disputed *ex tempore* with another student, Richard Carew, to great acclaim. He also spent time at court with Secretary of State William Cecil: in 1569, aged fourteen, Sidney was contracted to marry Cecil's eldest daughter Anne, but two years later she married Edward de Vere, seventeenth Earl of Oxford. In 1570 his father asked for Philip to come to Ireland, but the queen refused to license his travel. Sidney's Oxford days ended abruptly in April 1571, when plague shut down operations for nearly a year: he may have spent time at Cambridge, but no record survives.

On 25 May 1572 Elizabeth signed a passport for Sidney to travel abroad for two years with Lodowick Bryskett and three servants. He accompanied Edward Fiennes de Clinton, Earl of Lincoln, sent to Paris to sign the Treaty of Blois allying England and France against Spain, but Sidney stayed on when Lincoln left France in late June, lodging with the English ambassador Sir Francis Walsingham. Out of respect for the house of Sidney, and for his personal qualities, he was created Baron de Sidenay and Gentleman of the

Bedchamber to the French king, Charles X, on 9 August. In addition to celebrating the 18 August marriage of Henri de Navarre and Charles's sister, Marguerite de Valois, Sidney met in Paris leading Huguenot intellectuals, including logician Pierre de la Ramée (Ramus), theologian Philippe du Plessis Mornay, lawyer Jean Lobbet, printer André Wechel, Philip-Ludwig, Count de Hanau, and most influentially, the diplomat and political theorist Hubert Languet (Illustration 8), who would remain a close friend, correspondent, and mentor for the next eight years. On 24 August the St. Bartholomew's Day Massacre broke out, killing (among many others) de la Ramée, and Sidney took refuge in Walsingham's lodging. The Privy Council demanded that Sidney return home, but by the time the order reached Paris Walsingham had already dispatched Sidney with Francis Newton, Dean of Winchester, to the safely Calvinist Heidelberg (although Newton died *en route*).

Sidney would remain for three years in Europe, where he was accorded a status he did not enjoy in England. His father's position as Lord Deputy of Ireland made him in Latin a "Prorex" (viceroy), and Continental observers made much of the Lord Deputy as a person with royal powers, and at least quasi-royal status; by extension, Sidney was often eulogized as a quasi-prince. In addition, his proximity to Leicester rendered him attractive to the Protestant political cognoscenti. Traveling as a royal envoy in 1577, he displayed outside his lodgings a placard which proclaimed him (in Latin) as "The most illustrious and noble man Philip Sidney, Englishman, son of the Prorex of Ireland, nephew to the Earls of Warwick and Leicester, ambassador of the most serene Queen of England to the Emperor" (Collins 1:100).

In Heidelberg, Sidney met the scholar and printer Henri Estienne, who gave him a manuscript collection of Greek proverbs (and in 1576 dedicated to him his Greek New Testament), before traveling to Frankfurt, where he lodged with Wechel, met the Huguenot minister Théophile de Banos (who dedicated to Sidney his commentaries on Ramus's works), and Louis of Nassau, brother of William of Orange. In Strasbourg he met the educationalist Johann Sturm. Vienna introduced him to a new circle, including the French ambassador Jean de Vulcob, sieur de Sassy, the botanist Charles de l'Écluse, and the imperial physician Johannes Crato von Crafftheim. In September 1573 Sidney spent three days in Bratislava; in late October he left Vienna for Venice, where he joined the Count of Hanau. Between January and August 1574, Philip shuttled between Venice and Padua, with a side trip in March to Genoa via Florence. In Venice he met the poets Cesare Pavese and François Perrot de Mésières, and chose Veronese over Tintoretto to paint his portrait (see Goldring *ARC* 1:20). In July 1574 he may have met the new French king, Henri III, in Venice, as Henri made his way home from Poland. Sidney arrived back in Vienna in late August, where he became friendly with the English diplomat Edward Wotton.

In October–November 1574 Sidney traveled to Cracow, for reasons still unclear. In a 1587 elegy Robert Dowe wrote of the possibility that Philip might succeed to the Polish Crown, but there is no evidence this was ever seriously considered. With his passport now expired, Sidney planned his return home. With Languet he traveled to Prague for nine days in February 1575, where he was received kindly by the Holy Roman Emperor, before setting out for Frankfurt, where he received strict instructions to return to England immediately, "ordered by the Queen and by my family," as he wrote (*Correspondence SPS* 1:432).

Arriving in England on 31 May 1575, Sidney spent June in London before joining the queen's summer progress to Kenilworth and Woodstock, leaving briefly in August to see his father off to Ireland as he undertook another term as Lord Deputy. Although he corresponded with Continental friends and in spring 1576 considered joining the Loire revolt led by the French king's brother, François, Duc d'Anjou, Sidney spent his time primarily at Elizabeth's court. Around September 1576 he was appointed as Royal Cupbearer, a position his father had held. His closest new court friend was Edward Dyer, a Somerset gentleman and protégé of Leicester some eleven years Sidney's senior. Dyer, Greville, and

Sidney formed what Sidney celebrated as a "happy blessed Trinitie" (Sidney, *Poems* 260), writing verse together and becoming known as arbiters of courtly taste in poetry: in 1581 Thomas Watson hoped that his *Ekatompathia* might find a place in the book-chests of Sidney and Dyer, since they determined what constituted literary excellence at court (2r–v). When Geoffrey Whitney wrote a eulogy to Sidney's poetic skill, Sidney insisted he direct it to Dyer instead (Whitney b2v–b3r).

From this time on, Sidney displayed a consistent interest in projected voyages of discovery. On 16 January 1577 Sidney accompanied Leicester and Dyer to a meeting with John Dee, which may have touched on such matters. Sidney, his mother, and Dyer invested £25 in Martin Frobisher's voyage in the summer of 1576; for the 1577 voyage Sidney and Dyer doubled their investment, and several of his friends, including Dyer and Greville, went on the mission. On Frobisher's return in September 1577 Sidney considered sailing with him west, but ultimately invested £67 10s. in the third voyage; in March 1578 there was talk of an "Indian project." But Sidney's travels kept him closer to home.

In May 1576 Walter Devereux, Earl of Essex, was reappointed as Earl Marshal of Ireland; at the English court he and Philip became close, to the extent that Edward Waterhouse reported that Essex "by adoption calleth [Philip] his [son]" (Collins 1:168). In July Sidney accompanied Essex to Ireland, and in August was reunited with his father, staying with him at Dublin Castle, and accompanying him west to quell a revolt, during which he encountered the sea-captain Grania O'Malley in Galway. To Continental observers the move to Ireland seemed a natural playing out of Sidney's given role: in a Latin poem the diplomat Daniel Rogers exhorted him to "prepare yourself for the rule of Ireland, for you are the son of a viceroy, and born for command" (Van Dorsten, *Poets* 39). But nothing came of this excursion. In September Sidney was summoned back to Dublin, where Essex was gravely ill, but the earl died before he arrived; Sidney traveled on to England, arriving back at court in November.

In the autumn of 1576 the European political scene suddenly changed: on 12 October Holy Roman Emperor Maximilian II died, followed fifteen days later by the Elector Palatine Friedrich III. Maximilian's heir, Rudolf II, was a strict Roman Catholic, while Friedrich's successor, Ludwig, was nominally a Lutheran. But his younger brother, Johann Casimir, was a Calvinist, and quickly became a rallying point for German Protestantism. On 8 February 1577 Elizabeth chose Sidney as her special envoy to offer condolences on the deaths of Maximilian and Friedrich. Sidney prepared for the mission by calling on Leicester's scholarly adviser Gabriel Harvey to read Livy's Roman history with him. According to Greville, Sidney enlarged his official instructions to "give him scope (as he passed) to salute such *German* Princes, as were interested in the cause of our Religion, or their own native liberty" (*Life* E1r). *En route* to the imperial court, he met with Don John of Austria at Louvain, Johann Casimir at Heidelberg, and Languet and Philip Camarerius in Nuremberg. Arriving in Prague on 4 April, Sidney was received by the new emperor four days later, but claimed he was "sullen of disposition, very secret and resolute" (*Correspondence SPS* 2:731); he also met the Jesuit Edmund Campion, whom he may have encountered in Oxford in 1566. Sidney returned via Heidelberg, where he gave the queen's condolences to Elector Ludwig, the other palatine count; on 4 May he and Languet met with Casimir to discuss a general agreement between all reformed Churches.

During this time, at Mainz, Languet told Sidney that he had found him a worthy bride: a princess. The identity is unknown, but the foremost candidate is Casimir's sister, Ursula. Sidney asked for time to consider, and kept stalling, much to Languet's embarrassment; Languet claimed that their friends "are convinced that you have changed your mind in Holland" (*Correspondence SPS* 2:768). This must refer to what happened on the way back to England. In Brussels Sidney received the queen's instructions to return to England, but instead he traveled to Middelburg, perhaps on Leicester's orders, where he stood as Leicester's proxy as godfather to William of Orange's second daughter. Sidney's first meeting with William was a huge success: Sidney penned an analysis of the Low Countries ("Certain Notes") based on their discussion. Intelligence reports suggest that it was mooted that Sidney should marry William's elder daughter, Marie von Nassau—which might explain his hesitation with Languet's proposal. Ultimately, nothing came of either marriage plan, and Sidney reached England *c.* 8 June.

During his absence, Sidney's sister Mary (Illustrations 9 and 10) had married Henry Herbert, Earl of Pembroke. Sidney was to spend much time at the Pembrokes' Wiltshire estate of Wilton, which served as a meeting place for the Herbert, Dudley, and Sidney families, and where Mary became a noted literary patron. Sidney worked closely with his sister, claiming to write his *Arcadia* in her presence, and collaborating on a hugely varied set of translations of the Psalms, now popularly known as the "Sidney Psalter" (see Hannay *ARC* 1:5, Prescott *ARC* 2:18, Clarke *ARC* 2:19, and Hamlin *ARC* 2:20).

While Mary had married well, their father's position in Ireland had deteriorated. In the autumn of 1577 Elizabeth engaged Sir Henry in a tedious battle by letter over his imposition of a cess (land tax) on lords within the borders of the Pale; the eleventh Earl of Ormond had intervened directly with Elizabeth to claim exemption through customary use. In September Philip snubbed Ormond at court (by refusing to respond when the earl spoke to him) and wrote a "Discourse" defending his father. Ireland, he wrote, was an extreme country which required extreme action. There were three possible options for the queen: "by direct conquest to make the country hers," "diminishing that she doth send thither," and "to raise at least so much rents" to cover her expenses. On 1 November the Privy Council agreed that Sir Henry's policy was legal, but in February 1578 he received the call to come home; Sidney did his best to salvage this blow to the family's reputation. During this tense time in the family household Sidney wrote a strikingly violent letter to his father's secretary, Edmund Molyneux, accusing him of unsealing his letters to his father, and threatening that if he did it again, "I will thrust my dagger into you" (*Correspondence SPS* 2:844). It is a rare glimpse of a passionate side to Sidney's character.

Sidney now began to develop his own persona at court. In the Accession Day tilt of November 1577, for which he may have written three poems, he appeared as the shepherd Philisides bearing the *imprese* (devices) "Vix ea nostra voco" ("I scarcely call those things my own"), and "Sic nos non nobis" ("Thus we do [or are], not for ourselves"). He became a fixture at such chivalric entertainments, and some of his devices were to appear in his *Arcadia*. In May 1578 he wrote an entertainment to be staged during the queen's visit to Leicester's Essex estate of Wanstead. In *The Lady of May* Elizabeth is accosted by a countrywoman who asks her to choose between her daughter's two suitors, the forester Therion and the shepherd Espilus; this is followed by a debate between the old shepherd Dorcas and the young forester Rixus, moderated by the pedant schoolmaster Rombus. The entertainment pitted action against security, with the former clearly being favored: it has been suggested that this entertainment alluded to a then possible Low Countries expedition, desired by Johann Casimir, who wanted Sidney to lead the English forces. There is evidence that it was believed Sidney would go—Gabriel Harvey dedicated an elogium to Sidney "a little before his departure" (*Gratulationum Valdinensium libri quatuor* K4r–v), and Abraham Fraunce prepared a manuscript of Ramist logic with a collection of *imprese* alluding to his voyage (Bodl. Rawlinson MS D. 345). But in *The Lady of May* Elizabeth chose the safety of Espilus; in reality, she agreed (belatedly, in July) to let Sidney go only as a private person, not as her representative; and in August she added the uncomfortable task of informing Johann Casimir that he had overstepped the line by publicizing her (secret) support. Leicester persuaded Sidney that he could not undertake this mission.

In January 1579 Johann Casimir decided to appeal in person to Elizabeth. The queen commissioned Sidney to meet him as he disembarked, and Sidney accompanied the retinue—which included Languet—as Casimir was wined and dined in London and at court. This visit was the last time Sidney saw Languet (who died in September 1581); Casimir made a sudden departure on 14 February, and the two men did not have a chance to say goodbye.

While Casimir was in England, the French king's brother, François, Duc d'Anjou, was making a final bid to marry Elizabeth. On 5 January 1579 his agent, Jean de Simier, arrived in London to pursue negotiations; from late March to early May the Privy Council debated the marriage, with Leicester, Walsingham, Pembroke, and Sir Christopher Hatton firmly in the opposition camp (William Cecil, Lord Burghley led another group that was more even-handed in its response). With feelings running high during Anjou's visit, Sidney had a dangerous encounter, probably in August, with the pro-marriage Earl of Oxford. As Sidney was playing tennis watched by members of the French embassy, Oxford ordered him off the court; when Sidney refused, Oxford twice called him "by the name of Puppy" (Greville, *Life* F6v), and Sidney in turn "gave my Lord a Lie impossible ... in respect all the world knows, Puppies are gotten by Dogs, and Children by men" (F7r). A challenge was subsequently sent (although by which man is disputed); Elizabeth lectured Sidney on "the respect inferiors ought [owed] to their superiors" (F8r), but he remained unrepentant.

A more direct hit at the marriage plans came in the form of Sidney's "A Letter to Queen Elizabeth Touching her Marriage with Monsieur"; not intended for print, this nevertheless became his most widely circulated writing (at least twenty manuscript copies survive). It argued that Anjou could not be trusted, and that the queen should not change her unmarried state, which had been good for the country so far: "What makes you in such a calm to change course (*Miscellaneous Prose* 47)?" It is often assumed that writing this "Letter" forced Sidney to quit the court—a printed anti-marriage tract by John Stubbes, *The Discoverie of a Gaping Gulfe*, led to Stubbes's and his publisher's loss of their right hands in November 1579—but there is no direct evidence that Elizabeth was offended. Indeed, Sidney spent much of the winter of 1579–80 at court and in London, making an appearance in the Accession Day tilts.

It is probably between 1578 and 1582 that Sidney produced much of his literary work, and certainly when he acquired a reputation as a poet and a literary patron. In 1579 alone, Sidney was the dedicatee of Edmund Spenser's *The Shepheardes Calender*, Stephen Gosson's *The Schoole of Abuse* and *The Ephemerides of Plato*, a translation of Philips van Marnix van Ste. Aldegonde's *The Bee Hive of the Romish Church*, and Richard Robinson's translation of Philipp Melanchthon's *Godly Prayers*. Sidney later praised Spenser's work as one of only four worthwhile vernacular verse works in the English canon (*Miscellaneous Prose* 112), and the two men may have had a closer relationship: in 1580 Spenser and his Cambridge friend Gabriel Harvey published an exchange of *Three Proper, and Wittie, Familiar Letters* in which Harvey claimed to be part of an "Areopagus" (academy) with Sidney and Dyer, dedicated to the composition of English verse in classical meter. Gosson's *Schoole of Abuse*, an "inuectiue against poets, pipers, plaiers, iesters, and such like caterpillers of a commonwealth," is sometimes credited with having provoked Sidney's *The Defence of Poesie*, a full-length analysis of the importance of poetry, which Sidney now identified as "my unelected vocation." He claimed that he had "just cause to make a pitiful defence of poor poetry, which from almost the highest estimation is fallen to be the laughing-stock of children" (*Miscellaneous Prose* 72–3).

Sidney's most ambitious work was apparently underway when he wrote to his brother Robert (Illustrations 13, 14 and 15) on 18 October 1580, promising to send him "My toyful book" (*Correspondence SPS* 1:1009): the *Old Arcadia*, an epic romance in five "acts" interspersed with eclogues and songs. In a dedicatory epistle to his sister Mary, Sidney writes that "You desired me to do it," claiming that the work was written in her presence, presumably at

45

Wilton. The *Old Arcadia* circulated in select circles in manuscript only: Edmund Molyneux wrote in 1586 that "a speciall deere freend he should be that could have a sight, but much more deere that could once obteine a copie of it" (Holinshed, *Chronicles* 1587 3:1554). This elite circulation encouraged the belief that it must be hiding a closely kept secret, and for centuries readers have interpreted the *Arcadia* as an allegory—of European Protestantism, of the English succession, of the threat of a French marriage—but these interpretations may miss the point of the work. In what he called his "imaginative groundplot" (Sidney, *Miscellaneous Prose* 103) Sidney raises moral, philosophical, political, and ethical issues to be debated, on a range of topics, including government, tyranny, gender, and marriage.

In addition to writing, Sidney juggled multiple other roles. In January 1581, for example, he was both chivalric courtier and working parliamentarian, as MP for Shrewsbury: on 25 January he sat on a committee for the subsidy, and on 1 February on one dealing with slanderous speeches and seditious practices against the queen. But in the midst of the Parliament, on 22 January, he was the "Blue Knight" in a court entertainment known as the "Callophisus Challenge," part of Philip Howard's campaign to win back the disputed earldom of Arundel (Stewart 234–5).

Much more elaborate was the tilting and rhetorical sparring put on at Whitehall on 15–16 May for another Anjou-related French embassy, in which four "Foster Children of Desire" assault the "Fortress of Perfect Beauty" (where the queen sat). The "Children" were Sidney, Arundel, Greville, and Edward, Lord Windsor, but Sidney also seems to have been heavily involved in planning and writing this piece. Since the January tilt Sidney's status had changed drastically. In September 1578 Leicester had secretly married Lettice Knollys Devereux, widow of the Earl of Essex; in April 1581 she gave birth to a son, Robert, Baron Denbigh; from that point Sidney was no longer Leicester's heir. According to William Camden, "at the next tilt-day" Sidney replaced his "SPERO ['I hope']" with "~~SPERAVI~~ ['I hoped'] thus dashed through, to show his hope therein was dashed" (*Remaines* Z3v).

Dashed hopes featured in another literary enterprise that was probably born in 1581. In January Sidney's aunt Katherine, Countess of Huntingdon, brought the Devereux sisters, Penelope and Dorothy, whom she had raised, to court. There had been talk in the mid-1570s that Sidney would marry Penelope, then only a child; by the end of 1581, however, Penelope was married to the newly titled and very wealthy Robert, third Lord Rich. Whether or not Sidney was interested in marrying Penelope Devereux, the situation seems to have inspired him to write *Astrophil and Stella*, a sequence of 108 sonnets, interspersed with eleven songs, which tells of the unhappy and unresolved love of Astrophil ("star-lover," but also "Phil") for the married Stella ("star"). The sequence contains some easy autobiographical references: in sonnet 30 he refers to his father's imposition of the cess ("that same golden bit" to "Ulster"); sonnet 65 contains a reference to the silver arrowhead in the Sidney arms; Penelope's married name "Rich" is mentioned three times, and riddled upon at length in sonnet 37. But Stella is often a cipher, a means to explore the many sides of Astrophil—lover, poet, and courtier—and to allow Sidney's dazzling play with language, meter, and imagery (see Sokolov ARC 2:14).

In May 1581 Sidney received a letter from Dom Antonio, the pretender to the Portuguese throne, then in Tunis, asking him to join his campaign. When Antonio arrived in England in June, Elizabeth allowed him to stay at Pembroke's London base, Baynard's Castle. A plan was hatched whereby Sir Francis Drake would seize the Azores in Antonio's name, but Elizabeth stalled and finally reneged on the scheme. Sidney (along with Pembroke) was chosen by the queen to escort Antonio to his ship, and then to chase after him to Gravesend with a last-minute message. Sidney was embarrassed by this treatment of his friend—and financially embarrassed by the cost of the mission. In late 1581 he dashed off begging letters to many patrons, but only the queen offered him something: income from recusancy fines, and property seized from Catholics—once again an uncomfortable solution for Sidney, as he lamented to Leicester: "Truly I like not their persons and much worse their religions, but I think my fortune very hard that my reward must be built upon other men's punishments" (*Correspondence SPS* 2:1049–50).

Through the early 1580s various careers—and their attendant incomes—were suggested for Sidney. He was appointed steward to the Bishop of Winchester in 1580. In spring 1582, after spending time in Hereford and the Welsh marches with his son, Sir Henry Sidney offered to undertake another term as Lord Deputy of Ireland if Philip were guaranteed to succeed him; nothing came of the plan. In March 1583 it was rumored that Sidney would be appointed as Captain of the Isle of Wight. Angling for a post in the Ordnance Office (where his uncle Warwick was master), Sidney spent the summer of 1584 doing appropriate work, strengthening the defenses of Dover harbor; only in July 1585 was he finally granted a post.

Another route to financial stability was marriage. After a series of failed possibilities—in addition to Anne Cecil, Penelope Devereux, and various European princesses, Sidney was hypothetically matched with a daughter of Henry, Lord Berkeley, and with Penelope's sister, Dorothy Devereux—Sidney finally contracted on 19 March 1583 to marry Frances, the fifteen-year-old daughter of Sir Francis Walsingham. The marriage took place on 21 September; through it, Sidney acquired homes in London (Walsingham House), and Surrey (Barn Elms), and Walsingham underwrote £1,500 of his debts.

Sidney was frequently called on to entertain foreign dignitaries. In February 1582 Sidney was among the 600-man envoy accompanying the Duc d'Anjou out of England, and continued with a party led by Leicester to Antwerp; Sidney was able to introduce Leicester to William of Orange in Flushing. In spring 1583 Sidney spent time with the Polish Prince Olbracht (Albert) Laski, who was visiting England: the two men witnessed Giordano Bruno's controversial disputation with the rector of Lincoln College, Oxford in May 1583, and visited John Dee on 15 June. Henri de Navarre's agent, Jacques Ségur-Pardailhan, visited Wilton with Sidney in July. And Sidney owed his knighthood to a foreign acquaintance: Johann Casimir named him as his proxy for his installation as Knight of the Garter, requiring Elizabeth to knight Sidney on 13 January 1583. In June 1584 Sidney seemed about to renew his diplomatic career, as the queen appointed him to convey her condolences on the death of her former suitor, Anjou, to his mother, Catherine de' Medici—and at the same time to urge France to support the Low Countries against Spain. However, the embassy was called off when the French king declared he was no longer in mourning, and no longer in Paris. Sidney also took an increasing interest in Scottish affairs: as early as 1576 he had developed a friendship with the Scot Sir John Seton, who presented his respects to the young King James VI. In the summer of 1585 he brokered negotiations between Elizabeth and the Scottish ambassador in the case of three banished Scottish nobles seeking asylum in England; he also obtained an opinion from civil lawyer John Hammond on the legality of the imprisonment and potential execution of Mary, Queen of Scots.

Sidney's reputation among Continental intellectuals was undiminished. During the 1580s books were dedicated to him by Franciscus Junius, Lambert Daneau, Scipione Gentili, Henri Estienne, Charles de l'Écluse, Timothy Bright, Alberico Gentili, Janus Dousa, and Justus Lipsius. Giordano Bruno, who spent 1583–85 largely in London, dedicated two printed works to him: *Spaccio de la bestia triofante* (1584) and *De gl'heroici furori* (1585); Sidney may have been present at the Ash Wednesday meal in Greville's house on 15 February 1584, the setting for Bruno's *La cena delle ceneri* (1584). And he remained a noted literary patron at home, where dedications included books by William Blandy, John Derrick, Nicholas Lichfield, David Powel, Thomas Lodge, William Temple, Thomas Washington, and Simon Robson, and manuscript works by Temple and Henry Finch.

Sidney's final literary endeavor presumably dates from 1583–85: the revision of the *Old Arcadia* into what became known as the *New Arcadia*. Massively expanding the work, he played with the story's chronology, cut many of the songs, introduced new characters, and provided heroic adventures of his princes only gestured at in the original version. In Greville's words: "His intent and scope was to turn the barren philosophy precepts into pregnant images of life" (*Life* C1v). The revision remained incomplete: Sidney broke off work mid-sentence, halfway through a fight scene in Book Three.

On 19 July 1584 Sidney's personal fortunes changed when Leicester's son Robert died at the age of three, leaving Sidney once again his uncle's heir presumptive. He stressed his Dudley credentials by penning a *Defence of the Earl of Leicester*, responding to the notorious attack (probably by exiled English Catholics) known as *Leicester's Commonwealth*, and stressing the ancient nobility of the Dudley family. He would be closely associated with Leicester for the rest of his life.

He continued to express interest in colonial ventures. In early 1582 Richard Hakluyt dedicated his *Divers Voyages touching the Discouerie of America* to Sidney, painting a picture of boundless possibilities for his nation. In July Sidney was granted three million acres of undiscovered lands in North America, part of Sir Humphrey Gilbert's scheme to establish a colony for English Catholics, and in 1583 drafted 10 percent of his grant to Sir George Peckham to furnish a ship for a forthcoming expedition. In a letter to Sir Edward Stafford dated 21 July 1584 Sidney revealed that "We are half persuaded" to join Gilbert on an expedition to Newfoundland (*Correspondence SPS* 2:1083). When he represented Kent in the parliamentary session of November 1584, he sat on a Commons committee on Ralegh's letters patent for exploration. In August 1585 Ralph Lane wrote from America to urge Sidney to act as "chief commander" in the new colony at Roanoke (*Correspondence SPS* 2:1107).

This long-standing interest provides the context for Sidney's involvement in Sir Francis Drake's 1585 West Indies mission. Throughout that summer Sidney used his Ordnance Office position to deliver materials to Drake; he chose officers and commanders for key positions on Drake's ships. When the fleet arrived in Plymouth, Sidney was alerted by letter; claiming to be meeting a returning Dom Antonio, Sidney and Greville set off for Plymouth. When the fleet sailed a week later, Sidney and Greville were on board Drake's ship, yet after an hour or two they were returned to shore. A "more Imperiall Mandate" had arrived, "carrying with it in the one hand grace, the other thunder": the thunder was presumably Elizabeth's anger, the grace the command that Sidney was to serve immediately under Leicester in the Low Countries (Greville, *Life* G4v). Greville was not allowed to go, and the two schoolfriends never met again.

Sidney's only child, Elizabeth, was born in October 1586 and baptized on 20 November at St. Olave's in Hart Street: the queen herself was present as godmother, but Sidney missed the baptism, since he had been granted letters patent for his appointment on 9 November (see Ioppolo *ARC* 1:6). He arrived in Flushing on 18 November, and was sworn in as governor four days later; he then accompanied Leicester (who joined him on 10 December) on his progress to The Hague, arriving on 28 December. In nearby Leiden, on 7 January Sidney was part of the four-man English team who met with six deputies from the States General to hammer out the technicalities of the agreement; on 24 January they decided that Leicester should take on the title of governor general. This bluntly contradicted Elizabeth's wishes, and she soon made known her anger, not just with Leicester, but also with Sidney, whom she saw as one of the "principal actors and persuaders thereof," as William Davison reported to Leicester (Stewart 289)—a matter not helped when Leicester appointed Sidney colonel of the Zeeland regiment, and rumors flew that he might be made governor of all the Isles (Stewart 294). Sidney was deputed to plead Leicester's case with a special envoy, Sir Thomas Heneage, who arrived in Middelburg in early March.

The campaign was slow, costly, and largely unsuccessful. In February Sidney's plan to besiege Spanish-held Steenbergen failed. He blocked an attempt to send his wife to join him. On 13 May he learned that his father had died eight days earlier: the queen rejected his request to return home to put his estate in order. But the tide seemed to turn as summer progressed. With the Count Hohenloe and his brother Robert, Sidney overthrew a cornet of horse belonging to the garrison at Breda on 30 June, and on 7 July, with Prince Maurice, launched a successful assault on the town of Axel. On 16 July he was nearly caught in an ambush at Gravelines, where about forty of his troops were killed. Returning to Flushing, Sidney found a seriously deteriorating situation; he dispatched missives to Burghley, Walsingham, and the Privy Council on 14 August, in which a newly desperate tone is evident. News of his mother's death on 9 August came to Sidney with the additional information that his sister Mary was ill and not expected to recover, although ultimately she did.

In early September Sidney was involved in the capture of the stronghold of Doesburg (although Leicester did not allow him to lead the assault). After Doesburg, the next target had to be Zutphen, on the River Ijssel; it was decided to ambush a supply convoy that an intercepted message revealed was expected in Zutphen. On the morning of 22 September, in thick mist, the English attacked the convoy, only to discover that the Spanish force numbered 3,000 foot soldiers and 1,500 horsemen. On the second charge Sidney had a horse killed under him, and on the third charge, while rescuing Peregrine Bertie, Lord Willoughby, he was hit by musket shot that shattered the bone above the left knee: he was not wearing cuisses (thigh armor). The wounded Sidney was taken by barge down the Ijssel to Arnhem, where he spent twenty-five days in the house of a Madame Gruithuissens. Although there were hopes of recovery, Sidney's leg developed gangrene. On 16 October he wrote to the Duke of Cleves's physician Jan Weyer asking for his help: "Weyer mine, come, come, I am slipping away from life and I want you" (*Correspondence SPS* 2:1320). But it was too late: after adding a codicil to his will, Sidney died the following afternoon. That will divided most of his estate between his widow and his brother Robert, although he left his books to Greville and Dyer. Most emblematically, he bequeathed his finest sword to Robert Devereux, Earl of Essex—Essex would go on to inherit much of Sidney's chivalric reputation, and to marry his widow, Frances.

The body was taken back to England, where it lay in the Minories for three months before a lavish funeral on 16 February 1587, in which some 700 mourners processed to St. Paul's Cathedral, where Sidney was buried without a memorial. The herald Thomas Lant produced an account and a remarkable set of drawings of the procession, which were engraved by Theodore de Bry: placed together, they form a continuous image some 35 feet (10.7 meters) long (*Sequitur & pompa funeris*, 1587). Sidney's death, and his funeral, produced an outpouring of elegiac verse, including collections from Cambridge and Oxford Universities, New College, Oxford, and the University of Leiden, represented by Georgius Benedicti (Neville, *Lachrymae*; Gager, *Exeqviæ*; Lloyd, *Peplvs*; Benedicti, *Epitapha*).

History of Life-Writing about Philip Sidney

The preceding account synthesizes the current knowledge of Sidney's life. Despite significant differences in interpretation and emphasis, recent full-length studies like Katherine Duncan-Jones's *Sir Philip Sidney, Courtier Poet* (1991) and Alan Stewart's *Philip Sidney: A Double Life* (2000) draw on much of the same material, as do encyclopedia and dictionary articles by H. R. Woudhuysen (2004), Roger Kuin (2006), and R. W. Maslen (2012). But this state of knowledge has come to exist in a lengthy, complex process. In what follows, I trace the history of the life-writing about Philip Sidney, and in so doing suggest the shifts and innovations that have come to produce our current understanding of his life story.

During and immediately following Sidney's life, any biographical information was confined to brief references in eulogies. In his 1576 twenty-line Latin poem "On Philip Sidney, a most promising and talented young man," for example, Daniel Rogers eulogizes Sidney as a European traveler who is about to take up his proper status as a commander in Ireland: "Now that you have roamed through the country of Italy, now that you have met the people of France and have with wandering steps explored the states of Bohemia after seeing the towns of Germany, was it Ireland that was left for you to inspect …?" (Van Dorsten 39). Despite its brevity, this life has a grasp of the geographical range of Sidney's 1570s travels that would be lost to biographers for many years.

Sidney was still alive when Edmund Molyneux mentioned him in his account of his former employer Sir Henry Sidney in Raphael Holinshed's *Chronicles* as "a gentleman of great hope, and exceeding expectation," sent on an embassy to Rudolf II before the age of twenty-one (*sic*), and whose *Arcadia* was a hidden treasure. Following Sidney's death, the passage was rewritten: no longer the author of *Arcadia*, Sidney becomes the martial hero, glimpsed in action at Flushing, Axel, and Gravelines, before being wounded above the left knee at Zutphen (Holinshed, *Chronicles* 1587 3:1554; Donno).

In the abundance of *post mortem* verse elegies, most focus on his valor, chivalry, and lost promise, rather than on details of his life. John Phillips (*The Life and Death of Sir Phillip Sidney*) refers to the war and Sidney's death in Flanders, and his funeral at St. Paul's, and implies he has a wife, uncle, and brother whom the reader should know; Thomas Churchyard (*The Epitaph of Sir Phillip Sidney Knight*) hints that his sister is now dying; Angel Day (*Vpon the Life and Death of … Sir Phillip Sidney*) refers to the *Arcadia* and Zutphen.

By contrast, in the fifty seven-line stanzas of *Sir Phillip Sidney, his honorable life, his valiant death, and true vertues* George Whetstone lays out the trajectory of Sidney's life: his Sidney and Dudley ancestry; his time as "the best scholar in Cambridge" (a rare claim); his travels abroad in France, Italy, and Germany; his time in Ireland with Essex; his embassy to condole the death of the emperor; his emblem "spero"; the *Arcadia* and other unknown writings—"If men but knew, the halfe that he did write"— suggesting that "The last shepards calenders" were "the reputed worke of S. Phil. Sydney" (B2r), as well as a partial translation of du Plessis Mornay's *Verité de la religion chrestienne*. Whetstone's account is most detailed about Sidney's Low Countries adventures, listing thirty English soldiers, dealing with the Axel and Zutphen skirmishes and the musket shot to the thigh, and ending with a lengthy account of the twenty-six days between his injury and death, in which Sidney is given an eloquent death speech.

A fuller life was provided by *Nobilis*, written at Wilton by physician Thomas Moffett in 1593. This Latin tract, "sent by way of an example to Sidney's most honorable nephew William Herbert" (67), probably as a New Year's gift in 1594, is clearly designed to mold the behavior of a young man. Moving through Sidney's seven ages, Moffett concentrates on Sidney's childhood, adolescence, and time at university. In boyhood, the three-year-old Philip "beheld the moon, with clean hands and head covered he used to pray to it and devoutly to worship" (70). Uninterested in games, Sidney was deeply bookish, showing prowess in grammar, mathematics, and composition (71–3). The adolescent Philip twice fell ill with fever. He wrote poetic, comical, and even musical work, but felt shame at such trivial output; at Oxford he rejected only astrology, and showed a particular interest in chemistry, which he pursued with Dee and Dyer. In later life Sidney was chosen to be sent to Rudolf II, and was praised by "the rich Germans," "the Emperor's noblemen—especially Casimir and the Counts of Palatine and Hanau" (81). Moffett also relates—presumably for Herbert's benefit—how Sidney kept aloof from unintellectual noblemen, befriending instead Dyer, Greville, Sir Henry Brouncker, Essex, and Willoughby.

Two other early lives are lost: Sir William Herbert's *Sidney, or Baripenthes, Briefely Shadowing out the Rare & Neuer ending Laudes of that most Honorable & Praise-worthy gent. Sir Philip Sidney knight*, supposedly published in 1586/87, is presumably the "Poem intituled Sir William Herbertes Sydney" licensed by the Stationers' Company to John Windet on 16 January 1587 (Arber 2:463), and Sir James Perrot's *The History of the Noble Birth, Education and Singular Good Parts of Sir Philip Sidney*, probably written *c*. 1600, and mentioned in 1615 (Stow 806). None of these early lives had much impact on the biographical tradition that emerged.

A portrait (in Latin) appears in Henry Holland's sequence of brief lives, the *Herωologia Anglica* (1620). Sidney is here the son and heir of Henry Sidney, an accomplished member of Elizabeth's court, and the author of the *Arcadia*. The sketch highlights his embassy at twenty-one (*sic*) to the Holy Roman Emperor in Austria, his appointment in the Low Countries, his fatal wounding at Zutphen, and his lavish funeral and burial at St. Paul's (F6r–G1v). Holland's sketch forms the basis for Samuel Clarke's biography in *The Second Part of the Marrow of Ecclesiastical History* (1650), in which Sidney became one of the few secular men and women added to Clarke's ecclesiastical lives (3I3v–3K2r). Clarke supplements Holland by describing Sidney's excelling performance at (an unnamed) university, his writing of the *Arcadia* at twenty-one (*sic*), his proposed election to the Polish throne, his marriage to Frances Walsingham, and his friendship with Fulke Greville. He lingers on the details of the Zutphen skirmish, and devotes almost half the entry to an account of Sidney's deathbed, as recounted by Leicester's chaplain, Humphrey Fenn. As Sidney lies wounded for twenty-five days, he thinks better of the "divers light, & amorous passages" of the *Arcadia*, "which might tend to the corrupting of the incautious reader," and writes to Greville to command him to burn the sole manuscript; Greville is only prevented by "the importunity of some around him" (3K1r–v).

Perhaps the most influential life of Sidney was written by his friend Fulke Greville, later Lord Brooke. Although published as *The Life of the Renowned Sir Philip Sidney* in 1652, it was written in the early Jacobean period as "A Dedication to Sir Philip Sidney" for a projected volume of Greville's own writings, and the text deals with Greville as much as Sidney. Greville claims a privileged entry into Sidney's life: "For my own part, I observed, honoured, and loved him so much; as with what caution soever I have passed through my dayes hitherto among the living, yet in him I challenge a kind of freedome even among the dead" (B2r).

In lieu of a chronological survey of Sidney's life, Greville's *Life* is structured around episodes. After locating Sidney's qualities in his father and mother, Greville presents the boy Philip as serious: "though I lived with him, and knew him from a child, yet I never knew him other than a man: with such staiednesse of mind, lovely, and familiar gravity, as carried grace, and reverence above greater years" (B3v). He presents the Languet–Sidney relationship as "this harmony of an humble Hearer to an excellent Teacher" (B4v). Greville claims that Sidney "purposed no monuments of books to the world, out of his great harvest of knowledge," although "his Arcadian Romanties live after him, admired by our foure-eyd Criticks" (B2v).

Greville recounts meeting in Delft with William of Orange (ch. 2), who told him "her Majesty had one of the ripest, and greatest Counsellors of Estate in Sir *Philip Sidney*, that at this day lived in *Europe*" (C6r). Hearing this from Greville, Sidney urges him not to tell Elizabeth—an example, Greville claims, of "the clearness, and readiness of this Gentlemens judgement, in all degrees, and offices of life" (C6v). Character references are also supplied by Leicester and Walsingham; Greville claims Sidney was prized by James VI of Scotland, Henri de Navarre (later Henri IV of France), Don John of Austria, the Spanish ambassador

Bernardino Mendoza, and by "[t]he Universities abroad" which "accompted him a generall *Maecenas* of Learning" (D1r).

Greville devotes chapters to Sidney's embassy to Rudolf II (ch. 4), the *Letter to Elizabeth* (ch. 5), his dispute with Oxford (ch. 6), and Sir Francis Drake's West Indies voyage (ch. 7), which he claims was "an expedition of his own projecting; wherein he fashioned the whole body, with purpose to become head of it himself" (G1r–v); Greville proudly recalls that "I that had the honour as of being bred with him from his youth; so now (by his own choice of all *England*) to be his loving and beloved *Achates* in this journey" (G3v). He channels Sidney's analysis of the European political situation (chs. 8–10) before moving on to the Low Countries campaign (ch. 11), Sidney's wounding at Zutphen (ch. 12), and his final suffering and death (ch. 13). At Zutphen Greville includes the most famous Sidney anecdote: as he was being carried from the battlefield, bleeding and thirsty, he called for drink,

> but as he was putting the bottle to his mouth, he saw a poor Souldier carried along, who had eaten his last at the same Feast, gastly casting up his eyes at the bottle. Which Sir Philip perceiving, took it from his head, before he drank, and delivered it to the poor man with these words, *Thy necessity is yet greater than mine*. (L3r)

Although the authenticity of this anecdote has been challenged (Gouws), biographers continue to quote Greville—often at great length—to the present day.

In 1655 "Φιλοφιλιππος" (Philophilippos, thought to be Thomas Fuller) signed a "Life and Death of Sir Philip Sidney," prefixed to the latest edition of the *Arcadia*. Apparently unaware of Greville's version, it gives a brief tour of highlights of Sidney's life: his Sidney and Dudley ancestry, education at Oxford (a4v), unspecified travel "beyond the Seas," an embassy to Vienna (b1r), his marriage to Frances Walsingham (strikingly out of sequence, b1v), his being offered the Polish throne (b2r–v), the *Arcadia*, depicted as "a continual Grove of moralitie, shadowing moral and politick results under the plain and easie emblem of Lovers" (b3r), the Low Countries campaign and Zutphen (b4r–v), and the mourning for his death. Twice during the short life the author alludes to "Corrivals" (b1r) and envy directed at Sidney by "some surlie, and ill natur'd Criticks" (b2v). Fuller repeated much of the same information in his entry on Sidney in his *The History of the Worthies of England* (1662), commenting that Sidney, "in relation to my book, may be termed an *Ubiquitary*, and appear amongst *Statesmen, Souldiers, Lawyers, Writers*, yea *Princes* themselves" (2L2r).

During the late seventeenth century John Aubrey compiled notes on Sidney, taken from his own knowledge and conversations with others (later published as *Aubrey's Brief Lives*). Dubbing him "the most accomplished Cavalier of his time" (278), Aubrey comments on Sidney's looks ("extremely beautifull … not masculine enough"), his travels to "France, Italie Germany," and presence "in the Poland warres" (278). When hunting at Wilton Sidney would "write down his notions" for *Arcadia* into a table-book "as they came into his head" (like Clarke, Aubrey further claims that Sidney, dying, "desired his follies might be burnt"). Testifying to his "very munificent spirit" to "all Lovers of Learning," Aubrey recounts how Spenser presented to an appreciative Sidney his *Faerie Queene*, and he recalls Sidney's passion for tilting and inventing devices (279); he also records how Wilton's library possesses "a Manuscript very elegantly written, viz., all the *Psalms of David* translated by Sir Philip Sidney, curiously bound in crimson velvet" (139). Aubrey's notes tend to the salacious: he claims that Sidney died of his wound because "he would not (contrary to the injunctions of his Physitians and chirurgions) forbeare his carnall knowledge of [his wife], which cost him his life" (280); in his notes on Mary Sidney Herbert, Aubrey alleges that "there was so great love between him and his faire sister that I have heard old Gentlemen say that they lay together, and it was thought the first Philip Earle of Pembroke was begot by him" (139). Significantly, none of Aubrey's anecdotes has had a healthy afterlife.

Arthur Collins's two-volume edition of *Letters and Memorials of State* (1746), "Faithfully transcribed from the Originals at *Penshurst Place* in *Kent*, the Seat of the Earls of *Leicester*, and from his Majesty's Office of Papers and Records for Business of State" (title page), provides a wealth of information about the Sidney family, although Philip is less well represented than his father and his brother Robert (1:98–113). Collins prints for the first time correspondence between Sidney and his father, Edward Waterhouse, Edmund Molyneux, Dom Antonio, and Edward Stafford, as well as the documents relating to his French honors in August 1572, the *Letter to Elizabeth*, and his will.

In *The Memoirs of the Life and Writings of Sir Philip Sydney* (1808), rebutting a negative assessment of Sidney by Horace Walpole, Earl of Orford (vii, 155), the churchman Thomas Zouch presents Sidney as an outstanding Protestant diplomat and soldier with "uniform zeal for the reformed religion" (91). Zouch relies heavily on the letters from Languet to Sidney, published abroad in 1633 and 1646, but newly available in David Dalrymple's 1776 edition, depicting Languet influentially as Socrates to Sidney's Alcibiades, Mentor to Sidney's Telemachus (Zouch 58). He also draws on the Penshurst papers, printed dedicatory epistles to Sidney, and most notably the British Museum's Cotton manuscript collection, from which he prints George Gifford's account of Sidney's final weeks (266–79). While the Languet correspondence allows Zouch to outline Sidney's European travels in 1572–75 and 1577, the detail is often sketchy; when that correspondence ends (in 1580), Zouch's account of Sidney's movements flounders. Much of the fourth chapter, supposedly dealing with the period 1577–85, is given to a defense of the *Arcadia* (Zouch knows only the *New Arcadia*), which "now lies neglected on the shelf, and has almost sunk into oblivion" (146). *Astrophil and Stella* and the *Letter to Elizabeth* are surprisingly absent, and some assertions are compromised by Zouch's failure to realize that in most sixteenth-century English documents the new year starts on 25 March—Sidney's 1577 embassy therefore takes place in 1576 in Zouch's telling (Fox Bourne, *Memoir* vi). And the Velazquez portrait of Sidney that prefaces the book is neither by Velazquez nor of Sidney. Despite its flaws, Zouch's account was for a while the "standard" life, informing, for example, William Gray's biographical notice in the 1829 *Miscellaneous Works* (1–66).

Steuart A. Pears appended "The Life and Times of Sir Philip Sidney" to his 1845 English translation of the Sidney–Languet correspondence (ix–lxxxii). His memoir, though informed and colorful, is chronologically vague: biographers are indebted to his translations and his bringing to light of sixteen letters from Sidney, which he located in the Wolff collection at Hamburg's Public Library.

In 1862 H. R. Fox Bourne published his sixteen-chapter *Memoir of Sir Philip Sidney*. Undertaking extensive archival research in the State Paper Office and the British Museum, Fox Bourne notably introduced to the telling of Sidney's life his presence at the 1575 Kenilworth celebrations, his 1576 visit to Ireland, his defense of his father's Irish policy, his colonial aspirations, and his appointment to the Ordnance Office; in his account of the Low Countries expedition he made telling use of John Lothrop Motley's recent work *The Rise of the Dutch Republic* (1856). In Fox Bourne's account, Sidney is taken seriously by Elizabeth: his retirement from court in 1580 is due not to a spat with the Earl of Oxford, but to a "patriotic dispute" with the queen. While easily the fullest account to date, Fox Bourne's *Memoir* displays a difficulty of dealing simultaneously with Sidney's life and his writings: often a single chronological period is represented by two chapters: 1578–79, for example, has "Under royal rule" and "Literary beginnings," while 1580–82 has both "Courtly bondage" and "Authorship as courtier." This splitting of Sidney into life and works would become a pattern in later biographies.

Publishing his *Life of Sir Philip Sidney* months after Fox Bourne's volume, Julius Lloyd could do little but carp that Fox Bourne's reading of *Astrophil and Stella* was based on an erroneous marriage date for Penelope Devereux. (Fox Bourne corrected himself in the 1891 revision of his book published as *Sir Philip Sidney: Type of English Chivalry in the Elizabethan Age*, highlighting "the chivalrous aspect of Sir Philip Sidney's life" [v]). Otherwise, Lloyd used many of Fox Bourne's sources, but did provide a different way of dealing with the life versus works issue: after three chapters on his life to 1580, Sidney returns to Wilton and writes *Arcadia*, which is given an entire chapter to itself; then, in chapter 5, Sidney makes a "return to public life."

The late nineteenth and early twentieth centuries saw several other biographies, most of which were openly dependent on Greville, Zouch, and Fox Bourne. Some are nostalgic and panegyric: the tone of the anonymous *Life and Times of Sir Philip Sidney* (1859) can be gauged by its opening line: "In the queenly days of Elizabeth, the soil of England was trodden by noble men, whose footprints will be revered until the sun shall gild for the last time the dominions on which it has been said, he never sets" (1). But others were increasingly diffident about their supposed hero. John Addington Symonds's *Sir Philip Sidney* (1886) admitted that "his renown transcends his actual achievement. Neither his poetry nor his prose, nor what is known about his action, quite explains the singular celebrity which he enjoyed in his own life" (1). Symonds dwells on two episodes in which Sidney displayed unmerited anger towards servants—a trait "not altogether pleasing in our hero's character" (50). Similarly, Percy Addleshaw's *Sir Philip Sidney* (1909) complains of Sidney's aloofness—"Noble he was, generous he was, quixotically honest he was; but also the qualities of the prig and the bigot are apparent" (1)—and especially his religious bigotry: "The greatest blot on his career is his loathing—it was little less—for those of the old faith" (3). By contrast, Anna M. Stoddart's short *Sir Philip Sidney Servant of God* (1894) aimed a Christian message at the youthful reader: "if boys and girls in Sidney's England will learn from its pages that obedience to the will of God alone can mould a life into immortal example, [the author] will reap a rich reward" (viii). Sidney Lee's 1897 entry for the *Dictionary of National Biography* relies on Fox Bourne's *Memoir of Sir Philip Sidney* as "[t]he fullest modern biography," and presents, more even-handedly, a Sidney with "a naturally chivalric, if somewhat impetuous, temperament."

Perhaps the most archivally based account to date was the life Ewald Flügel prefixed to his 1889 edition of *Astrophil and Stella* and *The Defense of Poesie* (1:lxvi), which draws on documents at Hatfield House, the State Paper Office, and the British Museum. But since Flügel wrote in German (and quoted documents in German translation), his influence on the mainstream tradition of Sidney biography was limited. Instead, the next great advance came with Canadian academic Malcolm William Wallace's *The Life of Sir Philip Sidney* (1915), revised from his PhD. While Wallace modestly describes his contribution to knowledge as "a number of facts which are interesting rather than significant" (vi), his biography is still widely regarded as the definitive life of Sidney. Wallace was the first biographer able to take advantage of the Victorian calendaring of the state papers (he draws on the calendars, rather than the papers themselves), and his mastery of this archive renders his work by far the most thorough and chronologically confident account of Sidney's life to date. The book has a distinct bias, with six of its twenty-one chapters devoted to Sidney's life before 1572 (by contrast, his Continental travels from 1572 to 1575 merit only one chapter). Drawing on a manuscript accounts book by Thomas Marshall discovered at Penshurst, Wallace throws light on Sidney's time at Shrewsbury and the 1566 excursion to Oxford. But Wallace believes that "[Sidney's] greatness was not in his works but in his life" (402), and his treatments of the *Arcadia*, *Defence of Poesie*, and *Astrophil and Stella* are confined to two chapters that interrupt the narrative *c.* 1580. Wallace's Sidney is marked by a "simplicity and serenity of outlook upon life" (402): "To do some worthy service for Queen and country was his highest aim—to translate his ideals into noble action … his countrymen hailed him as the president of noblesse and of chivalry" (403).

Publishing his biography during the first year of the Great War, Wallace was well aware that his subject "too, died in the Netherlands in defence of ideals strangely similar to those for which the British nation is to-day engaged in a life-and-death struggle" (vii). That connection was also made by Sidney's school, Shrewsbury School, when it commissioned a statue of Sidney by A. G. Walker RA to serve as the School's war memorial. In armor but without his helmet and cuisses, Sidney's statue is accompanied by a bronze relief that shows on one side Sidney giving his water bottle to a wounded soldier, and on the other the trenches of France.

After Wallace's achievement, much major Sidney scholarship lay outside life-writing. The biographies recycled existing materials, concentrating instead on interpretation. In 1931 Mona Wilson saw Wallace's book as "primarily historical," and aimed instead to produce an account "dealing more particularly with Sidney and the dawn of Elizabethan literature" (11); accordingly, four of her fourteen chapters are concerned with the literary works, but again, they form a discrete section of the book (chs. 7–10) between "Anjou's courtship" and "Politics and marriage." Feeling that Wilson had not gone far enough, C. Henry Warren's 1936 biography insists on Sidney as "a poet—and therein lies his claim on the world's attention" (4). For Warren, poetry did not live only on the page: "It was Sir Philip's innate ability to carry this invincible innocence of the poet into any phase of life—even on to the battlefield—that has established him in the favor of posterity" (7). Frederick F. Boas's 1955 life saw Sidney as a "representative Elizabethan," but this account of "life and writings" once again dealt with the writings in a separate, central chapter ("Philip Sidney: Representative Elizabethan: His Life and Writing"). Roger Howell's *Sir Philip Sidney: The Shepherd Knight* (1968) asks, "What … did his contemporaries see in him that made him at his death the subject of such mourning and regret?" (7), and sees the answer in "[t]he character of Philisides the Shepherd Knight," which Sidney was developing as early as 1579, and which was "[a] very definite part of his purpose and plan." Howell's account effectively starts in 1575, and focuses on the English Sidney, with his European travels compressed into a single chapter; again, the literary works are treated in a separate section, sandwiched between two slices of life. Almost alone, John Buxton's 1954 study *Sir Philip Sidney and the English Renaissance* offered something new to the Sidney biography. Although at heart a study of literary patronage, it is structured on Sidney's life story, serving almost as a literary complement to Wallace's biography, and notably enhancing our knowledge of Sidney's literary relations.

In 1962 J. A. van Dorsten suggested a new direction with his study of Sidney, Daniel Rogers, and the Leiden University humanists (*Poets, Patrons, and Professors*). While not a full biography—it focuses on the years from 1580, and is very much a study of Anglo-Dutch literary relations—it constitutes a valuable supplement to Buxton's Sidney. Van Dorsten's emphasis on the Dutch Sidney continued with his 1986 volume *Sir Philip Sidney: 1586 and the Creation of a Legend*, co-edited with Dominic Baker-Smith and Arthur F. Kinney. Drawing on this research, the slim but generously illustrated Dutch-language *Sir Philip Sidney 1554–1586* by Dorothee Cannegieter and Diederike van Dorsten-Timmerman presents Sidney as "the English poet, courtier, soldier and statesman, who played such an important part in the history of the Netherlands" (15).

The focus was widened from the Low Countries to Europe more generally by "the sudden recovery" of seventy-six letters to Sidney, previously unknown, throwing light on his "formative years," which provided the basis of James M. Osborn's 1972 study *Young Philip Sidney 1572–1577* (xi). The letters, apparently preserved by Sidney's secretary, Stephen Lesieur (xii), survived in a volume owned by Sir Thomas Phillipps, purchased by Osborn in 1967 (xi). Dating from 1573–76, with one outlier in 1581, the letters are virtually all from Sidney's

Continental acquaintances, led by law professor Jean Lobbet and newsbroker Wolfgang Zünderlin. Osborn used these letters to structure a narrative of Sidney's European travels in 1572–77, adding other letters, including eleven from Christ Church tutor Robert Dorsett to Philip concerning his brother Robert. Osborn's Sidney is "the promising young aristocrat whose character and abilities, especially his powers of mind, astounded the experienced and learned men who came to know him" (xi), thoroughly enmeshed with intellectual, political and religious culture on the Continent, engaging in correspondence in Latin, French, and Italian (although Osborn rendered all the letters into English; only with Roger Kuin's 2012 edition of the *Correspondence* were these texts published in their original languages).

The two most recent full-length biographies present opposing ends of the spectrum of life-writing about Sidney. Lamenting the penchant of previous biographers for "discussing the poetry separately from the documented, external events" (x), Katherine Duncan-Jones sets out in *Sir Philip Sidney Courtier Poet* (1991) to prioritize "his development as a writer" (xi), by "mov[ing] continually to and fro between Sidney's outward and inward lives," and thereby "to suggest many connexions which have not hitherto been noticed" (xi). This is not always easy: in attempting to understand *The Defence of Poesie* and *Astrophil and Stella* in terms of Sidney's life in 1582–83, years of "[t]ime-wasting and disappointment," she laments that "[e]xternally documented events provide an unpromising context for these two brilliant works" (223). Yet Duncan-Jones provides a persuasive account of the *Defence*, showing "Sidney's most irresistible public face" (238), designed to assure prospective father-in-law Walsingham that he "need not worry about his head being too full of poetic fancies for him to be a worthy successor to a vital post like his own First Secretaryship" (233), while she promotes the speculation that Sidney wrote *Astrophil and Stella* "because Penelope Devereux, to whose family he had long-standing obligations, had asked him to do so" (246). Resolutely committed to presenting Sidney as a "born poet" (xi), a man of "literary genius" (306), Duncan-Jones even reinstates Greville's story of Sidney's giving his water-bottle to a dying soldier, claiming it has a "higher truth" for this *"vir generosus"* (304).

Conversely, Alan Stewart's *Philip Sidney: A Double Life* (2000) seeks to illuminate two outward lives—one in England, the other in Europe. Building on the work of Osborn and Van Dorsten, Stewart presents Sidney on the Continent as "a name to conjure with, long before his death." Son of the "Prorex" of Ireland and Wales and the Dudley heir, Sidney met with French honors, royal marriage proposals, and offers of commands of English troops on the Continent. In England, by contrast, "he remained just another courtier, often too impecunious even to *be* a courtier" (6). Firmly focused on the details of the life, and with a strong Continental bias, Stewart's biography reduces discussion of Sidney's literary works to a few pages.

With the publication of Roger Kuin's edition of the complete *Correspondence* (2012), future biographers have a huge body of primary material easily to hand. It remains to be seen whether new information comes to light, and whether the various split Sidneys—posthumous versus living reputation, Continental versus English, life versus literature—will continue to structure, or to hinder, future lives of Philip Sidney.

Bibliography

Primary and Secondary Sources

Addleshaw, Percy. *Sir Philip Sidney*. London: Methuen, 1909.

Arber, Edward, ed. *A Transcript of the Registers of the Company of Stationers of London, 1554–1640*. 5 vols. London: privately printed, 1875–94.

Aubrey, John. *Aubrey's Brief Lives*. Ed. Oliver Lawson Dick. London: Secker and Warburg, 1950.

Benedicti, Georgius. *Epitaphia in mortem nobilissimi et fortissimo viri D. Philippi Sidneij equitis*. Leiden: J. Paedts, 1587.

Boas, Frederick S. *Sir Philip Sidney, Representative Elizabethan: His Life and Writings*. London: Staples Press, 1955.

Brennan, Michael G., and Kinnamon, Noel J. *A Sidney Chronology 1554–1654*. Houndmills: Palgrave Macmillan, 2003.

Bruno, Giordano. *De gl'heroici forori*. Paris: Antonio Baio [i.e. London: John Charlewood], 1585.

—. *Le cena de le Ceneri*. London: John Charlewood, 1584.

—. *Spaccio de la bestia triofante*. Paris [i.e. London: John Charlewood], 1584.

Buxton, John. *Sir Philip Sidney and the English Renaissance*. London: Macmillan, 1954; 2nd ed., 1965; 3rd ed., 1987.

Camden, William. *Remaines of a Greater Worke, concerning Britaine*. London: Simon Waterson, 1605.

Cannegieter, Dorothee, and Diederike van Dorsten-Timmerman. *Sir Philip Sidney 1554–1586*. Amsterdam: Uniepers/Zutphen: De Walburg Pers, 1986.

Clarke, Samuel. *The Second Part of the Marrow of Ecclesiastical History, Containing the Lives of Christians of Inferiour Ranks*. London: Robert White, 1650.

Collins, Arthur, ed. *Letters and Memorials of State* …. 2 vols. London: T. Osborne, 1746.

[Davis, Sarah Matilda Henry, Mrs.]. *The Life and Times of Sir Philip Sidney*. Boston, MA: Ticknor & Fields, 1859.

Donno, Elizabeth Story. "Some Aspects of Shakespeare's 'Holinshed.'" *HLQ* 50 (1987): 227–48

Duncan-Jones, Katherine. *Sir Philip Sidney, Courtier Poet*. New Haven, CT: Yale UP, 1991.

Flügel, Eward. *Sir Philip Sidney's Astrophel and Stella und Defence of Poesie nach den ältesten Ausgaben mite inter Einleitung über Sidney's Leben und Werke*. Halle: Max Niemeyer, 1889.

Fox Bourne, H. R. *A Memoir of Sir Philip Sidney*. London: Chapman and Hall, 1862.

—. *Sir Philip Sidney: Type of English Chivalry in the Elizabethan Age*. London: G. P. Putnam's Sons, 1891.

Fuller, Thomas. *The History of the Worthies of England*. London: Thomas Williams, 1662.

Gager, William, ed. *Exeqviæ illvstrissimi eqvitis, D. Philippi Sidnaei, gratissimæ memoriæ ac nomini impensæ*. Oxford: Joseph Barnes, 1587.

Gouws, John. "Fact and Anecdote in Fulke Greville's Account of Sidney's Last Days." *Sir Philip Sidney: 1586 and the Creation of a Legend*. Ed. Jan van Dorsten, Dominic Baker-Smith, and Arthur F. Kinney. Leiden: E. J. Brill and Leiden UP, 1986. 62–82.

Gray, William, ed. *The Miscellaneous Works of Sir Philip Sidney*. Oxford: D. A. Talboys, 1829.

Greville, Fulke. *The Life of the Renowned Sir Philip Sidney*. London: Henry Seile, 1652.

[Hakluyt, Richard]. *Divers Voyages Touching the Discouerie of America*. London: Thomas Woodcocke, 1582.

Harvey, Gabriel. *Gratulationum Valdinensium libri quatuor*. London: Henry Bynneman, 1578.

—. *Three Proper, and Wittie, Familiar Letters* …. London: Henry Bynneman, 1580.

Holinshed, Raphael. *Chronicles of England, Scotlande, and Irelande*. 3 vols. London: Henry Denham et al., 1587.

Holland, Henry. *Herωologia Anglica*. Arnhem: Jan Jansson, 1620.

Howell, Roger. *Philip Sidney: The Shepherd Knight*. London: Hutchinson, 1968.

Kuin, Roger. "Philip Sidney." *The Oxford Encyclopedia of British Literature*. Ed. David Scott Kastan. 5 vols. Oxford: Oxford UP, 2006. 5:10–14.

Languet, Hubert. *Epistolae politicae et historicae ad Philippum Sydnaeum*. Ed. Claude Sarrau. Leiden: Elzevir, 1646.

—. *Huberti Langueti viri clarissimi epistolæ politicæ et historicæ. Scriptæ quondam Ad Illustrem, & Generosum Dominum Philippum Sydnæum* …. Ed. William Fitzer. Frankfurt [i.e. Heidelburg]: William Fitzer, 1633.

Lant, Thomas. *Sequitur celebritas et pompa funeris ….* London, 1587.

Lee, Sir Sidney. "Sir Philip Sidney." *Dictionary of National Biography.* Ed. Leslie Stephen and Sir Sidney Lee. London: Smith, Elder & Co, 1885–1900.

Lloyd, John, ed. *Peplvs illvstrissimi viri D. Philippi Sidnaei svpremis honoribvs dicatvs.* Oxford: Joseph Barnes, 1587.

Lloyd, Julius. *The Life of Sir Philip Sidney.* London: Longman, Green, Longman, Roberts, and Green, 1862.

Maslen, R. W. "Sidney, Philip (1554–86)." *The Encyclopedia of English Renaissance Literature.* Ed. Garrett A. Sullivan, Jr. and Alan Stewart. 3 vols. Oxford: Wiley-Blackwell, 2012. 3:883–90.

Moffet, Thomas. *Nobilis or A View of the Life and Death of a Sidney and Lessus Lugubris.* Ed. and transl. Virgil B. Heltzel and Hoyt H. Hudson. San Marino, CA: Huntington Library, 1940.

Neville, Alexander, ed. *Academiae Cantabrigiensis Lachrymæ tvmvlo Nobilissimi Equitis, D. Philippi Sidneij Sacratæ.* London: ex officina Ioannis Winet impensis Thomæ Chardi, 1587.

Osborn, James M. *Young Philip Sidney 1572–1577.* New Haven, CT: Yale UP, 1972.

Pears, Steuart A., ed. *The Correspondence of Sir Philip Sidney and Hubert Languet.* London: William Pickering, 1845.

Φιλοφιλιππος (Philophilippos). "The Life and Death of Sir Philip Sidney." *The Countess of Pembroke's Arcadia Written by Sir Philip Sidney.* London: William Du-Gard for George Calvert, 1665.

Phillip, John. *The Life and Death of Sir Philip Sidney, Late Lord Gouernour of Flvshing.* London: Robert Waldegrave, 1587.

Sidney, Philip. *The Correspondence of Sir Philip Sidney.* 2 vols. Ed Roger Kuin. Oxford: Oxford UP, 2012.

—. *Miscellaneous Prose of Sir Philip Sidney.* Ed. Katherine Duncan-Jones and Jan van Dorsten. Oxford: Clarendon P, 1973.

—. *The Poems of Sir Philip Sidney.* Ed. William A. Ringler, Jr. Oxford: Clarendon P, 1962.

[Spenser, Edmund]. *The Shepheardes Calendar Conteyning Twelve Æclogues Proportionable to the Twelve Monethes.* London: Hugh Singleton, 1579.

Stewart, Alan. *Philip Sidney: A Double Life.* London: Chatto & Windus, 2000.

Stoddart, Anna M. *Sir Philip Sidney Servant of God.* Edinburgh: W. Blackwood and Sons, 1894.

Stow, John. *Annales, Or a General Chronicle of England.* Ed. Edmund Howes. London, 1631.

[Stubbes, John]. *The Discoverie of a Gaping Gulf whereinto England is Like to be Swallowed by an Other French Marriage.* London: Hugh Singleton, 1579.

Symonds, John Addington. *Sir Philip Sidney.* London: Macmillan, 1886.

Van Dorsten, J. A. *Poets, Patrons, and Professors: Sir Philip Sidney, Daniel Rogers, and the Leiden Humanists.* Leiden: Leiden UP, 1962.

—, Dominic Baker-Smith, and Arthur F. Kinney, eds. *Sir Philip Sidney: 1586 and the Creation of a Legend.* Leiden: E. J. Brill and Leiden UP, 1986.

Wallace, Malcolm William. *The Life of Sir Philip Sidney.* Cambridge: Cambridge UP, 1915.

Warren, C. Henry. *Sir Philip Sidney: A Study in Conflict.* London: Thomas Nelson, 1936.

Watson, Thomas. *The Ekatompathia or Passionate Centurie of Loue.* London: John Wolfe for Gabriell Cawood, 1581.

Whetstone, George. *Sir Phillip Sidney, his honorable life, his valiant death, and true vertues.* London: Thomas Cadman, [1587].

Whitney, Geoffrey. *A Choice of Emblemes, and Other Devises.* Leiden: Christopher Plantin, 1586.

Wilson, Mona. *Sir Philip Sidney.* London: Rupert Hart-Davies, 1931.

Woudhuysen, H. R. "Sidney, Sir Philip (1554–1586)." *ODNB.*

Zouch, Thomas. *The Memoirs of the Life and Writings of Sir Philip Sydney.* York: unknown publisher, 1808.

Mary Sidney Herbert (1561–1621), Countess of Pembroke

Margaret P. Hannay

Mary Sidney Herbert, Countess of Pembroke (Illustration 9), became famous during her lifetime as a patron, poet, and translator. She was also praised for her beauty, musical ability, and needlework, as well as for her religious devotion and her familial connections at court. As the daughter of Sir Henry Sidney and Mary Dudley Sidney, she was related to the prominent Dudleys; her grandfather John Dudley, Earl of Warwick and Duke of Northumberland, attempted in July 1553 to place Lady Jane Grey on the throne instead of Queen Mary, and then was executed, as were Lady Jane and her husband Guildford Dudley. Mary's surviving Dudley uncles were Ambrose, Earl of Warwick, and Robert, Earl of Leicester. Having been friends with Elizabeth from childhood, they emerged in importance after her accession, as did Katherine Dudley Hastings, Countess of Huntingdon; all three supported the Sidneys.[1]

Mary was born on 27 October 1561, just three years into Elizabeth's reign. Her father had recently begun serving as Lord President of the Council in the Marches of Wales (from 1559 until his death in 1586), and she was born at one of the official residences, Tickenhall Palace, on the hill above Bewdley, Worcestershire, recorded in the family records inscribed into the fifteenth-century manuscript known as the Sidney Family Psalter (Cambridge, Trinity College Library R.17.2 fol. 5v). Her godfather, William Herbert, first Earl of Pembroke (husband of Anne Parr, sister of Queen Katherine), was particularly important as a military commander and a landowner in Wales as well as Wiltshire and London (he had been the previous President of the Council in the Marches of Wales, 1550–58), and an ally of the Dudleys. Mary Sidney's mother was in such close service to Elizabeth that in 1562 she nursed the queen through smallpox, and then caught that dangerous disease herself. Henry Sidney later wrote to Sir Francis Walsingham that she was a "full faire lady in mine eye," but she became "as foul a lady as the smallpox could make her" (*Memoir* 105). Nonetheless, Henry and Mary Sidney had three more children after the smallpox attack. (Philip later portrayed her in his *New Arcadia* as Parthenia, whose facial disfigurement was miraculously healed [30].)

Young Mary was the fourth of seven children in her family—Philip, Mary (Margaret), Elizabeth, Mary, Robert, Ambrosia, and Thomas. Her father served as Lord Deputy of Ireland from 1565 to 1571 and from 1575 to 1578, in addition to his position in Wales (see Brennan *ARC* 1:1, McGowan-Doyle *ARC* 1:2, Herron *ARC* 1:13, and Maley and Schwyzer *ARC* 1:14). The family occasionally went to Ireland with him, but seem to have spent considerably more

---

1   Although Katherine Dudley had no children of her own, she was proud of educating others, including Margaret Dakins, who married Mary's youngest brother, Thomas Sidney, also for a time in Huntingdon care. Thomas died suddenly in 1595, and Dakins was forced to marry Posthumous Hoby; she is now known as the diarist Margaret Hoby.

time in Wales, particularly at Ludlow Castle (or Shrewsbury School for Philip and Thomas), although their home remained Penshurst Place. The brothers each went to Christ Church, Oxford, and each traveled abroad. None of Mary's three sisters survived, and none were included in the Sidney Family Psalter entries supervised later by Lady Mary Sidney, listing her living children and grandchildren. Mary (Margaret) had died at the family home of Penshurst when she was just about two and before Mary's birth; her sister Elizabeth, just a year older than Mary, died at age six in Dublin and seems to have a tablet in Christ Church Cathedral there (Kinsella 117–8). Her sister Ambrosia, a year or two younger than Mary, was close to her, and they often dressed alike; the accounts record such outfits as their matching crimson silk, or their warm winter "purple and white purled mockadore." They studied with the same governess and tutors who taught them the classics, rhetoric, and the languages of Latin, French, and Italian; the family financial records show that they also learned the female aristocratic arts of lute, needlework, and archery (Hannay, *Philip's Phoenix* 24–32). Ambrosia's death in Ludlow Castle in February 1574/75 was a great loss to the family; she received remembrance from her godfather, Ambrose Dudley, Earl of Warwick, by a magnificent monument (still visible) at the parish church in Ludlow. Queen Elizabeth sent her father a generous note of mourning, which offered that his one remaining "daughter of very good hope" would receive "a special care" if she came to court (TNA SP 40/2 fol. 83). In July Mary processed in honor with her mother and Queen Elizabeth to Leicester's Kenilworth and then to Warwick's Woodstock, where she received her first poetic tribute, which praised her for being "yonge in yeares yet olde in wit" (*Philip's Phoenix* 35).

Within two years Mary had an arranged marriage to the wealthy Henry Herbert (*c*. 1538–1601), second Earl of Pembroke, a colleague and close friend of her father and her uncles; Pembroke had inherited his father's rank and property, dominating Glamorganshire, and increasing his properties in England and in Wales. Pembroke, a childless widower, had recently lost his wife, Katherine Talbot, from a family closely connected with the Herberts.[2] Although Pembroke was in his forties and Mary just fifteen, Henry Sidney told Leicester: "I am made very happy by the match" (*Philip's Phoenix* 38). The £3,000 dowry was difficult for Henry Sidney to raise, but he was eventually successful. Mary's considerable settlement gave her life-interest in numerous territories, recorded in a lengthy jointure manuscript of nearly ninety leaves (Harvard, Houghton Library fMS Eng 725). When she was married on 21 April 1577, her mother gave her elegant clothes to fit her new position as countess, including some with gold and silver embroidery. (Her later version of Psalm 45 emphasizes gold cloth worn by the royal bride.)

Her first extant letter, "[sc]ribled in hast" after she had been sharply rebuked for not sending Leicester word of her husband's recovery from a minor illness, is nervously marked by deletions and additions, and perhaps tears. As a young bride she was learning the requirements of her position as she crossed out a reference to "he" and wrote the appropriate "my lord" (MSH, *Collected Works* 1:285). Technically, she immediately became the estate mistress at Wilton, along with several additional estates in Wiltshire like Ivychurch and Ramsbury, and also Baynard's Castle in London. Living with Pembroke and his young wife for a decade, however, was his widowed stepmother Anne Talbot Herbert, Dowager Countess of Pembroke (d. 1588), and later also his aunt Anne Herbert Talbot, who would have become Countess of Shrewsbury if not widowed first (d. *c*. 1590). They would have taught young Mary how to be hostess at Wilton and on other estates, though perhaps there was some resentment of the beautiful and talented teenage bride. She soon became accustomed to her

---

2   See Brennan *ARC* 1:1. Henry Herbert's youthful arranged marriage, which he had annulled for "whoredom," was with Katherine Grey, who loved and married Edward Seymour, son of the Duke of Somerset (Bodl. MS Tanner 193 fols. 226–7; Hannay, *Philip's Phoenix* 37).

position of wealth and social power, serving as hostess to many prominent political and artistic figures, including her powerful Dudley relatives. Her in-laws included the extended family of Herberts, the most important family of mid Wales, especially Pembroke's younger brother Edward and his wife, Lady Mary Stanley Herbert.

There was a family celebration of the Countess of Pembroke's seventeenth birthday in 1578 with the Herberts, Sidneys, and Dudleys all at her home at Wilton. (Following aristocratic custom, Pembroke may have waited for that age before marital sexual consummation.) He was so elated at the birth of William in April 1580 that he had a still visible panel installed in St. Mary's Church, Wilton, praising his "most Dere Wyfe" and the family heritage (*Philip's Phoenix* 50). Simon Bowere, a Groom of the Queen's Chamber and Wardrobe, brought "the Quenes Maiesties guifte from the Courte of Whitehall to Wilton ... for the Cristeninge of the Lorde Harberte, sonne and heire to the Earle of Pembroke" (Rye 293). The queen served as his godmother, represented by Anne Russell Dudley, Countess of Warwick. Pembroke later gave a celebratory dinner to the entire parish, and wrote happy responses to congratulations from English, Welsh, and European friends (*Philip's Phoenix* 51). After Pembroke finally had a son in his late forties, it was clear that his brother Edward would not inherit the earldom; Sir Edward Herbert then bought the "Red Castle" in Powis, and the Grey lordship.

In these early years a most frequent visitor was her brother, Philip Sidney, who apparently began writing *The Countess of Pembrokes Arcadia* in her company (see Woudhuysen *ARC* 2:3). His sonnet sequence *Astrophil and Stella* was circulated at Wilton, and he may have begun paraphrasing the *Psalmes* there as well (see Prescott *ARC* 2:18). Certainly, he was present to write her charming riddles about pregnancy, later echoed in "The Doleful Lay of Clorinda" as having been written "unto your selues, to make you mery glee" (*Philip's Phoenix* 48). During 1581–84 Mary bore three more children, also listed in the Sidney Family Psalter at the direction of her mother, Lady Sidney: Katherine, Anne, and Philip. Sadly, Katherine, "a child of promised much excellencie," as her distressed grandmother seems to have added in her own hand, was just "threyeare olde and one daie" when she died within hours of Philip's birth on 16 October 1584 (5v). The godparents at that sad occasion were just family—his grandmother Lady Sidney, and his Sidney uncles Philip, for whom he was named, and Robert. The Pembrokes had at least one other baby, who had died by 1590. The Countess of Pembroke's only extant family letter is after the death of this child, when she sent her baby nurse to her pregnant sister-in-law Barbara Gamage Sidney, who was then in Flushing; she also sent her "blessing to my pretty [God]Daughter"—that is, Mall, later Lady Mary Wroth (MSH, *Collected Works* 2:286). No babies born after 1586 were recorded in the family Psalter, for that was the year of their grandmother Lady Sidney's death. (Her death thus prevented her inclusion of the births of Robert and Barbara Sidney's subsequent eleven children.)

The year 1586 brought devastation for Mary Sidney Herbert. All three of her brothers were serving under their uncle Leicester in the Low Countries' struggle against Spanish occupation. Her father died that May in Wales; his heart was buried in Ambrosia's tomb, and his body carried to London for a formal funeral and then to burial at Penshurst. After Henry Sidney's death Pembroke became Lord President of the Council in the Marches of Wales, so that the Countess of Pembroke held the same position in Wales as had her mother, including hostess at Ludlow Castle; their physician, Thomas Moffett, writes of the family presence there in *Health's Improvement*. Her mother died in London in August, and Edmund Molyneux reported her as a model Christian and praised her eloquent speaking.[3] The Countess of Pembroke herself was dangerously ill. Then she heard the worst news: the lingering death of

---

3   The casket containing Sir Henry Sidney's heart is now at the British Museum. Extensive accounts of both parents' funerals are in MS Ashmole 836 fol. 253 (Hannay, *Philip's Phoenix* 230). Joseph Black has recently discovered two 1586 editions of Raphael Holinshed's *Chronicles* including

her brother Philip after the battle of Zutphen, where his leg injury became gangrenous. His pregnant young wife, Frances Walsingham Sidney, came to be with him as he was dying, but lost their second child to miscarriage. Both Philip's brothers were devastated, as is apparent in Robert's later poems and his probable portrait in mourning (Goldring; see Illustration 14). They came back with Philip's body for the magnificent funeral at St. Paul's, but as a woman, Mary could not join them. Instead, her brothers were in the procession as chief mourners, and her husband and uncles rode behind the casket, leaders among the 700-man cortege. Unable to contribute to Philip's memory there, or to the four university volumes of elegies published, she later encouraged the celebration of his life through patronage of writers who praised him, as well as through her own translation and poetry.

Mary Sidney spent two years in mourning for her little daughter, her parents, and her brother Philip. If that were not enough tragedy, there was then the danger of the Spanish Armada. Her husband was given the dangerous position of defending Milford Haven, Wales, where the Spanish might first attack. Her uncle Leicester led the English soldiers, including her brother Robert; Elizabeth made her famous speech to the English forces assembled at Tilbury. Mary helped Robert by inviting his wife Barbara and their baby Mall to Wilton, where they spent about six months avoiding the potential battle areas. Her own children were eight-year-old William, who would recently have begun studying Latin, four-year-old Anne, and three-year-old Philip. This lengthy time together began their lifelong affection. Then, in time to celebrate the defeat of the Spanish Armada in November 1588, the Countess of Pembroke went to London, traveling with her children (and probably also Barbara Sidney and little Mall), surrounded by some eighty servants in Pembroke livery. This journey began her public emergence as the prime celebrator of her brother Philip; she served as a patron to those who praised Sir Philip, published his works, made appropriate translations, composed two elegies for him, and completed the *Psalmes*. Her own literary reputation owes much to her self-identification as the "sister of Sir Philip Sidney" (MSH, *Collected Works* 1:294). Her heritage as a Sidney, and as her brother's literary heir, allowed her to circumvent some gender restrictions. Thomas Churchyard, for example, makes her unique position explicit when he presents her as "a *Sidney* right" who "shall not in silence sit" (B1v), and Nathaniel Baxter implies a similar emphasis when he praises her as a poet: "rare are her gifts full of *Sydneian*-fyres" (B1).

She was at first dismayed by the unprecedented publication of *The Countess of Pembrokes Arcadia* (1590) at a time when aristocrats did not seek publication and instead only allowed friends to copy manuscripts; Robert Sidney had received a copy *c.* 1581, as had other members of the Sidney circle including Sir John Harington, Abraham Fraunce, and George Puttenham in the late 1580s (*Philip's Phoenix* 70). After her brother's death she disapproved of certain editorial elements done by Philip's friend Fulke Greville, such as adding chapter headings; she therefore had *Arcadia* republished in 1593 in a different form, using the unfinished *New Arcadia* and then the conclusion of the *Old Arcadia*, attempting to control his literary legacy (Davis). In 1598 she supervised another edition including *Arcadia*, *Certain Sonnets* (many as songs), *Defence of Poetry*, *Astrophil and Stella*, and *Lady of May*, and making it, in a sense, his collected secular work. The first published mention of *Arcadia* was in a dedication to her in Thomas Howell's *Devises* (1581), and she was praised by Hugh Sanford in her 1593 edition as "done, as it was for her: as it is, by her" (*Philip's Phoenix* 70), yet there were quarrels with those involved in Fulke Greville's 1590 edition, notably John Florio. Since the *Old Arcadia* was rediscovered in 1909 by Bertram Dobell, her editorial work with *Arcadia* was viewed negatively until fairly recently. Danielle Clarke, for example, argues that her primary

---

Molyneux; presumably it is the second edition that celebrates Lady Mary Sidney's life and her exemplary death (see Black *ARC* 2:1).

position is as Philip's "literary executor" ("Mary Sidney Herbert" 184), and Patricia Pender that she "played a crucial role in the construction of the English author function" (65).

Certainly, her first efforts of patronage were to encourage Philip's praise, which shifted from military to literary compliments, notably in the collective *Phoenix Nest*, and in Edmund Spenser's "Ruines of Time" and his *Astrophel*. She was termed as Philip's "phoenix" in continuing his patronage, as by Nicholas Breton using that phrase to praise Philip notably in *The Phoenix Nest*, but also by Thomas Nashe and in her own "Angell Spirit." More amusing are frequent comparisons of the Countess of Pembroke to gold and jewels, hinting at the rewards sought by those who dedicated works to her, like Spenser's praising her mind as a "golden coffer" in *Colin Clouts Come Home Again*, or Gabriel Harvey as gems; cleverly, Michael Drayton and William Smythe each used marigolds as a pun on seeking "Mary's gold" (*Philip's Phoenix* 82, 114–15).

As the wife of one of the wealthiest men in England, one who had the right to bestow numerous clerical offices, the Countess of Pembroke was also called upon to serve the Church. Gervase Babington, who was the family chaplain at Wilton while she was in her early twenties, prays that she will "studie of his worde, and all other good learning" and "of the practise of duty to your God" (*Philip's Phoenix* 133). Others used admonitory flattery to instruct her on these religious duties, as when Breton termed her "the Nourisher of the Learned and favorer of the Godly." Because of her literary and religious patronage, he says, "the wise admire, the learned followe, the vertuous love and the honest serve" her (1.j).

Mary Sidney Herbert's encouragement of poets and story-tellers, particularly at Wilton, is most noted from Philip Sidney's dedication of *The Countess of Pembroke's Arcadia*, saying that "you desired me to do it, and your desire to my heart is an absolute commandment," and that he wrote on "loose sheets of paper," mainly "in your presence," and when he was away, sent sheets to her "as fast as they were done" (*Old Arcadia* 3). Samuel Daniel, apparently present at least from 1592 to 1594 to tutor her daughter Anne (her sons had left for Oxford), later praised her "best school"; her home was called the "College" by Thomas Churchyard and by John Aubrey (*Philip's Phoenix* 109). Fluent in Italian like her mother, Lady Sidney, she was compared by Breton to Elizabetta Gonzaga, Duchess of Urbino, praised in the Castiglione's familiar *Courtier*. Aubrey notes her "noble libraries of bookes," including literary, scientific, historical, and political, with many in Italian, as well as ancient manuscripts in Latin (*Natural History* 96). Her brother Robert, who visited on many occasions, wrote his autograph manuscript of poems "For the Countess of Pembroke," as Philip had addressed *The Countess of Pembroke's Arcadia* (Robert Sidney, *Poems* 127). The Wilton physician Thomas Moffet begins *The Silkewormes and their Flies* (1599) by celebrating her as a poet and leader of a literary group, emphasizing family:

> *Sydneian Muse*: if so thou yet remaine,
> In brothers bowels, or in daughters breast,
> Or art bequeath'd *the Lady of the plaine*,
> Because for her thou are the fittest guest .... (B1)

While this reference may first mention her brother Philip, so familiar because of her role in publishing his work, more likely it describes her living brother Robert. Next is her daughter, Lady Anne, praised later as Panclea, "*Miraes* chiefe delight" (*Silkewormes* F4v). Lamb discusses the intriguing possibility that the Bright MS includes anonymous poems written by a woman in the Sidney circle, likely Lady Anne or one of her cousins (194–8). Whether or not Anne wrote, Mary Sidney Herbert's most important female protégé was Mary Sidney Wroth, her namesake, niece, and god-daughter. Not only the family, but also much of the household wrote poetry—the children's tutors, the secretaries, the family physician, and even old retainers like Thomas Howell, who claimed ironically that he wrote "to avoyde greater ydlenesse" (6). Her leadership and encouragement of writing are noted by Samuel Daniel in her role as "[t]he happie and iudiciall Patronesse of the Muses (a glory hereditary to your house)" (A2), and later he thanked her for encouraging his progress to more serious work, presumably his *Civile Wares Betweene … Lancaster and Yorke* (Klein 136–70). She is also portrayed as patron and writer even by those who did not know her, like Francis Meres, who praised her hopefully as "very liberal unto poets. Besides, she is a most delicate poet" (*Philip's Phoenix* 110).

The presentation of Mary Sidney Herbert as a leader of literary sessions, mostly honoring her brother, is also emphasized by Abraham Fraunce, especially in the three volumes of *The Countess of Pembrokes Ivychurch*. Others who dedicate or allude to her include William Camden, John Davies, John Donne, Michael Drayton, Gabriel Harvey, William Gager, George Herbert, Aemilia Lanyer, Henry Parry, and William Shakespeare (Brennan, *Literary Patronage* ch. 5; Lamb ch. 1; *Philip's Phoenix* ch. 5). The Countess of Pembroke was thus usually represented as a literary figure by those who sought to win her patronage. Most extensive is the *Urania* of her niece and god-daughter Lady Mary Wroth, who presents the Queen of Naples as Pamphilia's mentor and literary companion (Hannay, "Mentor"), as well as shadowing her in other characters such as Clorina and perhaps Melissea (Wroth, *Urania* 1:lxxxvi). She was also praised for her music by Thomas Morley and for her needlework by John Taylor; they are obvious in their attempts to gain her support and also to gain sales from her fame. As Franklin D. Williams computed, she was the greatest sixteenth-century aristocratic female English patron. Drayton, for example, presents her as "learnings famous Queene" (*Works of Michael Drayton* 1:74, 76). More famously, Samuel Daniel said that she would be known by her Psalms and her honor would endure "even when Wilton lies low levell'd with the ground" — certainly true since the fire there in 1647 (H6v).

Original Poems of Mourning and Dedication

Fairly early in this period Mary Sidney Herbert wrote a poem mourning her brother's death. In 1591 Spenser, seeking her patronage, in *Ruines of Time* praised an unpublished elegy that she had written for her brother Philip: "who can better sing / Than thine owne sister … Which to thee sings with deep harts sorrowing" (Smith and de Selincourt 471). In 1594 she wrote asking Sir Edward Wotton to return a copy of her writing that was in memory of their love for Philip Sidney (MSH, *Collected Works* 286), probably the same poem praised by Spenser. This poem is either not extant, or it is "The Doleful Lay of Clorinda," a Spenserian-style poem in *Astrophel* (1595) that may have been the Countess of Pembroke's early poem of mourning. Early editions typically presented her as the author until Ernest de Selincourt in 1912 claimed it as Spenser's, an attribution continued by Spenserians through Hadfield's 2012 *Edmund Spenser* (see Bond ARC 2:4). In contrast, Gary Waller includes it as Mary Sidney's in his 1977 edition of *Triumph of Death*, and describes it as "not up to Spenser's standard of competence" in his 1979 *Mary Sidney* (91–6). Clorinda's poem of mourning appears with a separate page of introduction, a double border that matches the title page (Waller, *Mary Sidney* 92). This poem is thus treated like the work attributed to "Thestylis" (Lodovick Bryskett), which may imply that Spenser was in contact with her as well as with Bryskett when setting up the *Astrophel* volume, and he may well have helped her revise her early poem for publication. The style of the "Lay" is certainly Spenserian, as are her allusions to *The Shepheardes Calendar* in "A Dialogue between Two Shepherds, Thenot, and Piers, in Praise of Astrea," her Spenserian sonnet Psalm 100, and her *Faerie Queene* references in Psalms 78, 104, and 107 (Hannay, "Spenserian Poet"). The debate now focuses on whether it is Spenser's representation of a Continental male tradition of creating fictionalized female poets (Hadfield), or whether we cannot know (Clarke, "In Sort"), or whether it is indeed by the Countess of Pembroke.

In any case, she later wrote "To the Angell Spirit of the most excellent Sir Philip Sidney" as a dedicatory poem to their Psalms. Her earlier draft, found in the works of Samuel Daniel, is in deeply religious mourning; in the revision, the manuscript dated 1599, she also portrays herself as a writer, with these "dearest offrings of my hart / dissolv'd to Inke" (MSH, *Collected Works* 1:112). The poem echoes classical elements, such as Niobe's speech in Aphthonius' *Progymnasmata* (Jardine 143–6), and the traditional pattern of three stages of elegy—lamentation, praise of the deceased, and consolation. It also employs such Petrarchan metaphors as "broken bodies, monetary expenditure, emotional reckoning, eternizing conceits, and hyperbolic praise" (Wall 315). Her poetic style includes elements also in her Psalms, such as internal rhyme, compound words, polyptoton, and parallel restatement.

Like the dedicatory poem to her brother, her dedication to Queen Elizabeth is extant only in the Psalms manuscript previously owned by the late Bent E. Juel-Jensen and now at the Bodleian Library. Now frequently available in print, it may have been written only for the eyes of Elizabeth herself, beginning with the queen's governing "Care" in England and actions in Europe, and praising her able mind that made what was "toile" for others just "Exercise" for her. Mary Sidney's own mourning for Philip led her to complete the Psalms, as "hee did warpe, I weav'd this webb to end," and to present the "Cloth in both our names" as a "liverie robe" that the queen can distribute. She then continues to compliment Elizabeth by comparing her to King David, emphasizing "Men drawne by worth a woman to obey." The poem ends with the wish that the queen will "Sing what God doth and do what men may sing" (MSH, *Collected Works* 102–4). This dedicatory poem to the queen is now probably the work of hers most often printed and taught, frequently appearing in anthologies, and may be read as a personal, devotional, political, literary work, or as an exemplar of the voice and accomplishment of early modern women.

Mary Sidney Herbert's "Dialogue betweene Two Shepheards, Thenot, and Piers in Praise of Astrea" is another poem in praise of Elizabeth, printed in Francis Davison's 1602 *Poetical Rapsody* (MSH, *Collected Works* 1:89–91, 302–3). This poetic argument between Thenot and Piers was apparently written to be enacted when Elizabeth intended to visit Wilton in 1599 as part of her summer progress (Erler), as Philip Sidney had written "A Lady of May" for her 1575 visit to Wanstead. Apparently written about the time that the Countess of Pembroke wrote an eloquent and beautifully transcribed autograph letter of 2 July 1599 thanking Queen Elizabeth for her son William's entrance into court (MSH, *Collected Works* 1:290–91), the poem welcomes the queen as "Astrea" with praises that argue about whether language and metaphor are able to express the divine represented by Elizabeth as monarch. Piers, as Helen Hackett suggests, "represents a dogmatic Protestant poem of view," whereas Thenot is more subtle (177). Nine times Piers, arguing that language is not up to expressing the divine, gives Thenot the lie. Mary Sidney thus gives the queen a poem of sophisticated philosophical questions, and she also deftly uses many of the traditional images of Elizabeth's praise (such as beauty, wisdom, virtue, eternal youth, and military and literary accomplishment), and then says that those traditions are inadequate to equal her. The poem concludes "But silence, naught can praise her," which can also be read as a command to Thenot, "But silence! ..." (*Selected Works* 146–7).

Translations: *Discourse, Antonius,* and *Triumph of Death*

In 1590 Mary Sidney formally translated from the French two works appropriate to her situation, completing at Wilton on 13 May the Senecan and Christian meditation on life and death written by Philip's friend Philip Duplessis-Mornay, and then at Ramsbury, their northern Wiltshire estate, on 26 November the dramatic tragedy *Marc Antoine* by Robert Garnier. Both works were published in 1592 under her own name as *A Discourse of Life and Death, Written in French by Philip Mornay; Antonius: A Tragedy Written Also in French by Robert Garnier. Both Done in English by the Countess of Pembroke. A Discourse* warns against a selfish life; *Antonius* gives a dramatic example.

Of particular interest during her life, her translation of Philippe Duplessis-Mornay's *Discourse of Life and Death* was reissued four times by 1608 (MSH, *Collected Works* 1:311–12). Structured around the Senecan pattern of human life of infancy, youth, maturity, and old age, *Discourse* combines classical and biblical writers, notably Seneca and "Solomon," presenting the Stoic emphasis on reason and public responsibility. It particularly emphasizes the *ars moriendi*, as Lamb notes (206–7). This elegant translation, much better than that of her only predecessor, Edward Aggas (Bornstein, *Life and Death*), obviously enhanced her religious reputation, as later did her completion of the Sidney Psalms. "Die to live, Live to die," it concludes, as quoted by contemporaries, probably including Shakespeare (MSH, *Collected Works* 1:254; Duncan-Jones). Wroth plays with the phrase when Urania explains her new love—"Who dies to live, find change a happy grace" (*Urania* 1:332)—a sly allusion to those concluding lines of Christian Stoicism.

The popular contemporary use of this meditation on the trials of their lives is vividly demonstrated by the summary account that Victoria Burke and I discovered in Elizabeth Ashburnham Richardson's "Motherlie Endeavours" as her treatise of "the troble of life, and profit of death" (Folger MS V.a.511, reprinted now in *Selected Works* 130–35). Richardson used Mary Sidney's *Discourse* as an important source of spiritual instruction for her children and other Christians, although she includes only biblical citations and none of the classical, omits the court emphasis on ambition and avarice, and reduces thirty-one pages to a summary on four handwritten leaves (Burke; Hannay, "Elizabeth Ashburnham Richardson's Meditation"). Another demonstration of the personal importance of *Discourse* is the Folger's recently acquired 1600 personalized edition that Heather Wolfe and I examined. Compiled in an aristocratic household, it adds gold and silver ink in its elegant transcriptions of verses from the Geneva Bible and the Latin quotations on parallel pages, adds elegant transcriptions of English and Latin works that reflect on death, writes in some apparently original verses, and glues in hand-colored reflections on death, including *memento mori* emblems by Crispin van de Passe and poised skeletons from a prayer book. The immediate reception of *Discourse* in these copies was thus spiritual instruction and meditation on mourning; scholarly work on religious meditations is currently a major topic, so the *Discourse* is likely to receive increasing consideration, and additional personalized copies like those at the Folger may perhaps emerge.

Antonius, republished in 1595 as *The Tragedy of Antony*, has received considerably more scholarly attention (see Weller *ARC* 2:12). In 1600 John Bodenham included several excerpts from *Antonius* in his collection of verses entitled *Bel-vedere*; she was the only woman to be listed beside such male authors as Spenser, Philip Sidney, and Shakespeare—except for Queen Elizabeth, who is presented with King James of Scotland as a royal author (MSH, *Collected Works* 1:31–2). Dramatizing the tale of Antony and Cleopatra primarily from Plutarch and from Dio Cassius, *Antonius* follows the Senecan model of historical tragedy and is often read as reflecting on politics.

Discourse and *Antonius* are apparently samples of her translations, rather than a complete collection, because John Harington sent a manuscript of her "Triumph of Death" with a letter in December 1600 to their relative Lucy Harington Russell, Countess of Bedford, along with Mary Sidney Herbert's Psalms 51, 104, 137, and poems by others. This inferior transcription is the only extant copy,[4] so she may have translated all of Petrarch's *Il Trionfi*—the *Triumph of Love* of Laura, followed by his description of her *Triumph of Chastity*. His *Triumph of Death* seems to have been written in 1348, the year of Laura's death, and would have been of particular interest because she is given a voice. The final three poems show Laura's *Triumph of Fame*, apparently defeated by the *Triumph of Time*, which is finally conquered by the *Triumph of Eternity*. The poems thus presented allegorical figures for Love, Chastity, Death, Fame, Time, and Eternity, typically each shown as enthroned on a chariot pulled by allegorical beasts (see *Selected Works* pl. 7). The English and Europeans were familiar with these images on tapestries, paintings, glass cups, marriage chests, statues, and so on. Mary Sidney apparently knew some previous English *Trionfi* translations—Surrey's short passage from the *Triumph of Love*, Queen Elizabeth's youthful translation of the first ninety lines of the *Triumph of Eternity*, and the long couplets version of Henry Parker, Lord Morley, of the *Triumph of Death*. She was the first to follow Petrarch's original *terza rima* form (aba, bcb, and so on), and as Bornstein ("The Style") observes, her translation is significantly poetically superior to Morley.

    Triumph of Death is of particular interest because, as Petrarch mourns for Laura, she appears to him from heaven and explains that she loved him also, but to be virtuous, she had to say "no." Yet, she says: "My heart meane-while with love did inlie burn / But never will; my reason overcame" (MSH, *Collected Works* 1:280). As Ilona Bell and William Kennedy note in their studies of women poets and the Petrarchan tradition, Mary Sidney removed Petrarch's adjective "almost" from their flames of love, so that Laura tells Petrarch that "in equale flames our loving hearts were tryed" (MSH, *Collected Works* 1:281). Kennedy examines Protestant adoption of Petrarch, as well as sexual implication. Elaine Beilin demonstrates that Laura is virtuous, unlike Cleopatra; Pamela Benson emphasizes the moral instruction, and Lamb connects the Stoic virtues as in *Discourse* (139–41). Danielle Clarke sees "a deeply nuanced translation that ... provides a veiled and ambiguous critique of literary discourses surrounding the aging Elizabeth" (*Politics* 138), and also notes connections with her metrical Psalms, her most noted poetical work.

Psalms

Mary Sidney's Psalms present themselves as an act of pleasurable composition and religious devotion, basing her scholarship on most extant versions and commentaries in English, Latin, and French, and engaging her as a devout Christian, scholar, and accomplished poet. Maintaining appropriate humility in sacred text, she says: "And I secure shall spend my happie tymes / in my, though lowly, never-dying rymes" (*Collected Works* 2:100).[5] As Beth Quitslund observes, the Sidney Psalms now seem "not only canonical but counted among the major works of English Renaissance poetry" (83). Philip had written poetic versions

---

4   See Gavin Alexander's improvement online at http://www.english.cam.ac.uk/ceres/sidneiana/triumph.htm.

5   Noel Kinnamon admirably transcribed and gave the textual studies on the Sidney Psalms; see MSH, *Collected Works* vol. 2.

of Psalms 1–43; Mary completed the 150 Psalms, including the twenty-two sections of Psalm 119. Like Philip, she used a wide range of poetic forms.

Her versions are notable for two joyous sonnets, Psalm 100 in Scottish (Spenserian) form, and concluding with Psalm 150 in Sidneian form; she also has more then 120 other poetic forms (Woods 290–302; *Collected Works* 2:4–32). She presented the historically most studied penitential Psalm 51 in the elegant *rhyme royal* form (seven lines of iambic pentameter rhymed ababbcc). Its contemporary popularity is seen as one of the two known musical versions for her Psalms (see Larson *ARC* 1:21), and it is one of three sent to Lucy, Countess of Bedford, as we have seen. It seems also to be her most studied poem, often in connection with other poets like Anne Vaughan Lock and Sir Thomas Wyatt who preceded her, and by her influence on seventeenth-century devotional poetry. Mary Sidney's connections with Philip are particularly notable in her Psalm 53, which, as in the original, nearly repeats Psalm 14, and her Psalm 73, "It is most true," based on Philip Sidney's *Astrophel and Stella 5* (Zim 193–4). Also striking are the wedding poem in Psalm 45 and the position of women (weakened in revision) in Psalm 68, George Herbert's parallels to Psalm 71, reflections on rules in Psalm 77, instructions for the appointed king in Psalm 101, the alphabetic acrostic in Psalm 111 and as "Praise the Lord" in acrostic Psalm 117, the image of a weaned child in 131, the lament for exile (used also in Geneva) in Psalm 137, and the celebration of God's people in Psalm 148. Much of the extensive commentary on the Sidney Psalms includes her poetics, politics, scholarship, gender, and religion (Hamlin; Clarke, "Mary Sidney Herbert"; Coles; *Philip's Phoenix*; Quitslund; and Sidney, *Psalter*.)[6]

Life at Wilton

The Countess of Pembroke was known for her outstanding correspondence, though only a few letters are extant (*Collected Works* 1:285–98). Thomas Moffet praised her correspondence with Philip Sidney; all those letters should "go into the everlasting memory of his race and of the republic of letters" (*Nobilis* 74, 115n). Her letters to her brother Robert were frequently mentioned, and Robert's agent, Rowland Whyte, wrote praising her letter to help her brother with the Lord Treasurer: "I never read anything that could express an earnest desire, like unto this" (274). She also sent an "order" to her steward at Baynard's Castle to make rooms ready for Robert and his whole family; they were then able to spend court seasons there for more than twenty years. Apparently, many hundreds of her letters disappeared, but Steven May discovered a "warm and playful" letter to her neighbor John Thynne in October 1595, and another when she was a countess dowager with less influence in September 1603 (88–97).

By the mid-1590s the Earl of Pembroke was frequently ill, although he had seemed to recover in September 1594 (Robert Sidney, *DPFA* 56). During the later 1590s Mary Sidney was much concerned by her husband's failing health. She helped her husband with a tactful letter to Essex during their quarrel over property (1596). She wrote to Lord Burghley hoping to arrange a marriage between her son William and Cecil's granddaughter Bridget de Vere (1597); that same year she wrote a tactful thank you to Robert Cecil, although the marriage did not go through, and then in September an apology, basically, for her husband's crossness (*Collected Works* 1:288–90). (Her son Philip later married Bridget's younger sister Susan, who became Countess of Montgomery.) Her husband was so ill that Mary Sidney stayed at Wilton to care for him; Barbara Gamage Sidney helped by supervising young William and

---

6   See also Larson *ARC* 1:21; Kinnamon *ARC* 2:2, Bond *ARC* 2:4, Prescott *ARC* 2:18, Clarke *ARC* 2:19, and Hamlin *ARC* 2:20.

Philip Herbert in London during court activities, and Robert Sidney became almost like a father to them.

With her husband's death on 19 January 1601, Mary Sidney became the Dowager Countess of Pembroke a month before the court became preoccupied with the execution of the Earl of Essex on 25 February 1601. With no daughter-in-law yet, she probably continued as the mistress of Wilton, and perhaps also Baynard's Castle. William was under the Wards of Court until he came of age that April. The dowager countess herself wrote a model letter of thankfulness to the queen for accepting William at court in 1601 (*Collected Works* 1:290–92). Some time shortly after his father's death in January 1601, William had gotten into a quarrel by rejecting care of the maid of honor Mary Fitton who was bearing his child; he was pleased that the baby died, and did little to help his mistress. Elizabeth sent him to Fleet Prison, until apparently his mother and their family physician managed to get him home based on a "medical" problem: "he is fallen into an ague" (*Acts of the Privy Council* 31:299). Her father, Sir Edward Fitton, implies a *de praesenti* marriage that William no longer admits ("my daughter is confident in her claim before God"), but he anticipates "no good from him." The letters young Pembroke sends to Robert Cecil include fawning praises of Queen Elizabeth, but mostly whining in self-pity and bitter jests about himself punished like a galley slave or "in hell" (Hannay, *MSLW* 80–83).

John Chamberlain said that as a widow, the dowager countess was left almost penniless (1:116), but the reverse happened, with her extensive jointure, a generous will, and the support of her sons. As soon as William became the third Earl of Pembroke in 1601, aged twenty, he began to assume her previous role of literary patron, and subsequent poems of praise to her tended to group her with other family members, frequently seeking young Pembroke's favor by also including praise of his mother. He rapidly became a supporter of writers such as John Donne, George Herbert, Ben Jonson, and many others, evidently including Shakespeare (see Lamb *ARC* 2:17).

During her son's first years as earl, the dowager countess was still engrossed in family business problems. In August 1602 she wrote to Cecil from the Herbert Cardiff Castle "from the want of thos frends of myne long since lost" (*Collected Works* 1:292), including all her male relatives of the previous generation, as well as her brothers Philip and Thomas; Robert was then not in real favor at court, and her young Earl William was in disgrace with the queen.

After Elizabeth's death on 24 March 1603 Mary Sidney and her daughter Anne went to greet Queen Anne on her way south from Scotland to the English court in London, while her young sons joined King James. She tried to receive justice from what had befallen her in Wales. Rushing back to the queen's funeral, she had been caught in a brutal attack developing from the long argument in Wales between the Mathews and the Herberts; she then appealed to Sir Julius Caesar four times, apparently on her journey to meet with the new Queen Anne (July–September 1603), and finally to William's prospective father-in-law, the Earl of Shrewsbury (*Collected Works* 1:292–7). The quarrel in Cardiff included pirates, rioting and destruction of walls at Cardiff Castle, the theft of her jewelry being brought for the court event, and the murder of her servant Hugh Davyd (*Philip's Phoenix* 173–84). Her letter to Gilbert Talbot, Earl of Shrewsbury, her son's prospective father-in-law, praises her new "daughter," but worries about "such a monster as hath devided myne owne from me (he that was held the deerest part of me" (*Collected Works* 1:297). Little further evidence survives, but this is usually read as a temporary quarrel with the young Pembroke (Waller, *Sidney Family Romance* 79–80). Under King James and Queen Anne, the Sidney–Herbert royal favor increased in position, income, and titles; Mary and her daughter went to the Feast of St. George when William was made Knight of the Garter, and they were both apparently at Wilton when the king came on several visits, trying to avoid the plague in London. Both her sons were later involved in tilts, as well as hunting and hawking with the king. Even though Philip was involved in violent reactions at court that supposedly meant his mother "Tore her Hair at the Report of her Son's Dishounor" (Osborn 408), he remained a favorite of King James, who gave him important positions, including Knight of the Garter and Lord Lieutenant of Kent, and then made him, as the younger Pembroke son, Earl of Montgomery.

In 1604 both her sons and god-daughter married, although as early as 1599/1600 there had been a murmured suggestion that Lady Anne was being courted, ironically, by the elderly Earl of Hertford, who had married Katherine Dudley, whom Anne's own father had long ago divorced; by March, Hertford said that he "never moved any such thing," no doubt after Anne's refusal (Whyte 399, 433, 436). The dowager countess and her daughter Anne and her son William were at Penshurst in September 1604, preparing for Mall's wedding to Sir Robert Wroth, arranged long before. Each of her sons took charge of their own marriages, with William's long-negotiated arranged marriage with Mary Talbot like so many other connections with that family, including his stepgrandmother Anne Talbot, aunt Anne Herbert Talbot, and his father's second wife, Katherine Talbot Herbert. Lady Mary Wroth later portrays the marriage as a trick by Forsandurus (*Urania* 2), but there is no Herbert or Talbot family criticism of this traditional connection. Philip's desired marriage with Susan de Vere, daughter of Anne Cecil and Edward de Vere, Earl of Oxford, and niece of Robert Cecil, was given praised anticipation by William: "after long love," he said, they were "privately contracted without the knowledge of any of his or her friends," apparently a *de praesenti* marriage (*Philip's Phoenix* 190–91). Then King James approved an extravagant formal celebration at court, saying she was such a bride that "if he were not married he would not giue her but keep her himself" (Carleton 66).

In 1605 the dowager countess watched her daughter Anne, daughter-in-law Susan, and niece Mary Wroth perform with the queen in the *Masque of Blackness*. It seemed like a cheerful time, but Mary Sidney's life was much saddened by the recurring illness of her daughter Anne, noted in the correspondence of her uncle Robert with William Brown and with Hugh Sanford at Wilton (*MSLW* 132). Lady Anne was in such danger that her mother took her to Cambridge for special medical care (perhaps with her own doctor, Matthew Lister), but Anne died there in 1606 and was buried at the Cambridge church of St. Mary's rather than taken back to Wilton. Mary Sidney's last autograph letter extant is written to Cecil, then Earl of Salisbury, in 1607 about gaining the "wardship" of the son of Sir John Gennings (*Collected Works* 1:297).

The Countess of Pembroke continued to receive acclaim as a poet, notably by Aemilia Lanyer (1611), who praises "Her love, her zeale, her faith, and pietie" as shown in her Psalms as "th'eternall booke / Of endlesse honour, true fames memorie" (29). Wroth may have become increasingly important to her, because she served as a literary mentor as well as a godmother and aunt. She was noted primarily for her Psalms and *Discourse* by others, but Wroth portrays her as a love poet, the Queen of Naples, who is "perfect in poetry" and presents a poem on a nightingale; she "knew when she did well, and would be unwilling to lose the due unto her selfe" which she did receive (*Urania* 1:371, 490). Wroth hints that meekness need not have been one of her aunt's characteristics, after receiving a lifetime of praise.[7]

In the years 1608–13 there is, except for poetic tributes, no extant record of Mary Sidney's actions, probably suggesting that she was not doing anything distinctive enough to be recorded. But then she attracted considerable attention with her extended journey to Spa and other places on the Continent, including the poetic praise on her journey by William Basse. Three printed letters are attributed to her by John Donne the younger (who printed poems

---

7   June and Paul Schlueter have recently discovered poems on the Continent that were associated with (or perhaps even by) Mary Sidney.

by her son William plus others—see Lamb *ARC* 2:17). These letters to Sir Tobie Matthew celebrate their time at Spa and then speak of writings that they exchanged (*Collected Works* 1:298–301). She is more appealingly human than ideal in the letters of those cheerful gossips John Chamberlain and Dudley Carleton, who note the dowager countess's concern with her fading beauty, discuss her amusements of taking tobacco, playing cards, and dancing, stress that she enjoyed being with the Countess of Barlemont, wife of the Governor of Luxembourg, and mention her flirtation with her handsome and learned physician, Sir Matthew Lister (Carleton 209; see Kuin *ARC* 1:15). That Lister romance was reflected in Lady Wroth's pastoral drama *Loves Victory* (see Findlay *ARC* 2:13). She quickly left for England in September 1616 to be the godparent of Philip's baby James, but arrived too late, much frustrated by the unusually stormy two months of travel. She subsequently developed her own mansion in Houghton House; its magnificent ruins can still be visited. Set on the top of the hill in Bedford, it is perceived as "House Beautiful" by the locals there, as named by John Bunyan in *Pilgrim's Progress* (*Philip's Phoenix* 203). Her son Philip visited her in July 1617, and probably family members came each summer.

Her most familiar image is from the Simon van de Passe engraving, made in 1618, when she was aged fifty-seven (Illustration 10). Latin and English inscriptions identify her both as a Sidney and as the Countess of Pembroke, but the portrait itself represents her as a devout writer, as she holds out to the viewer her rendition of "Davids Psalms." At the top of the architectural frame, prominently displayed above the portrait, is the Sidney family device of the pheon (an arrowhead) crowned by a coronet to demonstrate her rank. Above these symbols of her position as a Sidney and as a countess is a laurel wreath. She thus presents herself as the male poets had described her and as female poets had emulated her; like Drayton, she wears "the Laurell crowne" (Drayton 1:74, 76).

She participated in the May 1619 funeral of Queen Anne, over which her brother Robert, now Earl of Leicester, presided. The following year she assisted her daughter-in-law in the birth of Pembroke's son Henry in March 1620, and she was his godmother at his christening in later April (Chamberlain 2:302; George Owen WSA MS 2057 F1/2). William Herbert profusely praised his heir in correspondence with friends, but lost him shortly thereafter; Pembroke may have had a second infant son named for James who died the following year (Vincent 3H3r). King James visited her Italianate Houghton House in July 1621 (Nichols 4:671).

The Dowager Countess of Pembroke was fashionably back in her London home at Aldersgate Street that autumn, when she died of smallpox on 25 September 1621. Her sons gave her a magnificent service at St. Paul's, followed by a long formal night procession to Wilton, and then she was buried next to her husband under the choir steps in Salisbury Cathedral. Late in her life and shortly after her death she was praised for her religious devotion by writers including Robert Newton in his 1620 dedication (A4v). Henry Holland and William Camden include praise of her in biographical entries on her husband's death. Frances Osborn, equating her with her brother Philip, claims that "her Pen" was "nothing short of his" (77). Donne equates the Sidneys in "Upon the translation of the Psalmes by Sir Philip Sydney, and the Countesse of Pembroke his Sister"; both the Sidneys present models for divine verse in English: "They shew us Ilanders our joy, our King, / They tell us *why*, and teach us *how* to sing" (Donne, *Divine Poems* 34). Her most famous eulogy is by William Browne, describing her as "the subject of all verse," identifying her as "Sydneys sister Pembrokes mother," and "faire and Learn'd," as well as "good" (*Philip's Phoenix* 206). More surprising is Thomas Archer, the rector in Houghton Conquest in 1760, who records her death and identifies Sir Philip Sidney primarily as the brother of the Countess of Pembroke. Like many other aristocratic women, the Countess of Pembroke became involved in court politics, assisted her husband with his business correspondence, supported public works, helped arrange marriages and positions for her children, encouraged the spiritual instruction of her family and retainers, and oversaw the household administration for enormous establishments in London, in Wiltshire, and in Wales. Celebrated during her own life and thereafter, she was prominent for her roles as patron, translator, and writer.

Biography and Bibliography

In the eighteenth- and nineteenth-century studies of women writers, the Countess of Pembroke is almost invariably praised as the sister of Sir Philip Sidney and as a poet and patron. For example, George Ballard's 1752 *Memoirs of Several Ladies of Great Britain* devotes descriptions to her family, poems dedicated to her, her role as patroness, her *Discourse*, *Antonie*, and Psalms, her Simon van de Passe engraving, and her famous Browne epitaph (incorrectly attributed to Ben Jonson) (Ballard 249–52). Many such reference works are similar, although some are much shorter and less informed, such as Giles Jacob's 1720 *Historical Account of ... Our Most Considerable Poets* (201), whereas the 1766 *Biographium faemineum* stresses her "natural genius" and adds to Ballard's account (2:189–92). Mary Hays's 1803 *Female Biography* describes her as Sir Philip's sister, with "a highly cultivated mind and superior talents," who "possessed a talent for poetical composition, which she assiduously cultivated," as well as serving as "a patroness of letters" (6:417). Mary Sidney is thus traditionally included and praised during this period. Her influence may even have been international, given her European travel in 1614–16.

The first full-length biography, *Mary Sidney, Countess of Pembroke*, is by Frances Young (1912), followed by Margaret Hannay's *Philip's Phoenix: Mary Sidney, Countess of Pembroke* (1990). Among the earlier scholarship, Pearl Hogrefe included a chapter on her in *Women of Action in Tudor England* (1977), and Waller a biographical introduction to her works, alluding to John Aubrey's scandalous account of incest (*Mary Sidney*, 1979), as did Jonathan Crewe (82–8). Her poetry is analyzed by Woods, who notes her being "largely uncredited" in 1985, and by Beilin in *Redeeming Eve* (1987). Brennan placed her in family context as a patron (*Literary Patronage*, 1988), and later as part of her family's relationship to their monarchs (Brennan, *Sidneys of Penshurst*, 2006); Lamb analyzed her as a woman writer and patron (*Gender and Authorship*, 1990). Most biographies of Sir Philip Sidney mention her, at least in passing.

Her critical heritage is discussed at length by Hannay in the lengthy introduction to *Mary Sidney, Countess of Pembroke* (xv–lxii), Volume 2 of *Ashgate Critical Essays on Women Writers in England, 1500–1700* (2009); the volume includes twenty-five scholars' essays. Also important are the seven essays in the *Sidney Journal*, Volume 23 (2005). Mary Sidney currently appears in standard reference works such as the *Oxford Dictionary of National Biography*, the *Oxford Dictionary of Literary Biography*, and most anthologies including early modern writers; her works have been analyzed in more than 250 modern articles and studies. Online bibliographies on her include Modern Language Association bibliography, Hannay's annotated entry at *Oxford Bibliographies Online*,[8] and Betty Travitsy's annotated bibliography at *Bibliography of English Women Writers (1500–1640)*.[9]

Now, as in her own day, Mary Sidney Herbert, Countess of Pembroke, is known for her patronage, translation, and authorship, expressing her roles in politics and in religion.

---

8   http://www.oxfordbibliographies.com/view/document/obo-9780199846719/obo-9780199846719-0053.xml.

9   http://www.itergateway.org/resources/beww.

Bibliography

Manuscript Sources

Cambridge, Trinity College Library
    R.17.2 Sidney Family Psalter
Folger Shakespeare Library
    V.a.511 (Richardson)
Harvard, Houghton Library
    fMS Eng 725 (jointure MS)
The National Archives, Kew (TNA)
    SP 40/2 fol. 83

Primary and Secondary Sources

Acts of the Privy Council of England. Ed. J. R. Dasent. 32 vols. London: HMSO, 1890–1907.

Aubrey, John. *Aubrey's Brief Lives.* Ed. Oliver Lawson Dick. London: Secker and Warburg, 1949.

—. *Aubrey's Natural History of Wiltshire.* 1685. Rpt. New York: Kelle, 1969.

Ballard, George. *Memoirs of Several Ladies of Great Britain.* 1752. Ed. Ruth Perry. Detroit, MI: Wayne State UP, 1985.

Baxter, Nathaniel. *Sir Philip Sydneys Ourania, that is, Endimions Song and Tragedie, Containing all Philosophie.* London: Edward White, 1606.

Beilin, Elaine. *Redeeming Eve.* Princeton, NJ: Princeton UP, 1987.

Bell, Ilona. *Elizabethan Women and the Poetry of Courtship.* Cambridge: Cambridge UP, 1998.

Benson, Pamela Joseph. "The Stigma of Italy Undone: Aemilia Lanyer's Canonization of Lady Mary Sidney." *Strong Voices, Weak History: Early Women Writers and Canons in England, France, and Italy.* Ed. Pamela Joseph Benson and Victoria Kirkham. Ann Arbor, MI: U of Michigan P, 2005. 146–75.

Biographium faemineum. 2 vols. London: printed for S. Crowder and J. Payne; J. Wilkie, and W. Nicoll; and J. Wren, 1766.

Bornstein, Diane. "The Style of the Countess of Pembroke's Translation of Philippe de Mornay's *Discours de la vie et de la mort.*" *Silent but for the Word: Tudor Women as Patrons, Translators, and Writers of Religious Works.* Ed. Margaret P. Hannay. Kent, OH: Kent State UP, 1985.

Brennan, Michael G. *Literary Patronage in the English Renaissance: The Pembroke Family.* London: Routledge, 1988.

—. *The Sidneys of Penshurst and the Monarchy, 1500–1700.* Aldershot: Ashgate, 2006.

Breton, Nicholas. *The Works in Verse and Prose of Nicholas Breton.* Ed. Alexander B. Grosart. 2 vols. 1879. Rpt. New York: AMS, 1966.

Burke, Victoria E. "Elizabeth Ashburnham Richardson's 'Motherlie Endeauors.'" *English Manuscript Studies 1100–1700* 9 (2000): 98–113.

Carleton, Sir Dudley. *Dudley Carleton to John Chamberlain 1603–1624: Jacobean Letters.* Ed. Maurice Lee, Jr. New Brunswick, NJ: Rutgers UP, 1972.

Chamberlain, John. *The Letters of John Chamberlain.* Ed. Norman Egbert McClure. 2 vols. Philadelphia, PA: American Philosophical Society, 1939. Rpt. Westport, CT: Greenwood Press, 1979.

Churchyard, Thomas. *A Pleasant Conceit Penned in Verse.* London: Roger Warde, 1593.

Clarke, Danielle. "'In Sort as She It Sung': Spenser's 'Doleful Lay' and the Construction of Female Authorship." *Criticism: A Quarterly for Literature and the Arts* 42 (2000): 451–68.

—. "Mary Sidney Herbert and Women's Religious Verse." *Early Modern English Poetry: A Critical Companion*. Ed. Patrick Cheney, Andrew Hadfield, and Garrett A. Sullivan, Jr. Oxford: Oxford UP, 2007. 184–94.

—. *The Politics of Early Modern Women's Writing*. London: Longman, 2001.

Coles, Kimberly Anne. *Religion, Reform, and Women's Writing in Early Modern England*. Cambridge: Cambridge UP, 2008.

Crewe, Jonathan. *Hidden Designs: The Critical Profession and Renaissance Literature*. New York: Methuen, 1986.

Daniel, Samuel. *Delia. Contayning Certayne Sonnets*. London: Simon Waterson, 1592.

Davis, Joel. "Multiple Arcadias and the Literary Quarrel between Fulke Greville and the Countess of Pembroke." *Studies in Philology* 101 (2004): 401–30.

Dobell, Bertram. "New Light Upon Sir Philip Sidney's 'Arcadia.'" *Quarterly Review* 211 (1909): 74–100.

Donne, John. *The Divine Poems*. Ed. Helen Gardner. Oxford: Clarendon P, 1952.

Drayton, Michael. *The Works of Michael Drayton*. Ed. J. William Hebel. 5 vols. Oxford: Basil Blackwell, 1931–41.

Duncan-Jones, Katherine. "Stoicism in *Measure for Measure*: A New Source." *Review of English Studies* 28 (1977): 441–6.

Erler, Mary C. "Davies's *Astraea* and Other Contexts of the Countess of Pembroke's 'A Dialogue.'" *SEL* 30 (1990): 41–61.

Goldring, Elizabeth. "'So lively a portraiture of his miseries': Melancholy, Mourning and the Elizabethan Malady." *The British Art Journal* 6.2 (2005): 12–22.

Goodblatt, Chanita. "'High Holy Muse': Christian Hebraism and Jewish Exegesis in the Sidneian *Psalmes*." *Tradition, Heterodoxy and Religious Culture: Judaism and Christianity in the Early Modern Period*. Ed. Chanita Goodblatt and Howard Kreisel. Beer-Sheva, Israel: Ben-Gurion U of the Negev P, 2006. 287–309.

Hackett, Helen. "Courtly Writing By Women." *Women and Literature in Britain 1500–1700*. Ed. Helen Wilcox. Cambridge: Cambridge UP, 1996. 169–89.

Hadfield, Andrew. *Edmund Spenser: A Life*. Oxford: Oxford UP, 2012.

Hamlin, Hannibal. *Psalm Culture and Early Modern English Literature*. Cambridge: Cambridge UP, 2004.

Hannay, Margaret P. "Elizabeth Ashburnham Richardson's Meditation on the Countess of Pembroke's *Discourse*." *English Manuscript Studies 1100–1700* 9 (2000): 114–28.

—. "The Countess of Pembroke as a Spenserian Poet." Rpt. *Ashgate Critical Essays on Women Writers in England, 1550–1700, Volume 2: Mary Sidney, Countess of Pembroke*. Ed. Margaret P. Hannay. Aldershot: Ashgate, 2009. 343–64.

—. *Mary Sidney, Lady Wroth*. Farnham: Ashgate, 2010.

—. *Philip's Phoenix: Mary Sidney, Countess of Pembroke*. Oxford: Oxford UP, 1990.

—— "'Your Vertuous and Learned Aunt': The Countess of Pembroke as a Mentor to Mary Wroth." Rpt. *Ashgate Critical Essays on Women Writers in England, 1550–1700, Volume 5: Mary Wroth*. Ed. Clare Kinney. Aldershot: Ashgate, 2009. 388–408.

Hays, Mary. *Female Biography*. 6 vols. 1803. Ed. Gina Luria Walker. London: Pickering & Chatto, 2013.

Herbert, Mary Sidney, Countess of Pembroke. *The Collected Works of Mary Sidney Herbert, Countess of Pembroke*. Ed. Margaret P. Hannay, Noel J. Kinnamon, and Michael G. Brennan. 2 vols. Oxford: Clarendon P, 1998.

—. *The Countess of Pembroke's Translation of Philippe de Mornay's Life and Death*. Ed. Diane Bornstein. Detroit, MI: Michigan Consortium for Medieval and Early Modern Studies, 1983.

—. *Selected Works of Mary Sidney Herbert, Countess of Pembroke*. Ed. Margaret P. Hannay, Noel J. Kinnamon, and Michael G. Brennan. Tempe, AZ: Arizona Center for Medieval and Renaissance Texts and Studies, 2005.

—. *The Triumph of Death*. Ed. Gavin Alexander. *COPIA: CERES Sidneiana*. Web. 20 September 1999. http://www.english.cam.ac.uk/ceres/sidneiana/triumph.htm.

—. *The Triumph of Death and Other Unpublished and Uncollected Poems by Mary Sidney, Countess of Pembroke (1561–1621)*. Ed. Gary F. Waller. Salzburg: U of Salzburg, 1977.

Hogrefe, Pearl. *Tudor Women: Commoners and Queens*. Ames, IA: Iowa State UP, 1975.

Howell, Thomas. *Howell's Devises 1581*. Oxford: Clarendon P, 1906.

Jacob, Giles. *An Historical Account of ... Our Most Considerable Poets*. London: E. Curll, 1720.

Jardine, Lisa. *Reading Shakespeare Historically*. London: Routledge, 1996.

Kennedy, William J. *Authorizing Petrarch*. Ithaca, NY: Cornell UP, 1994.

Kinsella, Stuart. "Colonial Commemoration in Tudor Ireland: The Case of Sir Henry Sidney." *SJ* 29.1–2 (2011): 105–46.

Klein, Lisa M. *The Exemplary Sidney and the Elizabethan Sonneteer*. Newark, DE: U of Delaware P, 1998.

Lamb, Mary Ellen. *Gender and Authorship in the Sidney Circle*. Madison, WI: U of Wisconsin P, 1990.

Lanyer, Aemilia. *The Poems of Aemilia Lanyer: Salve Deus Rex Judaeorum*. Ed. Susanne Woods. Oxford: Oxford UP. 1993.

May, Steven W. "Two Unpublished Letters by Mary Herbert, Countess of Pembroke." *English Manuscript Studies 1100–1700* 9 (2000): 88–97.

Moffet, Thomas. *Nobilis or a View of the Life and Death of a Sidney and Lessus Lugubris*. Ed. Virgil B. Heltzel and Hoyt H. Hudson. San Marino, CA: Huntington Library, 1940.

—. *The Silkewormes and their Flies* (1599). Ed. Victor Houliston. Binghamton, NY: MRTS, 1989.

Molyneux, Edmund. *Holinshed's Chronicles of England, Scotland and Ireland*. 1586. Ed. H. Ellis. London: Johnson, 1807–8. Rpt. New York: AMS, 1965. 4:869–80.

Newton, Robert. *The Countess of Montgomeries Eusebia: Expressing briefly, The Soules Praying Robes*. London: George Purston, 1620.

Nichols, John. *The Progresses, Processions, and Magnificent Festivities, of King James the First*. 4 vols. London: J. B. Nichols, 1828.

Osborn, Frances. *Historical Memoires on the Reigns of Queen Elizabeth and King James*. London: T. Robinson, 1683.

Pender, Patricia. "Mea Mediocritas: Mary Sidney and the Early Modern Rhetoric of Modesty." *What is the New Rhetoric?* Ed. Susan E. Thomas and John O. Ward. Newcastle upon Tyne: Cambridge Scholars, 2007. 104–25.

Quitslund, Beth. "Teaching Us How to Sing? The Peculiarity of the Sidney Psalter." *SJ* 23 (2005): 83–110.

Roberts, Josephine A. "The Huntington Library Manuscript of Lady Mary Wroth's Play, *Loves Victorie*." *HLQ* 46 (1983): 156–74.

Rye, Constance E. B. "Queen Elizabeth's Godchildren." *The Genealogist* n.s. 2 (1885): 293.

Schlueter, June, and Paul Schlueter. "Halfe maim'd? Five Unknown Poems by Mary Sidney Herbert, Countess of Pembroke." *Times Literary Supplement* Jul. 23, 2010.

Sidney, Henry. *A Viceroy's Vindication? Sir Henry Sidney's Memoir of Service in Ireland, 1556–1578*. Ed. Ciarán Brady. Cork: Cork UP, 2002.

Sidney, Philip. *The Countess of Pembroke's Arcadia (The New Arcadia)*. Ed. Victor Skretkowicz. Oxford: Clarendon P, 1987.

—. *The Countess of Pembroke's Arcadia (The Old Arcadia)*. Ed. Jean Robertson. Oxford: Clarendon P, 1973.

The Sidney Psalter: The Psalms of Sir Philip and Mary Sidney. Ed. Hannibal Hamlin, Michael G. Brennan, Margaret P. Hannay, and Noel J. Kinnamon. Oxford: Oxford UP, 2009.

Sidney, Robert, first Earl of Leicester. *Domestic Politics and Family Absence: The Correspondence (1588–1621) of Robert Sidney, first Earl of Leicester, and Barbara Gamage Sidney, Countess of Leicester.* Ed. Margaret P. Hannay, Noel J. Kinnamon, and Michael G. Brennan. Aldershot: Ashgate, 2005.

—. *The Poems of Robert Sidney.* Ed. Peter J. Croft. Oxford: Clarendon P, 1984.

Smith, J. C., and Ernest de Selincourt. *Spenser: Poetical Works.* Oxford: Oxford UP, 1912. Rpt. Oxford: Oxford UP, 1969.

Vincent, Augustine. *A Discovery of Errors in the First Edition of the Catalogue of Nobility, Published by Ralphe Brooke in 1619.* London: William Jaggard, 1622.

Wall, Wendy. *The Imprint of Gender: Authorship and Publication in the English Renaissance.* Ithaca, NY: Cornell UP, 1993.

Waller, Gary. "The Countess of Pembroke and Gendered Reading." *Women Editing/Editing Women.* Ed. Ann Hollinshead Hurley and Chanita Goodblatt. Newcastle upon Tyne: Cambridge Scholars, 2009. 35–54.

—. *Mary Sidney, Countess of Pembroke: A Critical Study of Her Writings and Literary Milieu.* Salzburg: U of Salzburg P, 1979.

—. *The Sidney Family Romance: Mary Wroth, William Herbert, and the Early Modern Construction of Gender.* Detroit, MI: Wayne State UP, 1993.

Whyte, Rowland. *The Letters (1595–1608) of Rowland Whyte.* Ed. Michael G. Brennan, Noel J. Kinnamon, and Margaret P. Hannay. Philadelphia, PA: American Philosophical Society, 2013.

Williams, Franklin D. "The Literary Patronesses of Renaissance England." *Notes & Queries* 207 (1962): 364–6.

Wolfe, Heather. "Dye to live, live to dye." *The Collation: A Gathering of Scholarship from the Shakespeare Folger Library.* Web. 19 April 2012. http://collation.folger.edu/2012/04/dye-to-live-live-to-dye/.

Woods, Susanne. *Natural Emphasis: English Versification from Chaucer to Dryden.* San Marino, CA: Huntington Library, 1984.

Wroth, Lady Mary Sidney. *The First Part of The Countess of Montgomery's Urania.* Ed. Josephine A. Roberts. Tempe, AZ: Arizona Center for Medieval and Renaissance Texts and Studies, 1995.

—. *Lady Mary Wroth's Love's Victory: The Penshurst Manuscript.* Ed. Michael G. Brennan. London: The Roxburghe Club, 1988.

Zim, Rivkah. *English Metrical Psalms: Poetry as Praise and Prayer, 1535–1601.* Cambridge: Cambridge UP, 1987. 185–210.

Those Essex Girls:
The Lives and Letters of Lettice Knollys, Penelope Rich, Dorothy Perrott Percy, and Frances Walsingham

Grace Ioppolo

She was married at least twice: once scandalously in secret for love, and at least once formally for dynastic allegiance, power, and wealth. She incurred the wrath of her monarch for at least one of her marriages, and never fully recovered her privileged status at court. She was accused of promiscuity and adultery, and her husband's paternity of her children was questioned in court gossip. She was beautiful, seductive, intelligent, and charming, and she manipulated the most important royal officials of the realm, most notably Queen Elizabeth I, William Cecil, Lord Burghley, and Sir Robert Cecil, Earl of Salisbury. She was at the center of dazzling literature, drama, spectacle, and art, as well as political intrigue, and she was probably complicit in the notorious treason of her husband, son, or brother. Most remarkably, she insisted that her mind, body, and sexuality were her own, and not the property of men.

To which of the women of the Essex family—Lettice Knollys, her daughter Penelope, her daughter Dorothy, or her daughter-in-law Frances Walsingham—does this description pertain? Remarkably, each of these women fits this description. Each was the maker and beneficiary of political and cultural influence and power, and each suffered royal condemnation and national scandal for choosing to think that she could live her life as she chose, regardless of what a royal patriarchy or matriarchy and peers insisted on. Although many historians and literary critics since the sixteenth century have referred to these women merely in the reflections of their politically powerful fathers, husbands, sons, or brothers, each woman in fact wielded considerable influence and authority in her own right, especially in ignoring myths about the boundaries of behavior for early modern aristocratic women.

Ironically, each of these women was a true "Essex girl," which the *Oxford English Dictionary* calls a "derogatory" and "contemptuous term applied to a type of young woman, supposedly to be found in and around Essex, and variously characterized as unintelligent, promiscuous, and materialistic." This late twentieth-century slang word, especially the labeling of an Essex girl as "promiscuous," could ironically be applied to these sixteenth-century true Essex girls from the family of the Earls of Essex. Lettice, Penelope, Dorothy, and Frances were each born into wealth, status, and political power derived from their fathers. But each woman acquired even more from her successive husbands. To begin to understand the female dynastic power they assumed, wielded, and only occasionally lost in the age of the Sidneys, we need to begin with its matriarch, who worked at great cost for so long to establish this power: Lettice Knollys, Countess of Essex and Countess of Leicester.

Lettice Knollys

Lettice (1543–1634) was the daughter of Sir Francis Knollys (1514–96), one of Elizabeth I's most loyal courtiers, and his wife Katherine (c. 1523–69), who was the daughter of Anne Boleyn's sister Mary Stafford, the mistress of Henry VIII during her first marriage to William Carey, and mother of Henry's illegitimate son.[1] Lettice's political relationship through her father and her blood relationship through her mother to the queen brought her early influence at court. In 1560 Lettice made a successful dynastic first marriage, probably to suit her family, to Sir Walter Devereux, second Viscount Hereford and later first Earl of Essex. But within a few years, and apparently no later than 1565 (Peck 267), Lettice seems to have begun a romantic relationship, and probably a sexual affair, with Robert Dudley (c. 1532–88), Earl of Leicester, which apparently intensified after her husband Walter Devereux departed for long periods to lead the queen's troops in Ireland beginning in 1573. According to court gossip, Lettice became pregnant more than once by Leicester during her husband's absence. One of those children, a daughter, was rumored to have survived and been raised by Lettice's relatives,[2] although there is no way to prove this claim. Further rumors suggested that some of her surviving four children with Devereux were indeed fathered by Leicester—a fear her husband may have shared, particularly in regard to the true paternity of his heir, Robert (1565–1601).

After Sir Walter's death in Ireland in 1576, Lettice appears to have entered into a clandestine marriage with Leicester, the ceremony for which may have taken place at Leicester's home at Kenilworth and became immediately known, at least to his nephew Sir Philip Sidney (Peck 202). However, Lettice's father insisted that, to protect her reputation, she and Leicester had to have a formal marriage service. On 20 September 1578, two years to the day of her first husband's death, and thus at the end of the formal mourning period, she married Leicester again at his London-area home Wanstead House, but without the permission or knowledge of Queen Elizabeth, who was away on progress at Loughton, the home of Francis Stonor (Peck 202). Due to Lettice's pregnancy the marriage was finally acknowledged, but its validity was contested by Lady Douglass Howard, Baroness Sheffield, who claimed that she had married Leicester in May 1573 and was the mother of his two legitimate children (Peck 269, 86).[3] The baroness also claimed that, when she refused to accept Leicester's bribe of £700 to disclaim the marriage, he attempted to poison her, and that for her own "safety" she later married Edward Stafford (Peck 270). Leicester denied the Baroness's claims and continued his married life with Lettice, although the couple suffered the tragedy of the early death of their son, the only one of his own children whom Leicester acknowledged as a legitimate heir. The author of *Leicester's Commonwealth*, which attacked Leicester's behavior in private

---

1   For a succinct account of Lettice's life, see Adams. Many popular history accounts of Lettice are sensational rather than scholarly.

2   The anonymous author of *Leicester's Commonwealth*, claimed that because Walter Devereux "was coming home from Ireland with intent to revenge himself upon my Lord of Leicester for begetting his wife with child in his absence (the child was a daughter and brought up by the Lady Shandoies, W. Knooles his wife)," Leicester had his friends administer Devereux with "an extreme flux" that killed him (Peck 82).

3   As Margaret Hannay has privately pointed out to me, Lady Douglas Howard's mother was a Gamage, so her "illegitimate" sons were Sidney cousins on that side as well as Leicester's.

and at court, was one of many who repeated the scurrilous claim that the boy had suffered from a "falling sickness," commenting that it "well may be a witness of the parents' sin and wickedness and of both their wasted natures in iniquity" (Peck 89). Both Leicester and Lettice may also have been chastised for their apparent licentiousness in Edmund Spenser's *The Shepheardes Calendar* (Mounts 195ff.)

Lettice continued to attempt to control her own life, regardless of her monarch's and her family's objections, because one year after Leicester's death in 1588 she married Sir Charles Blount, who was fifteen years her junior. She thus had moved up from Countess of Essex to Countess of Leicester and then down simply to Lady Blount, suggesting that love, or sexual desire, may have been more important to her than aristocratic standing. But, having been accused of poisoning her first husband, Walter Devereux, so that she could marry Leicester, as repeatedly stated in such texts as *Leicester's Commonwealth* and William Camden's *Annales*,[4] Lettice was then accused of poisoning her second husband Leicester so that she could marry Blount. Lettice survived such scandalous gossip and seemed remarkably uninterested in placating the wrath that her second and third marriages had provoked in Elizabeth, although her son Robert, second Earl of Essex, attempted several times to reconcile the two women. On one occasion in March 1598 Robert was so angry that Elizabeth had failed to receive Lettice, who had positioned herself in the queen's way with a proffered jewel, that he daringly left his chamber in the castle and "in his night gown went up to the queen the privy way" (Whyte 304). He failed on this and every other occasion to convince Elizabeth once again to formally acknowledge her cousin Lettice.[5]

The scandal of Lettice's third marriage only intensified when Blount was tried and executed in 1601 as a conspirator in the rebellion of Lettice's son Robert Devereux. Although both her husband and her son were executed for a treasonous plot that was planned and managed from Robert's London home, Essex House, where she was a frequent visitor, Lettice seemed not to have been formally implicated or even suspected of being a conspirator. However, Lettice and her daughter Penelope had been shrewd enough to ingratiate themselves for many years with King James VI of Scotland and his wife Queen Anne of Denmark, thereby guaranteeing their protection when the monarchs came to the English throne. But even after 1603, Lettice's life of scandal was still not behind her: she spent years involved in protracted legal battles with Leicester's illegitimate son Robert Dudley over Essex family estates, which were finally decided in her favor, but not before Lettice was charged with defending the legitimacy of her marriage to Leicester and disproving yet again charges of adultery before and during her years as Countess of Leicester. Her final years were spent in the company of her grandson, Robert, third Earl of Essex, who survived his own sexual scandal during the annulment proceedings of his marriage to Lady Frances Howard, in which he was required through a series of physical tests to prove that he could, in theory, consummate his marriage, but in practice had not succeeded in doing so. Lettice outlived most of her children, dying a rich woman, as demonstrated by her still-extant household inventory (BL Add. MS 18985) at

---

4   McGurk disputes the idea that Lettice poisoned Walter Devereux, as: "a rumour that the earl had been poisoned proved groundless, as attested by the post-mortem examination ordered by Sir Henry Sidney. Sidney's report to Walsingham gives a detailed description of Essex's last days, and likewise his secretary, Edward Waterhouse, wrote a sad account, printed in William Camden's *Annales* (as edited by Thomas Hearne, 1717). A manuscript copy of the latter, erroneously attributed to Thomas Churchyard's hand and once belonging to William Cole, the Cambridge antiquary, is now in the British Library (BL, Add. MS 5845 fols. 337–49)."

5   For a discussion of the relationship between Essex and Elizabeth, see esp. Hammer, *Political Career*, and Ioppolo, "'Your Majesties.'"

the age of ninety-one in 1643. Judging from letters dating from 1626 and 1629, she may have suffered from palsy in the last two decades of her life.[6]

In many ways Lettice set the standard of the powerful matriarch, female aristocrat, and irrepressible woman for her own children and for those in her court circle. Elizabeth reportedly referred to Lettice in the 1580s as a "she-wolf" (*CSP Spain (Simancas) 1550–86* 3:477), but never punished her with anything other than banishment from her presence. No matter what the political or personal scandal, intrigue, or plot in which Lettice was involved, she survived all attempts to silence or punish her, largely because she pretended, at least, to use discretion and decorum to ignore such attempts. Her sister, Lady Anne West, seems to have been as judicious, or at least fortunate. At one point she was supposedly overheard telling Lady Anne Askew that "one day she should see her sister, upon whom the queen railed so much (for so it pleased her to term her Majesty's sharp speech) to sit in her place and throne, being much worthier of the same for her qualities and rare virtues than was the other" (128). Judging from the fact that Lettice continued a cordial friendship with Robert Cecil, who had prosecuted and helped to execute her son Robert and her husband Charles, she must have learned to leave personal grudges and resentments behind her. She appeared expertly to understand that aristocratic women could only wield direct power by seeming to wield it indirectly through men. Perhaps her relationship to Queen Elizabeth through her parents, her second husband, and, for several years, her traitorous son Robert protected Lettice from recrimination. Perhaps, more simply, Elizabeth grudgingly respected Lettice's success in manipulating power in a culture that denied woman so much of it. Certainly, what Lettice gained through her daring and boldness was worth this sacrifice.

Penelope and Dorothy Devereux

If Lettice's sexual scandals and intrigue seem remarkable, they pale in comparison to those in the lives of her daughters Penelope and Dorothy and her daughter-in-law Frances. As the daughter of Sir Walter Devereux and later the stepdaughter of Leicester, Penelope (1563–1607) was certainly not without male power and influence, even as a child. She first married, or was forcibly married off to, Lord Robert Rich in 1581, in a union engineered by two of her guardians, the Earl of Huntingdon and Lord Burghley,[7] and on 26 December 1605 she married secondly, and illegally, Charles Mountjoy (1563–1606), Duke of Devonshire, her lover for the previous twelve years and father of six of her eleven children. Although King James I approved Rich's suit for divorce from Penelope, the king forbade them afterwards to marry their long-term partners. Both defied James, forcing him to banish them from court, despite Mountjoy's attempts to petition James to recognize the unhappiness of Penelope's first marriage. Her private joy at her marriage to Mountjoy ended in grief, however, when he died on 3 April in the following year, so perhaps the couple's reckless defiance was prompted by their knowledge that Mountjoy did not have long to live. In the end Penelope did get what she wanted for so very long—the titles of wife to Mountjoy and Countess of Devonshire, the latter title being held for only slightly longer than one year until her death on 7 July 1607.

Leicester seemed similarly ambitious in providing a first husband for Penelope's sister Dorothy (1564–1619). He made an attempt to match Dorothy with his nephew, Sir Philip

---

6   Her handwriting is notably shaky in these letters: State Papers 16/44/137 and 16/154/82.
7   See Henry Huntingdon's letter of 20 March 1580 to Burghley about the match: BL Lansdowne MS 31 fol. 105.

Sidney, in January 1582, and possibly with King James VI of Scotland (later King James I), the latter attempt purportedly provoking Elizabeth's ire (Freedman 70; Hammer, *Political Career* 53). Yet Dorothy seemed intent on not being forcibly married off to suit dynastic concerns, as her sister had been, and defied convention, control, and her own family and the queen in 1583 by eloping, evidently with Penelope's assistance,[8] with Sir Thomas Perrott, son of Sir John Perrott, after explicitly being denied permission to do so. As the story was later reported, "that unequal marriage" took place in the chapel at the home of Dorothy's guardian, Sir Henry Coke, at Broxbourne in Hertfordshire, where "they were married by a strange Minister, whom they had procured, two Men guarding the Church Door with their Swords and Daggers under their Cloaks, as the rest of the Company had, to the Number of five or six." When Reverend Lewis, the local vicar, repeatedly tried to stop the wedding, claiming that the marriage by special license "without the Banns asking" violated Church law, he was assaulted and told that John Aylmer, the Bishop of London, had provided the license. After a series of threats, Lewis finally became silent and watched as the wedding proceeded while Sir Henry's servants failed to break down the chapel's doors. Aylmer was later disgraced for his role in the secret wedding, and Dorothy was shunned not only by her new father-in-law, but the queen (Strype 327–9; Freedman 71). Perhaps Coke and Burghley felt that Perrott was a fortune hunter of too low a status who was taking advantage of a naive Dorothy, but more probably the two men had recognized that she was a commodity to be sold to a much higher bidder.

One of Essex's male biographers, Robert Lacey, asserted that this disastrous wedding should be blamed on "the inadequacies of Lettice's own relationship with her first husband" and the lack of "warmth or strength of affection" of either of Dorothy's parents, which left her and her brothers and sister "emotional cripples" (23). However, female biographers may see things differently: rather than using a long-outdated Freudian approach to blame Lettice for bad mothering, we can suggest that Dorothy was determined to avoid the types of marriages of convenience that her mother and sister had been forced to accept. As two letters to Burghley demonstrate (see below), although Dorothy was grateful that Thomas had been released from Fleet Prison after the wedding, she continued to defy Burghley after he attempted to annul the marriage. Dorothy similarly tried the patience of her cousin Queen Elizabeth, at one point going to stay at a stately home that was also hosting the queen, who insisted Dorothy stay out of her way and in her room despite the angry objections of her brother Robert, who blamed his rival, Sir Walter Ralegh, for inciting the queen against Dorothy, whose presence was taken as a mark of disrespect. As Ralegh had probably planned, the entire visit seems to have devolved into a number of arguments between Robert and Ralegh, and between Robert and Elizabeth, who took the opportunity of further attacking Lettice (Lacey 44; Freedman 73). Finally, Essex forced his sister to pack up and leave in the middle of the night, and he followed her shortly afterward.

But Dorothy's defiance did not need to last much longer. By 1594 she had become the mother of four daughters, but her husband was dead and her father-in-law had died in 1592 in political disgrace. Despite inheriting from Perrott's family substantial lands and property, including Syon House, Dorothy had evidently learned her lesson and became acquiescent and obedient, for within a year, and probably for dynastic reasons, she married Henry Percy (1564–1632), who soon became the ninth Earl of Northumberland, later known as the "Wizard Earl" for his interest in alchemy. His later comments to his son on his choice of Dorothy were not flattering: he specifically wanted an heiress who could breed male heirs (Freedman 95). Not surprisingly, the marriage was soon in trouble, and the couple separated in 1599 (see Nicholls), probably because their two sons and heirs had died as infants, and Dorothy had

---

8   See John Perrott's letter to Penelope, SP 12/161/22.

only managed to produce a daughter named Dorothy, who survived, and would later marry Sir Robert Sidney, second Earl of Leicester. Dorothy and William Percy were reconciled after Dorothy's brother Robert told her that she would have to live with the consequences of her choice of husband, although there is no way to tell if she did indeed choose him. Although now Countess of Northumberland, and by 1604 the mother of several more children, including the all-important male heir Algernon, her life would never achieve the domestic happiness of her sister's with Mountjoy, for Percy was implicated in the Gunpowder Plot of 1605 and imprisoned in the Tower of London for life. However, he was eventually released in 1621, two years after Dorothy had died. Dorothy had demonstrated herself to be a loyal and evidently loving wife who visited her husband nearly daily, and at least one of their children was conceived during his imprisonment. But perhaps her cordial relationship with her husband from 1605 stemmed from the fact that due to his incarceration, she was able, at last, to run the Northumberland estates in her imprisoned husband's stead and was the earl in all but name. Political intrigue finally allowed her to assume the role of a man.

Frances Walsingham

It would be unfair to suggest that the standard successively set by Lettice, Penelope, and Dorothy was one to which Frances Walsingham (1566?–1632) was bound once she became one of the Essex women. In fact, Frances did not seem bound to anything or anyone except what she desired. The daughter of Ursula St. Barbe (d. 1602) and Sir Francis Walsingham (1532–90), Elizabeth I's spymaster, Frances married first Sir Philip Sidney in 1583, then Robert Devereux, second Earl of Essex, *c.* 1590, then Richard de Burgh, fourth Earl of Clanricarde, in 1603. Frances's last marriage to a Catholic and her own conversion to Catholicism further scandalized her at court, from which she finally retired to her third husband's estates in Ireland. Penelope also converted to Catholicism later in her life, but by that time she had become so infamous for her sexual behavior that her religious conversion seemed trifling in comparison.

Unlike Penelope, Frances did not need a divorce to enter into second or third marriages, for Sidney, her first husband, died nobly after being wounded in the thigh in battle at Zutphen in 1586. Essex, her second husband, died ignobly in 1601 by the executioner's axe after failing in his rebellion against Queen Elizabeth. In a sense, Frances lost her first husband as recklessly as her second, for Sidney received his fatal wound only because he had failed to cover his legs with armor. Through Sidney and Essex, Penelope and Frances shared at least three psychologically complicated and somewhat incestuous bonds. First, if Penelope indeed had been Sidney's mistress before his marriage to Frances, and not just his poetic muse "Stella" in *Astrophil and Stella*, Penelope and Frances physically shared the body of the same man, Sidney. Secondly, as Penelope was the very dominant and controlling sister of Essex, Penelope and Frances came to share, emotionally, the mind and heart of another man, Essex. Third, as Essex allowed Penelope and Mountjoy to live openly and shamelessly as lovers, long before their illegal marriage, at the homes he shared with Frances, the bond between Penelope and Frances came to be not only sexually promiscuous, but voyeuristic and illicit. While Lettice and Dorothy used their voices to claim and exert power as daughters, sisters, wives, mothers, and aristocrats, Penelope and Frances most directly serve as synergistic symbols of the intellectual authority of women and how that authority was portrayed by and through men. Thus these two women offer the most persuasive, successful, and underappreciated range of representations of early modern women as peers not only to Elizabeth, but to the men who controlled her court, culture, and kingdom.

It is mainly through the sexual lives, words, and actions of Sir Philip Sidney and Robert, second Earl of Essex, that most scholars have represented Penelope. Scholars have not bothered to represent Frances at all. The only information available about Frances thus far has come through discussion of her father and first two husbands. Lytton Strachey naively stated in 1928 that:

> A shrouded figure, moving dubiously on that brilliantly lighted stage, Frances Walsingham remains utterly unknown to us. We can only guess, according to our fancy, at some rare beauty, some sovereign charm—and at one thing more: a superabundant vitality. For, two years later, the widow of Sidney and Essex was married for the third time—to the Earl of Clanricarde. And so she vanishes. (270)

Biographical information about Penelope is much more readily available; during her lifetime she was commonly known as "an Harlot, Adulteress, Concubine and Whore," due to her relationship with Mountjoy, and King James described her as "a fair woman with a black soul" (Freedman 179, 168). Her feckless brother Robert had called her an emasculating shrew, claiming at his 1601 trial: "[she] did continually urge me on with telling me how all my friends and followers thought me a coward, & that I had lost all my valour" (Goodman 2:17). We can only wonder what Frances made of the ruination of her first and second husbands by the same woman: Penelope. As Frances was at the bedside of the dying Sidney in October 1583, she may have overheard him when he reportedly uttered the words, "There came to my remembrance a vanity wherein I had taken delight, whereof I had not rid myself. It was my Lady Rich. But I rid myself of it, and presently my joy and comfort returned" (Gifford 169). Even if Frances had not actually heard these words or Sidney had not actually uttered them, she could not have helped hearing them later reported as truth in various forms of court gossip.

Reading Penelope and Frances Through Their Letters

All these anecdotes about Penelope and Frances exist in third-hand accounts by men. Very little attention has been paid to letters in Penelope's own hand, and apparently no attention paid to the letters in Frances's own hand. None of Penelope's or Frances's letters appeared in the 1853 standard printed edition of Devereux family letters which Strachey had used,[9] so perhaps that was why he declared Frances an unknown figure who vanished into the mists of time. Although far more autograph letters survive from Penelope than from Frances, there are certainly enough for both women (at least thirteen for Frances and twenty-one for Penelope) to understand their lives, words, and actions.[10] These letters do not include scribal copies of Penelope's notorious letter to the queen in 1600 pleading for her brother to be forgiven for his unauthorized return to England from the Irish wars. As I have argued elsewhere, Essex, and not Penelope, almost certainly wrote that letter to the queen—a belief

---

9   Walter Devereux, editor of *Lives and Letters of the Devereux*, includes letters from the queen and other important women of the period, but reduces mention of Rich to biographical information involving her brother and other male relatives.

10   The majority of the autograph letters of Penelope and Frances are among the Cecil family papers at Hatfield House. Other letters in Rich's hand are in the Anthony Bacon papers at Lambeth Palace, in various collections at the British Library, and among State Papers at The National Archives, the Bodleian Library, and at least one is in a Continental library.

that Elizabeth and Sir Robert Cecil, her principal secretary, also apparently shared (Ioppolo, "I desire" 299–325). Rather than relying on that letter to the queen to understand Penelope, we can let her and Frances use their own voices in their autograph letters to represent themselves not merely as objectified women, notorious only for the sexual and dynastic use of their bodies (especially evidenced by their multiple pregnancies), but as commanding and powerful aristocrats, known for the political use of their minds.

There is certainly much more known, or perhaps mis-known, about Penelope than Frances. No poems or other literary works attributed to Penelope are extant, although she may have been involved in some way as author or co-author of works written by the Sidney Circle (Lamb 15). Well educated and intellectually sophisticated, she was the patron of poets, translators, and musicians (Duncan-Jones 246).[11] Two letters about her can offer two contemporary views of her: the first letter is from the third man she and Frances came, figuratively, to share—Robert Cecil—and the second letter is from Lord Mountjoy.

In the first letter, from 1600, Cecil discusses with Thomas Sackville, Lord Buckhurst, the investigation into Penelope's letter to the queen, which had been printed without permission. Cecil chastises Buckhurst (a cousin of Penelope, as was the queen) for failing to extract the truth from Penelope during an interrogation. Cecil claims that Penelope has "shewed a proud disposition & not much better then a plain contempt of her Majesty and yourselfe that was used in the Cause." According to Cecil, the queen was shocked that Penelope, "being a Lady to whom it did not appertain so to meddle in such matters, would be so bold to write in such a style to her, especially when the best interpretations which Penelope doth make can not free her from stomach & presumption when she writ" (Cecil Papers 181/62). Cecil peevishly notes that the queen has obeyed Penelope's request to read and then burn a private letter of apology before he or anyone else could read it. As Cecil's letter is heavily revised, it seems that he took particular care in choosing his words here, perhaps to disguise his own anger.

The queen soon forgave Penelope for her pride, meddling, "stomach and presumption" for this potentially treasonous episode, and for another such episode in 1601, when she was arrested as a co-conspirator in her brother's rebellion and placed under the charge of Henry Sackford, Keeper of the Privy Purse. Penelope was eventually released without further charge,[12] perhaps in deference to her relationship with Mountjoy, who had more obediently replaced her brother as successful leader of the army in Ireland. In his letter to King James in 1606 and his "Discourse in defense of his Marriage with the Lady Rich," Mountjoy claimed that Penelope, as "[a] Lady of great Birth and virtue being in the power of her frends, was by them married against her will unto Lord Rich, one against whom she did protest at the very solemnity, and ever after; between whom from the first day there ensued continual Discord." Mountjoy adds that "[i]nstead of a Comforter Rich did study in all things to torment her …. After Rich had not for the space of twelve years enjoyed her he did by persuasions and threatnings move her to consent unto a Divorce and to confess a fault with a nameless stranger" in order to secure a divorce (BL Lansdowne MS 885 fol. 86).[13] Of course, Mountjoy does not admit his part in Penelope's adultery during those twelve years, which was so bold that the six illegitimate children he had by Penelope all had the surname of Rich, and two sons, Mountjoy Rich and Charles Rich, had names that continuously advertised Rich's cuckoldry.

---

11   Duncan-Jones offers a number of important readings of Rich's abilities in several articles and in introductions to various editions of Sidney's work, as does Woudhuysen.

12   See, for example, Hatfield House Cecil Papers 43/30 (in HMC, *Salisbury* 11:44), in which Captain Thomas Lee includes "La. Rich" in a list of conspirators of 12 February 1601. Her arrest is also documented in various 1601 State Papers at The National Archives.

13   Other copies of this text are extant in manuscript.

So was Penelope "virtuous" and abused by the loathsome Lord Rich, as Mountjoy claimed, or "proud," disobedient, and presumptuous, as the queen claimed? If neither speaks about Penelope without prejudice, we can listen to Penelope speak for herself. In her letters, written, as is usual with women of this age, in an Italic, or more properly "Roman" hand, she speaks without pride, but with some presumption and at least some affection for Lord Rich. In the late 1590s she solicited help at court on Rich's behalf to resolve a financial crisis. As she explained to the Earl of Southampton:

> the cause of Rich's earnest desire to have me come up is, his being so persecuted for his land, as he is in fear to lose the greatest part he hath, this next term who would have me a solicitor to bear part of his troubles, and is much discontented with my staying away so long. (Cecil Papers 101/25; see Illustration 11)

The unusually indulgent Rich surely had a right to reclaim her on occasion. She nursed Rich through at least one serious illness, and in fact mentions him without rancor throughout her letters, mostly dating from 1588 to 1605.

Penelope presents herself as an affectionate and loyal friend, and indeed a solicitor on behalf of those facing penury or prison, and a truly gracious benefactress. For example, in December 1595 she refused to allow possible exposure to measles to prevent her attending the baptism of a godson, Robert Sidney, later second Earl of Leicester, who would eventually marry her niece Dorothy (Whyte 103–4). This letter from July 1596 to Cecil is typical of Penelope's self-representation:

> Worthy Sir Roberte, the oblygation you haue tyed me in, by your Noble and Kinde frendship, doth increase so much, as though I knowe not how to aquit my selfe, of so greate a dett, yet my affection to honor, and estime you euer, shall be as assured vnto you, as your fauours hath bine to me, who desires to merit them. (Cecil Papers 43/30)

Penelope ensured that each of her letters took up only one page, even if this required her to write circularly around the margins when she ran out of room. Even when writing on a bifolium, which provides four pages, with the fourth page available for the address, she does not venture farther than one page. It appears that she did this to represent herself as one single, visual image, as in a painting or portrait. King James, for one, commended her fineness of wit and her inventive and "well" writings (Cecil Papers 18/50).[14] However, her solipsism in self-representation does not support William Ringler's still-influential 1962 assertion that "we are left partly admiring her courage, partly deprecating her departure from the moral standards of the day."[15] For Ringler, Penelope only exists in relation to Sidney, not in her own right; whether his departure from moral standards was less remarkable than hers is not easy to ascertain.

Penelope did use seduction in her life and in her letters. When Edward, Earl of Bedford, confessed on 9 February 1601 to the Privy Council about his part in Essex's rebellion, he claimed that he had been at home that day with his family at Sunday service, when at 10 a.m.:

---

14   For a transcription, see HMC, *Salisbury* 3:438.
15   For Ringler's commentary, see *Astrophil and Stella* in Sidney, *Poems* 443, 446. For a more recent study of Rich's possible involvement in the publication of Sidney's poems, see Woudhuysen.

> prayer being ended & a sermon begun the Lady Riche came into my house, desiring to speak with me speedily ... her lady then telling me the Earl of Essex would speak with me, whereupon I went presently with her in her coach .... About 11 of the clock I came to Essex house where shortly after the Earle of Essex with others of his company drew themselves into secret conference. (Cecil Papers 76/67)

It is not clear whether Penelope dragged Bedford away from his family, his house, and Sunday service at her brother's request or her own, but Bedford was certainly seduced by her solicitations to return immediately with her in her own coach to Essex House. At least this is what he claimed when pleading for his life. But perhaps he left so willingly in her coach because he thought her interest in him was personal, not political. Obviously her rhetoric in her speech was as persuasive as in her letters.

Penelope could be openly self-centered: after Frances successfully lobbied Cecil to be allowed access to the ailing Essex during his 1599 imprisonment, Penelope lobbied Cecil for the same privilege, pleading:

> [H]er Majesty told me if she granted me leave, my sister would look for as much, which need be no argument against me, since her Majesty being content to permit that favor but to some few, I may if please her obtain it before others, because I have humbly and earnestly made the first suit. (Cecil Papers 68/10)

Penelope does use a form of logical argument here, but her backstabbing of her sister Dorothy suggests a woman who is used to exerting complete control, and succeeding at it.

Actually, Penelope failed here, for she was not granted access to Essex, unlike her sister-in-law Frances. Perhaps Frances was more selfless or shrewd, or simply considered less dangerous to Elizabeth and Cecil. While Penelope made demands, Frances's letters suggest that she made requests. Not only is Frances's writing style distinctive, so too, evidently, were her writing implements, for in March 1597 Essex told Robert Sidney in a letter: "You know by my hand that this is my wife's pen and ink" (HMC, *De L'Isle and Dudley* 2:242). As a child, Frances, her father Sir Francis Walsingham, and her future husband, Sir Philip Sidney, were together in Paris in 1572 during the St. Bartholomew's Day massacre of Protestants; what she witnessed with them in looking out of her Paris window is tantalizingly unknown. Nor was that her only encounter with the greatest political debacles of the day: the first mention of her in any letter appears to come on 12 June 1583 from an anonymous correspondent to the imprisoned Mary Queen of Scots. The correspondent urges Mary, finally, to make her peace with Elizabeth, and to "bestow some favorable message upon Mr Secretary Walsingham and Mr Sidney who is shortly to be married to his only daughter and heire" (Cecil Papers 162/105). It is unclear here whether Mary was to bestow this message to Walsingham and Sidney in person or by letter, but in any case Frances's marriage to Sidney rated the attention of one of the most politically astute and dangerous women of the age.

Sidney probably married Frances at the explicit request of his close friend and mentor Walsingham, and thus, in a sense, Sidney married Francis, not Frances. If, as Katherine Duncan-Jones suggests, Sidney's sexual interest was primarily homosexual, and not heterosexual (240), his choice of bride would always have been political and dynastic, not personal. Nevertheless, the marriage appears to have been happy, but perhaps Sidney learned to love her while she had always loved him. Their still-extant marriage settlement, almost certainly negotiated by her father, allowed her to derive income on rents from Sidney family properties for many years. When Frances rushed to Holland in 1586 to the deathbed of Sidney, she was pregnant, but suffered either a miscarriage or a stillbirth shortly afterward. Also at Philip's deathbed was Robert, second Earl of Essex, to whom Philip bequeathed his best sword and, it was rumored, Frances herself—or at least Sidney extracted Essex's promise to protect Frances and her surviving child, Elizabeth. Perhaps in some way Essex thought that by owning Frances's body and mind he could own the soul of his great hero, Sidney.

By 1590 Frances was pregnant by Essex, and their son Robert was born in January 1591. The date on which Frances formally married Essex is not known; however, their secret marriage, probably no later than October 1590, so displeased Queen Elizabeth that she banned Frances, one of her maids-in-waiting, from court for some time afterward. Thus Frances suffered the same punishment as her mother-in-law Lettice after her marriage to Leicester, and Dorothy after her marriage to Thomas Perrott. Frances was pregnant by Devereux at least seven more times by late 1600, although only two of these children survived (see Hammer, *ODNB*). After Essex's execution, his property was confiscated, leaving Frances and her three "poor orphans," as she called them, penniless. Frances must have been incredibly resilient because she had also been left in a precarious financial state at the death of Sidney and of her father Walsingham, who died bankrupt due to outstanding debts. Within two years of Robert's death she married Richard de Burgh, fourth Earl of Clanricarde, although some had gossiped that she had taken up with him even before Essex was cold in the ground. Clanricarde, who had served as courtier to Elizabeth, was rewarded for his, and perhaps his wife's, loyalty to James I by being appointed Governor of Connaught in 1604. He eventually received the titles of Viscount Tunbridge and Baron of Somerhill, as well as Viscount Galway and Earl of St. Albans, and thus probably provided Frances with the type of stable life and status that she had been denied with her previous two husbands.

Perhaps, having learned secrecy from her spymaster father, Frances knew that subtlety often succeeded where boldness did not. Whether acting in her husband's absences to lobby Cecil to favor or protect a relative, Frances wrote with persuasive, if quiet, passion. Unlike Penelope, Frances was not arrested after Essex's rebellion, even though the two women were both in Essex House that day, although Richard London reported to Cecil on 22 February 1601, three days before Essex's execution:

> [A] fellow goeth about the street selling the Ballads, (whereas here is a copy enclosed) & giveth it out that the Countess of Essex hath made it, which procureth many to buy it. I have sent diverse up & down ye City to see if they can meet with him I am told that the ballad was made half a year since, & upon some other occasion. (Cecil Papers 77/1)

Richard London seems to apologize to Cecil for the accusation that Frances wrote the ballad to defend her condemned husband, as if Frances is not capable of sedition or treason, or at least Cecil will not have it so. The enclosed copy of the ballad must have been confiscated, for it is no longer with London's letter.

Although frequently contemptuous of Essex, Cecil had assisted Frances numerous times, especially, as noted above, enabling her to have access to her husband during his imprisonment. According to one account, Essex spent this time walking in the garden "with his wife, now he, now she, reading one to the other" (Whyte 461). No wonder, Frances had then written to Cecil in one of her most moving letters:

> Simple thanks is a slender recompence (good Mr Secretary) for so honorable a kindness as you have done me in procuring her Majesty's gracious consent for my infinitely wished access to my weak lord: yet when they come from a

> mind truly desirous to deserve it, and from a person that only wants ability to
> requite it: I doubt not but the same virtue that led you to so charitable a work,
> will likewise move to you accept in good part so beggarly a tribute. (Cecil
> Papers 74/79)

Apparently Cecil was moved by her sincerity here: all of his other letters to her have been
endorsed by one of his servants by writing "The Countess of Essex to my Master"; however,
this letter has been endorsed in his own hand with the comment: "The countess of Essex to
me." Evidently Cecil did not wish to share this very private letter by having it docketed by a
secretary. As usual, Cecil was also acting expeditiously here, for in November 1599 Frances
had turned up at court dressed all in "black of the meanest price," for "all she wore was not
valued at *vl*," and begging to be admitted to the queen. But Frances was turned away and
told to "come no more" (Whyte 378, 382). So Cecil may have been acting at the behest of the
queen, and not Frances, in finally allowing her access to Essex.[16]

Cecil came to Frances's aid several more times, particularly after Essex's death, when,
unlike in 1599, she had actually become the grieving, poor widow in black. In 1601 Frances
described in detail to Cecil a ruthless blackmail plot against her. Her servant Daniel had
stolen Essex's private letters to her while she was in childbed and was demanding that
Frances buy them back or he would distribute forged copies. She did so, pawning her jewels
and raising nearly £2,000 in cash. In a series of long pleading letters about Daniel, whom
Frances terms "the most perfidious and treacherous wretch that did ever infect the air
with breath," Frances pleads for Cecil's intercession in returning her money, so that he can
"punish falsehood, encourage truth, relieve the widow, cherish orphans, execute your own
decrees and bind me to add somewhat if it be possible to my humble thankfulness for your
other honorable favors" (Cecil Papers 90/82, 86/123; see Illustration 12). What stands out in
this series of letters to Cecil, her late husband's chief prosecutor, is not only Frances's moral
indignation at Daniel's treachery, but her guilt in being punished for her "sins" in relation
to Essex's treachery. In fact, she piously quotes Psalm 58:10 in telling Cecil: "I will kiss the
rod and bear my burden with humility and patience as becometh me" (Cecil Papers 90/82).

But this was not the first time that Cecil had been privy to Frances's most intimate
thoughts, for in 1598 she addressed a letter to Essex in care of Cecil. However, the letter
is among the Cecil Papers, suggesting that Cecil did not send it on to Essex in Ireland, as
Frances had requested. Frances's excruciatingly private letter to her husband reads in full:

> deare lord I did think this bearer would have gone sooner which made me
> make ready this enclosed letter 4 days ago and since that time I have had the
> good fortune to receive two letters from you. The first came when I was so
> sick that I could not speak with Mr Dary which brought it. But the joy which
> I took in receiving news from you did deliver me out of a fever which held
> me 3 hours, without any intervening, in great extremity but now I thank my
> god am free from it but so much weakened by it that I am not able to come of
> my bed: none that sees me would believe I were with child, for I am less then
> I was to months ago. Your son Robin is better then ever he was. I fear I shall
> never receive so great comfort of my other little one unless I quickly mend. I
> will for this time take my leave being not able to endure long writing. But by
> the next messenger I hope to write you word of my amendment.

---

16   Roland Whyte reported in a letter of 3 May 1600 to Sir Robert Sidney that "Lady Essex came this
afternoon to see my Lady and her children. Methought to see her clad as she was, was a pitiful
spectacle" (474); evidently she continued to demonstrate her penury.

The letter is signed, "your fathful wife, Fra*nces* Essex" (Cecil Papers 63/84). Such intimacy did not guarantee Essex's fidelity during his marriage to Frances, for in 1591 he fathered a child by Elizabeth Southwell, and in 1596 to 1597 he had an affair with Elizabeth Stanley, Countess of Derby. It was also reported on 12 February 1598 both that "Essex is again fallen in love with his fairest B," possibly Elizabeth Brydges (Hammer, *ODNB*), and that "Frances hears of it, or rather suspects it, and is greatly disquieted." If Frances had not yet heard it, this type of irresponsible gossip in a letter to her former brother-in-law Robert Sidney would certainly ensure that she would.

By April 1601 Frances had become so ill with "weak sinews" and a "distempered brain" that she tells Cecil that she could not write out the letter he is reading, but had to use a scribe (Cecil Papers 85/139). Although continually plagued with debts, Frances lived long enough to see her children marry into the most prominent families in England. However, she did have to bear the exceptionally humiliating gossip about her son Robert's unconsummated marriage to Frances Howard and their subsequent annulment.

Reading Dorothy and Lettice's Letters

If the letters of Penelope and Frances seem extraordinary in their demands that as women they should have the same status as men, the letters of Dorothy are no less commanding, although they lack the charm of those of her sister and her sister-in-law. For example, after Dorothy was reprimanded for her elopement with Perrott in 1583 she writes two letters to Lord Burghley, demanding first in September that he be "an erneste meanes vnto the quenes mayesty to voutesafe her gratious letter to S*ir* Ihone perrott as well for a relese for his promis made to her hyghnes not to do vs any good without her consente." Dorothy apologizes by stating: "I am lothe to troble your L*ordship* with my disgracefull fortune but that I haue a great hope of your L*ordship* tendering my estate, which betterred to be, I desire by your L*ordships* means but worse then it is it cannot bee" (BL Lansdowne MS 39 fol. 172). But the tone of the letter makes clear that Dorothy is impatient and reckless, and it is no surprise that Burghley's secretary has docketed the letter with the notation: "To intercede with ye Queen on her & her husbands behalf, who had married, being a Mayd of honour, without ye Queens consent." In a more audacious letter on 24 October Dorothy admits that she has been "bolde" with Burghley, but nevertheless states:

> I know your L*ordship* is so entertained with great publike causes as myne though in respecte of ther vnhappynes as great as priuate causes may be, yet in so much as it is very harde for any other to haue the feling of our owne esstate as wee haue our selues.

Dorothy eventually comes to the point but in a manner and tone that expect deference be paid to her: "I thought it not amis to be my owne solicitor once againe vnto your L*ordship* besetching our L*ordship* to haue a fauorable care of me concerning the well payment of my mariage monye" (BL Lansdowne MS 39 fol. 181). She then more strongly asserts: "Whereof the tyme is now to determine that it will pleas your L*ordship* to geue your good aduise in any way that in reson may be most for myne auayle." Dorothy does act in desperation here, citing the debts owed by her husband, and she presumes to address Burghley as her surrogate father, to whom her own father had awarded guardianship upon his death. But unlike her sister Penelope and her sister-in-law Frances, Dorothy dares to presume that familial loyalty, as cousin to Elizabeth and adopted daughter to Burghley, outweighs political status—a belief that often proved dangerous at Elizabeth's court, given the long imprisonment since 1568 and eventual execution in 1587 of her other cousin, Mary Queen of Scots. Unsurprisingly, Dorothy's letters apparently failed to obtain the queen's permission or Burghley's agreement for the payment of her dowry.

Dorothy appears to have lacked the graceful letter-writing skills not only of her sister and sister-in-law, but of her mother. As Lettice was the matriarch and role model for these women, it is fitting to end this discussion with a brief look at her own letters. In a 1608 autograph letter to Robert Cecil, by this time the Earl of Salisbury, Lettice begins with this charming sentence: "Noble Lord, I beseech you geue Leue to your poore absente frende to present hur faithfull loue to your honourable memorye, with desyre to hold styll a hyghe place in our fauoure." While the body of this fair copy letter, written in a careful, near-calligraphic hand, continues in this ingratiating fashion, Lettice finally makes her main point in a cramped marginal note on the left in which she suggests that her grandson Walter Devereux would be a good match for Lord Stallenge's daughter (TNA SP 14/40/3). Whether this bit of business, in which she feels free to indulge, was an afterthought and late addition, or was the main point from the beginning is not clear. However, Lettice has been shrewd enough to de-center and marginalize her real demand of Cecil in the letter and thereby represent herself as someone on the periphery of power. Her other extant letters include two from 1626 and 1629 (TNA SP 16/44/137 and 16/154/82) to the husbands of her granddaughters, in which she manages to express her affection while insisting on reminding them of her status as matriarch of a large family which had intermarried into the most powerful families of the realm, including the Sidneys and Cecils, and of the estates to which they eventually succeeded. Lettice's scandalous rise and fall as Countess of Leicester, a title she continued to claim even after her third marriage to Sir Charles Blount, was redeemed and legitimized in her granddaughter Dorothy Percy Sidney's eventual succession to the same title.[17]

This study of representative lives and letters of Penelope and Frances and this brief account of Lettice and Dorothy suggest that early modern women in the age of the Sidneys have been unfairly constrained in the boundaries and bonds in which modern scholars have forced them. Although in 1983 Sylvia Freedman produced a fine biography of Penelope subtitled *Lady Penelope Rich, an Elizabethan Woman*, Freedman's choice of *Poor Penelope* (originating from a contemporary comment) as the main title exemplifies the way in which even feminist scholars have stripped Penelope and the women of her age of power and authority. In truth, Penelope saw herself as an equal, not a "poor" or unfortunate inferior by virtue of her sex, to her brother and her husbands. Penelope created scandals that would have far-reaching implications for poets, dramatists, and pamphleteers. However, Frances unwittingly did the same, on a far wider scale. Due to the marriage of her daughter Honora de Burgh into the Seymour family, Frances came to be the tenth great-grandmother of the current Prince Charles. And because the Seymour family married into the Spencer family, Frances also came to be the tenth great-grandmother of the late Lady Diana, Princess of Wales. Dorothy could also lay claim through her daughter Dorothy Percy Sidney to being part of the ancestry of Lady Diana. When it comes to spawning scandals with far-reaching political, historical and cultural consequences, then, Frances, her two sisters-in-law, and her mother-in-law certainly had what Strachey called a "superabundant vitality."

---

17   On the life of Dorothy Percy Sidney, the daughter of Dorothy and the Earl of Northumberland and the wife of Robert Sidney the younger, see *Correspondence DPS*.

Bibliography

Manuscript Sources

British Library
    Add. MS 5845, 18985
    Lansdowne MS 31, 39, 885
Hatfield House
    Cecil Papers 18/50, 43/30, 63/84, 68/10, 74/79, 76/56, 77/1, 85/139, 86/123, 90/82, 101/25,
        162/105, 181/62
The National Archives, Kew (TNA)
    SP 12/161/22, 16/44/137, 16/154/82.

Primary and Secondary Sources

Adams, Simon. "Dudley, Lettice, Countess of Essex and Countess of Leicester
    (1543–1634)." *ODNB.*
Calendar of State Papers, Spain (Simancas). Vol. 3: 1580–1586. Ed. Martin A. S. Hume. London:
    Longman, Green, Longman, & Roberts, 1896.
Camden, William. *Rerum Anglicanum et Hibernicarum Annales.* Ed. Thomas Hearne.
    Oxford, 1717.
Devereux, W. B., ed. *Lives and Letters of the Devereux, Earls of Essex, in the Reign of Elizabeth,
    James I., and Charles I.* 2 vols. London, 1853.
Duncan-Jones, Katherine. *Sir Philip Sidney, Courtier Poet.* New Haven, CT: Yale UP, 1991.
Freedman, Sylvia. *Poor Penelope: Lady Penelope Rich, an Elizabethan Woman.* Abbotsbrook:
    Kensal P, 1983.
Gifford, George. "The Manner of Sidney's Death." *Miscellaneous Prose of Sir Philip Sidney.* Ed.
    Katherine Duncan-Jones and Jan Van Dorsten. Oxford: Clarendon P, 1973. 161–72.
Goodman, Godfrey. *The Court of King James I.* Ed. John S. Brewer. 2 vols. London: Richard
    Bentley, 1839.
Hammer, Paul E. J. "Devereux, Robert, Second Earl of Essex (1565–1601)." *ODNB.*
—. *The Political Career of Robert Devereux, 2nd Earl of Essex, 1585–1597.* Cambridge: Cambridge
    UP, 1999.
HMC. *Calendar of the Manuscripts of the Most Hon. The Marquis of Salisbury, K.G. ... Preserved
    at Hatfield House, Hertfordshire.* 24 vols. London: HMSO, 1883–1976.
—. *Report on the Manuscripts of Lord de L'Isle and Dudley Preserved at Penshurst Place.* 6 vols.
    London: HMSO, 1925–66.
Ioppolo, Grace. "'I desire to be helde in your memory': Reading Penelope Rich Through Her
    Letters." *The Impact of Feminism in English Renaissance Studies.* Ed. Dympna Callaghan.
    London: Palgrave Macmillan, 2007. 299–325.
—. "'Your Majesties Most Humble Faythfullest and Most Affectionate Seruant': The Earl
    of Essex Constructs Himself and His Queen in the Hulton Letters." *Elizabeth I and the
    Culture of Writing.* Ed. Peter Beal and Grace Ioppolo. London: British Library, 2007. 43–69.
Lacey, Robert. *Robert, Earl of Essex: An Elizabethan Icarus.* London: Phoenix P, 1971.
Lamb, Mary Ellen. *Gender and Authorship in the Sidney Circle.* Madison, WI: U of Wisconsin
    P, 1990.
McGurk, J. J. N. "Devereux, Walter, First Earl of Essex (1539–1576)." *ODNB.*
Mounts, Charles. "Edmund Spenser and the Countess of Leicester." *English Literary History*
    19.3 (1952): 191–202.

Nicholls, Mark. "Percy, Henry, Ninth Earl of Northumberland (1564–1632)". *ODNB.*

Peck, D.C., ed. *Leicester's Commonwealth: The Copy of a Letter Written by a Master of Art of Cambridge (1584) and Related Documents.* Athens, Ohio: Ohio UP, 1985.

Sidney, Dorothy Percy. *The Correspondence (c. 1626–1659) of Dorothy Percy Sidney, Countess of Leicester.* Ed. Michael G. Brennan, Noel J. Kinnamon, and Margaret P. Hannay. Farnham: Ashgate, 2010.

Sidney, Philip. *The Poems of Sir Philip Sidney.* Ed. William A. Ringler, Jr. Oxford: Clarendon P, 1962.

Strachey, Lytton. *Elizabeth and Essex: A Tragic History.* New York: Harcourt, Brace, 1928.

Strype, John. *The Historical Collection of the Life and Acts of the Right Reverend Father in God John Aylmer.* London: W. Boywer, 1701.

Whyte, Rowland. *The Letters (1595–1608) of Rowland Whyte.* Ed. Michael G. Brennan, Noel J. Kinnamon, and Margaret P. Hannay. Philadelphia, PA: American Philosophical Society, 2013.

Woudhuysen, H. R. *Sir Philip Sidney and the Circulation of Manuscripts, 1558–1640.* Oxford: Clarendon P, 1996.

The Life of Robert Sidney (1563–1626), First Earl of Leicester

Robert Shephard

Robert Sidney, first Earl of Leicester (Illustrations 13, 14 and 15), was a man who eventually achieved almost all of his dreams, but only after extensive delays and disappointments. From his own day down to the present he has stood in the shadow of his older brother, the dazzling Philip Sidney (Illustration 7), who was nine years his senior and who took an affectionate interest in his younger brother's education and development (*Correspondence SPS* 877–82, 1005–10). But Robert Sidney's life has significance on its own terms. As a soldier and a poet, and as a courtier and royal governor, he followed in his elder brother's footsteps in many ways, but he learned from his brother's missteps, and as a result was able to navigate his way safely through the dangerous waters of the late Tudor and early Stuart courts. In addition, Robert Sidney's life is exceptionally well documented, and therefore gives us a well-rounded portrait of the activities and interests of a well-connected courtier in the decades *c.* 1600.

When Robert Sidney was born on 19 November 1563, his father Sir Henry Sidney (Illustration 5) was already well ensconced through ties of blood and marriage in the inner circle of the then five-year-old Elizabethan regime. Of those connections, the closest and most important was with the Dudley family, through Sir Henry Sidney's wife and Robert Sidney's mother, Mary Dudley Sidney. Robert Sidney was named for his uncle and godfather, Lord Robert Dudley, later Earl of Leicester, Elizabeth's first and greatest favorite (Collins 1:74).

During his childhood Robert Sidney probably saw little of his father, who served as the queen's Lord Deputy in Ireland from 1565 to 1571 and again from 1575 to 1578. Although Robert Sidney was the third child and second son of the family—Mary Sidney Herbert, later Countess of Pembroke (Illustrations 9 and 10), was two years older than he was—his parents provided him with a high-quality humanist education. Robert Sidney followed Philip Sidney to Christ Church, Oxford, in 1575, and then from 1579 to 1582 he too engaged in an extensive period of study and travel on the Continent, staying for periods in Strasbourg, Prague, Frankfurt, and Paris (Hay 20–26; Shephard and Kinnamon 43–56). Along the way, he was welcomed by many who had met Philip Sidney on his earlier European excursions, and his older brother's mentor, Hubert Languet (Illustration 8), supervised Robert Sidney's education from a distance (*Correspondence SPS* 875–961). At Oxford, and almost certainly during his travels on the Continent as well, Robert was accompanied by an entourage that included Rowland Whyte, who would become Robert Sidney's long-time man of business and confidential agent (Brennan, "Your Lordship's" 3–5, 16–18; Shephard and Kinnamon 56–61).

Little documentation survives about Robert Sidney's life between 1582 and 1585, after his return from the Continent, except for one important event: his marriage to Barbara Gamage on 23 September 1584 (Illustrations 17 and 18). Barbara Gamage Sidney had recently become the heiress to extensive properties in Wales, and her hand in marriage had thus become subject to intrigues all the way to the royal court. One of Robert Sidney's rivals, almost certainly Herbert Croft, secured an order from the queen that Barbara should marry no one and come to court. Sir Francis Walsingham covertly encouraged the match to proceed, however, "for that I know her Majesty will no way mislike thereof," and the wedding took place two hours before the messenger arrived with the queen's order (*Stradling Correspondence* 3–11, 20–24, 27–30). It is not clear whether Robert and Barbara were personally acquainted before their conveniently well-timed marriage, but they developed a close and affectionate relationship over the ensuing thirty-seven years of their married life, and the Gamage estates provided around half of the family's income during the next two decades (Hay 54).

The Sidneys had long been aligned with the faction at court led by Leicester and Walsingham that favored a more active English role internationally in support of Protestantism and in opposition to Spain. Late in 1585, following the assassination of William of Orange and the Spanish capture of Antwerp, Elizabeth finally authorized direct English intervention in the Low Countries. Leicester took command of the English forces, and all three of the Sidney brothers—Philip, Robert, and their youngest brother Thomas—obtained positions under him. Robert Sidney participated in several military engagements, and on 7 October 1586 Leicester knighted him for the valor he had shown at the Battle of Zutphen a few weeks earlier. During that same battle, of course, Philip Sidney had received what proved to be his fatal wound. Robert Sidney remained with his brother as the wound became infected and gangrene set in. In the biography of Philip Sidney that Fulke Greville wrote much later, he described the stoical older brother admonishing his younger brother for his "abundance of childish tears" (Greville 158–9). This account may have owed more to rhetorical purposes and poetic license than to historical accuracy, but the circumstances were harrowing enough. The death of his older brother on 17 October 1586—following the deaths of both his father and his mother earlier that year—unexpectedly left Robert Sidney the head of the Sidney family at the age of twenty-two.

Robert Sidney returned to England to straighten out his debt-encumbered inheritance. In 1588, when the Spanish Armada threatened, he reported to the camp at Tilbury, where Leicester was mustering the queen's forces to defend against a possible Spanish invasion (*DPFA* 25–6). Soon after the danger receded, the queen sent him on a diplomatic mission to King James VI of Scotland. His tasks were twofold: first, to secure James's commitment to solidarity against Spain, and second, to disentangle Elizabeth from some financial commitments that the previous envoy had made when the threat from the Armada appeared direr. James had admired Philip Sidney, and Robert Sidney was the sort of handsome, poised young man to whose charms James was always susceptible. Robert Sidney accomplished his mission quickly and with complete success, and returned to England in early September 1588 (*CSP Scotland* 9:599–620). The positive impression he made on James at this time eventually became the basis for his future prosperity after James became king of England in 1603.

Robert Sidney received his first official post in the royal government in 1589, when Elizabeth appointed him Governor of the town of Flushing (Vlissingen) in Zeeland in the Dutch Republic. Flushing was one of the towns that the States General had handed over to the English in 1585 for an indefinite period as security for a large loan that Elizabeth had granted the Dutch. Flushing was an important port, and its location at the mouth of the Scheldt, blocking Antwerp's access to the sea, made it strategically crucial as long as the conflict with Spain continued. It was also a convenient entry point to the Continent for English merchants and travelers, and a useful post for gathering intelligence. The governorship was therefore an important and honorable office, which Philip Sidney had briefly held before his death. Robert no doubt saw it as a starter office, a stepping stone on the way to more significant posts closer to the center of power. As the years passed with no advancement, however, he came to see Flushing more and more as a place of exile, far distant from the opportunities available at the royal court.

The pattern of Robert's life was now set for the remainder of Elizabeth's reign, during which he alternated residence in Flushing and in England. As Governor of Flushing, he commanded the English troops stationed there, tried to maintain the town's fortifications and arsenal, and cultivated relations with Dutch officials at the local and national levels. In the process, he developed a particularly close relationship with Count Maurice of Nassau. He sometimes joined Dutch forces in the field against the Spanish, and he played a major role in the battle at Turnhout in 1598. This victory was celebrated in a play on the London stage, in which an actor played the role of Sir Robert Sidney (Whyte 362–5). In early 1594 he had traveled as a special envoy to consult with the recently converted Henry IV of France. However, the security of Flushing remained his primary concern, and his letters to Lord Burghley and the Privy Council are peppered with requests for powder, additional troops, and funds to maintain the town's crumbling defenses.

During the periods when Robert Sidney resided in Flushing, Barbara Sidney and the rest of the family typically remained in England. Considerations of safety and health were the usual reasons: "Though I want your company exceedingly and shall do every day more and more," he wrote to his wife on one occasion, "yet I would not for anything that you were here yet, this town and Middelburg being both full of violent agues and of the small pox also and measles" (*DPFA* 82–3). To these lengthy separations we owe one of the great collections of correspondence associated with Robert Sidney, the more than three hundred letters he wrote to Barbara Sidney at Penshurst, first from Flushing and later from the court of James I's Queen Anne. His wife did, however, join him in Flushing for several extended stays between mid-1590 and the end of 1592, and again in 1597–98. Their eldest son William was born in Flushing in November 1590, with Princess Louise de Coligny, the widow of Prince William the Silent of Orange, standing as his godmother (Hay 172–3, 181–2; *DPFA* 110n; Hannay 29–35, 59–66).

Each time Robert Sidney arrived in Flushing, he almost immediately began a new campaign to receive leave to come back to England, where family business and the quest for political advancement exerted a strong attraction. Absence from the royal court was always detrimental to those who had political ambitions, as his father's career had proved. This truism was even more valid in the 1590s, when the polarization of politics at Elizabeth's court reached extreme levels, producing tension and gridlock. The two main factions at court arranged themselves around the Cecils—William Cecil, Lord Burghley, and his son, Sir Robert Cecil—and around Robert Devereux, the second Earl of Essex. These two rival alignments dated back three decades and more, and the one now led by Essex was the direct descendant of the grouping formerly headed by Leicester and Walsingham, who had died in 1588 and 1590, respectively. In the 1590s the main issues of substance between them revolved around the strategy to be followed in the war against Spain, with the Cecils favoring a defensive orientation and Essex a more active, offensive approach. But patronage decisions soon became caught up in the rivalry, with intense lobbying directed at the queen regarding every appointment and grant.

Robert Sidney naturally gravitated toward the group aligned with Essex, given the ties of blood, marriage, and ideology that he and Essex shared. Leicester had been Robert Sidney's uncle and Essex's stepfather, and Essex was the inheritor of Philip Sidney's best sword, and also eventually his widow, Frances Walsingham Sidney, who became the Countess of Essex. Robert Sidney developed a close relationship with Essex, and the two of them received master of arts degrees—presumably honorary in nature—together at Oxford in 1588 (Brennan, *Sidneys of Penshurst* 99–100). When it came to advancement in his career, however, Robert

Sidney's membership in the circle around Essex proved a double-edged sword at best. In the mid-1590s especially, Essex provided strong and even vehement support for Robert Sidney's efforts to obtain a variety of appointments or promotions, including Lord Warden of the Cinque Ports, Vice-Chamberlain, and a barony. Yet the very fact of Essex's support tended to provoke an opposite and more than equal reaction from the Cecilian faction. As Rowland Whyte told him in 1597: "I hear the Queen uses him [Essex] very graciously in his own person, but in all other things his desires prevail little, either in matters of great or little moment" (149). And in fact, the more Robert Sidney tried to push his ambitions forward, the more his enemies at court tried to block his efforts to obtain leaves from his post at Flushing. It was no accident that his longest continuous residence in Flushing fell between August 1596 and March 1598, precisely when his efforts to secure advancement were at their peak. As he commented to his wife: "[H]erein I well perceive the practice of those, which like not my company at the Court" (*DPFA* 103). In the end, Essex's support gained him nothing.

Robert Sidney's enforced residences in Flushing were also responsible for the other famous collection of correspondence associated with him, the more than three hundred letters addressed to him from Rowland Whyte, his trusted agent at court. As mentioned earlier, the two had known each other from childhood. During Robert Sidney's stays in Flushing, Whyte sent him regular, detailed reports of political developments, court gossip, and Whyte's conversations with courtiers, together with news of his wife and children. Whyte's letters are thus an invaluable source on the activities and ambiance at the late Elizabethan court. They also provide insights into the stratagems Robert Sidney was using to try to achieve his goals, and the frustrations he was facing during these years at the end of Elizabeth's reign.

The surviving correspondence from this period makes it clear why Robert Sidney—despite having his advancement blocked—was able to avoid the disasters that befell so many of the Essex circle. The portrait that emerges is of a cautious and savvy political operator who kept channels of communication open and avoided needless provocations. In his letters to Essex he sought Essex's help, but avoided making inflammatory comments about the leaders of the opposing faction—which was wise, since some of these letters ended up in the hands of the government (and Cecil) after the Essex Revolt of 1601. (Robert Sidney himself, more discreet than Essex, evidently destroyed most of Essex's letters to him, for only a handful survive.) In addition, his duties in Flushing required frequent communication to the Privy Council, mainly through first Lord Burghley, and then Sir Robert Cecil. He used these letters to maintain a respectful and professional relationship with the heads of the Cecilian party. The contrast with Philip Sidney's more provocative and outspoken style as a courtier could not be stronger. This circumspect approach sometimes paid off in practical ways; for example, after the death of Robert Sidney's cousin in 1595 Lord Burghley, the Master of the Court of Wards, granted him the wardship of his cousin's son and heir (*DPFA* 66–7). In 1599 Rowland Whyte summed up Robert Cecil's attitude toward his master by saying that Cecil would help him as a Privy Councillor when it came to government business, although in matters of patronage his own followers would have priority (Whyte 334).

It was during these troubled and frustrating years toward the end of Elizabeth's reign that Robert Sidney became most active as a poet and writer. P. J. Croft has dated to 1595–98 the sonnets and other poems he wrote and revised in a manuscript in his own hand (Robert Sidney, *Poems*, xiv). Croft also comments on the parallels between Queen Elizabeth and the cruel mistress of the poems who betrays her faithful servant and refuses to reward him as he deserves (*Poems* 101–3; see Moore *ARC* 2:15). In addition, by 1600 at the latest Robert Sidney had begun compiling a series of commonplace books, in two of which he collected and organized political events from history pertaining to monarchies and their problems, expressing some criticisms of absolutism along the way (Shephard 1–30). Finally, the songs among his poems point to Robert Sidney's deep involvement with music, which Gavin Alexander has elucidated (68–90). In one of Philip Sidney's letters to his younger brother about his education he had written: "Now sweete brother take a delight to keepe and increase yowr Musick, yow will not believe what a want I find of it in my Melancholie times" (*Correspondence SPS* 1009). One hopes that Robert Sidney found some delight in his music during these melancholy years in the 1590s.

The climax of political risk and danger toward the end of Elizabeth's reign came in the year and a half following Essex's unauthorized return from Ireland in September 1599. For once, it was an advantage to be in Flushing; as Whyte wrote to Robert Sidney from court: "For here is such observing and prying into men's actions, that I hold them happy and blessed, that live away" (Whyte 343). After Essex's disgrace, Robert Sidney cautiously distanced himself from Essex and the more hotheaded members of his circle. For their part, they did not seek to involve him in the plotting that led to the Essex Revolt in February 1601. Robert Sidney, who was in London on leave at the time, joined the other loyal courtiers who rallied at Whitehall and participated in the siege of Essex House on the evening of 8 February 1601. Before the final assault was going to begin, the queen's forces sought a peaceful surrender. Because of his close ties to both sides, Robert Sidney became the crucial mediator between the besiegers and the besieged. Addressing Essex as "brother"—Essex's wife was his former sister-in-law—he persuaded Essex and his followers to surrender, on the promise that the queen would treat them honorably (HMC, *Bath* 5:278–81). Robert Sidney thus avoided the calamity of Essex's shipwreck, but with the Cecilians now firmly in control, his life went back to its familiar frustrating patterns for the remainder of Elizabeth's reign (Brennan, "Sidney and Essex" 1–38).

Robert Sidney's fortunes changed dramatically after Elizabeth died and James VI of Scotland became king of England as well. James had retained his positive impression of Robert Sidney ever since his embassy to Scotland in 1588, and the rewards that Elizabeth had granted so stingily or not at all soon began flowing in his direction. When James arrived in London in May 1603 he bestowed upon Robert Sidney the title of nobility he had sought for so long, and soon afterward he named the new Baron Sidney of Penshurst to be the Lord Chamberlain to Queen Anne. This meant that he became the second-ranking official at the queen's court and a member of her council, a position he retained until Anne's death in 1619. Two years later Robert Sidney received another promotion when James granted him the title of Viscount Lisle that his maternal grandfather John Dudley had once held (Nichols 1:119, 268n, 510–11). According to the Venetian ambassador, in 1605 Robert Sidney was also under consideration to become a member of the Privy Council (*CSPV 1603–07* 271). At that point, however, an unfortunate accident sank those ambitions. On his way to visit the garrison at Flushing, stormy weather forced him to land in the Spanish Netherlands, whence he proceeded overland through Spanish territory to Flushing. Although England and Spain were at peace by this time, the sensitivities of the Dutch and rumor-mongering by enemies at court turned the incident into a minor diplomatic and political imbroglio, to the annoyance of the current Privy Councillors. They ordered Robert Sidney to return to England immediately, but not to come to court until summoned (HMC, *Salisbury* 17:390–416). The episode was soon forgotten, but his opportunity of joining the Privy Council had passed, never to return.

The sources for Robert Sidney's life are far fewer during James's reign than they had been during Elizabeth's. He remained the Governor of Flushing, but as his new duties kept him in England, his visits to Flushing became brief and infrequent. Rowland Whyte's letters to Robert Sidney therefore ceased or have been lost, although the position Whyte obtained as postmaster to the royal court along with other grants demonstrated his master's enhanced capacity to secure patronage (Brennan, "Your Lordship's" 32). Robert Sidney's reports from Flushing to the secretary and council also came to an end, and instead he became the recipient of frequent reports from the deputy governors he appointed. His letters to his wife Barbara continued, however, because his duties at the queen's court often kept him away from Penshurst and his wife.

The paucity of surviving records from Queen Anne's court and council makes it difficult to know exactly what her lord chamberlain's duties were. Until his death in 1612, the top official at her court, the Lord Steward, was Robert Cecil, Earl of Salisbury after 1605. Cecil's other responsibilities as Lord Treasurer and Privy Councillor normally kept him occupied elsewhere, however, so Robert Sidney was often the ranking official actually present at the queen's court. At the monarch's court the Master of the Revels worked under the supervision of the Lord Chamberlain. It would be interesting to know if the same pattern applied at Queen Anne's court, because the Children of the Queen's Revels—one of the fashionable children's companies of the sort mocked by Shakespeare in *Hamlet*—produced a number of politically controversial plays in the early years of James's reign. These works, including *Philotas* and *Eastward Ho*, contained satirical commentary on Robert Cecil and even King James himself. Samuel Daniel, who was authorized to censor and approve the productions of the Children of the Queen's Revels, had been part of the literary circle at Wilton sponsored by Robert Sidney's sister, Mary Sidney Herbert, Countess of Pembroke (Tricomi 42–50). Be that as it may, Robert Sidney appears to have suffered no direct retribution when the company lost the queen's patronage after they staged John Day's *Isle of Gulls*, although these circumstances may account for Cecil's noticeable failure to defend his colleague during the incident in the Low Countries recounted above. Ben Jonson's association with Robert Sidney and Penshurst, which Jonson commemorated in several poems, including the famous "To Penshurst," probably began at this time (Brennan and Kinnamon 430–37).

During James's reign Robert Sidney's finances gradually stabilized, and he was able to provide dowries of several thousand pounds each for his four surviving daughters as they reached marriageable age: Mary to Sir Robert Wroth in 1604; Katherine to Sir Lewis Mansell by 1607; Philippa to Sir John Hobart in 1614; and Barbara to Thomas Smythe in 1619 (Hay 225). The relationships that he and his extended family had been cultivating with Prince Henry, the heir to the throne, promised to sustain the political influence of the Sidneys and Herberts into the next generation. Unfortunately for those plans, Prince Henry died in November 1612, and Robert Sidney's eldest son William died of smallpox the following month.

In 1613 Robert Sidney was one of the royal commissioners who accompanied Princess Elizabeth on her journey to Heidelberg following her marriage to the Elector Palatine Frederick V. During this excursion he was able to visit various friends on the Continent, and his only surviving son Robert joined the entourage and then accompanied him on a leisurely trip back to England, which included a stay in Spa to treat the arthritis and gout that increasingly plagued him in his later years (*DPFA* 182–5). In 1616 the younger Robert Sidney, now his heir, married Dorothy Percy, the daughter of the Earl of Northumberland, connecting the Sidneys with another aristocratic family.

Among Robert Sidney's enemies at court were the pro-Spanish former Essexian Henry Howard, Earl of Northampton, and his protégé Robert Carr, King James's favorite and eventually the Earl of Somerset. The personal and political enmity between Northampton and Robert Sidney ran so deep that Northampton pleaded successfully on his deathbed in 1614 that his office as Lord Warden of the Cinque Ports, which Robert Sidney had long coveted, not be granted to him following Northampton's death (Chamberlain 1:541–2; Peck 62–3). Robert Sidney and his allies therefore encouraged the rise of a new royal favorite, George Villiers (Lockyer 18–20). As Anne's Lord Chamberlain, he was well placed to help secure the queen's acceptance of Villiers's relationship with James, and close ties developed between Robert Sidney and Villiers. The two were installed together as Knights of the

Garter in July 1616, and the following month Robert Sidney participated in the ceremony of Villiers's creation as Viscount Villiers (Chamberlain 2:16, 22). Several years later John Chamberlain reported that Villiers (by then Marquis of Buckingham) had snubbed the Earl of Rutland at the St. George's Day feast to socialize with Robert Sidney instead (2:301). Given these circumstances, it seems likely that Buckingham played a role along with Queen Anne in securing Robert Sidney the honor he had been seeking for decades as the closest legitimate surviving male relative of the Earls of Warwick and Leicester: an earldom. He received the title Earl of Leicester on 2 August 1618, and proudly informed his wife in a letter the following day that "now you may boldly say yourself Countess of Leicester" (*DPFA* 217).

As the midpoint of James's reign passed and Robert Sidney's health slowly declined, he gradually withdrew from his public roles. In 1615, when the Earl and Countess of Somerset were accused of having murdered Sir Thomas Overbury in the Tower of London by sending him poisoned pastries, Robert Sidney had the satisfaction of serving as one of the peers commissioned to try the pair. At the hearing he delivered one of the more memorable lines from that notorious episode: when Somerset protested that the tarts he had sent to Overbury were all wholesome, Robert Sidney responded: "If you had sent him good tarts, you should have seen them conveyed by a trusty messenger" (Howell 2:994). In 1616, with the royal government desperately short of money, James compounded with the Dutch for the debt they owed, and Robert Sidney went to Flushing in person for the ceremony returning the city to Dutch control. After nearly thirty years he was finally free of the ambivalent honor of being Governor of Flushing, and the loss of the title and income was sweetened by a generous financial settlement and annuity from James (Hay 222).

In March 1619 Queen Anne died, and Robert Sidney's service to the queen ended with the leading role he played in her funeral procession. A more shocking blow came two years later, with the sudden death of his wife Barbara (Chamberlain 2:379). Increasingly ill and still wrestling with chronic financial problems, in May 1623 Robert Sidney transferred Penshurst Place to his son, and thereafter resided principally in London. He survived into the reign of Charles I, and in April 1626 he even married a second time, his new wife being Sarah Smythe, the widow of Sir Thomas "Customer" Smythe, the Sheriff of London at the time of the Essex Revolt. However, in July 1626 he suffered an apparent stroke in London, and he died at Penshurst on 13 July 1626 (Birch 1:129; Collins 1:120). He was survived by his second wife, by his son Robert, now the second Earl of Leicester, and by two of his daughters, Lady Mary Wroth and Lady Barbara Smythe, having been predeceased by his other eight children.

Robert Sidney's own life was now over. Through his commonplace books, however, in which his son Robert, the second Earl of Leicester, continued to write, the anti-absolutist political tradition of the Sidney family passed down to future generations, including his son and his grandson Algernon Sidney. And in the works of his daughter, Mary Wroth, we can see his literary interests and those of his siblings Philip Sidney and Mary Sidney Herbert being carried on as well.

Today Robert Sidney remains an under-appreciated member of the Sidney family. However, with the superb scholarly editions in recent decades of his poetry, his domestic correspondence, and the political correspondence of Rowland Whyte, the material is available for wide-ranging reappraisals of Robert Sidney's life and literary works. These could well cast new light not only on his own career, but on the political culture of the late Elizabethan and Jacobean courts as well. The opportunity also beckons to examine Robert Sidney's poems in the context of our current understanding of the literary activities of the other members of the Sidney family and their circle.

A Note on Sources

The Sidney Papers, including many letters to Robert Sidney and other members of the Sidney family along with other documents, remain the property of Viscount De L'Isle. They are currently on deposit at the Centre for Kentish Studies, Maidstone (classification U1475); however, permission to examine them must be obtained from Viscount De L'Isle. In the eighteenth century Arthur Collins compiled and edited (with varying degrees of completeness and accuracy) a collection of letters from the Sidney Papers, found in the two volumes of *Letters and Memorials of State* (1746). The six Historical Manuscripts Commission volumes on the De L'Isle and Dudley MSS (1925–66) provide a more modern calendar.

The letters Robert Sidney wrote to the Privy Council as Governor of Flushing are collected among the Secretaries of State: State Papers Foreign, Holland, catalogued as SP 84 at The National Archives, Kew. His letters in this collection through 1596 are referenced in the seven published volumes of the *List and Analysis of State Papers, Foreign*, edited by Richard Bruce Wernham (1964–2000). Modern editions of Robert Sidney's manuscript writings include P. J. Croft's *The Poems of Robert Sidney* (1984) and an edition of Robert Sidney's letters to his wife Barbara, found in *Domestic Politics and Family Absence* (2005). The recent edition of *Letters (1595–1608) of Rowland Whyte*, edited by Michael G. Brennan, Noel J. Kinnamon, and Margaret P. Hannay (2013), finally provides reliable modern texts of these important letters from Whyte to Robert Sidney. These last three works are all copiously annotated.

Among secondary sources, the only book-length biography of Robert Sidney is by Millicent Hay, *The Life of Robert Sidney* (1984). It is solid on facts and details, but could be stronger in interpretation. Two chapters in Michael G. Brennan's *The Sidneys of Penshurst and the Monarchy* (2006) survey Robert Sidney's life from a political perspective. The first half of Margaret P. Hannay's *Mary Sidney, Lady Wroth* (2010) contains considerable information about Robert Sidney's household.

Scholarly articles that address various aspects of Robert Sidney's life and career include the following. On his interests as the most musical of the Sidneys, see Gavin Alexander, "The Musical Sidneys" (2006; see also Larson ARC 1:21). On Robert Sidney's commonplace books, see Robert Shephard, "The Political Commonplace Books of Robert Sidney" (2003). For his relationship with Rowland Whyte, see Michael G. Brennan, "'Your Lordship's to Do You All Humble Service'" (2003). For Robert Sidney's relationship with the Earl of Essex, see Michael G. Brennan, "Robert Sidney and the Earl of Essex" (2014). And for his family's relationship with Ben Jonson, see Michael G. Brennan and Noel J. Kinnamon, "Robert Sidney, 'Mr Johnson,' and Education of William Sidney at Penshurst" (2003).

Bibliography

Primary and Secondary Sources

Alexander, Gavin. "The Musical Sidneys." *John Donne Journal* 25 (2006): 65–105.
Birch, Thomas, ed. *The Court and Times of Charles the First*. 2 vols. London: Henry Colburn, 1849.
Brennan, Michael G. "Robert Sidney and the Earl of Essex: A Dangerous Friendship Viewed Through the Eyes of Rowland Whyte." *SJ* 32.1 (2014): 1–38.
—. *The Sidneys of Penshurst and the Monarchy, 1500–1700*. Aldershot: Ashgate, 2006.
—. "'Your Lordship's to Do You All Humble Service': Rowland Whyte's Correspondence with Robert Sidney, Viscount Lisle and First Earl of Leicester." *SJ* 21.2 (2003): 1–37.

—, and Noel Kinnamon. "Robert Sidney, 'Mr Johnson,' and the Education of William Sidney at Penshurst." *Notes & Queries* 50.4 (2003): 430–37.

Calendar of State Papers, Domestic .... London: Longman, Brown, Green, Longmans, and Roberts, 1856–72.

Calendar of State Papers ... Venice, 1603–1607. London: HMSO, 1900.

Calendar of State Papers relating to Scotland and Mary Queen of Scots, 1547–1603. London: HMSO, 1898–1969.

Chamberlain, John. *The Letters of John Chamberlain.* 2 vols. Ed. Norman Egbert McClure. Philadelphia, PA: American Philosophical Society, 1939; rpt. Westport, CT: Greenwood P, 1979.

Collins, Arthur. "Memoirs of the Lives and Actions of the Sidneys." *Letters and Memorials of State ....* Ed. Arthur Collins. 2 vols. London: T. Osborne, 1746; rpt. New York: AMS, 1973. 1:1–180.

Greville, Fulke. *Life of Sir Philip Sidney.* Oxford: Clarendon P, 1907.

Hannay, Margaret P. *Mary Sidney, Lady Wroth.* Farnham: Ashgate, 2010.

Hay, Millicent. *The Life of Robert Sidney, Earl of Leicester (1563–1626).* Washington, DC: Folger Shakespeare Library, 1984.

HMC *Calendar of the Manuscripts of the Most Hon. the Marquis of Salisbury Preserved at Hatfield House, Hertfordshire.* 24 vols. London: HMSO, 1883–1976.

—. *Manuscripts of the Marquis of Bath Preserved at Longleat.* 5 vols. London: HMSO, 1904–80.

—. *Report on the Manuscripts of Lord De L'Isle and Dudley Preserved at Penshurst Place.* 6 vols. London: HMSO, 1925–66.

Howell, Thomas Bayly. *Cobbett's Complete Collection of State Trials, and Proceedings for High Treason and Other Crimes.* 34 vols. London: R. Bagshaw, 1809–26.

Letters and Memorials of State .... Ed. Arthur Collins. 2 vols. London: T. Osborne, 1746; rpt. New York: AMS, 1973.

List and Analysis of State Papers, Foreign Series, Elizabeth I, Preserved in the Public Record Office. 7 vols. Ed. Richard Bruce Wernham. London: Public Record Office, 1964–2000.

Lockyer, Roger. *Buckingham: The Life and Political Career of George Villiers, First Duke of Buckingham, 1592–1628.* London: Longman, 1981.

Nichols, John, ed. *The Progresses, Processions, and Magnificent Festivities of King James the First.* 4 vols. London: J. B. Nichols, 1828; rpt. New York: AMS, 1968.

Peck, Linda Levy. *Northampton: Patronage and Policy at the Court of James I.* London: George Allen & Unwin, 1982.

Shephard, Robert. "The Political Commonplace Books of Sir Robert Sidney." *SJ* 21.1 (2003): 1–30.

—, and Noel J. Kinnamon. "The Sidney Family Correspondence during Robert Sidney's Continental Tour, 1579–1581." *SJ* 25.1–2 (2007): 43–66.

Sidney, Philip. *The Correspondence of Sir Philip Sidney.* 2 vols. Ed Roger Kuin. Oxford: Oxford UP, 2012.

Sidney, Robert, first Earl of Leicester. *Domestic Politics and Family Absence: The Correspondence (1588–1621) of Robert Sidney, First Earl of Leicester, and Barbara Gamage Sidney, Countess of Leicester.* Ed. Margaret P. Hannay, Noel J. Kinnamon, and Michael G. Brennan. Aldershot: Ashgate, 2005.

—. *The Poems of Robert Sidney.* Ed. P. J. Croft. Oxford: Clarendon P, 1984.

Stradling Correspondence: A Series of Letters Written in the Reign of Queen Elizabeth. Ed. John Montgomery Traherne. London: Longman, Orme, Brown, Green, and Longmans, 1840.

Tricomi, Albert H. *Anticourt Drama in England, 1603–1642.* Charlottesville, VA: UP of Virginia, 1989.

Whyte, Rowland. *The Letters (1595–1608) of Rowland Whyte*. Ed. Michael G. Brennan, Noel J. Kinnamon, and Margaret P. Hannay. Philadelphia, PA: American Philosophical Society, 2013.

Barbara Gamage Sidney (*c.* 1562–1621), Countess of Leicester, Elizabeth Sidney Manners (1585–1612), Countess of Rutland, and Lady Mary Sidney Wroth (1587–1651)

Margaret P. Hannay

These three Sidney women, beloved of their families and each other, were less famous or wealthy than their close relative Mary Sidney Herbert, Countess of Pembroke, the first celebrated non-royal woman writer in England. Yet each of the three was known at court, had an arranged marriage equal in rank to that of her father (or stepfather) at that time, and each was praised by Ben Jonson and other poets. Barbara Gamage Sidney was a Welsh heiress, Robert Sidney's wife, and mother of eleven children (Illustration 17 shows her with six of them); the eldest was Mary ("Mall"), later Lady Mary Wroth. Lady Sidney was known primarily for her skill as a mother and a hostess, including entertaining aristocrats and royalty, but she did carry on an extensive correspondence with her husband when he was away fulfilling his duties. Her niece Elizabeth ("Bess") was the child of Sir Philip Sidney and his wife, Frances Walsingham; Bess and Mall were closely related, had just a year between their ages, wrote poetry, and met often. They each had an arranged marriage. Elizabeth Sidney Manners and Mary Sidney Wroth both came to court as young married women, they each gained a reputation as a poet, acted in a masque, and frequently visited family; each became a widow when she was twenty-six. After that their lives were radically different, since Elizabeth died shortly after her husband, Roger Manners, Earl of Rutland, and Mary lived another thirty-seven years after the death of her husband, Sir Robert Wroth, continuing with her writing and then some publication. She also had an affair with her cousin, William Herbert, Earl of Pembroke, and raised their two children, William and Katherine, giving them significant social positions. Wroth is often mentioned as suffering from her arranged marriage, but her life was much happier and healthier than her cousin Elizabeth's, and not as deeply related to those in court crisis. From these Sidney women writers, only Wroth's works have been extant; her reputation is now considerable.[1]

---

[1] Their cousin, Lady Anne Herbert, may also have written some poetry, but little is known of her (see Moffett, *Nobilis*).

Beginning Connected Lives: Sidney Marriages

Elizabeth Sidney could not remember her famous father Philip, but her life was shaped by his reputation and his relations. Overcoming some opposition from Queen Elizabeth to the wedding, Philip Sidney had married young Frances Walsingham on 21 September 1583. Frances was the only living child of Sir Francis Walsingham, Ambassador to France, and then Queen Elizabeth's secretary (and spymaster). Philip had known the Walsinghams well; they and Philip Sidney had all managed to escape the St. Bartholomew's Massacre in Paris (1572). After his marriage to Frances, Philip followed English custom by moving to his wife's family homes at Walsingham House in London and Barn Elms in Surrey. His wife Frances was eighteen when Bess was born in October 1585 and christened on 20 November near Walsingham House, at St. Olave's on Hart Street, with Queen Elizabeth as godmother. As Alan Stewart notes, Philip Sidney was not at the christening, since he was forced to leave for the Low Countries and was on a ship by 18 November (275, 385 n. 115). None of his remaining letters mention her, probably because none of his letters to his wife or sister survive.[2] Yet Thomas Moffet's *Nobilis*, apparently written to give instruction to young William Herbert at his mother's request, presents Sir Philip as he "warmly greeted the little girl," thinking that she had "opened the way for a son who would be his heir" (85).

Unlike the marriage of Elizabeth's parents, the marriage of Mary's parents was hastily arranged shortly after her father's death in 1584. Robert Sidney married the heiress Barbara Gamage (c. 1562–1621), daughter of John Gamage of Coity Castle and of his wife Gwenllian, daughter of Sir Thomas ap Jenkin Powell of Glynogwr. Barbara was born in a family known for its patronage of Welsh poetry and music in Glamorganshire, like the Herberts, Mansells, and Stradlings. Welsh poets sang at Coity, and the noted Tomas ab Ieuan ap Rhys later wrote an elegy praising her father as an intellectual (Williams 4:564). Her father significantly modernized Coity Castle, which had been in the Gamage family since the beginning of the fifteenth century, and he also acquired several others, including the Old Castle and New Castle that were given to Barbara's illegitimate brothers Edward and Thomas Gamage (NLW MS 11964); despite their settlement, her cousin Charles Howard, Lord High Admiral, noted that he had been "a very dear friend unto her" by preventing John from leaving his legacy to anyone but his "right and lawful heir" Barbara (*Stradling Correspondence* 3–4). Barbara was trained largely at St. Donat's, home of another cousin, the noted scholar and patron Sir Edward Stradling (son of Barbara's aunt, Katherine Gamage Stradling), and his wife, Agnes Gage Stradling, who was praised by another of Barbara's aunts, Margaret Gamage Howard, Lady Effingham, for "bringing [her] up" (*Stradling Correspondence* 9). Barbara would have been familiar with Welsh music and tales, and had exposure to Italian architecture and other elements of international culture where she was raised, largely by the Stradling cousin in St. Donats, but her training does not seem to have been the same as the Sidney sisters in English and Continental literature, rhetoric, and the performance of the lute. Nor was her handwriting as elegant as that of the Countess of Pembroke or her own daughters, though it was perhaps as legible as her husband's, given his reputation for scribbling letters. Barbara was also trained for splendid hospitality, exhibited later by all the family and aristocratic visits to their home at Penshurst, or their entertainment of Queen Elizabeth, probably at Baynard's Castle, as Katherine Duncan-Jones suggests (41).

At the age of twenty-two Barbara Gamage, known for her wealth, beauty, and skill, was still being courted by three cousins—Thomas Jones, Sir James Whitney, and Herbert Croft, to whom the Crofts claimed she was already engaged. When her father died suddenly in London on 8 September, there was a dash to obtain by marriage her substantial inheritance.

---

2   Roger Kuin, private correspondence.

The Crofts were supported by the Cecils and Queen Elizabeth. The Earl of Pembroke's position as husband of Mary Sidney Herbert, with her father, Sir Henry Sidney, serving as Lord President of the Marches of Wales, and the quiet support of Walsingham, whose daughter Frances had recently married Sir Philip Sidney, made their family member Robert Sidney an important suitor. Despite Stradling's continuing quarrel with the Earl of Pembroke over various offices and property in Glamorganshire, he did support Barbara's marriage to Robert Sidney, and letters of thanks are preserved from Sir Henry Sidney, Sir Francis Walsingham, and Robert's aunt, Anne Russell Dudley, Countess of Warwick (*Stradling Correspondence* 21–30). The views of Barbara's cousins, Sir Walter Ralegh and Croft, Comptroller in the Queen's Household, prevailed in Elizabeth's expression of written disapproval of the marriage; that letter arrived, apparently after some clever planning, two hours after the wedding at St. Donats (Hannay, *MSLW* 7–12). Their daughter Wroth later gave a lively retelling of their wedding tale as Bersindor's in *Urania* (1:499), and Barbara Sidney had a long gallery built at Penshurst that echoed St. Donats; its exterior brick walls still retain the Sidney porcupine crest and the Gamage griffin.

Over three hundred extant letters from Robert Sidney to his "sweetheart" wife show considerable love for each other and their eleven children, beginning with their "little Mall" (*DPFA*). Barbara, trained in the Welsh system that gave many positions to servants (once she hired sixty in their London residence), often included workers from the Coity area, and apparently included as pages some children of her illegitimate brothers. In addition, a nurse was a Powell wife, and thus from her mother's family (*DPFA* 85). William Gamage and his brothers served under Robert Sidney in Flushing, and William wrote poems to Barbara Gamage Sidney and the family, particularly Katherine Sidney Mansell as a Welsh resident. Barbara Sidney had her Welsh pedigree elegantly drawn up, probably in connection with Katherine's marriage (De L'Isle MS U1500 F13). During her life, and even long afterwards, the Sidneys were responsible for helping the careers of people there, for example finding the Welsh-speaking vicar for Coity. Despite these efforts, William Gamage wrote an epigram against "World-wasting Time" which was allowing Coity Castle to decay, actually protesting against the Sidneys, who apparently never preserved it (C2v).

Just two years after the marriage of Robert and Barbara, the Sidney family mourned the death of Sir Philip, with male relatives and friends participating in the magnificent funeral in St. Paul's. His brother Robert is shown grieving in his poetry and perhaps in a reputed portrait (Goldring; see also Goldring *ARC* 1:20), and his sister, both in her own poems and in verses by those for whom she was a patron. Yet debts from Philip's will tangled much of Robert's affectionate relationships; in addition to the annual annuities left to various employees, his brother Robert and his wife Frances each inherited one half of his lands. Robert inherited the responsibility of paying Philip's major debts, and his wife Frances was the sole executor of his will (Hay 50–51). He also left £4,000 as a dowry for his daughter Elizabeth. Thomas Nevitt later included in Robert Sidney's accounts that, in addition, all moveables at Penshurst, worth £20,000, went with Frances (Nevitt 2r). Frances Walsingham Sidney's remarriage to Robert Devereux, Earl of Essex, involved more complexity. Financial problems meant that even while Frances was many times acting as Robert's advocate for aid from her husband Essex, and even as Barbara spent considerable time supporting Frances during Essex's incarceration, there were also financial arguments and lawsuits between the Sidney and Essex families, and ultimately (after 1603) with Frances's third husband, Richard Burke, the Earl of Clanricarde (see Ioppolo *ARC* 1:6).

Mary Sidney (later Wroth) was born on 18 October 1587, approximately nine months after Robert Sidney returned home for his brother Philip's funeral. Her mother took her to stay at Wilton for about six months at the time of the Spanish Armada in 1588. Little Mall, or Malkins, as she was known, probably walked her first steps and said her first words there about the time she turned one year old. Her three Herbert cousins—Will (age eight), Anne (age six), and Philip (age three)—thus knew her well from her infancy. Either her father was able to come to Wilton in the autumn, or Mall and her mother rode back with the Countess of Pembroke in her elegant coach and a litter for the children, surrounded by more than eighty servants in Pembroke livery. Barbara Sidney also remained friends with her sister-in-law Frances, and their little girls Bess and Mall were probably together quite frequently.

Childhood of Mall and Bess

Mary Sidney Wroth's childhood is more vividly known than almost any other early modern English writer, because of two lively sets of extant letters, specifically written while her father, Robert Sidney, was Governor of Flushing. His wife retained over three hundred letters from him dating from when little Mall was a baby in April 1588 until just before Barbara's own death in May 1621.[3] Written over a much shorter period, 1595–1602, Rowland Whyte's business letters to her husband Robert are full of vivid details of the family as well as official court news (Illustration 16). Whyte, in a servant capacity, was with Robert at Oxford, and their tutor noted that "Whyte is by far the more enthusiastic for the study of letters" (Whyte 7).[4] His later correspondence included not only political reports and advice, but also a lively prose style of description and dialogue at important events, both at court and in the Sidney family.

Wroth had an unusual level of travel abroad in her childhood. Her father, during his early period as Governor of Flushing, brought his family there in 1590. Pregnant Barbara received a letter from her sister-in-law, the Countess of Pembroke, sending her a nurse to help; this is the only extant copy of the many letters that must have circulated among these women in the family (MSH, *Collected Works* 1:286). Fortunately, baby William did well, though the Sidneys lost another son, Henry. The three eldest surviving children, Mall, Kate, and Will, were often invited places together, while the seven born later (1592–1602) were treated as much younger. They all typically stayed in the Prinsenhuis, a residence offered by Prince Maurice, and often the home of the prince's stepmother, Louise de Coligny. Therefore, when Mall was young she spent time in a prince's house with a view of the sea and the ships below that headed abroad, some even to the New World, and she heard the general use of the Dutch language, as well as Louise de Coligny's French (Couchman).[5] Given her time in Flushing and her parents' linguistic ability, Wroth probably spoke several languages, most notably French; her ship journeys and experience abroad, as well as court experience, strongly influenced adventure narratives in her later *Urania*. Mall may also have been rather shy as a child, unlike her sister Kate; the Countess of Huntingdon reported that "the Queen doth often speak of them, and that she never saw any child come towards her with a better or bolder grace than Mistress Kate did" (Whyte 152).

The family never returned to Flushing after 1597, and the Sidneys did everything they could for Robert Sidney to return to England. Even in the midst of financial discussions and

---

3   For speculation on Lady Sidney's replies, see Hannay, "High Housewifery."

4   Noel Kinnamon's transcription shows that the Historical Manuscript Commission volume of Whyte's letters has made some textual errors, some dates are wrong, and some letters are much condensed. On Arthur Collins's most problematic editorship of the letters, see also Whyte 35–6 and Illustration 16.

5   I am grateful to Jane Couchman for sharing her insights on Louise de Coligny in various discussions and emails. See also her analysis of Louise's political correspondence in "Give Birth Quickly."

arguments, he appealed to Lady Essex, asking for her help in convincing her husband to have him granted a better position than Governor of Flushing. Lady Essex and her sister-in-law, Barbara Sidney, were frequently visiting each other. On 19 October 1593, for example, a coach had been sent by Lady Essex for Barbara, and presumably her older children, to visit her at Barn Elms, the Walsingham country home. Robert was leaving to serve as the English Ambassador to France (exaggerated as the melodrama of Dettareus in *Urania*), and had borrowed £1,000 from Essex to fund that journey (*DPFA* 36). Yet Robert bitterly tells his wife in August 1594, "mine own rents of Kent and Sussex must go to the payment of my Lady of Essex and of the annuities"—everything else was waiting for "the rents of your lands" in Wales around Christmas (*DPFA* 55). They thus had no money to pay those undertaking building work at Penshurst, nor for other major expenses.

Family details appear in Rowland Whyte's first year of reports in 1595.[6] Because Barbara was too pregnant to travel with her husband, Whyte had helped find them a London residence (rented from Alderman John Catcher), and reported on family life, saying of Mall in particular: "God bless her, she is very forward in her learning, writing, and other exercises she is put to, as dancing and the virginals" (Whyte 67). He also gives in these earliest letters one of the most detailed and vivid Elizabethan accounts of labor and birth, in this case of Barbara Sidney's young Robert, later second Earl of Leicester. Her daughters and then Barbara herself came down with frightening bouts of measles, and Whyte sent her husband many pages detailing her labor, the use of medical help, and the safe birth of baby Robert, even with a measles rash: "He sucks as well as any child doth and cries as strongly" (Whyte 104). Then Whyte describes visits by various important people, including Barbara's cousin, Sir Walter Ralegh, just home from Guiana. Mall may even have met a young man from Guiana, if Ralegh brought to her residence Cayowaroco, son of Topiawari, Lord of Aromaia, for whom Ralegh had exchanged two of his own young men on the voyage; Ralegh took Cayowaroco home the following year (Vaughan). Probably many of Wroth's later comments on exotic countries in *Urania* included such memories.

Those celebrating little Robert's christening on 31 December included Mall and her siblings, the family giving welcome to many aristocrats, including Margaret, Countess of Cumberland, and her young daughter, Anne Clifford, as well as Frances, Countess of Essex, and her daughter, Elizabeth Sidney, demonstrating that from childhood all these women writers were friends, probably meeting often (*MSLW* 47–52).

The following winter season (1596/97) Barbara and all her children stayed at the Savoy with Robert Sidney's aunt, Katherine Dudley Hastings, Countess of Huntingdon, whose husband had died the previous December, and who was trying to make the Savoy Robert Sidney's preferred London home. So when Wroth was nine she and her siblings were taken to court for visits and celebrations, often by their great aunt or by their mother's cousin, Charles Howard, the Lord Admiral, who in 1588 had commanded the English fleet against the Spanish Armada.

An important change in the potential status of all three (Lady Sidney, Mall, and Bess) occurred in March of 1597, when Robert Sidney was working with both the Earl and Countess of Essex to obtain the position of Cinque Ports, formerly held by the father of Henry Brooke, eleventh Lord Cobham; Cobham was closely allied with Robert Cecil, whose sister Cobham had married. At the time the Sidney family thought they were making good progress through Essex support: "My Lady Essex doth continually put her Lord in mind

---

6   Whyte reports the death of Robert Sidney's younger brother Thomas in late July and the mourning of his widow, Lady Margaret Dakins Sidney, who was then pushed into a marriage with Posthumous Hoby. A noted diarist in later years, she would have been an intimate aunt of Wroth had Thomas Sidney lived.

of you" (Whyte 161). But Robert's alliance with Essex and frequent feuding with the Cobhams, as well as occasionally their relatives the Cecils, meant that he never gained another position or an aristocratic title during Elizabeth's reign. As Whyte's letters indicate and Michael Brennan notes, Whyte, "an unusually astute and informed court observer, at first viewed Robert Devereux as one of Sidney's most influential supporters and then as a dangerous liability" ("Robert Sidney").

After the quarrel with Cobham, and after the Countess of Huntingdon had lost the Savoy, Robert Sidney's family went again to Flushing in June of 1597. Mall was there for her eleventh birthday in October. For her and her siblings it was time for a more formal education, after a disagreement between their mother, who had wanted the children to stay with their family, and their father, who had wanted them accommodated for education in elite homes (*DPFA* 102–7). Whyte tells her father:

> I never saw one take it so unkindly as Mistress Mary doth, who every time she thinks of it doth fall a-weeping, and my Lady … doth bear her company. Mistress Mary came to me and prayed me to write to you for leave to come over to see your Lordship and that she was yet too young to part from her mother. (Whyte 191)

She prevailed. This time Mall and the two next children in age, William and Katherine, traveled on the queen's ship, with the younger children on board other vessels. The girls were to be taught by their governess, and young Will by a tutor. They may also have shared the residence with Louise de Coligny and her stepdaughters, regularly speaking French (*MSLW* 30–33).

Following their return home in March 1598, Barbara Sidney and her girls apparently never again left England, but were granted an apartment by the Countess of Pembroke primarily for the annual winter season (usually for most of November through April): Whyte prepared "all the rooms upon the waterside for my Lady [Barbara] and the children" (310). The Countess of Pembroke often stayed at Wilton, nursing her husband until his death in January 1601, and her sons William and Philip Herbert came to stay at Baynard's Castle under their aunt's care—a situation reciprocated as William came close to the earldom, given his father's illness and Essex's imperiled situation. Whyte recommended that Robert Sidney pull away from Essex as patron and rely on his nephew William: "I doubt not but you shall have great comfort by him, and I believe he will prove a great man in court. He is very well beloved, and truly deserves it" (451). Mall, who spent so much time with her parents, siblings, and cousins at Baynard's Castle, loved him as well (see Lamb *ARC* 2:17). She continued to spend the court season there, along with the Herberts and her parents and siblings, for more than twenty years.

Elizabeth Sidney was also involved in family visits, both at Penshurst and Wilton. For example, Robert Sidney tells his wife in autumn 1598, when Bess was visiting at Penshurst, that he is heading for Wilton, and:

> I send you here a letter … about Bess, from my Lady of Pembroke, by which you may see how much my Lord doth long for her. There is a coach and a gentlewoman come up of purpose for her, and therefore, I pray you let her be sent thither as soon as possibly you may. (*DPFA* 111)

So probably after a lengthy visit at Penshurst with Mall and the other children, Bess was then sent to Wilton, where she would have spent time with her cousin, Lady Anne Herbert, who was, like her, also interested in poetry, as praised by Thomas Moffett, resident physician at Wilton, in his *Silkewormes* (see Hannay *ARC* 1:5). This one extant praise of Lady Anne's poetry suggests that Bess's own love of poetry was encouraged there by her cousin as well as her aunt; no record survives of her mother or own half-sisters as poets.

Marriage to Rutland

Bess was married in 1599 to her stepfather Essex's follower, Robert Manners, fifth Earl of Rutland, who descended from a noble family that held the Norman castle Belvoir (pronounced "Beaver"). Rutland had seemed appealing to the Sidneys in his youth. In November 1595, when he was on his way to Flanders through Flushing, Robert Sidney wrote a letter of praise to his uncle, Roger Manners (Whyte 97). Within three years Essex was pushing an engagement between Bess and Rutland, though she was only eleven and Rutland was a decade older. By January 1598 Rutland had, not surprisingly, "waxen more cold in the matter of marriage" (Whyte 276). Essex proceeded to act as his mentor, sending his own cousin, Robert Vernon, to accompany him. Rutland traveled through most of Europe. After an illness in Italy at Padua University, he came back to go on Essex's ineffective expedition to the Azores. Then he married Elizabeth Sidney in 1599, when she was just twelve. By September Whyte reported that Rutland was at court and more often at her grandmother's Walsingham estate of Barn Elms, "and I hear hath created your niece Countess of Rutland, as young as she is" (327). Her new husband focused on having a good time in London that October with his friend Henry Wriothesley, third Earl of Southampton—"They pass away the time in London merrily in going to plays every day" (Whyte 352)—with no indication that his bride went as well.

This merriment was soon to cease. By that September Rowland Whyte reported to Robert Sidney that Elizabeth's stepfather Essex barged into the queen's private chamber on his return from Ireland about six months after the Rutland wedding. He fell into deep disgrace. Essex was already in a situation so dire that in November Elizabeth's mother "came to the court all in black, and all she wore was not valued at five pounds …. God comfort her, for I hear none can be more miserable" (Whyte 182). That same month Barbara Sidney asked Rutland to be godfather for her new child Barbara, but he had gone to Belvoir Castle, and presumably had taken his wife there. Most of the Countess of Rutland's married life was led in this massive castle near Nottingham, more than a hundred miles north of London. The generous money and properties that she had been left years ago in her father's will caused financial trouble with the Sidneys. On 3 March 1600 Whyte articulates the worry to Robert Sidney that Rutland, who was staying at Belvoir, intended to sell the Sidney properties to buy properties near his home, advising him to "suffer not yourself to be persuaded to confirm any act of your niece's, for until she be xxi (which will not be yet these 6 years) no act of hers is good, and you the assured heir in remainder" (437).

The women did not seem directly involved in these financial arguments. Barbara Sidney frequently visited her friend and former sister-in-law Frances, Countess of Essex, and the Countess of Rutland was frequently with her mother while her husband followed Essex to Ireland and then to London on his campaign to turn citizens against Queen Elizabeth. Whyte gave reports of such visits, but by autumn 1600 they grew more formal, with Essex and his family treated with some distance, given his arrest as a traitor. Even Lady Rutland is given less attention. That September Whyte reported that she "hath been much troubled with an ague, but I hear she hath shaken it off" (533). Rutland a few weeks later came with his lady to Walsingham House and then to court to support Robert Sidney's story of a serious illness in Flushing to convince the queen to let him come home. Shortly before Essex's execution in

February 1601, Rutland was imprisoned and then given the highest fine of £30,000. While it later dropped to £20,000, it remained enough to impoverish him.

His wife Bess's life already contrasted sadly to the cheerful life of Mall, who at Christmas 1602 was praised for her achievement in dancing well with a professional in front of Elizabeth (Whyte 552). That was just three months before the queen's death on 24 March 1603, and by this time the two oldest of Barbara Sidney's daughters were apparently engaged, Mall to Robert Wroth, and Kate to Lewis Mansell, eldest son of the Gamages' Welsh friends the Mansells (*MSLW* 89–91).

Shortly after Queen Elizabeth's death, the Earl and presumably the Countess of Rutland were visited by James VI and I in April 1603 on his way south. Rutland regained favor at court, and his remaining fine was cancelled. He stayed primarily in the country estate of Belvoir, except for his trip away as an ambassador to Denmark in July–August 1603 and his attendance at the installation of Henry as Prince of Wales in 1610. As we shall see, the Countess of Rutland still spent considerable time with Mall after her marriage.

Wroth Marriage

Under King James, Robert Sidney also prospered, and therefore so did his children (Brennan, *Sidneys of Penshurst* 114–32). Mary was married on 27 September 1604 to the eldest son of the prominent parliamentarian Sir Robert Wroth, the same season that her Herbert cousins married aristocratic women. William followed the Herbert tradition of connections with the Talbots, marrying Lady Mary Talbot (1580–1650), daughter of the Earl of Shrewsbury; Philip sought his own desire in marrying Lady Susan de Vere (1587–1629), daughter of Edward de Vere, seventeenth Earl of Oxford, and of Anne Cecil, daughter of Lord Burghley. Susan, later Countess of Montgomery, became Mary Wroth's closest friend, living at Elsings Palace in Enfield, near the Wroth estate of Durrance and not far from Loughton Hall. They often shared the Enfield church of St. Andrew's.

In the first years of marriage all three of these young couples stayed together frequently with their Sidney/Herbert relatives at Baynard's Castle for almost half the year, traveling to the wife's parents' or their own country estates in the summer; the Wroths hosted the men participating with the royal hunting group in Waltham Forest, now the Forest of Essex. Three of the related young women, Lady Anne Herbert, Lady Susan Herbert, and Lady Mary Wroth, were in Ben Jonson and Inigo Jones's first masque for Queen Anne, the *Masque of Blackness*, and must have enjoyed rehearsing and wearing their yellow and blue outfits that matched each other and also that of the queen. The audience was shocked by their black faces and arms, described by Dudley Carleton, for example, who also criticized "their apparel rich, but too light and courtesanlike" (68). The high office of Wroth's father gave her the opportunity to be received at court as "daughter of my Lord Chamberlain" (Winwood 2:39). For the queen's next masque at court (1608) Wroth was one of the audience, sitting with the royal family to watch Jonson's *Masque of Beauty* performers, including her friends Susan, Countess of Montgomery, and Lady Anne Clifford.[7] Later Wroth's sisters Philippa and then Barbara were also chosen for masques at the age of seventeen (*MSLW* 140).

Wroth's husband was often not with her during the winter court activities, because of his responsibilities for the king's hunting forest. He was locally prominent in an ancient and distinguished family that owned three miles of land along the River Roding, and for several

---

7   See Galli; Orrell. Ian Donaldson suggests that Wroth, Pembroke, and the Countess of Rutland did
     not perform Jonson's *The May-lord*, as is usually assumed (290–93).

generations had represented their area in Parliament. The families were mutually respected, and their grandfathers, Sir Henry Sidney and Sir Thomas Wroth, had served young King Edward VI together. The Wroths had emerged as Puritans during their time as Marian exiles, and returned to serve again in Parliament under Elizabeth. Robert Sidney and the older Robert Wroth were then on several of the same committees. These sixteenth-century alliances indicate that the Wroth family was at that time virtually equal to the Sidneys in social status (*MSLW* 109–21). But before the time of their marriage in September 1604, Robert Sidney had been created Baron Sidney and appointed as Queen Anne's Chamberlain; less than a year later he had become the first Sidney aristocrat, Viscount Lisle, at the same time that the king made his nephew, Philip Herbert, the Earl of Montgomery.

Had Wroth been younger, she would probably have married into greater court prominence, like her sister Philippa; after serving as Maid of Honour for the queen, Philippa married Sir John Hobart, son of Sir Henry Hobart, Lord Chief Justice of Common Pleas, in June 1614. Their youngest living sister Barbara, in 1619, a year after her father became Earl of Leicester and a Knight of the Garter, married Sir Thomas Smythe of the family of the wealthy East India Company; they later had a number of estates, and she traveled with more servants than aristocratic women had done. Their sister Katherine's earlier marriage to Sir Lewis Mansell (probably in 1605) meant that she lived in Glamorganshire in Wales, not far from her mother's Coity Castle. Katherine never served at court and was usually geographically isolated from her family; she had the sadness of the loss of her babies. Her health problems led to her own death in May 1616 on a visit to the family at Baynard's Castle; she was buried at Penshurst (Penshurst Parish Register).[8] Wroth also lost her cousin, Lady Anne Herbert, who was taken to Cambridge by her mother for special medical care, where she apparently died in December 1606.

Even before the 1606 death of her father-in-law, the Royal Forester, young Lady Wroth would have been the Wroths' hostess to royalty because in the two years before her marriage both of Robert Wroth's notable grandmothers had died; then shortly before her marriage her mother-in-law had died, probably from the plague then going through Essex. King James had knighted the younger Robert Wroth, and the king and/or his sons and friends were often Wroth guests during hunting seasons. Mary Wroth had been trained from early childhood how to act with royalty and aristocrats, and her poise surely enhanced the Wroth reputation. Yet the Wroth family may well have expected women on other occasions to dress more like sober Puritans, not in the colorful silk dresses of court life that we see in her portraits or described in *Urania* (*MSLW* 120). She might even have been expected to dress daily more like her former aunt, Margaret Dakins Sidney (currently Hoby), unlike her father, who spent more on his court clothes than on building the entire Long Gallery of Penshurst (Nevitt 4r–v, 6r). This may be a good subject for future research on possible conflicts in clothing between Sidney court practice and Wroth family expectations.

Wroth's hospitality and aristocratic forms of entertainment (Illustration 19 shows her with an archlute) are indicated by the music written for her, including "Durrants Masque" and "My Lady Wroth's Mascharada" (Sabol #119 and #401; Alexander 92; Larson, "Voicing Lyric"; Larson *ARC* 1:21). The frequent visits by royalty, aristocrats, family, and poets demonstrate that Robert and Mary Wroth were renowned for their hospitality at Durrance and then at Loughton Hall. William Gamage wrote an epigram "To the worthy Knight, Sir Robert Wroth, of his house called Durrance," describing him as "a famous housekeeper," much as Wroth later depicts the hospitality of the husbands of Pamphilia and Bellamira.

---

8   Four of Wroth's seven sisters had died at early ages. Little Bridget and Alice had both died at Penshurst in 1599. Elizabeth, old enough to come to court at age thirteen, died in 1605; the following year Vere, the youngest sibling, died.

Ben Jonson first praised the Sidneys who hosted him at Penshurst, honoring Barbara Sidney herself as "noble, fruitful, [and] chaste" (*Complete Poetry* 81–2). Similarly, in the accompanying poem "III. To Sir Robert Wroth," Jonson's praise for Wroth hospitality is comparable to his glowing account of Penshurst (*MSLW* 154–7). It is also notable that the Wroths were, as Jonson notes, "so neere the citie, and the court," and of superior living (*Complete Poetry* 81).

Wroth had far more involvement with the arts than did her cousin Elizabeth, who was also known in her own right as a poet and a friend to poets. This may have caused some marital strain. As Jonson told William Drummond of Hawthornden: "one day being at table with my Lady Rutland, her husband coming in, accused her that she kept table to poets" ("Conversations" 1:142). In contrast, as we shall see, Wroth's husband apparently supported her writing, as indicated through his will. While there may have been some marital tensions—Jonson observed that "my Lady wroth is unworthily married on a Jealous husband" ("Conversations" 1:142)—there are no known marital challenges to her writing.

The Countess of Rutland continued to have connections with both the Walsingham and Sidney families whenever possible, and obviously enjoyed spending time with Wroth and with her other cousins. When she was in London she often stayed with her mother's Walsingham family, but she also visited Wroth at Durrance and her aunt Barbara at Penshurst, and her uncle Robert Sidney and some of her cousins came to visit her at Belvoir. Yet despite the cancellation of her husband's Elizabethan fine, financial problems for the Rutlands continued. In October 1605 she was arrested by a goldsmith in Cheapside—then the goldsmith himself was fined in the Star Chamber for "arresting the Countesse of Rutland" (Chamberlain 1:211). The financial crush occasioned by her husband's association with Essex had made a severe impact on her life, but the Star Chamber protected her, and she started to advance at court. In January 1606 she danced in Jonson and Inigo Jones's *Masque of Hymenaei*, presented at the wedding of her half-brother, Robert Devereux, third Earl of Essex, to Frances Howard, daughter of the Earl of Suffolk (the bride was later to become infamously involved with Robert Carr, Earl of Somerset). Memorialized in an individual masque portrait, this seems to have been her most dramatic appearance at court.

Visits from the Countess of Rutland demonstrate her friendship with Lady Sidney, Wroth, and the rest of the family. July through November 1610 is their most documented time together (*DPFA* 153–63). Wroth's brother William and then her father had gone to meet Pembroke at Belvoir in August. On 4 October Wroth had written to her father that "this night my Lady of Rutland comes" (159). After two weeks together at the Wroth home of Durrance, they and Robert Sidney "set forth together" for London; the Countess of Rutland and Wroth then went together to Penshurst. Alluding to her father Philip Sidney's previous possession of Penshurst, Robert Sidney told his wife to let the Lady of Rutland know that "she is in her own house." He urged Wroth "to look well that my Lady of Rutland want nothing" (161–2). The foul weather and difficulty in traveling lengthened the trip into November, when she stayed at Durrance with Wroth before her journey home, having spent about six weeks with Wroth, including her Penshurst stay. The Countess of Rutland also praised Lady Sidney's excellence as a hostess. Robert Sidney says: "She took her entertainment at Penshurst exceeding well: and commends her kindly unto you" (163).

Poetic Praise of Life and Death

All of these Sidney women received poetic praise. Lady Sidney was praised for roles as hostess and mother in Jonson's "To Penshurst," as we have seen. Her relative William Gamage praised Barbara as "the Omega," the last "of the Gamages" in *Linsi-Woolsie* (1613) and Wroth as "the most famous, and Heroike Lady." Wroth's sister Kate was more important to him as his Welsh "heroic, and splendent Patronesse, Katherine, Lady Mansel," a "Rare paragon of virtue" (A2, D3v, A6r–v). She lost all her children when they were very young, and she died herself at Baynard's Castle in May 1616 (*MSLW* 178).

Elizabeth Sidney Manner's connection to the muses is praised by Jonson in "XII: Epistle To Elizabeth Countesse Of Rutland" (from *The Forest*), in which he first describes those who care only about gold, and turns to her, who will honor his poetic gift because she has inherited her father's "love unto the Muses, when his skill / Almost you have, or may have, when you will?" In his Epigram "LXXIX—to Elizabeth, Countess of Rutland" Jonson wrote that the saying "That poets are far rarer births than kings" was proven by her "noblest father," whose "most masculine issue of his brain" led only to a female child. "Destinies" thought that only males would achieve, but "Nature" was incensed by the anti-female, so Nature "happily displeased, made you." That is, while Jonson believed that men are better poets in general, Philip Sidney would be so impressed by his daughter's writing "those rare, and absolute numbers" that they would lead him to "burn, or better far his book" (*Complete Poetry* 33–4). These tributes suggest that she, Wroth, and a number of Sidney siblings and friends were writing poetry at that time. (There may be two forthcoming poems by Elizabeth Sidney Manners, cited by Donald Foster and Tobian Banton.) Had the Countess of Rutland better health, longer life, and a supportive husband, she might well have emerged as Wroth's poetic equal. Unfortunately, the other poems praising her are elegies.

Elizabeth Sidney Manners's husband, Roger Manners, Earl of Rutland, died on 26 June 1612 in Cambridge and was buried at St. Mary's in Bottesford in an elegant tomb designed for him and his wife.[9] Elizabeth's death followed her husband's within weeks; he had perhaps given her syphilis. Rumors that her death was hastened by medicine supplied by Sir Walter Ralegh were unfounded (Chamberlain 1:374). She had presumably been in the care of her London relatives, for she was buried in St. Paul's near her father and her grandfather, Sir Francis Walsingham.[10] Francis Beaumont's "An Elegy on the Death of the Virtuous Lady Elizabeth, Countess of Rutland" expresses anger at doctors who freed "the looser sort of people in the street," the wicked, from this disease and did not acknowledge that her husband might have inflicted it on Elizabeth. Beaumont's elegy describes a marital unhappiness that seems to have been common knowledge: God did not give her "the chief / Blessing of women, marriage," which "was to thee / Nought but a sacrament of misery" (Beaumont and Fletcher 11:508).[11] Jonson had also observed that she had to live as "a widow'd wife" (*Complete Works* 8:224–5; 11:88).

Wroth's marriage was much happier than her cousin Elizabeth Sidney Manners's, although she was apparently not content. Some of the portrayals of unhappy arranged marriages in *Urania* seem to reflect her preferred choice of William Herbert, Earl of Pembroke. Arranged marriages were not, however, uncommon in her circle; her sister Katherine as well as some of her cousins and friends at court also entered into such alliances. While she may have experienced the occasional loneliness expressed by her avatar Pamphilia, Wroth was also frequently with her family, whether at court, Baynard's Castle, or Penshurst. Her family often came to Durrance or Loughton Hall, and Wroth visited Cecil at Hatfield House. Friends including Lady Anne Clifford and Lucy, Countess of Bedford, visited Penshurst with her, and she went to see her aunt, the Countess of Pembroke, at least until 1619 (*DPFA* 225). Wroth knew Queen Anne well enough to request her support for her husband's petition

---

9   For the Rutland tomb at St. Mary's in Bottesford, see Sparham.

10   Since the burial area of St. Paul's was destroyed by the Great Fire of London in 1666, there is a modern inscription for Sir Philip Sidney, but none for his daughter.

11   See both Beaumont poems and a list of the many other copies in Denbo 103–7, 290–91.

to the king for a longer lease on Loughton Hall, promising its refurbishment to make it suitable for royal visits; her request noted a personal benefit: "it will be much for my good, Mr. Wroth having promised to add it to my jointure, all the rest of his lands being entailed" (Cecil Papers 130/174). The king's approval led to several years of elegant rebuilding. Wroth may well have been thinking of Loughton Hall in her description of a forest lodge, much visited by the country's king, in the *Urania*: "Situated on a hill a fair house," with "a delicate walk" from the river up through the garden, and then to the " House ... with furniture fit for a Court" (1:344).

Wroth was beginning to emerge in published poetry first as a supporter of the arts, receiving dedications to her "worth" as offered by John Davies of Hereford in his *Scourge of Folly* (S1r–v). George Chapman's dedicatory poems in the Homer translation praised her virtuous mind, "Reason, and Religion" (2B6v). George Wither described her as "Arts sweet lover" in *Abuses Stript and Whipt* (1613). Ben Jonson treated her as a poet. Dedicating *The Alchemist* (1612) to her, he approved her literary "judgment (which is a Sidneys)", identifying her with other family writers ("To the Lady"). In these years Wroth became known for her poetry, some of which was set to music, probably by Alfonso Ferrabosco, who was also staying at Baynard's Castle (Alexander 99–102). Ben Jonson highly praised her writing, which he may have read as he associated with the Sidneys at Penshurst in 1611 (Brennan and Kinnamon, "Robert Sidney"). The epigram "CIII: To Mary Lady Wroth" praises her particularly as a Sidney (as does his poem to her sister Philippa), and "CV: To Lady Mary Wroth" praises her mythologically, perhaps as a reflection of her appearance in his first masque for Queen Anne. He also praises her primarily as a Sidney in his dedication of *The Alchemist*, as "The Lady Most Deserving Her Name and her Blood: Lady Mary Wroth." In his "A Sonnet, to the Noble Lady, the Lady Mary Wroth" Jonson adopts her preferred poetic form to praise her, asserting that since he copied out her poetry, he has "become / A better lover and much better Poet"; "readers" take her lines as reflecting Venus, whose "joyes, her smiles, her loves" all appear in her verse, along with "All Cupids Armorie" (*Complete Poetry* 49, 50, 166). She and Jonson remained friends; James Loxley ("New Light") has recently noted that they met on Jonson's way north to visit Drummond in Scotland in 1618.

Deaths of Robert and James Wroth

In late 1613 Wroth was pregnant with her first known child, although she and her husband had apparently lost at least two daughters in infancy. Since her husband was close to death, James's birth in February 1614 was of exceptional significance as the last chance for this branch of the Wroth family to produce an heir. Robert Wroth wrote his will on 2 March 1614, the day before little James's christening took place, probably in the church of St. Nicholas at Loughton Hall, with just family serving at the ceremony: the Sidney grandparents, Robert and Barbara, and the Earl of Pembroke serving as proxy for the king as ceremonial godfather (William Holman, "Pedigree," ERO MS D/Y/1/3/52). While Robert Wroth's will was as generous as possible to his wife and his new baby, his estate was tied up by the recurring debts of his father and his grandfather. Two-thirds of Wroth properties were to remain in trust for another seven years to pay off his father's debts before James would have fully inherited. John Chamberlain's estimate of £23,000 of debt for Lady Mary Wroth was actually understated for the Wroth family (1:519). That debt did not directly involve her, but she had a personal debt of about £2,000, still difficult for her. Her husband left her lifetime residency at Loughton Hall, a few smaller properties, and £1,000 for her other bills and the cost of remodeling Loughton Hall. His generous stipulation emphasized she would retain all her apparel and jewelry, the furniture of her room, and his "best coach." His inclusion of "all her books and furniture of her study and closet" indicates appreciation for her writing and love of literature. He asked his "dear and loving wife" to accept the will as "a testimony of my entire love and affection towards her," noting that "her sincere love, loyalty, virtuous conversation, and behavior towards me have deserved a far better recompense," if it were not for "the care of satisfying of my debts and supporting my house [the Wroth family]" (TNA Prob 11/123).

Robert Wroth left the care of young James to both families, Robert Sidney and Pembroke, and the three John Wroths—his brother, uncle, and cousin. Lady Mary Wroth herself was much worried by this arrangement, since James was under the Wards of Court until he was twenty-one, and so she asked her father to become his legal guardian (MS Crawford 177, Kansas). As Queen Anne's Lord Chamberlain and a Herbert family relative, Robert Sidney had enough influence finally to become James's guardian. Technically, little James was the inheritor of the Wroth legacy. In practical terms, however, most of this income was taken by the rest of the family, and her husband's royal positions in the forest were assumed by others. Tragically, James died in July of 1616; his sad death is recorded in the Wroth chapel in St. Andrew's in Enfield (*MSLW* pl. 14).[12] At James' death the substantial Wroth estate was transferred to his uncle, Sir John Wroth. Subsequently, Mary Wroth's finances became difficult enough that she was obliged to beg Sir Edward Conway for the king's protection from debt enforcement; she received yearly protection, as noted in the 1623–31 *Acts of the Privy Council* (*MSLW* 249–51).

Wroth's Primary Literary Decade

As Jonson's poetry suggests, Wroth wrote poetry from a young age. Her published works and extant manuscripts, however, seem to date from after the death of her son in 1616 and to conclude about a decade later. Wroth's first extant piece appears to be her formal presentation of poems in her manuscript that begins "Pamphilia to Amphilanthus" (Folger MS V.a.104), a manuscript that seems to have been written in sequence and perhaps for her lover Pembroke; we know it precedes the 1621 printed *Urania* because of authorial changes in the printed version (Wroth, *Poems*, "Textual Notes"; Bell, "Autograph Manuscript"). The first manuscript group of fifty-five poems seems to be the most formal; all of it is incorporated into the published version, though seven poems are exchanged with the second section of fifty-five poems. With its sequence of ten numbered sonnets or five songs and, most notably, the corona of the fourteen poems "Labyrinth," the second section of poems conforms to the French model of varying sequences. Both of these sections are concluded with the "signature" of Pamphilia, surrounded by fermesse, or slashed S. The third section seems to be a later addition, concluding with a final note of the speaker's grief at the loss of her beloved when she complied with his desire. Lacking the bottom-ruled margin for the first two sections, the final paper matches paper used in *Love's Victory* (Bell, "'A too curious secrecie'"; Hannay, "Ending End"). The next extant work may well be *Love's Victory*, her original drama that exists in two autograph manuscripts (complete copy in Penshurst

---

12 The Wroth family is now extinct there and forgotten at the church in Enfield. Fortunately, Sue Taylor, a local historian in Loughton, has generated interest in Wroth as a prominent writer by producing her booklet *Lady Mary Wroth* (2005) and by featuring Wroth in local literary celebrations. Rev. Sue Brewster, vicar of St. Nicholas next to Loughton Hall, opened the church for us to visit.

MS, incomplete in Huntington MS 600; see *Love's Victory*, ed. Brennan). It may have been written for the marriage of Barbara, her youngest surviving sister, to Sir Thomas Smythe in April 1619.

Throughout most of this period of Mary Wroth's copious writing Lady Sidney continued to offer gracious hospitality, especially during summer visits by her surviving daughters Mary Wroth, Philippa Hobart, and Barbara Smythe, and other visitors, including Lady Isabella Rich and Lucy, Countess of Bedford. Wroth continued to stay close to her parents; she traveled from court to Penshurst in July 1618, bringing her mother Robert Sidney's letter announcing his new title, so that "now your Ladyship is Countess of Leicester" (*DPFA* 216). In September 1620 Barbara and Robert Sidney were crushed by the death of their "worthy and loving" daughter Philippa (*DPFA* 227), a loss that appears in *Urania* 2:1 as the death of Philistella. Wroth continued to help her father in hiring a keeper from Loughton on 12 May 1621 (*DPFA* 232–3). The Countess of Leicester died later that month and was buried at Penshurst chapel on 26 May. The most expansive details of Wroth's life end at that point because, with the death of her mother, her father's family letters ceased. Her mother's death must have caused Wroth considerable mourning; their family letters and their joint portrait (Illustration 18) demonstrate their closeness. Wroth's beloved aunt and literary mentor the Countess of Pembroke died in October of that same year.

Events occurring in Wroth's family life appear, often in distorted form, in her *Urania* (1621). The families of the major characters generally parallel the organization of the Pembroke and Sidney families, who were so often together: the King and Queen of Naples and their children Amphilanthus, Urania, and Leonius, who shadow the Earl and Countess of Pembroke and their children William, Anne, and Philip Herbert; and the King and Queen of Morea and their children Pamphilia, Parselius, Rosindy, Philarchos, Philistella (and in *Urania* 2, Bardariana) who shadow Wroth's own family. Wroth dramatizes some family events: for example, her father's embassy in France is reflected in the ambassadorship of Dettareus, before his melodramatic narrative veers off into pure fantasy. The suffering caused by the death of her siblings William and Philippa is reflected in the characters' grief over the deaths of Parselius and Philistella. In several ways her romance with her cousin Pembroke is somewhat shadowed by the major characters Pamphilia and Amphilanthus. As Helen Hackett observes, the process of fictionalizing her life in *Urania* is itself fictionalized, as when Dorolina notes that Pamphilia feigns Lindamira as a "French story," but knows that it "was some thing more exactly related than a fiction" (45–69; *Urania* 1:499, 505). But readers should be cautious. Equating all the details of the romance with her biography can lead to misunderstandings (Hannay, "Sleuthing").

Contemporary readers at court treated *Urania* (1621) as topical. An exchange of bitter letters and satiric poems with Wroth shows that Edward Denny, Baron of Waltham, read her treatment of Sirelius as satire about his recently deceased daughter (Wroth, *Poems* 32–5, 237–42). He also disapproved of Wroth's role as an author (Lamb, *Gender* 156–9). John Chamberlain wrote to Dudley Carleton about the "bitter verses" Denny wrote "upon the Lady Marie Wroth" describing how she "doth palpable and grossely play upon him and his late daughter the Lady Hayes, besides many others she makes bold with." Chamberlain discounted Wroth's clever and satiric answering verse, claiming that only Denny's verse was worth copying to send (Chamberlain 2:427).[13]

---

13   The three extant copies of the exchange have survived: a copy in the Cecil Papers (MS 130/117–21); a copy in the Clifton manuscripts at the University of Nottingham (MS Cl LM 85/1–5), and a holograph copy that Wroth made for the Earl of Denbigh, now in the Warwickshire Record Office (MS CR2017/C48/2/1–4). In addition, copies of Denny's poem appear in Huntington Library MS HM 198/64, and British Library Add. MS 22603/64v–65 (Wroth, *Poems* 33; see also Roberts).

Since Wroth's *Urania* 2 does not represent Pamphilia's father as either remarried or dead, it was probably completed before the remarriage of her father to Sarah Blount Smythe on 25 April 1626, followed by his death less than three months later. It may have ended in Wroth's pregnancy or shortly after the birth of her natural children William and Katherine *c.* 1624.

Katherine and William [Herbert]

About a decade after her husband's death Wroth bore Pembroke two children, apparently twins born in the spring of 1624. William was named for his father and also, with Katherine, for Wroth's closest siblings; the three of them had traveled together as the older children, while the younger ones remained in the nursery. Wroth's young William and Katherine were well known among neighbors and family. Judith Foxe, Wroth's neighbor in Woodford Bridge near Loughton, included in her will "dear friend Mistress Katherine Herbert" and "the honorable Mr. William Herbert," as well as leaving her house of Prouts Place to Wroth and then to Katherine (TNA Prob 11/175).

Beyond a poem on their birth by their relative Sir Edward Herbert, there are no surviving references to their childhoods. Their father, dying in 1630, never knew them as adults. His brother Philip, now fourth Earl of Pembroke and Earl of Montgomery, provided them an excellent chance for a successful future. Philip convinced the king to give young Will an estate in Ireland. Unfortunately for him, the estate was lost with the Irish rebellion, and the rapid descent into the conflicts of the English Civil War. Young Will served as captain in the one military campaign of his relative and neighbor, Sir Henry Herbert, and then later in the elite cavalry of Prince Maurice, the king's nephew. Although Loughton Hall was in a strongly parliamentarian area of Essex, Wroth's son was clearly a royalist, as was his patron Philip Herbert in the early days of the war. Young Will's fate is not known. He may have been an early war casualty, or he may have remained with his commander Maurice until his ship went down in the Caribbean, or he may have transferred to parliamentarian troops. More is known about his sister Katherine. She married John Lovet (not Lovel), the eldest son and heir of a prominent royalist family. Her husband soon inherited the home and extensive lands of Lovet; but, even more rapidly than in Wroth's own life, Katherine lost her fortune when her husband quickly became ill and died (his burial is recorded for 14 September 1643 in the parish register of Sparsholt Holy Cross, near Oxford). Since no children were yet born, all the property except her dowry was transferred to his younger brother. The Lovet location was in the midst of civil war strife, so it is unclear where the young widow lived. Two documents note her second marriage. First is her inheritance of Prouts from her mother, listed in the Woodford Manor Rolls, which give her name as "Katherine Parry widow daughter of Dame Marie … Late wife of James Parry deceased" (ERO MS D/DCw M23). Second is the Welsh genealogy that lists her husband James Parry and their sons James and Phe (Philip). Katherine is listed as the daughter of the Earl of Pembroke, accompanied by her family crest, the Pembroke coat of arms with a small aristocratic gold bar sinister signifying her illegitimacy. Their home was in the Parry family at Llandefaelog Tre'r Graig, Breconshire (NLW GTJ08715; *MSLW* 292–7).

Wroth died in the spring of 1651, apparently at Loughton Hall in late March (*MSLW* 304–5). Katherine, who seems to have been with her in her final illness, may well have brought some of her mother's possessions back to Wales, including the working manuscript

---

The exchange in the Clifton manuscripts at the University of Nottingham (MS Cl LM 85/1–5) can be seen at http://wroth.latrobe.edu.au/row-117.html.

of *Urania* 2 (Newberry Library, Newberry Case MS f.Y 1565 W95), eventually purchased in the nineteenth century from a nearby estate sale at Tredegar Park, owned by the Morgan family, which had intermarried with the Parrys. Wroth's other extant manuscripts have not yet been traced that far back, but perhaps Katherine brought several home, along with her mother's additional works that we do not yet know; there may well be other Wroth manuscripts that will be found by scholars sleuthing in the archives. Certainly Wroth is emerging as an important writer, gaining much scholarly attention in teaching, conference sessions, articles, books, online manuscripts and studies, and the 2014 performance of her "Love's Victory" at Penshurst.[14] She now considerably outranks her remarkable Welsh mother Barbara Gamage Sidney, Countess of Leicester, and her literary cousin Elizabeth Sidney Manners, Countess of Rutland.

Bibliography

Manuscript Sources

Centre for Kentish Studies, Maidstone
De L'Isle MS U1500 F13
Essex Record Office (ERO)
ERO MS D/DCw M23
ERO MS D/Y/ 1/3/52, William Holman, "Pedigree of the Wroth Family"
Folger Shakespeare Library
Folger Shakespeare Library MS V.a.104
Hatfield House
Cecil Papers 51/25, 130/117–21, 174
Newberry Library
Newberry Case MS f.Y 1565. W95
National Library of Wales (NLW)
"The descendants of Idio Wylht." *Golden Grove Book of Pedigrees.* Vol. 2, image 52.
GTJ08715. http://education.gtj.org.uk/en/item6/16713
NLW MS 11964
The National Archives, Kew (TNA)
Prob 11/123 Will of Sir Robert Wroth
Prob 11/175 Will of Judith Foxe
Penshurst Parish Register
Sparsholt Holy Cross Parish Register
University of Nottingham
MS C1 LM 85/1–5 Copy of correspondence of Wroth and Denny, "Mary Wroth's Poetry: An Electronic Edition." *LaTrobe University Humanities and Social Sciences.* Web. 15 June 2012. http://wroth.latrobe.edu.au/row-117.html
Warwickshire Record Office (WRO)
WRO MS CR2017/C48/2/1–4
Wiltshire and Swindon Archives (WSA)
WSA MS 2057/F1 and F1/2

---

14   See Bell *ARC* 2:5; Hackett *ARC* 2:8; Findlay *ARC* 2:13, Salzman *ARC* 2:16, and Larson, "Recent Studies."

Primary and Secondary Sources

Alexander, Gavin. "The Musical Sidneys." *John Donne Journal* 25 (2006): 65–105.

Beaumont, Francis, and John Fletcher. *The Works of Beaumont and Fletcher*. Ed. Alexander Dyce. 11 vols. London: Edward Moxon, 1846.

Bell, Ilona. "The Autograph Manuscript of Wroth's *Pamphilia to Amphilanthus*." *New Ways of Looking at Old Texts, V: Papers of the Renaissance English Text Society, 2007–2011*. Tempe, AZ: Arizona Center for Medieval and Renaissance Texts and Studies, 2012.

—. "'A too curious secrecie': Wroth's Pastoral Song and *Urania*." *SJ* 32.1 (2013): 23–50.

Brennan, Michael G. *The Sidneys of Penshurst and the Monarchy, 1500–1700*. Aldershot: Ashgate, 2006.

—, and Noel J. Kinnamon. "Robert Sidney, 'Mr Johnson,' and the Education of William Sidney at Penshurst." *Notes & Queries* 50.4 (2003): 430–37.

—. "Robert Sidney and the Earl of Essex: A Dangerous Friendship Viewed Through the Eyes of Rowland Whyte." *SJ* 32.1 (2014): 1–38.

Carleton, Sir Dudley. *Dudley Carleton to John Chamberlain 1603–1624: Jacobean Letters*. Ed. Maurice Lee, Jr. New Brunswick, NJ: Rutgers UP, 1972.

Chamberlain, John. *The Letters of John Chamberlain*. Ed. Norman Egbert McClure. 2 vols. Philadelphia, PA: American Philosophical Society, 1939; rpt. Westport, CT: Greenwood Press, 1979.

Chapman, George. *The Whole Works of Homer ... in his Iliads and Odysses*. London: printed by Richard Field and William Jaggard for Nathaniell Butter, 1616 (?).

Couchman, Jane. "'Give Birth Quickly and Then Send Us Your Good Husband': Informal Political Influence in the Letters of Louise de Coligny." *Women's Letters Across Europe, 1400–1700: Form and Persuasion*. Ed. Jane Couchman and Ann Crabb. Aldershot: Ashgate, 2005. 163–84.

Davies, Sir John of Hereford. *The Scourge of Folly*. London: Edward Allde for Richard Redmer, 1611.

Denbo, Michael, ed. *The Holgate Miscellany: An Edition of Pierpont Morgan Library Manuscript, MA 1057*. Tempe, AZ: Arizona Center for Medieval and Renaissance Texts and Studies, 2012.

Donaldson, Ian. *Ben Jonson: A Life*. Oxford: Oxford UP, 2012.

Duncan-Jones, Katherine. "'Almost Always Smiling': Elizabeth's Last Two Years." *Resurrecting Elizabeth I in Seventeenth-Century England*. Ed. Elizabeth Hageman and Katherine Conway. Madison, NJ: Farleigh Dickinson UP, 2007. 31–47.

Foster, Donald W., with Tobian Banton, ed. *Women's Works, Volume 3: 1603–1625*. New York: Wicked Good Books, 2013.

Galli, Antimo. *Rime di A. G. all'Illustrissima Signora Elizabetta Talbot-Grey*. London, 1609.

Gamage, William. *Linsi-Woolsie, or Two Centuries of Epigrammes*. London: Joseph Barnes, 1613.

Goldring, Elizabeth. "'So Lively a Portraiture of His Miseries': Melancholy, Mourning and the Elizabethan Malady." *British Art Journal* 6.2 (2005): 12–22.

Hackett, Helen. "'Yet Tell Me Some Such Fiction': Lady Mary Wroth's *Urania* and the 'Femininity' of Romance." *Women, Texts and Histories 1575–1760*. Ed. Clare Brant and Diane Purkiss. London: Routledge, 1992. 39–68.

Hannay, Margaret P. "The 'Ending End' of Lady Mary Wroth's Manuscript of Poems." *SJ* 32.1 (2013): 1–2.

—. "'High Housewifery': The Duties and Letters of Barbara Gamage Sidney, Countess of Leicester." *Early Modern Women: An Interdisciplinary Journal* 1 (2006): 7–36.

—. *Mary Sidney, Lady Wroth*. Farnham: Ashgate, 2010.

—. "Sleuthing in the Archives." *Re-Reading Mary Wroth*. Ed. Katherine R. Larson and Naomi Miller, with Andrew Strycharski. New York: Palgrave Macmillan, 2015. 19–36.

Hay, Millicent V. *The Life of Robert Sidney, Earl of Leicester (1563–1626)*. Washington, DC: Folger Shakespeare Library, 1984.

Herbert, Mary Sidney, Countess of Pembroke. *The Collected Works of Mary Sidney Herbert, Countess of Pembroke*. Ed. Margaret P. Hannay, Noel J. Kinnamon, and Michael G. Brennan. 2 vols. Oxford: Clarendon P, 1998.

Jonson, Ben. "Ben Jonson's Conversations with William Drummond of Hawthornden." *Ben Jonson*. Ed. C. H. Herford and Percy Simpson. 11 vols. Oxford: Clarendon P, 1925. 1:128–78.

—. *The Complete Poetry of Ben Jonson*. Ed. William B. Hunter, Jr. New York: W. W. Norton, 1963.

—. "To the Lady, Most Deserving Her Name, and Blood: Mary, Lady Wroth." *The Alchemist*. Ed. Alvin B. Kernan. New Haven, CT: Yale UP, 1974. 19.

Lamb, Mary Ellen. "The Biopolitics of Romance in Mary Wroth's *Countess of Montgomery's Urania*." *ELR* 31 (2001): 107–30.

—. *Gender and Authorship in the Sidney Circle*. Madison: U of Wisconsin P, 1990.

Larson, Katherine R. "Recent Studies of Mary Wroth." *ELR* 44.2 (2014): 328–59.

—. "Voicing Lyric: The Songs of Mary Wroth." *Re-Reading Mary Wroth*. Ed. Katherine R. Larson and Naomi Miller, with Andrew Strycharski. New York: Palgrave Macmillan, 2015. 19–33.

Loxley, James. "New Light on Ben Jonson's Walk to Edinburgh." *Times Literary Supplement* Sept. 11, 2009.

Moffet, Thomas. *Nobilis or a View of the Life and Death of a Sidney and Lessus Lugubris*. Ed. Virgil B. Heltzel and Hoyt H. Hudson. San Marino, CA: Huntington Library, 1940.

—. *The Silkworms and their Flies* (1599). Ed. Victor Houliston. Binghamton, NY: MRTS, 1989.

Nevitt, Thomas. "Nevitt's *Memorial*." Ed. Gavin Alexander and Barbara Ravelhofer. *COPIA: CERES Sidneiana*. Web. 27 May 1999. http://www.english.cam.ac.uk/ceres/sidneiana/nevitt.htm.

Orrell, John. "Antimo Galli's Description of *The Masque of Beauty*." *HLQ* 43 (1979–80): 13–23.

Roberts, Josephine A. "An Unpublished Literary Quarrel Concerning the Suppression of Mary Wroth's *Urania* (1621)." *Notes & Queries* 222 (1977): 532–5.

Sabol, Andrew J., ed. *Four Hundred Songs and Dances from the Stuart Masque*. Providence, RI: Brown UP, 1978.

Sidney, Robert, first Earl of Leicester. *Domestic Politics and Family Absence: The Correspondence (1588–1621) of Robert Sidney, First Earl of Leicester, and Barbara Gamage Sidney, Countess of Leicester*. Ed. Margaret P. Hannay, Noel J. Kinnamon, and Michael G. Brennan. Aldershot: Ashgate, 2005.

—. *The Poems of Robert Sidney*. Ed. Peter J. Croft. Oxford: Clarendon, 1984.

Sparham, Bob. "St Mary's Bottesford Phase V.V, Monument to Roger Manners, 5th Earl of Rutland." *Bottesford Living History*. Web. 28 April 2007. http://www.bottesfordhistory.org.uk/page_id__96_path__0p3p77p.aspx.

Stewart, Alan. *Philip Sidney: A Double Life*. London: Random House, 2000.

Stradling Correspondence: A Series of Letters Written in the Reign of Queen Elizabeth. Ed. John Montgomery Traherne. London: Longman, Orme, Brown, Green and Longmans, 1840.

Taylor, Sue. *Lady Mary Wroth*. Loughton: Loughton and District Historical Society, 2005.

Vaughan, Alden T. "American Indians in England (act. *c*. 1500–1609)." *ODNB*.

Whyte, Rowland. *The Letters (1595–1608) of Rowland Whyte*. Ed. Michael G. Brennan, Noel J. Kinnamon, and Margaret P. Hannay. Philadelphia, PA: American Philosophical Society, 2013.

Williams, Glanmor, ed. *Glamorgan County History*. 6 vols. Cardiff: Glamorgan County History Trust, 1971–88.

Winwood, Sir Ralph. *Memorials of Affairs of State in the Reigns of Queen Elizabeth and King James I.* 3 vols. London: T. Ward, 1725.

Wither, George. *Abuses Stript and Whipt: or Satirical Essayes.* London: Printed by Richard Badger for Robert Allot, 1613.

Wroth, Lady Mary Sidney. *The First Part of The Countess of Montgomery's Urania.* Ed. Josephine A. Roberts. Tempe, AZ: Arizona Center for Medieval and Renaissance Texts and Studies, 1995.

—. *Lady Mary Wroth's Love's Victory: The Penshurst Manuscript.* Ed. Michael G. Brennan. London: The Roxburghe Club, 1988.

—. *Mary Wroth: The Countess of Montgomery's Urania (Abridged).* Ed. Mary Ellen Lamb. Tempe, AZ: Arizona Center for Medieval and Renaissance Studies, 2011.

—. *The Poems of Lady Mary Wroth.* Ed. Josephine A. Roberts. 2nd ed. Baton Rouge, LA: Louisiana State UP, 1992.

—. *The Second Part of The Countess of Montgomery's Urania.* Ed. Josephine A. Roberts, completed by Suzanne Gossett and Janel Mueller. Tempe, AZ: Arizona Center for Medieval and Renaissance Texts and Studies, 1999.

Robert Sidney (1595–1677), Second Earl of Leicester

Germaine Warkentin

Robert Sidney, second Earl of Leicester (Illustration 23), is perhaps the least-known of the early modern Sidneys, but he made a significant contribution to our understanding of their world. Leicester left no "works" to stand beside those of his uncle Sir Philip Sidney, his father Robert, his aunt the Countess of Pembroke, his sister Lady Mary Wroth, or his son Algernon. But in his twenties—perhaps earlier—he began to buy books, assembling over forty years a collection that absorbed and then massively exceeded his father's smaller one. The resulting library at Penshurst represented in its richness and diversity the intellectual life of a gifted magnate family during more than a century of political and intellectual crisis. Leicester's library, or what remained of it, was sold at auction in 1743, but the catalogue his servant Gilbert Spencer prepared *c.* 1652, and which various hands (including Leicester's) added to up to 1665, still exists to give us entry to that world (CKS U1475 Z45/2). Leicester read intensively among his books, for from young manhood he recorded what he read in heavy, vellum-bound folios, six of which, plus some loose collections, are still among the family papers deposited in the Centre for Kentish Studies, Maidstone. If Leicester left us no works of poetry or fiction, he nevertheless produced an exceptional record of how a seventeenth-century English nobleman—courtier, soldier, ambassador, and eventually bitter recluse—interpreted the works of others and the world in which he read them.

Robert, second Earl of Leicester, was born at Baynard's Castle in London on 1 December 1595, the second son of Sir Robert and Barbara Gamage Sidney. Among his godparents was Penelope Rich, the "Stella" of his uncle Philip Sidney's sonnet sequence *Astrophil and Stella*. His life thus forms a bridge between two ages: that of the notable Sidneys of the sixteenth century, and that of their often troubled seventeenth-century descendants. Like his brother William and his numerous sisters, Robert was initially taught at home, and the letters of his parents testify to the care they took with their children's education; for some months in 1611–12 the learned poet and dramatist Ben Jonson was almost certainly tutor to their two sons (Brennan and Kinnamon). In 1607, aged eleven, Robert and his elder brother matriculated at Christ Church, Oxford, as had their father and uncle. In 1612 William died of smallpox, and the younger brother found himself heir to Penshurst and the titles his father would accumulate over the next decade.

In 1614 Robert served as MP for Wilton in the Addled Parliament. In the same year he was given command of a company of foot, and from 1616 into the 1640s he served as titular colonel of the English regiment in the United Provinces. In 1616 his father became Viscount Lisle, and in 1618 was created Earl of Leicester, drawing the Sidneys into the higher reaches of the aristocracy. Like his father, Robert married ambitiously: in 1616 he secretly wedded Dorothy, daughter of Henry Percy (1564–1632), the ninth ("Wizard") Earl of Northumberland, and granddaughter of the Earl of Essex—a marriage that allied the Sidneys with two powerful noble families. It also brought him close to the circle of Queen Henrietta Maria, for the ninth earl's daughter Lucy Hay and younger son Henry were members of her household. His brother-in-law, Algernon Percy (1602–68), later tenth Earl of Northumberland and eventually Lord High Admiral, would remain Leicester's lifelong friend and ally.

Robert (after 1618, Viscount Lisle) was able to cultivate his intellectual interests among the learned circle of the Wizard Earl during the latter's imprisonment in the Tower (1605–21). There he made friends with the mathematician Thomas Harriot (*c.* 1560–1621), whom in one of the rare personal observations among his papers he calls "Mr. Harriote that same Mathematician, and admirable Scholler, my particular frend and preceptor" (CKS U1475 Z1/4, 478). Lisle was to serve as one of the executors of his mentor's will. Whether Harriot initiated his interest in mathematics or cultivated one already flowering, the evidence of his book collecting shows that throughout his life the second earl maintained an intense interest in current developments in arithmetic, geometry, algebra, navigation, optics, artillery practice, mensuration, and astronomy.

Viscount Lisle and his wife seem to have been typical young courtiers of the era, praised, for example, in verses by the otherwise unknown George Tashe printed in William Camden's *Remaines* (151–3): "He that was borne vertues select, hath got / A rare choice gemme; divinest lovers lot" and "Where hands and hearts in sacred linke of love / Are joined by Christ: that match doth happy prove." In the manuscript continuation of her *Urania* (1621) Lady Mary Wroth depicted them as Rosindy and Meriana, "the happiest Couple in all things, being in the highest of contents blessed of any living" (*Urania* 2:353). Their first child, Dorothy (Edmund Waller's "Sacharissa"), was born in 1617 (see Akkerman *ARC* 1:10). Eight girls and five boys followed, of whom eight lived to maturity. Among them were Philip (1619–98), eventually the third earl; Algernon (1622–83), political theorist and republican martyr, and Henry Sidney, Earl of Romney (1641–1704), who in 1688 would craft William IV's invitation to take the throne of England (see Brennan *ARC* 1:12).

In 1619 Robert's brother-in-law, James Hay, Viscount Doncaster (1590–1636), led an embassy sent by James I to Germany in an attempt to mediate between the Emperor Matthias and Protestant rebels in Bohemia after the Defenestration of Prague. Lisle attached himself to the group for a period and visited the Palatine Library in Heidelberg, the most important scholarly collection in Northern Europe. Its supervisor was Janus Gruterus, a Continental intellectual from circles familiar to the generation of Lisle's father and uncle. The meticulous accounts kept by Robert's servant Phillip Maret from 1618 to 1626 (CKS U1475 A41/1–14) document Robert's regular purchase of volumes of history, theology, mathematics, and philosophy. At his death in 1626 the first earl owned at least forty books on history and contemporary affairs (Shephard), and probably two or three times that number. When his son assumed the title he already owned many more, and his interests were clearly much wider than those of his father. Maret's accounts ceased when his master became earl, but later book bills, letters, and the catalogue itself indicate that by 1652 the second Earl of Leicester's library catalogue contained about 4,927 entries (including a number of cross-references). Between then and the cessation of entries in 1665 another 871 titles were added. By that time the library at Penshurst was one of the most substantial yet assembled for the use of a great English family.

The elder Robert Sidney had accumulated heavy debts during his lifetime, and in 1626 he died intestate. As a mortgage transfer (CKS U1500 C292/79) and an inventory of 1623 (CKS U1500 E120) show, three years before he died he transferred Penshurst to his son, who had a growing family, moved to London, and became a mere sojourner on his own estate. When he succeeded to the title, Leicester had to devote much time and ingenuity to repairing the family's financial situation. His role was still that of a rising courtier, however, and he was clearly ambitious. In 1630 he acquired four acres (1.6 hectares) in St. Martin's Fields, north-west of Charing Cross, and in 1631–35 he and his wife erected a mansion on the north side. The building of Leicester House asserted their claim to elite status just as the palaces along the Strand had done for earlier magnates.

In September 1632 Leicester was appointed ambassador extraordinary to Denmark, ostensibly to condole with King Christian IV on the death of the Dowager Queen Sophia (Charles I's grandmother), and privately to encourage Christian to become involved on the side of the Protestant interest in the Thirty Years' War. The ambassador found himself at a raucous, disorderly court, presided over by a crude, stubborn, and dismissive king. Leicester held his own ably in the constant drinking bouts, but returned to England with relief after two wearying months. The little he had achieved was wiped out four days after his return by the death in the Battle of Lützen of the king of Sweden, Gustavus Adolphus, as a result of which Lutheran religious hegemony in Europe fell back before the rising force of the Catholic Reformation.

Leicester, a firm opponent of Catholic Spain and the reigning Habsburgs, was closely allied with the anti-Spanish interest at Charles I's court, particularly among the circle of Queen Henrietta Maria, where his Percy connections gave him influence. In 1636 the queen pressed for his appointment as ambassador extraordinary to France. The emissary already in place, Viscount Scudamore, was pro-Spanish, whereas Leicester favored an alliance between England and France against the Habsburgs. Unfortunately, he and Scudamore could not abide each other, a situation aggravated not only by Leicester's firm Protestantism (he worshiped with the Huguenots at Charenton), but also by his ability to outwit the less able Scudamore. The correspondence of the second earl offers painful insight into their disagreements, the sometimes ludicrous juggling for place among courtiers, the financial cost of court service, and the sheer tedium of ambassadorial life (Collins 2:374–666). Leicester's sons Philip and Algernon accompanied him, but his wife, Dorothy, Countess of Leicester, chiefly remained in England defending the family interest, which she did vigorously, as her letters show (*Correspondence DPS*; see Akkerman *ARC* 1:10). Though Leicester made friends with his fellow ambassador Hugo Grotius, there is no evidence he attempted to contact Parisian intellectuals who would have shared his interests, for example the distinguished mathematician Marin Mersenne or members of his circle. Nor did he seek out a literary milieu; apart from his daughter Dorothy's admirer Edmund Waller, the only writer he is known to have patronized was the French Protestant scholar David Blondel (1591–1655), who, at the author's request, he haplessly tried to recommend to Archbishop Laud; six of Blondel's books were in his library. As the tone of his letters occasionally suggested, Leicester may have been too conscious of his high status as an ambassador; when his friends were campaigning to have him appointed secretary in place of the pro-Catholic Sir Francis Windebanke, Charles I is said to have remarked of the earl (possibly sarcastically) that he was "too greate for that Place" (Collins 2:664, and see Adams 92–3).

By 1637 Leicester's mission to Paris was changing; he became involved in secret intrigues between Louis XIII's mother, Marie de Médicis, and his queen, Anne of Austria, to undermine Cardinal Richelieu and paradoxically hinder the very Anglo-French agreement for which he had originally pressed. He was recalled from his futile mission, briefly in 1639 and finally in 1641. Leicester returned to England still seeking advancement; he had already been sworn a Privy Councillor in May 1639. The project to appoint him secretary had failed, but his friends, including Northumberland, were campaigning to make him Lord Lieutenant of Ireland, the role his grandfather, Sir Henry, had filled and his sons would hold, Philip in 1646–47 and Henry in 1692–93. Archbishop Laud, friend to Scudamore, exerted every effort to block the appointment, unjustly accusing Leicester of being a severe puritan, but by 1641 the Earl of Strafford, whom he was to succeed, had fallen, Laud was about to be impeached, and the appointment was finally Leicester's.

During 1641–43 Leicester struggled to prepare himself to serve in Ireland, but was unable to arbitrate between the conflicting demands of the king and Parliament. In 1642 Charles called him back to Oxford, where he waited in frustration until in 1644 the king withdrew the appointment in favor of the more decisive Earl of Ormond, with whom he had been in secret correspondence. Leicester had written loyally to Northumberland in 1642, "your lordship knowes I am a servant, and I could not run away if I would" (Blencowe 265), but in 1642 he wrote desolately to James Hay's widow, his sister-in-law Lucy, Countess of Carlisle:

> I am environed by such contradictions, as I can neither get from them, nor reconcyle them. The Parliament bids me go presently; the King commands me to stay till he dispatch me. The supplyes of the one, and the authority of the other, are equally necessary. I know not how to obtain them both, and am more likely to have neither; for now they are at such extremes, as to please the one is scarce possible, unless the other be opposed …. How soon I shall get myself out of this labyrinth I cannot tell your ladyship. (Blencowe xxi–xxii)

Constantly weighing possibilities in the balance without having to act was an asset to an ambassador, but a fatal flaw in a king's counselor.

A similar ambivalence would mark Leicester's life as an intellectual, for he was of a very different temperament from his amiable father: melancholy, and more combative. Leicester was a rigid man in his habits; among his early acts on succeeding to the title had been to issue a detailed list of rules for the conduct of his household (HMC, *De L'Isle and Dudley* 6:1). He was also endowed with a good measure of the hot Sidney temper. In 1620 he struck his brother-in-law, the royal favorite James Hay, who had snubbed him unmercifully for reasons still uncertain. To strike a Privy Councillor was a serious offense, and only the Marquis of Buckingham's intervention saved him from disgrace. Robert left what proved to be a symptomatically woeful and puzzled account of the altercation in a letter to his father (Collins 1:121–7). It was the first of several occasions when his combination of hauteur, uncertainty, and self-absorption became evident—characteristics that eventually affected both his public and his personal life. By the 1640s he found himself in a situation neither rigor nor temper could resolve. That shrewd observer Edward Hyde, Earl of Clarendon, saw him as "a man of honor and fidelity to the king," but one hampered by the "staggering and irresolution in his nature." Leicester "expected a greater certitude in the consultation of business than the business of this world is capable of: which temper proved very inconvenient to him through the course of his life" (2:531). In June of 1644 Leicester retired to Penshurst, perhaps hoping to live at last among his books and satisfy his speculative nature. His ambitions in tatters, though sworn into the Privy Council at the Restoration in 1660 he took almost no part in political life henceforth.

Leicester's retirement from public duties did not, however, protect him from private turmoil over the next three decades. During his French embassy he had left his wife entirely in charge of the estate's finances, but later accused her of exploiting his revenues to enrich herself (HMC, *De L'Isle and Dudley* 6:554–9). However, her letters show that knowing his ambassadorial expenses would be great and the king slow to reimburse him, she managed the estate shrewdly (*Correspondence DPS*). Originally the two had been very attached, but by the time she died in 1659 they were considering separation. Leicester nevertheless wrote a moving account of her death (Blencowe xxxv–xxxvi), and to Northumberland wrote how much he lamented her passing (Collins 2:682). A second tempest arose when Leicester took on the wardship of his nephew, Philip Smythe, Lord Strangford, who despite the earl's disapproval in 1650 married his daughter Isabella. Strangford's dissolute life and tangled finances would burden Leicester and his son Algernon for years (Scott, *Algernon/Republic* 63–6; Scott, *Algernon/Restoration* 99–103). Algernon was the brightest and most able of Leicester's sons, and they were very close (see Scott *ARC* 1:11). His heir, Philip, was more distant, less likeable, and not as clever. In 1645 Philip married Catherine Cecil, and Leicester secured the estate and title to him, but asserted his right to charge the estate with up to £29,000 before he could take possession (Scott, *Algernon/Restoration* 90). In 1652, when Catherine died, he cut off Philip's allowance on the grounds that he now needed less support. At this Philip struck the old man, a heinous offense for two reasons: Leicester was not only his father, but a peer of the realm. By the time of Leicester's death a series of codicils to his will had left Philip with almost no room to move financially. Leicester quarreled stubbornly with others as well: with John Maudit, the intruded minister of Penshurst Church (Warkentin, "The Magnate"), and seemingly with others in the neighborhood, for some time in the mid-1670s men he named only as "the spoylers" invaded Penshurst and took away a number of his books, though they were later returned "from Mr. Alston, by Alexander Bell's cart" (CKS U1500 E112, E113).

These unhappy conflicts make more curious the perspective presented in the anonymous political romance *Theophania*, written *c.* 1645, but published a decade later. Like the other romances of the period (and with some resemblance to Sir Philip Sidney's very popular *Arcadia*), the characters of *Theophania* bear classicizing names and undergo remarkable adventures. However, the setting in which events are recounted is clearly Penshurst, and the protagonists the Sidney family and their circle; chief among them is Leicester, portrayed as the wise Synesius. Someone who knew the second earl well enough to refer obliquely to his public life and personal interests chose the name, for the original Synesius (373–414) a Greek philosopher and bishop, like Leicester was of noble descent, a soldier, an ambassador, and a mathematician, who gave wise advice to the rulers of his time, chiefly of a mediating nature. *Theophania* was evidently written by a moderate royalist—Sir William Sales has been suggested (*Theophania* 12)—but Leicester's actual position was much more ambiguous. His sons Philip and Algernon were forthrightly of the republican party, but his son-in-law Sunderland died at Newbury in 1643, fighting on the royalist side. In the midst of these differences the second earl's obligation was to secure his legal position (in 1650 he signed the Engagement to ensure it), and to safeguard his estates, briefly sequestered in 1643 until his wife and her brother Northumberland managed to get the order quashed by Parliament. The journal Leicester kept between 1646 and 1655 (with one added entry for 1660 on the new king's return) charts the earl's views during that time.

Leicester's *Journal* is devoted almost exclusively to events in Parliament, initially at first hand, but later chiefly drawn from newsbooks and diurnals. Leicester watches his fellow aristocrats—men he knew well—compromising with the new regime after the abolition of the House of Lords by taking up a seat in the Commons, or alternatively facing execution because they refused to bend. His few comments are sardonic, and he does not spare the kind of man who "loved his interest better then honesty" (HMC, *De L'Isle and Dudley* 6:566). Nor does he disguise his loathing of Cromwell, observing sourly that his commission as Governor General in Ireland was simply copied from that of his son Philip. He also keeps his distance from the monarchy, referring at one point to Charles II as "theyr king" (meaning the Scots), but showing sympathy for Charles I during the days before his execution. The *Journal* is not a personal record; Leicester briefly records the births and deaths of children and grandchildren, but almost always with chill detachment; his mourning for "the sweet boy, little Harry Spencer, my grandchilde" (HMC, *De L'Isle and Dudley* 6:587) is a rare exception. What chiefly emerges is his stiff pride and his persistent sense of the injustices afflicting himself and his sons. Leicester's political views were probably those of a moderate Presbyterian; like Synesius he sought a middle way between ruler and people. Yet his position was not the result of a coherent view of policy. In July 1649 he recorded a sarcastic passage from the *Moderate Intelligencer* on Cromwell's journey to Ireland, adding symptomatically: "And now that action begins again, it is fit to observe how Cromwell and the rest will prosper after the taking away of the late Kings life, and other persons, lords, etc., and abolishing kingly government, and house of Peeres, and erecting a Commonwealth" (HMC, *De L'Isle and Dudley* 6:590). Whatever his views about the responsibilities of the individual, the orderliness and stability of the system of kingly government, as he understood it, was crashing about him. The *Journal* lapsed between 1655 and 1660, but was briefly revived with the return of the king. The final entry records Leicester's evident pleasure (and probable relief) when he was treated with kindly respect by the new monarch, sworn again of the Privy Council, and allowed to depart for Penshurst "for my health" (HMC, *De L'Isle and Dudley* 6:623).

If the search for—and failure to find—just such a coherent pattern in human action is the key to how Leicester's mind worked, it is also the foundation of his legacy: not only the library he accumulated, but the record of his method of reading preserved in his commonplace books. The elder Robert Sidney had kept commonplace books as well, four of them, accumulating material that he must have hoped would educate his sons as they entered the treacherous world of English and (for a Sidney, it would be assumed) European court life (Shephard). The second earl revered his amiable father; with a sense of continuity exceptional among commonplacers, he retained the four great folios, sometimes adding entries to what his father had written, and for forty years wrote his own observations in volumes closely resembling them in size and binding. His reputation for learning was apparently well known: even to Clarendon he was "a man of great parts, very conversant in books, and much addicted to the mathematics … in truth rather a speculative than a practical man" (2:531). A neo-Latin poem addressed to him on his appointment to Paris praises him as just such a figure: "With your talent you surpass the ancient glory of your family, and your ancestors, whom your image praises … And you defend, with fair laws, the paths of justice, To which you devote your study night and day" (Heffernan, ll. 7–14, transl.). In 1683 Leicester's son Algernon would tell the judge trying him for treason: "I believe there is a brother of mine here has forty quires of paper written by my father, and never one sheet of them was published; but he writ his own mind to see what he could think of it another time, and blot it out again, may be" (*Cobbett's Complete Collection*, 9 col. 878). This constant activity (evident in Illustration 24) was characteristic of the late humanist practices of copying, collation, and evaluation of sources so typical of the encyclopedic intellectual culture of the mid-seventeenth century. For Leicester, however, it also appears to have constituted an important aspect of his inner life. In his vast annotations the second earl conducted a four decades-long dialogue with himself.

Six volumes and some loose collections are still extant (CKS U1475 Z1/4–9, Z/9 [part of Z1/9] and Z/47). Traces of another survive in excerpts made in the eighteenth century by Thomas Birch (BL Add. MS 4464). They are much alike: vellum-bound, about 35 cm (13.8 in.) tall, most comprising hundreds of pages, sometimes empty or only partly filled. When Leicester's possessions were seized at Chester by royalist forces in February 1644, the inventory of what was taken lists three trunks of printed books, including "9 greate Bookes covered with vellom" (U1500 E96). If these were the commonplace books and there were indeed nine in all, the two now missing may have been the "collections on Livy" Leicester speaks of in one entry (CKS U1475 Z1/9, slips g and h) and possibly the records of his reading in mathematical sources, for which our only evidence is the remarkable number of such books listed in the library catalogue.

Each of the commonplace books differs from the others: some collect miscellaneous notes, others are more consistent. U1475 Z1/4 is laid out in two columns and has miscellaneous topic headings; U1475 Z1/8 is ruled in three columns and collects readings on law, politics, and problems of rule. Another book, U1475 Z1/9, is also tightly organized under headings: "Authors and Learned Men," "Church," "Pope," "Law," "Money," "Scotland and France," "Rule of Sea," and "Variae." There are loose slips in several volumes, and a file of loose sheets, U1475 Z47, contains notations undigested or awaiting entry. As a few overlapping datable references show, Leicester kept several volumes in progress at the same time; the latest citation, from 1662, actually appears in a volume chiefly compiled in the 1640s (CKS U1475 Z1/9). Note-taking ceased after the early 1660s, apparently when his hands became arthritic. All of this material, except for some late excerpts from European newsletters copied by a servant, is in his own hand; he worked, it seems, in solitude. To manage his large volumes and habitual small slips of paper (some still extant), Leicester developed extensive cross-references, a practice that also characterizes his library catalogue. Leicester's note-taking Buckinghamshire contemporary Sir William Drake cautions himself: "Be sure not to study much books of learning for they divert business, take up the memory too much, and keep one from more useful things" (Sharpe 125). Yet it was precisely the meditative perusal of learned writings scorned by Drake that was central—perhaps even psychologically necessary—to Leicester's later life. Whether in residence at Penshurst, serving his country in Denmark or Paris, or cooling his heels in Oxford awaiting the king's instructions, Leicester labored over his huge folios; the margins of his personal Bible (a heavily used volume still at Penshurst) show the same intense activity.

Despite his excellent collection of canonical Latin texts, Leicester showed little interest in Latin literature for its own sake. He almost never cited the poets, but made many references to ancient historians, biographers, and anecdotalists: Tacitus, Livy, Plutarch, Josephus, Aulus Gellius, often citing them from a single source, Pierre Ayrault's *Rerum ab omni antiquitate judicatorum pandectae*; he owned the edition of 1615 (Warkentin, Black, and Bowen 3v28). This vast historical compendium on civil law was replete with citations from classical authors, all thoroughly indexed. For Leicester, "Aerodii pandect." must have provided not only a source, but a model of organization. Classics aside, his reading was chiefly among contemporary authors, both Continental and English. Here too Leicester showed no interest in poetry, preferring the drama, to judge from the contemporary play-books he purchased, along with folio editions of Shakespeare, Jonson, and Beaumont and Fletcher. For English history and controversy he turned to Bede, Matthew Paris, William of Malmesbury, Hooker, Camden, Coke, and William Prynne.

But the intellectual world in which Leicester moved with greatest ease was that of the historians, chronographers, and court gossips of sixteenth- and early seventeenth-century Continental Latin culture, authors such as Giovanni Catena, Jean de Serres, Nicolas Vignier the Elder, Laurent Bouchel, Sethus Calvisius, and Johann Carion. Few of these authors, classical or contemporary, seem to be cited because Leicester agreed or disagreed with their ideas. Like Ayrault, they were used as source books for the collation and comparison of the ideas of different authors and for the evaluation of their authority. Leicester's method is evident in one comment on "Mr. Prynne, whose authority I do not valew, but only make use of his citations to see if they be right when I have time to looke upon the authors" (U1475 Z1/8, 156, margin). He saw his authors less as making an argument than as a source of learning to be situated in a complex of related ideas. The excerpts he quarried are often very long, as for example an exceptional body of selections in U1475 Z1 8 from the letters of Cardinal Arnaud d'Ossat. They must have taken him many weeks, perhaps months, to copy out. Evidently the very activity of copying was essential to him, for he possessed two printed copies of the text. The library was thus not exploited as the basis for either a chronological or discursive approach to the record of human knowledge. Rather, to Leicester it was "method," the ongoing activity of organization and annotation, that mattered, the constant process of assimilation during which one authority was compared with another (often with some skepticism) and where words and concepts were subjected to etymological, if not genuinely philological, analysis.

His many biblical and theological references reveal the rationale for Leicester's attempt to systematize the record of history as he understood it, and perhaps his seeming lack of concern, given the varying organization of his commonplace books, for bringing his system to perfection. A favorite book was St. Augustine's *De civitate dei*, where the insistence on the separation between the city of man and the city of God would have established for Leicester a fundamentally eschatological vision of the order of history, one which justified both his absorption in memoirs of court intrigue and his devout study of God's word. For this angry, reclusive man the central activity of philosophical and moral humanism could only take the form of exegesis, and it was in his great folio notebooks that he conducted that constant labor.

Though Leicester traveled between Penshurst and Leicester House regularly in the 1650s, after the early 1660s he resided at Penshurst, apparently sleeping in a study-bedroom off his library. In 1660 he complained to the exiled Algernon that his son had left him "sick, solitary and sad at Penshurst" and grumbled that "Disus of wryting, hath made it uneasy to me, age makes it hard, and the weakenes of sight and hand makes it almost impossible" (Blencowe 205). Algernon would return to Penshurst and his father's sickbed only weeks before the reclusive old earl expired. For unknown reasons, additions to the library catalogue ceased abruptly in 1665, but Leicester continued for some years to revise the will he had made in the same year, attempting to keep estate revenues, if not the title, from his heir. In the 1665 will, however, he had outlined a more generous plan for his intellectual heritage. Leicester left:

> the said bookes papers and other thinges ... to be used by my said son Viscount Lisle during his life. And after his decease I will and give the same to my grandchild Robert Sidney his eldest sonne for his use during his life and after to remaine from one heire Male to another. ... And I desire and require ... that every of them in his tyme do carefully look to and preserve the same for the good and benefitt of those that shall succeed them as I have done in my time and larger increased them. (CKS U1475 F32/4)

The inclusion of Leicester's papers in the legacy as well as his printed books projected the significance of his encyclopedic writings into the future, and signaled his hope that later Sidneys would benefit from them just as his father had preserved his readings for his own sons.

The second Earl of Leicester died at Penshurst on 2 November 1677, plunging his sons into a series of suits in Chancery as Algernon (supported for a time by Henry) fought Philip for his share of the estate (Scott, *Algernon/Restoration*). Leicester's later successors proved more interested in paintings than in their dusty library; decades later the unhappy seventh earl, in desperate financial straits, viewed the books simply as a commodity, and in 1743 sold what was left of them at auction (Warkentin, Black, and Bowen 38–40). But the papers Leicester sought to preserve as a legacy—including the library catalogue and the commonplace books—remained among the family muniments, to be deposited in 1923 with the Historical Manuscripts Commission, and in 1966 transferred to the Kent archives. There the great vellum folios remain, one of the last untapped resources for studying the intellectual world of the Sidneys.

Bibliography

Manuscript Sources

British Library, London
    Add. MS 4464 (excerpts by Thomas Birch from the lost commonplace book of Robert Sidney, second Earl of Leicester)
Centre for Kentish Studies, Maidstone
    CKS U1475 A41/1–14 (accounts of Philip Maret, 1618–26)
    CKS U1475 F32/4 (Robert Sidney, second Earl of Leicester's, will)
    CKS U1475 Z1/4–9, Z/9 [part of Z1/9] and Z/47 (Robert Sidney's commonplace books and papers)
    CKS U1475 Z45/2 (library catalogue)
    CKS U1500 C292/79 (mortgage transfer, 1623)
    CKS U1500 E120 (inventory, 1623)
    CKS U1500 E112, 113 (lists of books stolen and returned)

Primary and Secondary Sources

Adams, Simon. "Spain or the Netherlands?" *Before the English Civil War: Essays on Early Stuart Politics and Government*. Ed. Howard Tomlinson. London, Macmillan, 1983. 79–101.

Blencowe, R. W., ed. *Sydney Papers, Consisting of a Journal of the Earl of Leicester, and Original Letters by Algernon Sidney*. London, 1825.

Brennan, Michael G., and Noel J. Kinnamon. "Robert Sidney, 'Mr Johnson,' and the Education of William Sidney at Penshurst." *Notes & Queries* 50.4 (2003): 430–37.

Camden, William. *Remaines of a Greater Worke, concerning Britaine*. London: Simon Waterson, 1605.

Clarendon, Edward Hyde, Earl of. *The History of the Rebellion and Civil Wars in England Begun in the Year 1641*. Ed. William Dunn Macray. 6 vols. Oxford: Clarendon P, 1888.

Cobbett's Complete Collection of State Trials. Ed. Thomas Bayley Howell. 34 vols. London, 1808–28.

Collins, Arthur. *Letters and Memorials of State …*. 2 vols. London: T. Osborne, 1746.

Heffernan, Roger. *Illustrissimo nobilissimoque domino D. Roberto Sydnaeo Lecestriae comiti … ad Ludovicum XIII legato*. Paris (?), 1638 (?).

HMC. *Report on the Manuscripts of Lord De L'Isle and Dudley Preserved at Penshurst Place*. 6 vols. London: HMSO, 1925–66.

Scott, Jonathan. *Algernon Sidney and the English Republic 1623–1677*. Cambridge: Cambridge UP, 1988.

—. *Algernon Sidney and the Restoration Crisis 1677–83*. Cambridge: Cambridge UP, 1991.

Sharpe, Kevin. *Reading Revolutions: The Politics of Reading in Early Modern England*. New Haven, CT: Yale UP, 2000.

Shephard, Robert. "The Political Commonplace Books of Sir Robert Sidney." *SJ* 21.1 (2001): 1–30.

Sidney, Dorothy Percy. *The Correspondence (c. 1626–1659) of Dorothy Percy Sidney, Countess of Leicester*. Ed. Michael G. Brennan, Noel J. Kinnamon, and Margaret P. Hannay. Farnham: Ashgate, 2010.

Theophania: Or, Several Modern Histories Represented by Way of Romance, and Politickly Discours'd Upon. Ed. Renée Pigeon. Ottawa: Dovehouse Editions, 1999.

Warkentin, Germaine. "The Magnate and the Minister: Power and Property at Penshurst 1651–59." *SJ* 24.2 (2006): 1–13.

—, Joseph L. Black, and William R. Bowen, eds. *The Library of the Sidneys of Penshurst Place ca. 1665*. Toronto: U of Toronto P, 2013.

Wroth, Lady Mary. *The Second Part of the Countess of Montgomery's Urania*. Ed. Josephine A. Roberts, completed by Suzanne Gossett and Janel Mueller. Tempe, AZ: Arizona Center for Medieval and Renaissance Texts and Studies, 1999.

A Triptych of Dorothy Percy Sidney (1598–1659), Countess of Leicester, Lucy Percy Hay (1599–1660), Countess of Carlisle, and Dorothy Sidney Spencer (1617–1684), Countess of Sunderland

Nadine Akkerman[1]

While no expense was spared introducing the eminently marriageable Percy sisters Dorothy and Lucy (Illustration 26) at court during the festivities that accompanied the Palatine wedding in 1612/13, the attempts of Henry Percy (1564–1632), ninth Earl of Northumberland, and Dorothy Devereux (1563/65–1619) to control the love interests of their teenage daughters were in vain. The young Dorothy caught the eye of the much older Frederick Henry, future Prince of Orange, who had accompanied his nephew, the Elector Palatine, from the Low Countries to the Stuart court. John Chamberlain wrote to Dudley Carleton: "Here is whispering that the Count [Frederick] Henry of Nassau hath a month's mind to my Lord of Northumberland's daughter, which if it should fall right might prove a great match for her" (1:441). A year later, Walter, second Lord Scott of Buccleuch, also showed some interest (Betcherman 30). Dorothy, however, had fallen in love with Robert Sidney, heir to Viscount Lisle. Her mother conducted negotiations, but Robert's father did not feel the proposed dowry of £5,000 sufficient. He entered into negotiations with the Watson family instead, but his son was not keen, as Chamberlain noted: "It is thought the young gentleman inclines to a daughter of the Earl of Northumberland … [Robert] grows weary of hunting in a foiled scent, that hath been haunted by so many others" (2:571). Robert and Dorothy took matters into their own hands, marrying without either settlement or full parental consent; the marriage was kept secret, possibly for over a year (Betcherman 34; Atherton). Like her sister, Lucy also got engaged without first informing her father of her attachment to the fashionable spendthrift James Hay, a match brokered by her mother's friend Lucy Harington Russell, Countess of Bedford, Queen Anne's First Lady of the Bedchamber, who presumably envisioned a court career for Lucy similar to her own.

Both Dorothy and Lucy chose marriage candidates in the absence of their father, whom the Star Chamber had convicted as an accomplice in the Gunpowder Plot in 1606 and subsequently incarcerated in the Tower of London, where their grandfather had committed suicide. As a nobleman, Northumberland enjoyed relatively luxurious lodgings,

---

1   This research has been made possible by a VENI grant from the Netherlands Organisation for Scientific Research (NWO).

but remained an inmate until June 1621. His love of "scientific" instruments, medicine, anatomy, and alchemy earned him the epithet "the Wizard Earl" (Nicholls), but he took little interest in his daughters until they both visited the Martin Tower to announce their marriages. Dorothy's husband, noble scholar and diplomat Robert Sidney, was a match that the earl approved, raising the dowry to £6,000. Lucy's engagement to a recently widowed Scot twice her age with two young children was less popular, however, and he endeavored to detain her in the Tower, offering £20,000 to choose another. It was in vain, however, and the marriage went ahead when Lucy turned eighteen, the ceremony attended by her father, with grudging approval, as well as by the king and her future lover Buckingham.

As the title of Lita-Rose Betcherman's 2005 double biography *Court Lady and Country Wife* suggests, the adult lives of these sisters could barely have been more different. Lucy came to live in London's Upper Thames Street, where her husband, as Master of the Wardrobe, had luxurious lodgings: set on the path of a glittering court career, she attained the position of Lady of the Bedchamber by July 1626, having secured her place at court by the time her husband was called upon to travel the Continent as ambassador. Dorothy, on the other hand, had married the down-to-earth, studious Robert Sidney, a man accustomed to spending his days abroad as diplomat in Denmark, and later France. She led a relatively solitary existence, from 1623 running the country estate of Penshurst in his absence (*Correspondence DPS* 31). In a typical letter she writes of "the wood that has been sold at Penshurst these 3 years," how she had "mended the windows," that "the park is in very ill condition," and of the deer "killed by [her] appointment" (10 December 1638, *Correspondence DPS* 134).[2] In another letter to him, she plainly chokes back her envy of her sister's glamorous life:

> It is a month since I expected my sister's company, but my Lord Deputy is still thereabouts, and till he be gone I must not look for her … I will … content myself the best I can with this lonely life without envying the[ir] greatness, their plenty or their jollity. (10 November 1636, *Correspondence DPS* 74–5)

While Dorothy was pregnant for more than eleven years of her life, delivering fifteen children, of whom eight survived infancy, only in November 1618 would Lucy give birth to a son, who died within the month (Schreiber, *ODNB*). Reports of returning illnesses suggest possible miscarriages after her first pregnancy, with Thomas Wentworth receiving a letter saying in January 1633 that "[m]y Lady Carlile also hath not been well of late, looks well, but hath utterly lost her Stomach [that is, her appetite (*OED* n.5a) or her sexual lust (*OED* n.1g)], insomuch that she is forced to leave the Court for awhile, and lye at [her] House in the Strand" (Strafford 1:177). The following lines of William Cartwright's "A Panegyrick to the Most Noble Lucy Countess of Carlisle" comment upon Lucy's possible sterility, connecting it to her career as "court beauty":

> Oh had you Of-spring to resemble you,
> As you have Vertues, then—But oh I do
> Complain of our misfortunes, not your Own,
> For are bless'd Spirits, for less happy known
> Because they have not receiv'd such a Fate
> Of Imperfection, as to Procreate?
> Eternall things supply themselves; so we
> Think this your Mark of Immortalitie. (ll. 129–63)

---

2 All quoted letters from *Correspondence DPS* are to her husband Robert Sidney, second Earl of Leicester, unless otherwise noted.

The letters that passed between the sisters suggest that Dorothy felt the strain of keeping up the "high huswifery" Ben Jonson had praised in her mother-in-law, keeping Penshurst ready for unexpected visits, such as those from her sister: "To have her linen, plate, and all things, nigh / When she was far: and not a room but dressed / As if it had expected such a guest!" (Jonson, "To Penshurst" ll. 84–8). While Dorothy played "the ill housewife" (*Correspondence DPS* 103), letters she received from Lady Carlisle suggest that her sister was using her influence at court to obtain Robert Sidney an office which would free him from ambassadorial missions.

When it came to Lucy's own husband, however, different rules seemed to apply. A mere two years into her marriage it appeared that her father's misgivings had proved correct, with Lucy reportedly acting coldly on her husband's unexpected return from an embassy to Heidelberg and Vienna in January 1620. This news was swiftly communicated abroad, as Tobie Matthew noted in a postscript to an undated newsletter to Hay:

> It hath been written hither [on the Continent], that there is grown some little disgust between your noble Lady & your selfe, sauinge that no disgust xx ^can be^ little, between such a couple of creatures, as you two[)].[3] But for my part, I am resolued not only that it is (excuse the fouleword word) a Lye; but that, it shall euer be so ^so^. (Tobie Matthew to Doncaster, undated, BL Egerton MS 2595 fol. 164v)

The French ambassador to the Stuart court, Comte de Tillières, reported to his officials that it was the Marquis of Buckingham, royal favorite and the most powerful man in England, excepting perhaps King James himself, who stalled the then Viscount Doncaster's revocation in order to create an opportunity to seduce his wife: "They say that it is not the King's business that necessitates the ambassador's return visit to the Emperor ... but to consummate a love that the Marquis of Buckingham has for someone very close to him" (Betcherman 63). Lucy's adulterous affair with Buckingham was common knowledge, but her marriage does not seem to have suffered as a result.

Her infidelity did cause its share of salacious gossip, however, the undated and anonymous libel "The Progress" drawing a humorous and not entirely flattering bibliographical comparison between the now Earl of Carlisle's public generosity to his houseguests and his private entertainment of his wife:

> My Lord Carliles voluminous boord
> And dishes in folio do affoord
> Great entertainment to his friends
> Whom virtue, or his wife commends. (Bellany and McRae, libel R5 ll. 37–40)

Whether wittingly or unwittingly, the balladeer picks up the hospitality motif of Jonson's country house poem, but these relations of the Sidneys have become over-liberal. The earl's public hospitality comes in folio, the biggest, most lavish and costly printed format, paving the way for a simultaneously lewd and denigrating metaphor:

> But shee poore Lady must bee fed
> With decimo sexto in his bed
> And takes no pleasure to read int
> Beecause it is too small a print. (ll. 41–4)

---

3   There is one closing parenthesis missing in the MS.

Whereas the earl's friends feast on the grandest of "dishes" (l. 38), his wife is "fed" (l. 41) "in his bed," with a mere "decimo sexto" (l. 42), a far smaller and cheaper format whose multiple folds squeeze sixteen leaves from a single broadsheet: the folio's single fold provides but two. It is no surprise, the poet intimates, that Lady Carlisle seeks a format she can get her teeth into when fed such a meager diet at home. Her husband—whose 1628 portrait, by an unknown artist, now hanging in the National Portrait Gallery, illustrates vividly why Elizabeth Stuart, sometime Queen of Bohemia, called him "filthy, ugly Camel's face," albeit teasingly (Stuart 1:824)—was no match for the dashing young Buckingham.

When Buckingham installed his wife and other relatives as ladies-in-waiting in Henrietta Maria's household so that he could effectively spy on the queen, he put forward Lucy for the office of Lady of the Bedchamber. Initially, Henrietta Maria objected to the appointment because her Grand Almoner, Daniel du Plessis, Bishop of Mende, had informed her that the Earl of Carlisle and Buckingham schemed to make Lucy Charles's mistress.[4] Still, the appointment was made in July 1626 and Lucy quickly became the queen's favorite. Mistress to the powerful Buckingham and favorite of the queen was an irresistible combination, and Lucy became both exceptionally influential and hated by Buckingham's wife and female relatives. His wife Katherine, Duchess of Buckingham, wrote to him in La Rochelle:

> I hope you will remember your promise in making hast home for I will assure you both ^for^ the publicke and our privat good here in cort ^ther is great neede of you^ for xxxx your great lady that~you take so~ you beleeue is so much your frend uses your frends somthing worse then when you were here and your fauour has made her so great as now shee cares for nobody. ([October?] 1627, TNA SP 16/81 fol. 49r)

If telling her husband that his mistress cannot be checked is not enough to persuade him to end the affair, the duchess concludes by reminding him of his familial obligations: "my child begines to stere~well~ strongly" (fol. 48v).[5]

Not even the resentment of Buckingham's wife, however, could alter Lucy's position at court, where immediate access to the queen's ear allowed her to press her husband's suits. A letter from Secretary of State Sir Edward Conway to Carlisle shows her brokering did not go unnoticed:

> I knowe nothinge that should haste you hither ... Sure I am your Lordship can finde nothinge here comparable to the noble gracious Societie of your excellent Ladie, the glory of her Sexe, and ornament of the Age; and your excellent help. (5 June 1626, BL Egerton MS 2597 fol. 13r)

Yet such influence had a price: Carlisle's tacit acceptance of her continued relations with the duke. On his appointment as Stuart ambassador extraordinary to France in January 1628, rumors quickly arose that Carlisle was again being: "sent awaie only to be put out of the waie, & to be saued from doeing the Duke ill offices or not good offices ... but for that end of putting him off for the better access to his Ladie in his absence." However, the letter writer scornfully added that such measures were to no real purpose, as the earl had

---

4 Schreiber, "First Carlisle" 97 refers to Bishop of Mende to Cardinal Richelieu (24 July 1626, TNA PRO 31/3 no. 64 fol. 114r); Wolfson 318 transcribes Mende's letter as: "Son soin principal est maintenant de donner à son maistre de nouvelles affections: à cet effet, il fait ses efforts pour establir la Comtesse de Carlisle, Dame du lict, espérant que l'occasion luy en fera naistre le dessein." See also Betcherman 86, 89.

5 Buckingham's male heir and namesake was born on 30 January 1628.

always turned a blind eye to his wife's sexual liaison: "[I]n truth it needed not for he was quyett enough with all was done by her." When the sitting Parliament assigned Lucy a pension of £2,000, presumably at Buckingham's behest, Carlisle's acquiescence meant he was effectively operating as her pimp. Yet, the writer speculated, Carlisle and his wife would never see a penny:

> [F]or my opinion is he shall not be halfe his iourney before she be turnd out of the Court, for both the Dukes mother, his Ladie, and his Sister doe hate her euen to death not merely for my Lo Dukes lying with her but also for that she hath the ~~Dukes~~ Queenes hart aboue them all so as in comparison she valleweth them at nothing—she hath alredie brought her to paynt [that is, to use make-up] & in tyme she may by her example be ledd vnto more debauchednes. (John Hope to "some at Brussels," TNA SP 16/101 fol. 93)

By 1628 Lucy was as dangerously influential as the hated Buckingham—an influence she established by moving in Buckingham's orbit and so securing the queen's favor. When he was assassinated in August that year, all this changed.

Lucy's own feelings for the duke or her reaction to his murder are not recorded, but his loss left her vulnerable: with her husband away from court, she became seriously ill. Her brother Henry wrote to her stepson at Turin: "I had heard the day before being the 2 of Sep*tember* that she was past all hope, ~~and~~ her doctors had giuen her ouer." As a last resort, physicians decided "to let her bloud under the tounge, from ~~it~~ which place they^re^ came a quart of bloud mingled with filthy matter, w^h^ich was the sole cause of her health," according to a letter sent by Henry Percy to James Hay (4 September 1628, TNA SP 16/116 fol. 51r). Two months later she was able to write to her husband that she was recovering from the smallpox (23 November 1628, TNA SP 16/120 fol. 89v). This disease was much feared, especially by court ladies, as those who did not figure in the 30 percent mortality rate were often left with severe facial scarring. Lucy wore a mask from the moment she had become ill, and insisted on wearing it for months after, noting that the queen has given her "leaue to keepe one my maske & which wase neuer of sence my siknes." In the same letter she urged her husband to come home quickly because the signs were fading: "I wishe you maye find sume markes of my uilanus [that is, villainous] diseas; which you shall not do with^out^ you returne uerie shortlie; I wase by euerie creatur not thought posible to recouer, and am mutch satisfyd with my self for I find I fear not death" (3 October 1628, TNA SP 16/118 fols. 19v–20r). Within a month Lucy appears to have recovered fully: "My Lady mistris is now at Penshurst very well in health and in noe danger of an imprinted face" (George Goring to Carlisle, 29 September 1628, TNA SP 16/529 fol. 36v).

Dorothy not only nursed her sister at Penshurst and later Essex House, but might have looked after her in other respects as well. Carlisle's absence meant that he could not take part in the power struggle that ensued as courtiers fought over Buckingham's now-vacant offices. Lucy was too weak to protect her husband's interests, but in December 1628 a letter writer tried to assure Carlisle, then in Brussels, that they were in hand:

> There hathe beene some secret woorking, for your continewance abroad by those who caryeth an outward shew of frendship to your lo: … (you are wyse anewgh and doeth well know your haters and your lovers) but your Master is faythfull and loving and you need not feare there malice) and as I am informed fayre *Lucibella* or rather *Philoclea* hathe played her trew part which doeth still more and more procure my trew loue and respect you will know muche more at your returne. (TNA SP 16/123 fol. 10r)

Lucibella translates as "the beautiful Lucy," but it is not Lucy/Lucibella who "played her trew part," but "rather *Philoclea*," a character from Sidney's *Arcadia*; Philoclea's identity is revealed in one of Edmund Waller's poems, "On My Lady Dorothy Sidney's Picture":

> Such was Philoclea, and such Dorus' flame!
> The matchless Sidney, that immortal frame
> Of perfect beauty, on two pillars placed;
> Not his high fancy could one pattern, graced
> With such extremes of excellence, compose;
> Wonders so distant in one face disclose! (ll. 1–6)

Waller later immortalized the Sidneys' eldest daughter, Dorothy Sidney Spencer (later Smythe), Countess of Sunderland (Illustration 27), or Doll, as Sacharissa, but here addresses her as Philoclea. (The affectionate nickname "Doll" for Dorothy was a common enough contraction, but also carried the slight scent of something a little less savory, as two literary Dolls, *The Alchemist*'s Doll Common and *Henry IV Part 2*'s Doll Tearsheet, attest). How the eleven-year-old Doll might have served as proxy to her inconvenienced aunt Lucy is difficult to imagine, but years later Doll's husband Sunderland would also link the two ladies and their affinity for politics, excusing himself for not writing to Lady Leicester ("Pray let my Lady Leicester know that to write news, without or with a cypher, is inconvenient"), but in the same letter full of military and political news, assuring his Doll "I am your and Lady Carlisle's servant" (Ady Cartwright 31).

Salon Culture

Without Buckingham's protection, the Carlisles were vulnerable, albeit temporarily. Lucy was banished from court in January 1630 following an altercation with Charles de l'Aubespine, Marquis de Châteauneuf, the French ambassador, but by the following February she was back in the queen's bedchamber, her influence at court reasserted (*CSPV* 22:264; Smuts, "Puritan"; Smuts, "Religion"; Wolfson 327–9; Betcherman 119). Courtiers flocked to Whitehall to pay their respects, increasingly so as her influence grew:

> [M]ore pleasure it were to me to perform this duty in your lodginge at Court when you see your perfections in ~~in~~ the glasse [that is, the mirror] addinge perfection to perfection ~~to perfection~~ aproouing the *bonne mots* there spoken in your presence, moderatinge the exscesse [*sic*] of compliments, passinge ouer a dull gest, without a sweete smile, giuinge a wise answer to an extrauagant question.

The sixty-year-old earl wished to be "yonge againe," then he "shuld be a most humble sutor," wishing her "lodginge might be [his] Academie quittinge [that is, leaving] to the rest both Italie and France" (William, Earl of Exeter, to Lucy, undated [1634?], TNA SP 16/280 fol. 30r). The Sidneys also benefited from the Carlisles' newly-regained influence: in 1631 the earl assisted them in getting a license from the king to build their own grand London mansion, Leicester House, near Covent Garden, with Dorothy overseeing the design (*Correspondence DPS* 31).

Betcherman rejects the idea, propagated by Erica Veevers and Julie Sanders, that Lucy formed "a rival salon to the Queen's at her house in the Strand," suggesting that "[r]ather than competing with the Queen, Lucy's gatherings may be said to have been the anteroom to Henrietta Maria's salon for aspiring dramatists and poets. A well-phrased tribute to Lady Carlisle could have served as a letter of recommendation to the royal patron" (165–6). This seems plausible, as it would have resembled Lucy's duties as Lady of the Bedchamber, such as accepting petitions and passing them and other messages on to her mistress if deemed worthy. The fact remains that whether rivaling or complementing each other, there were two literary salons at the Caroline court by the 1630s: one presided over by the queen, the other by Lady Carlisle. Henrietta Maria embraced *préciosité*, "the set of manners and literary tastes that had developed in France during the opening years of the seventeenth century" (Veevers 14), rooted in the notion of *honnêteté*, a religious fashion appropriate to a queen:

> The concept of *honnêteté* ... invested women with the Neoplatonic qualities—Beauty, Virtue, and Love—... it recommended a conservative [proto-]feminism, in which women exercised their beauty and virtue in such a way as to make for cordial relations between the sexes and for a general social harmony governed by religion. (Veevers 2–3)

As Lady of the Bedchamber, Lady Carlisle stuck to the more traditional, secular strand of *préciosité*: in an atmosphere of platonic love, men worshipped her as the epitome of a French *salonnière*—in this context, there was endless sexual teasing without the promise of consummation (Veevers 3). Poets portrayed the queen as "affectionate and demonstrative ... as giving, as well as receiving virtuous love," whereas they portrayed Lady Carlisle as one of the "cold-hearted shepherdesses of the romances": Henrietta as "soft" and "sweet"; Lady Carlisle as "dazzling and disdainful" (Veevers 35).

Sir Tobie Matthew's prose work "A Character of the Most Excellent Lady, Lucy Countess of Carlisle" (1636), published posthumously by John Donne Junior as prefatory to a collection of Matthew's letters, paints Lady Carlisle in the Petrarchan mold. According to Matthew, Lady Carlisle's friendships are self-serving: "She is too high a mind and dignity, not onely to seek, but almost to wish, the friendship of any Creature: They whom she is pleased to chuse, are such, as are of the most eminent condition, both for Power and Employments ..." (A4r–v). Incapable of loving another:

> she will freely discourse of Love, and hear both the fancies and powers of it; but if you will ... boldly direct it to her self, she is likely to divert the discourse, or, at least, seem not to understand it ... since she cannot love in earnest, she would have nothing from Love. So contenting her self to play with love, as with a child. (A5v)

Disdainful to the point of arrogance, "She believeth nothing to be worthy of her consideration, but her own imaginations ... since, in the world, she cannot find any thing worthy of her loving" (A7v). Her wit, "kindle[d]" by a "cholerick disposition," "hath a sharpnesse, and strength, and taste, to disrelish, if not to kill, the proudest hopes which you can have, of her value of you" (A8r). "She more willingly allowes of the conversation of Men, than of Women" (A5r). Because of this and because of the fact that her wit and beauty "far exceeds" the wit and beauty of all other women, "She is more esteemed than beloved by her own Sex" (A7r).

For Matthew, Lucy's understanding of love is only skin-deep. This accords with John Suckling's thoughts, who, excluded from her inner circle, must, along with other men pour scorn on the veneer they can see. His sensual, witty poem "Upon My Lady Carliles Walking in Hampton-Court Garden" (written *c.* 1628–32), a barely disguised dialogue between himself and fellow poet Thomas Carew, sees the two poets undressing Lucy with their eyes, taking advantage of her reputation as sexual temptress as well as the *salonnière* who, placed on a pedestal, encourages sexual banter. (As such, it would not have roused her anger; if it had been set in the context of the queen's salon, however, it would have been highly inappropriate to the point of treason.) Still, it is hard to imagine that Suckling would have written the following final stanza had Buckingham still been alive:

> 'Troth in her face I could descry
> No danger, no divinity.
> But since the pillars were so good
> On which the lovely fountain stood,
> Being once come so near, I think
> I should have ventur'd hard to drink.
> What ever fool like me had been
> If I'd not done as well as seen?
> There to be lost why should I doubt,
> Where fools with ease go in and out? (ll. 40–49)

Lucy's appearance is deceptive. Thom points out that there is "great danger" (l. 33) behind the mask. While the innuendo mounts, Lucy's actual character remains as elusive as her thirst for political intrigue was notorious. J. S. can neither discern "danger" nor "divinity" (l. 41); he can neither see her as a *femme fatale* nor as a saint, the two literary appearances granted her. On the one hand, these last lines describe a fantasy of oral sex; on the other, they comment upon the privileged access to the chambers of power granted only to some. Lady Carlisle controlled patronage and access.

One of the most passionate admirers frequenting Lucy's salon was her cousin Henry Rich, first Earl of Holland. Dorothy thought Holland's attempts to become one of her sister's servants ludicrous: "Many verses he has lately written to her which are the worst that ever were seen," she wrote (*Correspondence DPS* 115; see also Strafford 2:48). Holland started paying compliments to Lucy in December 1631, around the same time as Thomas Wentworth. Wentworth seems to have been so smitten by her that one of the first paintings he shipped from England to Ireland when he was installed as Lord Deputy was one of Lady Carlisle.[6] Wentworth despised Holland; they inhabited opposing court factions—Holland's pro-French, Wentworth's pro-Spanish. Wentworth's jealousy was apparent when he wrote to Carlisle in June 1633:

> [W]ee heare ther is greate curtesye spasse betwixt your Lordship and my Lord of Hollande, and heare all his freinds make ~~great~~ ^mighty^ addresses to my Ladye but weather out of true respectts [*sic*] to you two singly; or complicated wth sum secrett designe to fortifie themselues the better, to make themselues more all to ballance, to doe the Treasurer a shrewde sume; I conceaue may in good iudgmentt be doubted; for I am one of this that beleeue noe miracles, but that freindshipps which are to be trusted, growe vp *per media*, vpon sum noble precedent existent matter, wheare thes which ^are^ skiped into >thus< *per salta*, are for the most partte only to serue turnes, and deceatfully temporary, and therfore euer to be suspected. It must be time and your owne wisedomes which must discouer this mistery … hauing my self noe other interest then to

---

6   In 1636 Wentworth and Lady Carlisle also exchanged Van Dyck portraits of themselves: see Shaw nn38, 75.

> desire that all may succeede to the honoure and happinesse of your Lordship
> and my Ladye. (25 June 1633, BL Egerton MS 2597 fol. 140v)

Wentworth competed for her attention, writing to Conway in March 1635: "You might tell her sometimes when she looks at herself at night in the glass that I have the ambition to be one of those servants she will suffer to honour her" (Betcherman 138). When the Earl of Carlisle was dying, Lucy humbly wrote to Wentworth, soliciting "an absolut security" of his protection. Wentworth replied courteously: "Surely Madam there were many of Greater vnderstanding and power you might haue Commanded, but not any that will more readily and Chearfully serue you then myself" (7 September 1635, Sheffield Central Library, Strafford Papers, Fitzwilliam MSS 15 fol. 211r; and his answer of 14 October 1635, 8 fol. 287r). In fact, both Holland and Wentworth became her protectors when she was widowed in April 1636. Lady Carlisle had no difficulty playing them, ensuring that she had friends in both court factions. Dorothy writes: "My sister … is greater in her own conceit than ever she was, for her two gallants are more her slaves than I think ever men were to any woman" (17 November 1636, *Correspondence DPS* 77). Together with the sisters' brother Northumberland, Holland was made Keeper of Nonsuch, an office coveted by Carlisle since May 1620: this ensured Lucy's continued use of her lodgings in the palace (Betcherman 152). Wentworth, as Lord Deputy of Ireland, became her trustee and financial adviser, and managed her Irish wine customs and interests from the lands in the County of Wicklow, the so-called Birnes Country, which she had inherited from the Earl of Carlisle (Betcherman 169). In return, Lucy used her influence with the queen, with Archbishop William Laud, for example, writing to Wentworth to ask if Lucy could smooth the way when he needed to confront Henrietta Maria about the increasing numbers of courtiers converting to Roman Catholicism in 1637. Wentworth approved, writing to Laud:

> I judge her Ladyship very considerable; for she is often in Place, and is extreamely well skilled how to speak with Advantage and Spirit for those Friends she professeth unto, which will not be many. There is this further in her Disposition, she will not seem to be the Person she is not, an Ingenuity I have always observed and honoured. (Strafford 2:120; see also Betcherman 175)

Those whom Lucy favored were few, but well served: her husband's death presented a new opportunity for writers and those with suits to press. For instance, William Davenant wrote "To the Countess of Carlile, on the Death of the Earle Her Husband," William Habington "To the Right Honourable the Countesse of C.," and Robert Herrick "Hesperides".

While powerful men protected her and poets sang her praises, her sister Dorothy grew increasingly impatient:

> [My sister] is here [fu]ll of ill humour … Her great fortune, the observations of powerful men, and the flatteries of some mean ones doth make her less sufferable than ever she was. And though I believe she might do us man[y] courtesies on diverse occasions ye[t] is it impossible for me to stoop s[o] to her as I think she expects, but I will keep myself from being at any great distance with her if I can. (*Correspondence DPS* 82)

Dorothy had expected Lucy to ensure Leicester would succeed Sir John Coke as Secretary of State or Wentworth as Lord Deputy of Ireland. While Lucy waded in luxury, she and Leicester struggled to make ends meet, Leicester being sent away on embassies without a decent salary. Dorothy blamed Coke, whom she dismissively called an "old man"

(17 November [1636], *Correspondence DPS* 77) for failing to ensure that gratuities were paid or writing letters to friends in high places, such as Holland, to get her husband another appointment: "God grant he [Leicester] may speedily and well acquit himself of this employment, and it shall be part of my litany to deliver all my friends from embassies till Secretary Coke be laid down in peace" (undated [between October 1636 and January 1637?], *Correspondence DPS* 72). She grew bitter, writing in partial code to her husband in France:

> I shall be in much hope that you will succeed 200 [Thomas Wentworth], whom they say will only stay the accomplishment of what he has undertaken, but I fear that 154 [the Countess of Carlisle], who has more power with him than any creature, will do nothing for our good. (10 January [1636/37], *Correspondence DPS* 95)

In the mid-1630s Dorothy was concerned not only with her husband's advancement, but with that of her eldest daughter, Doll; in this she would again feel unsupported by Lucy. Several matches for the young Dorothy faltered. (While Edmund Waller made her the object of his affection, as evidenced by the approximately twenty poems he wrote in her honor, he was never considered a truly eligible marriage candidate.) When Doll was only nineteen her mother grew desperate: "It grieves me often to see that our poor Doll is sought by none and that she will be shortly called a stale maid" (25 October 1636, *Correspondence DPS* 69). Accordingly, the family worked anxiously to find her a suitable husband. She spent three years in the hope of concluding a match between her daughter and William Cavendish (1617–84), in 1628 third Earl of Devonshire, brother of Doll's close friend Anne (the "Amoret" of Waller's poetry—Chernaik).

The search for a suitable match for Doll was much aided by Dorothy's taking up residence in London in order to oversee the construction of Leicester House, the license for which had been granted in 1631. Leicester House, constructed in lavish style in what is now London's Leicester Square, was something of a double-edged sword for Dorothy. It was an expensive business, designing and building a new home, and in a letter dated 26 September (1636?), she writes:

> And now I will tell you of our works at London. The great chamber, the anteroom and the stairs are very handsomely fretted after a new way which cost about 80*ll*. … All this I fear will not be done for the money which we reserve only for these purposes. The smith's work also will take away some of it. But I will take the best care that I can that it may go as far as it is possible. (*Correspondence DPS* 61–2)

A London residence was an opportunity to entertain, and the family spent every winter there, with Lucy numbering among their most regular visitors. Indeed, in 1637 Dorothy was "put out to hear that Lucy was stabling her horses and keeping her servants at Leicester House without even asking her" (Betcherman 169). Leicester House became something of a salon, with Sir Edward Hyde noting in 1641 that she "drew the principal persons who were the most obnoxious to the Court and to whom the Court was most obnoxious, to a constant conversation" (Clarendon 1:434–5), with one of her anti-royalist visitors, John Pym, being the later object of Lucy's largesse. Within six years of its construction the house was under repair, the workmen languishing unpaid—Leicester House revolved around money, and it took all of Dorothy's skills to keep estate and London residence out of the hands of creditors.

As for finding a husband for the young Dorothy in London, Doll's maternal uncle Henry did not believe a suitable husband could be found in England, concluding his letter to

Doll's mother: "Give me leave to present my humble service to my Lady Dorothy, and tell he[r sh]e must go into France; [w]hat [h]er beauty and father's wisdom [will] do, the Lord knows" (Henry Percy, Baron Percy of Alnwick, to Dorothy, undated [4 February 1636/37], *Correspondence DPS* 102). Doll did not join her father's embassy in France, remaining with her mother in London. Increasingly desperate, her mother ill-advisedly attempted to marry off Doll to John Lovelace (1615/16–70), second Baron Lovelace, but found herself in a quandary when he showed his libertine streak:

> And now concerning Doll, of whom I can neither say what I desire, nor what I thought I should have done, for I find my Lord Lovelace so uncertain and so idle, so much addicted to mean company and so easily drawn to debauchery as it is now my study how to break off with him in such a manner as it may be said that we refused him. ... Many particulars I could tell you of his wildness ... though his estate is good, his person pretty enough, and his wit much more than ordinary, yet dare I not venture to give Doll to him. (18 May 1637, *Correspondence DPS* 127)

The negotiations with Devonshire also foundered, an outcome potentially damaging to Doll's reputation because Henry Rich, Earl of Holland, had already advertised the match as going ahead:

> And concerning my Lord of Devonshire I can say as little to please you, for though his mother and sister made fair shows of good intentions to us, yet in the end we find them just as I expected, full of deceit and juggling. The sister is gone from this town but the young lord is still here, who never visited us but once and yet all the town spoke of a marriage which I think came upon my Lord of Holland's divulging his confidence that it would be so. (18 May 1637, *Correspondence DPS* 127–8)

Rightly sensing that negotiations with Devonshire would come to nothing (he married Elizabeth Cecil in March 1639), Dorothy blamed Lucy, thinking she had placed courtly politics over familial concerns, luring Devonshire away from Doll to persuade him to marry Mademoiselle de Rohan instead (Ady Cartwright 19).

With Dorothy's failure, Henry Percy's suggestion became irresistible, and matters were handed over to her husband in France. Robert Sidney invited the nineteen-year-old Henry Spencer, who had hoped to marry Elizabeth Cecil, the lady for whom Devonshire had turned down Doll, to take an interest in his daughter instead. A Van Dyck painting was sent to France so that Leicester could show off his daughter to her potential suitor: "Doll's picture shall be sent to you immediately after we come to London," his wife wrote (9 December 1638, *Correspondence DPS* 133; Betcherman 189). Dorothy's high hopes become apparent from her ordering sheets from France in "yellow damask," writing "if it please God to bless our endeavours it may come seasonably for Doll" (15 January 1638/39, *Correspondence DPS* 142). The painting of Doll (Illustration 27) as a shepherdess was indeed captivating enough to persuade Spencer to propose marriage. Wounded in his pride by her engagement to another man, the ultimate rejection by Sacharissa, Waller wrote his last poem to Doll, "At Penshurst":

> To thee a wild and cruel soul is given,
> More deaf than trees, and prouder than the heaven!
> Love's foe professed! Why dost thou falsely feign
> Thyself a Sydney? ... (ll. 7–10)

Such deafness to his professions of love, such coldness, was unworthy for a Sidney, Waller claimed. She betrayed the spirit of Jonson's "To Penshurst," where ladies were "noble, fruitful, chaste withal" (l. 90) and welcoming to their guests. Despite Waller's cry from the heart, Doll and Henry married at Penshurst on 11 July 1639 (*Correspondence DPS* xxv).

If failed marriage negotiations had strained relations between the sisters, the Wars of the Three Kingdoms would again unite them, even as it divided the family at large.

The Bishops' Wars

When the clashes which became known as the Bishops' Wars began, as Charles I tried to impose an episcopal system upon the Presbyterian-inclined Church of Scotland, bringing the subject of curtailing the powers of the Crown into relief, all pensions were suspended. Dorothy wrote to her husband: "I hear the King has forbidden the payment of any pension till the affairs of Scotland be composed … how 154 [Countess of Carlisle] takes this restraint I do not know" (4 December 1638, *Correspondence DPS* 131).

Times grew increasingly desperate for Lucy. Even though Wentworth claimed he did all he could, her Irish lands rendered little profit. Perhaps she had to pawn the £1,500 diamond necklace Holland bestowed on her in 1639 as a New Year's gift (Donagan 339), just as Dorothy had pawned her jewellery to keep Penshurst running and build Leicester House (*Correspondence DPS* 99). Lucy corresponded more frequently with Dorothy and Leicester, mostly about the Scottish conflicts—a precursor of the Civil Wars in England. Lucy instructed Leicester to send her a cipher key so that she could communicate more freely (Leicester to Lucy, 16 August 1639, KHLC U1475 C.87/1A).[7] Secrets of state, which the queen had communicated to Lucy in confidence, such as that Ireland was gathering an army of ten thousand soldiers to rise against Scotland in name of the king, thus found their way to the Stuart embassy in France.[8] Richelieu's spies had won over Leicester's secretary, René Augier (Atherton). Leicester's letters were read by the cardinal. It is tempting to speculate that Lucy might have been aware of Richelieu's infiltration of her brother-in-law's embassy, and purposely fed Richelieu state secrets. After all, Richelieu was in close contact with the leader of the Scottish Presbyterians, the Earl of Argyll, who tried to foment rebellion against their king. Lucy neither addresses nor signs these coded letters to Leicester, which are unmistakably in her hand. Politically astute and fully aware that letters could be intercepted, she writes to her sister:

> Let me know whether you understand my writing this way [in cipher] and whether there be danger of having the letters either lost or intercepted, for I have some things that I dare scarce write you, and I am not certain that you understand them when I do, and my heart would not conceal anything from you, so much it love and trust you. (5 December 1639, *Correspondence DPS* 148)

Wentworth, by then Earl of Strafford, was the first of Lucy's friends lost in the conflict between king and Parliament. Her brother Henry Percy had failed to organize his escape;

---

7   Leicester's endorsement reads: "To my Lady of Carlisle 16: Aug: 1639. with a cipher sent vnto her by her commandements."

8   Lucy to Dorothy, 5 December 1639, *Correspondence DPS* 147. Even though the letter was written to Dorothy, the endorsement in Leicester's hand suggests that Dorothy forwarded the letter to her husband.

members of the First Army Plot fled to France, where Dorothy, who had joined her husband's embassy, tried to offer them refuge. After Wentworth's execution in 1641, her brother-in-law succeeding him as Lord Lieutenant of Ireland, Lucy warmed to John Pym and betrayed the king's party. Even contemporaries were mystified by this change of allegiance, as the memoirs of Sir Philip Warwick testify: "that busy Stateswoman, the Countess of Carlisle (who had now changed her Gallant from Strafford to Mr. Pym, and was become such a She-Saint, that she frequented their sermons, and took notes)" (Warwick 204). Perhaps disappointed that the king could not even protect those closest to him, or perhaps seeing Wentworth in a different light when she discovered during his trial that he had skimmed profits from her Irish interests (Betcherman 229), Lucy started to play a double game. She frequented Viscount Mandeville's estate in Chelsea, where parliamentary leaders such as Essex, Warwick, and Newport, and those disaffected with the king's party, such as her old admirer, Holland, gathered. She returned to court with secret papers, deemed valuable enough for Sir Edward Nicholas to wish to print them, letting her mistress Henrietta Maria believe that she, as her cunning and faithful Lady of the Bedchamber, obtained intelligence from the parliamentarians (Evelyn 4:75). Instead, she was providing the queen misinformation to create unrest, possibly on Pym's orders (Betcherman 236).

Like secretaries, ladies-in-waiting were close to the source of power, able to follow the queen's every move and eavesdrop effectively. Lucy overheard that Charles wanted to impeach Pym, Denzil Holles, John Hampden, William Stroud, and Sir Arthur Haselrig. She warned Pym. John Rusworth relates how Pym stood up in the House stating he had "private intimation from the Countess of Carlisle that endeavours would be used this day to apprehend" him and his four companions (Betcherman 237; Warwick 204). Having obtained leave from the House, they scurried away moments before the king stormed in to do just that. While the parliamentarians were forever grateful (see Bulstrode Whitelocke in Betcherman 238, and Haselrig's 1658/59 confession in Burton 3:93), the king's party had seen the true colors of a treacherous spy. Lady Carlisle tried to convince Charles not to leave London, but to no avail (Donagan 347); the king moved his court to Oxford. The Civil War had begun.

The Civil War

In January 1643 Parliament took measures to control communication between parliamentarian London and royalist Oxford. Two laws were passed: the first stating "That no Carriers, Waggoners, carts or waggons, or horses laden with any commodities whatsoeuer, shall be permitted hereafter to go from hence or elsewhere to Oxford, or any part of the Kings Army ... without the special license [of parliament]," while the second deemed "That if the Agent or Servant to any person that bear Arms against the Parliament, shall presume hereafter to come to Westminster, or reside here about London, That he shall be forthwith apprehended as a Spy" (*House of Commons Journal* 2:17 January 1643). The fact that Lady Carlisle was allowed to continue to rent Little Salisbury House suggests that all believed her a parliamentarian. Lucy had the perfect cover to turn again, to act as intelligencer for the royalist cause.

Meanwhile, her sister Dorothy used similar tactics, but playing the other side. While her family fought for the king, there was no cause to suspect her of keeping contact with Roundheads. She encouraged Pym to write to her: "Mr Pym need not fear the miscarriage of his letters to me, for they have not opened any one of mine since I left London" (Dorothy to William Hawkins, 31 August [1642], *Correspondence DPS* 167). Her affections might have changed when the twenty-three-year-old Spencer, Doll's husband, newly created Earl of Sunderland, the son-in-law she had always craved, lost his life at the First Battle of Newbury, his body so desecrated by parliamentarians as to be unfit for burial (Betcherman 256). When the news of his death reached her, "through the extremity of her sorrow she fell into a swoune" (J. Sudbury to the Earl of Leicester, 24 September 1643, HMC, *De L'Isle and Dudley* 6:434). Also, Dorothy could only just prevent Penshurst from being sequestered by the parliamentarians (*Correspondence DPS* 40).

In 1644 Lucy's London residence, Little Salisbury House, became a hotbed of royalist plotters. Denzil Holles sat in the House of Commons and as a member was thus forbidden by order "to visit foreign representatives" (Crawford 109). Yet he, Holland, and Sir Philip Stapleton met Sabran, a French agent, at Lucy's residence; Sabran was to persuade Charles I first to accept Presbyterianism in exchange for back-up of a Scottish army, and later, when this plan failed, to comply with peace negotiations with Parliament (Crawford 109). In 1647 the army charged Denzil Holles and ten others "for meeting together at the Lady Carlisles Lodgings in White-hall; and other places, with other disaffected persons" (Prynne 8). They declared:

> that within the time there limited for those meetings to have bin, and at no time before or since, they have at all bin at her Ladiships lodgings: only Mr. Holles, Sir William Lewis, and Sir Philip Stapleton do acknowledg, that by her Ladiships favour, they have many times waited upon her both at her own Lodgings in Whitehall, and elsewhere, yet never to any such [foul] intent … but only to pay unto her Ladiship that respect which is due unto her (a person of so great honor and desert) from them, and in truth from all others who are wel wishers to the welfare of this Kingdom. (Prynne 8; Crawford 109)

Lucy's reputation as a *salonnière* had been the perfect cover for organizing "secret cabals" (Betcherman 263).[9] It is not difficult to see how, as Julie Sanders observes, having a salon "was … a highly convenient means of developing a powerful court faction and the semi-emotional, semi-intellectual structures of such a movement should not blind us to the political intrigues and manipulations they enabled and facilitated" (453–4).

The schemes at Lady Carlisle's home were to prove fruitless. Charles was not to be convinced. When he finally surrendered himself to David Leslie of the Scottish army, he was immediately sold out to Parliament. Years of imprisonment would follow: four months in Northampton, three months in Hampton Court, and finally Carisbrooke Castle in the Isle of Wight. Royalists tried to organize his escape. Lady Carlisle's London home became a clearing house. Believing Thomas Witherings, the postmaster, had discovered the cover under which his letter passed to the Queen in France, Charles ordered Henry Firebrace: "Do not send that letter of mine to the posthouse, but either to Dr. Fraiser [Alexander Fraser] or my Lady Carlisle, with a caution not to trust the postmasters" (Hillier 90). When one of the escape plans was discovered, however, Lady Carlisle was immediately suspected of betrayal. In his memoirs Bishop Warburton claimed that Lucy had acted as a double-agent. Warburton's claims cannot be substantiated, but have ensured that Lucy is seen as false by historians. As Raymond A. Anselment states, his "unsupported insistence that 'lady Carlisle' was the unnamed source of 'information and intelligence what his majesty intended to do' added substance to the impression of a career in double-dealing" (213).

Prince Charles thanked Lucy days before his father's execution. The fact that Parliament incarcerated her shortly after Holland's execution suggests that it was assumed she had

---

9   In 1660 Holles is still plotting with Lady Carlisle: see Crawford 187, referring to Bodl., Clarendon MS 71 fol. 339v, Coventry to Hyde, 20 April 1660.

not played the royalists, but had aided them instead. On 20 March 1649, the Council Day's proceedings noted that papers had been taken from Lady Carlisle's house, and that they awaited a report the following day. On 21 March 1649 she was committed to the Tower on "suspicion of treason" (*CSPD 1649–50*), apparently under severe conditions ("up to her final hours in the Tower, Lucy had been under close restraint and had had no visitors"; Betcherman 312), but it was as early as 26 April 1649 that the Lieutenant of the Tower issued a warrant "to permit the Countess Dowager of Carlisle to take the air, and see her friends within the Tower, in his presence or that of his deputy" (*CSPD 1649–50*, warrant dated 26 April 1649).

In mid-June 1649 the parliamentarians approached the Leicesters as guardians for the royal children Princess Elizabeth and Prince Henry, Duke of Gloucester. Dorothy took care of them at Penshurst. However, in August 1650 they were removed to Carisbrooke Castle, with their uncle having landed in Scotland (*Correspondence DPS* 42). Perhaps Lucy's release on bond a few months previously, in March 1650, was an extra incentive to remove them. Even though Lucy was not granted full freedom until March 1652, to have her, a possible royalist plotter, in such close proximity to the royal children would have been considered a hazard.

If this is why the children were moved, evidence supporting these precautions was not long in coming. In March 1651, while Lucy was out on bail, royalist Thomas Coke was incarcerated and broke during cross-examination:

> The ladies looked upon as active in the Presbyterian design are the Lady Carlisle and the Lady Peterborough, the former, though in prison, yet kept weekly correspondence by ciphers till the King went into Scotland, with her brother, the Lord Percy, who always acquainted the King therewith, and sometimes me, with his intelligence. (Betcherman 313)

The "Presbyterian design" Coke referred to was a plot to have Charles II lead a Scottish army into England; having crossed the border, he would find the assistance of English Presbyterians whom Coke had stirred up, along with royalist refugees returned from the Continent (Betcherman 307). Despite this fresh incriminating information, the Council of State did not retract Lucy's probation, possibly because Coke had listed dozens of names.

Lucy was released in time to witness the second marriage of her niece, Doll, to Robert Smythe. The women in the family attended the wedding at Penshurst; Doll's disapproving father stayed away (*Correspondence DPS* 43). Like Dorothy Osborne, he could not see what his widowed daughter possibly gained by the union. Osborne commented:

> My Lady Sunderland is not to bee followed in her marrying fashion .... Whoe would ere have dreamt hee should have had my Lady Sunderland, though hee bee a very fine Gentleman … I shall never forgive her one thing she sayed of him, which was that she married him out of Pitty … To speak truth 'twas convenient for neither of them … She has lost by it much of the repute she has gained, by keeping herself a widdow. It was then believed that Witt and discretion were to be Reconciled in her personne that have soe seldome bin perswaded to meet in any Body else: but wee are all Mortall. (Osborne 52–4)

Following female tradition in the family, Doll had chosen her own husband and married for love. However, even though her parents' marriage had the appearance of a love match, it might have been about securing alliances for Robert as well. In the final years, when the long-sought office of Lord Lieutenant of Ireland had disheartened him and he retreated to

Penshurst, he fell out with his wife. He wrote to her brother Northumberland: "I have paid her all civilities due to the Earl of Northumberland's daughter, and I have loved her better for being your sister than I could have loved any woman that was not so" (17 February 1658, *Correspondence DPS* 43). While Dorothy had been fortunate to marry into the Sidney family, Robert had praised himself for securing an alliance with the Percys. From the letter it appears that he was preparing a separation, pondering leaving Penshurst to his wife: "I am thinking of a retreat for myself that your sister may live somewhere being secure from my passions and all disturbances by me" (44). But his consideration was rendered moot as Dorothy died of cancer at Penshurst on 20 August 1659, followed fourteen months later by her sister Lucy, who died at her London residence, Little Salisbury House, on 5 November 1660. Robert Sidney never left Penshurst, dying there in 1677.

Doll was widowed once more in the mid-1660s, by which time she had become a skillful estate manager, like her mother, and an able politician not afraid to express her opinions, like her aunt. It seems that her romantic side revisited her in later life. When she asked her old admirer Waller in 1680 when he would again address "beautiful verses" to her, he answered, with biting sarcasm: "When, Madam, your Ladyship is as young and as handsome again" (Chernaik).

Bibliography

Manuscript Sources

British Library
    Egerton MS 2595; MS 2597
Kent History and Library Centre (KHLC)
    U1475 C.87/1A
The National Archives, Kew (TNA)
    PRO 31/3 no. 64
    SP 16/81; 16/101; 16/116; 16/118; 16/120; 16/123; 16/280; 16/529
Sheffield Central Library
    Strafford Papers, Fitzwilliam MS 8; MS 15

Primary and Secondary Sources

Ady Cartwright, Julia Mary. *Some Account of Dorothy Sidney, Countess of Sunderland, Her Family and Friends, 1617–1684*. London: Seeley, 1901.
Anselment, Raymond A. "The Countess of Carlisle and Caroline Praise: Convention and Reality." *Studies in Philology* 82.2 (1985): 212–33.
Atherton, Ian. "Sidney, Robert, Second Earl of Leicester." *ODNB*.
Bellany, Alastair, and Andrew McRae. *Early Stuart Libels: An Edition of Poetry from Manuscript Sources*. Web. 2005. http://purl.oclc.org/emls/texts/libels/. Libel R5.
Betcherman, Lita-Rose. *Court Lady and Country Wife: Two Noble Sisters in Seventeenth-century England*. New York: HarperCollins, 2005.
Burton, Thomas. *The Diary of Thomas Burton, esq.* Ed. John Towill Rutt. 4 vols. London: H. Colburn, 1828.
Calendar of State Papers Domestic: Interregnum, 1649–50. Ed. Mary Anne Everett Green. London: HMSO, 1875.

Cartwright, William. "A Panegyrick to the Most Noble Lucy Countess of Carlisle." *The Plays & Poems of William Cartwright*. Ed. G. Blakemore Evans. Madison: U of Wisconsin P, 1951. 441–5.

Chamberlain, John. *The Letters of John Chamberlain*. Ed. Norman Egbert McClure. 2 vols. Philadelphia, PA: American Philosophical Society, 1939; rpt. Westport, CT: Greenwood P, 1979.

Chernaik, Warren. "Spencer [née Sidney], Dorothy, Countess of Sunderland [Known as Sacharissa]." *ODNB*.

Clarendon, Edward Hyde, Earl of. *The History of the Rebellion and Civil Wars in England Begun in the Year 1641*. Ed. William Dunn Macray. 6 vols. Oxford: Clarendon P, 1888.

Crawford, P. *Denzil Holles, 1598–1680: A Study of His Political Career*. London: Royal Historical Society, 1979.

Donagan, Barbara. "A Courtier's Progress: Greed and Consistency in the Life of the Earl of Holland." *The Historical Journal* 19.2 (1976): 317–53.

Evelyn, John. *Diary and Correspondence of John Evelyn*. Ed. William Bray. 4 vols. London, 1859.

Hillier, George. *A Narrative of Attempted Escapes of Charles I from Carisbrook Castle*. London: Richard Bentley, 1852.

House of Commons Journal 2 (January 1643). London: HMSO, 1802.

Jonson, Ben. "To Penshurst." *The Cambridge Edition of the Works of Ben Jonson*. Ed. David Bevington, Martin Butler, and Ian Donaldson. 7 vols. Cambridge: Cambridge UP, 2012. 5:209–14.

Matthew, Tobie. *A collection of letters made by Sr Tobie Mathews. With a Character of the Most Excellent Lady, Lucy Countess of Carlisle ...* [1636]. London: Printed for Henry Heringman, 1660.

Nicholls, Mark. "Percy, Henry, Ninth Earl of Northumberland." *ODNB*.

Osborne, Dorothy. *Letters to William Temple*. Ed. K. Parker. London: Penguin, 1987.

[Prynne, William]. *A Full Vindication and Ansvver of the XI. Accused Members; viz. Denzill Holles, Esq; Sir Philip Stapleton, Sir William Lewis, Sir John Clotworthy, Sir William Waller, Sir Iohn Maynard Kts Major Gen. Massey, Iohn Glynne Esq; Recorder of London. Walter Long Esquire Col. Edward Harley, Anthony Nichols Esq to a Late Printed Pamphlet Intituled, A Particular Charge or Impeachment ...* London, 1647. Wing (2nd ed.)/P3968; Thomason/E.398[17].

Sanders, Julie. "Caroline Salon Culture and Female Agency: The Countess of Carlisle, Henrietta Maria, and Public Theatre." *Theatre Journal* 52.4 (2000): 449–64.

Schreiber, Roy E. "The First Carlisle Sir James Hay, First Earl of Carlisle as Courtier, Diplomat and Entrepreneur, 1580–1636." *Transactions of the American Philosophical Society* n.s. 74.7 (1984): 1–202.

—. "Hay [née Percy], Lucy." *ODNB*.

Shaw, Dougal. "Thomas Wentworth and Monarchical Ritual in Early Modern Ireland." *The Historical Journal* 49.2 (2006): 331–55.

Sidney, Dorothy Percy. *The Correspondence (c. 1626–1659) of Dorothy Percy Sidney, Countess of Leicester*. Ed. Brennan, Michael G., Noel J. Kinnamon, and Margaret P. Hannay. Ashgate: Farnham, 2010.

Smuts, Malcolm R. "The Puritan Followers of Henrietta Maria in the 1630s." *The English Historical Review* 93 (1978): 26–45.

—. "Religion, European Politics and Henrietta Maria's Circle, 1625–1641." *Henrietta Maria: Piety, Politics and Patronage*. Ed. Erin Griffey. Aldershot: Ashgate, 2008. 13–37.

Strafford, Thomas. *The Earl of Strafford's Letters and Despatches*. Ed. William Knowler. 2 vols. London: Robert Owen, 1740.

Stuart, Elizabeth. *The Correspondence of Elizabeth Stuart, Queen of Bohemia*. Ed. Nadine Akkerman. 3 vols. Oxford: Oxford UP, 2011–.

Suckling, John. *The Works of Sir John Suckling*. Ed. Thomas Clayton. 2 vols. Oxford: Clarendon P, 1971.

Veevers, Erica. *Images of Love and Religion: Queen Henrietta Maria and Court Entertainments*. Cambridge: Cambridge UP, 1989.

Waller, Edmund. *The Poetical Works of Edmund Waller and Sir John Denham*. Edinburgh: Nichol, 1857.

Warwick, Sir Philip. *Memoires of the Reign of King Charles I*. London: R. Chiswell, 1701.

Wolfson, Sara J. "The Female Bedchamber of Queen Henrietta Maria: Politics, Familial Networks and Policy, 1626–1640." *The Politics of Female Households: Ladies-in-Waiting Across Europe*. Ed. Nadine Akkerman and Birgit Houben. Leiden: Brill, 2013. 311–41.

Algernon Sidney's Life and Works (1623–1683)

Jonathan Scott

More than three decades ago I decided on Algernon Sidney (Illustration 25) as a doctoral topic after reading a collection of his letters published in 1825. From Hamburg on 30 August 1660 he wrote to his father, Robert Sidney, second Earl of Leicester:

> I knowe the titles that are given me of fierce, violent, seditious, mutinous, turbulent …. I know people will say, I straine at knats, and swallow camels; that it is a strange conscience, that lets a man runne violently on, till he is deepe in civill blood, and then stays at a few words and complements; that can earnestly endeavour to extirpate a long established monarchy, and then cannot be brought to see his error, and be persuaded to set one finger towards the setting together the broken pieces of it …. I cannot helpe it if I judge amisse; I did not make myself, nor can I correct the defects of my own creation. I walk in the light God hath given me; if it be dimme or uncertaine, I must beare the penalty of my errors: I hope to do it with patience, and that noe burden shall be very grievous to me, except sinne and shame. (Blencowe 194–8)

I was moved by the content and the powerful, classically educated prose. But I had no idea, and could not until recently have recognized, the extent to which most of Sidney's life and writings are here encapsulated. Now, after two books (Scott, *Algernon/Republic* and *Algernon/Restoration*) and important work by many others, a great deal has been explained, but relatively little added. Here is the republicanism, never abandoned, and the mutiny which brought him to the scaffold. Violence and blood knit the life and writings together in the service of a cause about the rightness of which he agonizes. Part of that morality was classical, both Greek and Roman. But it has taken a long time for scholars to recognize, as they now have, how deeply it was anchored in religion. Sidney knew Plato and Livy by heart, but did not die for them. He died for "the people of God" (*Apology*, in Sidney, *Works* 30–32): "God direct us in that which is for our good, and prepare us well to defend our cause, or willingly to suffer for it, if he please to call us unto it" (East Sussex Record Office, Hampden Letter 5, 2–3).

Something else strikes me over twenty years later, which is how many important questions remain unanswered. For long periods Algernon is largely, though not entirely, absent from the record (1623–42; 1653–58; 1666–77; 1681–82). We have no corroborated information about sexual partners, marriage, or children, though there is this, among the *Discourses Concerning Government*'s many indictments of the "ingratitude and treachery" of Charles II:

> It is ill, that men should kill one another in seditions, tumults and wars; but … there is a way of killing worse than that of the sword … by taking from men the means of living, bring some to perish through want, drive others out of the country, and … dissuade men from marriage, by taking from them all ways of supporting their families. (*Discourses*, in Sidney, *Works* 194, 223–5)

In relation to the *Discourses*, the most intriguing question remains: How did it survive its use as evidence for the prosecution in a successful treason trial to be published fifteen years later? The holy grail of future Sidney discoveries would be discovery of the manuscript of the *Discourses*, which has disappeared, leaving ground for legitimate questions about the integrity of the publication. Indeed, neither of Sidney's major works (*Court Maxims*; *Discourses*) survive in his hand—a potentially significant fact to which I will return.

This is in striking contrast to his letters (over a hundred survive), the majority of which have been published. During my research I came across the most dramatic collection until then unused (East Sussex, Hampden Letters). Ten in number, and long, these were written during his final months in the Tower of London. They deserve an edition, because of their content and the still inadequately researched importance of their context (Sidney's trial, execution, and the use of the *Discourses* in the process, laid the basis for two hundred years of fame). Letters 1–9 are written to a fellow prisoner also awaiting trial, almost certainly John Hampden Junior. But the last, and the last letter Sidney ever wrote (on 22 November 1683), is to a "most deare freind [*sic*] and kinsman" on the outside, and encloses money. It is sobering for the historian and biographer both, as well as for the now broad community of Algernon Sidney scholars, that his closest friend—and a relative—remains unidentified.

Laying out these loose ends retrospectively suggests that perhaps they form a common tapestry. This essay will conclude by offering a possible collective answer to them. But let us first return to the beginning: of Sidney scholarship, and then of Sidney.

Algernon Sidney Scholarship

When I traveled to Cambridge in 1982 I thought that I was the first historian since Alexander Ewald (two volumes in 1873) to undertake sustained research on the topic. Sidney's fame as author of the *Discourses* and martyr for liberty had led to a string of biographies—many appended to editions of his works—of which the best was published in 1813 (Meadley). All, however, were Whig hagiographies, leaving a need to locate the man who died before Whiggism was formed (Scott, *Algernon/Republic* Introduction; Scott, *Algernon/Restoration* pt. 1). None incorporated the manuscript resources which had since become available to modern scholars. None, finally, had attempted a sustained analysis of Sidney's political works and thought.

I soon discovered that in all of these areas I had a distinguished contemporary predecessor. Blair Worden, indeed, had discovered an entirely new work by Sidney, *Court Maxims*, written in exile in the Netherlands almost twenty years before the *Discourses* in 1665 (Worden, *Literature and Politics*; Ludlow Introduction). He subsequently published in 1985 an essay on his life and writing (Worden, "Commonwealth"), and returned to Sidney's thought and/or /bibliography in later more general works (Worden, "English Republicanism" 443–75; Wootton pt. 1; Worden, *Roundhead Reputations*; Worden, *English Civil Wars*). In much of this work Worden was building on two earlier classic intellectual histories which established the most important framework for the subsequent interpretation of Sidney's thought. This was classical republicanism (Fink; Pocock, *Machiavellian Moment*;

see Scott, *Commonwealth Principles* ch. 1). Another important predecessor had been Caroline Robbins ("Algernon/Discourses"; *Two English Republican Tracts*).

There remained a need, however, for a full-length modern intellectual biography. By the time this was completed (Scott, *Algernon/Republic*; Scott, *Algernon/Restoration)*, three other single-volume studies had appeared, or were about to (Carrive; Houston; Carswell), the first two focusing on Sidney's thought, and the third on his life. John Pocock reviewed these works in 1994 ("England's Cato"). Other studies followed, either of Sidney in particular or of the body of republican writing to which he contributed. From being historiographically marginal, Algernon had emerged for a second moment "on the stage," this time as a republican rather than a Whig. Historiographically, republicanism remains hot stuff (Fink; Pocock, *Machiavellian Moment*; Wootton; Rahe, *Against Throne*; Rahe, *Republics*; Skinner, *Hobbes*; Norbrook; Nelson; Mahlberg; Hammersley). What has emerged more recently is the importance to it in general, and to Sidney's life and thought in particular, of radical Protestantism (Scott, *Commonwealth Principles*; Winship).

The details of Sidney's life, as far as they have been established, are summarized in Scott (*ODNB*). This is a more reliable guide than Carswell in *The Porcupine*, who did not distinguish sufficiently carefully between established fact and hoary legend. There are undoubtedly further discoveries to be made, particularly concerning the very significant proportion of his life spent outside England in Ireland, Scandinavia, Denmark, Sweden, Germany, Italy (especially Rome), and France. Historians of England, the present writer included, are notoriously limited, as Algernon was not, by their language skills. Gaby Mahlberg's forthcoming study of English republicans in exile may well shed new light.

Algernon was born at Baynard's Castle, London, on 14 or 15 January 1623. He died almost sixty years later, on 7 January 1683, by beheading on Tower Hill. He was the second surviving son of Robert Sidney, second Earl of Leicester (1595–1677), and Dorothy Percy (d. 1659), daughter of Henry Percy, ninth Earl of Northumberland (see Warkentin *ARC* 1:9; Akkerman *ARC* 1:10). One of fourteen children, his oldest brother was Philip Sidney (1619–98), Viscount Lisle and later third Earl of Leicester, a Cromwellian politician with whom he vied bitterly for his father's favor, and later for his inheritance. One of the principal themes of the *Discourses*, a refutation of Sir Robert Filmer's *Patriarcha*, that power should be determined by merit rather than heredity in general, and primogeniture in particular, owed as much to this family as to his political experience (Scott, *Algernon/Republic* ch. 4; *Algernon/ Restoration* ch. 2). His older sister was Dorothy Spencer (1617–84), Countess of Sunderland and Waller's Sacharissa; and his youngest brother, Henry Sidney (1641–1704), later Earl of Romney and intimate of William III (see Brennan *ARC* 1:12).

From the Sidneys Algernon inherited a humanist culture and militant Protestant cause; from the Percys an ancient lineage and ungovernable pride. It was because he saw his own struggle against counter-reformation and arbitrary power as continuing that of his famous great uncle Sir Philip—whose martyrdom he would come to see himself as emulating—that he wrote in the signature book of the University of Copenhagen in 1659: "PHILLIPUS SIDNEY MANUS HAEC INIMICA TYRANNIS EINSE PETIT PLACIDAM CUM LIBERTATE QUIETEM" ("Philip Sidney this hand always an enemy to tyrants seeks by the sword peace under liberty") (Bibliothèque Nationale, Lantiniana 101), thus furnishing the state motto of Massachusetts to this day. His *Court Maxims* described the "powerful, gallant" nobility of "the Plantagenet Age" when Percy power was at its zenith (67); his *Discourses* the king-making prowess of the first Earl of Northumberland "and his brave son Hotspur" (205). Thus Gilbert Burnet commented that on the one hand Algernon "had studied the history of government in all its branches beyond any man I ever knew," and that on the other he was "a man of most extraordinary courage … but of a rough and boisterous temper, that could not bear contradiction" (2:34).

153

Sidney was raised at the beautiful family seat of Penshurst Place, Kent. With his brother Philip he accompanied his father on embassies to Denmark in 1632 and France from 1636. He remained in France for five years, continuing his education either in Paris or at the Huguenot academy at Saumur, founded by Sir Philip Sidney's friend Philippe Du Plessis Mornay. In Paris the Sidneys attended services at Charenton, where the minister was Jean Daille, formerly chaplain to Du Plessis Mornay, and praised by Algernon in the *Maxims*.

In 1641 the family returned to an England in crisis. On 14 June Leicester was appointed Lord Lieutenant of Ireland in the place of the executed Earl of Strafford; a few months later Ireland was convulsed by rebellion. In February 1642, under parliamentary authority, the oldest brothers arrived in Dublin, Philip Lord Lisle in command of a cavalry regiment, Algernon captain of a troop of horse. Both saw action in this exceptionally brutal theater of war; in June 1643 Algernon wrote to his mother of his desire to leave

> that which is bad for that which may be better, I think not possibly worse …. Nothing but extreame necessity shall make me think of bearing arms in England, and yet … theare is so few that abstaine from warre for the same reason I doe, that I doe not know wheather in many mens eyes it may not prove dishonourable to me. (Gilbert 1:xlviii–xlx)

The nature of this desired abstention remains unclear, and whether for reasons of honor, necessity, conviction, or family connection (Northumberland was a parliamentarian), on 15 April 1644 Algernon was appointed colonel in the Earl of Manchester's regiment of horse in the Eastern Association.

On 2 July at Marston Moor he charged "with much gallantry at the head of my lord's regiment of horse, and came off with much honour, though with many wounds, to the grief of my Lord, and many others, who is since gone to London for the cure of his wounds" (*Ash's Intelligence* no. 6). In April 1645 he declined a command in the New Model Army with "extreame unwillingnesse … by reason of my lamenesse" (BL Sloane MS 1519 fol. 112). Forty years later, following his execution, he was depicted in a ballad declaiming "View my Hack'd Limbs … my numerous Scars in Hell's best Cause the old republic wars" (*Sydney's Farewell*). Despite three subsequent military governorships, of Chichester (appointed May 1645), Dublin (February 1647), and Dover Castle (mid-1648 until mid 1651), this was the sum total of Sidney's active military service. Yet if forced by injury to exchange sword for pen, he proved unique in his subsequent commitment to wield the latter on behalf of—sometimes almost as—the former. As he put it in 1660: "I did not take the warre in which I was engaged to be a slight matter, nor to be done by halfes. I thought it undertaken upon good grounds, and that it was the part of an honest man to pursue them heartily" (Blencowe 222). This was partly an outgrowth of his analysis of the causes at stake, and the contemporary means necessary to secure them. But it was also—as the mentions of honesty and honor suggest—a placement at their service of the military function and ideals of the "ancient" aristocracy he venerated.

Algernon has been called an "aristocratic" republican—a misleading depiction of his constitutional preferences, which were distinctly Machiavellian (for Rome at its most popular and expansive, rather than peace-mongering aristocratic Venice). Machiavelli was, indeed, on behalf of military power, unambiguously anti-aristocratic. Sidney was similarly scathing about the "effeminate" contemporary nobility. But as a description of his temper, his admiration for less submissive elites like the French (see below), and his account of Anglo-Saxon and Plantagenet history, "aristocratic" retains its usefulness.

Between sword and pen came that which bound them together and accompanied nearly all Sidney's writing: political engagement. This was, in order, parliamentary, republican, and finally insurrectionary. He entered the House of Commons in December 1645 as a "recruited" Member for Cardiff. He remained there until Oliver Cromwell's dissolution of the "Rump" on 20 April 1653. Until 1652 his attendance was irregular, and during Pride's Purge and the regicide (3 December 1648–30 January 1649) he absented himself altogether. As in the case of the man who was to become his closest colleague, Sir Henry Vane Junior, this was because Algernon was as opposed to military as to royal "arbitrary" interference in parliamentary politics. Thus, although a decade later as the republic's un-diplomatic envoy to the Baltic he was credibly reported to have defended the regicide as "the justest and bravest act … that ever was done in England, or anywhere" (BL Add. MS 32680 fols. 9–10), there is little reason to doubt his claim in self-defense to his father that at the time he had personally "alleged in vaine" to Cromwell that "First, the King could be tried by noe court; secondly, that noe man could be tried by that court" (Blencowe 236–7).

To reconcile these statements might involve holding that Sidney believed the regicide to have been illegal but just. Put differently, there is no evidence that he opposed the beheading of the king, still less the abolition of monarchy, as opposed to the military takeover of civilian politics which preceded and accomplished it. An alternative or additional explanation, with much evidence in support, is that between 1649 and 1659 his beliefs developed. As was the case among so many of his colleagues, it is less clear that republicanism made the republic, as that the republic made republicanism. His *Discourses*, written thirty years later, still rings with pride and praise. This was the republic which Cromwell ended in April 1653 as he had ended the monarchy which preceded it, before a brief revival in 1659. For those who had "sat at the helm" between 1649 and 1653, the Protectorate was a tyranny.

Thus Algernon and other colleagues returned to the purged Commons during 1649 because they were attempting to restore civilian government. As in the aftermath of most revolutions, government policies hinged upon military security. Between 1649 and 1651, with no less brutality than efficiency, the New Model Army conquered Ireland and Scotland. Within three years of an unprecedented political transformation England had achieved a no less unparalleled mastery of the British Isles. Meanwhile, less well documented by historians, a parallel revolution was underway. In part this was a matter of political economy: obsolete royal systems of taxation were replaced by new ones. Secondly, it was administrative: dynastic government by individuals and their dependants was replaced by government by committee. Then, in an equally startling reversal of policy, and reflecting the government's close relationship to the City of London, there was a new emphasis on trade (marked by the Plantation Act of 1649 and the Navigation Act of 1651). This meshed with a no less crucial domain for the achievement of security, which was maritime. Whereas during wartime Charles I had built one or two ships a year, the republic built dozens—twenty-two in 1654. While it had taken the early Stuarts a year to plan a summer cruise in the narrow seas, the republic patrolled the Channel, Irish Sea, Mediterranean, and Caribbean simultaneously. The completion of this military revolution at land and sea was signaled by the astonishing defeat of the Dutch in 1654. Europe had acquired a new superpower (Scott, *When the Waves* 74–5).

The causes of this transformation were administrative, cultural, and financial. They were also social, in that following the Self-Denying Ordinance of 1643–44 command of the army and navy ceased to be aristocratic (Scott, *When the Waves* ch 4). In addition to new taxes, Parliament and then the republican government funded their military ventures with the proceeds of delinquency compositions and the sale of royal and episcopal property. Between 1642 and 1660, it has been estimated, government income from these sources totaled £95,000,000—an annual income more than five times that available to Charles I in his best year (Oppenheim 303–43).

Sidney's role within the republican government centered on the settlement (I think we should understand it as colonization) of Ireland (culminating in 1651) and then foreign relations in general, and management of the Anglo-Dutch war in particular. Thus, following his election, alongside Vane, to the government's Council of State in 1652, he found himself at the locus of its new-found international achievement and prestige. Thus it was from his pen that there emerged some of the most stirring utterances of a newly created ideology. It was not that the republic's military successes reflected an array of new-found resources, but rather that it was a consequence, as Machiavelli had insisted it would be, of the replacement of a monarchy by a republic. It was a direct effect of the acquisition of liberty and its management by men selected not by birth, but for ability and merit:

> When Van Tromp [the Dutch Admiral] set upon Blake in Foleston-Bay, the parliament had not above thirteen ships against threescore … to oppose the best captain in the world …. But such was the power of wisdom and integrity in those who sat at the helm, and their diligence in chusing men only for their merit was blessed with such success, that in two years our fleets grew to be as famous as our land armies; the reputation and power of our nation rose to a greater height, than when we possessed the better half of France …. All the states … of Europe … sought our friendship; and Rome was more afraid of Blake and his fleet, than they had been of the great king of Sweden, when he was ready to invade Italy with a hundred thousand men. (*Discourses* 278–99)

Reputation, which had always concerned Algernon and always would, pertained to nations as well as persons. With England's at its zenith, it was henceforth intertwined with the republican cause.

It was no coincidence that when in April 1653 Oliver Cromwell forcibly dissolved the Rump, those responsible for making "its fleets … as famous as its land armies" attracted his particular personal ire. Algernon reported to his father that he pointed "particularly upon somme persons, as Henry Vane to whome he gave very sharpe language … [and when] Algernon Sydney … sayd he would not go out … Harrison and Wortley putt theyr hands upon Sydney's shoulders, as if they would force him to go out" (Blencowe 140–41). The war was not over, but the revolution was. Yet arguably the foundations of the British empire had been laid.

In this dramatic confrontation we see juxtaposed two enduring reference points of Sidney's career. During his subsequent exile this was underlined by his composition of "Characters" of both Cromwell and Vane. The former has been lost; the latter has survived and is reproduced as an appendix to Rowe's *Sir Henry Vane the Younger*, "The Character of Henry Vane Jnr.," which presents an archetype of incorruptible virtue: Sidney's mentor and model. It praises Vane's godly work in Massachusetts, his naval leadership thereafter, and his steadfast resistance to the tyrant by whom the glorious experiment would be destroyed. In his *Court Maxims* Vane's judicial murder is emotionally lamented and the full extent of his religious influence on Sidney becomes clear. In his final months in the Tower Sidney re-examines Vane's trial and assumes, correctly, that it will be used as a model for his own (Scott, *Algernon/Restoration* 316). When he went to the scaffold thanking "The Lord … that at the last thou hast permitted me to be singled out as a witness of thy truth, and even by the confession of my opposers, for that OLD CAUSE in which I was from my youth engaged, and for which though hast often and wonderfully declared thyself," this was a cause for his understanding of which Vane was by far his most influential and inspirational colleague (Sidney, *Last Paper*, in *Works* 40).

In the absence of Sidney's "Character of Cromwell," we must settle for Milton's Satan in *Paradise Lost* (Scott, *Commonwealth Principles* 174–7, 217–20). At his trial in 1683 he said: "[Y]ou need not wonder that I called him a tyrant, I did so every day in his life, and acted against him too." If the action in question was political, no trace of it has been recovered. If, however, it was dramatic, Algernon's brother Lord Lisle complained on 17 June 1656 to his father of "a play acted" at Penshurst "of publike affront" to the Lord Protector, during which the audience were so "exceedingly pleased with the gallant relation of the chief actor in it … that by applauding him they put him several times upon it" (HMC *De L'Isle and Dudley* 6:400). From this grew the legend of Algernon playing Brutus in Shakespeare's *Julius Caesar*—a story perhaps too good not to be true.

In general, between the Rump's dissolution in 1653 and its re-establishment in May 1659 Algernon appears to have retired to concentrate on family and financial business, moving between Penshurst, his uncle Northumberland's house at Petworth in Surrey, and Sterry in Kent (details in Scott, *Algernon/Republic* ch. 4). When he answered the call back to political action in 1659, it was to enact a new post-Protectoral foreign policy managed by Henry Vane. Characteristically, this was Anglo-Dutch and naval in character. At the entrance to the Baltic, of vital strategic importance to England for naval supplies, Cromwell had supported Charles Gustavus X of Sweden and the United Provinces Denmark. Now, with Sweden threatening to overrun its neighbor, Vane agreed with the United Provinces that the two republics had a joint interest in keeping control over the Straits divided. Following in the footsteps of his father, Algernon arrived at Elsinore on 20 July 1659 as ambassador plenipotentiary aboard an English fleet.

There Sidney's strategy, in concert with the Dutch, of combining diplomatic and military measures ("a few shots of our cannon would have made this peace") was at the very least unorthodox. Venetian observers reported: "We shall soon see the results of such unprecedented methods of negotiation" (*CSPV 1659–61* 64). It was, on the other hand a more or less direct continuation of Algernon's style in co-managing the Anglo-Dutch war in 1652–53. Alas, it was a high-risk approach which came unstuck. Charles X reacted with "great choler," only to be told by Algernon to behave himself (Scott, *Algernon/Republic* 131–5). As the Danes recovered their courage, Anglo-Dutch relations began to fray. Crucially, however, the English fleet, under the command of the Cromwellian Edward Montagu and encouraged by the Swedes, decided to return to England, where the political situation was unraveling and Restoration in the air. Algernon was up the Baltic without a paddle.

Charles X turned out to prefer Sidney without his fleet, and when the Swedish king died suddenly on 12 February 1660, Sidney preferred him without his life. He reported that the departed monarch had been "a man of exceeding good wit, valiant, industrious, vigilant … whoe, by the many and great actions of his short reign deserves to be remembered with honour" (Blencowe 174–8). Meanwhile, with accounts of his strident republicanism reaching England, Algernon could not immediately return. As it turned out, his exile would last seventeen years.

In retrospect, one can see this period of Algernon's life falling into three subchapters. During the first, one of political retirement, he visited Hamburg and then traveled south to live in Rome. Most remarkably, his time there was spent primarily among papal Cardinals "which some," reported one observer, "impute to his own Parts and wit, others to some recommendation from [Christina] the [ex-]Queen of Sweade" (Scott, *Algernon/Republic* 156). Sidney had indeed left Sweden with a letter of introduction to Roman Catholic convert Christina, whom he visited in Hamburg, and he was among the Cardinals close to her friend Azzolini. By April 1661, however, he was in a position to send his father "Characters" of all the Cardinals (Collins 2:705–20). A few months later he was summering at the Villa de Belvedere at Frascati, at the invitation of Prince Pamphili, nephew of the previous pope, in the magnificent library in which "I have applied myself to studdy" (Collins 2:718–21).

In addition to Rome he visited Venice, and he next appears on the historical record in mid-1663, visiting his fellow republican exile Edmund Ludlow in Vevey, Switzerland. This was the end of his "retirement" and a turn towards action, the springs of which can be divined from two sources. The first is Ludlow's diary, in which the author recorded that Algernon "[n]ow thinks it seasonable to draw towards his Native Country, in Expectation of an Opportunity wherein he might be more active" (*Voyce* 977). What underlay this decision is made clear in *Court Maxims* and subsequent correspondence: the execution of the regicides, the passage of the Act of Uniformity (1662), and above all the judicial murder of Vane. After presenting Ludlow with a pair of Italian pistols, Sidney visited the Calvinist academy at the University of Geneva, where he inscribed the visitor's book: "SIT SANGUINIS ULTOR JUSTORUM" ("Let there be revenge for the blood of the just") (Borgeaud 442–3). In the *Maxims*, begun two years later, Sidney wrote: "noble Vane … thy death gave thee a famous victory and a never perishing Crown" (49).

From Bern, Sidney traveled to Brussels and then to the United Provinces, where, having found "no rest in my owne spirite, because I lived only to myself, and was in no ways useful unto God's people, my country and the world," he nevertheless found "the spirits of those who understood seasons farre better than I … not to be fully prepared" (Blencowe 259–60). He retreated to Augsburg, returning, however, to the United Provinces in mid-1665. The political context for this move was probably the approaching Second Anglo-Dutch War (1665–67). His Dutch host may have been Benjamin Furly, an English Quaker living in Rotterdam, and two decades later also host to John Locke. Sidney's correspondence with Furly has survived in the Beinecke Library at Yale, and it was to him that he wrote: "I do not knowe what success God will give unto our undertakings, but I am certaine I can have no peace in my own spirite, if I doe not endeavour by all meanes possible to advance the interest of God's people" (Blencowe 259–60).

Algernon's strategy over the following eighteen months was twofold. In the context of war between the Dutch republic—surviving embodiment of the religious and political principles recently overthrown in England—and the restored English monarchy, he attempted to rally republicans and Nonconformists on both sides of the Channel. At the same time he lobbied the Dutch government for backing for a planned republican invasion. Gilbert Burnet recorded: "Algernon Sidney … came to de Wit, and pressed him to think of an invasion of England and Scotland … and they were bringing many officers to Holland to join in the undertaking" (BL Add. MS 63057 1:393). In this context Sidney made strenuous and eventually splenetic but unsuccessful attempts to summon Ludlow (*Voyce* 1079–80, 1105). Nor could De Wit, remembering the Dutch defeat of 1652–54, be convinced that restoring an English republic would be in the interest of the United Provinces. Finally, in 1666 Sidney personally met the Dutch ally French king Louis XIV to seek support. Having been offered only a fifth of the financial backing he was seeking, Algernon accepted instead royal permission to begin a third retirement in Montpellier.

Sidney's first major work, *Court Maxims*, composed in 1665–66, unfinished and unpublished, was written in the service of this design. It makes the case for joint Anglo-Dutch republican action to "destroy the detested Houses of Stuart and Orange." A platonic dialogue, it works its way through the "maxims" of the English monarchy to reveal it as in every respect a tyranny animated by interests "irreconcilably contrary" to those of the public. Once this has been revealed to the English people, "nothing is more reasonable than that they should repent of their choice *and endeavour to unmake what they have made*" (7).

Detailed analyses of the *Maxims'* argument and content are available in Scott, *Algernon/ Republic* (ch. 12) and Scott, *Commonwealth Principles* (in particular, but not only, ch. 15). This being the case, what seems more valuable here is to review the dramatic history of historical interpretations of it and its place within Sidney's *oeuvre*. As explained, the manuscript was discovered by Blair Worden in Warwick Castle. It is a little over two hundred pages (brevity was not Algernon's specialty: the *Discourses*, at over five hundred, was also unfinished) and in the handwriting of two copyists, with Sidney's name on the cover. The discovery was itself dramatic, but also intellectually challenging. By comparison to the later *Discourses*, the first impression is of dissonance, because it is so comparatively emotional, violent, and saturated by biblical and religious imagery. Worden's response was to attribute this tone to the intended Nonconformist audience, Ludlow included, and to see the more humanist *Discourses* as closer to Sidney's real voice (*Voyce*, Introduction).

The difference in tone between the two works is indeed notable. But there were and are two problems with Worden's interpretation. One is that the more one studies their *content*, the clearer their affinity—indeed, continuity—becomes. This involves both their overall insurrectionary objective and countless specific turns of phrase, arguments, sources, and examples. Because neither has survived in Sidney's hand, we cannot be sure that either is unadulterated. But it cannot reasonably be doubted that both are the works of the same author. The other problem with seeing the emotional devotional content of the *Maxims* as exceptional in Sidney's *oeuvre* is that, as we have seen, it is precisely replicated in his final writings: the letters in the Tower, the *Apology*, and *Last Paper*. The first survive in Sidney's hand, and the last he carried by hand and owned upon the scaffold.

Thus, what has become clear is not that the *Maxims* is anything other than the real Sidney; it is that even after its discovery, there was no more place for that Sidney in the Romanized Enlightenment stoic so influential throughout the eighteenth century than there was for the real Ludlow, whose *Voyce*, Worden showed, was entirely rewritten (as *Memoirs of Algernon Sidney*) for publication; however, that such a place needs to be created is evident simply from Sidney's political formation as a fervent Vanist and his thinking about Vane even up to and including his own trial. Vane was driven, as actor and writer, by a deep and complicated set of religious beliefs that have taken some unraveling (Parnham). Until very recently no Sidney scholar attempted anything comparable, partly because none were qualified, and partly because few understood or accepted the central importance of Algernon Sidney's religious beliefs.

This situation has been transformed by a single article, Michael Winship's "Algernon Sidney's Calvinist Republicanism" (2010). This showed—as chronology might suggest—that the *Maxims* is the key interpretative lens for understanding the *Discourses*, rather than the other way around. That Sidney's use of "the heady religious language of mid-century radical Puritanism … in *Court Maxims* has never been given close examination" is both "unfortunate in its own terms" and has meant that the scattered but critical traces of this language in *Discourses* have gone unnoticed (Winship 4). Far from being a proto-Enlightenment free-thinker or anti-predestinarian "arminian," Sidney:

> was, and acknowledged himself to be, a Calvinist. His theological assertions … mirror those of the orthodox Independent divines whose company he favoured (the Independents' congregationalism was an offshoot of Presbyterianism). Sidney was willing to call himself a "Puritan" and his religion was grounded [—like Vane's—] in the crowning creation of Puritanism: "experimental" Calvinism, the translation of the theology of predestination and absolute depravity into conversionist piety. (Winship 2–3)

All of this explains the ferocious religious and political binaries by which the *Maxims* is actuated. These dramatize the struggle between the "prophets, apostles, and all the saints from the beginning of the world"—the godly laity, "Joining in prayer and holy exercises"—and the "powers of earth and hell united … the 'tyrants and priests.'" The former are animated by the "spirit of God"; the latter are instruments of Satan. The struggle between them is inescapably violent, and "[m]any signs" portend its approaching climax: "The blood of the saints … cries aloud against you … and God will not long delay his appointed vengeance" (*Maxims* 191).

This is not only an interpretation which makes sense of the *Maxims* and other utterances, both private and public; it also makes biographical sense as an outgrowth of Sidney's formative experience as a parliamentary soldier, with its associated religious culture. But does it make sense of the *Discourses*? Acknowledging a change of tone Winship nevertheless sees continuity of purpose: "To put it crudely, *Court Maxims* is about why God's laws require that saints should kill kings, while the *Discourses* is about why those laws require that everyone else should join in" (13). More importantly: "Since there is no obvious polemical incentive for the expression of Calvinism in *Discourses*, any evidence of it there can be taken as a reflection of Sidney's personal conviction. The evidence, in fact, is there … terse but emphatic" (13–14). The book is a response to Filmer's *Patriarcha*. When Filmer attacks Calvin, Sidney responds that he was a "glorious servant of God," and when insisting that the observation of the Sabbath is a perpetual divine law, he is willing to take the "reproach" of being called "a Puritan and a Calvinist" (Winship 15). More important, Winship explains, is Sidney's response to Filmer's claim that humanity has a natural propensity to monarchy. This he dismisses, while adding that "Even if humanity did have that propensity … it would demonstrate nothing. Men have always been wicked liars, none do good, and evil thoughts proceed out of their hearts continually," Sidney claims, stringing together Genesis 6:5, Psalms 116:11 and 14:3, and Matthew 15:19 without acknowledgment. He then loosely channels Romans 6 to demonstrate that grace alone can deliver people from this corruption. The spiritual man's "proceedings can only be referred to God, and that only so far as he is guided by the spirit." The "natural man," by contrast, "is in perpetual enmity against God without any possibility of being reconciled to him, unless by destruction of the old man, and the regenerating or renewing him through the spirit of grace" (Winship 15).

This and other crucial theological argumentation has escaped analysis in a work dominated on the one hand by references to God's natural gift of liberty (natural law theory) and on the other by classical and humanist sources (classical republicanism) (Scott, *Algernon/Restoration* chs. 10–11; *Commonwealth Principles* chs. 5, 8, 15). But it is this which connects Sidney's life and writing as a whole, and it is this which explains the *Discourses'* similarly "starkly dichotomized" argumentative structure, for which a response to the Laudian Filmer is a perfect vehicle. Perhaps if Filmer had not attacked Machiavelli and Grotius and grossly misrepresented Aristotle, the *Discourses* would not have devoted so much time to defending and extrapolating upon their claims. But in a violent confrontation between good and evil, their utility, and that of Machiavelli in particular, was obvious.

This recovery of Sidney's religious identity and cause is the most important historiographical development since the sudden renaissance in studies of Algernon between the early 1980s and 1990s. It has taken us some way ahead of his retreat to Montpellier, Languedoc, in 1666. This began the most significant of his retirements, not only because it was the longest, but because it formed the centerpiece of a much longer-lasting French biographical dimension, both before and after. Sidney's father had been Ambassador to Paris; Algernon had lived and perhaps been educated there between 1636 and 1640. By the early 1670s he had moved from Montpellier to the picturesque village of Nerac, near Agen, in Guyenne/Bordeaux. This was within the Duchy D'Albret of Maurice-Godefroi, Duc de Bouillon. De Bouillon was nephew of the Huguenot Turenne, mareshal de France and the king's own military instructor. Turenne recorded a visit by Sidney to his residence in Paris in 1670 (other visits to Paris occurred in 1676 and 1677). Later the *Discourses* referred to "the brave Monsieur Turenne." It praised the readiness of the French nobility to act "in the defence and vindication of their violated liberties," and listed among those families having taken up arms in the past fifty years "the houses of Conde, Soissons, Montmorency,

Guise, Vendome, Angoulesme, Bouillon, Rohan, Longueville, Rochefoucault, Espernon" (*Discourses*, in *Works* 254–5). During the treasonous discussions which preceded Algernon's arrest in 1683, he is quoted as having informed his fellow conspirators of the French saying that "He who draws his sword against his prince ... ought to throw away the scabbard" (Scott, *Algernon/Restoration* 289).

From his rural fastness in Nerac, Algernon wrote to Monsieur de Bafoy, agent of de Bouillon, "[t]o acquit myself of the promise I made you to give news of the affairs of this country" (Paris Archives Nationales R 2/82; my transl.). As to be expected from the theological assumptions just discussed, the duc's local employees turn out to be *trop mauvaise*: "The first is simply an idiot, who signs false [acquittances] when Masselieres orders him to do so, and the other serves him in the villanies of the town house." Hunting resources are severely depleted because "there is no one who wishes to conserve the game ... d'Orient is not around for a quarter of the year, and that is only to collect the wood revenues or to insult somebody, but as for his job, when he is sitting with a bottle in front of the fire, he does not even take the trouble to get up at all the gunshots he can hear" (R2/82). More happily, we learn that Algernon has himself been riding and hunting, and has visited the author De la Rochefoucauld at his seat at Verteuil.

Remarkably, by 1677 Sidney had secured a conditional pardon and pass—in exchange for a vow to strictly abstain from actions prejudicial to the Crown—to return to England. This was the work of Sidney's grandnephew and the current Ambassador to Paris, Henry Savile, with whom Algernon maintained a subsequent correspondence reprinted in many editions of his *Works*. From Nerac on 18 December 1676 he wrote to Savile that he did "not value the leave you have obtained for me to return into my country after so long an absence, at a lower rate than the saving of my life" (*Works* 56–7). Algernon's immediate motivation appears on this occasion to have been personal and not political. He explained: "my desir of being ... somme service unto my old father perswaded me to ask leave to comme over" (*Original Letters* 79–80). He returned in early September, and the second Earl of Leicester died on 2 November.

In the background, however, was a family contestation concerning the earl's inheritance centered upon rivalry between Algernon and Philip, now third earl. This had its roots in the interregnum, and had involved a subsequent meeting between Algernon and his younger brother Henry at Limoges in 1675 (Scott, *Algernon/Republic* ch. 4 and 236–8; *Algernon/Restoration* ch. 5). In 1678 he wrote to Furly:

> I have no other business heare then to cleare some small contests that are growne between one of my brothers and me concerning that which he hath left me, and [then to] retire from hence ... to purchase a convenient habitation in Gascony ... where I may in quiet finish those days that God hath appointed for me. (*Original Letters* 79–80)

Later, he lamented in his *Apology*:

> When I prepared myself to return into Guascony ... I was hindered by the earl of Leicester my brother, who questioned all that my father had given me for my subsistence; and by a long and tedious suite in chancery, detained me in England, until I was made a prisoner. (in Sidney, *Works* 30–32)

While not strictly correct (Algernon received £5,000 immediately, and the use of the family's London seat, Leicester House), the Chancery suits in question furnish a trove of previously unknown biographical and emotional detail (see the preceding Scott references). Meanwhile, the idea of double imprisonment, first by a legal dispute, and then by an accusation of treason, is worthy of reflection. Writing to John Hampden Junior from the tower on 18 October 1683, Sidney said:

> I did yesterday receive a letter from a friend in Guascony, who tells me … he had tow houses … which should be at my disposal: one … I knowe very well … a good one, about twelve leagues above Bordeaux, the other … much better, and in a better country, is eight or ten leagues higher. If you can for a while content yourself with a country life, and it please God to deliver us from hence, wee may probably expect as much peace, safety and convenience ther as in any place I knowe. (Glynde Place Archives no. 794, Lewes Hampden Letter 6:3–4)

Thus Sidney probably expected his return to England to be temporary. However, when a major religious and political crisis broke out in late 1678, forcing Charles II to dissolve the Cavalier Parliament in December and imprison his chief minister, Danby, what followed was electrifying.

Between 1679 and 1681 three more Parliaments were called, eventually prorogued (in one case for a year), and finally dissolved. The underlying trigger for the crisis—its beginning and its end—was a rupture between Louis XIV and Charles II which led the French king to have read in Parliament deeply incriminating correspondence between the two monarchs exposing the secret monetary payments received by Charles since the signing of the Treaties of Dover in 1670 (Scott, *England's Troubles* chs. 7–8). The result was England's second seventeenth-century crisis of "popery and arbitrary government," only brought under control with the resumption of French funding, and consequent abandonment of Parliaments in 1681.

This was a revival of what we have heard Sidney's *Last Paper* call that "OLD CAUSE in which I was from my youth engaged." It was a "struggle to uphold the Common rights of mankind, the lawes of this land, and the true Protestant religion, against corrupt principles, arbitrary power and Popery …. I doe now willingly lay down my life for the same; and having a sure witness within me, that God doth … up hold me …am very little solicitous, though man doth condemne me" (*Apology* 27).

Refusing to remit his execution after an extremely doubtful trial, the king remarked: "Algernon Sidney had, on his return to England, promised him to behave blamelessly towards him; how was he to spare men who would not have spared him had he fallen into their hands?" (Von Ranke 4:188).

Algernon Sidney's involvement in the crisis, as shown below, may be said to have moved in stages from the overt and legal—and so arguably blameless—to the covert and conspiratorial. Nevertheless, that he broke the terms of the conditional pardon that permitted him to return is as clear as the reason: that his duty to God could not and would not be secondary to his promises to man. Returning to England, he had not expected this call; when it arrived, the king discovered that the pardon had been a bad idea.

Algernon's involvement seems surprising unless viewed in these terms and in the context of his own previous political experience. Assisted by the Quaker leader William Penn, to whom he had been introduced by Furly—and the three would collaborate on the first draft of the Frame of Government of Pennsylvania—he contested the parliamentary elections of both January and September 1679 (for Guildford and Amersham, respectively), as well as a subsequent by-election in Amersham (December 1680) (Scott, *Algernon/Restoration* 135–78). These attempts to secure a parliamentary seat were unsuccessful, though not by much, and meanwhile Sidney provided a continuing commentary upon the political situation in 1679 in his letters to Henry Savile in Paris.

It was during the thirteen-month prorogation of the House elected in September 1679 that the focus of political agitation turned to the City of London. The king's opponents could be forgiven for taking the view that parliamentary politics having been stifled, extra-parliamentary measures for defending Protestantism and Parliaments were now in order. One of these was to capture the government of the City and its judicial institutions (as in 1641), and it is from the French Ambassador to London, Barillon, that we learn in mid-1680 (reinforcing the analysis of Winship) that Algernon "is in the party of the independents and other sectaries ... [who] were masters during the late troubles ... they are strong in London ... and it is through the intrigues of ... Sidney that one of the two sheriffs, named Bethel, has been elected" (PRO Baschet Correspondence 147:402–3). Bethel, a republican writer and co-conspirator in the Netherlands, had been a member of the English Republic's Council of Trade.

A further avenue of influence was through Barillon himself, who reported on 6 October that:

> At the moment my most intimate liaison is with Mr. Algernon Sidney; he is the man in England who seems to me to have the greatest understanding of affairs; he has great relations with the rest of the Republican party; And nobody in my opinion is more capable of rendering service than him. (Archives du Ministère des Affaires Etrangères, Paris Correspondence Politique Angleterre 40)

In accounting for this startling estimate of Sidney's understanding, it is useful to bear in mind that these conversations were probably conducted in French; that Sidney would have known many senior figures in Barillion's French, as well as the English, political world (he was uncle of both the Earls of Halifax and Sunderland, equally important in this period), and that Sidney understood, as perhaps few English contemporaries below the king did, and even fewer subsequent historians have, with the exception of Leopold Von Ranke, the extent to which the current crisis hinged upon Anglo-French relations. Thus, with Barillion, Sidney applied himself negatively to emphasize to the ambassador the importance of not restoring to the king French funding; and positively to bring him to see what an error it was to believe the restoration of an English republic to be antithetical to French interests. This latter effort foundered on the same rock as the earlier courting of De Witt. The republic of 1649–53 had become much too powerful for French or Dutch comfort (Scott, *Algernon/Restoration* 124).

Sidney's closest allies in the Parliament eventually permitted to meet in October 1680 were Attorney General Sir William Jones and Colonel Silius Titus. They dominated the session in the Commons as Halifax did in the Lords. Following the king's dissolution of his subsequent and last Parliament at Oxford in April 1681, a pamphlet appeared titled *A Just and Modest Vindication of the Proceedings of the Two Last Parliaments*, described by Burnet as "the best writ paper in all that time ... at first penned by Sidney ... and corrected by Jones" (2:276–7). The *Vindication* anticipated various arguments and turns of phrase in the *Discourses* which Sidney began writing in the same year. The latter was a notably eloquent, deeply learned, and overly long argument in favor of insurrection. Amid a religious and political emergency, and given the chief magistrate's refusal to summon Parliament to counter the danger, there was no alternative.

Sidney was still writing the *Discourses* in May 1683 when he was arrested and imprisoned in the Tower. The manuscript was taken to be one of the two witnesses necessary to his treason on the grounds that "Scribere est agere" ("to write is to act")—an early and infamous application of Austin's Speech Act Theory. At the same time, from early 1683 and following the death in exile of his rival the Earl of Shaftesbury, Algernon had almost certainly played a leading role in organizing a joint Anglo-Scots uprising. This role was like the last. Crucial arguments were beginning to break out among the conspirators, insufficiently republican, obedient or godly, at the time of his arrest.

For the nature of the conspiracy and Algernon's subsequent imprisonment, trial and execution, readers may find details in Scott, *Algernon/Restoration* (chs. 12–14). Although all such plans have been conflated into the picturesque but distinct and possibly fictional "Rye House Plot," the outlines of Sidney's own design seem clear. In 1640 Charles I had been forced to end the Personal Rule and capitulate to Parliament by a successful Scots invasion. In 1679 the same thing had almost happened to Charles II. This was what Sidney and others were trying to re-animate in 1683.

Algernon was beheaded on Tower Hill on the morning of 7 December during a winter so cold that the Thames froze over. On the scaffold he explained that he had given a copy of his *Last Paper* to a friend, but meanwhile he had come "not to talk, but die … I have nothing to say to men" (Account 1683). In a privilege accorded to the brother of an earl, his body was released to be buried in "the sepulchar of his family" in the parish church at Penshurst.

This brings us back to the unanswered questions posed at the beginning of this chapter concerning sex life, children, the survival of the *Discourses*, and the unknown recipient of Algernon's last letter. In 1682 a satirical *Elegy* was published on the death of the republican Thomas Merry. To his deathbed Merry called "The Noble Peer / With Tap in Side[;] the Salamanca Seer / In his Geneva Cassack[; the] Colonel / with Cobs, with Scabs, with Cloak, with Sword most fell." These are, without question, Shaftesbury, Titus Oates, and Sidney. "To thee my colonel" Merry then bequeathed "my Arms and Armour … [and] into thy hands I do commit my spouse, whose Life I sav'd, yet ne'r read Aristotle … She's as Blithe, as Brisk and Debonair, as she thou hast of Danish Race and Hair" (Scott, *Algernon/Restoration* 85–6).

Who was "she"? A woman born to Sidney when he was in Denmark in 1659–60 would be in her early twenties by this time. In 1680—perhaps when it became clear that his stay in London would be prolonged—Sidney obtained permission for Joseph Ducasse, his "valet" in Nerac, to join him. Ducasse was a Huguenot, and so his arrival was part of a gathering tide of such immigration in the years leading up to the Revocation of the Edict of Nantes (1685). It was Ducasse who waited on Sidney throughout his imprisonment, and who was responsible for the hiding and safekeeping of his *Apology*, which he must have spirited out of the Tower, appearing with it before a committee of the House of Lords established to investigate the 1683 executions in 1690. *The Registers of the French Church, Threadneedle St London* show him married to one "Marie," and eventually the father of a number of children (Scott, *Algernon/Republic* 244n49, 50). Finally, a single letter from James Vernon to the Duke of Shrewsbury in 1697 refers to Ducasse as the Frenchman who "married Algernon Sidney's daughter" (James 273).

As explained earlier, the recipient of Sidney's last letter has until now proved impossible to identify because it survives in a bundle of letters to Hampden, but farewells "My most dear friend and kinsman," and Hampden was not a relative. It continues:

> When I first grew acquainted with you, I discovered those qualityes in you, that I had most loved in men, and by experience finding that I had judged rightly, grew to have more kindnesse unto you than ever I had to any man, and doe not think that any thing could break it, but that which is now shortly to ensue. For want of a better way of expressing it, when I made my will in March I gave you all I had. (East Sussex Hampton Letter 10, 1)

That will now being forfeit to the Crown, Sidney enclosed "as a token one bill for 1376 pounds upon a very honest merchant in London, and tow bills of exchange from Holland for 507 pounds" (Letter 10, 2). This is Algernon at his most attractive and touching.

It now becomes clear that the recipient was probably Ducasse. I confess to having been blinded, as the Crown was, by the fiction of his status as "valet." But a woman of Danish race and hair born to Sidney and subsequently married to Ducasse would make the latter a kinsman, and this friendship has remained obscure because it was a product—initially—of the years in Nerac. Sidney would not have consented to his daughter's marriage to anyone he did not admire, and of course he would thereafter attempt to make the couple the recipients of his will. During his sojourn in Nerac, on 13 May 1674, two English travelers, Suzanne Groundon and Oliver Cheyney, were married by a Huguenot pastor in the Comte de Sidney's house (Archives de Lot-et-Garonne, 4E 199/17). Was this a practice run, or were these pseudonyms?

Thus Algernon was attended in the Tower, and entrusted copies of the *Apology* and *Last Paper* not to his valet, but to his son-in-law and closest friend. And did he have a copyist produce a second version of the *Discourses* as he wrote, which was safely kept by the same person, making possible its publication in 1698? The publisher emphasizes—as publishers did, three years after the expiry of the Licensing Act—the unimpeachable integrity of his source.

It owed much to the high profile given to the *Discourses* by Sidney's martyrdom that for subsequent influence in Enlightenment Britain, America, the United Provinces, Germany, and France he had no rival alongside John Locke. After 1698 the text was reproduced in five further editions in London, two in the Netherlands, two in Paris, one in Edinburgh, and two each in Germany and the United States. In particular, we know that Sidney and Locke were by far the most widely read English sources in eighteenth-century America, including by the founding fathers, particularly John Adams and Thomas Jefferson. In that way, and perhaps in others, his influence, and those which shaped him, remain with us.

Bibliography

Manuscript Sources

Archives de Lot-et Garonne, Agen, France
  "Registre des mariages benie en l'eglise reformee de Nerac"
Archives Nationales, Paris
  R2/82
Bibliothèque Nationale, Paris
  Fr MS 23254 "Lantiniana"
British Library, London
  Add. MSS 32680, Sidney Papers
  Add. MSS 63057, Burnet Transcript (2 vols.)
  Sloane MSS 1519, Letters of State, Sidney to Fairfax, 1645
East Sussex Record Office, Lewes
  Glynde Place Archives no. 794, Sidney to Hampden and Ducasse
Ministère des Affaires Etrangères, Paris
  Correspondance Politique, Sous-serie Angleterre vols. 99, 102
Public Record Office (PRO), London
  Baschet Correspondence, PRO 31/3

Primary and Secondary Sources

Account of the Arraignment, Trial and Execution of Algernon Sydney Esq. London, 1683.

Ash's Intelligence from the North. London, 1644.

Blencowe, R. W., ed. *Sydney Papers, Consisting of a Journal of the Earl of Leicester, and Original Letters by Algernon Sidney.* London, 1825.

Borgeaud, C. *Histoire de L'Université de Genève: 1. L'Académie de Calvin 1559–1798.* Geneva, 1900.

Burnet, Gilbert. *History of My Own Time.* 2 vols. Oxford: Oxford UP, 1823.

Calendar of State Papers … Venice 1659–61. London: Longman Green, 1864–1947.

Carrive, Paulette. *La pensée politique d'Algernon Sidney 1622–1683. La querelle de l'absolutism.* Paris, 1989.

Carswell, John. *The Porcupine: The Life of Algernon Sidney.* London: John Murray, 1989.

Collins, Arthur, ed. *Letters and Memorials of State ….* 2 vols. London: T. Osborne, 1746.

Colyer-Fergusson, T. C. *London Huguenot Society Publications 16: Registers of the French Church, Threadneedle St., Volume 3.* London: Huguenot Society, 1906.

Ewald, A. C. *The Life and Times of Algernon Sidney.* 2 vols. London: Tinsley Brothers, 1873.

Fink, Zera. *The Classical Republicans: An Essay in the Recovery of a Pattern of Thought in Seventeenth Century England.* Evanston, IL: Northwestern UP, 1945.

Gilbert, J. T. *History of the Irish Confederation and the War in Ireland 1641–43.* 7 vols. Dublin, 1882–87.

Hammersley, Rachel. *The English Republican Tradition and Eighteenth Century France: Between the Ancients and the Moderns.* Manchester: Manchester UP, 2010.

HMC. *Report on the Manuscripts of Lord De L'Isle and Dudley Preserved at Penshurst Place.* 6 vols. London: HMSO, 1925–66.

Houston, Alan Craig. *Algernon Sidney and Republican Heritage in England and America.* Princeton, NJ: Princeton UP, 1991.

James, G. P. R., ed. *Letters Illustrative of the Reign of William III.* London, 1841.

Ludlow, Edmund. *A Voyce from the Watchtower Pt 5 1660–62.* Ed. A. B Worden. London: Camden Society, 1979.

Mahlberg, Gaby. *Henry Neville and England Republican Culture in the Seventeenth Century: Dreaming of Another Game.* Manchester: Manchester UP, 2006.

Meadley, G. W. *Memoirs of Algernon Sidney.* London: Cradock and Joy, 1813.

Nelson, Eric. *The Greek Tradition in Republican Thought.* Cambridge: Cambridge UP, 2004.

Norbrook, David. *Writing the English Republic: Poetry, Rhetoric and Politics 1627–1660.* Cambridge: Cambridge UP, 1999.

Oppenheim, H. *A History of the Administration of the Royal Navy and of Merchant Shipping in Relation to the Navy.* London: J. Lane, 1896; rpt. Hamden, CT: Shoe String P, 1961.

Parnham, David. *Sir Henry Vane, Theologian: A Study in Seventeenth-century Religious and Political Discourse.* London, 1997.

Pocock, J. G. A. "England's Cato: The Virtues and Fortunes of Algernon Sidney." *Historical Journal* 37 (1994): 4.

—. "Historical Introduction." *The Political Works of James Harrington.* Ed. J. G. A. Pocock. Cambridge: Cambridge UP, 1977.

—. *The Machiavellian Moment: Florentine Politics and the Atlantic Republican Tradition.* Princeton, NJ: Princeton UP, 1975.

Rahe, Paul A. *Against Throne and Altar: Machiavelli and Political Theory under the English Republic.* Cambridge: Cambridge UP, 2008.

—. *Republics Ancient and Modern, Volume 2: New Modes and Orders in Early Modern Political Thought.* Chapel Hill, NC: U of North Carolina P, 1994.

Robbins, Caroline. "Algernon Sidney's Discourses Concerning Government: Textbook of Revolution." *William and Mary Quarterly* 4.3 (1947): 267–96.

—, ed. *Two English Republican Tracts*. Cambridge: Cambridge UP, 1969.

Scott, Jonathan. "Algernon Sidney (1623–1683)." *ODNB*.

—. *Algernon Sidney and the English Republic, 1623–1677*. Cambridge: Cambridge UP, 1988.

—. *Algernon Sidney and the Restoration Crisis, 1678–83*. Cambridge: Cambridge UP, 1991.

—. *Commonwealth Principles: Republican Writing of the English Revolution*. Cambridge: Cambridge UP, 2004.

—. *England's Troubles: Seventeenth Century English Political Instability in European Context*. Cambridge: Cambridge UP, 2000.

—. *When the Waves Ruled Britannia: Politics and Political Identities 1500–1800*. Cambridge: Cambridge UP, 2011.

Sidney, Algernon. "The Character of Henry Vane Jnr." F. V. Rowe. *Sir Henry Vane the Younger: A Study in Political and Administrative History*. London, 1970. Appendix.

—. *Court Maxims*. Ed. Hans Blom, Eco Haitsma Mulier, and Ronald Janse. Cambridge: Cambridge UP, 1996.

—. *Discourses Concerning Government*. Ed. T. West. Indianapolis, IN: Liberty Fund, 1996.

—. *Original Letters of Locke, Algernon Sidney, and Anthony Lord Shaftesbury*. Ed. T. Forster. London, 1830.

—. *Sydney on Government: The Works of Algernon Sydney*. Ed. J. Robertson. London: W. Strahan, 1772.

—. *Sydney's Farewel*. London, 1683.

Skinner, Quentin. *Hobbes and Republican Liberty*. Cambridge: Cambridge UP, 2006.

—. *Liberty Before Liberalism*. Cambridge: Cambridge UP, 1998.

Von Ranke, Leopold. *A History of English Principally in the Seventeenth Century*. 6 vols. Oxford: Clarendon P, 1875.

Winship, Michael P. "Algernon Sidney's Calvinist Republicanism." *Journal of British Studies* 49.4 (2010): 753–73.

Wootton, David, ed. *Republicanism, Liberty and Commercial Society*. Stanford, CA: Stanford UP, 1994.

Worden, Blair. "The Commonwealth Kidney of Algernon Sidney." *Journal of British Studies* (1985): 241.

—. *The English Civil Wars: 1640–1660*. London: Weidenfeld & Nicolson, 2009.

—. "English Republicanism." *The Cambridge History of Political Thought*. Ed. J. H. Burns and Mark Goldie. Cambridge: Cambridge UP, 1990.

—. *Literature and Politics in Cromwellian England: John Milton, Andrew Marvell, Marchamont Nedham*. Oxford: Oxford UP, 2007.

—. *Roundhead Reputations: The English Civil Wars and the Passions of Posterity*. London: Penguin, 2001.

Henry Sidney (1641–1704), Earl of Romney, and Robert Spencer (1641–1702), Second Earl of Sunderland

Michael G. Brennan

Henry Sidney and the House of Orange

The crucial role of Colonel Henry Sidney (Earl of Romney from 1694) during the 1680s in supporting the claims of the House of Orange and William III to the English throne is now often underestimated and merits reassessment. In May 1678 Colonel Sidney, the fourth surviving and youngest son of Robert Sidney, second Earl of Leicester, and Dorothy (Percy) Sidney, Countess of Leicester, led an infantry regiment in the British expeditionary force to Flanders. These circumstances provided him with an opportunity to begin cultivating a lasting friendship with the Protestant William III, Prince of Orange (1650–1702), the future King William III. The time was ripe for the active fostering of Anglo-Dutch relations because on 4 November 1677 William had married Princess Mary, daughter of James, Duke of York, and thereby became a likely candidate for the English throne if his father-in-law was excluded because of his Catholicism. Henry Sidney's personal contacts with the prince were judged so promising that in June 1679 he was appointed as Envoy-Extraordinary to the States General of the United Provinces with a brief to maintain a defensive alliance with the Dutch against France. Sidney family connections proved crucial to this political appointment since it had been engineered largely through the influence of two close associates: his own nephew and coeval, Robert Spencer (from 1643, second Earl of Sunderland), and the preceding English envoy at The Hague, Sir William Temple (1628–99), who was the grandson of Sir Philip Sidney's trusted secretary during the 1580s, William Temple, and the nephew of Henry Hammond, formerly Rector of Penshurst, 1633–42.

Henry Sidney's relationship with William III, Prince of Orange, flourished during the next two decades, and he became a valuable conduit for diplomatic negotiations between the English and Dutch. The two men often dined and hunted together, and Sidney was treated by the prince and his family as a trusted confidant. On 11 August 1680, for example, he accompanied William on a poignant trip to view "the fortifications of Zutphen" (Sidney, *Diary* 2:94), where his great-uncle, Sir Philip Sidney, had received his mortal wound in September 1586. Another typical reference in one of his letters, dated 17 December 1680, records how that evening: "the Prince and Princess of Orange and Prince of Hanover do me the honour to come to my house. They shall have music and dancing, and the best entertainment I can give them" (*Diary* 2:146).

This level of personal intimacy between Henry Sidney and Prince William III was also founded upon a century of mutual respect and friendship between the Sidneys and the

House of Orange. The prince's great-grandfather, William I ("the Silent"), Prince of Orange (1553–84), had hoped in 1577 to marry his daughter, Marie of Nassau, to Henry Sidney's great-uncle, Sir Philip Sidney, who during the early 1580s had been keen to join William I's military forces. Philip's younger brother, Robert Sidney, served as Governor of Flushing from 1589 until 1616, and when his eldest son and heir, William, was born in November 1590, Louise de Coligny, Princess of Orange—the fourth and last wife of William I—had stood as godmother for the christening. Fifty years later Henry Sidney's older brother, Algernon (see Scott *ARC* 1:11), sought in late 1640 a military appointment in the forces of William II, Prince of Orange, in advance of the prince's marriage on 2 May 1641 to Mary Henrietta Stuart, the Princess Royal and eldest daughter of King Charles I. When addressing the Dutch Assembly at The Hague in August 1679, Henry Sidney was justifiably proud to recall:

> I am very glad to be employed in a service of so great importance to both nations, and I shall not fail to contribute all my endeavours towards it; and your Lordships having had so many of my family engaged formerly in employments here, will, I hope, take it as an earnest of my own good affection to the service of the State. (*Diary* 1:58)

On 28 January 1690 Henry Sidney also cryptically noted in his diary that "Monsieur Zulestein was married" (*Diary* 2:162)—an event that provided yet another Sidney family connection since William Frederick van Nassau van Zuylestein (later Earl of Rochford) married Jane Wroth (1659–1703), a Maid of Honour to Mary, Princess of Orange, and the daughter of Henry Wroth (a nephew of Henry Sidney's aunt, Lady Mary Wroth).

Following the death of King Charles II in February 1685, Henry Sidney crossed once again to the Low Countries in the following November and renewed his friendship with the Prince of Orange and his Protestant wife, Princess Mary. By 1688, the year of the "Glorious Revolution" when the prince was poised to invade England to support his claim to the throne, Henry Sidney was firmly established as his chief intermediary with supporters in England. He was prominent in the drafting of the formal letter (the final version was in his hand) that was delivered to William on 30 June 1688, inviting him to cross over to England. Gilbert Burnet, who was then serving as William's personal chaplain, recorded that Sidney was the "man in whose hands the conduct of the whole design was chiefly deposited, by the prince's own order" (*Bishop Burnet's History* 3:264). He landed with the prince at Torbay on 5 November (as his senior commanding officer in the field with the rank of major-general) for the House of Orange's largely peaceful claiming of the English throne.

Henry Sidney prospered during the reign of King William III, and on Coronation Day (9 April 1689) was created Baron Milton and Viscount Sidney of Sheppey. In 1689 he was appointed as a Privy Councillor, First Gentleman of the Bedchamber, and Lord Lieutenant and Vice-Admiral of Kent, followed by the Wardenship of the Cinque Ports and Constable of Dover Castle (1691), along with generous royal grants of extensive lands in Ireland. Most prominently, he occupied the public and symbolic role of one of the king's most experienced military commanders, echoing his family's proud tradition of royal military service stretching back to the distinction achieved by his great-great-grandfather, Sir William Sidney, at the Battle of Flodden (1513). During summer 1690 he served during the Irish campaign, culminating in his participation at the Battle of the Boyne and the Siege of Limerick. In May 1691 he was named, during William III's absence in Flanders, as overall commander of all foot regiments, and in March 1692 was appointed as Lord Lieutenant of Ireland, where his brother Philip, third Earl of Leicester, his father Robert, the second earl, and his great-grandfather, Sir Henry Sidney, had all held high office (see Warkentin *ARC* 1:9; McGowan-Doyle *ARC* 1:2). Recalled to England in 1693, he was chosen as Master-General of the Ordnance—a key post in relation to both national security and William III's military plans on the Continent. In May 1694 he was promoted to the rank of lieutenant-general and created first Earl of Romney.

By now in his mid-fifties, Henry Sidney retired from active field service, but remained prominent in military procurement and pageantry. He took a leading role in the London celebrations following the English triumph at the Siege of Namur (1695) and the signing of the Treaty of Ryswick (1697), which concluded the Nine Years' War and which had been managed by his nephew, Robert Spencer. This period marked the apogee of the royal court careers of both Henry Sidney and Robert Spencer, and they were named together among the Lord Justices to govern the country during William III's absence in 1697. Henry Sidney remained on intimate personal terms with the king, accompanying him on three separate visits to The Hague between 1699 and 1701. King William III died on 8 March 1702; on 28 September of the same year Robert Spencer died of heart failure and was succeeded as third Earl of Sunderland by Charles (c. 1674–1722), his only surviving son. The accession of Queen Anne effectively ended Henry Sidney's public career, and he died of the smallpox on 8 April 1704.

Education, Continental Travel, and Court Careers of Henry Sidney and Robert Spencer

Henry Sidney's distinguished court career during the last quarter of the seventeenth century often interlinked with that of his nephew and coeval Robert Spencer, Earl of Sunderland, with whom he had grown up as a child. However, even though Sidney and Spencer, as noted, were named together among those appointed in 1697 to govern the country while William III was abroad, their earlier careers during the reigns of Charles II and James II had sometimes taken divergent paths. Let us now look back in time to examine their shared childhood, youth, and early court experiences, and in particular their sometimes starkly contrasting personal affiliations with James II and William III.

Henry Sidney was born during his father's Paris embassy in spring 1641, and his nephew, Robert Spencer, was also born at Paris on the following September. They were to become lifelong friends and court associates, demonstrating yet again the political potency of Sidney family networks (see Brennan ARC 1:1). Robert was the eldest surviving son of Henry's sister, Dorothy, who had been widowed when her royalist husband, Henry Spencer, first Earl of Sunderland, was killed in 1643, aged twenty-two, at the Battle of Newbury. The two boys were educated together at Penshurst under the charge of Thomas Pierce, an ejected fellow of Magdalen College, Oxford. As political conditions grew uncertain in 1658, they were sent with Pierce to broaden their education by traveling on the Continent, where they stayed until Charles II's restoration was certain. They were abroad again for much of the first half of the 1660s. Robert traveled extensively through France (with William Penn, later the founder of Pennsylvania), Spain, Switzerland, and Italy, only returning briefly to England in 1663. Henry was in Italy again for most of 1664 with a cultured group of young Englishmen, including Henry Savile, Sidney Godolphin, William Trumbull, and his nephew Sunderland. When both young men finally returned to England in 1665, their court careers began in earnest. They were to prove themselves two of the most adaptable, pragmatic, and shrewd courtiers of their generation, even if they tended occasionally to overstretch themselves, both on the personal and political levels, and expressed differing political and royal loyalties.

Renowned for his good looks and social charms, Henry Sidney secured a position as Groom of the Bedchamber to James, Duke of York, and was soon appointed as Master of the Horse to the duke's wife, Anne, the daughter of Charles II's chief minister, Edward Hyde, Earl of Clarendon. Unfortunately, his flirtatious relationship with the duchess led to his dismissal, and he is known to have had liaisons at this period with other women, including Anne Temple (1649–1718) and Grace Worthley, by whom he had an illegitimate son, Henry (Sidney, *Diary* 1:xxvii–xxxv). By 1667 he was reduced to accepting a commission in a regiment under the command of his older brother, Robert Sidney (1626–68), in the United Provinces. After a failed attempt to gain a parliamentary seat in 1668, he returned to France in the following year. He was there again in 1672, this time to deliver a message of condolence from Charles II over the death of Louis XIV's daughter, Marie-Thérèse. Still ambitious for a formal presence at the English court, Henry purchased in 1675 the position of Master of the Robes, thereby gaining his first major post at the royal court.

Robert Spencer's court career also began in 1665, when he returned to England and married Anne, daughter of George Digby, Earl of Bristol, whom he had previously courted in 1663, but then suddenly fled abroad when a marriage was arranged. Apparently now happily married, Robert and Anne took up residence at the family's seat at Althorp, Northamptonshire. This union brought Robert into useful contact with his brother-in-law, George Savile, Earl of Halifax, who in 1656 had married Robert's sister, Dorothy Spencer (1640–70; see Akkerman *ARC* 1:10), and also with the Dukes of York and Monmouth. Through his wife's family he was on friendly terms with Henry Bennet, Earl of Arlington, Charles II's former agent at Madrid and his Secretary of State (1662–74). Arlington sponsored his introduction to diplomatic affairs, arranging for him to be sent in 1670 to Louis XIV to offer Charles II's thanks after the signing of the Treaty of Dover. In the following year Spencer went to Madrid as an envoy-extraordinary with the difficult brief of attempting to prevent an Hispano-Dutch alliance against the French. Although this mission achieved little, with Arlington's patronage he secured the English ambassador's post at Paris in 1672. Taken conveniently ill in March 1673 when about to depart on yet another taxing and expensive embassy to Cologne, he was able to shed his diplomatic duties and move back to London, where he secured a position as a Gentleman of the Bedchamber. By this time Arlington had fallen from royal favor, but Spencer deftly secured the personal support of Charles II's then most influential mistress, Louise de Kéroualle, Duchess of Portsmouth. He regularly acted as a verbal intermediary between the king and the duchess, and assisted in gaining royal assent in 1675 for the ennobling of her son as Duke of Richmond. He undertook two other brief diplomatic missions to the court of Louis XIV in 1667/68 before achieving genuine political potency in February 1679, when Charles II appointed him as his Secretary of State of the Northern Department.

Henry Sidney's father, Robert, second Earl of Leicester, died on 2 November 1677, and his will provided generous provision for both Henry and Algernon (see Scott *ARC* 1:11), to the detriment of their eldest brother, Philip, now third Earl of Leicester, who had fallen out with his father in 1652. A protracted chancery case ensued, with Henry residing at Penshurst and Algernon at Leicester House in London. The aftermath of the Popish Plot in 1678 and the beginnings of the Exclusion Crisis in 1679, focusing on the problems of the probable succession of Charles II's Catholic brother James, placed Henry Sidney and Robert Spencer at the very heart of governmental intrigues. Sunderland was active in trying to placate those most hostile to a Catholic succession, notably the Earl of Shaftesbury, and led an attempt to gain support for a scheme of limitations, under which James as a Catholic king would vow to uphold the Church of England and respect the authority of Parliament. Henry Sidney was simultaneously continuing to court the trust of William III, Prince of Orange, and now considered it imperative that William should either personally come to England or declare publicly his claim to the English throne. Sunderland's public support for the second Exclusion Bill in late 1680 led to his own temporary exclusion from royal favor; however, by September 1682 he had regained a seat on the Privy Council, and he was again named as Secretary of State on 31 January 1683.

In the aftermath of the Rye House Plot, which was supposedly planned to murder both Charles II and his brother and heir James, Duke of York, Henry Sidney's elder brother Algernon was executed on Tower Hill on 7 December 1683. Although his nephew, Robert Spencer, had distanced himself from the trial, Henry Sidney was allowed to bury Algernon's body at Penshurst and to inherit his estate. Sunderland's influence at court was still very much in the ascendant during 1684, and he was poised to become chief minister when Charles II unexpectedly died on 6 February 1685. Although his personal contacts with James had diminished during the Exclusion Crisis, his skillful manipulation of the House of Commons to ensure its support for the new king rapidly gained him royal favor, and he retained his post as Secretary of State. Renowned for his "time-serving and double-dealing" (Kenyon 21) and regarded as the "most political animal in late Stuart England" (Speck), two key elements facilitated Sunderland's political survival and prosperity under James II. Unencumbered by any strong religious convictions, he readily went along with plans for the re-establishment of the Church of England. But he was also ready to cultivate the most ardent Catholic faction rather than more moderate elements, calculating that their intimacy would propel him more rapidly into the king's innermost circle. Secondly, through his undoubted personal charms, he was soon able to exert a strong influence over James II's queen, Mary of Modena.

In 1685 the king entrusted Sunderland with presiding over the brutal legal repression of the Monmouth Rebellion led by Judge Jeffreys (who had sent his uncle Algernon to execution), and Sunderland rewarded Jeffreys by persuading James to appoint him as Lord Chancellor. With the Earl of Halifax dismissed for not supporting the repeal of the Test and Habeas Corpus Act, Sunderland became the most powerful man at court when he succeeded him as Lord President. During mid-1686 Sunderland completed his political metamorphosis by secretly converting to Catholicism, followed by the public conversion of his eldest son, Robert, in April 1687. Ever the deft courtier, the latter conversion meant that he could now show more sympathy towards moderate Catholics and Nonconformists by lending his full support to the royal Declaration of Indulgence for toleration of worship of April 1687. Following the birth of a son, James (later the "Old Pretender"), to James II and Mary on 10 June 1688, Sunderland publicly declared his earlier conversion to Catholicism.

When rumors escalated in the following September that William was poised to invade, both King James and Sunderland hastily sought to forge bonds of support with the formerly despised Anglican Tories. But when storms turned back William's first invasion force in mid-October, James was furious at having been persuaded to grant concessions to the Anglicans, and promptly sacked Sunderland as the scapegoat to placate Catholic resentment towards the policy of appeasement. Following William's successful landing at Torbay on 5 November, Sunderland immediately sought refuge in Catholic France, but was spurned by Louis XIV and instead spent the rest of the month raising funds for his exile abroad. To the surprise of many at court, Sunderland and his Protestant wife finally fled to Rotterdam, although his wife soon returned to England on 19 December with the manuscript of a "Letter to a Friend in London" for an English printer (Henry Sidney's copy, in Sunderland's hand, is BL Add. MS 32681 fols. 326–9), which simultaneously defended Sunderland's dealings with James II and lavishly praised the new king, William III. The Countess of Sunderland returned to Rotterdam in January 1689, but her husband was arrested and briefly imprisoned before his resourceful wife engineered his freedom by appealing to William's consort, Mary. They were able to return to England in April 1690 to reside on their Althorp estates, and Sunderland quietly resumed his seat in the House of Lords in January 1692. When James, from his exile in France, pointedly excluded Sunderland from his Proclamation of Pardon in April 1692, he was able to offer his absolute allegiance to William, and his tacitly given advice on the management of parliamentary and court affairs grew steadily more influential. He continued to exert considerable influence behind the scenes, and on 19 April 1697 was appointed Lord Chamberlain.

His opponents at court, however, sought his resignation in the following December, and although the king was unwilling to allow him to step down, he never again performed the duties of this office. He was also caught up during 1698 in an unpleasant scandal surrounding his Jacobite son-in-law, the Earl of Clancarty, who had deserted his first wife, Sunderland's daughter Elizabeth, and returned to Ireland to live as a Catholic and marry for a second time, only to then abandon this second marriage and to return to England to reclaim his first wife. Sunderland's eldest son, Charles, had him thrown into Newgate Prison, and this messy affair was finally solved by the departure abroad of Clancarty and Elizabeth to live in Germany on a royal pension. By now Sunderland preferred to spend most of his time on his Althorp estates, although he returned to London in December 1699 for the second marriage of his son Charles in the following January to Lady Anne Churchill, the daughter of the Earl of Marlborough, whom his uncle Henry Sidney had known well from visits to The Hague with William III. During the first two years of the eighteenth century Sunderland was influential in the negotiations for the Act of Settlement (1701) that led to the accession of the House of Hanover in 1714, but as his health rapidly failed, he died on 28 September 1702.

Diary and Correspondence of Henry Sidney

In 1843 a two-volume edition was published of the *Diary of the Times of Charles the Second by the Honourable Henry Sidney, (Afterwards Earl of Romney)*, edited by Robert Willis Blencowe, which also contained selections from his correspondence with his sister, the Countess of Sunderland, and other prominent court figures. Henry Sidney's diary covers the period 1 June 1679–18 January 1682, and Blencowe transcribed and interspersed with letters within its text at appropriate dates. Samples of Sidney's outgoing correspondence from this period include letters addressed to William III, Prince of Orange; James, Duke of York (the future King James II); Arthur Capel, Earl of Essex; William Savile, Viscount Halifax; and Sidney's nephew Robert Spencer, Earl of Sunderland. Copies of other letters from Sidney include those sent to Edward Conway, Earl of Conway; Laurence Hyde (later Earl of Rochester); Sidney Godolphin (later Earl of Godolphin); and the Welsh lawyer and diplomat Sir Leoline Jenkins.

Blencowe included samples of incoming correspondence from Henry Sidney's sister, the widowed Dorothy (Sidney) Spencer, Dowager Countess of Sunderland (see Akkerman *ARC* 1:10); the Earl of Sunderland and his countess, Anne Digby Spencer; the Duke of York; George Savile, Earl of Halifax; James Butler, Earl of Ormonde (also known as the Earl of Ossory); Ralph Montagu (later Duke of Montagu); Laurence Hyde; the politician and diplomat William Harbord (Herbert); Sidney Godolphin; John Mounsteven (Secretary to the Earl of Sunderland); William Savile; Sir William Temple; Gilbert Spencer (steward to Henry Sidney's father, the second Earl of Leicester); the diplomat Sir Richard Bulstrode; Sir Henry Capel (later Baron Capel of Tewkesbury); Sir Gabriel Sylvius (Chamberlain to the Prince of Orange); Sir Leoline Jenkins; and William Penn. A shorter concluding selection of letters covers the period February 1684–June 1689, with correspondence to Henry Sidney from Hans Willem Bentinck (later Earl of Portland); the diplomat Sir Robert Southwell; the Prince of Orange; the Countess of Sunderland; Princess Anne (later Queen Anne, the daughter of James II); Charles de Schomberg (later Duke of Schomberg); Bishop Gilbert Burnet; and the Earl and Countess of Sunderland.

Although these two early Victorian volumes still remain an invaluable primary source for the life and political career of Henry Sidney, many other relevant manuscript documents are now known, and there is a pressing need for a new edition of his correspondence. There is also a good case to be made for the undertaking of what would be the first book-length biography of this shrewd and ambitious individual. Henry Sidney's reputation is still a matter of historical controversy, as is demonstrated by the concluding paragraph of David Hosford's excellent *ODNB* article, explaining how he:

> has been the subject of widely divergent views about both his capacity and character. Macaulay dismissively described him as "incapable, ignorant, and dissipated" …. In turn, Macaulay seems to have been influenced by Jonathan Swift's disparaging references, one differing only slightly from the other, to the effect that Romney was "an idel, drunken, ignorant rake, without sense or honour" …. Thomas Bruce, second earl of Ailesbury, hardly a friendly witness, took a much more charitable view of his character, while John Macky called him the linchpin of the planning effort for the revolution, a man of honour and honesty who served William to the best of his ability. Both Burnet's *History* and the supplement to that work provide an even fuller portrait. It is certainly one of an individual with flaws, but also remarkable for his even temper, straight dealing, good judgement, and a knack for gaining the trust of others.

A wide range of other significant items from Henry Sidney's life and correspondence are now preserved at The National Archives, Kew, and at the Centre for Kentish Studies in the Sidney family's private archive, but generally these documents have not been utilized in previous assessments of his political importance. Apart from Blencowe's 1843 introduction to his *Diary* and David Hosford's informative entry in the *ODNB*, there is still no substantial study of the life and public career of Henry Sidney, Earl of Romney. His posthumous reputation remains controversial, but through his personal friendship with the Prince of Orange and his undoubted diplomatic skills, it may be argued that he did more than any other member of the Sidney family to define the future of the British monarchy for his own and succeeding generations.

Bibliography

Manuscript Sources

British Library, London
    Add. MS 4197 (extracts from correspondence)
    Add. MS 15914 fols. 120–27 (personal papers)
    Add. MSS 32680–83 (diary, correspondence and personal papers)
    Althorp Papers, Add. MSS 61126, 61486–90, 61501
Centre for Kentish Studies, Maidstone
    U1475 A47, A75, C163, E124–9, F8, O102–31, T332
    U1500 C2/47, E31–2, E71 (personal papers)

The National Archives, Kew (TNA)
    ADM 106/486/312, 106/492/90, 106/494/397
    C6/82/52–6; SP 44/43, 44/55–65, 44/71, 87/3, 87/5, 89/16
    PC 1/1/137–8
    SP 34/1, 34/1/8, 36/19, 41/3/1, 41/3/6–7, 41/34/1

Primary and Secondary Sources

Brennan, Michael G. *The Sidneys of Penshurst and the Monarchy, 1500–1700.* Aldershot: Ashgate, 2006.

Burnet, Gilbert. *Bishop Burnet's History of His Own Time.* Ed. M. Routh. 6 vols. Oxford: Oxford UP, 1823.

Hosford, David. "Henry Sidney, First Earl of Romney (1641–1704)." *ODNB.*

Kenyon, J. P. *Robert Spencer, Earl of Sunderland, 1641–1702.* 1958; rpt. Aldershot: Ashgate, 1992.

Macaulay, T. B. *The History of England From the Accession of James II.* Ed. C. H. Firth. 6 vols. London: Macmillan, 1913–15.

Sidney, Henry. *Diary of the Times of Charles the Second by the Honourable Henry Sidney, (Afterwards Earl of Romney) Including his Correspondence with the Countess of Sunderland and Other Distinguished Persons at the English Court; to which are Added Letters Illustrative of the Times of James II and William III.* Ed. Robert Willis Blencowe. 2 vols. London: Henry Colburn, 1843.

Speck, W. A. "Robert Spencer, Second Earl of Sunderland (1641–1702)." *ODNB.*

Swift, Jonathan. *The Prose Works of Jonathan Swift.* Ed. H. Davis. 14 vols. Oxford: Blackwell, 1939–68.

PART III
The Sidneys in Ireland and Wales

The Sidneys in Ireland

Thomas Herron

The Sidney family have had a powerful impact on the history, monuments, and letters of early modern Ireland. Most important among them, in terms of his military and administrative legacy, was undoubtedly Sir Henry Sidney (1529–86) (Illustration 5). He helped to lead the re-conquest, colonization, and administrative reforms of the country during the reigns of Queens Mary and Elizabeth I, with often bloody results. Historians, art historians, archaeologists, and literary scholars continue to study his acts in Ireland and the monuments he left behind.[1]

The importance of his son, Sir Philip Sidney (1554–86), to Ireland's literary legacy in the English language was also surprisingly influential and enduring, despite the brief time he spent there. A spirit of militant Protestantism with Philip at its center infuses the poetry of Edmund Spenser (c. 1552–99) and Lodowick Bryskett (c. 1546–c. 1612), for example, both New English administrators and planters in Ireland. Sir Philip's influence can be felt in John Milton's pastoral elegy "Lycidas" in turn.

This chapter will provide an overview of Sidney family activity in Ireland, focusing mainly on Sir Henry, before stressing the importance of his son Sir Philip in subsequent literary developments involving New English letters there. As their lives and works demonstrate, the legacy of the Sidneys was truly international, and Ireland plays a significant role in building that legacy.

The Sidneys in Ireland: Military and Administrative Roles

The military history of the Sidneys in Ireland is extensive. When Lord Philip John Algernon Sidney, second Viscount de L'Isle (1945–), became an Additional Member of the Military Division of the Most Excellent Order of the British Empire on 11 January 1977, in recognition of his distinguished service as a captain in the Grenadier Guards in Northern Ireland,[2] he followed in the footsteps of his ancestors who had fought with and without distinction in Ireland in the early modern period. The Sidney men, and at least one woman, who bolstered armies at that time include the current Viscount de L'Isle's namesakes Sir Philip (d. 1586), who toured Ireland with his father in 1576 (see below and Stewart *ARC* 1:4); Philip Sidney, Viscount de L'Isle and third Earl of Leicester (1619–98), who came to Ireland at the head of 600 horse in 1642 and served as Lieutenant-general of Horse under the Earl of Ormond (Illustration 28), and Algernon Sidney (1623–83), the republican martyr (Illustration 25),

---

1   See, most recently, Herron and Maley.
2   *The London Gazette, Second Supplement* no. 47118, 10 January 1977.

who accompanied his brother Philip to Ireland in 1642 as Captain of Horse (see Brennan *ARC* 1:12). Algernon's service was clouded by a court martial for cowardice in Dublin in 1643; he and four other commanders of cavalry were cleared of all charges (Scott). Other Sidney soldiers in Ireland included Sir Henry (d. 1586) (see below) and Henry Sidney, Earl of Romney (1641–1704), who accompanied William of Orange on campaign in 1690 and fought at the Battle of the Boyne and later at the siege of Limerick. He also served in the Grenadier Guards (Scott; Firth; Hosford). Mary Dudley Sidney (1530/35–86) called in troops to break the siege of Drogheda by Shane O'Neill in 1566; her husband absent, O'Neill reputedly wanted to kidnap her (Holland 58–9; Brennan 51; see McGowan-Doyle *ARC* 1:2).

Except for the first and last Philips, the above-mentioned Sidney men were also Irish administrators: Sir Henry (d. 1586) served as Vice-Treasurer and Lord Deputy (see below). Philip, the third Earl of Leicester, resumed his seat in the English Parliament in 1643 and became an "adherent of the Independent faction at Westminster, a group that advocated radical religious views, a drastic curtailment of the Crown's powers, and, more pertinently, the establishment of English hegemony over Ireland and Scotland" (Cronin 944). He and his circle were closely associated with the publication of the hard-line anti-Catholic Irish tract *The Irish Rebellion* (1646) by Sir John Temple (Cronin 944). These radical politics in London did not translate into effective governance among the New English in Ireland, however; Philip was appointed Lord Lieutenant in 1646, arrived in 1647, "accomplish[ed] nothing," and left the same year (Firth). As "the do-nothing figurehead of a do-nothing Irish policy," he aggravated the "adventurers, Army, and the Protestants in Munster" in particular, including the native Irish Earl of Inchiquin (Bottigheimer 97, 103–6).

Algernon Sidney was Commissioner for Irish Affairs in the English Parliament in 1652, where he played a "major role" in Cromwell's post-conquest settlement, "for the satisfaction of those adventurers who had lent money to Government to quell the Irish rebellion on an assignment of the confiscated lands" taken from the Irish (Ewald 1:143). Henry Sidney, Earl of Romney, was temporarily a Lord Justice of Ireland in 1690, and was sent there in 1692 as Lord Lieutenant, a post in which he fared poorly. He was unpopular among the governing class in Ireland for his excessive sympathy for the defeated Jacobites and Catholics, for assigning forfeited estates to Williamite cronies, and for resisting efforts to increase Irish parliamentary authority (which was dominated by the New English faction). He was charged with corruption and lost (or sold) most of his own 50,000 confiscated acres in Ireland in 1699—a huge amount of land (McGrath; Hosford; Lenihan 202–3). In addition, Robert Sidney, second Earl of Leicester (1595–1677), was appointed Lord Lieutenant of Ireland in the wake of the fall of Thomas Wenworth, Earl of Strafford (1593–1641), but never traveled to Ireland (unlike his sons Philip, Algernon, and Henry, above; and see Warkentin *ARC* 1:9). The poet Sir Philip, had he lived past Zutphen, might well have become governor there (see below).

Sidney women with connections to Ireland included Frances Sidney Radcliffe, Countess of Sussex (1531/32–89), and Anne Sidney Fitzwilliam (1526–99), both sisters of Sir Henry (d. 1586). They resided with their Lord Deputy husbands periodically in Dublin (Holland). Philip the poet's widow, Frances Walsingham (1567–1633), married Robert Devereux, second Earl of Essex (1565–1601), Lord Lieutenant of Ireland and commander of the queen's forces there in 1599. Frances's third husband was the Irishman Richard Burke, Earl of St. Albans and fourth Earl of Clanricarde (1573–1635), another administrator and veteran of Irish wars. Frances lived with him in London, Kent, and on occasion (beginning in 1604) in Ireland, where he had various estates, including a fine early modern house (recently restored and open to the public) at Portumna, Co. Galway (Fenlon; Wilks 16–17). She joined her husband by becoming Catholic (see Ioppolo *ARC* 1:6). Philip's poetic inspiration, Penelope Riche (1563–1607), became the mistress (then wife) of Charles Blount, eighth Baron Mountjoy and first Earl of Devonshire (1563–1606), who served as field commander and Lords Deputy, Justice and Lieutenant of Ireland (1600–04). Blount famously won the Battle of Kinsale; the fourth Earl of Clanricarde, known as "Richard of Kinsale," fought alongside him and earned distinction there.

Sir Henry Sidney

Both a proper biography and an archaeological survey of the works of Sir Henry Sidney (d. 1586) and of his wife Mary have yet to be written. Ample correspondence between them and their works, including their children, some of whom lived (and one of whom died) in Ireland, would seem to warrant such labor. Sidney served as Vice-Treasurer and General Governor of Revenues (1556–69) and three-time Lord Deputy (1565–67, 1568–71, and 1575–78) of Ireland,[3] while also serving as Lord President of the Council in the Marches of Wales (1560–86) and in other capacities (see McGowan-Doyle *ARC* 1:2). His reward for governing Ireland was occasional success, further rebellion, immortality in verse, and (according to him) penury.

Sir Henry's rule as Lord Deputy has garnered extended historical attention. A long-running debate begun in the 1970s focuses on the degree to which his reforms on a national scale were indeed truly innovative. Whereas Ciarán Brady, for example, sees Sidney's reforms as intensifications of policies of his predecessor as Lord Deputy, Thomas Radcliffe, Earl of Sussex, and hence in line with a gradual process of English rule over the Ireland, albeit heavily reliant on coercive means and the power of individual viceroys (*Chief Governors*), Nicholas Canny emphasizes a renewed wave of colonization, Protestantism, and ethnic stereotyping that accompanied Sidney's rule, which he sees taking on new form and intensity during Sidney's first and third deputyship ("Review Article"; *Making Ireland British* 53–54). Canny, Brady, Brendan Bradshaw, and others have also debated the character and influence of "humanism" as an agent of sometime violent reform in early modern Ireland, including Sidney's role therein (Canny, *Making Ireland British* 37; Bradshaw; Brady, "Spenser's Irish Crisis"; see also Carey, "The Irish Face"). The well-educated Sidney emulated classical models in word and deed: not only Julius Caesar conquering the Gauls (Sidney, *Memoir* 8–10; Siegfried), but also the ancient Roman general and governor of Celtic Britain Agricola, celebrated by Tacitus. Agricola demonstrated a "central axiom of Roman imperialism: brutal and bloody repression was necessary before peaceful colonial governance could be established" (Brennan 52).

Sidney's efforts to transform the country on a national scale placed both the native Irish and Old English establishments there in turmoil.[4] His humanist reform agenda included military campaigns, colonization, new taxation, and promotion of provincial presidencies at the expense of local lords. To what extent Sidney promoted an "absolutist" agenda

---

3   Sidney's lord deputyship is divided by many historians into two terms, not three. For these dates (which follow the timeline in *The New History of Ireland*) and discussion, see Herron and Maley (1n). Thomas White states that he was "three times Lord Deputy in the Irish parts" (B3v).

4   Ireland's inhabitants in the period are usually classified according to three main cultural groupings: the "native Irish," who spoke Irish as their primary language and were of Gaelic descent from prehistory; the "Old English," who were descendants of the original twelfth-century Anglo-Norman conquerors of much of Ireland, and the "New English," or the newcomers and settlers who arrived as part of the sixteenth-century English re-conquest and re-administration of the country. The first two groups were predominantly Catholic; the third group was predominantly Protestant and far less integrated into native Irish language and culture than the second one was.

avant la lettre is also debated.[5] The Old English of the Dublin Pale, England's traditional stronghold of loyalty in the country and a close-knit civic identity, feared for their traditional liberties and independence in the face of Sidney's princely prerogatives. The Old English greatly resented Sidney's effort to impose the cess (land tax) on them in order to pay for the government, including armies. Nor did they generally support Sidney's reformed religious views, given their own majority Catholic status and the strong influence of the Counter-Reformation in Ireland. Recent work on Sidney has emphasized his persistent evangelical efforts in the country (Hutchinson). Again, he was an innovator in this regard. He patronized a Church primer of the reformed religion, the *Aibidil Gaoidheilge & Caiticiosma* ("Gaelic alphabet and catechism") (1571) by Seán Ó Cearnaigh. It was the first book published in Irish in Ireland, and has been described as "the most lasting product of Sidney's subtle but ambitious religious agenda" (Caball 298). It includes a translation of Sidney's declaration on the articles of religion, proclaimed at Dublin in 1566–67.

Sidney's relations with the Old English beyond the Dublin Pale were no better. Sidney's reforms helped to provoke the Butler revolt of 1569, which only further cemented the powerful tenth Earl of Ormond's animosity towards Sidney (Edwards, "The Butler Revolt"). Sidney's efforts to reform the Pale and the rest of the country coalesced during his Dublin Parliament of 1569–71. Sidney convened the Parliament so as "to promote the policy of conquest," and it included the retrospective attainder of the already dead Shane O'Neill as another vital part of his reform and propaganda campaign (Hayes-McCoy 3:92–3; Treadwell; McGowan-Doyle 88–94). The Parliament lasted for three years, and while the attainder passed, other reforms were frustrated or compromised, mainly due to Old English resistance.

Sidney's attitudes towards the native Irish were sometimes extreme, egged on by colonial or ethnic prejudice. His campaigns against Shane O'Neill in Ulster were brutal and earned acclaim on the London stage in the 1590s (Heywood 178).[6] He described the chronically rebellious O'Byrne clan of Wicklow as "those caniballs of Goulranell" who deserve "extirpinge" (Egerton 70), and he treacherously massacred many of the midland O'Mores at Mullaghmast (Carey, "John Derricke's *Image*"). Indeed, his nonchalance over killing so many people on his campaigns, expressed in his *Memoir*, is deeply disturbing (Maley, "The Name"). Studies of atrocity, memory, and trauma in early modern Europe can profit from following Sidney and his bloody paper trail (Palmer 30–31). Overall, Sidney's tenures as Lord Deputy came well along the road of a long-term escalation of state-sponsored violence that he, arguably, intensified (Edwards, "Beyond Reform"; Edwards, "The Escalation"; Palmer). Sidney promoted a harsh agenda against those he perceived as resisting Crown authority.

As part of his colonial reform, Sidney patronized expert cartography in Ireland (including associations with Daniel Rogers and Robert Lythe) and proudly renamed Ulster's largest lake, Lough Neagh, Lough Sidney (Morgan, "Overmighty Officers"; Smyth 36–43). A polymath, he patronized the arts, which celebrated his rule. Both monuments and books emphasized how he reformed and scourged the Irish and the Old English in Ireland. Many monuments, some still standing, can be found in Ireland and await a programmatic

---

5   For example, Ciarán Brady writes that Sidney's reforms included "proposals to impose taxation without parliamentary consent," the "establishment of powerful regional governors," and "a willingness to exempt compliant nobility from taxation," all of which demonstrate "a drift in his thinking on Ireland toward a form of government that would later be recognised as absolutism. But if so, Sidney himself was largely unconscious of it" (Brady, "Sidney, Sir Henry"; see also Sidney, *Memoir* 35–6; Herron and Maley 7–9; Morgan, "Overmighty Officers").

6   Given the date of the play's likely composition and first performance (*c.* 1596), the threatening Shane O'Neill must have reminded viewers of Hugh O'Neill, Earl of Tyrone (O'Neill 127–8).

catalogue.[7] Most dramatically, Sidney built bridges with sophisticated propaganda schemes and continued the restoration of Christ Church, Dublin, begun by his predecessor, Lord Deputy Sussex, including a substitute tomb to replace the destroyed tomb of Strongbow, the original twelfth-century Anglo-Norman conqueror of Ireland. Sidney erected a stone plaque celebrating his own deeds above it (Bradley; Manning; Kinsella 109, 113, 137; Morgan, "Giraldus" 30–31; Herron and Maley 3–7).

Sidney had literary ambitions as well. His extraordinary *Memoir*, written *c.* 1582–83 but unpublished until the late nineteenth century and only recently edited into a stand-alone volume, is a lengthy account of his service in Ireland. It shows a heroic Caesar on constant campaign, but its immediate purpose was strategic and courtly. Sidney wrote the so-called memoir not for its own sake as a memorial for all time, but primarily as a compendium of talking points and refutations of criticisms for Sir Francis Walsingham and Sir Henry's son Philip Sidney to use in support of his candidacy for a fourth term as the queen's Governor of Ireland (Shephard 174).

It would appear, in this regard, to complement John Derricke's lavishly illustrated *Image of Irelande with a Discoverie of Woodkarne* (1581), which may have been published with Sidney's preferment to greater office in mind. Sidney had hoped to be appointed by the queen to a more lucrative and powerful post, Lord Lieutenant, for a fourth tour; his request was turned down (Brennan 75). Ireland, like so many divided and ill-funded places, was an opportunity for enrichment and status for bold, harsh, and ambitious outsiders. Sidney is patron and heroic subject of Derricke's book, which is best-known for its twelve spectacular, high-quality woodcuts of the native Irish in their element and Sidney on campaign against them. It also has a lengthy, little-studied poem attached, with a rambling, disjunctive narrative and poor-quality verse. Its bigoted anti-Irish message and apocalyptic overtones seem alarming today. Nonetheless, the *Image* has great value as a cultural resource. Given its detailed prints, the book may have been intended in part for a sophisticated international audience eager to inquire about Irish customs, and not only to abolish them (Moroney 155–7; Herron and Maley 13–17).[8] While it may have compromised Sidney's position at court, exposing him as an ambitious over-reacher (Brennan 75), it persists as his most effective and visible monument.

Sidney therefore had an antiquarian as well as authoritarian streak. *The Image* should be further studied in this dual regard, and the woodcuts themselves deserve proper art-historical analysis. In a similar paradox, Sir Henry not only vanquished his Irish foes and accelerated Protestant reform, but he patronized Catholic writers, such as Richard Stanihurst, who dedicated his history of Ireland to him.[9] Sidney also patronized Stanihurst's tutor and authorial source the martyr Edmund Campion. Campion's history of Ireland, Ireland's first early modern history in English, was researched in Ireland under Sidney's protection in 1571, and praises Sidney's government therein.

Sir Henry's dual reputation as colonial governor and humanist therefore persists beyond his own time thanks to high-quality monuments in stone and paper. Richard Robinson dedicates his translation of John Leland's *A Learned and True Assertion of the Original Life, Actes, and Death of the Most Noble, Valiant, and Renowned Prince Arthure, King of Great Brittaine* (1582) to Sir Henry and to Arthur, Lord Grey (A1–A2). After Sidney's death the aptly named *Englands Hope, against Irish Hate* (1600) by "J. G. E." (John Egerton?) celebrates him as a

---

7   See Kinsella for the best overview so far, with a focus on Sidney monuments in Christ Church
     Cathedral, Dublin in particular.
8   For further discussion of Henry and his family's patronage and use of New World tracts, see Kuin.
9   Raphael Holinshed dedicated the Irish section of the 1577 edition of his *Chronicles* to Sidney. These
     dedications were repeated in the 1586 edition.

conquering reformer for the English Protestant cause, alongside the Earl of Essex and Lord Grey (D1). Sir Henry built impressive monuments and provoked rebellion in Ireland while helping to shape an enduring legacy of sharply partisan and sectarian reform.

Sir Philip in Ireland

Sir Henry's son Philip was considered a suitable replacement for his father as Viceroy of Ireland. His father suggested the idea in a letter of advice to Lord Deputy Arthur, Lord Grey (Duncan-Jones, "*Discourse*" 6).[10] The humanist Daniel Rogers wrote a Latin poem praising the young man for the position of viceroy, "For the house of Sidney was destined for the land of Ireland, a house that is indeed worthy to prescribe the law to a state" (Brennan 71).

Philip and his mother were slated to join his father there in 1570, but were prevented from doing so by Henry's recall in 1571. Undeterred, Philip visited briefly in the summer of 1576, probably in the company of Walter Devereux, the first Earl of Essex (who was to die in Dublin Castle while Sir Philip was still in the country) (Woudhuysen; Maley, "Sir Philip Sidney"; Duncan-Jones, *Sir Philip Sidney* 108–12). While there, Sir Philip traveled west and met the famous female sea-captain and chieftain Grace O'Malley.

Little remarked on or downplayed is his participation campaigning with his father against the rebel sons of the Earl of Clanricarde, which makes him yet another military veteran among the Sidneys there (Duncan-Jones, *Sir Philip Sidney* 109–10), particularly ironic given his widow's marriage into that family (see above). Nicholas Lichefield demonstrates Sir Philip's potential interest in Irish military affairs when he dedicates his translation (from Spanish into English) of *De Re Militari* by Luis Guiterres de la Vega to Sir Philip. Lichefield in his dedication notes that his copy-text was acquired from the "fort" in Ireland occupied by Spanish and Italians, which must refer to the Fort d'Oro at Smerwick, Co. Kerry (captured by Lord Grey in 1580). The translation is appended to the second edition of Thomas Styward's *Pathwaie to Martiall Discipline* (1582), which also declares on its title page where de la Vega's work was found: "where the Spaniards and Italians had fortified themselves."

George Whetstone's praise poem *Sir Phillip Sidney, His Honorable Life, His Valiant Death, and True Vertues. A Perfect Myrror for the Followers both of Mars and Mercury* places Ireland as a shaping force in Philip's martial knowledge:

> He oft did reade, which well he did regarde,
> That prudent Peace, had still to Warre an eye:
> And therefore he the souldier good prefarde,
> Whose life, himselfe, in *Ireland* did trye,
> Till Essex di'de the flower of Chiuallry,
> And euermore, the Lawrell with the Launce:
> He excerside his Honour to aduaunce. (B2v)

According to Whetstone, Sidney was inspired by the first Earl of Essex's own heroic efforts and death in Ireland; Sidney inherited the earl's sword and martial spirit. Sidney's

---

10 See also Henry Sidney, "Sir Henry Sidney to Arthur Lord Grey, Lord Deputy of Ireland; How to Proceed in his Government of that Kingdom" (1580), in Egerton 70. Nicholas Canny suggests that Sir Philip wrote his policy tract on Ireland in part to promote himself for the position of Lord Deputy, succeeding his father (*Making Ireland British* 62).

example as soldier would live on in the memory of the Irish-based versifiers Bryskett and Spenser.

Philip fully supported his father's endeavors at subduing the native Irish and bringing the Old English to heel. In a rare mention of his father in his poetry, he boasts that Sir Henry's is the "golden bit" that "once made [Ulster] half tame." The "golden bit" could refer to the cess, or taxes, imposed by Sir Henry with varying success in order to raise armies to tame O'Neill in the north (Sidney, *Astrophil and Stella* #30; Westerweel). Writing from Wilton House in 1577, Philip wrote a "strikingly Tacitean" policy tract, "Discourse on Irish Affairs" (1577), of which only a fragment survives (Brennan 51, 73; Duncan-Jones, *Sir Philip Sidney* 114–15). It defends his father's imposition of the cess and his "severe means" in government. According to Philip, the Irish "choose rather all filthiness, than any law," live under petty tyrants, are dangerous supporters of the pope, and could at any time side with a foreign—that is, non-English—invading force (11), as indeed they would.

Sidney likewise inspired those who followed him to the country. His widow became deeply involved with men deeply involved in Ireland's wars, and lived there (see above). His friends Edward Denny and Lodowick Bryskett, as well as the poet Edmund Spenser, whom he patronized, became Protestant settlers and administrators in Ireland. Bryskett and Spenser lionized Sidney in their verse as a great intellectual and poetic inspiration, as well as an example of the virtuous soldier who shone in difficult circumstances. Sidney's martyrdom fighting for the Protestant cause in the Netherlands inspired their own artistic and political purpose in Ireland.

Sir Philip's Irish Legacy: Bryskett, Spenser, and Milton

In 1568 Sir Henry Sidney briefly owned Kilcolman, Co. Cork, which would eventually become Edmund Spenser's home (Jones 239). The coincidence is one of many that encourage further research into the legacy of the Sidneys in Spenser's life and works. Spenser moved into Kilcolman some time in the late 1580s as an undertaker (or principal owner/settler) on the Munster Plantation, and he can be said to have inhabited Sidneian spaces in more ways than one.

Spenser, like the Sidneys, was a partisan and beneficiary of the Earl of Leicester's militant Protestant faction at court. He began living in Ireland when he followed his employer Arthur, Lord Grey to Dublin in 1580; Spenser may have served Sir Henry in Ireland earlier, however, in 1577, and Sir Henry (if not Leicester himself) likely played a role in placing Spenser into Grey's service (Brennan 74; Maley, "Spenser's Life" 18; Judson 11:71–2).

Spenser regularly evoked the heroic spirit of Sir Philip. Spenser celebrates international, militant Protestantism in chivalric guise in *The Faerie Queene*, a poem fraught with Irish politics; in his dedicatory sonnet to Philip's sister Mary, Countess of Pembroke, appended to the 1590 edition, Spenser emphasizes the debt he feels to an unnamed "most Heroicke spirit … His goodly image liuing evermore, / In the diuine resemblaunce of your face; / Which with your virtues ye embellish more."[11] Philip's loss is lamented and his spirit celebrated in Spenser's poem "Colin Clouts Come Home Againe" (1595), which prominently situates Spenser as

---

11　"To the Right Honourable and Most Vertuous Lady, the Countesse of Penbroke" (Spenser, *The Faerie Queene* 734). The spirit could also conceivably refer to that of her father, Henry. In the sixth Commendatory Sonnet appended to the same volume, the author "W. L." refers to "Sidney" three times as patron of Spenser. Sidney's first name is not specified (724). Sir Sergis in *The Faerie Queene* V.xi.38ff. might allegorize Sir Henry Sidney (589n).

a complaining shepherd-poet in Munster. Colin Clout, Spenser's alter ego, laments "Now after *Astrofell* is dead and gone: / But while as *Astrofell* did liue and raine, / Amongst all these was none his Paragone" (ll. 449–51). In these three succinct lines Sidney is lost, resurrected (in parallel syntax to the previous line), and his fame bruited. Sidney's life, death, and fame are resurrected later in the same volume, in Spenser's epyllion "Astrophel," a retelling of the Venus and Adonis myth, wherein Sidney at Zutphen is allegorized as Astrophel, and the Spanish as the boar that destroys him. Astrophel's love Stella joins him in death, and both are resurrected as a flower. Tellingly, the woods where Astrophel encounters the boar are compared to those of Spenser's foreboding "Arlo wood" near Kilcolman (l. 96). The poem is dedicated to Sidney's widow, Frances Walsingham, then Countess of Essex. Spenser thus reminds her and the reader to keep his Irish situation in mind as he tells the sad story of a hero, a primary literary patron, and inspiration who could once have been his Lord Deputy. Instead, the second Earl of Essex would eventually take up that office (as Lord Lieutenant of Ireland).

The volume *Colin Clouts Come Home Againe* concludes with various elegies to Philip, including two by his bosom companion, Lodowick Bryskett, another planter and administrator in Ireland (these poems may be co-written by Spenser; Hadfield 314; Cheney 251–2). In one of these, "A Pastorall Aeglogue Upon the Death of *Sir Philip Sidney Knight, &c.*," the character Colin Clout (that is, Spenser) laments Sidney's death in pastoral guise in back-and-forth dialogue with Bryskett's own alter ego, Lycon (an anagram of "Colin"). The setting is clearly Ireland, the speakers New English, and the message is that Sidney's loss will not go unfelt on the edges of the empire. Laments Colin:

> Unhappy flock that wander scattred now,
> What maruell if through grief ye woxen leane,
> Forsake your food, and hang your heads adowne?
> For such a shepheard neuer shall you guide,
> Whose parting, hath of weale bereft you cleane. (100)

The Protestant flock has lost its shepherd, but the poets are inspired by and will immortalize him as they tend their own sheep.

Deeply affective is the repeated refrain "Phillisides is dead," which likely inspired John Milton's "For Lycidas is dead" (l. 8). Milton's "Young Lycidas" of line 9 echoes the "Young Astrophel" of Spenser's poem as well ("Astrophel" ll. 8–9) (Elledge 255). "Lycidas" mourns the death of young Edward King, scion of a powerful New English settler family in Connacht. Edward drowned while sailing home to Ireland *en route* from Cambridge University. King was planning to serve in the Protestant ministry; the "blind mouths" of the Church that are targeted for reform in "Lycidas" therefore refer to both Irish and English Churches threatened by the "Woolf with privy paw" (ll. 119–28). In "Lycidas" the Protestant ghost of Philip is happily transformed across time and place into the name "Lycidas," with a further pun on *felicity*, lost by Bryskett and, at a further remove, by Milton. So, too, Irish waters lament the loss of Sidney in Bryskett's "Pastorall Aeglogue" (95), thus foreshadowing the dangerous waters and weeping nymphs of Milton's poem.

Milton's poem nonetheless promises future action. Sorrow continues yet consolation comes knowing that King has earned his place in heaven. Such consolation is standard for the genre; it occurs in "Colin Clouts Come Home Againe" and "A Pastoral Aeglogue" regarding the lost shepherd Sidney. As in "Lycidas," the shepherds rise purposefully at the end of the poems and drive their flocks to shelter. In Bryskett's poem a lingering "feruent zeale and pure" keeps the flowers strewn upon Phillisides' grave from wilting entirely (100).

186

Milton, in turn, keeps an Irish militant Protestant, imperial, Elizabethan spirit alive in his picture of the flower-strewn hearse of "Lycidas." Its "daffadillies" and "cowslips" (150, 146) echo details from the flower-catalogue in the fourth (April) eclogue of Spenser's *Shepheardes Calendar* (ll. 140–41), which heralds Elizabeth in Virgilian terms as an ideal queen (Browne, cited in Elledge 299–300). Spenser will later rewrite this ideal image of the fertile queen into the pastoral Irish countryside in "Colin Clouts Come Home Againe": when Colin is dead and gone, "shepheardes daughters dancing rownd ... with flowry gyrlonds crownd" will forever sing his verse in praise of Cynthia (that is, Queen Elizabeth) (ll. 641–3). Milton resurrects Bryskett's Phillisides within the afterglow of the divine glory of this same queen, Spenser's queen, in a bold statement of imperial poetry facing westward towards Ireland—and guarding against Spain's incursions into England—with an ambitious but mournful hope of epic works to come.

Bibliography

Primary and Secondary Sources

Bottigheimer, Karl S. *English Money and Irish Land: The "Adventurers" in the Cromwellian Settlement of Ireland*. Oxford: Clarendon P, 1971.

Bradley, John. "Sir Henry Sidney's Bridge at Athlone, 1556–67." *Ireland in the Renaissance, c. 1540–1660*. Ed. Thomas Herron and Michael Potterton. Dublin: Four Courts P, 2007. 173–94.

Bradshaw, Brendan. "Sword, Word and Strategy in the Reformation in Ireland." *Historical Journal* 21 (1978): 475–502.

Brady, Ciarán. *The Chief Governors: The Rise and Fall of Reform Government in Tudor Ireland, 1536–88*. Cambridge: Cambridge UP, 1994.

—. "Sidney, Sir Henry (1529–86)." *Dictionary of Irish Biography: From the Earliest Times to the Year 2002*. Ed. James McGuire and James Quinn. Cambridge: Cambridge UP, 2009. 938–41.

—. "Spenser's Irish Crisis: Humanism and Experience in the 1590s." *Past and Present* 111 (May 1986): 17–49.

Brennan, Michael. *The Sidneys of Penshurst and the Monarchy, 1500–1700*. Aldershot: Ashgate, 2006.

Browne, R. C., ed. *English Poems by John Milton*. Oxford: Oxford UP, 1866; 1894.

Bryskett, Lodowick. "A Pastorall Aeglogue Vpon the Death of Sir *Phillip Sidney Knight, &c.*" (1595). Scott Elledge, *Milton's "Lycidas"*. New York: Harper and Row, 1966). 95–101.

Caball, Marc. "Print, Protestantism, and Cultural Authority in Elizabethan Ireland." *Elizabeth I and Ireland*. Ed. Brendan Kane and Valerie McGowan-Doyle. Cambridge: Cambridge UP, 2014.

Canny, Nicholas. *Making Ireland British, 1580–1650*. Oxford: Oxford UP, 2001.

—. "Review Article: Revising the Revisionist." *Irish Historical Studies* 30 (1996): 242–54.

Carey, Vincent. "The Irish Face of Machiavelli: Richard Beacon's *Solon His Follie* (1594) and Republican Ideology in the Conquest of Ireland." *Political Ideology in Ireland, 1541–1641*. Ed. Hiram Morgan. Dublin: Four Courts P, 1999. 83–109.

—. "John Derricke's *Image of Irelande*, Sir Henry Sidney, and the Massacre at Mullaghmast, 1578." *Irish Historical Studies* 31 (1999): 305–27.

Cheney, Patrick. "*Colin Clouts Come Home Againe, Astrophel, and The Doleful Lay of Clorinda* (1595)." *The Oxford Handbook of Edmund Spenser*. Ed. Richard A. McCabe. Oxford: Oxford UP, 2010. 237–55.

Cronin, John. "Sidney, Philip (1619–98)." *Dictionary of Irish Biography: From the Earliest Times to the Year 2002*. Ed. James McGuire and James Quinn. Cambridge: Cambridge UP, 2009. 943–44.

Duncan-Jones, Katherine. "*Discourse on Irish Affairs*: Introduction." *Miscellaneous Prose of Sir Philip Sidney*. Ed. Katherine Duncan-Jones and Jan Van Dorsten. Oxford: Clarendon P, 1973. 3–7.

—. *Sir Philip Sidney: Courtier Poet*. New Haven, CT: Yale UP, 1991.

Edwards, David. "Beyond Reform: Martial Law and the Tudor Reconquest of Ireland." *History Ireland* 5.2 (1997): 16–21.

—. "The Butler Revolt of 1569." *Irish Historical Studies* 28.111 (1993): 228–55.

—. "The Escalation of Violence in Sixteenth-century Ireland." *Age of Atrocity: Violence and Political Conflict in Early Modern Ireland*. Ed. David Edwards, Padraig Lenihan, and Clodagh Tait. Dublin: Four Courts P, 2007. 34–78.

Egerton, Sir Philip de Malpas Grey, ed. *A Commentary of the Services and Charges of William Lord Grey of Wilton, K.G., by His Son Arthur Lord Grey of Wilton, K.G.* London: Camden Society, 1848; rpt. 1968.

Elledge, Scott. *Milton's "Lycidas."* New York: Harper and Row, 1966. 95–101.

Ewald, A. C. *The Life and Times of Algernon Sidney*. 2 vols. London, 1873.

Fenlon, Jane, ed. *Clanricard's Castle: Portumna House, Co. Galway*. Dublin: Four Courts P, 2012.

Firth, C. H. "Sidney, Philip, Third Earl of Leicester (1619–1698)." Rev. by Sean Kelsey. *ODNB*.

Hadfield, Andrew. *Edmund Spenser: A Life*. Oxford: Oxford UP, 2012.

Hayes-McCoy, G. A. "Conciliation, Coercion, and the Protestant Reformation, 1547–71." *Early Modern Ireland (1534–1691): A New History of Ireland*. Ed. T. W. Moody, F. X. Martin, and F. J. Byrne. 9 vols. Oxford: Clarendon P, 1976. 3:69–93.

Herron, Thomas, and Willy Maley. "Introduction: Monumental Sidney." *SJ* 29.1–2 (2011): 1–25.

Heywood, Thomas. *Famous History of the Life and Death of Captain Thomas Stukeley*. Ed. Charles Edelman. Manchester: Manchester UP, 2005. 129–230.

Holland, Karen. "The Sidney Women in Ireland, *c.* 1556–1594" *SJ* 29.1–2 (2011): 45–69.

Hosford, David. "Sidney, Henry, First Earl of Romney (1641–1704)." *ODNB*.

Hutchinson, Mark A. "Reformed Protestantism and the Government of Ireland, *c.* 1565 to 1582: The Lord Deputyships of Henry Sidney and Arthur Grey." *SJ* 29.1–2 (2011): 71–104.

J. G. E. *Englands Hope, against Irish Hate*. London, 1600.

Jones, Walter A. "Doneraile and Vicinity." *Journal of the Cork Historical and Archaeological Society* 2.7 (1901): 238–42.

Judson, Alexander C. *The Life of Edmund Spenser. The Works of Edmund Spenser: A Variorum Edition*. 11 vols. Baltimore, MD: Johns Hopkins P, 1945. 11.

Kinsella, Stuart. "Colonial Commemoration in Tudor Ireland: The Case of Sir Henry Sidney." *SJ* 29.1–2 (2011): 105–45.

Kuin, Roger. "Querre-Muhau: Sidney and the New World." *RQ* 51.2 (1998): 549–85.

Leland, John. *A Learned and True Assertion of the Original Life, Actes, and Death of the Most Noble, Valiant, and Renoumed Prince Arthure, King of Great Brittaine*. Transl. Richard Robinson. London, 1582.

Lenihan, Pádraig. *Consolidating Conquest: Ireland 1603–1727*. Harlow: Pearson Longman, 2008.

Maley, Willy. "'The Name of the Country I Have Forgotten': Remembering and Dismembering in Sir Henry Sidney's Irish *Memoir*." *Ireland in the Renaissance, c. 1540–1660*. Ed. Thomas Herron and Michael Potterton. Dublin: Four Courts P, 2007. 52–73.

—. "Sir Philip Sidney and Ireland." *Spenser Studies* 12 (1998): 223–7.

—. "Spenser's Life." *The Oxford Handbook of Edmund Spenser.* Ed. Richard A. McCabe. Oxford: Oxford UP, 2010. 13–29.

Manning, Conleth. "Arms and the Man." *Archaeology Ireland* 24 (2010): 8–11.

McGowan-Doyle, Valerie. *The Book of Howth: The Elizabethan Re-conquest of Ireland and the Old English.* Cork: Cork UP, 2011.

McGrath, C. Ivar. "Sidney (Sydney), Henry (1641–1704)." *Dictionary of Irish Biography: From the Earliest Times to the Year 2002.* Ed. James McGuire and James Quinn. Cambridge: Cambridge UP, 2009. 941–3.

Morgan, Hiram. "Giraldus Cambrensis and the Tudor Conquest of Ireland." *Political Ideology in Ireland, 1541–1641.* Ed. Hiram Morgan. Dublin: Four Courts P, 1999. 22–44.

—. "Overmighty Officers: The Irish Lord Deputyship in the Early Modern British State." *History Ireland* 7.4 (1999): 17–21.

Moroney, Maryclaire. "'The Sweetness of Due Subjection': John Derricke's *Image of Irelande* (1581) and the Sidneys." *SJ* 29.1–2 (2011): 147–71.

Ó Cearnaigh, Seán. *Aibidil Gaoidheilge & Caiticiosma.* Dublin, 1571.

O'Neill, Stephen. *Staging Ireland: Representations in Shakespeare and Renaissance Drama.* Dublin: Four Courts P, 2007.

Palmer, Patricia. "'An headlesse Ladie' and 'a Horses Loade of Heades': Writing the Beheading." *RQ* 60.1 (2007): 25–57.

Scott, Jonathan. "Sidney, Algernon (1623–1683)." *ODNB.*

Shephard, Robert. "The Motives of Sir Henry Sidney's *Memoir* (1583)." *SJ* 29.1–2 (2011): 173–86.

Sidney, Henry. *A Viceroy's Vindication? Sir Henry Sidney's Memoir of Service in Ireland, 1556–1578.* Ed. Ciarán Brady. Cork: Cork UP, 2002.

Sidney, Philip. *Astrophil and Stella* (1591). *Sir Philip Sidney: The Major Works.* Ed. Katherine Duncan-Jones. Oxford: Oxford UP, 1989; 2002. 153–211.

—. "Discourse on Irish Affairs." *Miscellaneous Prose of Sir Philip Sidney.* Ed. Katherine Duncan-Jones and Jan Van Dorsten. Oxford: Clarendon P, 1973. 8–12.

Siegfried, Brandie R. "Rivaling Caesar: The Roman Model of Sir Henry Sidney's *Memoir* (1583)." *SJ* 29.1–2 (2011): 187–208.

Smyth, William J. *Map-making, Landscapes and Memory: A Geography of Colonial and Early Modern Ireland c.1530–1750.* South Bend, IN: U of Notre Dame P, 2006.

Spenser, Edmund. *Edmund Spenser: The Shorter Poems.* Ed. Richard McCabe. New York: Penguin, 1999.

—. *The Faerie Queene* (1590; 1596; 1609). Ed. A. C. Hamilton. 2nd ed. Edinburgh: Pearson, 2007.

Styward, Thomas. *The Pathwaie to Martiall Discipline.* 2nd ed. London: 1582.

Treadwell, Victor. "The Irish Parliament of 1569–71." *Royal Irish Academy Proceedings* C.65 (1966–67): 55–89.

Westerweel, Bart. "Astrophel and Ulster: Sidney's Ireland." *The Clash of Ireland: Literary Contrasts and Connections.* Ed. C. C. Barfoot and Theo D'haen. Amsterdam: Rodopi 1989. 5–22.

Whetstone, George. *Sir Phillip Sidney, His Honorable Life, His Valiant Death, and True Vertues. A Perfect Myrror for the Followers both of Mars and Mercury.* London, 1587.

White, Thomas. *A Godlie Sermon Preached the xxj. Day of Iune, 1586. at Pensehurst in Kent, at the Buriall of the Late Right Honourable Sir Henrie Sidney Knight ....* London, 1586.

Wilks, Timothy. "Richard, Fourth Earl of Clanricard, and the English Court." *Clanricard's Castle: Portumna House, Co. Galway.* Ed. Jane Fenlon. Dublin: Four Courts P, 2012. 8–31.

Woudhuysen, H. R. "Sidney, Sir Philip (1554–1586)." *ODNB.*

The Sidneys and Wales

Willy Maley and Philip Schwyzer

The Heart of the Matter

It was Henry Sidney's (Illustration 5) last wish that his heart be buried in the church at Ludlow, next to his daughter Ambrosia.[1] He might have had less fondness for the country he served for half his life had he known that a century after his death his great-grandson, Algernon (Illustration 25), would be sent to the scaffold by a Welsh judge. Henry Sidney served as Lord President of the Council of the Marches of Wales from 1560 to 1586, the second longest holder of that office after Bishop John Alcock, its first incumbent. The policies and persons he supported over this quarter-century had a profound and lasting impact on the political and literary history of the Principality; the fact that Henry supported the major early modern history of Wales, Llwyd and Powel's enduringly influential *Historie of Cambria*, is but one testament to this impact. Nor does the story of "The Sidneys and Wales" conclude in 1586. Henry's long service in Ludlow had a ripple effect on the story of the Sidneys for another hundred years. Through intermarriage with the Herberts, the Sidneys gained their long association with the Welsh earldoms of Pembroke and Montgomery. Three successive generations of Henry Sidney's descendents married into Welsh families (the Gamages, Mansells, and Parrys; see Hannay *ARC* 1:8).

Henry Sidney served as chief governor of Ireland on three separate occasions during his tenure as Lord President of Wales, and the vexed nature of Irish history means that his Irish service has received more attention than his period of Welsh governance. Thomas Fuller notes that Sidney was "Lord President of *Wales*, and for eleven years (*off* and *on*) Deputy of *Ireland*," but the entire entry is given over to his Irish service (*Worthies* 74). Sidney himself is largely responsible for the disproportionate emphasis on his time in Ireland. Ciarán Brady, who has shown the extent to which the governance of the two countries was intertwined, points to the paradox of Sidney's choosing to write a memoir of the country in which he had the less sustained, more vexatious experience:

> [I]n almost thirty-six years of public life Sidney spent most of his time in Wales, much else at court or on diplomatic service abroad, and in all no more than thirteen years in Ireland, during only eight of which he served as Lord Deputy. Yet curiously in a memoir promising at the outset an account of all his achievements, Sidney spends hardly any time at all discussing his career in Wales. (Sidney, *Memoir* 5)

---

[1] The lead casket in which the heart was interred, bearing the inscription "HERLITH THE HARTE. OF SYR HENRYE. SYDNY. L.P. ANNO," is now in the British Museum (no. OA.4280).

Sidney's allusions to the "sweet marches" of Wales in his Irish *Memoir* of 1583 are favorable, if fleeting (*Memoir* 104). He speaks of his progress through Kildare and King's and Queen's Counties, and concludes that he "in all those counties took orders between party and party, as quietly as presently I can do in Wales" (76). Revealingly, William Gerard's notes on Ireland from 1577–78 include the observation that until the time of Henry VIII Ireland and Wales presented similar problems for the English Crown, but thereafter "Wales was reclaymed a notable president for Ireland" (McNeill 291). The Welsh precedent for Ireland benefited from sharing, in Henry Sidney, Gerard's mentor, a Welsh President.

Henry Sidney found it convenient to proffer Wales as the poster-child for successful Anglo-British imperialism. Until quite recently historians and critics have tended to follow in his lead. There was a time when it was tempting to speak of Wales as having been absorbed into the English state, or the Tudor state, a dragon slain by its own mythmaking. But this conceals a range of complexities. These complexities include the fact that the Tudors were of Welsh origin, a lineage Shakespeare extends to their predecessor Henry V when he has that king declare: "For I am Welsh, you know, good countryman" (*Henry V*, Act 4, Scene 7 1. 94). This was a time when the Welsh were asserting their British identity, and therefore claiming to be a key part of any future United Kingdom. Between 1536 and 1542 a series of acts bound Wales to England in new ways as part of a policy of assimilation that included the suppression of the Welsh language. Yet the survival of Welsh as a living language down to the present day also owes much to Tudor policy, which supported the translation of scripture into Welsh even as it banished the language from the council chamber and court of law. It was during Sidney's tenure as President of the Council that *Testament Newydd* (1567), William Salesbury and Richard Davies's groundbreaking Welsh translation of the New Testament, was printed.

There is less recent scholarship on Sidney's Welsh experiences than on his Irish exploits. Wallace MacCaffrey's *ODNB* entry typically understates the Welsh context, as Sidney is there described as "lord deputy of Ireland and courtier," with scant regard to Wales. Yet the chapter on Sidney in Penry Williams's *The Council of the Marches in Wales* (249–75) suggests that Sidney made a substantial contribution to the country's governance, reinforcing Caroline Skeel's earlier findings that Elizabethan Wales was a place of peace in comparison to the preceding period (*Council* 19). A memorandum on Welsh government submitted prior to Sidney's appointment demanded "wide powers" and "severe repression of theft and disorder" (Williams, *Council* 250). Williams divides Sidney's Welsh tenure into two distinct phases. The first period, 1560–75, was relatively successful, but marked by sustained absences, so that between 1562 and 1571 Sidney was "almost continuously absent on various missions" (252). In the second phase, 1575–86, Sidney became a victim of faction, facing increasing hostility from council and court, suffering the twin threats of "personal animosities" and "the old handicap of absence abroad" (257). By 1577 Sidney had fallen out with Gerard, and was assailed on all sides. Walsingham, who remained sympathetic, wrote a warning letter to Sidney in August 1580: "Your lordship had neade to walke warely, for your Doings are narrowely observed, and her Majestie is apt to geve Eare to any that shall yll you. Great Howlde is taken by your Ennemyes, for Neglectyng the Execuytyon of this Commission" (267).

The leaders of the council faction opposed to the Lord President had, like Sidney himself, a foot in two camps, and three countries. Sir James Croft (*c.* 1518–90), "the malcontent magnate on the council" of Wales (MacCaffrey), served as Lord Deputy in Ireland in 1551–52. Croft, "the eldest surviving son of Richard Croft (d. 1562) of Croft Castle, Herefordshire, and his second wife, Katherine, daughter of Sir Richard Herbert of Montgomery" (Ellis), was one of many Elizabethans of Welsh—or Marcher—provenance who saw Irish service. James Croft's grandson Herbert was a thwarted suitor of Barbara Gamage, so the Crofts had good reason to resent the Sidneys, and the arena of their antipathy straddled Wales and Ireland (Williams, *Council* 270). William Herbert, a fellow Munster undertaker alongside Edmund Spenser, who wrote in praise of Croft in his Latin text *Croftus sive de Hibernia Liber* (1588), was "the great-grandson of Sir George Herbert, third son of William Herbert, first Earl of Pembroke (*c*. 1423–69), a pedigree upon which he placed considerable emphasis" (Maginn). Herbert mortgaged his Monmouthshire land and other property in North Wales, "possibly to support the Munster venture" (MacCarthy-Morrogh 123).

Sir Henry drew on his experience in Wales in order to suggest regional presidencies or provincial councils for Connaught and Munster (Canny 93). Wales provided the prototype for the shaping and shiring of Ireland (Highley 106). In 1569 Sir Edward Fitton became Lord President of Connaught. Fitton was a protégé of William Cecil, Lord Burleigh. The Cecils were of Welsh provenance, and there are many ways in which, just as Scotland was used in the settlement of Ulster in the seventeenth century, Wales was used in the settlement of Munster in the sixteenth century. Sidney's chosen man for the job of Lord President of Munster was his Welsh ally Sir John Perrot, but that posting drew objections, and Sidney was frustrated in his attempts to put his man in place (Turvey). The Cambro-Hibernian web was further strengthened by the fact that William Fitzwilliam, who had married Sidney's sister Anne in 1543, became Lord Deputy of Ireland in Sidney's stead in 1572.

Henry Sidney's association with Ireland is often thought to pre-date his Welsh experiences, since he was serving under the Earl of Sussex in Ireland in 1556, while he did not take up his Welsh post for another four years. Elizabeth saw a danger that between Henry's Irish and Welsh posts, the Sidneys could become too powerful. This anxiety intensified after 1577, when William the Silent tried to have his daughter, Marie of Nassau, marry Philip Sidney, cementing Sidneian connections in the Low Countries. Elizabeth may have feared that "Philip had contrived to become something of an intimate of Orange, and even to inveigle his way into the Orange royal family" (Stewart 189). Such anxiety is palpable in the queen's comments concerning "the provinces of the Low Countries" conveyed to Daniel Rogers on 22 June 1577: "For we could not like that any foreign prince should enter into any such secret combination with our President of Wales or Deputy of Ireland or any other governor under us, which might any way estrange him from th'obedience he oweth us" (Stewart 189–90).

As Michael Brennan says of Sir Henry: "As both Lord Governor in Ireland and Lord President of Wales, he had been placed ... by Elizabeth in overall administrative control of approximately one-quarter of her entire domestic territories" (46). How "domestic" or "domesticated" these territories were is a matter of dispute. In their attempt to suppress one kind of over-mighty subject (Irish magnates, Marcher lords), the Tudors risked creating another (bureaucrats like Sidney combining powerful posts in Ireland and Wales). On 11 June 1567 Elizabeth wrote to Sidney spelling out her anxiety about Sidney's occupation of both offices and his viewing of the posts as interlinked:

> In some other your letters also we fynde that which we cannot lyke, that so small regard shuld be had of us, as you cannot content your self, if we shuld dispose the office which you had to be President of our Counsell in Wales, upon any other person, but that you wold also thereupon be ready to leave that which you have. We thinke you ar not ignorant, but that these officers ar to be disposed at our pleasure, and never grauntid to any during lief, nor hitherto ever grauntid to any one person jointly. And therfore we allowe not of such precise tearmes as you use. For we meane therin to alter change, or contynue those offices as to us shall seeme meete. And so also it is meete for you to think, and conforme yourself. (Ó Laidhin 68)

Penry Williams, citing this letter, observes that Sidney "committed the tactical error of asking the queen for a life patent of the presidency," and suggests that "Elizabeth took his request, or pretended to take it, as a slight on her prerogative" (*Council* 255–6). Elizabeth's concern is also clearly focused on Sidney's efforts to link the two posts in ways that prevent either being reassigned.

The queen wrote to Sidney again a month later, linking Ireland and Wales in a different manner while asking after the safekeeping of Shane O'Neill's son:

> We think good that the soone of the late rebell now in prison at Dyblyn wer surely lookid to for escaping and if you think the same doubtfull by his abode in Irland, we wold have you advertise us whether it wer not better he wer kept in some castell in Wales and where you think the same meete to be. (Ó Laidhin 75)

Here, Wales provides a potential safe house for an Irish prisoner, and Sidney's knowledge of both neighbor nations is a boon for the English court he serves.

Writing Wales

Henry Sidney played a major part in the mapping of and musing on Wales. He acted as patron for *The Historie of Cambria, Now Called Wales* (1584), published during his tenure as Lord President. The core of the text was Humphrey Llwyd's translation of medieval Welsh chronicle matter, completed and much expanded by Sidney's Ludlow chaplain, David Powel. In his dedication "to the sonne and heire of him that was the procurer and bringer of it to light," Powel urges Philip Sidney to "Labour by the example of your father to discover and bring to light, the acts of the famous men of elder times" (3v). Powel makes clear the extent of Philip's father's input into the enterprise:

> Your father, with his great expenses and labour, having procured & gotten to his hands the histories of Wales and Ireland (which countries for manie yeeres with great love and commendation he governed) committed unto me this of Wales, to be set foorth in print, with direction to proceed therein, and necessarie bookes for the dooing thereof. (3v)

Philip Schwyzer notes that "Powel's reference to the history of Ireland is to John Hooker's continuation of Richard Stanihurst's Irish history, in Raphael Holinshed's *Chronicles* (1577)" ("'A Happy Place'" 208n11). Stanyhurst had dedicated his labors in the first (1577) volume of the *Chronicles* to Henry Sidney, reproduced in the second volume (unpaginated), and Sidney supported the translation into English by John Hooker of Gerald of Wales's Irish chronicle *Expugnatio Hibernica* as part of the second volume of Holinshed's *Chronicles*: "In the dedication of *Pontici Virunnii … libri sex*, Powel refers to Sidney's patronage of Hooker, and describes his Irish history as imminently forthcoming" (Schwyzer, "'A Happy Place'" 212–13n20). Hooker dedicated his work to the Earl of Oxford, but Holinshed dedicated the second volume of the *Chronicles* as a whole to Henry Sidney (A2r–v):

> Sidney seems to have taken the view that English readers needed to know what Gerald had written about Ireland, but not necessarily what he had written about Wales. Given that Gerald's views on English dominion in Wales

were far more equivocal than his support for the conquest of Ireland, this is hardly surprising. (Schwyzer 213)

The important point here is that Gerald of Wales, when it came to Ireland, was a Welsh colonist; when it came to Wales, he was a Welsh patriot (Bartlett 56).

Sidney's involvement in the writing of Wales may go back further still. In 1573 Thomas Twyne had translated Llwyd's *Commentarioli Britanicae descriptionis fragmentum*, first printed in Cologne in 1572. Twyne's translation was published under the title *The Breviary of Britayne* in 1573. It is possible that Henry Sidney may have met Llwyd before his death in 1568. He certainly supported the translation and publication of "Llwyd's major unpublished work, the *Cronica Walliae* … a translation of the medieval Welsh chronicle, *Brut y Tywysogion* (The Brute of the Princes), covering the history of Wales from the seventh century to the 1270s, when the last independent Welsh principality succumbed to England's Edward I" (Schwyzer, "'A Happy Place'" 207). Sidney seems to have found something both attractive and useful in Llwyd's firm conviction that the Welsh experience provided the key to British history and identity. His Tudor masters, after all, founded their claim to British dominion in their Welsh descent. Henry Sidney created an archive at Ludlow Castle curated by his chaplain, David Powel (Ludlow's status as a "lost capital" makes it a fascinating location; Dodd, "Lost Capital"). When Powel published Llwyd's *Cronica Walliae* as *The Historie of Cambria* in 1584, it was both a translation and a work of original scholarship (Schwyzer, "'A Happy Place'" 207–8). The volume also included *A Description of Wales*, begun by Sir John Price and completed by Llwyd. In an edition of *A Description of Wales* published in 1663, the printer's preface by William Hall retold the story of how Llwyd's translation saw the light of print:

> The Right Honourable *Sir Henry Sidney* Lord President of Wales, having had a Copy of his *Translation* a great while lying by him, employed *David Powel* Doctor of Divinity to Peruse, Correct, Augment, and Continue it in order to the setting of it out in Print. The *Doctor* at his request compared the translation with the *British* Booke, whereof he had two ancient Copies, and corrected it where he saw cause.

Powel went on to publish two British/Welsh histories, a digest of Geoffrey of Monmouth's *History of Britain*, and Gerald of Wales's two Welsh works. These two texts presented by Powel for publication are in Latin. Schwyzer contends that *The Historie of Cambria*, "the standard history of medieval Wales," exerted influence on later writers such as Spenser, Drayton, and Milton, so that "Henry Sidney's narrow, politically-motivated quest for Welsh antiquities helped shape Welsh and English futures" ("'A Happy Place'" 213). Sidney's reputation as a champion of Welsh culture survived into the seventeenth century. In his 1630 history of the principality, John Dodridge described Sidney as one "whose love to learning, & favour to learned men, need not here to be spoken" (53).

As well as supporting Powel's efforts in publishing Llwyd's Welsh history, Sidney also patronized Christopher Saxton in the production of his Welsh maps in 1579 (Hannay, *Philip's Phoenix* 27). This was a period when Welsh and Anglo-Welsh writers were patriotically asserting the value of the nation. Thomas Churchyard's *The Worthines of Wales* (1587) is a case in point. As one of Henry Sidney's loyal Welsh servants, Churchyard had praised Lady Mary Sidney in his ballad *A Farewell Cauld, Churchyeards, Rounde. From the Courte to the Cuntry Grownd* (1566). In *The Worthines of Wales* Churchyard praises Henry Sidney's additions to Ludlow Castle (82–3), and mentions in particular a fascinating "device of the Lord Presidents" which exemplifies Sidney's Cambro-Hibernian interface: "At the end of the dyning Chamber, there is a pretie device how the Hedgehog brake the chayne, and came from *Ireland* to *Ludloe*" (83). Churchyard had served Sidney in Ireland and Wales in the 1560s and 1570s. The extent of that Cambro-Hibernian interface can be gauged from the fact that Sidney's ally on the Council of Wales, William Gerard, served under Sidney in Ireland as Lord Chancellor from 1576 (Williams, "Gerard," *ODNB*). Indeed, Gerard's Irish appointment created unease in the Welsh Council, which feared its authority might be undermined by Sidney's extension of his power base there (Williams, *Council* 262).

In his *Apology for Poetry* (1595) Philip Sidney extolled the virtues of Welsh verse:

> In Wales, the true remnant of the ancient Britons, as there are good authorities to show the long time they had poets, which they called *bards*, so through all the conquests of Romans, Saxons, Danes, and Normans, some of whom did seek to ruin all memory of learning from among them, yet do their poets even to this day last; so as it is not more notable in soon beginning than in long continuing. (83)

Sidney's source for this knowledge could well be Llwyd's *Breviary*, which he had joked about in his correspondence with Hubert Languet years before (Schwyzer, *Literature* 76–9). In this jesting epistolary exchange Sidney's Welsh servant Griffin Madox is at once the font of historical information and the butt of the joke, in that his credulous acceptance of ancient British lore permits Sidney to adopt a more nuanced and ironic stance while remaining a British patriot. We may perhaps see the interplay between Philip Sidney and Griffin Madox reprised in the relationship between Henry Sidney and David Powel. Humphrey Llwyd could have been thinking of the culturally complex Sidney–Madox relationship when he observed that many English gentlemen preferred Welshmen as their personal servants.

Welsh Weddings and Wooing

Henry Sidney's wife, Mary Dudley (Illustration 6), gave birth to her daughter Mary in the Welsh marches at Tickenhall in 1561. In 1577 young Mary Sidney (Illustration 9) married Henry Herbert, second Earl of Pembroke, who later succeeded Henry Sidney as Lord President of Wales (*Philip's Phoenix* 15, 38–42). Indeed, Penry Williams notes that despite having limited administrative experience, Sidney's son-in-law proved a worthy successor, helped by his familiarity with Wales through his Glamorgan estates, and by an ability to speak Welsh, so that he "was eulogistically called *Llygad holl Gymru*—the eye of all Wales" (Williams, *Council* 276). Sidney's second son, Robert Sidney (1563–1626), married wealthy Barbara Gamage of Glamorgan (Illustrations 13 and 17), served as MP for Glamorgan in 1584 and 1593, and went on to become Earl of Leicester (Shephard; see Shephard *ARC* 1:7 and Hannay *ARC* 1:8). The Welsh marriages of Henry Sidney's children were major means by which he bought into the politics of that country (Hannay, *MSLW* 9–17, 97–8). Within this tight weave of Welsh weddings and wooing, Sidney was able to exert considerable authority and influence. This web of Welsh relations throws up some fascinating entanglements. For example, when Sidney successfully negotiated the marriage of his son Robert to Barbara Gamage, he did so in the face of stiff competition from her Welsh cousins. Vying for land and power among England's new nobility made negotiating marriage alliances absolutely crucial, and there are other instances where Cambro-Hibernian interfaces were vital.

In her *ODNB* entry on Mary Sidney Herbert, Margaret Hannay speaks of Mary's marriage to "one of the wealthiest landowners in Britain." This is fair comment, but it should be acknowledged that whatever the desires of patriotic Welshmen, Wales was not Britain, and Henry Herbert, second Earl of Pembroke, was one of the wealthiest landowners in Wales. Henry Herbert is described as "the weightiest of the south Wales magnates" (MacCaffrey). The marriage of Mary and Henry was the starting point of a Sidney–Herbert dynasty in Wales. The Welshness of *The Countess of Pembroke's Arcadia* (1593) may be confined to its title, yet intriguing parallels have been spied between Philip Sidney's work and contemporary Welsh bardic literature (Jones). The Welsh connection forged by the marriage of Mary Sidney to the second Earl of Pembroke, like her brother Robert's marriage to Barbara Gamage, might have been supplemented by another Anglo-Welsh alliance, because in 1569 Philip Sidney was engaged to William Cecil's daughter Anne (Woudhuysen) but in 1571 Anne married the Earl of Oxford, Sidney's rival. Philip Sidney was acquainted with another prominent Welshman, John Dee. Philip was temporarily displaced as his uncle's heir to the earldom of Leicester when his uncle's wife gave birth to a son, Robert, given the Welsh title of Baron Denbigh. The child died in 1584, but again the child's title reinforces the Welsh inheritance. According to Woudhuysen: "As early as 1564 Philip Sidney received the income of a church benefice in Wales; to this he added a Welsh prebend in the next year, and more may have followed."

Lady Mary Wroth (1587–1651) is another pivotal figure for the Sidneys and Wales (Illustrations 18 and 19). She was the eldest daughter of Robert Sidney, first Earl of Leicester, and Barbara Gamage. Their next daughter, Katharine, married Lewis Mansell and moved to Wales. As a widow, Mary Wroth had two children by her cousin William Herbert, third Earl of Pembroke (1580–1630) (Illustrations 20 and 21). One of Mary's children by William Herbert was given property there, and then served on English battlefields in the civil wars (*MSLW* 20–21, 283–91). If *The Countess of Pembroke's Arcadia* is one key text for the Sidneys and Wales, then Wroth's *The Countess of Montgomery's Urania* is another. That these two great prose romances take their names from family women married to earls named after Welsh counties is not unimportant. Mary Ellen Lamb in her entry on Wroth calls *Urania* "the first extant romance written by an Englishwoman," yet Mary Wroth's mother and the title of her romance were both Welsh. Margaret Hannay's magisterial biography puts enlightening emphasis on Mary's Welsh ancestry and her mother's use of the Welsh language. In the next generation, Mary's daughter Katherine would marry the Welshman James Parry and move to Wales, where she had two sons (*MSLW* 295–7). Mary's grandsons were thus predominantly Welsh in both ancestry and residence.

The congeries of Cambrian connections in the Sidney family have their end point in the 1680s, when two events tied together different dimensions of the Sidney dynasty. This nodal point requires some needlepoint. In 1683 the last English republican, Algernon Sidney (Illustration 25), was sent to the scaffold by Judge George Jeffreys, a Welshman (Halliday). As Jonathan Scott notes, the astonishing decision at Algernon's trial was taken "to use the manuscript *Discourses* as the second witness against Sidney: in the famous ruling of Lord Chief Justice Jeffreys: 'Scribere est agere' ('to write is to act')." Two years later Jeffreys was the judge who presided over the prosecutions of the Monmouth rebels. James Scott (formerly Crofts), Duke of Monmouth and first Duke of Buccleuch (1649–85), was a complex figure (Harris). Duke of Monmouth was a title he was given by Charles II, and he was rumored to be that king's illegitimate child from a liaison in The Hague in 1649 with a Welshwoman, Lucy Walter. She was a cousin of the Sidneys who was also rumored by James II, for his own obvious reasons, to have had a relationship with Colonel Robert Sidney (1628–68). Indeed, "Charles tended to treat Monmouth as if he were a prince of Wales" (Harris). James II clearly wanted Monmouth out of the picture as a pretender accepted as legitimate by his royal father (Harris). When Jeffreys presided over the prosecution of the Monmouth rebels with a severity that earned him the nickname "The Hanging Judge," he did so under the auspices of Robert Spencer, another of the Sidney dynasty. Spencer, second Earl of Sunderland, was the nephew of Henry Sidney, Earl of Romney (1642–1704), as the son of Romney's sister, Dorothy (see Brennan *ARC* 1:12). Robert Spencer's daughter Elizabeth married the fourth Earl of Clancarty, Donough MacCarthy. Spencer's son Charles married Anne Churchill, whose father, John, first Duke of Marlborough, also put down the Monmouth rebellion.

According to Wallace MacCaffrey, Elizabeth "preferred that [Henry] Sidney should serve her in remote Ludlow or transmarine Dublin. He thus remained on the outer edge of the court solar system where the sun's warmth was hardly felt." But if the queen wanted him on the outskirts of her imperial monarchy, then Sidney strove to place those margins at the heart of an expanding state, as well as of his personal dynasty. Whether or not his Lord Presidency was successful in terms of cementing ties between England and Wales, Henry's policies and patronage while in office would have a long-term impact on Welsh literature and historiography. As noted earlier, when Sidney died on a boat journey on the Severn on 5 May 1586, his body was sent for burial at Penshurst, but his heart was interred at Ludlow, on his instructions (Sidney, "Sir Henry Sidney's Heart" 1903). In choosing his heart's resting place, Sidney may have been moved more by proximity to his daughter Ambrosia than to the Principality. Nonetheless, Wales remains at the heart of Henry Sidney's life, and is a haunting presence as well as a source of income and inspiration in the careers of his heirs and successors.

Bibliography

Primary and Secondary Sources

Adams, Simon. "Sidney [*née* Dudley], Mary, Lady Sidney (1530x35–1586)." *ODNB*.

Atherton, Ian. "Sidney, Robert, Second Earl of Leicester (1595–1677)." *ODNB*.

Bartlett, Robert. *Gerald of Wales, 1146–1223*. Oxford: Oxford UP, 1982.

Boling, Ronald J. "Anglo-Welsh Relations in *Cymbeline*." *Shakespeare Quarterly* 51.1 (2000): 33–66.

Brady, Ciarán. "Comparable Histories? Tudor Reform in Wales and Ireland." Ed. Steven G. Ellis and Sarah Barber. *Conquest and Union: Fashioning a British State, 1485–1725*. London: Longman, 1995. 64–86.

Brennan, Michael G. *The Sidneys of Penshurst and the Monarchy, 1500–1700*. Aldershot: Ashgate, 2006.

Canny, Nicholas. *The Elizabethan Conquest of Ireland: A Pattern Established 1565–76*. Hassocks: Harvester Press, 1976.

Chernaik, Warren. "Spencer [*née* Sidney], Dorothy, Countess of Sunderland [*known as* Sacharissa] (1617–1684)." *ODNB*.

Churchyard, Thomas. *The Worthines of Wales*. London, 1587; rpt. 1776.

Cull, Marisa R. "'Prince of Wales by Cambria's Full Consent?': The Princedom of Wales and the Early Modern Stage." *Writing Wales: From the Renaissance to Romanticism*. Ed. Stewart James Mottram and Sarah Prescott. Farnham: Ashgate, 2012. 75–90.

Davies, R. R. "Colonial Wales." *Past and Present* 65 (1974): 3–23.

Dodd, A. H. "A Lost Capital." *Studies in Stuart Wales*. Cardiff: U of Wales P, 1952. 49–75.

—. "North Wales in the Essex Revolt of 1601." *English Historical Review* 59.235 (1944): 348–70.

Dodridge, John. *The History of the Ancient and Modern Estate of The Principality of Wales, Duchy of Cornewall, and Earldome of Chester*. London, 1630.

Ellis, Steven G. "Croft, Sir James (c.1518–1590)." *ODNB*.

Firth, C. H. "Sidney, Philip, Third Earl of Leicester (1619–1698)." Rev. Sean Kelsey. *ODNB*.

Fuller, Thomas. *A History of the Worthies of England*. London, 1662.

Gray, Madeleine. "Sidney [*née* Gamage], Barbara, Countess of Leicester (*c.*1559–1621)." *ODNB*.

Gurr, Andrew, ed. *King Henry V*. Cambridge: Cambridge UP, 1992; rpt. 2005.

Halliday, Paul D. "Jeffreys, George, First Baron Jeffreys (1645–1689)." *ODNB*.

Hannay, Margaret P. "Herbert [*née* Sidney], Mary, Countess of Pembroke (1561–1621)." *ODNB*.

—. *Mary Sidney, Lady Wroth*. Farnham: Ashgate, 2010.

—. *Philip's Phoenix: Mary Sidney, Countess of Pembroke*. Oxford: Oxford UP, 1990.

Harris, Tim. "Scott [*Formerly* Crofts], James, Duke of Monmouth and First Duke of Buccleuch (1649–1685)." *ODNB*.

Highley, Christopher. *Shakespeare, Spenser, and the Crisis in Ireland*. Cambridge: Cambridge UP, 1997.

Holinshed, Raphael. *The Second Volume of Chronicles*. London, 1586.

Hosford, David. "Henry Sidney, First Earl of Romney (1641–1704)." *ODNB*.

Huws, Daniel. "Gwyn [White], Richard [St Richard Gwyn] (*c.*1537–1584)." *ODNB*.

Jones, J. Gwynfor. "Braint, awdurdod a chyfrifoldeb uchelwriaeth: agweddau ar waith Syr Philip Sidney (1554–1586) a Beirdd yr Uchelwyr." *Llên Cymru* 16 (1989–91): 212–14.

Lamb, Mary Ellen. "Wroth [*née* Sidney], Lady Mary (1587?–1651/1653)." *ODNB*.

MacCaffrey, Wallace T. "Sidney, Sir Henry (1529–1586)." *ODNB*.

MacCarthy-Morrogh, Michael. *The Munster Plantation: English Migration to Southern Ireland, 1583–1641*. Oxford: Oxford UP, 1986.

McNeill, C., ed. "Gerrard Papers: Sir William Gerrard's Notes of His Report on Ireland, 1577–8." *Analecta Hibernica* 2 (1931): 93–291.

Maginn, Christopher. "Herbert, Sir William (*c.*1553–1593)." *ODNB*.

Oakley-Brown, Liz. "Writing on Borderlines: Anglo-Welsh Relations in Thomas Churchyard's *The Worthines of Wales*." *Writing Wales: From the Renaissance to Romanticism*. Ed. Stewart James Mottram and Sarah Prescott. Farnham: Ashgate, 2012. 39–57.

Ó Laidhin, Tomás, ed. *Sidney State Papers 1565–70*. Dublin: Irish Manuscripts Commission, 1962.

Palmer, Patricia. "'An Headlesse Ladie' and 'a Horses Loade of Heads': Writing the Beheading." *RQ* 60.1 (2007): 25–57.

Powel, David. *The Historie of Cambria, Now Called Wales*. London, 1584.

Price, John. *A Description of Wales*. Oxford, 1663.

Roberts, Peter. "Tudor Wales, National Identity and the British Inheritance." *British Consciousness and Identity: The Making of Britain, 1533–1707*. Ed. Brendan Bradshaw and Peter Roberts. Cambridge: Cambridge UP, 1998. 8–42.

Saxton, Christopher. *Atlas of the Counties of England and Wales*. London, 1579.

Schwyzer, Philip. "'A Happy Place of Government': Sir Henry Sidney, Wales, and *The Historie of Cambria*." *SJ* 29.1–2 (2011): 209–17.

—. *Literature, Nationalism and Memory in Early Modern England and Wales*. Cambridge: Cambridge UP, 2004.

Scott, Jonathan. "Sidney [Sydney], Algernon (1623–1683)." *ODNB*.

Shephard, Robert. "Sidney, Robert, First Earl of Leicester (1563–1626)." *ODNB*.

Sidney, Henry. *A Viceroy's Vindication? Sir Henry Sidney's Memoir of Service in Ireland, 1556–1578*. Ed. Ciarán Brady. Cork: Cork UP, 2002.

Sidney, Mary. "Sir Henry Sidney's Heart." *Notes & Queries* 9.12 (1903): 307.

Sidney, Philip. *An Apology for Poetry (or A Defence of Poesy), by Philip Sidney*. Ed. R. W. Maslen. Manchester: Manchester UP, 2002.

Skeel, Caroline A. J. "The Council of the Marches in the Seventeenth Century." *English Historical Review* 30.117 (1915): 19–27.

—. *The Council in the Marches of Wales: A Study in Local Government During the Sixteenth and Seventeenth Centuries*. London: Hugh Rees, 1904.

Stewart, Alan. *Philip Sidney: A Double Life*. London: Chatto & Windus, 2000; London: Pimlico, 2001.

Turvey, Roger. "Perrot, Sir John (1528–1592)." *ODNB*.

Williams, Glanmor. *Renewal and Reformation: Wales c. 1415–1642*. Oxford: Oxford UP, 1987; 2002.

Williams, Penry. *The Council in the Marches of Wales Under Elizabeth I*. Cardiff: U of Wales P, 1958.

—. "Gerard, William (d. 1581)." *ODNB*.

—. "Herbert, Henry, Second Earl of Pembroke (*b.* in or after 1538, *d.* 1601)." *ODNB*.

Woudhuysen, H. R. "Sidney, Sir Philip (1554–1586)." *ODNB*.

View of BAYNARD's CASTLE.

Wooding Sculp.

Illustration 1 View of Baynard's Castle, copper engraved print by John G. Wooding for *The New, Complete, and Universal History, Description, and Survey of the Cities of London and Westminster* (London, 1784) and *Picturesque Views of the Antiquities of England & Wales* (London, 1786). Private collection.

Illustration 2 View of London, 1616 (cartographic material), by Nicholas John (Claes Jansz) Visscher, showing the position of Baynard's Castle on the River Thames. Map L85c no. 28. By permission of the Folger Shakespeare Library.

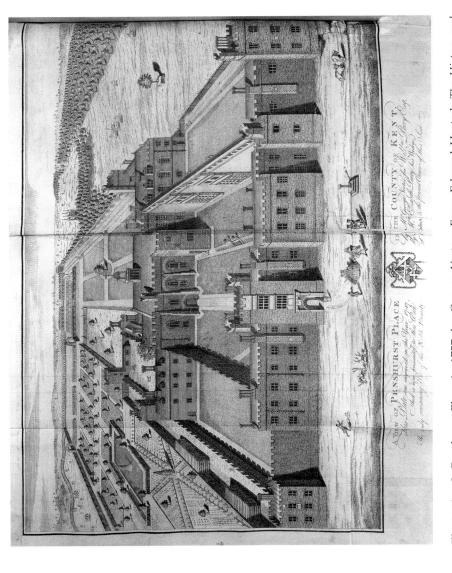

Illustration 3 Penshurst Place in 1757, by George Vertue. From Edward Hasted, *The History and Topographical Survey of the County of Kent* (Canterbury, 1778–99). Private collection.

Illustration 4 Penshurst Place, copperplate engraving by Johannes Kip from a drawing by Thomas Badeslade. From John Harris, *The History of Kent* (London, 1719). Private collection.

Illustration 5 Sir Henry Sidney, English School. By kind permission of Viscount De L'Isle from his private collection at Penshurst Place, Kent.

Illustration 6 Lady Mary Sidney (*née* Dudley), by Henry Bone, after unknown artist, pencil drawing squared in ink for transfer. NPG D17112. © National Portrait Gallery, London.

Illustration 7 Sir Philip Sidney, by unknown artist, oil on panel, *c.* 1577. NPG 5732.
© National Portrait Gallery, London.

Illustration 8 Portrait of Hubert Languet, tutor to Sir Philip Sidney, with identifying inscription and date "ANN° DOMINI 1564, ÆTATIS SVÆ 51," English School, oil on panel. By kind permission of Viscount De L'Isle from his private collection at Penshurst Place, Kent.

Illustration 9   Mary Sidney Herbert, Countess of Pembroke, by Nicholas Hilliard, watercolor on vellum, *c.* 1590. NPG 5994. © National Portrait Gallery, London.

Illustration 10   Mary Herbert, Countess of Pembroke, engraving by Simon de
Passe, 1618, sold by John Sudbury, sold by George Humble.
NPG D19186. © National Portrait Gallery, London.

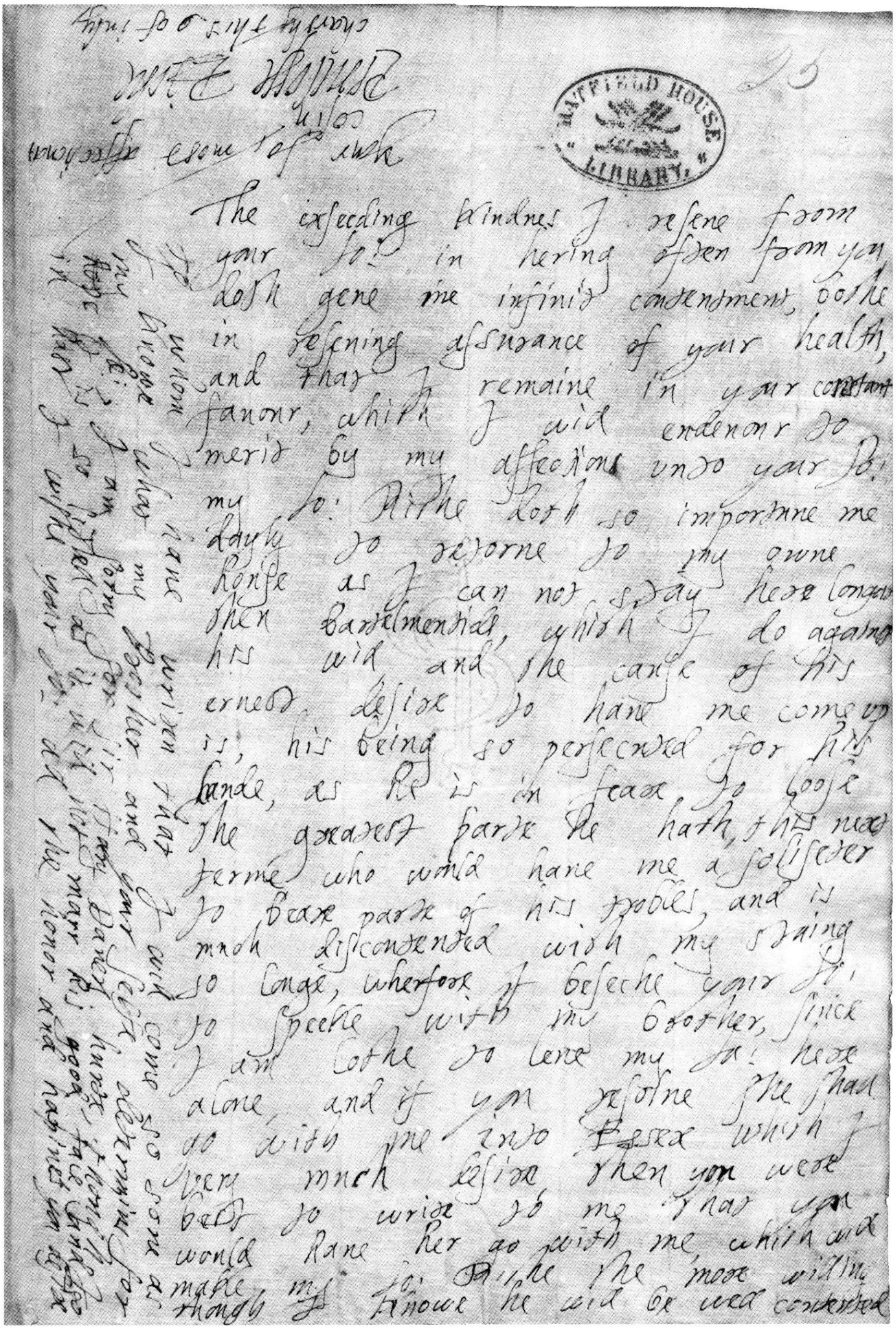

The exceeding kindnes I resene from
your lo: in hering ofden from you
dosh gene me infinit contenment, oohe
in resening assurance of your health,
and thay I remaine in your constant
fauour, which I wid endeuor do
merid by my affeciond vndo your lo:
my lo: Rithe Lost so importune me
dayly do reiorne do my owne
honse as I can not sday here longer
shen Candelmenhas, which I do againd
his wid and she cange of his
erned desire do hane me come vp
is, his being so persecuted for his
lande, as he is in feare, do loose
the greatest parte he hath, & his neas
ferme who would hane me a solisceter
do beare parte of his spoiles, and is
much disconsended wish my sdaing
so longe, wherfore I beseche your lo:
do speetle wish my brother, since
I am lothe do lene my lo: here
alone, and if you resolue she shad
do with me in do Essex which I
very much desire, then you weae
best do wrise do me shas you
would Rane her go wish me, which wid
make my lo: Rithe she moore willing
though I Rnowe he wid be wed content

Illustration 11 Letter from Penelope Rich to Robert Cecil, CP101/25. Hatfield House,
Hatfield. Reproduced by permission of Hatfield House.

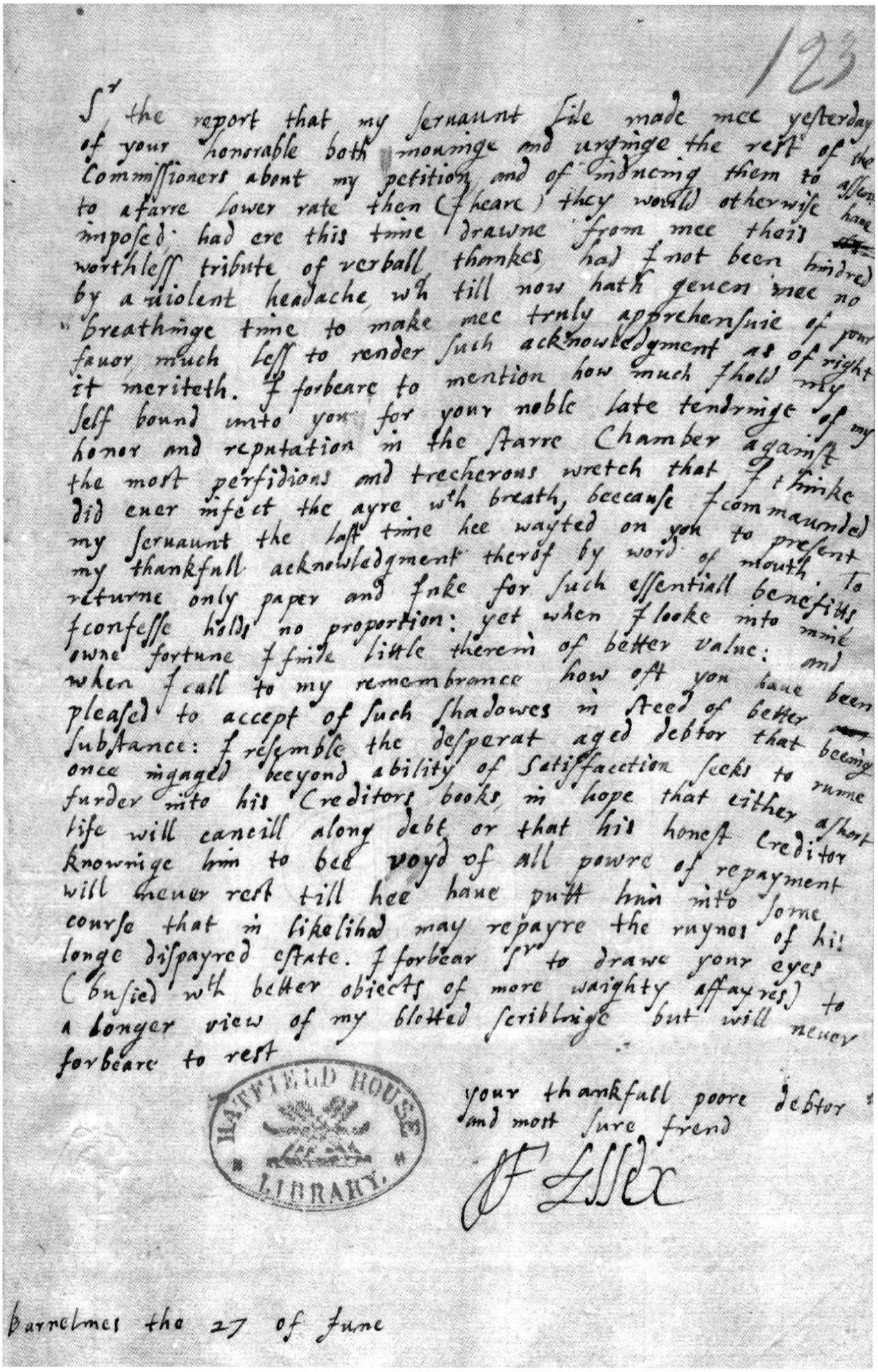

S.r the report that my seruaunt Gile made mee yesterday
of your honorable both moaninge and urginge the rest of the
Commissioners about my petition, and of induceing them to assent
to a farre lower rate then (I heare) they would otherwise haue
imposed: had ere this time drawne from mee their
worthlesse tribute of verball thankes, had I not been hindred
by a uiolent headache, wh till now hath geuen mee no
breathinge time to make mee truly apprehensiue of your
fauor much lesse to render such acknowledgment as of right
it meriteth. I forbeare to mention how much shold my
self bound unto you, for your noble late tendringe of my
honor and reputation in the starre Chamber against
the most perfidious and trecherous wretch that I thinke
did euer infect the ayre wth breath, beecause I commaunded
my seruaunt the last time hee wayted on you to present
my thankfull acknowledgment therof by word of mouth, To
returne only paper and Inke for such essentiall benefitts
I confesse holds no proportion: yet when I looke into mine
owne fortune I finde little therein of better value: and
when I call to my remembrance how oft you haue been
pleased to accept of such shadowes in steed of better
substance: I resemble the desperat aged debtor that beeing
once ingaged beeyond ability of satisfaction seeks to runne
furder into his Creditors books, in hope that either a short
life will cancell along debt or that his honest Creditor
knowinge him to bee voyd of all powre of repayment
will neuer rest till hee haue putt him into some
course that in likelihod may repayre the ruynes of his
longe dispayred estate. I forbear S.r to drawe your eyes
(busied wth better obiects of more waighty affayres) to
a longer view of my blotted scriblinge but will neuer
forbeare to rest

your thankfull poore debtor
and most sure frend

Essex

barnelmes the 27 of June

Illustration 12 Letter from Frances Essex to Robert Cecil, CP86/123. Hatfield House,
Hatfield. Reproduced by permission of Hatfield House.

Illustration 13 Sir Robert Sidney, unknown artist, oil on canvas, *c.* 1588. NPG 1862.
© National Portrait Gallery, London.

Illustration 14 Sir Robert Sidney in mourning for Sir Philip
Sidney, unknown artist, oil on canvas, *c.* 1587–88.
Private collection, courtesy of The Weiss Gallery.

Illustration 15 *Robert Sidney, first Earl of Leicester, depicted (as described in a Penshurst inventory of c. 1623) "at length in his vicounte Robes,"* attributed to Robert Peake, oil on canvas, *c.* 1605. By kind permission of Viscount De L'Isle from his private collection at Penshurst Place, Kent.

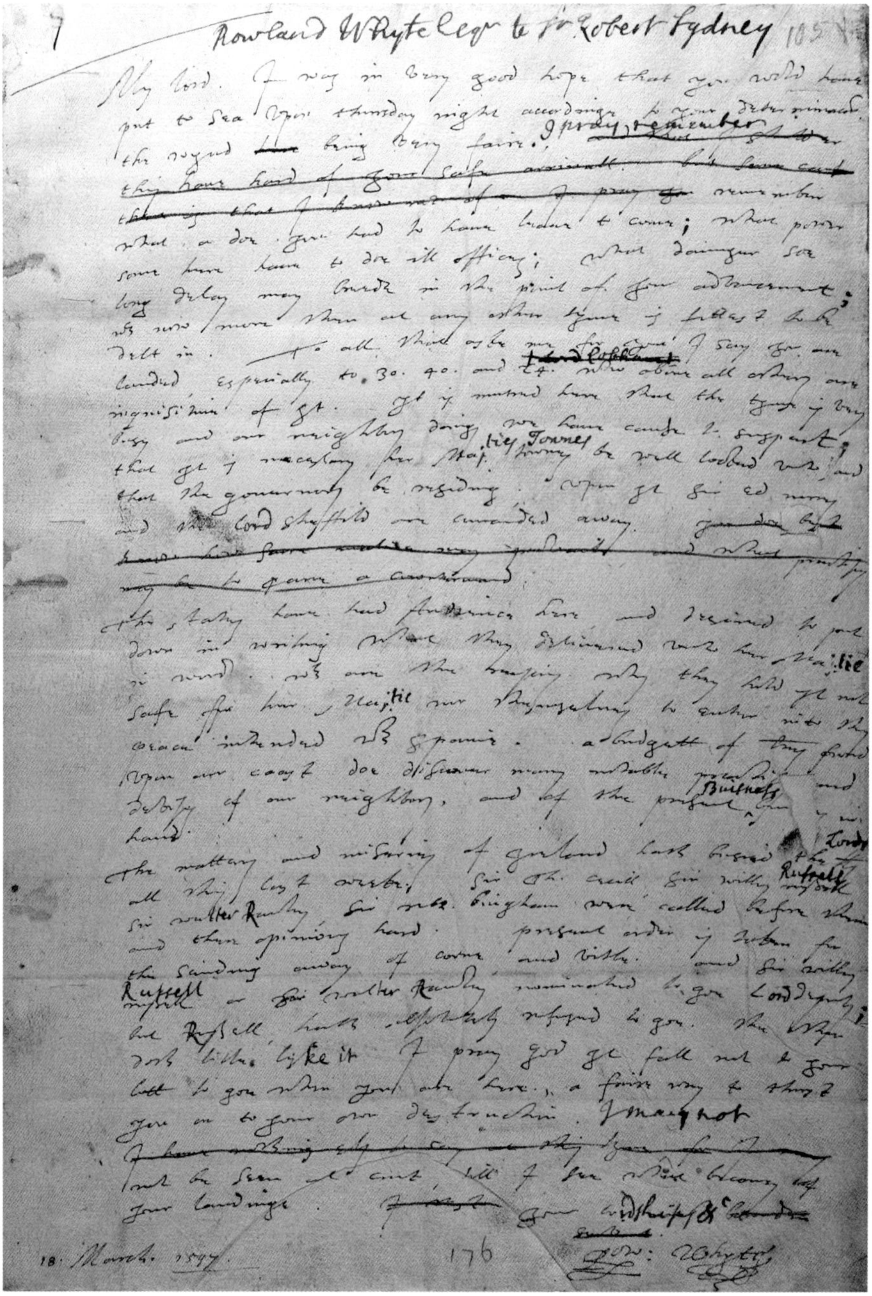

Rowland Whyte Esqr to Sr Robert Sydney

18. March. 1597

Illustration 16 An example of Arthur Collins's intervention in the text of a letter from Rowland Whyte, to Robert Sidney. Kent History and Library Centre (formerly Centre for Kentish Studies), Maidstone, Kent. KHLC U1475 C12/147. By kind permission of Viscount De L'Isle from his private collection.

Illustration 17 *Portrait group of Barbara, Countess of Leicester (née Gamage) with six of her children: Elizabeth, Robert, Philippa, William, Mary, Katherine*, by Marcus Gheeraerts II, oil on canvas, *c.* 1596. Barbara has her hands on Robert and William. By kind permission of Viscount De L'Isle from his private collection at Penshurst Place, Kent.

Illustration 18 *Double portrait of two ladies (probably) Lady Mary Wroth and Lady Barbara
Sidney, the landscape with haymakers. With inscription Lady Wroth and Lady
Gamage dated 1612*, by Marcus Gheeraerts II, oil on panel. By kind permission
of Viscount De L'Isle from his private collection at Penshurst Place, Kent.

Illustration 19 *Portrait of Lady Mary Sidney (1587–1651), daughter of Sir Robert Sidney 1st Earl of Leicester and wife of Sir Robert Wroth*, full-length, holding an archlute, attributed to John de Critz, oil on canvas. By kind permission of Viscount De L'Isle from his private collection at Penshurst Place, Kent.

Illustration 20   Miniature by Isaac Oliver, traditionally described as William Herbert, third
Earl of Pembroke, but possibly Philip Herbert, fourth Earl of Pembroke.
Folger FPm10. By permission of the Folger Shakespeare Library.

Illustration 21 William Herbert, third Earl of Pembroke, after Daniel Mytens, oil on canvas, *c*. 1625. NPG 5560. © National Portrait Gallery, London.

Illustration 22   Philip Herbert, fourth Earl of Pembroke, attributed
to Alexander Cooper, watercolor on vellum.
NPG 4614. © National Portrait Gallery, London.

Illustration 23 Robert Sidney, second Earl of Leicester, by Cornelius Janssens (Jonson). By kind permission of Viscount De L'Isle from his private collection at Penshurst Place, Kent.

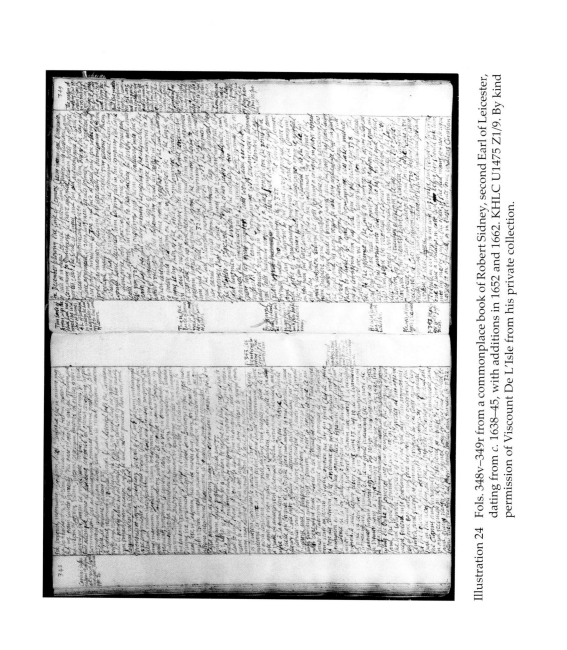

Illustration 24 Fols. 348v–349r from a commonplace book of Robert Sidney, second Earl of Leicester, dating from c. 1638–45, with additions in 1652 and 1662. KHLC U1475 Z1/9. By kind permission of Viscount De L'Isle from his private collection.

Illustration 25 Algernon Sidney, after Justus van Egmont, oil on canvas. NPG 568.
© National Portrait Gallery, London.

Illustration 26 Double portrait of Lucy Percy Hay, Countess of Carlisle, and Dorothy Percy Sidney, Countess of Leicester, after Sir Anthony Van Dyck. By kind permission of Viscount De L'Isle from his private collection at Penshurst Place, Kent.

Illustration 27 Lady Dorothy (Sidney) Spencer, Countess of Sunderland, by Anthony Van Dyck and studio. Private collection, by courtesy of Hoogsteder & Hoogsteder, The Hague.

Illustration 28 Philip Sidney, third Earl of Leicester, attributed to Gerard Honthorst. By kind permission of Viscount De L'Isle from his private collection at Penshurst Place, Kent.

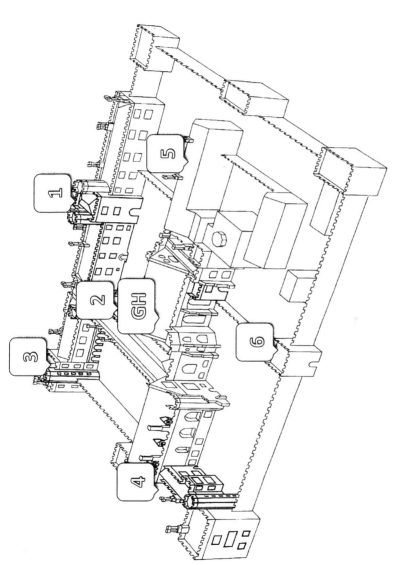

Key: GH. Great Hall. 1. King's Tower. 2. West range. 3. President's Tower. 4. Nether gallery, upper hall over. 5. Service wing. 6. Garden Tower.

Illustration 29 Penshurst Place, Kent, *c.* 1600, centered on the Great Hall, after *The Architectural Development of Penshurst Place* (IPC Business Press Ltd., 1975). © Susie West.

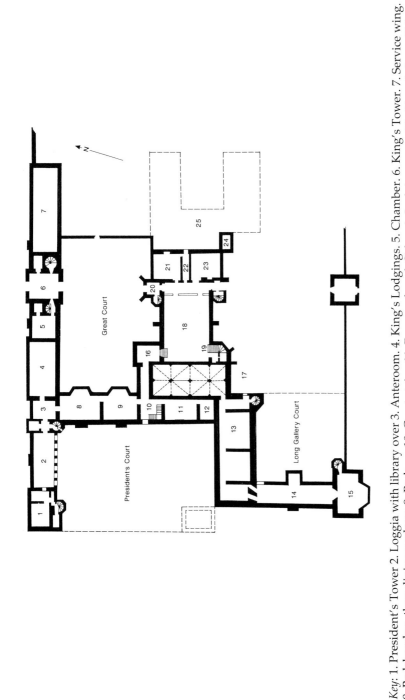

Key: 1. President's Tower 2. Loggia with library over 3. Anteroom. 4. King's Lodgings. 5. Chamber. 6. King's Tower. 7. Service wing. 8. Bedchamber, then dining parlour. 9. Parlour. 10. Great stairs. 11. Former chapel, Sidney's Lodgings over. 12. Chapel closet, Sidney's Lodgings over. 13. Buckingham Building, Leicester's Lodgings with Gloucester's Lodgings over. 14. Nether gallery, upper hall over. 15. Record Tower. 16. Lobby Tower 17. Undercroft, solar/great chamber over. 18. Great Hall. 19. Medieval stairs. 20. North porch. 21. Pantry. 22. Passage. 23. Buttery. 24. Sunderland Lodgings. 25. Kitchen and service areas.

Illustration 30   Penshurst Place, reconstructed ground-floor plan *c.* 1600. © Susie West.

Illustration 31 Leicester House, London, artist unknown, watercolor on paper, c. 1720. Private collection. Looking north, the house is enclosed to west and east after the land was developed during the 1680s, although some formal gardens are visible at the rear. The gallery wing has three windows below the break in the roof line. © Bridgeman Education.

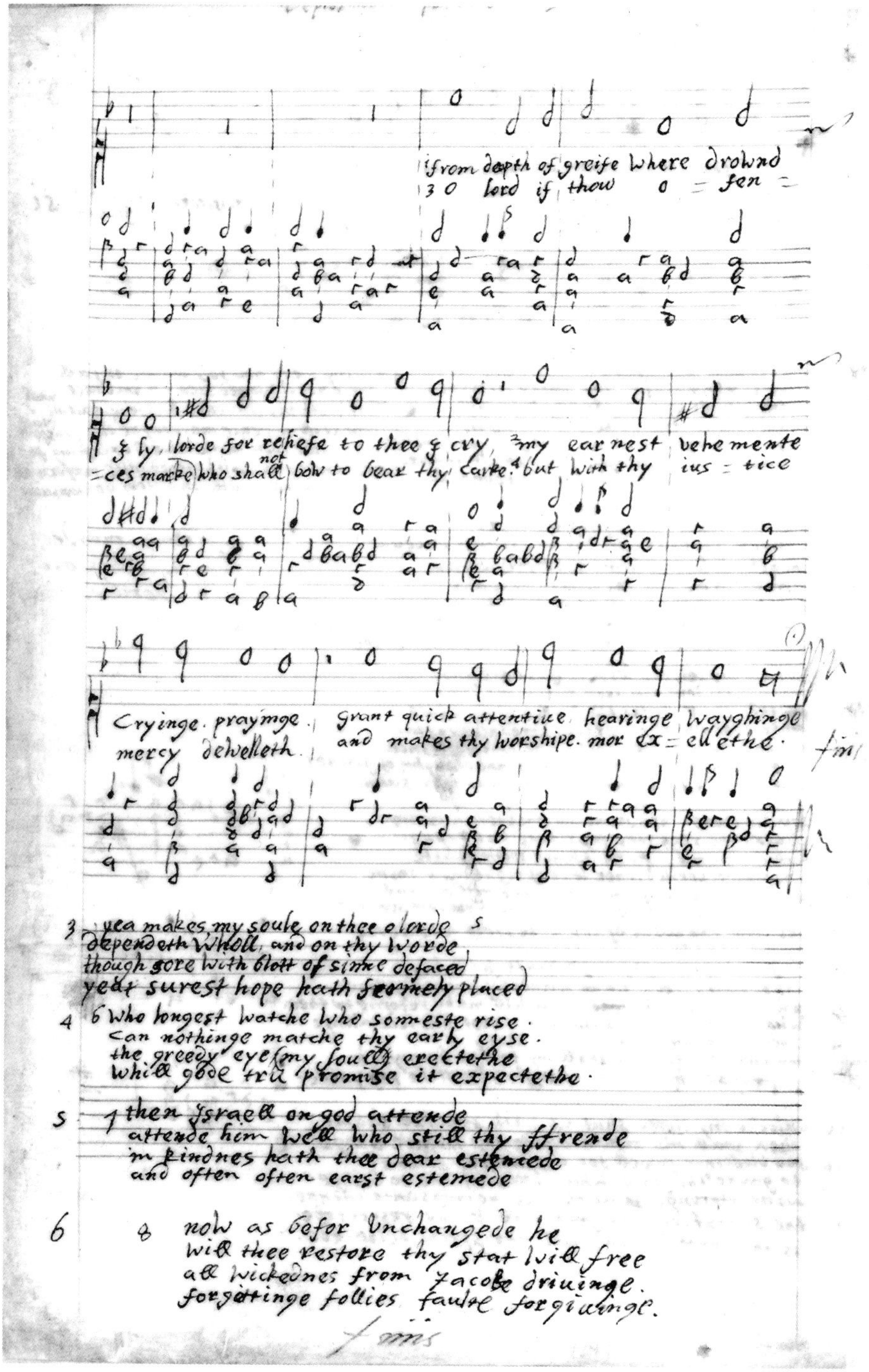

Illustration 32 Musical setting of Mary Sidney's Psalm 130. British Library Add. MS 15117 fol. 5. © The British Library Board.

PART IV
The Sidneys and the Continent

The Sidneys and the Continent:
The Tudor Period

Roger Kuin

In the 1930s the London *Daily Mirror* tabloid is said to have featured the headline "FOG IN CHANNEL—CONTINENT CUT OFF." While this is probably apocryphal, Prime Minister Neville Chamberlain's reaction to the Sudeten Crisis in 1938 is not: he referred querulously to "obscure conflicts in faraway lands between people of whom we know nothing." Such notorious insularity was not the norm in Elizabethan England, at least among the ruling class. While they would not have thought of it as "the Continent" (that term was first used in the modern sense by Edmund Waller in 1655[1]), but rather as France, Spain, Italy, the Netherlands, and the Empires, both Holy Roman and Ottoman, they were familiar with it through trade and travel, and conscious of its importance for English policy. The Sidney family is a good example (see MacCaffrey; Brennan; Stump).[2] In the five generations of their prominence—from Sir William, the chamberlain to young Edward VI, to Algernon the revolutionary—they were intimately linked to the Continent, in diplomacy, in the *res militaria*, in politics, in literature, and in thought (Prescott, *French Poets* is good on such non-insularity).

In 1580 Sir Henry Sidney (Illustration 5), until recently Lord Deputy of Ireland, had the senior Herald of the South, Clarenceux King of Arms Robert Cooke, draw up a family pedigree in the approved heraldic manner, with coats of arms from the simple medieval down to the complex ones of recent generations.[3] This pedigree has been shown in modern times to be largely fanciful in its beginnings, whether deliberately on Cooke's part or not cannot now be determined. At the time it was believed. The probable truth is that the Sidneys were ordinary landowning gentry until, *c.* 1470, Sir Nicholas Sidney, a gentleman from Surrey, married Anne Brandon (Gunn).

This was a considerable step up in the world, for Anne was the sister of Sir William Brandon, who was standard bearer to Henry Tudor, Duke of Richmond, at the Battle of Bosworth, where he was cut down by Richard III in person. And her other brother,

---

1   "Holland, to gain your Friendship, is content / To be our Out-guard on the continent" (*A Panegyrick to my Lord Protector* 6). The capital C in "Continent" was first used in the nineteenth century.

2   *ODNB* is good on all the Sidneys. A useful modern study is Michael G. Brennan's *The Sidneys of Penshurst and the Monarchy*, and perhaps the most useful research tool is St. Louis University's online *Sir Philip Sidney World Bibliography*, edited by Donald Stump: http://bibs.slu.edu/sidney/. For reasons of space and immediate relevance, I omit Algernon Sidney from this chapter, although his relations with the Continent were lifelong, extensive, and important (see Scott *ARC* 1:11).

3   This pedigree, long lost, has now resurfaced and been acquired by the Bodleian Library, Oxford, where it can be examined.

Sir Thomas Brandon, became a courtier and a diplomat in the service of Henry VII (as he became) and briefly of Henry VIII, dying in 1510.

William Sidney

Nicholas and Anne Sidney's firstborn was named William; he was taken into his uncle Thomas Brandon's household at an early age, and lived with him until the uncle's death. So William—who of course became Philip Sidney's grandfather—was schooled in court manners and diplomacy by his mother's brother, who was also Royal Master of the Horse. William was about eighteen in 1500, so we can reasonably assume that he was part of all Thomas Brandon's diplomatic activities for the next ten years; and many of these involved the Continent.

The first was a mission in 1502 to Cologne and Antwerp, to persuade Maximilian, King of the Romans and co-ruler of the Holy Roman Empire, not to support the exiled Yorkist pretender Edmund de la Pole, Earl of Suffolk, in any attempt he might make to win the English throne. The aftermath of the Wars of the Roses clearly still bedeviled English foreign policy. This was successful: Maximilian signed a treaty to that effect.

Four years later Maximilian's son Philip the Fair and his wife Joanna of Castile, sailing to Spain to assume the contested Castilian crown, were shipwrecked on the Dorset coast, and Brandon was sent to Melcombe Regis to receive them. The diplomatic situation was delicate: although officially the guests of Henry VII, the couple were virtually hostages. After six weeks it was only by surrendering the Earl of Suffolk that they were allowed to leave. Again, it seems certain that William Sidney was part of the team.

And in October 1507 Sir Thomas Brandon, newly decorated with the Order of the Garter, was delegated to welcome to England none other than Baldassare Castiglione, who had been sent over to receive the Garter on behalf of his master, the Duke of Urbino.

Significantly, when Thomas Brandon died in 1510, the person who carried the Great Banner of his arms in his funeral procession was none other than William Sidney. All this explains why the Brandon arms—"a barry of ten argent and gules, overall a lion rampant or, ducally crowned[4] per pale argent and gules"—were ever after joined most closely to the family pheon in the Sidneys' arms: they were not just those of a great-grandmother, but of a mentor, almost a second father, who had schooled William Sidney in the skills of a courtier and in the conduct of foreign affairs and diplomacy. Nicholas Sidney appears to have spent his life in England, but his son was in constant contact with the Continent.

After his mentor's death, William Sidney joined Lord Darcy on his ill-conceived and ill-fated expedition to Spain. King Ferdinand had asked for some English archers to help him against the Moors; but by the time Darcy's expedition reached Cadiz, Ferdinand had made peace with them, and the English behaved so badly that they were urged to leave. William Sidney, however, stayed behind for some time, and Holinshed claims that he was offered a Spanish knighthood, but "William Sidneie so excused himselfe, that he was not made knight," probably for fear of offending King Henry.[5]

---

4   Thomas Brandon's younger brother Charles (1484–1545) became a favorite of Henry VIII, who made him Duke of Suffolk. Thenceforward the lion in the family's arms received a ducal crown.

5   "After this, vpon request made by the lords of Spaine, the lord Darcie and all his men the same night went aboord their ships, but Henrie Guilford, Weston Browne, and William Sidneie, yoong and lustie esquiers, desired licence to see the court of Spaine: which being granted, they went thither, where they were of the king highlie interteined. Henrie Guilford and Weston Browne were made knights by the king, who also gaue to sir Henrie Guilford a canton of Granado, and to sir

At the naval Battle of St. Mathieu off Brest in 1512, William Sidney captained one of the king's ships, and was knighted after the victory. The following year he distinguished himself in the vanguard at the Battle of Flodden; and a year later he went to the Netherlands with the king's letter of recommendation, officially to learn the language, and acted as agent for his ducal cousin Charles Brandon. When Brandon secretly married the recently widowed Queen of France, Henry VIII's sister Mary, in Paris in February 1515, Sir William Sidney was again of the party.

By now he seems not only to have learnt excellent French, but to have become known as an expert on France, because in the following years he acted as agent for Wolsey in various French negotiations. On the Field of the Cloth of Gold in 1520 he was a prominent jouster, and three years later he was a captain in Suffolk's (Brandon's) 11,000-strong army that, urged by Emperor Charles V, briefly invaded France and got within eighty miles from Paris before being forced to retreat by the season and lack of support.

This seems to have been Sir William's last role on the Continent. In the 1530s he helped, as a magistrate, suppress the Pilgrimage of Grace, and by 1538 he had become Chamberlain to the young Prince Edward. As such, he added his nine-year-old son Henry to the Prince's household as a playmate; and Henry remained with Edward, as one of the principal Gentlemen of the Privy Chamber, until the sixteen-year-old king died in his arms.[6]

Henry Sidney

Henry Sidney by then was twenty-four, and had spent his formative youth at the very heart of power and court life. In 1551 he had been knighted, at the same ceremony that created John Dudley Duke of Northumberland: that same Dudley was by then his father-in-law, whose daughter Mary he had married nine months earlier.[7]

Sir William had seen to it that from his earliest years Henry became fluent in French and Italian, and accordingly, at the age of twenty-two he was sent on a diplomatic mission to Paris, to sound out King Henri II of France on the possibility of England acting as mediator in the conflict between that king and Emperor Charles V. (Sir Andrew Dudley was simultaneously sent on a similar mission to the emperor.)

Henry weathered the storms following Edward's death with skill and with considerable success: the episode of Lady Jane Grey, the Privy Council's sudden change of mind, the fall of his father-in-law Northumberland, and the accession of Mary. From her he obtained a pardon before the end of 1553, and he served her well. Early the following year he accompanied the Earl of Bedford's mission to Spain to obtain the signature of King Philip II to the treaty for his marriage to Mary: some historians think that he was included in the mission because of his language skills. Philip married Mary on 25 July of that year, and he seems to have liked Sir Henry Sidney: in early December he stood godfather to his first son, to whom his name was given.

It is possible that one reason for Sir Henry's ready acceptance by Mary and her entourage was the queen's fondness for his cousin, Jane Dormer, nine years younger than Sir Henry

---

Wolston Browne an egle of Sicill on a chefe, to the augmentation of their armes. William Sidneie so excused himselfe, that he was not made knight. When they had soiourned there a while, they tooke their leaue of the king and quéene, and returned through France into England" (Holinshed 6:810).

6   On Edward and his entourage, see, *inter alia*, Alford; on the religious aspect, see McCulloch.

7   Almost all the published material about Sir Henry Sidney concerns his work in Ireland. Some balance is provided by MacCaffrey (see also McGowan-Doyle *ARC* 1:2).

and one of the queen's favorite ladies-in-waiting. When King Philip came over to be married, Jane fell in love with one of his attendants, Don Gomez Suarez de Figueroa of Cordova, Duke of Feria. Mary was much in favor of their union, but wanted the marriage put off until Philip should return to England. This never happened, and the couple did not marry until after Mary's death in 1558, when Feria briefly became the first Spanish ambassador to Queen Elizabeth. By this time Sir Henry's career, under the influence of his new brother-in-law, Thomas Radcliffe, Earl of Sussex, had turned definitively to Ireland, where Sussex was Lord Deputy, but he and Jane continued to correspond. At this time, then, the Sidney family's Continental connection was no longer based on France or on diplomacy with the Holy Roman Empire, but on Spain. Before moving to Philip Sidney, we may perhaps look briefly at the influence and effect of religion on the family's Continental relations. Sir William Sidney had joined the Reformation, and was accepted by Henry VIII and Cranmer into the Protestant household of Prince Edward. We know that he was maintained in that household when Edward became king and his entourage became increasingly Puritan, and so may assume that Henry was brought up in this atmosphere and with this outlook. When Mary came to the throne, Henry Sidney did not join the Protestant Marian exiles. Why not? Nothing we know of his character suggests that he was a time-server. Perhaps we have been conditioned by hard-line Puritans and equally hard-line Catholics (and perhaps by some twentieth-century attitudes) to forget a more complex attitude to religion—shown also by Elizabeth after her accession. While Philip in particular tended to frequent some fairly uncompromising Protestants, and claimed not to like his Catholic acquaintances' persons, "and much worse their religions" (letter to Leicester, 28 December 1581), this did not mean that he, and his father, boycotted them in civil life, either in England or on the Continent. Sir Henry seems to have got on well with Queen Mary, and maintained a correspondence with his devoutly Catholic (and now Spanish) cousin, Jane Dormer; Philip wrote a kindly letter to Lady Kytson about her recusant father (28 March 1585), and while in Venice was on good terms with Edward, Lord Windsor, and with Cesare Caraffa (*Correspondence SPS*). It is perhaps significant that neither Sir Henry nor his eldest son left any utterance at all about their private religious faith. The openness they showed served them well in dealing with the Continent.

Philip Sidney

Of all the Sidney family, it was Philip (Illustration 7) who entertained the most extensive relations with the Continent. And these relations—educational, diplomatic, military, and literary—were rich and varied enough to make him very much the center of this chapter (for Philip in this context, see Wallace; Buxton; Osborn; *Correspondence SPS*). In the tradition of his father and his grandfather, he laid the groundwork by learning languages—not only Latin, like every schoolboy, but also French and Italian. The family had at least one French tutor, Jean Tassel,[8] and when Philip went to France at the age of seventeen, an eyewitness claimed that the French were greatly surprised at the quality of his spoken French. This journey, the beginning of his Continental experience, he took as a junior member of a large special embassy under Edward Fiennes de Clinton, Lord Lincoln, to congratulate the French king on his sister's imminent marriage to King Henri of Navarre. When, after sumptuous entertainments, the embassy returned home, Philip stayed behind, as his grandfather had

---

8   Not much is known about him: the family came from Langres, and is better known for two seventeenth-century painters. He was almost certainly a Huguenot.

done in Spain. And, as if history were determined to repeat itself, the king, Charles IX, was much taken with him and offered him a title. Unlike his grandfather, Philip accepted; and so, before he was eighteen, he was made Baron de Sidenay and a Gentleman of the King's Bedchamber.

Not only had he made the king's acquaintance, but also that of Hubert Languet (Illustration 8), a fifty-four-year-old political observer and "intelligencer," who took him under his wing and introduced him to intellectuals and scholars with political connections (for Languet and his "network," see Nicollier-De Weck). As is well known, however, the Continent rapidly turned very bad for Sidney, who was staying as a royal guest in the old Louvre palace: it was there that, in the early hours of 24 August 1572, the killing began that would turn into the St. Bartholomew's Massacre. Philip was too important a foreigner to be in serious danger; he was taken to Sir Francis Walsingham's Embassy on the Left Bank's Quai des Bernardins, where he spent a nervous week cooped up with other English refugees. His uncle, the Earl of Leicester, wanted him back, but he had already left, with a small party, for Heidelberg, and was not to return to England for nearly three years.

The first year, from the autumn of 1572 until that of 1573, he spent in Heidelberg, Frankfurt, Strasbourg, and especially Vienna—an extraordinary learning experience that went well beyond what was slowly becoming the usual Grand Tour. For Languet had made him free of a remarkable network of learned and influential people, all of whom seem to have enjoyed his company. There was Zacharias Ursinus, the gentle theologian from Heidelberg; André (now Andreas) Wechel, the French-born printer in Frankfurt; Jean Sturm, the celebrated educator whose Strasbourg Academy so impressed Philip that he later sent his younger brother there; and in Vienna a host of contacts, from the kindly Emperor Maximilian II to his Imperial Librarian Hugo Blotius, his physician Johann Crato von Krafftheim, his general Lazarus von Schwendi, and many more. The experience taught Philip not only how an empire was run, but how the interaction worked between learned men and those in power; how the Reformation had come to be divided within itself into strict Lutherans on the one hand and Calvinists and Melanchthonians on the other, and how all foreign policy was overshadowed by the fact that the Turkish Empire began only eighty miles from Vienna.

After a September excursion into Hungary, during which he may have met Bálint Balassi, the dashing young poet who was his Magyar counterpart, Sidney headed across the Predil Pass to Padua and its university. Padua, even more than others, was a kind of international university, because on the one hand it was in Italy, while on the other it was in the Veneto, where the new Post-Tridentine rigor of the Inquisition was mitigated by Venetian independence and internationalism (Woolfson). Although we know where Philip lodged—with one Hercole Bolognese at the Pozzo della Vacca, or Cow's Well—we have no direct knowledge of his studies there, which in any case do not seem to have been formally intense. Padua, we should remember, also meant Venice, where he spent a good deal of time, staying at the French Embassy near the Jewish ghetto, and where he met new and interesting people: Wolfgang Zündelin, a political intelligencer not unlike Languet; François Perrot, an Italophile Frenchman who may have given him the idea of versifying Psalms; Edward, Lord Windsor, an English Catholic; quite possibly Veronica Franco or one of her poetically minded *consœurs*, and the French ambassador himself, Arnaud du Ferrier, an almost-Protestant who had attended the Council of Trent. It was in Venice that Philip had himself painted by Paolo Veronese, and we may assume that it was in Padua and Venice that he read a certain amount of Italian literature, as well as the political and historical works he himself mentions in his letters. Apart from quick visits to Florence and Genoa, he saw no more of Italy, and claimed—like any good Protestant Englishman of his time—not to have been impressed with the Italians. Yet his time there did bring him closer to Mediterranean affairs, where details of religion were less important than the major danger of the Turkish navy.

In the autumn of 1574 Philip went back to Vienna, to spend the winter there. It was during this time that he and his friend Edward Wotton enrolled in the recently created Imperial Riding School to learn the Italian "new horsemanship," very much aimed at new techniques of cavalry warfare on light, athletic horses bred in Spain from Arab stock. This is not a historical aside: it was part of what the Continent gave Sidney, and what Sidney then, through his example, propagated. The *res militaria*, after all, was diplomacy by other means; Philip, writing to young Robert, advised him to go to any good wars he might hear of. And Philip himself was fatally wounded during a cavalry charge (for the new horsemanship, see Franz 119–29).

In October he visited Poland at the invitation of a young aristocrat, but returned unimpressed; in February he and Languet followed the emperor to Prague. This visit taught him much about Bohemia, a proud and ancient kingdom where the ruling class was mainly Protestant and the populace largely Hussite or Catholic. It gave the emperor problems similar to those the English Parliament gave Elizabeth: while he needed money to fight the Turks, the Bohemians wanted to talk about something else, in this case not the succession, but religion.

The spring was spent traveling slowly westward, to Leipzig in Saxony, where he met the Camerarius brothers, learned friends of Languet's who also became friends of his, and to Kassel in Hessen, where he was warmly received by Landgrave William, a Protestant but cautious ruler rather in the manner of Queen Elizabeth, sympathizing with foreign causes, but hesitant to employ scarce resources in their active support. He then went to Frankfurt, whence he was abruptly called home by a messenger from the queen, for reasons we still do not know.

What had been the effect of these two-and-a-half years on the Continent? It was twofold. In the first place, and most importantly, it had taught him about governance: about politics, statesmanship, and diplomacy. He had met and discussed with monarchs, courtiers, high functionaries, humanists, diplomats, and political observers. As someone who learned a second language, his own country's way of doing things was no longer self-evident: he had seen, and pondered, others. Moreover, he had discovered books that supported this, his reigning passion: historians especially, but also more theoretical thinkers.

Secondly—and this derives more from inference than evidence—he had absorbed important information about religion and its role in civic life. He had seen Catholicism at its worst, and yet befriended Catholics; he had learnt that a Gnesio-Lutheran did not agree with a Lutheran moderate, and why; he had learnt that while Lutherans called Philippists (followers of Melanchthon) "crypto-Calvinists," there was much that separated these two Reformed currents; he had learnt about the Augsburg Confession, about Ubiquity, Utraquism, and *adiaphora*. He had seen the intolerance born of theological strife, and agreed with Languet (a Philippist) that no theological "correctness" should be allowed to interfere with common solidarity against militant Tridentine Catholicism and its mailed fist, Spain. And he had begun to see the importance of that solidarity and that struggle, to which he was henceforth to devote so much of his energy, and for which he lost his life.

From now on the Continent was always present to him in the form of correspondence; and in the spring of 1577, at the age of twenty-two, he was sent by the queen as envoy extraordinary to congratulate the new emperor, Rudolph II, and sound out a number of princes on the possibility of a Protestant counter-organization to the newly formed Catholic League. It was in many ways the high point of his career as a courtier and diplomat: he acquitted himself in exemplary fashion, though the mooted Protestant League fell victim to the quarrels, caution, and cowardice of the proposed participants.

The Continent's next irruption into his life came in the form of a royal marriage project, in which Queen Elizabeth was to wed the King of France's youngest brother, the Duc d'Anjou, formerly d'Alençon. This set England by the ears: some, like Burghley and the Earl of Sussex, were in favor as it might be a bulwark against Spain; others, like the Earl of Leicester and Sir Francis Walsingham, were against it because of French unreliability in general and Anjou's personal irresponsibility in particular. These last two—Sidney's uncle and his future father-in-law, respectively—persuaded him to write an open letter to the queen arguing against the marriage. This, while Elizabeth seems not to have condemned it, earned him the enmity of the "pro" faction, and especially that of the profligate Earl of Oxford, who tried to have him murdered.

Sidney went to ground for a year at Wilton, where his sister Mary—of whom more presently—lived, married to the Earl of Pembroke. As far as we know, it is during this year, 1580, that he wrote at least the first complete drafts of the works that made him famous: the *Defence of Poesy*, the sonnet sequence *Astrophil and Stella*, and the first version of the *Arcadia*, as well as possibly a beginning to the versified Psalms. In all of these, his experiences of, and on, the Continent were prominently reflected.[9]

The *Defence* is based in part on the works of Italian theorists. This was shown as early as the 1930s by Kenneth Myrick in his influential *Sir Philip Sidney as a Literary Craftsman*. He traced elements of Sidney's apology to Julius Caesar Scaliger's 1561 *Poetices*, to Antonio Minturno's 1559 *De Poeta* and his 1563 *Arte Poetica*, and to Lodovico Castelvetro's 1576 *Poetica d'Aristotele*. However, Stillman convincingly argued for an additional, and perhaps even more important, influence of Melanchthon, whose 1542 *Elementorum rhetorices libri duo*, Stillman claims, accompanies Sidney's critical thinking at crucial points. Where Sidney breaks new ground is in his unvarnished claim that secular fiction, *poesis*, if both made and absorbed in the right spirit, can itself be a moral education (see Borris ARC 2:6; Stillman ARC 2:9).

It is in this way that we should best approach his romance *Arcadia*, written (in its first form) at Wilton, so the author's preface claims, for his sister Mary and her friends. This prose tale interspersed with pastoral poetic interludes introduced into England something of its Continental models, chiefly Jacopo Sannazaro's *Arcadia* (begun in the 1480s and published in 1504), Jorge de Montemayor's 1559 *Diana*, and its 1564 continuation by Gaspar Gil Polo, *Diana enamorada*. In a rare epistolary reference to his literary work, Sidney called *Arcadia* a "toyfull book," but a fruitful combination of continuing interest and dissatisfaction led him to begin a revision, left uncompleted at his death, which deepens and expands the moral elements of the original. It is in the revised version (now usually called the "New Arcadia," the earlier one being the "Old Arcadia") that we most clearly sense the thoughts on governance—from self-governance in private morals to the governance of kingdoms—Sidney derived not only from written sources, but from his own Continental experience and observation (Genouy; Hamilton, "Sidney's *Arcadia*"; Lindenbaum; Schneider). In fact, governance was Philip Sidney's overriding interest and concern, and in contemplating it we should constantly bear in mind, as he did, his family's history, its closeness to the centers of power, the vicissitudes of its close relation to that power, and the internationalism of its political experience.

It was probably also during this year of rustication at Wilton that he completed his sonnet sequence *Astrophil and Stella*, the characters of which have clearly decodable names. It was an open secret that this work, circulated in manuscript, but not printed until after his death, concerned his love for Penelope Devereux, the daughter of the first Earl of Essex, recently married to Robert, Baron Rich. More pertinent to our topic here is that the sequence was a bold and unusual reworking of the Continental Petrarchan model in the

---

9   Hamilton's *Sir Philip Sidney* is still one of the best all-round studies on Sidney's life and work.

light of English Protestant values (Kalstone; Roche; Kennedy). The adulterous nature of its European forebears, never there questioned, now becomes a stumbling block, treated with defiance by the lover, but definitively preventing his success. It allows Sidney brilliantly to demonstrate his principle of "moving the reader" in the touching speech by Stella, who admits that she returns Astrophil's love, but insists that "tyrant Honor" must have the last word. Sidney's sequence set off a decade of sonneteering in England. Spenser's *Amoretti*, ending in an epithalamion, could be seen as a reply to it, while Shakespeare's *Sonnets* and *Lover's Complaint* might be interpreted as an answer to Spenser (see Sokolov *ARC* 2:14).

Sidney is also likely to have begun at Wilton his experiment of casting the Psalms into varied and complex forms of English verse—an exercise that may have originally been suggested to him by a friend and correspondent in Venice, the Italophile Frenchman François Perrot, who had in 1576 published *Perle elette di Francesco Perrotto, cavate da quel tesoro infinito di CL. salmi di David* ("Chosen pearls of Francesco Perrotto, taken out of that infinite treasure of the 150 Psalms of David"), three series of 150 poems each, based on the Psalms. I will return to these versifications presently when dealing with the Countess of Pembroke.[10]

Returning to court, Sidney passed through a frustrating period of inaction and financial difficulties. We know little about the precise dates of his literary work, but it seems safe to assume that it continued, off and on, through the early 1580s. Apart from the *Arcadia*'s revision, he worked on some translations of works by Continental Protestants. Guillaume de Salluste du Bartas, a Huguenot Gascon gentleman, had written the *Sepmaine, ou Creation du Monde*, an epic poem on the Creation which enjoyed immediate popularity among literary Protestants, and even some Catholics. Sidney rendered its nearly 6,500 lines in an English translation which, alas, is not known to have survived. He also began the translation of an important prose treatise by his Huguenot friend Duplessis-Mornay, the *Verité de la religion chrestienne*. This was completed by Arthur Golding, and published as *A Woorke Concerning the Trewnesse of the Christian Religion* in 1587.[11] In 1583 he was made Joint Master of the Ordnance with his uncle, Ambrose, Earl of Warwick. A project to join Drake on an expedition to the New World together with his friend Fulke Greville was disallowed by the queen at the last minute (they were already on board). Instead, she named Sidney Governor of the Dutch cautionary town of Flushing (Vlissingen), thus inaugurating his final Continental experience.[12]

The situation he now entered was complex and important enough to warrant a brief explanation, the more so as his brother Robert eventually succeeded him in the post. The Netherlands, once part of the old Duchy of Burgundy, was now part of the Holy Roman Empire. When Charles V abdicated in 1555 he divided the empire between his son, Philip II, and his nephew, Maximilian II. Maximilian inherited the empire's Central European part, while Philip's portion was Spain and Burgundy. Philip was a modern, centralizing ruler who found the Netherlands' dizzying congeries of towns and regions, all semi-autonomous by virtue of ancient liberties, an anachronism, and the adherence of many of them to the Reformation intolerable. His hard-line policy of repression had durably alienated the Protestant regions, notably Holland and Zeeland, which were now in a state of open if unacknowledged revolt, led by the capable and diplomatic William of Nassau, Prince of Orange, officially the "Stadhouder" (lieutenant-governor) for the king. Orange was assassinated in 1584, and the Protestant regions were hard pressed by the new Spanish general Alexander Farnese, Duke of Parma, who was operating a threateningly successful

---

10   For Philip's Psalms, see Martz 261–82; Freer 63–78; Greene 19–40; see also Prescott *ARC* 2:18.
11   There is, as far as I know, no modern French edition of the *Verité*. Sypher edited a good facsimile edition of the English translation.
12   For Sidney in the Netherlands, see Van Dorsten, *Poets*; Dop; Van Dorsten, Baker-Smith, and Kinney; the best general introduction is still Parker.

reconquista. They had for some time been asking Queen Elizabeth for aid, as the only powerful and independent Protestant monarch, but she had been reluctant to commit scarce resources to an unpredictable adventure that would certainly win her the enmity of Spain without the counterweight of a French alliance. In the face of Parma's success, however, she finally agreed to send some troops on condition that the States of the Netherlands cede her three cautionary towns,[13] to be garrisoned with English soldiers and commanded by an English officer. The towns were carefully chosen: Flushing, which dominates the estuary of the Western Scheldt; the sea-fort of Rammekens, which controls the passage from the narrower Eastern Scheldt to the Western; and Den Briel ("the Brill"), which dominates the Meuse. Flushing was by far the most important of these, as all waterborne traffic to and from Antwerp—the Netherlands' major city, recently taken by the Spaniards—had to pass by it. It was the cork in the bottle, and Sidney was made its governor.

The last year of his life he spent, first, trying to improve the conditions of the troops under his command; second, touring Holland and Zeeland with his uncle Leicester, now the head of all English operations in the Netherlands; and third, on military operations, first in Zeeland, then farther East. It was now that he met and conversed with a number of important Dutch humanists: Justus Lipsius the philosopher, Janus Dousa the neo-Latin poet, and others (Van Dorsten). A few intriguing moments stand out at this time. Sidney and Leicester, in Leiden, went to hear Lipsius lecture on Tacitus and took him to dinner, during which Sidney asked him for some advice on the correct modern pronunciation of Latin. Lipsius responded with a brief treatise on the subject, *De recta pronunciatione Latinae linguae dialogus*, eventually printed in 1599. And Jérôme Groslot, a bright young Frenchman who had barely escaped the St. Bartholomew's Massacre, gone to Scotland, become a protégé of George Buchanan and been brought up with young James VI, was now in Leiden with his friend Paul Schede or Melissus, the German neo-Latin poet. They, Daniel Rogers, and Sidney seem to have spent one or more pleasant evenings drinking and writing poetry. And in an epitaph after Sidney's death, Groslot claims that he was second to none in the arts of the Muses, "as witness the British Muse, the Tuscan, the Roman, the French, and the Greek"—in other words, he had written poetry in English, Italian, Latin, French, and Greek; and it was this, said Groslot, that would make him live for ever (Van Dorsten, *Poets* 185). Even if we take the French as referring to the Du Bartas, this still leaves unaccounted-for some Sidneian verse in Italian, Latin, and Greek that it would be pleasing to recover.

The brief remainder of Philip's time on the Continent was spent dealing with more mundane subjects, mainly military, which need not be gone into at length here; but it may be worth quoting a letter he wrote to Sir Francis Walsingham, by now his father-in-law, who was attempting to deal with the queen's fury at learning that Leicester had made the diplomatic blunder of accepting the Governor-Generalship of the Netherlands. It gives a good insight into both the problems he was facing and the mentality he brought to bear upon them:

> I receive divers letters from you full of the discomfort which I see, and am sorry to see, that you daily meet with at home. And I think—such is the goodwill it pleaseth yow to bear me—that my part of the trouble is something that troubles you. But I beseech you, let it not. I had before cast my count of danger, want and disgrace, and before God, sir, it is true that in my hart the love of the cause doth so far overbalance them all that with God's grace they shall never make me weary of my resolution.

---

13   These were granted to Elizabeth as security for the Dutch Estates' repayment of her assistance's costs. They were eventually returned to Dutch control by James I.

If her Maiesty were the fountain I would fear, considering what I clearly find, that we should wax dry; but she is but a means whom God useth, and I know not whether I am deceaved, but I am faithfully persuaded that if she should withdraw herself other springs would rise to help this action. For methinks I see the great work indeed in hand, against the Abusers of the world, wherein it is no greater fault to have confidence in man's power, than it is too hastily to despair of Gods work.

I think a wise and constant man ought never to grieve while he doth play, as a man may say, his own part truly, though others be out; but if himself leave his hold because other mariners will be idle, he will hardly forgive himself his own fault. For me, I know I cannot promise of my own course, no, not of the mind, because I know there is a higher power that must uphold me or else I shall fall; but certainly I trust I shall not by other men's wants be drawn from myself.

Therefore, good sir, to whom for my particular I am more bound than to all men besides, be not troubled with my troubles, for I have seen the worst in my judgment beforehand, and worse than that cannot be. If the queen pay not her soldiers she must lose her garrisons: there is no doubt thereof. But no man living shall be able to say the fault is in me. What relief I can do them I will: I will spare no danger if occasion serve.

I am sure no creature shall be able to lay injustice to my charge, and for further doubts, truly I stand not upon them. I have written by Adams to the council plainly: thereof let them determine.

It hath been a costly beginning unto me this war, by reason I had no thing proportioned unto it: my servants inexperienced and myself every way unfurnished, and no helps. But hereafter, if the war continue, I shall pass much better through with it.[14]

The story of the final cavalry charge at Zutphen and of his death from gangrene three weeks later is too well known to repeat here; in the present context, suffice it to say that this least insular of Englishmen fought and died on the Continent for an international cause and in an international context (see Stewart *ARC* 1:4).

One of the men who mourned for Sidney was his Huguenot friend Philippe de Mornay du Plessis, known as Duplessis-Mornay, who was defending Montauban at the time against the League (see Daussy). He wrote to Walsingham: "Henceforth I am tempted either to love no man, or to hate myself." And it is Mornay—whose long fundraising visit to England, with his wife, in 1578–79 had been cheered by the friendship of Philip and Mary Sidney, and to whose second daughter Elisabeth Philip had stood godfather in the French Church in Threadneedle Street, London in June 1578—who may be allowed to lead us to the next Sidney who had relations, though very different ones, with the Continent: Philip's sister Mary, the Countess of Pembroke (Illustrations 9 and 10). For while Philip had translated one work of Mornay's, Mary had translated another.

---

14   Sidney to Francis Walsingham, 24 March 1586; *Correspondence SPS* 2:1212–16.

Mary Sidney Herbert, Countess of Pembroke

When, after the St. Bartholomew's Massacre, Mornay found himself in the Protestant city of Sedan, he met there a young widow, Charlotte Arbaleste, whose Huguenot husband had died in the wars five years earlier, and her little daughter Suzanne. Philippe and Charlotte became engaged, and it was for this delightful and intelligent bride that he wrote *Un excellent discours de la vie et de la mort* ("An excellent discourse of life and death")—less a repudiation of life than a celebration of the harbor to which our frail ships are bent. It was this work that Mary, Countess of Pembroke, decided to translate in 1590 as part of her immense effort to honor her brother's memory and at the same time help the cause of the Huguenots by making their texts better known in England (see Beilin *ARC* 2:11).

As Margaret Hannay has demonstrated in her admirable biography of the countess, she had had an excellent education, but had not previously been known to produce any written texts (Hannay, *Philip's Phoenix*; the Garnier translations are in MSH, *Collected Works* 1:208–55). Why then translation? In part because it was considered a humble and safe labor for women; but in recent years much more attention has begun to be paid to Elizabethan translations, and scholarship is becoming increasingly sensitive to the important part they played in the international movements of culture. Mary, not only by her sex, but because of her position, was better placed to receive European civilization in England than to go out and seek it where it lived; and once again the Sidney family's penchant for mastering foreign languages (especially French and Italian) stood her in good stead. Her translation of the *Discours* admirably captures the verve and charm of Mornay's French (Kuin 143–60). And it at once became popular: when it was printed in 1592; reprints followed in 1600, 1606, 1607, and 1608.

The Countess of Pembroke was a fine poet, probably the best woman poet of her age in England. And since we are here concerned with the Continent, we may consider her next translation, that of Robert Garnier's tragedy *Marc Antoine* (1578). Garnier, a magistrate close to King Henri III, wrote Senecan tragedies not unconnected with the turbulent times being experienced by his country. He was a Catholic, whose closeness to the king did not prevent him toying with support of the League; his tragedies are concerned with the ills of civil war and tyranny. For Philip Sidney's bereaved sister, this was of course a worthy choice: war, tyranny, and governance were subjects that had always fascinated her brother. Margaret Hannay has made it clear that Mary's *Antonius* reflected not so much an artistic choice of Senecan over popular theater as a Sidneian choice for a formally sophisticated, Continental theater with definite political overtones. She cites in support of this Samuel Daniel's dedication to Mary of his *Cleopatra*, conceived as a companion piece to *Antonius* and commissioned, says Daniel, by the countess herself.

What made Continental drama such as Garnier's attractive to the Countess of Pembroke and her circle? Theme, in the first place: Garnier was concerned with a ruler's, and a subject's, duty to the state, and with the horrors of civil war. In this context, it is interesting to note Garnier's dedication of the original, and the echoes it would have awakened in Mary's memory. For *Marc Antoine* was dedicated to "Monseigneur de Pibrac," and Guy du Faur de Pibrac (1529–84) was not only, like Garnier himself, a jurist and poet of considerable talent, but had been admired and befriended by Languet himself, who had gently upbraided Philip Sidney for scornful criticism of his defense of the king's actions at St. Bartholomew's. To Pibrac, Garnier wrote:

> But above all, to whom better than you should be addressed the tragic representations of Rome's civil wars? [You] who regard with such horror our civil dissensions and the unhappy troubles of this Kingdom, despoiled today

of its ancient splendor, and of the venerable majesty of our Kings, profaned by tumultuous rebellions? For those reasons, Monseigneur, and in order to rejoice together with all France at the new dignity with which our good King has recently decorated your virtue for the good of his people and as ornament of his justice, I consecrate this *Marc Antoine* to you .... (9; my transl.)

Virtually all Garnier's work is concerned with civil disturbance, war, violence, and the abuse of power. It has been suggested that *Marc Antoine*, with its passionate harangues against passion and moral license, was aimed at Henri III, whose behavior following the death of the Princess of Condé was increasingly criticized in France; but it seems more likely that Garnier, who after all was a supporter of the king, was not so much criticizing as uttering a grave warning, the more powerful for being applicable well beyond the royal person. And the theme of the monarch's duties as inseparable from the subject's was very much that of the *Arcadia*, and may have carried particular overtones *c.* 1590 with the rise of Essex as a royal favorite and pastime.[15]

A second reason for the Countess of Pembroke's choice was in all probability linked to Philip's attempt to rejuvenate English writing through the judicious emulation of Continental models. Garnier in his time was the most highly regarded dramatist in France. Praised by Ronsard for having "changed into gold" the French stage which hitherto "was mere wood," regarded by Robert Estienne as ranking with the Greeks and being "the ornament of French theater," he was compared by Dorat to Æschylus, Sophocles, and Euripides. In reality, he was influenced more by Seneca, of whom Scaliger had written in his *Poetice* that he considered "him in no way inferior to the Greeks in majesty, but in cultivation and luster greater even than Euripides. True, they have inventions; but he has majesty of verse, sonority and spirit" (Scaliger 375). And beyond Seneca, Garnier—his contemporaries found—had a temperate seriousness, an interest in character and motivation, and a moral gravity that greatly attracted the later sixteenth century: not only learned Frenchmen, but the sister of Sir Philip Sidney.

As in the case of Mornay's *Discourse of Life and Death* (together with which *Antonius* was published in 1592), Mary's translation was skillful and vivid. She manages to be both literal and forceful, as in this section from Act 2's chorus:

Il n'est puissance mondaine	Nothing worldly of such might,
Si grande que le Destin,	But more mightie Destinie,
Comme une moindre, n'ameine	By swift *Times* unbridled flight,
Avec le temps à sa fin.	Makes in ende his ende to see.
Le Temps abbat toute chose,	Euery thing *Time* ouerthrowes,
Rien ne demeure debout,	Nought to ende doth stedfast staie:
Sa grande faulx tranche tout,	His great sithe mowes all away
Comme le pié d'une rose:	As the stalke of tender rose:
La seule immortalité	Onlie Immortalitie
Du ciel estoilé s'oppose	Of the Heau'ns doth it oppose
A sa fort deïté.	Gainst his powerfull *Deitie*.
Il viendra quelque journee	One daie there will come a daie
Pernicieuse à ton heur,	Which shall quaile thy fortunes flower,
Qui t'abatra ruinee	And thee ruin'de low shall laie

---

15 Excellent on the countess's Garnier and its background is Prescott, "Mary Sidney's French Sophocles."

Sous un barbare seigneur:	In some barbarous Princes power:
De toutes parts ravageant,	When the pittie-wanting fire
O Romme, ira saccageant	Shall, *O Rome*, thy beauties burne,
Tes richesses orgeilleuses	And to humble ashes turne
Et tes bastimens dorez,	Thy proud wealth and rich attire,
Dont les pointes envieuses	Those guilt roofes which turretwise,
Percent les cieux etherez.	Justly making Enuie mourne,
	Threaten now to pearce the Skies.

This effort on the countess's part to import Continental drama into England had far-reaching consequences. Not only did Daniel's *Cleopatra* follow shortly after, in 1594, but in the same year Thomas Kyd published his translation of Garnier's *Cornelie* as *Cornelia*. Fulke Greville also practiced the Senecan form—with dire warnings to sovereigns—in his *Alaham* and his *Mustapha*, both written around the same time, but not published until later: *Mustapha* in 1609, and *Alaham* after the author's death in 1633. And finally, of course, Mary's Garnier translation was not without effect on the *Antony and Cleopatra* of an even greater playwright (see also Weller *ARC* 2:12).

The third Continental aspect of Mary's writing concerns her continuation of Philip's versification of the Psalms. (Here I will deal only with that aspect of the Sidney Psalms, as they are treated exhaustively in Prescott *ARC* 2:18.) The Reformation had instituted the singing of Psalms as an important part of the liturgy, and for a congregation to sing them in anything other than plainsong, some form of modern, preferably simple, verse was required. Accordingly, such versions began to appear all over Western Europe. One of the first in France was that of Clément Marot, published in 1530–43 (Wursten); when Marot was banished and went to Geneva, he continued the work, and after his death his forty-nine Psalm versifications were completed by Théodore de Bèze, or Beza, and the whole was published in 1562 as *Pseaumes de David*, with 123 different tunes (Austern, McBride, and Orvis).

While Robert Crowley's 1549 *Psalter of Dauid Newely Translated into Englysh Metre in Such Sort that it Maye the More Decently, and wyth More Delyte of the Mynde, be Reade and Songe of Al Men* was an entirely English affair in fourteeners with plainsong tunes, the collection published in the same year of forty-four Psalms versified by Thomas Sternhold and John Hopkins was taken to Geneva by Marian exiles, where it was revised and added to, so that in 1562 John Day could publish *The Whole Booke of Psalmes, Collected into English Meter*. Sternhold, Hopkins, and the others who had added Psalms had put them into Common Meter for ease of singing, and many of their tunes were Genevan ones from the Huguenot Psalter (Quitslund; see Kinnamon *ARC* 2:3, Prescott *ARC* 2:18, Clarke *ARC* 2:10, and Hamlin *ARC* 2:20).

I have already mentioned another Continental influence on Philip Sidney's Psalm work, to which it is now time to return. François Perrot, the Italophile Frenchman Sidney had met in Venice, wrote as Francesco Perrotto. When Sidney met him in 1573 he was secretary to the French Embassy in Venice, and had just begun work on the Psalms. With them he did two things. First, he versified them: by 1581 he brought out the first half as *Settantacinque Salmi di David, tradotti in lingua volgare Italiana*, using the Genevan tunes of the Marot-Beza version. Secondly, five years earlier, in 1576 he published that curious book the *Perle elette*. In it, all 150 Psalms are paraphrased, and paraphrased three times, in iambic pentameter octains rhyming ababababcc. They are condensations: in the margin of each, Perrot prints the verses he had chosen for his summary. The three sets are separate in purpose, as shown by their prefatory material: the first is presented to Venice as a remedy for its spiritual ills; the second appears to have been written during a plague year, similar to the first, but with more urgency; the third is in fact a long poem "on the First and Last War of the World," in which the individual Psalm paraphrases have become stanzas (Bettoni 71–95).

I dwell briefly on these poems because on 26 November 1574, while he was working on these, Perrot wrote to Sidney in a letter: "in response to what you write, I am sending you the Italian verses." While we cannot be sure that these were the *Perle elette*, there is a reasonable probability; and in that case, they are the only vernacular Psalm poetry that we know Philip, and therefore Mary, to have possessed.

It will be noted that virtually all the Continental models the Sidneys had were intended for congregational song and fitted to relatively simple meters. The notable exception is the Psalm translation of Jean-Antoine de Baïf, who in 1567 published sixty-eight Psalms in quantitative verse, and in 1573 the entire corpus (Maser 334–41). His meters are complex, his spelling peculiar, and his versions sometimes odd; but metrically he is closer to the Sidneys than anyone else. Nevertheless, his outspoken "anti-heretic" stance and his enthusiastic support for the St. Bartholomew's Massacre may have made him less attractive to Philip and Mary.

While Baïf's exercises seem to have been entirely academic and to have concentrated on the word as recited in speech, we are still faced with the question of the Sidney Psalter's forms. What did Philip and Mary have in mind? (When looking at Renaissance writers' formal choices, "What were they doing?" is often a less interesting question than "What did they *think* they were doing?") One clue may be provided by Marot, who in his prefatory address to the elegant ladies of François I's and Marguerite de Navarre's courts suggests that they can now pack that little wingèd inconstant god of love's madness off and, their fingers still on the keys of their "Espinettes," replace him in their songs with the loveable God of "amour non variable." No more of the little lad's useless songs that may be harmful to your health: here is far better matter to sing, and from a more reliable divinity.

The operative word is *sing*. When dealing with sung Psalms, we earnest academics tend to be preoccupied with the sturdy unison of stolid congregations. But although Philip and Mary most certainly went to church, they also lived in a very different world—a world that sang after dinner, played the lute, and was shortly to receive its greatest genius in John Dowland. One of Mary Wroth's portraits (Illustration 19) shows her with an archlute; Philip reminds Edward Denny to sing his songs; William Byrd's posthumous tribute to Sidney was the 1588 *Psalms, Songs and Sonnets*, and John Danyel, Thomas Campion, and Thomas Morley were close to the Sidney circle. Campion, in fact, has several very fine examples of religious lute songs; Rivkah Zim mentions a seventeenth-century manuscript with two of Mary Sidney's Psalms set for soprano and viols, and one of Morley's songs—"With my love my life was nestled"—almost perfectly fits Sidney's Psalm 42. The school of versification, I believe, was in fact a conservatory for the Christian ladies' (and gentlemen's) lute songs.[16]

Robert Sidney, First Earl of Leicester

With Robert Sidney, later first Earl of Leicester of the Jacobean creation, we return to an earlier kind of Sidneian relation with the Continent (Illustrations 13, 14 and 15). Chosen by

---

16   "Lutes were also used to accompany Psalms and other religious texts used for domestic purposes. The Dallis manuscript contains much of this sort of material. Along with courtly lyrics it contains fourteen Psalm-tune settings, ten workings of the religious song 'Leve le coeur', and two versions of Kinwelmarsh's 'O heavenly God,' which is also in the Giles Lodge book. Some of the religious pieces are settings for lute solo; others supply a vocal line, and in some cases words as well" (Spring 256–7; see Larson *ARC* 1:21).

the queen after the defeat of the Armada to succeed his brother as Governor of Flushing, he (like Philip) relied a good deal on the admirable water bailiff William Borlas or Burlas for the day-to-day work of the position, and spent much of his time and energy attempting to get back to England and the court. However, he did perform a useful embassy to the newly converted Henri IV of France in 1594, to obtain assurances of continued alliance; these he was given, and from the king's reactions we can conclude that Robert had inherited some of his late brother's charm. There is an interesting early seventeenth-century mention of two of his French trips in a manuscript in the Bibliothèque Nationale, which I quote *in extenso* because it is one of the few external descriptions of Robert's Continental diplomacy at work:

Mess^e. Robert Sidney, Chevalier, Viconte de l'isle, Gouverneur pour le Roy d'Angleterre a <u>Vlissinghe</u>, et ~~Cham~~ premier ou grand Chambellan de la Roine d'Angleterre est neveu et principal heritier des feues Contes de <u>Warwic</u> et /de\ <u>Leycester</u> freres, frere de ce tant renommé Caualier <u>Philippe Sidney</u>, qui fut tué d'vn coup de mousquet au genoil, comme il pensoit empescher le rauitaillement de Zutphen par les Espagnols, en Septembre ou Octobre 1586.

Ledict Sr Robert Sidney, a fait plusieurs legations pour la feu Roine d'Angleterre tant en France, que en Allemagne et païs bas. Sa premiere en france, fut sur la crainte que eurent ceux de la religion apres la conuersion du Roy, que Sa Majesté ne changeast de volonté enuers eux, comme il auoit changé de religion: pour prier & conuier sadicte majesté de la part de la Roine d'Angleterre de vouloir continuer sa bienueillance enuers lesdicts de la religion: et arriua a <u>Mantes</u>[?] aussitost apres la Conference. Delà le Roy le mena a <u>Chartres</u>, où il assista a son sacre, n'y ayant pour lors de la part des princes estrangers que luy, et l'<u>Ambassadeur de Venise</u>. Et peu apres accompagna le Roy, estant <u>toujours armé</u> et pres sa personne, a la <u>prinse de Paris</u>: d'où ayant eu fort fauorable response de Sa majesté il partit en Auril 1594. #

L'autre legation fut aussitost apres la <u>prise de Calais</u> en 1597, par les Espagnols, le Roy se trouuant alors au chateau de Bologne, où ledict Sieur Sidney proposa a Sa Majesté de la part de ladicte /feu\ Roine les conditions moyennant lesquelles elle vouloit donner a sadicte Majesté tout secours & assistance pour le recouurement dudict Calais et autres places prises et surprises par l'Espagnol.

Sir Robert Sidney, Knight, Viscount Lisle, Governor for the King of England in Vlissingen,[1] and first or great Chamberlain of the Queen of England, is nephew and chief heir of the late Earls of Warwick and Leicester, brothers, brother of that so famous horseman Philip Sidney, who was killed by a musket-shot to the knee, as he attempted to forestall the resupply of Zutphen by the Spaniards, in September or October 1586.

That same Sir Robert Sidney has undertaken several embassies for the late Queen of England, to France, to Germany and to the Netherlands. His first one to France concerned the Protestants' fear, after the King's conversion, that His Majesty might change his policy toward them as he had changed his religion: to beg and invite his Majesty, on behalf of the Queen of England, kindly to continue his goodwill toward the Protestants; and he arrived in Mantes directly after the Conference.[2] Thence the King took him to Chartres, where he was present at his coronation, when at that time he and the Venetian Ambassador were the only representatives of foreign princes. And soon thereafter he accompanied the King, always armed and near his person,[3] to the capture of Paris; whence, having received a very favorable reply from his Majesty, he left in April 1594. #

The second embassy was just after the capture of Calais in 1597 by the Spaniards, when the King was at the château of Boulogne, where Sir [Robert] Sidney laid out before his Majesty the late Queen's conditions for giving his Majesty all help and assistance for the recovery of Calais and other fortified towns captured and overpowered by the Spaniard.

# Et a marquer, que lors de la surprise de Paris M. Sidney sceut que le <u>Duc de Feria</u> y estoit auec les Espagnols qui y auoient tenu garnison: neanmoins, pour ne donner ombrage, nj au Roy, nj a la Roine sa maistresse, ne le voulut voir, bien qu'il fust <u>cousin germain</u> dudict Duc, ayant le pere du Duc de feria autreffois espousé la <u>tante paternelle</u> dudict Sieur de Sidney pendant le mariage et sejour du feu Roy d'Espagne auec Marie Roine d'Angleterre.	# And it is noteworthy that when, at the capture of Paris, Master Sidney learned that the Duke of Feria was with the Spaniards who had garrisoned it: nevertheless, in order not to offend either the King or the Queen his own mistress, he did not want to meet him, even though he was first cousin to that Duke, as the Duke of Feria's father had formerly married Sir [Robert] Sidney's paternal aunt at the time of the marriage and the stay of the late King of Spain with Mary Queen of England. (BnF MS Dupuy 348 fols. 205/244ff.)

Notes:

[1] Flushing.

[2] This was the Dispute of Mantes, in late 1593 and early 1594, where the Huguenots expressed their fears about the king's conversion and its possible consequences.

[3] A sign of great favor, particularly after the assassination of Henri III.

Robert also forged an excellent relationship with Count Maurice of Nassau, who was uniting the fractious Netherlands under strict rule and a rigorous Reformed Church.

His initial moderate support of Essex soon showed itself counter-productive, and Robert weathered the 1601 crisis with skill. He had earlier charmed James VI of Scotland, and on that monarch's accession to the English throne, Robert Sidney's English career took off. As Viscount Lisle he undertook one more important journey to the Continent, as part of the group that accompanied Princess Elizabeth to her new bridegroom, the Elector Palatine, and her new home in Heidelberg. His poetry, for him a private pastime, owes more to his brother's example than to direct Continental influence (see Moore *ARC* 2:15).

One light-hearted Continental interlude may be mentioned here: the healthful waters to be found in Spa, near Liège. These had become famous through a 1559 work by Gilbert Lymborh (a pseudonym for Gilbert Fuchs, the Prince-Bishop of Liège's personal physician), *De Acidis fontibus sylvae Arduennae, praesertim eo qui in Spa visitur*, and Sir Henry Sidney had taken the waters there in 1584. It was still a very small and rustic village around the *pouhon* (spring) (spurned by Queen Margot, who had the waters brought to her in Liège), but it was rapidly becoming fashionable, and in July 1613 Robert Sidney wrote to his wife Barbara from "Spaw." In the summer of 1614 the Countess of Pembroke went there, and clearly enjoyed it so much that she remained in the area for two years (*Philip's Phoenix* 196–201). She struck up a friendship with another countess, the thirty-six-year-old Marguerite de Lalaing, whose husband Florent de Berlaymont was Governor of Artois, Namur, Guelre-Zutphen, and Luxembourg. Marguerite was at Spa with her two little daughters, Isabelle-Claire (aged twelve) and Marie-Marguerite (aged nine), and a good time seems to have been had by all. The two countesses shot at targets with wheel-lock pistols, the first kind of firearm that could be carried on the person (and incidentally the kind with which William of Orange was assassinated). They also took tobacco, either by drinking it as an infusion or, more probably, by smoking it in clay pipes. And Mary was thought by some to have taken advantage of this Continental sojourn to have an affair with her physician, Sir Matthew Lister. What is interesting in the two countesses' relationship from the present chapter's point of view is that the Comtesse de Berlaymont was an intensely devout Catholic who went to Mass daily and only a few years later founded an order of nuns, the Dames de Berlaymont. And her father-in-law, Charles de Berlaymont, counselor to Margaret of Parma, is said to have coined the insult proudly borne by the Dutch rebels when he told Margaret: "N'ayez pas peur,

Madame, ce ne sont que des gueux" ("Be not afraid, Ma'am, they're nothing but beggars"). None of this appears to have bothered Mary in the slightest, reminding us that—like Sir Henry and like Philip—the Protestant piety of her Mornay and her Psalms did not make her a bigot in personal relations.

Lady Mary Wroth

Robert's daughter Mary (Illustrations 17, 18 and 19), married to Sir Robert Wroth, though she traveled to Flushing with her mother Barbara several times during her childhood, spent her adult life in England; and in her case, too, Continental influences in her writing—the romance *Urania* and the sonnet sequence *Pamphilia to Amphilanthus*—appear to be filtered through what had by now become a family tradition, begun by her uncle Philip. (The full title of the romance is *The Countess of Montgomery's Urania*, as Philip's was *The Countess of Pembroke's Arcadia*.) More potent, to contemporary readers at least, was the *roman à clef* aspect that hinted at goings-on among the great; and in the story itself, love has a far greater role than politics or governance.[17]

Although too wide for the Armada, for Napoleon, and for Hitler, the Channel is a narrow reach of water. The educated English of the sixteenth and seventeenth centuries were anything but insular, and the Sidneys are no exception. It may be useful to ask ourselves what the Continent meant to them. Their relations with it were of several kinds: diplomatic, military, religious, and literary. What appears from their lives and works is a clear indication that these kinds were indissolubly connected, and that relations with the Continent were for the Sidneys above all a learning experience. They mostly went there in their younger years, and whatever the tasks they performed there, they made human contacts and absorbed ideas. The human contacts were of two kinds: governmental and learned. They met monarchs, courtiers, functionaries, but also scholars, diplomats, theologians, printers, and even the occasional poet. The ideas they absorbed were very much those of their time, which inseparably joined politics with religion. William Sidney found himself, after diplomatic and military activity on the Continent, directing the severely Protestant household of young Edward VI, where "religion" meant something between Melanchthon and Calvin; Henry Sidney grew up there, but had to deal with Catholics and Catholicism, and learnt to do so without apparent pain; Philip, through his friendship with Languet, became a Philippist, but was never explicit about it; Mary seems to have followed Philip in this, while Robert's and Mary Wroth's religious stance appears to have been comfortably and unemphatically English, living as they did between the upheavals of the mid-sixteenth and those of the mid-seventeenth centuries.

What they learnt most of all from the Continent, I submit, is a concern with governance. They all supported the monarchy, but never uncritically; they worked and wrote in defense of an active and critically advising ruling class; they believed in the importance of public affairs and political duty. Part of the lessons were *a contrario*: contemplating the French religious wars led to thoughts about the Elizabethan settlement and policy. Some of them were direct: studying the rule of a William of Hessen or of William of Orange conveyed valuable insights into political compromise and caution. And though most of the lessons could and should be applied to their own country, some called for engagement elsewhere: in Dublin, in Flushing, or in Zutphen.

---

17   For Wroth, see especially Hannay, *MSLW*. Wroth used foreign romances—Montemayor, Ariosto, *Amadis de Gaule*, and Honoré d'Urfé's *Astrée*—but in English translations.

Bibliography

Manuscript Source

Bibliothèque Nationale
  BnF MS Dupuy 348 fols. 205/244ff

Primary and Secondary Sources

Alford, Stephen. *Kingship and Politics in the Reign of Edward VI*. Cambridge: Cambridge UP, 2002.

Austern, Linda Phyllis, Karl Boyd McBride, and David L. Orvis, eds. *Psalms in the Early Modern World*. Farnham: Ashgate, 2011.

Bettoni, Anna. "Le Perle elette di François Perrot." *Scrittori stranieri in lingua italiana, dal Cinquecento ad oggi. Atti del Convegno internazionale di studi (Padua, 20–21 March 2009)*. Ed. Furio Brugnolo. Padua: Unipress, 2009. 71–95.

Brennan, Michael. *The Sidneys of Penshurst and the Monarchy, 1500–1700*. Aldershot: Ashgate, 2006.

Buxton, John. *Sir Philip Sidney and the English Renaissance*. London: Macmillan, 1964.

Daussy, Hugues. *Les Huguenots et le roi: le combat politique de Philippe Duplessis-Mornay (1572–1600)*. Geneva: Droz, 2002.

Dop, Jan Albert. *Eliza's Knights: Soldiers, Poets, and Puritans in the Netherlands 1572–1586*. Alblasserdam: Remak [1981].

Duplessis-Mornay, Philippe. *Un excellent discours de la vie et de la mort*. Ed. Mario Richter. Milan: Editrice Vita e pensiero, 1964.

—. *Verité de la religion chrestienne*. Transl. Arthur Golding as *A Woorke Concerning the Trewnesse of the Christian Religion* (1587). Ed. F. J. Sypher. Delmar, NY: Scholars' Facsimiles and Reprints, 1976.

Franz, Patricia M. *The Horseman as a Work of Art: The Construction of Elite Identities in Early Modern Europe, 1550–1700*. Ann Arbor, MI: ProQuest, 2006.

Freer, Coburn. "The Style of Sidney's Psalms." *Language and Style* 2 (1969): 63–78.

Garnier, Robert. *Marc Antoine, Hippolyte*. Ed. Raymond Lebègue. Paris: Les Belles Lettres, 1974.

Genouy, Hector. *L'Arcadia de Sidney dans ses rapports avec l'Arcadie de Sannazaro et la "Diana" de Montmayor*. Paris: Henri Didier, 1928.

Greene, Roland. "Sir Philip Sidney's Psalms, the Sixteenth-century Psalter, and the Nature of Lyric." *SEL* 30 (1990): 19–40.

Gunn, Steven J. *Charles Brandon, Duke of Suffolk c. 1484–1545*. Williston: Basil Blackwell, 1988.

Hamilton, A. C. "Sidney's *Arcadia* as Prose Fiction: Its Relation to its Sources." *ELR* 2.(1972): 29–60.

—. *Sir Philip Sidney: A Study of His Life and Works*. Cambridge: Cambridge UP, 1977.

Hannay, Margaret P. *Mary Sidney, Lady Wroth*. Farnham: Ashgate, 2010.

—. *Philip's Phoenix: Mary Sidney, Countess of Pembroke*. Oxford: Oxford UP, 1990.

Herbert, Mary Sidney. *The Collected Works of Mary Sidney Herbert, Countess of Pembroke*. Ed. Margaret P. Hannay, Noel J. Kinnamon, and Michael G. Brennan. Oxford: Oxford UP, 1998.

Holinshed, Raphael. *Chronicles of England*. 1587. 6 vols. *The Holinshed Project*. Web. http://www.english.ox.ac.uk/holinshed/texts.php?text1=1587_6913. 6:810.

Kalstone, David. *Sidney's Poetry: Contexts and Interpretations*. Cambridge, MA: Harvard UP, 1965.

Kennedy, William. *The Site of Petrarchism: Early Modern National Sentiment in Italy, France and England*. Baltimore, MD: Johns Hopkins UP, 2003.

Kuin, Roger. "Life, Death, and the Daughter of Time: Philip and Mary Sidney's Translations of Duplessis-Mornay." *French Connections in the English Renaissance*. Ed. Catherine Gimelli Martin and Hassan Melehy. Farnham: Ashgate, 2013. 143–60.

Lindenbaum, Peter. *Changing Landscapes: Anti-Pastoral Sentiment in the English Renaissance*. Athens, GA: U of Georgia P, 1986.

MacCaffrey, Wallace T. "Sir Henry Sidney." *ODNB*.

Martz, Louis L. *The Poetry of Meditation: A Study in English Religious Literature of the Seventeenth Century*. New Haven, CT: Yale UP, 1954.

Maser, Simone. "La traduction des psaumes par J.A. de Baïf, restitution biblique." *Canadian Review of Comparative Literature* 8.2 (1981): 334–41.

McCulloch, Diarmaid. *The Boy King: Edward VI and the Protestant Reformation*. Berkeley, CA: U of California P, 2002.

Myrick, Kenneth O. *Sir Philip Sidney as a Literary Craftsman*. Cambridge, MA: Harvard UP, 1935.

Nicollier-De Weck, Béatrice. *Hubert Languet 1518–1581: un réseau politique international de Melanchthon à Guillaume d'Orange*. Geneva: Droz, 1995.

Osborn, Albert W. *Sir Philip Sidney en France*. Paris: Champion, 1932.

Parker, Geoffrey. *The Dutch Revolt*. Harmondsworth: Penguin, 1977; rev. ed. 1985.

Prescott, Anne Lake. *French Poets and the English Renaissance*. New Haven, CT: Yale UP, 1978.

—. "Mary Sidney's French Sophocles: The Countess of Pembroke Reads Robert Garnier." *Representing France and the French in Early Modern English Drama*. Ed. Jean-Christophe Mayer. Newark, DE: U of Delaware P, 2008. 68–90.

Quitslund, Beth. *The Reformation in Rhyme: Sternhold, Hopkins and the English Metrical Psalter, 1547–1603*. Aldershot: Ashgate, 2008.

Roche, Thomas P., Jr. *Petrarch and the English Sonnet Sequences*. New York: AMS, 1989.

Scaliger. *Iulii Caesari Scaligeri viri clarissimi Poetices libri septem*. [Geneva:] Petrus Santandreanus [Pierre de St. André], 1594.

Schneider, Regina. *Sidney's (Re)Writing of the "Arcadia."* New York: AMS, 2008.

Sidney, Philip. *The Correspondence of Sir Philip Sidney*. Ed. Roger Kuin. 2 vols. Oxford: Oxford UP, 2012.

Sidney, Robert, first Earl of Leicester. *Domestic Politics and Family Absence: The Correspondence (1588–1621) of Robert Sidney, First Earl of Leicester, and Barbara Gamage Sidney, Countess of Leicester*. Ed. Margaret P. Hannay, Noel J. Kinnamon, and Michael G. Brennan. Aldershot: Ashgate, 2005.

Spring, Matthew. *The Lute in Britain: A History of the Instrument and its Music*. New York: Oxford UP, 2006.

Stewart, Alan. *Sir Philip Sidney: A Double Life*. London: Chatto & Windus, 2000.

Stillman, Robert E. *Philip Sidney and the Poetics of Renaissance Cosmopolitanism*. Aldershot: Ashgate, 2008.

Stump, Donald, ed. *Sir Philip Sidney World Bibliography*. Web. 2001–2005. http://bibs.slu.edu/sidney/.

Van Dorsten, J. A. *Poets, Patrons and Professors: Daniel Rogers and the Leiden Humanists*. Leiden: Leiden UP, and Oxford: Oxford UP, 1962.

—, D. Baker-Smith, and A. F. Kinney, eds. *Sir Philip Sidney: 1586 and the Creation of a Legend*. Leiden: Brill, 1986.

Wallace, M. W. *The Life of Sir Philip Sidney*. Cambridge: Cambridge UP, 1915.

[Waller, Edmund] *A Panegyrick to my Lord Protector, by a Gentleman that loves the Peace, Union and Prosperity of the English Nation*. London: Thomas Newcomb, 1655.

Whyte, Rowland. *The Letters (1595–1608) of Rowland Whyte*. Ed. Michael G. Brennan, Noel J. Kinnamon, and Margaret P. Hannay. Farnham: Ashgate, 2013.

Woolfson, Jonathan. *Padua and the Tudors: English Students in Italy, 1485–1603*. Toronto: U of Toronto P, 1998.

Wursten, Dick. *Clement Marot and Religion: A Reassessment in the Light of His Psalm Paraphrases*. Leiden: Brill, 2010.

Zim, Rivkah. *English Metrical Psalms: Poetry as Praise and Prayer, 1535–1601*. Cambridge: Cambridge UP, 1987.

The Sidneys and the Continent: The Stuart Period

Michael G. Brennan

The Sidneys' involvement in Continental affairs during the seventeenth century through diplomacy, administrative appointments, and personal travel is central to an understanding of their public prestige and family lives. But while their court status was frequently enhanced by onerous duties abroad, the impact of these commitments on their family lives, especially in terms of their expense and a debilitating sense of being exiled from home and loved ones, was immense. The remarkable wealth and range of the Sidneys' family archive, published writings, and other surviving documents makes the narrative of their experiences from the accession of James I in 1603 until the death of William III in 1702 well worth exploring—and at times redefining—from the specific perspective of their Continental activities.

Robert Sidney, First Earl of Leicester

The new reign began promisingly for Robert Sidney (Illustrations 13, 14, and 15) as he had personally known King James VI of Scotland since 1588. On 4 May 1603 he was raised to the rank of Viscount Lisle, followed by his appointment on 13 May as Queen Anne's Lord Chamberlain. Given his productive dealings with King Henri IV during the last decade of Elizabeth's reign, Robert was a logical choice to be sent in early June 1603 to Canterbury formally to welcome to England the French ambassador, Maximilien de Béthune, Marquis de Rosny, whom he had known since 1593. It seems that he took this opportunity to discuss with him the need to reinforce the Flushing garrison. Certainly, when Rosny's brother-in-law, André de Cochefilet, Baron de Vaucelas, was passing through Flushing in mid-July, Sidney's deputy governor, Sir William Browne, invited him to dinner and then duly reported their discussions about the garrison back to Sidney. Vaucelas had been used in mid-June to deliver some correspondence from Henri IV to Queen Anne, and Browne also reported on 17 July 1603 French anxieties over the strong Continental sympathies of the new king and queen of England:

> He discoursed somewhat freely in private and told me … that our Queen was very goodly and beautiful lady and that he met her beyond Northampton but that he feared that she would be induced to procure our King to peace with Spain and that, as he said, haply by some propositions [which] might be made for some alliance of her children. I told him that I hope the contrary ….
> (HMC *De L'Isle and Dudley* 3:41–2; Hay 145, 217)

Robert Sidney had been appointed as successor to his eldest brother Philip as Governor of Flushing in 1589, and regarded this arduous posting as a personal exile from the English court. In a letter to the Earl of Essex dated 24 May 1597 Sidney had bitterly lamented: "I see Flushing must be the grave of my youth and I fear of my fortune." But under James I it became much easier for him to perform these duties as an absentee office-holder, especially after his appointment as Lord Chamberlain of Queen Anne's household and Surveyor of the Queen's Revenues and his nomination in July 1604 as a member of her council, since these posts required his regular attendance at court (HMC *Salisbury* 7:210–11; Levin, Carney, and Barrett-Graves 30–38; Shephard).

Nevertheless, Sidney's journeys to and from Flushing remained fraught with unexpected dangers. In August 1605, for example, his vessel was blown off course in a storm and was obliged to make an emergency landing at Gravelines, then under control of a Spanish governor, Archduke Albert, from where he hastily continued his journey overland, crossing through Spanish-held Flanders and Brabant on his way to Flushing. Rumors, certainly false, immediately began to circulate at the English court, suggesting that his landing at Gravelines had been deliberate and part of a secret mission to negotiate the handing over of Flushing to the Spanish. The Venetian ambassador reported on 14 September that King James had responded by issuing a peremptory order for Sidney to return home without delay, implying that he would be deemed a traitor, his estates confiscated, and under threat of execution if he failed to obey (*CSPV 1603–07* 271). In fact, the Privy Council had issued a more temperately phrased summons, and Sidney was obliged to write to King James and to solicit the support of the Earl of Salisbury so that he could conclusively establish his innocence. Although he was eventually able to clear his name, this misadventure may well have cost him a seat on the Privy Council (HMC *Salisbury* 17:380, 390–94, 403–4, 413–16). It was also damaging to his burgeoning reputation as Continental administrator and diplomat, as John Chamberlain's mocking comment to Ralph Winwood on 25 October makes clear: "I doubt not but you have heard how Viscount Lisle was called *coram* for his absurd journey by Flanders to Flushing; and how he was fain to cry *peccavi* and confess his error" (1:209; Hay 213–15).

In late June 1606 Queen Anne's brother, Christian IV of Denmark (1577–1648), made an official state visit to England, and as the queen's Lord Chamberlain, Robert Sidney was personally involved in the arrangements. The Danish king, then aged twenty-nine, and his entourage proved a bibulously riotous assembly, and the various court entertainments, which Sidney would have been obliged to attend in his official capacity, became notorious for their indecorous indulgence. He remained occupied with these celebrations during July and August. In early July, for example, military tilts were held in Christian IV's honor at Greenwich Park, with Sidney's nephews, the Earls of Pembroke and Montgomery, taking two of the four lead roles in an elaborate chivalric event, the "Four Knights Errant Dominated by the Fortunate Islands" (Brennan, *Sidneys of Penshurst* 119). Just over twenty-five years later Sidney's son, Robert, second Earl of Leicester (Illustration 23), was to encounter the drunkard Christian IV once again during a largely abortive 1632 embassy to Denmark.

Robert Sidney's dealings with the Continent took an unexpected turn of events in 1606 with the escalation of his ongoing disputes with Sir Robert (or Roberto) Dudley (1574–1649), the illegitimate son of his uncle, the Earl of Leicester (d. 1588), by Lady Douglas Sheffield. Dudley claimed that his mother had gone through a secret but lawful marriage ceremony with his father, and consequently he was the legal heir both to the Earl of Leicester and his brother, Ambrose Dudley, Earl of Warwick, rather than Robert Sidney. The case was rejected by the Star Chamber on 4 May 1605, and soon afterwards, on 25 June, Dudley obtained a license to travel abroad, leaving England in July and abandoning his wife Alice and their five surviving children. He traveled in the company of Elizabeth Southwell, a former Maid of Honour (disguised as one of his pages), with whom he later converted to Catholicism and had thirteen children. After spending some time in France, he took up residence in late 1606 at Florence, where he styled himself "Earl of Warwick and Leicester" and was employed as a naval engineer by Ferdinand I, Grand Duke of Tuscany, and later by his son, Cosimo II (Adams).

Emboldened by his new position at the Florentine court, Dudley revived his claims to the earldom of Warwick. In response, the Privy Council ordered his return home—an instruction which he arrogantly rejected because the summons did not formally style him as an earl. The legal wrangling then dragged on, to the mounting frustration of Robert Sidney, who recorded in a letter of 20 September 1607 to his wife Barbara that he was going directly to see "the King about Sir Robert Dudley's matters." A year later, on 8 September 1608, he was still complaining to Barbara that "that which stays me most" from returning from Hampton Court to Penshurst was "the commission" between "the King and Sir Robert Dudley." In the following summer, on 1 July 1609, he lamented to Barbara yet again that he was stuck in London and unable to return to Penshurst because Dudley's cause was about to be adjudicated upon, and he "must not be from the King till I have brought the business to an end." But even these expectations were premature, and on the following 1 November Sidney was reporting to Barbara that yet another hearing was about to be given to Dudley's suit. Dudley's hopes were not finally dashed until August 1618, when he learned that Sidney had been created Earl of Leicester and the earldom of Warwick had been bestowed on Robert Rich (*DPFA* 130, 136, 142–3, 149; *Sidneys of Penshurst* 120–21). Dudley's lifelong enmity with the Sidneys was revived in 1625, when Robert Sidney died and his son Robert, second Earl of Leicester, laid claim to Dudley's two remaining Warwickshire estates, Itchington and Balsall, resulting in a new set of legal proceedings. Finally, in May 1644, following a review of the original 1605 Star Chamber case, Dudley's legitimacy was retrospectively accepted by King Charles I, and his first wife Alice was created Duchess Dudley by Letters Patent. These decisions were reached primarily because the king had personally studied the files and felt that Dudley was indeed the first Earl of Leicester's legitimate heir and that he had not been paid the appropriate price for Kenilworth when it had been sold in 1611 during his father's reign (Adams; *Correspondence DPS* 75–6). As late as 1670 Dudley's son, Carlo, was still attempting to establish his ducal rights in England by writing personally to Charles II, and in 1677 he made an abortive visit to the House of Lords in pursuit of his claim (Lee 187–8, 216–21, 234).

Robert Sidney's eldest son, William (1590–1612), had been born at Flushing, and returned there as a child in 1597, where his father engaged a learned Dutchman as his tutor. He described this individual to Barbara in a letter of 9 May 1597, and also mentioned his plans for William to travel abroad when older:

> He is of a race of gentlemen of these countries, but poverty constraineth him
> to seek means to live. He speaketh both high Dutch and low Dutch, French,
> and some English, besides Latin and Greek, and thereby besides teaching of
> the boy, will be able to do me other good services. And when the boy shall be
> old enough to travel he will be very fit to go with him. (*DPFA* 106)

William was appointed in November 1606 as a commander in absentia of one of its garrisons before being sent off, along with his younger brother Robert, to the University of Oxford in February 1607. On 15 January 1610 a license was issued for William to travel (like his father and uncle Philip) on the Continent for a period of three years, not in the company of his former Dutch tutor, but one of the Earl of Pembroke's closest friends, Benjamin Rudyerd (*CSPD* 8:581). The purpose of these travels would have been entirely traditional—to gain valuable first-hand experience of foreign courts and international diplomacy. But whether through reasons of ill health, family finance, or his own reluctance, William never undertook this grand tour, and by May 1611 plans were being made for him to take over the position of Deputy Governor at Flushing. Nor did these plans come to fruition, and later that summer he was back at Penshurst being tutored by a "Mr Johnson," probably Ben Jonson, who wrote an "Ode to Sir William Sidney: on his Birthday" in November 1611 (Brennan and Kinnamon 430–37). Sadly, his father's ambitions for his eldest son's career in the administration of Flushing and Continental diplomacy were dashed when William died unexpectedly on 3 December 1612 from smallpox (*Sidneys of Penshurst* 124–5; Hay 182–5).

From the late 1590s there had been major developments in the political situation of Western Europe. The Franco-Spanish War had been concluded by Henri IV and Philip II in 1598 through the Peace of Vervins. In 1604 King James I and Philip III followed suit with the Treaty of London, ending the Anglo-Spanish War which had been initiated by the Earl of Leicester's Dutch campaign and had led to the death of Sir Philip Sidney in the Low Countries. At first, this latter treaty enabled the Spanish to concentrate more on their struggle with the Dutch Republic, but both sides steadily grew weary of these hugely expensive conflicts. In April 1609 a cessation of hostilities was agreed (later known as the Twelve Years' Truce) between the Spanish Habsburgs, the Southern Netherlands, and the Dutch Republic, leading to the formal recognition of the United Provinces. With more peaceful conditions now prevailing, Robert Sidney was able to use the excuse of his official court duties as a reason for acting largely as an absentee Governor of Flushing. Instead, he maintained regular correspondence with his deputies there over day-to-day administrative and military problems.

But during 1612 this convenient arrangement threatened to collapse, due to increasingly acrimonious tensions between the then deputy governor, Sir John Throckmorton, the Sergeant-Major of the Flushing garrison, Michael Everarde, and the widow of the previous deputy governor, Sir William Browne. On 7 March Sidney received a disturbing report from Throckmorton, lamenting the "desperate and distracted state" of "these disjointed and lacerated provinces" of the Low Countries. These problems rumbled on throughout the summer, and Sidney resisted returning to his governorship for as long as possible. Eventually, however, it became clear that he could procrastinate no longer, and he duly arrived back at Flushing at sunset on 11 August 1612. He took up residence in the house of the widow of the former deputy governor, Lady Browne—an arrangement which further aggravated Throckmorton's own sense of grievance. After finally establishing some sort of order, Sidney compiled a formal report addressed to James I which underlined the strategic importance of the Flushing garrison to national security and as a bulwark against the threat of Spanish Catholicism. He viewed control of the town as key to maintaining the security of the English Channel, the only route via which English could realistically be invaded (SP 84/68/297–9). Even though he was able to return back home after just over one month, this depressing trip to the Continent reaffirmed in Sidney's mind that the morale and military organization of Flushing were so poor that his governorship remained an ongoing liability which might at any moment entirely compromise his carefully cultivated reputation at the English court for administrative and diplomatic competency. Finally, in late April 1614 Sidney received reports of a drunken struggle between the still-feuding Throckmorton and Everarde, and he ratified the difficult decision to sack the latter (HMC *De L'Isle and Dudley* 5: 6–7, 18–20, 187–97; Hay 134–5, 221; *DPFA* 172–80; *Sidneys of Penshurst* 123–4).

On a more positive note, on 26 April 1613 Robert Sidney set out again for the Continent as one of the four royal commissioners with ambassadorial status appointed to accompany James I's daughter, Princess Elizabeth, to Germany following her marriage to Frederick V, Elector Palatine. Sidney's personal importance to this royal party was signaled by their galleon, the *Prince Royal* (so named after the princess's late brother Henry) and an accompanying fleet of over twenty other vessels, crossing directly to Flushing. Halfway across the Channel they were met by a Dutch fleet which accompanied them into the specially dredged Flushing harbor, where on 29 April they were welcomed by a military company under the command of Sidney's now eldest surviving son and heir, Robert (later second Earl of Leicester, see Warkentin *ARC* 1:9). Frederick left for The Hague on 30 April, and on 1 May Sidney and the princess moved on to Rotterdam and then The Hague and Bacharach, followed by a week-long journey, at the princess's personal invitation, up the Rhine to Heidelberg, where they arrived in mid-June. As was usual for such diplomatic missions, the personal costs for Robert Sidney were enormous, totaling close to £1,000. After several days of diplomatic niceties at Heidelberg, Robert senior and junior commenced their return journey. They passed through Cologne with the aim of spending some time at Spa, a favored Continental resort of the Sidneys. Meeting up with the Prince and Princess of Orange, they rested there for about three weeks before making a leisurely journey homewards via Liège, Aachen, Antwerp, and Flushing, arriving back in England in mid-August 1613 (Hay 218–20; *Sidneys of Penshurst* 126; Shephard).

Robert Sidney had been accompanied on the outward trip to Heidelberg by Thomas Howard, Earl of Arundel, and his countess, Aletheia, the most renowned aristocratic English female traveler on the Continent during this decade. After leaving Princess Elizabeth with her new husband in Germany, the Howards had traveled on to tour Italy with Inigo Jones, and her peregrinations may have inspired another senior member of the Sidney family to travel abroad for an extended period (Hannay, *MSLW* 175). On 25 June 1614 Throckmorton reported the arrival at the port of Flushing of Mary Sidney Herbert, Dowager Countess of Pembroke (Illustration 10), at the beginning of a Continental tour which then took her on to Antwerp:

> Your Lordship's right honourable and noble sister the Countess of Pembroke arrived here yesterday. I first sent unto her honour my son (her ship being yet under sail) to know here pleasure whether she would come ashore or form her ship embark into another, that might carry her for Antwerp. Her honour desired to go on her journey. (HMC *De L'Isle and Dudley* 5:217)

This itinerary was echoed in William Basse's "Eclogue V: Of Temperance," which recounted how Poemenarcha (identified in his Eclogue 8 as the sister of Philisides) had left the "chalky cheeks" of Dover to travel to the Continent where the "Belgique boats" came to meet her on her way to "famous Spa" (Basse 209–12; Hannay, *Philip's Phoenix* 195). Now in her early fifties, the dowager countess was presumably attracted to Continental travel by both its intrinsic stimulations and the Sidneys' long-standing pleasure in the health cures available at Spa among a cosmopolitan and high-ranking social set. Certainly, in early August 1614 Robert Sidney remarked in a letter to his wife Barbara that he had received correspondence while at London from his sister at Spa, "where she found herself agree very well with the use of those waters" (*DPFA* 185). The dowager countess usually transmitted her letters to her brother via Throckmorton and the Flushing postal service, and Robert sent his replies via the same means and then on to her residence at Antwerp once the summer season at Spa had ended. By 2 November he was able to report to Barbara that the dowager countess had moved on to Amiens, "where it is thought she will stay all the winter" (*DPFA* 187).

By December 1614 the dowager countess was at Mechelen, where she probably stayed to see out the winter period until spring 1615. The town enjoyed a vibrant social life, with a constantly changing range of English visitors. On 24 February 1615 Throckmorton reported from Flushing to Robert Sidney:

On Monday last here passed by us in her coach one Mrs Ann Stanley, the widow of Sir William Stanley's eldest son, and sister unto Sir William Herbert, with her 4 daughters and landed at Middelberg, for the coach was of that town. I went yesterday of purpose to salute her and to offer unto her (out of duty I owe unto your Lordship and my lord of Pembroke) my best service to assist her in her passage from hence to Antwerp …. She came into these parts very well and never sick at sea. She telleth me she will stay about Mechelen until the Countess of Pembroke doth return to the Spa, and that with her she will return back into England. (HMC *De L'Isle and Dudley* 5:275–6)

Dudley Carleton described to John Chamberlain on 2 August 1616 how he had met the dowager countess at Spa, and noted that she "complains chiefly of a common disease and much troublesome to fair women, *Senectus* [old age], otherwise we see nothing amiss in her." She was regularly socializing with another distinguished lady, the Countess of Barlemont, the wife of the Governor of Luxembourg, and both ladies enjoyed taking tobacco and shooting "at marks with pistols" (Carleton 209). She also encountered there the wealthy MP and comptroller of London customs Sir Arthur Ingram, and the Catholic diplomat Toby Matthew, with whom she may have corresponded over various now lost manuscript compositions. Rumors even circulated that she had formed a liaison with her handsome young doctor, Matthew Lister, and Lady Mary Wroth's *Love's Victory* may well shadow this relationship in the courtship of its central characters, Simeana and Lissius. Chamberlain even reported (erroneously) from London on 5 April 1617 that "Here is a suspicion that the old Countess of Pembroke is married to Doctor Lister that was with her at the Spa" (2:69; *Philip's Phoenix* 198–200; see Kuin *ARC* 1:15).

In autumn 1616 the dowager countess decided to return to England to attend the christening of her grandson, Philip Herbert's heir. On 25 August Robert Sidney advised his wife that the ceremony was being planned for 18 September: "where if my sister come not in the meantime, my Lady of Bedford shall be godmother. The godfathers are the King and my Lord Chamberlain [William Herbert, Earl of Pembroke]." Although the christening was delayed, it had become clear by 23 September that the dowager countess was not going to arrive back in time, and the Countess of Salisbury agreed to act as a replacement godparent. Still hindered by unfavorable winds, Robert Sidney reported on 1 October of the dowager countess's slow progress back home: "I think also that my sister is in England already, for a day or two ago she was at Calais, and sent to my Lord Zouche to borrow his pinnace to bring her over, which accordingly went for her" (*DPFA* 197–201). Another contemporary report suggested that she may have been delayed at Calais even longer. Back home in England, King James I granted to her a life interest in Houghton Park, Bedfordshire, where she built herself a three-story mansion, Houghton House (TNA SP 14/89; *Philip's Phoenix* 201–2).

Earlier, on 7 May 1616, Robert Sidney had been appointed as a Knight of the Garter, and during the following weeks he was closely involved in the Privy Council's plans, driven largely by financial considerations, finally to return Flushing to the Dutch. He crossed back there on 30 May to preside over the formal hand-over ceremony, and was granted a lump sum of £6,000 and a generous pension of £1,200 per annum in lieu of the governorship. The younger Robert, although often away from Flushing, remained in command of a new English regiment formed from the former garrison soldiers. After twenty-six years Robert Sidney was finally rid of this great administrative burden. He then traveled with his son to The Hague for the installation of the younger Robert as a colonel of an English regiment in the Low Countries (Hay 221).

Now in his early fifties and sometimes troubled by ill health, the remaining ten years of Robert Sidney's life were focused primarily upon court and family life rather than public service overseas. But he and his immediate family retained a strong interest in Western European politics, especially relating to the affairs of Princess Elizabeth and her husband Frederick. This context seems to be implicitly relevant to the mysterious circumstances surrounding the publication of the prose romance *The Countess of Montgomery's Urania* (1621) by Robert's eldest daughter, Lady Mary Wroth, and its apparently sudden withdrawal from circulation (*MSLW* 234–5). Although nominally intended as a homage to her uncle's *Arcadia*, Wroth's fictions clearly also reflected on various aspects of the Sidneys' own family history and Jacobean court life. In particular, Wroth's romance seems to have focused on one of the most intriguing political fantasies of the early seventeenth century: the revival of a Holy Roman Empire in the West. This concept appealed personally to King James I, who systematically adopted a quasi-imperial identity in his formal portraits, civic entries, masques, and coinage (Wroth, *Urania* 1:xxxix–liv). In her *Urania* Wroth probably intended to commend and respectfully promulgate the king's desire to cast himself as a peacemaker and the harbinger of a new golden age in Western European diplomatic relations. But, with hindsight, her casting of her fictional character Amphilanthus as an idealized Roman-style emperor was potentially dangerous. The problem lay in the fact (reasonably obvious to anyone close to Wroth and the Sidneys) that Amphilanthus was modeled on her cousin, William Herbert, Earl of Pembroke. By 1621 he was, along with his younger brother, the Earl of Montgomery, her father's most influential friend at court, and was already (or soon to become) Lady Mary Wroth's lover and the father of her two illegitimate children. The casting of Amphilanthus/Pembroke in such an imperial role could have suggested to the Sidneys' enemies at court (and probably also to King James himself) that they and their Herbert relatives were becoming far too politically ambitious in their scarcely veiled responses to royal international policy.

Although the Sidneys' and Herberts' concerns for the welfare of Elizabeth and Frederick were genuine, their position had become increasingly beleaguered. After the death of Emperor Matthias in March 1619, Frederick had accepted the throne of Bohemia in response to a Protestant uprising against the oppressive Catholic rule of Ferdinand of Styria. The Dowager Countess of Pembroke had grown friendly with Dudley Carleton during her time at Spa, and her niece, Lady Mary Wroth, maintained a correspondence with him while he served as English Ambassador at The Hague (Wroth, *Urania* 1:xlv). It seems that she was soon acting as a useful conduit for intelligence about Elizabeth and Frederick for her Sidney and Herbert relatives. But King James, ever the balancing peacemaker and already assiduously courting a Catholic Spanish spouse for his son, Prince Charles, had no desire, through Frederick's acceptance of the Bohemian crown, to be drawn into the Thirty Years' War. James was enraged by his son-in-law's lack of consultation and suspicious of those whom he regarded as Frederick's closest allies at the English court, especially the Sidneys and the Herberts.

Following the crowning of Frederick and Elizabeth at Prague as King and Queen of Bohemia in November 1619, Wroth's *Urania* represents Amphilanthus, Prince of Naples, being named King of the Romans and crowned at Frankfurt (the traditional location for installing Holy Roman Emperors). Amphilanthus then goes on to unify Wroth's imaginary Continental Europe in a period of halcyon religious toleration, an alluring counter-myth in poignant contrast to the reality of Frederick's beleaguered position as King of Bohemia. Within a year of his coronation Frederick's forces were crushed on 8 November 1620 at the Battle of White Mountain, resulting in his loss of the Bohemian crown and the invasion of the Palatinate by the Catholic imperialists. On 26 November Leicester wrote to his wife Barbara, lamenting how confusing and contradictory reports from the Continent had recently become:

> Here we have had pitiful news of the overthrow given to the King of Bohemia and the loss of the town of Prague: but since, news are come that Prague is not lost, but that the King and Queen are in it and both in good health, and that in the fight, the Emperor lost more men than the King did. (*DPFA* 230)

In April 1621 Elizabeth and Frederick fled to The Hague, and in the following month Leicester was appointed to serve on a Council of War to consider the feasibility of English military intervention on behalf of the elector. In another letter to Barbara written on 9 May he commented: "The King and Queen of Bohemia are still at The Hague, in very good health and much respected: and the war is like to grow on there very hotly" (*DPFA* 232). The Earl of Pembroke was also deeply concerned, and Sir Benjamin Rudyerd remarked: "Nothing makes him so sad or merry as the success of their affairs" (SP 81/18/155). Wroth's idealized depiction of her cousin as a quasi-imperial "King of the Romans," implicitly usurping James's own image as a beneficent dispenser of global peace, was as politically dangerous as it was unrealistic in terms of the sad reality of Frederick's and Elizabeth's true situation. Nor would James, along with those of his advisers who most keenly supported the proposed Spanish match, have welcomed Wroth's *Urania*, with its implied support for a militaristic English intervention into Protestant affairs on the Continent. Instead, in November 1624 a formal marriage agreement was reached on behalf of the heir to the English throne, Prince Charles, and the Catholic Princess Henrietta Maria, the daughter of Robert Sidney's former friend, King Henri IV of France (*Sidneys of Penshurst* 133–8).

Robert Sidney, Second Earl of Leicester

After Robert Sidney's death on 13 July 1626 the Leicester earldom passed to his eldest surviving son, Robert (1595–1677; see Warkentin *ARC* 1:9 and Illustration 23), although little is known about his court or other public activities until 1632. In April of that year, however, he was drawn into royal diplomatic service when he was appointed as ambassador extraordinary to the late Queen Anne's brother, Christian IV of Denmark. The public purpose of this mission was to offer English condolences on the death of King Charles I's maternal grandmother, Queen Sophia Frederica. But a more significant political intention was to enter discussions with Christian IV over English debts to the Danes and to establish whether Denmark was sympathetically disposed towards an anti-Habsburg league which had been proposed by the Swedes (Bodl. Library, Oxford, MS Rawlinson C 354; SP/75/12). Accompanied by his two eldest sons, Philip and Algernon (see Brennan *ARC* 1:12), the second Earl of Leicester left England on 15 September 1632 with an entourage of some fifty-five black-clad retainers. Also traveling with him was his personal secretary, James Howell, who was an experienced Continental traveler, and later the author of *Instructions for Foreign Travel* (1642). Robert Sidney compiled and preserved a journal of his Danish embassy, and his pride in being entrusted to undertake this delicate mission was evident in his arranging for a Frankfurt publisher to print the first edition of the correspondence of Hubert Languet and his uncle, Sir Philip Sidney, intended as a tribute to the Sidneys' long family tradition of diplomatic service.

Unfortunately, the business-like tone of Sidney's personal entourage was compromised by the boorishly drunken behavior of the Danish court. He would have already known of the Danish king's bibulous reputation from his father's reminiscences of the chaotic court entertainments which marked the young Christian IV's visit to the English court in 1606. Now in his mid-fifties, Christian kept Robert waiting until 1 October for his formal audience (with each side addressing the other in Latin and Dutch) which seemed strangely perfunctory and inconclusive. Sidney was far from impressed by the Danish king, as his brief journal sketch of his person and habits eloquently conveys:

> The King is a big, strong man, about 56 years of age, brown haired and but a little grey ["unless he use art" is scored through]. He is somewhat leaner than he was in England. A strange life he leads, for though he be careful of his business, yet he is very often drunk ... and every night he lies with a whore that he keeps, who follows him up and down where he goes and was a servant to Frau Christian, his last wife as most men say. (HMC *De L'Isle and Dudley* 6:19)

Sidney had another unproductive meeting with the king on 3 October, then six days later attended a formal banquet marking the conclusion of his brief embassy. At this riotous event Sidney's main achievement seems to have been to remain mobile after thirty-five toasts while the Danish king had to be carried from the table drunk and prostrate in his chair. Leaving Denmark with nothing achieved other than some minor trade concessions, he reached Hamburg on 25 October, where on the following 5 November he recorded in his journal: "We kept the remembrance of the Gunpowder treason, which the English at Hamburg yearly do and have a sermon" (*Sidneys of Penshurst* 140–41). Back in England by late November, and after submitting unavoidably high expenses to the Treasury, he took some solace in the general view that his embassy had failed entirely due to the Danish king's intransigence. The unexpected death on 6 November of King Gustavus II Adolphus of Sweden at the Battle of Lützen also stalled the earlier plans for an anti-Habsburg Protestant league. But the Sidneys, in the person of the second Earl of Leicester, had now been drawn once more into important royal service, and to commemorate this honor Van Dyck was commissioned to produce a series of lavish paintings of the Sidneys, with sittings at Penshurst and Eltham Palace (HMC *De L'Isle and Dudley* 6:12; *Sidneys of Penshurst* 140–41).

On the same day when Robert Sidney wrote in his journal about the Gunpowder Plot celebrations at Hamburg, his brother-in-law, Algernon Percy, succeeded to the earldom of Northumberland. Along with Robert's wife, Dorothy Percy Sidney (see Akkerman *ARC* 1:10), Northumberland and his other sister, Lucy Percy Hay, Countess of Carlisle, and his younger brother, Henry Percy (later Lord Percy of Alnwick), were to play a major role in Robert Sidney's next diplomatic appointment. The Percy sisters were assiduous in cultivating a friendly relationship with Queen Henrietta Maria, and Sidney readily described himself as her "Slave" (Collins 2:387). It was unsurprising, therefore, when in 1636 he was sent to France as an ambassador extraordinary with a brief to establish whether the French would be sympathetic towards English support for attempts to regain the Palatinate and to assess whether the earlier plans for an anti-Habsburg pact might be revived (SP 78/101–11). An English mission led by John, Viscount Scudamore, had been sent to France in the previous summer with virtually the same brief, but had met with no success. Robert Sidney arrived at Paris on 3 June 1636, again accompanied by his sons, Philip and Algernon, who continued their education at either Paris or the Huguenot Academy at Saumur (founded in 1602 by Philippe Du Plessis-Mornay). Robert was to be based mainly in France for the next six years, except for five months back in England during 1639.

This French embassy, although of high prestige for Sidney since it confirmed his importance within the circle of Queen Henrietta Maria, was fraught with problems, most of which revolved around Scudamore, who had also been retained as an ambassador-in-ordinary and bitterly resented his displacement. He did everything possible to hinder Robert's progress, and although both men were guilty of irascible intransigence, the

English king and queen were also clumsily culpable in forcing them to work together. Sidney's personal relationship with Scudamore floundered from the outset, and as early as 16 June 1636 he remarked in a letter to Henry Percy: "He is jealous of me, and thinks that I come to supplant him in his employment" (Collins 2:387). They were soon using different lawyers, arguing with one another in official meetings, and even choosing to worship at different churches. Robert reaffirmed his family's long-term support for the Huguenots by attending the Reformed Church at Charenton, while Scudamore dutifully conformed to the preferences of the king and Archbishop Laud in the English Chapel at Paris. His wife, Dorothy, was clearly also preoccupied with the problems over Scudamore, and advised on 26 September 1636:

> And if you know anything of importance against your companion [Scudamore] make the King acquainted with it and none else. For I am confident that if you had done so it would have been much the better for you and the worse for him. But if the things be trivial or cannot be proved I think it is best to say nothing of him …. (*Correspondence DPS* 62)

The key area of disagreement between the two men lay in their contrasting approaches to Continental policy. Scudamore loyally adhered to King Charles I's preference for a broadly neutral stance towards Spain, but Robert Sidney was obliged to support Henrietta Maria's closest associates at court, who favored a more militant anti-Habsburg alliance. Robert focused much of his diplomatic efforts on attempting to engineer an aggressive alliance between England and France against Spain, arguing that "nothing can be more glorious, nor more religious in the sight of God and man than such a war" (SP 78/101/400). Charles I and Scudamore, however, remained committed to securing a negotiated settlement—in contrast to the views of Henrietta Maria, who hoped to persuade her brother, Louis XIII, into a more militant stance.

While Leicester was away at Paris, the Percys promulgated at court his anti-Habsburg views, and Dorothy assiduously courted the friendship of Henrietta Maria. Her letters to Robert from this period are replete with telling details of the Sidneys' current intimacy with the royal families of both England and France, and in November 1636 she requested that her husband should provide her with a cipher so that she could keep him more fully briefed on English affairs while he was abroad (*Correspondence DPS* 77). On 4 January 1637 she reported giving a New Year's gift to the king, and in early February she was in earnest correspondence with Robert over selecting a suitable gift for the "Queen of France," Louis XIII's wife, the Spanish Anne of Austria (*Correspondence DPS* 103). Other lavish gifts followed, and on 5 May Dorothy was finalizing her "commodities for the Queen of France's present" (costing "about 120*ll*"), prior to sending it over to France (*Correspondence DPS* 124–5).

In April 1637, as plague spread rapidly through London, Dorothy informed Robert that she had been in discussions with Henrietta Maria over how Robert could best cultivate the political trust of her husband. She assured him of the queen's continuing high favor and absolute confidence in his loyalty to her. She also mentioned that her sister, Lucy, had been told by the queen that King Charles was "very well satisfied" with Sidney's diplomatic work in France (*Correspondence DPS* 93, 118). But both Robert and Dorothy remained nervous over exactly how the king viewed his embassy, especially in view of the unending clashes with Scudamore, as her letter of 20 April 1637 makes clear:

> I am infinitely desirous to receive from you some assurance of a happy success in those affairs that you have negotiated with so much pains, but howsoever the French behave themselves I hope you will acquit yourself so as the King

shall find cause to value your service and not to blame it. (*Correspondence DPS* 120)

Events were now moving rapidly in France, with the negotiations for an Anglo-French alliance remitted to a peace conference to be held at Hamburg in 1637. Robert Sidney then became ensnared by August 1637 in plots between King Charles I and the exiled court of Marie de Médicis at Brussels, who was intent on thwarting and overthrowing Cardinal Richelieu (whose personality overwhelmed that of Louis XIII). Anne of Austria was also determined to foil Robert's attempts to foster an Anglo-French alliance against the Habsburgs. He was fatally compromised by the fact that his French secretary, Réné Augier, was secretly forwarding copies of Anne's letters to the Spanish Netherlands, and French spies were very probably also intercepting his correspondence.

In February 1639 Leicester wrote to Charles to express his grave concerns over a rumored Catholic plot to forge an alliance between the pope and the kings of France, Spain, and Hungary. He was rapidly recalled to England, accompanied by his sons Philip and Algernon, and the respect in which Sidney was still held by both his king and queen is evident from his being sworn in as a Privy Councillor on 5 May. His enmity with Scudamore, however, had antagonized Archbishop Laud, who remained his most problematic opponent at court, and who was determined to block any further promotions for Leicester. In July 1639 he was able to attend the wedding of his daughter Dorothy to Henry Lord Spencer (Earl of Sunderland from 6 June 1643). When Sidney returned to his Paris embassy in August 1639 he was accompanied by his wife and the newly married couple, whose two eldest children, Dorothy and Robert, were both born there. They did not return to England until 1641, when they took up residence at Spencer's ancestral home, Althorp in Northamptonshire.

As Charles's dealings with Parliament grew steadily more fraught during the late 1640s, Hawkins kept Leicester briefed at Paris on the impeachment of Thomas Wentworth, Earl of Strafford, and Archbishop Laud. The Earl of Northumberland again pressed the king to appoint Robert as his Secretary of State, but Charles replied, cryptically, that he considered Sidney "too great for that place" (Collins 2:664). Finally, with Strafford's attainder and execution in May and Laud's committal to the Tower on a charge of High Treason, Robert's path to higher preferment at the English court was now clear. On 14 June 1641 he was duly appointed as Strafford's successor to the post of Lord Lieutenant of Ireland, thereby echoing the illustrious Irish role of his grandfather, Sir Henry Sidney, during Queen Elizabeth's reign (see Herron *ARC* 1:13). He briefly returned to France in August 1641 to complete his embassy, and was back in England by early October to prepare for his new duties (*Sidneys of Penshurst* 141–4; Atherton).

Philip Sidney, Third Earl of Leicester, and Algernon Sidney

The second Earl of Leicester's withdrawal from public life in the mid-1640s effectively ended his direct contacts with Western Europe, although his ongoing acquisition of books for his voluminous library continued to provide him with a range of intellectual interests in Continental affairs and scholarship (see Black *ARC* 2:1). The Sidney family's involvements in Continental travel now passed down another generation to Robert Sidney's children, and it was largely his wife's family, rather than Leicester himself, who sought to further their public careers. Her brother, Algernon Percy, Earl of Northumberland, was especially supportive towards his sister's sons. During the Second Bishops' War their eldest son, Philip (Illustration 28), commanded the cuirassiers who formed Northumberland's bodyguard, and in the Short Parliament of April 1640 Philip was elected, again through his uncle's influence, this time as Lord Admiral, as MP for the borough of Yarmouth on the Isle of Wight (Firth). Similarly, on 2 May 1641 King Charles I's daughter, Princess Mary, married William, the son of the Prince of Orange. In the preceding December Northumberland had been making determined attempts to secure a military post for Algernon in the service of the Prince of Orange, almost certainly as an opportunistic response to this intended marital union (CKS U1475 C85/7; C85/9; Scott, *Algernon/Republic* 43). Almost fifty years later the son of Mary and William would accede to the English throne as King William III, a succession which would depend heavily upon the support of Henry Sidney, later Earl of Romney (Robert Sidney's youngest son), and Robert Spencer, second Earl of Sunderland (Robert Sidney's grandson).

Following Robert Sidney's acrimonious split with the king in the mid-1640s, he maintained a studiously neutral political position, but his wife Dorothy and two sons Philip and Algernon overtly sided with the parliamentarians. During the early 1650s Algernon enjoyed an active and influential political career, especially after his election to the Council of State in November 1652 (Illustration 25). His work was mainly focused on foreign affairs, regularly meeting with ministers from Portugal, Spain, France, Sweden, Hamburg, Tuscany, Holland, and Austria, and the First Anglo-Dutch War (1652–54). But these involvements came to an unexpected halt in 1653. His father's diary contains a vivid account of Cromwell's expulsion of the Rump of the Long Parliament on 20 April, probably supplied by Algernon verbatim, for attempting to pass the Perpetuation Bill. Algernon had been involved only the previous evening in its final drafting and he was enraged by Cromwell's denunciation: "You are no Parliament, I say you are no Parliament." He steadfastly refused to vacate his place to the right of the Speaker, and only after Cromwell's command "Put him out" did he leave the chamber of his own accord (*Sidneys of Penshurst* 158–9). Algernon's parliamentary career was effectively over, and this crisis also impacted directly on his brother, Philip, who had been appointed in December 1652 as an ambassador to Sweden. Following his brother's ejection from Parliament, Philip also resigned from this mission just as his instructions were completed in late March 1653, but rather than risking another personal clash with Cromwell, he tactfully pleaded ill health.

The contrasting behavior of the two Sidney brothers at this period is revealing, both of their personal characters and political flexibility. Despite not carrying out his Swedish embassy, Philip managed to retain Cromwell's favor and was summoned to sit in the Barebones (or "Little") Parliament, serving as a member of both of its Councils of State. When the Barebones Parliament was dissolved in December 1653 the remaining MPs were obliged to resign all of their powers to Cromwell, who was installed on 16 December as Lord Protector of England, Ireland, and Scotland. Algernon's response to Cromwell's absolute ascendancy was in sharp contrast to Philip's quietly pragmatic approach. Although John Milton's *Defensio Secunda*, a strident defense of Cromwell's rule published on 30 May 1654, described Algernon as "Sidney (an illustrious name, which I rejoice has steadily adhered to our side)," he decided to leave the country, and by 31 July was at The Hague, where he stayed until the following September (*Sidneys of Penshurst* 159).

In May 1659 Algernon was chosen by the restored Rump Parliament to lead an embassy to Sweden, in view of the escalating risk of their current conflicts with Denmark impeding both English and Dutch trade via the Baltic Sound. His party arrived at Elsinore in Sweden on 20 July, but King Charles X Gustavus failed to agree to an audience quickly enough for Algernon's liking. Instead, he began impromptu discussions with the Dutch over assembling a joint fleet to impose a settlement on the Swedes. Naturally, the Swedish monarch was irate at Algernon's imperious behavior, a situation made even worse when he was handed by Algernon a draft treaty already signed by the Danes, with threats of war if Sweden did not also agree to it. With Charles X incredulously claiming that the English wished "to command all, as if they were masters" (*CSPV 1659–61* 66), Algernon later insisted that "a few shots of our cannon would have made this peace" (Scott, *Algernon/Republic* 129). On a visit during this mission to the University of Copenhagen Algernon signed its visitors' book with a pugnaciously proud Latin reminiscence (later adopted as the motto of the US state of Massachusetts) of the militarism in 1586 of his great-uncle, Sir Philip Sidney: "PHILIPPUS SIDNEY MANUS HAEC INIMICA TYRANNIS EINSE PETIT PLACIDAM CUM LIBERTATE QUIETEM" ("Philip Sidney, this hand, enemy to tyrants, by the sword seeks peace with liberty").

The unexpected death of Charles X on 12 February 1660, along with the departure of the English fleet, severely hampered the progress of Algernon's negotiations, but a treaty between the Swedes and Danes, mediated by England, France, and the Dutch, was finally agreed on 27 May. During his time in Sweden, however, Algernon had demonstrated himself to be a brusque and warlike diplomat, and more problematically in view of the changing English political landscape, an unrepentant upholder of the tenets of republican freedom (Scott, *Algernon/Republic* 127–35).

The resignation of Richard Cromwell on 24 May 1659 marked the beginning of another period of political uncertainty for the Sidneys. The Countess of Leicester died on 20 August 1659, and her husband Robert became even more introspective in his habits. Although he resumed his seat in the House of Lords in April 1660 and was named as a Privy Councillor on 31 May, as soon as Parliament adjourned in October he took the opportunity to plead ill health and withdrew permanently to Penshurst. He did not attend Charles II's coronation in April 1661. However, despite his unquestioning service to both Oliver and Richard Cromwell, Philip, Viscount Lisle, was not regarded as a political threat by Charles II. He was granted a pardon under the Great Seal on 30 October 1660 and took little part in public affairs before his father's death in 1677. In contrast, Algernon remained unapologetic, describing in 1659 the regicide as "the justest and bravest act … that ever was done in England or anywhere" (BL Add. MS 32680 fols. 9–10), and republicanism as "that cause, which by the help of God I shall never desert" (Blencowe 170–71). Following Charles II's restoration, Algernon lingered on in Scandinavia before moving to Hamburg, but his brusque treatment of the Swedish and Danish kings at Elsinore still rankled with the newly empowered royalists. Even his father, the Earl of Leicester, felt that Algernon's refusal to condemn the regicides remained so perilous that he should not return home since his presence could endanger the welfare of his entire family: "[H]e must not think of coming into England, when that action was so much abhorred by all men, and by me in particular, that am his father" (BL Add. MS 32680 fols. 9–10).

Although Algernon's father considered it wise for him to remain at Hamburg, where he met up with Christiana, ex-Queen of Sweden, he readily confessed: "I dislike all the drunken countries of Germany, and the north, and am not much inclined to France, I think I shall choose Italy" (Blencowe 195). Algernon remained in Italy from 1660 until *c.* 1663, first residing at Rome (Scott, *Algernon/Republic* 153). There he occupied himself with paying courtesy visits to various cardinals, whom in April 1661 he described in great detail to his father (Collins 2:711–15), and admiring the "Liberty and Quiet, which is generally granted to all Persons here" (2:700). Although he no longer found "those Signs of Ease, Satisfaction, and Plenty" which he had experienced on his first visit to Rome in 1638, he was duly grateful for the "Company of Persons excellent in all Sciences, which is the best Thing Strangers can seek." He also offered to supply his father with books from Rome, such as a copy of the Jesuit Cardinal Pallavicini's *Istoria del Concilio di Trento* (1656/57), which he felt would become "an Ornament to your Library" (Collins 2:700–702). During February 1661 he viewed with stern interest and characteristic disapproval, the various pre-Lenten festivities:

> All the Streets are full of Masquerades there, every Day public Comedies, and many in private Houses, but all of them as ill as ever was seen. There hath been two moral Representations in Music … which were very fine, and not to be equalled by any Persons out of Rome. The Jesuits have made many Plays in their Seminary, but they are exceeding cold and dull. (Collins 2:705)

During March 1661 he continued to compile a list of suitable books for his father (Collins 2:706–8), and by early April was also keenly hunting out other interesting objects to send back to Penshurst, noting:

> I have written to my Correspondent at Frankfurt, for Sir Philip Sidney his Picture. I could not send your Lordship a Thing of less Value then my own, but since Sir J. Temple says your Lordship would have it, I will send it. If you please to have any Thing else provided here, that will be an Ornament to your new Buildings, as Pictures, Statues, Marble Table, or of Mosaic Work, I shall most diligently provide such as your Lordship shall please to Command me. (Collins 2:709)

By mid-1661 Algernon was residing at the idyllic Villa de Belvedere at Frascati, at the invitation of Prince Pamphili, a nephew of the previous pope, where he lived a more solitary life and devoted himself to academic study.

In mid-1663 Algernon was passing through Switzerland and paused to visit other English republican exiles at Vevey, before heading on through Geneva and Brussels to Augsburg (where later in April 1665 he survived an assassination attempt). At the University of Geneva he inscribed their visitor's book with a haunting lament for the executed regicides: "SIT SANGUINIS ULTOR JUSTORUM" ("Let there be revenge for the blood of the just"). He then traveled on to the United Provinces and the commencement of the Second Anglo-Dutch War in 1665 led him to some overly optimistic hopes for an invasion of England (Scott, *Algernon/Republic* 171–3). During the summer he traveled from the United Provinces to the court of Louis XIV, seeking to secure French financial support for such a campaign. His hopes of military action, however, were confounded by both the French king's caution and Dutch skepticism over how a renewed commonwealth in England could, in reality, advantage the United Provinces. At this period he was also drafting his explosive *Court Maxims*, arguing for rebellion against the restored monarchy, which, fortunately for the rest of the Sidneys, were not published until the mid-1990s. Five of the fifteen dialogues included in the *Maxims* focus specifically on England's foreign policy and argue for a union of Protestant nations. Residing variously at Rotterdam and Montpellier, Algernon poignantly viewed himself as wandering like a "Vagabond through the World, forsaken of my Friends, poor, and known only to be a broken Limb of a Ship-wrecked Faction" (Collins 2:720). His period of French residence confirms this depressing sense of a rootless existence: "Sidney's time in France was divided between Languedoc in the south-east (from 1666 to some time between 1670 and 1672) and Guyenne/Bordeaux in the south-west (from 1672 or 1673 until 1677), with extended visits to Paris throughout the period (in 1666, 1670, 1676, 1677)" (Scott, *Algernon/Republic* 223).

In 1670 he traveled to Paris, where the Earl of Northumberland and his family were also visiting, and to Versailles, where he tried to offer his services to King Charles II via the Vicomte de Turenne, Marshal of France. About this time Algernon finally retired to Nérac in Gascony, where he spent most of the rest of his exile in France.

Algernon was not to return to England until early September 1677, only two months before his father's death. Leicester died on 2 November, and was buried at Penshurst.

Although Algernon originally intended a prompt return to France, his father's will provided generous provision for both himself and his younger brother Henry, to the detriment of Philip, now third Earl of Leicester, who had fallen out with his father in late 1652. A protracted chancery case ensued, with Henry residing at Penshurst and Algernon at Leicester House in London. In the mean time, Algernon was drawn once again into the center of political affairs, maintaining close personal links with the French, and leading attempts to formulate an Anglo-Dutch republican foreign policy as an alternative to a monarchic union of the Houses of Stuart and Orange. With the execution of Algernon on 7 December 1683, following his complicity in the Rye House Plot, which was supposedly planned to murder both Charles II and his brother and heir James, Duke of York, the future political and family fortunes of the Sidneys now lay in the hands three individuals: Philip, who succeeded his father as third Earl of Leicester in 1698; his younger brother, Henry Sidney, later Earl of Romney, and his nephew, Robert Spencer, later Earl of Sunderland. The Continental involvements and crucial importance of these two latter members of the Sidney family in ensuring the accession of Prince William III of Orange as King William III of England are traced in Brennan *ARC* 1:12.

Bibliography

Manuscript Sources

Bodleian Library, Oxford
  MS Rawlinson C 354
British Library, London
  BL Add. MS 32680
Centre for Kentish Studies, Maidstone
  CKS U1475 C85/7
The National Archives, Kew (TNA)
  SP 14/89; 75/12; 78/101–11; 81/18
  SP 84/68/297–9

Primary and Secondary Sources

Adams, Simon. "Sir Robert Dudley (1574–1649)." *ODNB.*
Atherton, Ian. "Robert Sidney, Second Earl of Leicester (1595–1677)." *ODNB.*
Basse, William. *The Poetical Works of William Basse.* Ed. R. Warwick Bond. London: Ellis and Elvey, 1893.
Blencowe, R. W., ed. *Sydney Papers, Consisting of a Journal of the Earl of Leicester, and Original Letters of Algernon Sidney.* London: John Murray, 1843.
Brennan, Michael G. *The Sidneys of Penshurst and the Monarchy, 1500–1700.* Aldershot: Ashgate, 2006.
—, and Noel J. Kinnamon. "Robert Sidney, 'Mr Johnson,' and the Education of William Sidney at Penshurst." *Notes & Queries* 50.4 (2003): 430–37.
Cant, Reginald. "The Embassy of the Earl of Leicester to Denmark in 1632." *English Historical Review* 54 (1939): 252–62.
Calendar of State Papers Domestic .... Ed. Martin A. S. Hume. 38 vols. London: HMSO, 1894.
Calendar of State Papers ... Venice, 1659–61. London: Longman Green, 1864–1947.
Calendar of State Papers ... Venice, 1603–1607. London: HMSO, 1900.

Carleton, Sir Dudley. *Dudley Carleton to John Chamberlain 1603–1624: Jacobean Letters.* Ed. Maurice Lee, Jr. New Brunswick, NJ: Rutgers UP, 1972.

Chamberlain, John. *The Letters of John Chamberlain.* Ed. Norman Egbert McClure. 2 vols. Philadelphia, PA: American Philosophical Society, 1939; rpt. Westport, CT: Greenwood P, 1979.

Collins, Arthur. *Letters and Memorials of State ….* 2 vols. London: T. Osborne, 1746.

Firth, C. H. "Philip Sidney, Third Earl of Leicester (1619–1698)." Rev. Sean Kelsey. *ODNB.*

Hannay, Margaret P. *Mary Sidney, Lady Wroth.* Farnham: Ashgate, 2010.

—. *Philip's Phoenix. Mary Sidney Countess of Pembroke.* Oxford: Oxford UP, 1990.

Hay, Millicent. *The Life of Robert Sidney Earl of Leicester (1563–1626).* Washington, DC: Folger Shakespeare Library, 1984.

HMC. *Report on the Manuscripts of Lord de L'Isle and Dudley Preserved at Penshurst Place.* 6 vols. London: HMSO, 1925–66.

—. *Calendar of the Manuscripts of the Most Hon. The Marquis of Salisbury, K.G. … Preserved at Hatfield House, Hertfordshire.* 24 vols. London: HMSO, 1883–1976.

Lee, Arthur Gould. *The Son of Leicester: Biography of Sir Robert Dudley.* London: Victor Gollancz, 1964.

Levin, Carole, Jo Eldridge Carney, and Debra Barrett-Graves. *Elizabeth I: Always Her Own Free Woman.* Aldershot: Ashgate, 2003.

Scott, Jonathan. "Algernon Sidney (1623–1683)." *ODNB.*

—. *Algernon Sidney and the English Republic (1623–1677).* Cambridge: Cambridge UP, 1988.

Shephard, Robert. "Robert Sidney, First Earl of Leicester (1563–1626)." *ODNB.*

Sidney, Algernon. *Court Maxims.* Ed. Hans W. Blom, E. H. Mulier, and R. Janse. Cambridge: Cambridge UP, 1996.

Sidney, Dorothy Percy. *The Correspondence (c. 1626–1659) of Dorothy Percy Sidney, Countess of Leicester.* Ed. Michael G. Brennan, Noel J. Kinnamon, and Margaret P. Hannay. Farnham: Ashgate, 2010.

Sidney, Robert, first Earl of Leicester. *Domestic Politics and Family Absence: The Correspondence (1588–1621) of Robert Sidney, First Earl of Leicester, and Barbara Gamage Sidney, Countess of Leicester.* Ed. Margaret P. Hannay, Noel J. Kinnamon, and Michael G Brennan. Aldershot: Ashgate, 2005.

Wroth, Lady Mary. *The First Part of the Countess of Montgomery's Urania.* Ed. Josephine A. Roberts. Tempe, AZ: Arizona Center for Medieval and Renaissance Texts and Studies, 1995.

PART V
The Sidneys and the Arts

The Sidneys and Public Entertainments

Arthur F. Kinney

Introduction

From five-act plays at the Theatre and royal masques at court to pageants at manor houses and tournaments in tiltyards, Robert Dudley, Earl of Leicester and his descendants shared patronage and participation in the public and private entertainments for three generations. Sir Philip Sidney's participation in *The Four Foster Children of Desire* and the authorship of *Astrea* by his sister Mary, Countess of Pembroke, are only two examples of such entertainments from an incomparable Sidney family legacy. Other entertainments supervised for Queen Anne by Robert Sidney and masques and tilts with his nephews William and Philip Herbert centered on Prince Henry from 1609 until his unexpected death in 1612, and thereafter on Prince Charles. Under both Elizabeth and James there were Accession Day tilts annually, but throughout the decade such chivalric remnants took various forms: there was the tilt, in which combatants rode against each other with lances separated by a palisade; the tourney, where mounted knights fought with rebated swords; and the barriers, often fought inside on foot with sword or pike. Annual Twelfth Night celebrations at court meant splendid feasting, dancing, and masques. Robert's daughter, Mary Wroth, brought them into the realm of fiction. Cumulatively, their involvement was unrivaled.

Robert Dudley, First Earl of Leicester

Tradition holds that Robert Dudley and Elizabeth Tudor were both born on the same day and, moreover, imprisoned in the Tower of London the same day for potential treason—Elizabeth as a suspected rival to her half-sister Mary, and Robert, son of John, Duke of Northumberland, as a close friend of the Protestant Edward VI, who supported Lady Jane Grey as his successor. Like his father, Robert was sentenced to death, but was later freed in 1554 (Osborne 108). Elizabeth and Dudley were attracted to each other from this start; in 1559, the year following Elizabeth's coronation, Dudley appeared with Lord Hunsdon wearing black and white scarves, her favorite colors, as her champion. She responded by making him Master of the Horse, a Privy Councillor and Knight of the Garter; in 1564 she made him Earl of Leicester, granting him the extensive estate of Kenilworth. Margaret Hannay reports that Leicester performed in a tilt before the queen at the third marriage of his brother Ambrose and conjectures that their niece Mary Sidney (named for her mother and for Mary Tudor) visited uncle Ambrose at the Feast of St. Michael in Warwick in 1571 and uncle Robert at Kenilworth in 1572 (Hannay, *Philip's Phoenix* 21), prompting Sir Philip

Sidney to write in Leicester's defense of "the nobility of that blood whereof I am descended" (*Miscellaneous Prose* 134).

As the family's progenitor for public entertainments, Leicester's influence and importance are immense, distinguished by his patronage of his nation's premiere theater company from its infancy. Sally-Beth MacLean has discovered the first reference to "your L[ordship's] players" in a payment of 20s. in the family household accounts book on 26 March 1559 ("Politics of Patronage" 177; but see also MacLean, "Tracking"), although she believes there were performances by the troupe around London for a month or two before (178). A letter to the Earl of Shrewsbury in mid-June 1559 asks for a license for Lord Dudley's players to perform there following a proclamation of May 1559.

Once established, Lord Dudley's players performed at Norwich in 1558–59; at Oxford, Saffron Walden, and Plymouth in 1559–60; in Bristol in July 1560; in Grimsthorpe, in 1561; in Oxford, Maldon, and Ipswich in 1561–62; and in Bristol in September 1562. They played at court during Christmas in 1560, 1561, 1562, and 1563. Then, as Leicester's Men, they went on to Maldon in 1564–65; York on 6 April; in Nottingham in August 1569; Bristol in January 1570; Oxford on 4 May 1570; Leicester in 1570–71; at Abington, Barnstaple, and Gloucester in 1570–71; and Saffron Walden in October (a full listing is in Gurr 193–5). Clearly touring was important—and so was Leicester: as patron, he arranged for performances in towns and private residences and provided protection. Other performances were staged at Oxford University and at the Inns of Court; in March 1565 Dudley brought players from Gray's Inn to Whitehall to entertain Elizabeth.

Leicester's Men, destined to become the first playing company for two decades, were established in 1572 when six members of Leicester's company—including James Burbage and Robert Wilson—joined his official patronage. On 19 May 1574 they were issued a patent "to vse, exercise, and occupie the Arte and faculties of playenge Comedies, Tragedies, Enterludes, stage playes, and such other like as they have alredie vested and studied" (Chambers 4:87). They reappeared at court at Christmas that year and each year through 1583. Leicester's Men was the first major dramatic company in Tudor England; they were the first to receive a royal patent; they set the model for all subsequent playing companies, and they were the first to occupy, in Burbage's Theatre, the first public playhouse on a permanent basis. They were, sums MacLean, "at the top of their profession" ("Politics" 180).

In March 1583 Leicester's Men suffered when the formation of the Queen's Men assembled the best actors of the London companies and took three of the best actors—John Laneham, Robert Wilson, and William Johnson, all of whom had signed the 1572 appeal to Leicester—from their company. Chambers thinks they also lost Burbage's Theatre and that the owner, James Burbage, retired (4:89). The first notice of a reconstituted company is in the household accounts book for 5 May 1585, when they were given £5 at Leicester House in London with an additional payment of 10s. to Will Kempe, now "one of the players" (MacLean, "Leicester and the Evelyns" 489). Subsequent records show that this reconstituted company went on a summer tour: they were in Dover in June and Bath in August, but this time Leicester was not with them; he was in Greenwich and Nonsuch, perhaps already turning his attention to the Low Countries. His fifteen players and twelve musicians were paid £5 on 4 December for "ther Ioyng to the seaye from Leaster house" (MacLean, "Leicester and the Evelyns" 490). There was a triumphant entry into The Hague on 29 December (detailed in Strong and Van Dorsten). Back home, Leicester's Men played at Exeter on 23 March 1586, at court that December, and in London until *c.* 25 January 1587, moving on to Abingdon, Bath, Latham, Coventry, Leicester, Oxford, Stratford-on-Avon, Dover, Canterbury, Marlborough, Southampton, Exeter, Gloucester, and Norwich during 1586–87. The following year they were at Coventry, Reading, Bath, Maidstone, Dover, Plymouth, Gloucester, York, Saffron

Walden, and probably Exeter: their return to a number of cities suggests they were once again a leading company. They kept at it, playing at Ipswich in September still wearing the badge of their patron, apparently unaware they had outlived him.

Leicester's historic patronage to public entertainment set the stage for the extraordinary patronage of later generations. Leicester was acknowledged by Geoffrey Whitney in *A Choice of Emblemes, and Other Devises* (1586) as "a bountifull Mecenas" (301). Dudley courted Elizabeth in 1562 with the masque *Desire and Lady Beauty*, Thomas Norton's and Thomas Sackville's *Tragedie of Gorboduc* (about succession), and the performance at Gray's Inn about Juno and Diana debating the wisdom of marriage. But his most ambitious entertainment, dedicated to the queen, was the 1575 entertainment at Kenilworth Castle recounted in a letter by the courtier Robert Laneham and in George Gascoigne's *Princely Pleasures*. This would be his crowning achievement, but ultimately one that suffered from bad luck.

The public entertainment at Kenilworth, Warwickshire in July 1575, unrivaled in her reign, lasted seventeen days. It began with a midday dinner at Long Itchington, seven miles from Kenilworth, and an afternoon of hunting. When they moved on to the castle, entering by way of the tiltyard, they were welcomed by a porter who stood on the wall, "huge and monstrous trumpets counterfeited," Gascoigne tells us. The gigantic pasteboard figures were reminders that Kenilworth had once been one of King Arthur's castles; shows drew on Arthurian traditions. Next the queen was presented with a floating island on the lake, from which the Lady of the Lake delivered an oration on the history and antiquity of the castle. The day ended with a display of fireworks and a great peal of guns.

The next day, Sunday, was given over to services in the parish church, music and dancing in the afternoon, and fireworks in the evening. Monday was hot and humid, and the queen stayed indoors until she went hunting at 5 p.m. Returning by torchlight, she was confronted by Gascoigne dressed as a woodwose (a wild man covered with moss), and speaking in verse dialogue with Echo: "And who gave all these gifts? I pray thee, Echo say, Was it not he who (but of later) this building here all day?" Echo replied: "Dudley." A deer was caught the following day, but then freed, and on Thursday there was a bear-baiting, with Leicester supplying thirteen bears; in the evening there were more fireworks and an Italian acrobat. It rained for the next two days, and then it was Sunday—a church service followed by a country wedding or bride-ale, Morris dancing, a pageant play, supper, another play, an ambrosial banquet, and a masque. For much of the day Elizabeth watched the festivities from an upper window.

On Monday five men were knighted, and the queen gave nine more the royal touch against scrofula. More hot weather kept her indoors until 5 p.m. once again, when she went hunting. On her return there was a water pageant with a large mermaid, the Lady of the Lake, and Sir Bruce Sans Pitee, followed by Arion singing on a twenty-foot (6.1-meter) dolphin containing a consort of six musicians. The next day—Wednesday—was the last full day, and Gascoigne wrote and rehearsed a masque in which Diana, goddess of chastity, lost her favorite nymph Zabeta (a partial anagram of Elizabeth) to Juno, the goddess of marriage. Mercury, a son of the woodwose, reappears in need of Zabeta. Iris, the goddess of the rainbow, is sent by Juno to tell the queen (Zabeta) that she should not leave with Mercury nor listen to Diana, but most reasonably follow Juno. This public entertainment, making a case for marriage with Leicester, was never performed due to wet weather—and perhaps at the queen's suggestion. At her departure, Gascoigne ran alongside her, praising Kenilworth. But she ignored him, as she ignored what seems to have been another marriage proposal from Leicester. But there may be a deeper meaning to Gascoigne's eclipsed entertainment. Subsequent interpretations by William Hunnish and more modern commentators see Sir Bruse's attempted rape of the Lady of the Lake, intending "by force her virgin's state / full folkie to deface," as a reference to Catholic Spain's attack on the Low Countries.

In interpreting the role of the Captain as the opponent of Sir Bruse and the defender of the Lady of the Lake, it supported Leicester as the leader of Protestant protection of the Netherlands and the enemy of Catholic expansion, and gave purpose to a new set of armor Leicester had made by the Royal Workshops in Greenwich. Freeing the Lady in the fiction, then, as he did at Kenilworth, anticipated—perhaps instructed—Elizabeth to come to the aid of the beleaguered Dutch. Either way, or both, the Kenilworth shows had far deeper significance than customary public entertainments.

And the double significance of marriage and military action were repeated two months later, in September 1575, when public entertainments at Woodstock "functioned as a coda," Elizabeth Goldring tells us, in the presentation of the knight Contarenus, who is also both suitor and soldier (186). Here the queen first saw a combat between two knights, Contarenus and Loricus (Sir Henry Lee, the Queen's Champion). This was followed by the tale of Hemetes the hermit, extant in a fragmented manuscript (the text is summarized by Yates 96–7). A banquet was followed by the "Song of the Oak," echoing the "Song of Deep Desire" sung in the holly bush at Kenilworth. Goldring adds that Leicester personally oversaw the last-minute preparations for the queen's visit (185). Although she declined his thoughts of marriage, in 1584 she named Leicester Lord Steward of the Household, an office he held until his death in 1588.

Ironically enough, Elizabeth herself took on the double roles of suitor and soldier when she donned military armor to address her troops at Tilbury as they awaited the arrival of the Spanish Armada in the summer of 1588. She remained there, nervously, concerned about her own safety, from 8 to 10 August, refusing to leave until 11 August, promising her troops that she had the heart and stomach of a king. It was her own military entertainment, realizing at last, in her own time and way, the invitation Leicester seems to have made at Kenilworth.

Sir Philip Sidney

"At jousts, triumphs, and other such royal pastimes," Edmund Molyneux, secretary to Sir Henry Sidney, Philip's father, wrote to him of his son, "he would bring in such a lively gallant show, so agreeable to every point which is required for the expressing of a perfect device, (so rich was he in those inventions) as, if he surpassed not all, he would equal or at least second the best" (Duncan-Jones 205). Philip's reputation as a skilled combatant was universal. He returned to England from his European Grand Tour on 31 May 1575 and went briefly to Penshurst Place before joining the queen's progress at Kenilworth. He left the royal party early in August to join his father in Shrewsbury, where Sir Henry had just been reappointed Lord Deputy of Ireland, and then rejoined the queen in time for the entertainments at Woodstock. He first entered the tiltyard there, or at the Accession Day tilt that 19 November. Around this time he was appointed Royal Cupbearer—a position once given his father (Illustration 7).

His debut at tilting at Whitehall came in the autumn of 1577 between visits to Wilton. He took a leading role in the Accession Day tournament of 1577. In May 1578 he wrote his own entertainment, *The Lady of May*. He participated in the Accession Day tilts in 1578 and 1579, this time with Oxford and the Catholic Lord Windsor. Leicester's wife gave birth to a son in April 1581 disinheriting Philip; he appeared next on the tiltyard with the impresa "Speravi" ("I hoped") with a line drawn through it. He continued entering Accession Day tilts, and on 22 January 1581 he took part in a court entertainment, *The Callophisus Challenge*, seeking the queen's favor as the Blue Knight. There was also a second tournament, *The Four Foster Children of Desire*, in which he appeared with Arundel, Windsor, and Greville on 15–16 May at a banqueting house in Whitehall before the French ambassadors. He probably took part in the 1581 Accession Day tilt before a returning Alençon, the queen's suitor, now Anjou. He also took a leading part in an elaborate 1584 tilt arranged by Sir Henry Lee, leading off the challenge by running the whole six courses along the tilt, and on 6 December he joined ten married men (including his brother Robert, the Earl of Cumberland, Lord Willoughby, and Sir Henry Lee) against ten bachelors (including Henry Brouncker and Edward Denny)."His profile as a tilter was now so high," Katherine Duncan-Jones sums up: "that a learned Italian Protestant refugee, Scipio Gentile, in dedicating a translation of twenty-five Psalms into Latin hexameters to him in 1584 described his 'most magnificent devising of shows and his equestrian feats' as the most striking achievement of his mature manhood" (271).

Sidney wrote two courtly entertainments. The first, *The Lady of May*, was written for the queen's visit to Wanstead, Leicester's home in Essex. It relies for its inspiration on the entertainments at Kenilworth and Woodstock, using the license allowed for festivities on May Day to reiterate the two earlier shows. Like them, it requires the queen to participate: "Her most excellent Majesty walking in Wanstead Garden … came suddenly [upon] an honest man's wife of the country … crying out for justice" (*Miscellaneous Prose* 21). Kneeling before the queen, the Lady of May remarks:

> With me have been (alas I am ashamed to tell it) two young men, the one a forester named Therion, the other Espilus a shepherd, very long even in love forsooth. I like them both, and love neither. Espilus is the richer, but Therion the livelier. Therion doth me many pleasures, as stealing me venison out of these forests, and many other such like pretty and prettier services; but withal he grows to such rages, that sometimes he strikes me, sometimes he rails at me. This shepherd, Espilus, of a mild disposition, as his fortune hath not been to do me great service, so hath he never done me any wrong, but feeding his sheep, sitting under some sweet bush, sometimes, they say, he records my name in doleful verses. Now the question I am to ask you, fair lady, is whether the many deserts and many faults of Therion, or the very small deserts and no faults of Espilus be to be preferred. (24–5)

> Espilus. tune up my voice, a higher note I yeeld,
>   To high concepts the song must needs be high,
>   More high then stars, more firme then flintie field
>   Are all my thoughts, on which I live or die:
>   Sweet soule, to whom I vowed am a slave,
>   Let not wild woods so great a treasure have.
> His thoughts ascend; he must feed his soul.
> Therion. The highest note comes oft from basest mind,
>   As shallow brooke's yield the greatest sound,
>   Seeke other thoughts thy life or death to find;
>   Thy stars be fal'n, plowed in thy flintie ground:
>   Sweete soule let not a wretch that serve th sheep,
>   Among his flocke so sweete a treasure keepe. (25–6)

Rather than establish a counter-argument, Therion's answer is unoriginal, earthbound mockery, uninspired imitation. Epsilius replies that his possessions are simple ones, grounded in nature which deserves the service; but he would gladly give them away; for him the greatest possession is not material, but grace freely given, but Therion's response is invective.

The subsequent debate between Dorcas and Rixus "does not merely repeat or elaborate the initial opposition of Espilus and Therion," Louis Montrose notes; "Instead, it moves the debate to a higher level of analysis. Sidney's rhetorical strategy is to unfold the implications of the objectionable appearances" (15). Critics have long argued that the contemplation of the shepherd's life is put against the rage and wealth of the settled courtier, and that Elizabeth's final decision to declare Espilus victor is a mistake on her part. But they are wrong. The aggressive plan of Leicester to invade the Low Countries is what really frightened her: "One of her most pressing domestic problems was effectively to check, control, and channel the talents and energies, the thirst for self-aggrandizement and the ideological zeal of men in the upper strata of a mobile, disequilibrious and intensely competitive society" (Montrose 21). She could not always trust even Leicester. In this, she was quite right. On 21 September 1578—less than a month after the queen departed Wanstead—Leicester was secretly married, on that very estate, to Lettice, Countess of Essex. Elizabeth did not know that for nearly a year.

Sidney's other entertainment was *The Four Foster Children of Desire*, which Henry Woudhuysen has called "the most important and exciting of the Queen's reign" (318). It was presented before the French ambassadors on Whit Monday and Tuesday, 15–16 March 1581, and like *The Lady of May*, seemed to propose marriage only to deny it. At the end of the tiltyard, in an addition to Whitehall, the queen sat in a gallery in what was labeled "The Fortress of Perfect Beauty." Elizabeth was portrayed as both unattainable and as celestial perfection: William Ringler conjectures it is the basis for *Astrophil and Stella*, Sonnet 14 (Sidney, *Poems* 474). Four knights would besiege the castle to win her: the Earl of Arundel, Lord Windsor, Sidney, and Fulke Greville. The first day they entered the tiltyard in turn, each accompanied by trumpeters, pages, grooms, and yeomen. They were joined by a boy who sang accompanied by cornets, and were elegantly dressed—Sidney in partly blue armor, gilt and engraved; he arrived with four spare horses with costly furniture of cloth of gold embroidered with pearls. That day each contestant ran six courses, attempting to attack the castle and failing. A boy, accompanied by cornets, sang this song:

> Heeled, yeels, O yeels, you that this FORT do holde,
> > Which seated is, in spotless honors fielde,
> Desires great force, no sources can withhold:
> > Then to DESIERS desire, O yeelde O yeelde.

Another boy, turning himself to the Foster Children, sang:

> Alarmed, allarme, here will no yeelding be,
> > Such marble ears, no cunning, works can charme,
> Courage therefore, and let the stately see,
> > That naught withstands DESIRE, Allarme, allarme. (Goldwell A8v–B1)

On the second day they entered the tiltyard seated in a single chariot around the Lady Desire, accompanied by mournful music. Jousting followed. In the evening a boy appeared with an olive branch, fell before the queen, and reported that all four Foster Children submitted to Beauty. Virtue stood over the queen, he said, and she would not be subject to desire nor marriage.

But military entertainments kept preoccupying Sidney's imagination, so that when he came to revise the *Arcadia*, they became a fundamental grid for his imaginative reformulation. At the start, Palladius/Musidorus is taken from Laconia to the house of Kalendar in Arcadia, where entertainment is a way of life, where "from high to low is given to those sports of wit," where "ordinary it is among [even] the meanest sort to make songs and dialogues in metre" (Sidney, *New Arcadia* 24). It follows, then, when the Helots revolt, Palladius, seeking some stratagem, suggests that all the men there should disguise themselves as poor Arcadians (35), and when this fails, to determine the outcome by representatives in single combat (37); in a later combat Amphialus kills his lifelong friend Philoxenes over Helen of Corinth (64–5). Such limited fights grow; Book I concludes with a tournament in which Philantas defends the honor of Artesia against five knights before being defeated by Pyrocles in disguise. Book II returns to such key actions. Another war is settled "when Tiridates [seeking to conquer Erona, heiress to Lycia] found [he] would make the war long … he made a challenge of three princes in his retinue against those two [Greek] princes and Antiphilus, and that thereupon the quarrel should be decided" (207). Pyrocles accepts the challenge of Anaxius to a single combat, which turns bloody (236–8) before proceeding, like the previous book, to the grand Iberian tournament (253) in which Duncan-Jones finds "clear allusions to Accession Day Tilts" (145). In fact, Sidney places himself here anagrammatically as the shepherd knight Philisides, accompanied by shepherds who, "attending upon Philisides went among them and sang an eclogue, one of them answering another, while the other shepherds, pulling out recorders which possessed the place of pipes, accorded their music to the others' voice. The eclogue had great praise" (255).

Clare Kinney has traced "the elaborate knightly devices and 'shows' [and] invites their demystification" (35). There is the single combat between the Black Knight, representing Basilius and Amphialus (345–6), followed by that of Amphialus and Phalanus of Corinth (365–70). Soon enough, Amphialus is in single combat with Argalus (371–9). After the death of Argalus, Amphialus fights the widowed Parthenia disguised as the Knight of the Tomb (396–8). Musidorus fights Amphialus disguised in turn as the Forsaken Knight (403–13). Then, in an unexpected change of pace, there is the gruesome spectacle of Pamela's staged beheading (525–6) and that of Philoclea's head in a bloody basin (430–31); both tricks are revealed soon after (436–7). Zelmane challenges Anaxius to single combat, although nothing comes of it (452–3), and then kills Anaxius' brother (459–62). Philisides makes two more appearances as shepherd rather than shepherd knight, supplying yet further entertainment as the Shepherd Knight singing the lovely "As I my little flock on Ister bank" in the eclogues to Book I, "to satisfy Basilius" (478).

Shortly after these revisions, Sidney abandoned the role of an entertaining shepherd knight named Philisides to join forces with his uncle Leicester in battling for the Protestant cause and against Catholic Spain, then invading the Low Countries. He died unexpectedly in the Netherlands, following the Battle of Zutphen, of an infected leg wound. In another month, he would have turned thirty-two.

Mary Sidney Herbert, Countess of Pembroke

Philip's sister Mary (Illustrations 9 and 10) became the third wife of Henry Herbert, the recently widowed second Earl of Pembroke, on 21 April 1577 in a wedding arranged by her uncle, Robert Dudley, and together they carried on the family traditions of providing entertainments. As Lord President of the Council of Wales, Herbert sponsored companies of players as Leicester had, and Mary herself patronized the Queen's Men in June 1590 and 1596, Lord Strange's Men (with which Shakespeare was associated) in August 1593, Worcester's Men in 1595 and 1596, and Essex's Men in 1596 in performances at Shrewsbury. Throughout the period Pembroke himself continued his patronage of Pembroke's Men. But Mary had also turned the Sidney home at Wilton, near Salisbury, into the most famous center of literary patronage from the late 1570s until the death of her husband in 1601. According to John Aubrey in his *Brief Lives*, "Wilton House was like a College, there were so many learned and ingenious persons. She was the greatest Patronesse of Witt and learning of any Lady in her time" (Waller 77)—of courtiers, teachers, playwrights, poets, and clergymen, most especially Abraham Fraunce and Nicholas Breton, but also Thomas Howell, Aemilia Lanyer, Henry Lok, Thomas Moffett, Thomas Morley, Robert Newton, Edmund Spenser, John Taylor, and Thomas Watson. It was "the equivalent of Baif's Paris academy," Gary Waller writes, "a workshop for poetical experimentation, the seedbed of a literary revolution" (45), testing quantitative meter and pastoral poetry on the one hand, and political and religious commentary on the other.

The day Mary was born, her uncle Leicester, as Master of the Revels, staged at the Inner Temple the political play *Gorbuduc*—an English play about the transfer of rule that her brother Philip praised in his *Defence of Poesie* (1580) for its "stately speeches and well-sounding phrases" as well as its "notable morality, which it doth most delightfully teach" (*Philip's Phoenix* 121); Mary herself translated Robert Garnier's play *Antonius* into *The Tragedy of Antonie* by 26 November 1590. Meant as a closet drama to be read aloud in great houses such as Wilton, the play was published in 1592 and went through five editions in fifteen years. Her translation shadows her uncle Leicester's entertainment at Kenilworth, her brother Philip's *Lady of May* in its political undercurrent, and still more closely, Seneca's *Octavia* in its analysis of moral behavior in a corrupt state. Mary's play follows Garnier in settling on a single event—the defeat of the forces of Antony and Cleopatra at Actium—and its aftermath in long speeches that, rather than advancing the plot, reflect on it prismatically. It is a play of emotion, but even more a play of the mind, a play of conscious reckoning with public events and the personal self: one of the characters is a philosopher who underscores the play's issues, while the five Choruses represent the common people acting concretely. The focus, therefore, is not on character or action, but on what we can (and should) make of what happens, make of interpretation and response to matters of value, life, and death. Amid the destruction of civil war, the play traces the destruction of family and (analogously) of state; Alexander Witherspoon notes the emphasis on "love of country, praise of freedom, and emulation of the stern virtues of the ancient Romans" (*Philip's Phoenix* 125). This very political play thus also deals with religion: in its portrayal of Cleopatra draws attention to Elizabeth, and in her love for Antony alludes to Essex. Clearly these were contemporary Renaissance claims that attracted Mary, but she adds to them an overlay of Garnier's stoicism, suggesting even more her attraction to him, in arguing the inescapable necessity of idealism and virtue for a committed soul in a time of chaos. Roman soldiers displace Egyptians in the final chorus:

> Shall Euer ciuile bate
> gnaw and devour our state?
> Shall neuter we this blade,
> Our blood hath bloudie made
> Lay downe? …
> But as from age to age,
> So passe from rage to rage! (N2; *Philip's Phoenix* 128)

Mary also translated an unpublished portion of Petrarch's *Triumph of Death* in 1599. Like Garnier's Cleopatra, Petrarch's Laura accepts death at the end with a kind of stoicism; her example, notes Mary Ellen Lamb:

> shows how any woman can fulfill the function of spiritual guide, molding her
> words and actions to benefit her man on the pilgrimage to heaven. … [She]
> presents a model if not of heroism, then at least of courageous intellectual
> assertion that was made possible by her creation of these Stoic heroines, from
> whose very self-effacements and beautiful deaths she created a viable version
> of authorship. (141)

Mary's final recorded literary work returns once again to the petitions at Kenilworth and the subsequent *Lady of May* by her brother. "A Dialogue between Two Shepherds, Uttered in a Pastoral Shew, at Wilton," popularly known as *Astrea* (1599), was written to welcome the queen to Wilton. But Elizabeth never came, and the entertainment remained unstaged. Astraea (the proper spelling) was a popular name for the queen, and fitting for her proposed August visit, since she was the Greek astronomical poet for Justice; her constellation was Virgo; her chief attribute was her virginity; her month was August; and she was due to return to England in its second Golden Age. Praise for Elizabeth as Astrea grew upon the defeat of the Spanish Armada in 1588. The two shepherds are Piers, a devout Protestant perhaps named for the fourteenth-century Piers Plowman, or John Piers, bishop of nearby Salisbury from 1577 to 1589, and Leicester's militant ally at court. Piers's opponent is the shepherd Thenot, a traditional name perhaps taken from Spenser's *Shepheardes Calender*. This very brief dialogue raises a theological problem—the inadequacy of language to speak about the divine—as well as the political—flattering the queen with outspoken praise leads to outrageous behavior. The two linguistic appeals meant to prove worthy remind us of *The Lady of May*, where language itself falls short. The only response proposed, then, is silence—not only a consequence, but a comment on the entertainments that preceded hers. This deliberately comic turn nevertheless does not deny, but reinforces, the religious and political issues of her three works.

Robert Sidney, Viscount Lisle and First Earl of Leicester

"Her Highness hath done honour to my poor house by visiting me," Sir Robert Sidney wrote to Sir John Harington in 1600:

> and seemed much pleased at what we did to please her. My son made a fair
> Speech, to which she did give a most gracious reply. The women did dance
> before her, whilst cornets did salute from the gallery; and she did vouchsafed
> to eat two morsels of rich confit cake, and drank a small cordial from a gold
> cup. She had a marvellous suit of velvet borne by four of her first women
> attendants in rich apparel; two ushers did go before, and going up stairs she
> called for a staff, and was much wearied in walking about the house, and said
> she wished to come another day. Six drums and six trumpets waited in the
> Court, and sounded at her approach and departure. (Osborne 81)

Together Sidney and Elizabeth I concocted a brief entertainment. But Robert knew such fragmentary features of entertainments: he and his older sister Mary had both been at their uncle Leicester's entertainment at Kenilworth in 1575; he had been to his sister's wedding in 1577, and in 1588 he had been at Tilbury with the queen as the Spanish Armada came up the Thames. At the age of twenty-five he was appointed Lord Governor of Flushing on 27 October 1588. On 28 December he was transferred from participant in an entertainment to a subject in one when his servant Rowland Whyte wrote him from London that "This afternoon I saw *The Overthrow of Turnabout* [*sic*] played and saw Sir Robert Sidney and Sir Francis Vere upon the stage, killing, slaying, and overthrowing the Spaniard" (Whyte 365; cf. Whyte 362–3n).

While succeeding his uncle Leicester as Governor of Flushing was the best office he could persuade under Elizabeth, Robert fared much better with King James and Queen Anne (Illustrations 13, 14, and 15). The king stopped at Wilton on his initial progress from Edinburgh to London. Just fifty days after Elizabeth's death—Robert was now forty—he was made Baron Sidney of Penshurst, and on 9 October he overcame strong opposition, perhaps with the aid of Mary's sons William and Philip Herbert and the queen's insistence, and was appointed Queen Anne's Lord High Chamberlain and Surveyor General at an annual salary of £30. Within two years he was made Viscount Lisle, a family title he had sought since 1597. The Sidney portrayed on the London stage was now removed to court, where, constantly in the presence of the queen, he supervised all her entertainments.

A comprehensive record of Robert's tasks in this new post is not extant, and we need to piece together our own inferences to realize at least part of it. Fortunately, British Library Add. MS 17520 is a careful record of Robert's expenses by the keeper of his wardrobe and his financial records, Thomas Nevitt, who concentrated largely on his vast expenditures for clothes. The initial listing there of Robert's activity is involvement with the marriage of the Earl of Derby (fol. 3), followed by a masque at Hampton Court after a royal visit to Wilton (fol. 4). He was at the opening of Parliament and the marriages of the Lords of Montgomery, Carlisle, and Essex (fol. 5). In 1604 Robert, his daughter Mary Wroth, and his nephew William Herbert danced in the first of the Queen Anne's masques, Samuel Daniel's *Vision of the Twelve Goddesses*. Robert and Mary danced in Ben Jonson's *Masque of Blackness*—she danced as a Moor with a blackened face—on Twelfth Night 1605. "When the late Queene [Anne] made a maske at Whitehall wherein the Maskers came in like Moores," Nevitt records, "your honor made a sute of Ashe coloured satten cutt with a peach couloir taffetie and laid. on thick with silver lace this sute cost your honor £80" (fol. 5). The marriages of the Queen of Bohemia, Lord Rockborough, and Lord Somerset followed (fol. 5), and his installation as Knight of the Garter and his advancement from viscount to earl (fol. 5v). Nevitt suggests that Robert did more than dance or attend the entertainments he supervised: "Your honor made you two barges with a barge cloth ymbrothered and cushions of velvet and two Turkie carpettes for them" (fol. 5v). In addition, there were many feasts and tilts.

The title page of the quarto of *The Characters of Two royall Masques, The one of BLACKNESSE, The other of BEAVTIE* claims they are "performed By the most magnificent of Queenes, ANNE," so Robert was necessarily involved in both. John Nichols's *Progresses, Processions, and Magnificent Entertainments* is another resource for data and grounds for inference. He gives the full text of an entertainment for the king and queen as she is given Theobalds by the Earl of Salisbury. The most elaborate entertainment of the queen was *Tethys' Festival; or, the Queen's Wake* by Daniel, performed on 5 June 1610 "to solemnize the Creation of the high and mighty Prince Henry of Wales" (Nichols 2:346); at the conclusion she "sodainely appears … In a most pleasant and artificiall grove" (2:357). Ben Jonson's slight *Love Freed from Ignorance and Folly* is labeled "A Masque of Her Majesty's, 1611"; Robert's daughter Philippa was one of the masquers. Daniel's "Hymen's Triumph, A Pastorall Tragicomaedie, Presented at the Queen's Court in the Strand" for the marriage of Lord Roxborough (Nichols 2:749) was performed on 3 February 1611 in Denmark House, the queen's new palace. *Cupid's Banishment* was a masque presented to Queen Anne by the young gentlewomen of the Ladies' Hall (Nichols 3:283). In our attempts to resurrect Robert's career as Lord High Chamberlain to Queen Anne, we can also refer to the lists compiled by John Astington in the appendix to his *English Court Theatre 1558–1642*, adding Thomas Heywood's *The Silver Age* (245) and *The Lords Masque* (247).

There were also bundles of entertainments on the king's and queen's progresses; Nichols provides a full account of their progress to Oxford in August of 1605 (1:530–62).

Yet whatever part the Queen's Lord High Chamberlain took in the shows, tournaments, and feasts Queen Anne proposed, music was likely to be a part of it. His songs, comments Gavin Alexander, "show an exceptional recognizable and lyric gift" (191). His Song 20, "Senses by unjust force banish'd," was set to music by Alfonso Ferrabosco and constituted the middle strophe of a song in three sections. He wrote at least two lyrics to music. Alexander adds:

> Another music manuscript, from c. 1600 and possibly representing the repertoire of the Children of the Chapel Royal (a company associated with Queen Anne), includes a setting of the first stanza of Sidney's witty dialogue Pastoral 2. The whole poem can be performed to the music, clearly strophic in design, and was probably intended to be (manuscripts of strophic songs often give the text of only the first stanza). We must wonder if Sidney's words came to be performed not only within the court masque but on the public stage (190).

Indeed, when Robert Dowland dedicated his music miscellany *A Musical Banquet* to his godfather Robert Sidney in 1610, his own father, the esteemed composer John Dowland, contributed a solo lute composition called "Sir Robert Sidney's Galliard." Held back by his political responsibilities in the Netherlands, Sidney came to a career of politics alongside ceremonies and entertainments in mid-life, but as Lord High Chamberlain to a monarch who welcomed him, he breathed new life into the Dudley-Sidney-Herbert-Wroth family traditions.

The Herbert Family

On 21 April 1577 Mary Sidney became the third wife of the aging Henry Herbert, who in 1570 had succeeded his father as the second Earl of Pembroke and Lord Lieutenant of Wiltshire. In addition, he inherited large estates such as Wilton in Wiltshire and Glamorgan in Wales for services rendered to Edward VI by his father. Henry's authority increased with the decline of the older gentry, but had its limitations because he was irascible and impatient, and suffered from feuds and hostility with major gentry. He once wrote a letter to Queen Elizabeth that was "so passionate" that his secretary refused to deliver it. In his later years he also worried about his ill health: "I dream of nothing but death. I hear of little but death, and … I desire nothing but death," he wrote a friend on Christmas Eve 1595. In time his elder son William asked the queen for permission to stay with his father at Wilton lest he give away all his money.

But there was another side to Henry Herbert. He also followed in the footsteps of his wife Mary in awarding patronage—appointing Fulke Greville as Secretary to the Council in the Marches, and Abraham Fraunce as the queen's solicitor. He may also have awarded the see of Llandaff to his chaplain, Gervaise Babington. Also in the tradition of Leicester, he became the patron of his own theater company in 1591 or early 1592. Pembroke's Men played at Burbage's Theatre in Shoreditch with Richard Burbage and Edward Alleyn (who had once been the leading player of the now defunct Leicester's Men), and were sufficiently professional that in their very first season, at Christmas 1592–93, they joined the older company of Lord Strange's Men, who played at the Rose, in an invitation to perform at court. The title pages of plays claiming to be performed by Pembroke's Men—*Edward II, Titus Andronicus, The Taming of the Shrew* and *Henry VI Part 3*—suggest that Pembroke's Men were associated with Marlowe and Shakespeare. They also played *Richard III* and the ill-fated *Isle of Dogs*. Their fall in 1593 was just as rapid; it was caused by the onset of plague and competition on the road from Strange's Men. The company reappear, however, traveling to Ipswich on 7 April 1595 and to Ipswich, Bath, Bristol, and Oxford in 1596, as well as to Ludlow, Shrewsbury, Rye, York, Coventry, Dover, Leicester, Norwich, and Hardwick. Their patent, moreover, survived such changes, and Francis Langley revived the company in his new Bankside playhouse in 1597. Their patron Henry Herbert, Earl of Pembroke, died on 9 January 1601.

Henry Herbert's two sons, William and Philip, combined family traditions (Illustrations 20. 21 and 22). Like their great-uncle Leicester, their uncle Philip, and their mother Mary, they performed in entertainments at court and in the tiltyard and they patronized the arts. G. F. Waller reminds us that in 1562 Elizabeth fostered the rules for armed combat dormant since 1466 and encouraged contests in full armor as a central part of court pageantry. Philip Sidney advised his brother Robert to practice jousting as a part of the essential skills at court (53). Chivalric shows were a throwback to an earlier time, but also a present means of resolving disputes and demonstrating aesthetic athleticism. It was also a means of courtiership advocated by Castiglione and "discussions of beauty, love, ambition, dissimulation, and public responsibility," according to Guazzi (Waller 55), done with *sprezzatura*, with nonchalance. In his first-hand account of his friend Sir Philip Sidney, *Nobilis, or A View of the Life and Death of a Sidney*, Thomas Moffet likened young William Herbert to Philip in a comparison that lasted Herbert's lifetime. He was the ideal courtier of his generation. Anthony Wood wrote at the time:

> He was the very picture and *viva effigies* of Nobility. His person was rather majestic than elegant, and his presence, whether quiet or in motion, was full of stately gravity. His mind was heroic, often stout, but never disloyal; and so vehement an opponent of the Spaniard, that when that match [of Prince Charles and the Spanish Infanta] fell under consideration in the latter end of the reign of James I, he would sometimes rouse to the trepidation of that King, yet kept in favour still; for his Majesty knew plain dealing (as a jewel in all men so) was in a Privy Counsellor an ornamental duty; and the same true-heartedness commended him to Charles I. (Nichols 1:255)

Philip's secretary Rowland Whyte remarked: "My Lord Herbert resolves this year to shew himself a man at armes, and prepares for yt"; "My Lord Herbert is practicing at Greenwich; I sent him word of this; he leapes, he dances, he singes, he gives counterbuffes; he makes his horse runne with more speed" (Nichols 1:255).

On 14 June 1600 William Herbert attended the wedding of his cousin Henry, Lord Herbert (heir to the Earl of Worcester), where he saw Mary Fitton perform in a masque and was instantly infatuated. There were rumors that she came to his rooms in men's clothing. In time, she was pregnant. Elizabeth ordered William to Fleet Prison on 25 March. Later that month his son was born, but died almost at once. On 26 April the queen released William and banished him to Wilton, just as she had banished his uncle Philip decades before. He spent his years in exile building a power base. On Queen Elizabeth's death on 24 March 1603 William and his brother Philip raced north to Edinburgh to welcome the new King James; as a result, the king made the first of his visits to William's Wilton on his journey from Edinburgh to London. It was the first of two visits there by the king that year. Their friendship remained, reversing William's life (and Philip Sidney's) under Elizabeth:

> Pembroke was well suited for the boisterousness of the Jacobean court. He participated enthusiastically in every accession day tilt until 1615, and performed in many masques celebrating courtly milestones. His personal relationship with James drew comment from the Venetian ambassador, who recounted a scene from the coronation: "The earl of Pembroke, a handsome youth, who is always with the king and always joking with him, actually kissed His Majesty's face, whereupon the king laughed and gave him a little cuff" .... On one of his many stays at Wilton, James, aware that Pembroke detested frogs, put one down his favourite's neck to general hilarity. Nothing abashed, Pembroke later took revenge by sneaking a live pig into the king's close stool (Slater).

William Herbert tilted for the first time in November 1600. Both William and his uncle Robert were invited to dance in Queen Anne's first masque, *The Vision of the Twelve Goddesses*, on New Year's Day 1604. On 27 December William, now the third Earl of Pembroke, wed Mary, the daughter of Gilbert Talbot, Earl of Shrewsbury; the following night he performed in a masque. His marriage was preceded by that of his cousin Mary Wroth, the daughter of his uncle Robert, and followed by the wedding of his brother Philip to Susan Vere. Other festivities followed, several of them reprinted or noted in Nichols. At the creation of Henry Stuart as the Prince of Wales in 1610, Pembroke was the prince's server, while his younger brother, now the Earl of Montgomery, was the cup-bearer. Then, in November 1615, he was at last appointed by the king to the position he had long sought—Lord Chamberlain to James, as his aging uncle Robert Sidney was Lord High Chamberlain to Queen Anne. In this position William would preside over the household above stairs, supervising six hundred officers. He was in charge of all court entertainments for King James—masques, plays, and concerts. He would supervise the office of works and license theaters. He began by organizing the Christmas revels of 1615, but he celebrated by presenting to the court on 1 January 1616 Ben Jonson's *The Golden Age Restored*, performed at the Banqueting Hall. On Twelfth Night 1616 he presented the masque once again, this time before a potentially contentious mix of ambassadors from France, Venice, and the Savoyard; they were led to their seats by the Lord Chamberlain himself, assisted by Lord Danvers. Later that year he was appointed to the committee planning the creation of Prince Charles, to include tilting, barriers, and a masque by the Inns of Court. And then, on 29 January 1617 he was elected Chancellor of Oxford University. Meanwhile, his friendship with the king, although he disagreed with the plan to marry Prince Charles to the Infanta, only deepened. The king visited Wilton again in the summer of 1620; in 1621 he appointed Pembroke Lord Lieutenant of Somerset and Wiltshire.

Pembroke inherited his courtly athletic and political skills from his great-uncle and his uncle, but his abiding concern with patronage of the arts was his mother's legacy. Edward Hyde, Earl of Clarendon, described Pembroke as "the most universally loved and esteemed of any man of that age," as: "[a] man very well bred, and of excellent parts, and a graceful speaker upon any subject, having a good proportion of learning, and a ready wit to apply it, and enlarge upon it, of a pleasant and facetious humour, and a disposition affable, generous, and magnificent" (Donaldson 268).

He was the patron of potentially dangerous plays like *The Isle of Dogs*, staged by Pembroke's Men, *Eastward Ho!* and Jonson's single-authored *Sejanus*—after which Pembroke gave Jonson an annual stipend of £20 to buy books—and *Cataline* (both plays were dedicated to him), and Middleton's *A Game at Chess*. He saw to it that his kinsman the poet and parson George Herbert received a church living at Bemerton and a seat in the House of Commons. He patronized the architect Inigo Jones as well as Jonson; commissioned portraits by Nicholas Hilliard, Marcus Gheeraerts the Younger, and Daniel Mytens, and supported two of the most prominent musicians, Thomas Tompkins and John Dowland. He also invested in the Virginia Company, the Guiana Company, the Somers Islands Company, the discovery of the Northwest Passage, and the East India Company. He argued on behalf of Ralegh for forays into Spanish America. "He was," sums Slater, "the best-known patron of his generation."

William Herbert inherited the generosity of his mother, but his brother, Philip Herbert, the first Earl of Montgomery and fourth Earl of Pembroke (Illustration 22), inherited his father's temper and irascibility. Although he was handsome and a sportsman, and especially attractive to King James, he could also erupt into fighting. In 1641 Queen Henrietta Maria recommended that he be dismissed from his post of Lord Chamberlain; on 19 July of that year, David Smith notes:

> he became involved in one of his periodic quarrels, this time with Lord Maltravers in a committee of the Lords; there was a violent altercation which culminated in his striking Maltravers twice with his staff. This episode provided the king with an excuse to demand Pembroke's resignation from his position.

In his earlier years Clarendon had been more positive, noting that Philip:

> had the good fortune, by the comeliness of his person, his skill, and indefatigable industry in hunting, to be the first who drew the king's eyes towards him with affection. ... He pretended to no other qualifications than to understand horses and dogs very well, which his master loved him the better for. (Smith)

Aubrey is more succinct: "His Lordship's chief delight was in hunting and hawking, both of which he had to the greatest perfection of any peer in the realm" (Smith).

So honors came quickly. He was made a Gentleman of the Privy Chamber in May 1603, Gentleman of the Bedchamber in 1605, and Baron Herbert of Shurland and first Earl of Montgomery in May 1605. Later, on his brother William's death in 1630, he became the fourth Earl of Pembroke and Lord Lieutenant of Wiltshire, Lord Lieutenant of Somerset (1630–43) and Cornwall (1639–42), and Lord Warden of the Stanneries; still other offices followed in 1641 when he succeeded his brother as Chancellor of Oxford. Aubrey estimated his annual income at £30,000. He lived lavishly, Smith records, said to spend £18,000 a year on hunting, maintaining a staff of 80 in his London home and 160 at Wilton, where he entertained the king every summer. Montgomery, wrote Aubrey, "did not delight in books or poetry: but exceedingly loved painting and building, in which he had singular judgement, and had the best collection of any peer in England, and was the great patron to Sir Anthony Van Dyck: and had most of his painting" (Smith). To his credit, he also patronized the playwright Philip Massinger, and when Massinger died, provided a pension for his widow.

Philip Herbert also followed the family tradition of participating in courtly entertainments. At Christmas 1604 there were not only plans for "a gallant Maske, which doth cost the Exchequer £3,000," but "In the mean time here is great provision for Cockpit, to entertaine [the King] at home, and of Masks and Revells against the marriage of Sir Philip Herbert and the Lady Susan Vere which is to be celebrated on St. John's day" (Nichols 2:468–9). Montgomery danced in Ben Jonson's *Masque of Hymenaei* on Twelfth

Night 1606, celebrating the marriage of Robert, Earl of Essex, to Frances, daughter of the Earl of Suffolk. Montgomery danced with Queen Anne at the Twelfth Night masque in 1617, acknowledging the new Earl of Buckingham. Along with ten others, he ran the tilt on King's Day 1618 and danced in the Prince's Masque on Twelfth Night 1618, about which John Chamberlain wrote to Dudley Carleton: "There was nothing in it extraordinary; but rather the invention proved dull" (Nichols 3:464). In 1619 Montgomery joined the prince and Buckingham in a masque on Twelfth Night.

But for the most part the two brothers seemed inseparable. This began on Sunday 24 July 1603, when Pembroke was made a Knight of the Garter and Philip was made a Knight of the Bath. They were together again in a masque of men in 1603. On New Year's Day 1604:

> William Herbert led the masquers in presenting the king "an impresa in a shield with a sonnet in a paper to express his device and presented a jewel of £40,000 value." His brother Philip caused much comment by his device of "a fair horse-colt in a fair green shield, which he meant to be a colt of Bucephalas race and had this virtue of his sire that none could mount him but one as great at least as Alexander." James was delighted. (Brennan 23)

Both Pembroke and Montgomery played two of the "Four Knights Errant, denominated of the Fortunate Island, servants of the Destinies" before Christian of Denmark, brother to Queen Anne, at Greenwich on 3 August 1606.

They accompanied Prince Henry at the ceremonies on the election of a new master and wardens at Merchant Taylor's' Hall in 1607. Both performed in Jonson's masque with nuptial songs for the marriage of Lord Haddington at Whitehall on 7 February 1608. They presented a masque at Queen's House, Greenwich in November 1613. On 13 December of that year they returned to the Banquetting-House at Whitehall to perform in a masque celebrating the marriage of the Earl of Somerset to Frances Howard written by Thomas Campion. And there were tilts such as the one the two brothers participated in on King's Day 1606. Both men performed before Lord Burghley, Lord Knolles, and Sir Henry Carey serving as judges at Whitehall on Monday 25 March 1606, where "the Earle of Montgomery, for a young beginner, did extraordinary" (Nichols 2:43), again on King's Day 1607 along with the Duke of Lennox, and on King's Day 1613 with the Earl of Arundel. There was a more elaborate ceremony in Jonson's *Challenge at Tilt* at a marriage in 1614. On King's Day 1615 he performed before the judgment of Lord Knolles, Sir Fulke Greville, and Sir Henry Carey, "To give greater lustre and honour to [the] Triumph and Solemnitie, in the presence of the King, Queen, Prince, and Lords" (Nichols 3:215), and there was a running of the ring at the creation of Charles as Prince of Wales on 6 November 1616. Together Pembroke and Montgomery formed "the incomparable pair of brethren" whom, a short time later, Hemings and Condell would memorialize in their dedication of the first folio of Shakespeare's works.

Lady Mary Wroth

When Robert Sidney's daughter Mary, named for his mother, attended Christmas celebrations at court at the age of fifteen, she "danced before the Queen two galliards with one Mr. Palmer, the admirablest dancer of this time," Rowland Whyte wrote to her father on 28 December 1602. "Both were much commended by her Majesty (Illustrations 18 and 19). Then she danced with him a courant" (Whyte 552). She had danced earlier for Elizabeth at Penshurst, and three years later she would return, this time dancing with Queen Anne on Twelfth Night

1605 in the *Masque of Blackness* by Ben Jonson and Inigo Jones, and three years later attended the companion *Masque of Beauty*. It is also possible she appeared in Thomas Campion's *Lord Hay's Masque* (1607), mentioned in her *Urania*, Samuel Daniel's *Tethys' Festival* (1610), and Jonson's *Hymenaei* (1606) and *Masque of Queens* (1609), which could have suggested the character of Melissea in the second book of *Urania*. But then, as Heather Weidemann observes, the *Urania* "construed social experience as theatrical" (192). In 1610 Jonson dedicated his play *The Alchemist* to her.

On 27 September 1604 this younger Mary Sidney married Robert Wroth; he died of gangrene on 14 March 1614. In time she gave birth to two children through a presumed liaison with her cousin William Herbert, according to Sir Thomas Herbert, Pembroke's cousin. During her lifetime she followed in the footsteps of her uncle Philip and aunt Mary, writing a play, *Love's Victorie*, a sonnet sequence, *Pamphilia to Amphilanthus*, and a massive prose romance in two books, *The Countess of Montgomery's Urania* (named for her cousin Philip's wife) with the same characters (shadowing her own life and William Herbert's). The five-act tragicomedy *Love's Victorie* (1620s) investigates different kinds of love, testing the powers of Venus and Cupid with four pairs of lovers: Philisses and Musella, who are virtuous; Lissius and Simeana, who are jealous; Silvesta, who is chaste, and Rustic and Dalina, who are sensual. Its central interest in licit and illicit love makes it social and personal—the very opposite of the intellectual and political concerns of her playwright aunt.

Wroth's major work, *Urania* (also 1620s), is marked by continual references to the theater. The first part has a full-blown wedding masque (*Urania* 1:41–2) preceded by "Justs, Tilts, and all other warlike exercises" and "dancing and feasting" (41), and a candlelight masque (185) as well as three "enchantments": the Three Towers of the House of Love (48–9), the Marble Theatre on an island in the gulf of Venice (373), and the crown of stone with Pamphilia's corpse (654–7). The three enchantments are succeeded in *Urania* 2 by three full masques. Marion Wynn-Davies notes that "The descriptions of costumes, scenery and music are reminiscent" of Jonson's masques (95). The first is to Rodomandro, who woos and wins the queen:

> Att last Rodomandro would needs present the Court with a show of theire Country fashion, in manner of a maske, which indeed was very pretty and pleasant, him self being one of the twelve maskers, and four and twenty torchbearers here had all apparelled like horse men in counterfeitt armes, bases, and boots with great longe spurs, faire plumes of feathers, vizards they had non, the most of them having faces grimm and hard enough to bee counted vizards. The maskers had a pretty kinde of vizards or slight coverings of their faces. (*Urania* 2:46)

The central masque, presented to Pamphilia, introduces the enchantress Melissea:

> ther appeerd a strange darkness, and in that darkenes a fearfull fire, which presented a chariott drawne with four firy dragons. The Chariott fire, yett in the body of itt (all the parts beeing howsoever fire satt an aged Lady. The chariots stopt at the foot of the estate. The Queenes were neither of them afrayed, parseaving itt to bee an incha(n)ment. The Chariott and horses vanisht, the Lady advanced to Pamphilia who she knew presently to bee the sage Melissea.

> Then a verre pretty show came in sight .... For ther appeered an aged shepherd a younge sea-faring lad in habits according. The youth extreamly amourous,

Cupid nott in jest having wounded him with his sharpest and killingst-steeled darts ..., beeng as it seemd the boys deerest love. (*Urania* 2:112–13)

This leads Wynne-Davies to see an authorial response in Pamphilia's "The instabilitie of this world is such as nott many minutes can bee left free in certainties to any" (115). "Obscurity, veilings, fantasy," she remarks, "all belong to the 'twilight content,' things which are half seen, not fully understood and delightful, perhaps because of that insubstantial quality, yet at the same time illusory, passing and mutable" (97)—to which we might add, "like masques, like theater, like entertainments."

Conclusion

An increasingly sophisticated court culture under Elizabeth I and James I, inspired by writers such as Castiglione and Guazzo, produced historically an exceptionally rich period of theater, music, and dance as well as jousting and feasting, as the successive royal lord chamberlains knew so well and practiced so assiduously. In that sense, we cannot be surprised to learn that performances of all sorts were central to the life and work of the Sidneys. What remains so very remarkable is that their occupations and contributions flourished so successively through three generations. Beginning with Leicester, who financed Kenilworth and patronized Leicester's Men, the family took on more and more responsibility. Philip wrote two political entertainments and entered his own *Arcadia* as the shepherd Philisides; Mary found in her entertainment and her play how a woman could be as politically poetic and succeed, paving the way for Robert, in middle age and home from the Netherlands, to become Queen Anne's Lord High Chamberlain. In time William Herbert would follow suit as the king's chamberlain, while his younger brother succeeded him, having enacted roles in court festivities. Yet it rested with the widowed Mary Wroth, in her way, to outdo them all by writing a book longer than the *Arcadia* in which she writes herself into the leading role. At first in imitation of her uncle's groundbreaking epic romance and conscious of her own gendered and biographical position, she found in thinly disguised fantasy ways to take political and poetic entertainment to its farthest reaches. Today we remain indebted to the Dudley-Sidney-Herbert-Wroth family, not only for supplying us with unrivaled entertainments of all sorts, but, thankfully, for patronizing books that recorded them for posterity.

Bibliography

Primary and Secondary Sources

Alexander, Gavin. *Writing After Sidney: The Literary Response to Sir Philip Sidney, 1586–1640*. Oxford: Clarendon P, 2006.
Astington, John. *English Court Theatre 1558–1642*. Cambridge, Cambridge UP, 1999.
Brennan, Michael. "Robert Sidney, King James I and Queen Anna: The Politics of Service (1588–1607)." *SJ* 15.1–2 (2007): 3–30.
Chambers, E. K. *The Elizabethan Stage*. 4 vols. Oxford: Clarendon P, 1923.
Donaldson, Ian. *Ben Jonson: A Life*. Cambridge: Cambridge UP, 2011.
Duncan-Jones, Katherine. *Sir Philip Sidney: Courtier as Poet*. London: Hamish Hamilton, 1991.

Gascoigne, George. *Gascoigne's Princely Pleasures, with the Masque: Intended to Have Been Presented Before Queen Elizabeth, at Kenilworth Castle in 1575.* London: J. H. Burn, 1821.

Goldring, Elizabeth. "Portraiture, Patronage and the Progresses: Robert Dudley, Earl of Leicester, and the Kenilworth Festivities of 1575." *The Progresses, Pageants of Elizabeth I.* Ed. Jayne Elizabeth Archer, Elizabeth Goldring, and Sarah Knight. Oxford: Oxford UP, 2007. 163–88.

Goldwell, Henry. *A Briefe Declamatio of the Shews*, 1581.

Gurr, Andrew. *The Shakespearian Playing Companies.* Oxford: Clarendon P, 1996.

Hannay, Margaret P. *Philip's Phoenix: Mary Sidney, Countess of Pembroke.* Oxford: Oxford UP, 1990.

—. "Sleuthing in the Archives." *Re-Reading Mary Wroth.* Ed. Katherine R. Larson and Naomi Miller, with Andrew Strycharski. New York: Palgrave Macmillan, 2015, 19–33.

Herbert, Mary Sidney. *Collected Work of Mary Sidney Herbert, Countess of Pembroke.* 2 vols. Ed. Margaret P. Hannay, Noel J. Kinnamon, and Michael G. Brennan. Oxford: Oxford UP, 1998.

Kinney, Clare L. "Chivalry Unmasked: Courtly Spectacle and the Abuses of Romance in Sidney's *New Arcadia.*" *SEL* 35.1 (1995): 35–52.

Lamb, Mary Ellen. *Gender and Authorship in the Sidney Circle.* Madison, WI: U of Wisconsin P, 1990.

MacLean, Sally-Beth. "Leicester and the Evelyns: New Evidence for the Continental Tour of Leicester's Men." *Review of English Studies* 39.156 (1998): 487–93.

—. "The Politics of Patronage Records in Robert Dudley's Household Books." *Shakespeare Quarterly* 44.2 (1993): 175-82.

—. "Tracking Leicester's Men: The Patronage of a Performance Troupe." *Shakespeare and Theatrical Patronage in Early Modern England.* Ed. Paul Whitfield White and Susan R. Westfall. Cambridge: Cambridge UP, 2002.

McGee, C. E. "Mysteries, Musters and Masque: The Import(s) of Elizabethan Court Entertainments." *The Progresses, Pageants and Entertainments of Elizabeth I.* Ed. Jayne Elizabeth Archer, Elizabeth Goldring, and Sarah Knight. Oxford: Oxford UP, 2007. 104–21.

Montrose, Louis Adrian. "Celebration and Insinuation: Sir Philip Sidney and the Motives of Elizabethan Courtship" *Renaissance Drama* n.s. 8 (1977): 3–35.

Nevitt, Thomas. "Nevitt's *Memorial.*" Ed. Gavin Alexander and Barbara Ravelhofer. *COPIA: CERES Sidneiana.* Web. 27 May 1999. http://www.english.cam.ac.uk/ceres/sidneiana/nevitt.htm.

Nichols, John. *The Progresses, Processions, and the Magnificent Festivities, of King James the First, His Royal Consort, Family, and Court Collected from Original Manuscripts, Scarce Pamphlets, Corporation Records, Parochial Registers, &&c comprising forty masqwues and entertainments, ten civic pageants.* 4 vols. London: Society of Antiquaries, 1828.

Osborne, James. *Young Philip Sidney 1552–1577.* New Haven, CT: Yale University P, 1972.

Sidney, Philip. *The Countess of Pembroke's Arcadia (The New Arcadia).* Ed. Victor Skretkowicz. Oxford: Clarendon P, 1987.

—. *Miscellaneous Prose of Sir Philip Sidney.* Ed. Katherine Duncan-Jones and Jan van Dorsten. Oxford: Clarendon P, 1973.

—. *The Poems of Sir Philip Sidney.* Ed. William A. Ringler, Jr. Oxford: Clarendon P, 1962.

Slater, David L. "Herbert, Philip, First Earl of Montgomery and Fourth Earl of Pembroke (1584–1650)." *ODNB.*

Smith, David. "William Herbert, Third Earl of Pembroke (1580–1630)." *ODNB.*

Stillman, Robert. "Justice and the 'Good Word' in Sidney's *The Lady of May.*" *SEL* 24 (1984): 23–38.

Strong, Roy C., and J. A. van Dorsten. *Leicester's Triumph.* London: Oxford UP, 1962.

Waller, G. F. *Mary Sidney, Countess of Pembroke: A Critical Study of Her Writings and Literary Milieu*. Salzburg: Institut für Anglistik and Amerikenistik—Universität Salzburg, 1979.

Weidemann, Heather L. "Theatricality and Female Identity in Mary Wroth's *Urania*." *Reading Mary Wroth: Representing Alternatives in Early Modern England*. Ed. Naomi J. Miller and Gary Waller Knoxville, TN: U of Tennessee P, 1991.

Whitney, Geoffrey. *A Choice of Emblemes, and Other Devises*. Leiden: Christopher Plantin, 1586.

Whyte, Rowland. *The Letters (1558–1608) of Rowland Whyte*. Ed. Michael G. Brennan, Noel J. Kinnamon, and Margaret P. Hannay. Philadelphia, PA: American Philosophical Society, 2013,

Wilson, Derek. *Sweet Robin: A Biography of Robert Dudley, Earl of Leicester 1533–1588*. London: Allison and Bushy, 1997.

Woudhuysen, H. H. "Leicester's Literary Patronage: A Study of the English Court 1578–1582." PhD thesis, University of Oxford, 1980.

Wroth, Lady Mary. *The First Part of the Countess of Montgomery's Urania*. Ed. Josephine A. Roberts. Tempe, AZ: Arizona Center for Medieval and Renaissance Texts and Studies, 1995.

—. *The Second Part of the Countess of Montgomery's Urania*. Ed. Josephine A. Roberts, Suzanne Gossett, and Janel Mueller. Tempe, AZ: Arizona Center for Medieval and Renaissance Texts and Studies, 1999.

Wynne-Davis, Marion. "The Queen's Masque: Renaissance Women and the Seventeenth-century Court Masque." *Gloriana's Face: Women, Public and Private, in the English Renaissance*. Ed. S. P. Cerasano and Marion Wynn-Davies. Detroit, MI: Wayne State UP, 1992. 63–78.

Yates, Frances A. *Astraea: The Imperial Theme in the Sixteenth Century*. London: Routledge & Kegan Paul, 1975.

The Sidneys and Literary Patronage

Lisa Celovsky

Following publication of his translation of Philip Melanchthon's *Prayers* in 1579, the scribe Richard Robinson noted that the volume was "Dedicated by mee to the Honorable vertuous and renowmed gent Mr. Philip Sydney Esq. who gave me for his booke 4 Angels, and his Honorable Father Sir Henry Sydney Knight gave mee for his boke x s [10 shillings]" (Vogt 632; Brennan, *Literary Patronage* 13–18; Woudhuysen, *Sir Philip Sidney* 195–203). This transaction exemplifies in its simplest form the patronage system that governed most kinds of literary production in the sixteenth and seventeenth centuries, with an author dedicating his work to a social superior in hopes of reward. As Robinson's complaints elsewhere in his accounts make clear, however, these hopes were often not fulfilled: gift exchanges can only imply obligation, not require it (Davis 3–14). That Henry and Philip Sidney responded generously to Robinson's offerings demonstrates how seriously they took their patronage responsibilities. Numerous other dedications and panegyrics reveal that the Sidneys, as well as their relatives the Dudleys and the Herberts, played prominent roles in the system of literary patronage. Philip Sidney, his uncle Robert Dudley, Earl of Leicester, and his nephew William Herbert, third Earl of Pembroke, were all honored by contemporaries as reincarnations of Maecenas, the famously generous patron of poetry in Augustan Rome (Rosenberg 203; Brennan, *Literary Patronage* 38, 150, 162). Philip received about forty dedications of printed and manuscript books, as well as numerous panegyric celebrations after his death (Williams, *Index*; Woudhuysen, *ODNB*; Brennan and Kinnamon, *Sidney Chronology*); Leicester was the dedicatee of over a hundred works (Rosenberg 355–62). The Herberts were celebrated by almost 250 writers, with Mary Sidney Herbert, Countess of Pembroke, earning more dedications than any other woman of her era, excluding only royalty and her cousin the Countess of Bedford, and her son William more than any other peer of his time (Williams, "Literary Patronesses" 366; Brennan, *Literary Patronage* xii). Henry Sidney, Robert Sidney, first Earl of Leicester, Robert Sidney, second Earl of Leicester, Philip Herbert, fourth Earl of Pembroke, and Lady Mary Wroth all received dedications, and even less prominent family members such as Mary Dudley Sidney, Barbara Gamage Sidney, Frances Walsingham Sidney, Elizabeth Sidney Manners, Dorothy Percy Sidney, and Katherine Sidney Mansell garnered tributes (Williams, *Index*; Brennan and Kinnamon, *Sidney Chronology*; see also Levin and Medici *ARC* 1:3, Ioppolo *ARC* 1:6, and Hannay *ARC* 1:8).

Yet "literary patronage" involved far more than rewards, dedications, or panegyrics, and the Sidneys, Dudleys, and Herberts participated in all of its broader manifestations. In an era without copyright and with relatively little income for writers from sales, a patron's interest provided clients with sustained protection and security. In return, writers offered patrons vehicles for enduring fame, the articulation of values and programs consistent with the patron's religious or political aims, and loyal service in roles potentially unrelated to literary production. The Herberts in particular not only dispensed one-time monetary rewards, but also provided employment within their household or through legal, administrative, and clerical appointments in the localities they oversaw in Wales and Wiltshire, as well as at Baynard's Castle in London (Illustrations 1 and 2). A writer might also value critical guidance provided by a patron, especially one possessing literary judgment. Furthermore, the Sidneys and their relatives sustained literary productivity by anchoring networks of writers and stationers, administering and honoring the missions of universities, helping to found libraries, and supporting theater companies and dramatic entertainments. Patronage systems could be complex and long-lasting, even inherited over generations—a particularly strong tradition in the Sidney-Herbert family (Brennan, *Literary Patronage* 12, 74–5). Literary patronage in this period is thus best imagined as a web of transmissions and mediated transactions among multiple stakeholders, rather than as a vertical line connecting socially prominent patron and starving artist.

Although the participation of the Sidneys, Dudleys, and Herberts in these more expansive aspects of the patronage system was consistent with that of their peers, familial involvement was in some respects atypical. While many patronage networks were wide-ranging, the literary and political legacies of Philip Sidney created especially sustained connections, influences, and obligations in the patronage relations established by family members. Moreover, some family members (in particular Philip, Mary Sidney Herbert, Mary Wroth, and William Herbert) experienced the patronage system from more than one perspective. As courtiers, they dispensed patronage; as literary artists in their own right, they pursued it with their own developing talents. Furthermore, they produced their own writing in a system of cross-fertilization wherein their literary tastes were attracted to and informed by the work of the writers they patronized. Family networks included a large number of writers who depended upon the patronage system and who are now recognized as fundamental to the development of English literature, among them Spenser, Jonson, Shakespeare, Donne, and Herbert, as well as figures such as Thomas Browne, George Chapman, Thomas Churchyard, William Browne, Samuel Daniel, Michael Drayton, John Ford, Philip Massinger, and Thomas Nashe. The Sidneys and their relatives both contributed to and were products of the evolution of the patronage system as defined in its widest senses from the mid-Tudor period to the civil wars.

Family Patronage in Context

Though we tend to think of the Sidneys primarily as writers of literature, and while some works dedicated to family members qualify as literary, most of what is termed the "literature of patronage" is not literary in our contemporary sense (Marotti, "John Donne" 207–8). Books dedicated to the Sidneys, Dudleys, and Herberts included examples not only of poetry and romance such as family members themselves wrote, but also of histories, handbooks, polemic, translations, treatises (scholarly and devotional), and works of exploration and scientific discovery. These books could be of general interest to nobles (on diplomacy, for example, or successful military strategy), or appeal to the specific interests of family members: antiquarian interests in Wales and Ireland, the championship of Protestant and anti-Spanish causes, and commercial ventures and exploration. That is, the writers the family patronized reveal as much about their lives as courtiers, public servants, and politicians as about their own work as artists. Family members engaged in patronage relationships with members of professions that could be serviceable to a noble family and that could serve mutually productive aims: with stationers, lawyers, clergymen and theologians, academics and propagandists, civil servants and secretaries, doctors and scientists, military experts, and explorers and adventurers.

The Sidneys and their relatives supported "letters" in this broad sense in three main ways. First, family members patronized not just individual writers, but also stationers and presses that produced numerous (non-Sidneian) works. Secondly, the family fostered scholarship in the universities, not only by supporting particular works of science or theology but also by nurturing scholarly exchange and influencing literary production in more indirect ways. Philip, for example, would become an influential figure among the scholar-authors of Oxford, which he attended, and Cambridge (Buxton 39–44; Stewart 52–67). As Chancellors of Oxford, both Robert Dudley and William Herbert placed followers there (including Continental Protestant refugees) whose presence informed the work of the scholarly community. Dudley authorized official establishment of the Oxford University Press; he also worked with Elizabeth to educate a cohort of appropriately trained and ideologically minded divines. Such men would go on to assume positions in the Church and teaching roles throughout the country, where they could advance Protestantism and inspire religious literary production (Rosenberg 102–3, 116–51; Brennan, *Literary Patronage* 160–67; Peacey 51–2). Herbert oversaw review of the university's statutes, creating revised regulations that remained in use for over three centuries and affected generations of writers from the institution. The Bodleian Library also benefited from family patronage, with major donations of books and manuscripts by Herbert and Robert Sidney, first Earl of Leicester (Brennan, *Literary Patronage* 162; Warkentin, Black, and Bowen 21). By these means, Sidneian patronage informed the production of letters well into and even beyond the seventeenth century.

Finally, the Sidneys and their relatives patronized dramatic performances, writers, and companies. Records show support of itinerant companies and players at holidays and at family residences: for example, Henry Sidney paid for Lord Sussex's Players at Ludlow Castle, and Robert Sidney's tutor made payments to Robin Hood performers on May Day and minstrels on Midsummer's Day (Brennan and Kinnamon, *Sidney Chronology* 28, 45). Family members also formally sponsored companies. Following the Act for the Punishment of Vagabonds (1572), theatrical players needed to prove that they nominally "belonged" to a noble household—a status that allowed a company to wear a nobleman's livery and thereby sanctioned their movements around the country. These companies included Leicester's Men, the company of James Burbage, and the Earl of Pembroke's Men, who had plays by Shakespeare in their repertoire (MacLean). Inherited familial interest may be discerned in the Herberts' support of Richard Burbage (son of James) until his death in 1619. Robert Dudley also protected the Children of the Chapel Royal and other children's companies. At the Stuart courts, the positions held by Robert Sidney as Lord Chamberlain to Queen Anne and William Herbert as Lord Chamberlain to King James made them responsible for court entertainments and pageantry, and thereby positioned them within the networks of writers, artisans, and companies who were employed to produce these events. The families also patronized the theater of their day by attending and performing in court entertainments and by their probable presence at the entertainments of the Inns of Court and elsewhere (Rosenberg 301–7; Wilson 151–6; Brennan, *Literary Patronage* 92–6, 176; Hannay, *Philip's Phoenix* 124–9; Hannay, *MSLW* 124–9, 216).

In all its various forms, both direct and indirect, the literary patronage system should be understood as an inseparable and constituent branch of the larger socio-political patronage system in which the Sidneys and Herberts participated at court and in their domains in Kent, Wales, and Ireland (Brennan, *Sidneys of Penshurst*). Patronage was the basis of advancement at court, where, like the hungry creatures of Sir Thomas Wyatt's lyric "They Flee from Me," courtiers were ever "busily seeking" the sustenance of political and social favor. Those at the apex of the courtly system received the allegiance of those seeking preferment, while those lower in the hierarchy earned honors, offices, and monopolies. In turn, successful courtiers circulated the fruits of these rewards within their own circles and home communities, where these same courtiers became recipients of gifts (sometimes literary) from those who had benefited or who hoped to benefit. In early modern England this system worked to bring regional patronage systems (political and literary) into the orbit of the centralized government, creating a web of interdependent networks motivated and fueled by related forms of patronage. Patronage was at once "symbiotic and symbolic," with ties developed through friends, kinship, and locality, and brokered through transactive agents as well as individual patrons and clients (Peck, *Court Patronage* 3; see also Rosenberg 6–12; Brennan, *Literary Patronage* 1–18; Marotti, "John Donne" 207–11).

The patronage system did evolve throughout the English Renaissance, and the story of this evolution is in many ways the story of the Sidneys, Herberts, and Dudleys themselves. In fact, critical history of literary patronage rests largely on studies of the family, its literary influence and development, and the evolving understanding of its patronage activities. Patronage under the early Tudors operated primarily through a "great house" system that Chaucer would have recognized, wherein leading aristocrats offered secure and long-term protection for writers. This system gradually eroded under Elizabeth and James: the explosive growth of printed texts, public theater, and the emergence of professional writers weakened the traditionally sustained and exclusive ties between writer and patron (Sheavyn, *Literary Profession* 8–38). Literary patronage consequently began to encompass the wider range of texts related to the many public roles played by courtier families, and extended to other activities and institutions whereby they could further religio-political or cultural agendas. In the later Elizabethan and Stuart eras the patronage system found new forms of expression as growing numbers of political and literary suitors sought to benefit from the trickle-down effect of increasingly limited resources (Peck, "Court Patronage" 41–6).

Critical focus has likewise shifted from Elizabeth's reign and theories of organized systems that operated mostly in top-down fashion (for example, Sheavyn, *Literary Profession*; Sheavyn, "Patrons") to the fluidly complex social, political, and cultural dynamics of the Stuart courts. Concomitantly, scholars have looked beyond a client's motivations for economic support and a patron's desire for fame to recognize a broader range of shared and competing socio-political incentives to participate in patronage transactions. Informed by New Historicism, recent scholarship has identified multiple stakeholders with powers and obligations to give and to receive, and has explored the processes of self-fashioning and self-display required of writers and courtiers in these environments (Gundersheimer; Jardine; Davis 37, 67, 75–80). Writer-courtiers like the Sidneys found themselves positioned not only as patrons but also as negotiating and sometimes spurned suitors—a role that Philip Sidney explores in *Lady of May* (Stewart 205–6) and couches in amatory sonnet language in *Astrophil and Stella* (Marotti, "'Love is Not Love'" 396–406). The patronage of drama, both public and private, has also been a subject of renewed study (Heinemann, *Puritanism*; White and Westfall; Somerset), while the development of feminist approaches has revealed the agency and influence of women as suitors and patrons. Finally, the emerging field of "history of the book" has helped to illuminate literary production and dissemination (in manuscript as well as print), the material conditions of textual production and circulation, and the social functions of "paratext" such as dedications and forewords. In general, the flourishing of literary patronage coincides with the growth of family participation in the system, and it can be difficult to distinguish the extent to which their participation depended upon patronage trends and conventions, upon inherited cultural and political obligations, or upon the literary and political agendas of individual family members.

The First Generation: Robert Dudley, Henry Sidney, and Henry Herbert

An "exemplification of the Elizabethan system of patronage" (Rosenberg xvi), Robert Dudley, Earl of Leicester, serves as a touchstone for the patronage activities of his generational peers Henry Herbert, second Earl of Pembroke, and Sir Henry Sidney (Illustration 5). This generation of patrons operated within a relatively established system wherein writers approached patrons, and patrons accepted dedications and thereby guaranteed license for publication and protection from censure and critics: title pages sometimes signify Leicester's endorsement by including his device, the bear with ragged staff. Some of these patronage relationships reflected traditional aristocratic support for the arts, as writers returned the favor of support by helping sustain the fame of the nobility. Others operated within a newer system that developed under the early Tudors to exploit the emerging medium of print: administrators such as Thomas Cromwell realized that selective support for the numerous religious, antiquarian, political, and scientific works coming off the presses could be used to advance and endorse religio-political programs. These co-existing approaches explain both the kinds of texts that Leicester and his peers patronized and their motives for doing so: these men functioned within an inherited system of *noblesse oblige* to protect their followers and to promote learning; they also operated as agents to bolster Elizabeth's power and initiatives as well as to promote their own educational, political, and religious interests (Rosenberg 3–18, 25–58, 186–7; Brennan, *Literary Patronage* 9–10, 32–7).

In addition to theater companies, Leicester's clients included "the translators Blundeville and Golding, the historians Grafton, Stow, Campion, and Holinshed, the teachers Mulcaster and Florio, and in belles-lettres the writers Gascoigne, Whitney, Greene, Harvey, and Spenser" (Rosenberg xiii). He employed Spenser as a secretary in his household in the 1570s, and debate continues on the extent to which Spenser's poetry offers veiled critique of his patron (for Leicester's secret marriage, for example, or his lack of political and military success in the Netherlands) (Greenlaw; Rosenberg 336–48; Hadfield 128–31, 275–80, 320). Some works Leicester sponsored spoke to the obligations and duties of nobility to behave appropriately (with piety in the "right" religion, for example) and to understand subjects such as warfare or diplomacy (Brennan, *Literary Patronage* 31–2). Others, such as histories with their stories of tyrants and rebellions, addressed both those in power and the wider population by providing moral exempla and reminding each group of its obligations to the other and the commonwealth (Rosenberg 60). Many of the works Leicester and his peers patronized provided expert opinions on useful subjects: law, medicine, martial skills and strategies, rhetoric, navigation, mathematics, and medicine (Wilson 162–8). Moreover, Leicester protected many translators and compilers who served humanist aims of recovering the classics and making them available in the vernacular. While such works helped develop a corps of skilled linguists and offered patrons proof of clients' suitability for secretarial or diplomatic commissions, they also offered mutually constitutive support for educational and nationalist ideals. In a related trend, Leicester, Henry Sidney, and Henry Herbert promoted antiquarian works such as regional histories, geographies, and lexicographical works that explored national origins, created cultural identity, offered explanations and solutions from the past for problems of the present, and supported the regions these men protected (Rosenberg 59–115; Oakley-Brown 49–52; Peck, "Court Patronage" 35; Schwyzer).

Civil love and duty could be local as well as national, and patrons linked to both spheres of influence connected provincial areas to a national "English" center (Peck, "Court Patronage" 27–31). The cultural and geographic character of Wales and Ireland attracted the particular interest of Henry Sidney, Henry Herbert, and his father William Herbert. The Herberts patronized Griffith Roberts's Welsh grammar, and John Gwynne, "Surveyor of

North Wales, and servant to the right honourable Earl of Pembroke," presented a historical and topographical study of Wales to William Cecil in the 1560s (Brennan, *Literary Patronage* 98–100). Henry Sidney's tastes also ran to geography and cartography. He was the dedicatee of the first surviving map by an English cartographer printed in England, Anthony Jenkinson's map of Russia. As Lord President of the Council of the Marches of Wales, Henry encouraged Christopher Saxton to publish his maps of Wales (1597) and arranged for his chaplain, David Powel, to revise an English translation by Humphrey Llwyd of an important medieval Welsh chronicle. Published as *The History of Cambria* (1584) and dedicated to Philip Sidney, this book would remain the standard history of medieval Wales for the next three centuries. As Lord Governor of Ireland, Henry undertook the preservation, collation, and publication of historical and legal records, initiated John Gough's survey of Ireland, and sponsored Robert Lythe's surveys of 1567–70 (Andrews; *Philip's Phoenix* 27; Herron and Maley 14–15). He was praised by Edmund Campion in his *History of Ireland* (written in 1570) and earned the dedication of the Irish section of the 1577 edition of Holinshed's *Chronicles*. The text and woodcuts of John Derrick's *Image of Irelande* (1581), dedicated to Philip Sidney, celebrate Henry's military prowess and just rule (Moroney). A special issue of the *Sidney Journal* (29.1–2, 2011) illuminates these activities by showing how Henry earned his reputation as a patron, and how he and his clients fashioned memorials (textual and otherwise) that represented him as a fatherly savior-reformer and connected his literary interests to his governing agendas in Wales and Ireland. Did Henry's antiquarian and patronage initiatives associate him more with traditional colonialist ideologies or with radical change? The collection does not settle the debate, but does demonstrate how, for example, Henry functioned in networks that included individuals who supported both views and attracted both Protestant and Catholic clients. Seen through this new lens, Ireland was a gateway to globalism and world ventures, with Henry as the apex patron. He operated at its center yet also figured boundary-crossing: not only between Ireland and its English communities and among England, Wales, and Ireland, but also extending these connections to the Continent and beyond, to Antarctica and China, through sponsorship of texts of cartography and discovery (Kuin 549–54; Kuin and Prescott 11–12; Herron and Maley 3–17).

Finally, an important strain of the patronage activities of this first generation was religion. The stage for Leicester's activities in this area was set by the first dedication he received: John Aylmer's response (1559) to John Knox's attack (1558) on female rulers. As he developed as a leader, first of Reformed religion in England and later of pan-Protestant causes in the Low Countries and throughout Europe, Leicester sponsored writers—or was solicited as a potentially sympathetic sponsor by writers—of sermons, devotional commentaries, polemical tracts, and anti-Catholic propaganda. Leicester's brother, Ambrose, Earl of Warwick, and his wife, Anne Russell, a much beloved and supportive kinswoman to the Sidneys (*Sidneys of Penshurst* 44, 109), likewise sustained Puritan divines and Protestant devotional works (Adams, *ODNB*). Henry Herbert was also an active patron of religious writers and texts, especially in Wales, where he operated as President of the Council charged with ensuring uniformity in the Welsh Church and guarding against recusancy (Brennan, *Literary Patronage* 88). Even in the early Tudor reigns, the Herberts had a strong tradition of supporting the Church, as the first earl negotiated the line between Protestant and Catholic in his patronage activities (Brennan, *Literary Patronage* 28–38). Following the Reformation, patronage was funded more by lay sources than ecclesiastical ones, leading to more messages (in paratextual materials, dedications, and elsewhere) praising nobles who excelled in their religious duties (such as the Dudleys and Herberts) and blaming those who allowed corruption to creep into the system by issuing patronage for personal gain rather than for advancement of Protestant causes (Lytle 72–3). Such criticism is evident, for example, in criticism of the Welsh Church and patronage networks by Gervase Babington, the Herbert family chaplain who was associated with Henry and Mary Sidney Herbert's networks at Wilton and who was granted the livings of several parishes in Wiltshire and eventually the bishoprics of Llandaff, Exeter, and Worcester (Brennan, *Literary Patronage* 88–91; *Philip's Phoenix* 132–5). Thus the activities of family forebears laid a foundation for literary patronage that would be inherited and sustained by future generations of Sidneys and Herberts.

Philip Sidney

Philip Sidney understood his inherited responsibilities to patronize literature and became an unusually active linchpin of patronage networks during his relatively short life. Though lacking the means or status to bestow much patronage in conventional ways (such as employment), Philip more than made up for that limitation by offering clients the benefit of his artistic taste and the chance to become part of the networks associated with his literary and political interests (Illustration 7). In addition, even as a quite young man Philip was widely perceived as a figure of great expectations. Scholars and stationers, particularly on the Continent, hastened to attach themselves to his rising star, and when Sidney believed in the intellectual importance of a proposed project, he emulated his patron forebears as best he could: "write me your estimate of the cost of publishing them," he informs Joachim and Philip Camerarius in 1578, referring to their father's commentaries on Aristotle's *Politics* and *Ethics*, "I should gladly contribute to the expenses" (*Correspondence SPS* 2:837–8). Unusually, Philip's patronage activities continued and even increased after his death, as Leicester and other relatives became surrogate recipients for posthumous dedications and tributes to a figure celebrated as literature's most devoted patron and Protestantism's great hero. Philip became regarded as an exemplary patron of scholarship, politics, and arts. According to Fulke Greville, "The universities abroad and at home accounted him a general Maecenas of learning, dedicated their books to him, and communicated every invention or improvement of knowledge with him":

> his heart and capacity were so large that there was not a cunning painter, a skilful engineer, an excellent musician or any other artificer of extraordinary fame that made not himself known to this famous spirit and found him his true friend without hire, and the common rendezvous of worth in his time.
> (Greville 21)

Sidney's activities as a patron have been detailed comprehensively (Van Dorsten; Buxton; Osborn; Woudhuysen, *Sir Philip Sidney*; Stewart). That some of these studies focus as much on Renaissance literary and book history as on Philip himself points to the extent to which Philip's own reading and writing arose from and influenced the mechanisms and systems for creating and disseminating "English literature."

Philip's reputation as a patron of learning began early in his career, as he became acquainted with a wide range of men of letters during his university studies and travels abroad. He drew praise from such English and Continental intellectuals as Giordano Bruno, Justus Lipsius, Petrus Ramus, William Camden, Lambert Daneau, Janus Dousa (the Elder and the Younger), Domenicus Baudius, Alberto Gentili, Pieto Bizari, and Paulus Melissus, who described Philip as "renowned for [his] study of the Muses" after his visit to Heidelberg in 1577; Philip was twenty-three at the time (Van Dorsten 50; Buxton 33–94; Stewart, 139–40, 246–7, 254). In 1573 Philip met Hubert Languet (Illustration 8), who would make introductions

267

and mentor his reading and studies for years to come; Philip also established contact with scholar-printers such as Andreas Wechel and Henri Estienne, who presented Sidney with a manuscript volume of Greek maxims "in anticipation of later dedications of scholarly productions from his own press" (Van Dorsten 30). These connections often led to later patronage activities or helped spur the formation of patronage networks. The dedication of a Latin life of Ramus published in Frankfurt in 1576 resulted in other dedications to Sidney of Ramist works in English, for example, and Philip's sponsorship of the schoolboy Abraham Fraunce encouraged Fraunce to place himself later at the service of Mary Sidney Herbert (Buxton 146–8; Brennan, *Literary Patronage* 75). From the 1560s and into the 1580s Leiden and its university were a Continental locus of the patronage activities of Philip and his uncle Leicester; their networks included Daniel Rogers, Jean Hotman, George Gilpin, Baudius, the Dousas, and Lipsius (whom Philip invited to England and undertook to provide for in the event of his death), as well as the English writers Geoffrey Whitney, who dedicated to Sidney *A Choice of Emblemes*, the first emblem book in English, and George Whetstone, whose *Honorable Reputation of a Soldier* (1585) was translated into Dutch in 1586 with accompanying English, Dutch, and Latin verse that reflected these networks (Van Dorsten). While early studies focused on Philip's literary "taste" and his role in developing English literature (Sheavyn, "Patrons" 306, 334–5; Buxton 2), more recent scholarship has built on work by Van Dorsten to explore Sidney's Continental connections and their mutually constitutive influences, expanding his artistic interests to include patronage of Protestant and humanist political philosophy and the cultivation of chivalric competency in such subjects as history, logic, or law (Skretkowicz, "Sidney's *Defence*"; Kuin and Prescott; Stewart; Stillman). The recent publication of Sidney's *Correspondence* establishes a foundation for further work on these Continental contexts for his patronage activities.

While early praise of Philip was offered more "as tokens of friendship and in admiration of his youthful promise rather than in recognition of" actual status as a writer or viable patron (Brennan, *Literary Patronage* 50), by the time of his death in 1586 Philip had become regarded as the primary patron of the "new poetry" in England (Buxton 102–12, 173–204; Brennan, *Literary Patronage* 55–63). The term "new poetry" originates in Spenser's *Shepheardes Calender* (1579) with its dedication to Philip. With the *Calender* and subsequent *Familiar Letters* (1580), Spenser and Gabriel Harvey secured Sidney's public reputation as a man of letters. The *Letters* positioned Philip at the center of the "Areopagus," a group of literati interested in experimenting with English versification and nurturing vernacular literature. Scholars continue to debate the extent to which this Areopagus existed as an informal academy, with Philip at the center before his death and his sister Mary posthumously sustaining it. Had Sidney even met Spenser and Harvey by this point? The question arises because the Spenser–Harvey correspondence is in many ways a sophisticated (and self-promoting) literary game. But even as scholars have become more circumspect about reading published praise as evidence of actual relationships, they have compiled greater evidence for the existence of networks that would have linked Sidney to Spenser and Harvey through mutual associations with Edward Dyer, Richard Mulcaster, the Dousas, Daniel Rogers, and Ludowick Bryskett. These linkages have encouraged Spenser's most recent biographer, Andrew Hadfield, to suggest that, even if Spenser and Harvey were exaggerating the degree of their acquaintance with Sidney, a "casual symposium" may indeed have existed (Hadfield 37–8, 63, 106–8, 179). However active this Areopagus was, Sidney's role in the campaign for vernacular literature prompted numerous tributes that extolled Sidney as an exemplary scholar who knew at first hand the struggles necessary to achieve perfection and who gave every deserving writer and text its deserved rewards (Brennan, *Literary Patronage* 53).

Sidney's reputation as a patron also grew after his death. Writers mourned his passing and praised his generosity in four collections of memorial verse as well as in numerous separately published laments. Many of these posthumous tributes celebrated Sidney for his liberality, discerning taste, and critical eye, as well as for the inspiration provided by his own writing. Some adopted the dedicatory forms and rhetoric that clients might use to appeal to a living patron, while others came in the form of imitations of the patron's work (Buxton 173–7; Brennan, *Literary Patronage* 51–4; Alexander 56–75). These tributes raise the question of what a deceased person can offer in a system of cultural exchange and implicit obligation. If the early praise Sidney had received outstripped his abilities to dispense much actual patronage, these posthumous tributes celebrated a patron now incapable of bestowing any rewards at all. Some incentivize their audience to live up to religio-political ideals Sidney had exemplified or the literary causes he had championed; others effect transfers of their writers' connections to Philip to other potential patrons (such as the Earl of Essex) by depicting them as Sidney's heirs (Norbrook 195–234; Brennan, *Literary Patronage* 83–7). Well into the Stuart era Sidney would be invoked as a model to emulate, a figure who could authorize literary and political projects and create textual community (Brennan, *Literary Patronage* 115–18, 132–43; Marotti, "Patronage" 37–44; Alexander). His memory could also serve as an ever-contemporary warning. Published decades after Sidney's death, Fulke Greville's *Dedication* (1633), for example, not only protected his friend and patron's reputation, but also offered critical commentary on the mistrustful present: communicating with the idealized dead was safer than negotiating with unreliable patrons in the dangerous present (Skretkowicz, "Greville").

Philip's Siblings: Robert Sidney and Mary Sidney Herbert

In a patronage system dependent on inherited obligations and networks, an obvious candidate to continue family legacies after Philip Sidney's untimely death was his brother Robert, himself a poet and musician (Alexander 151–65). On a par with peers of his rank, Robert did achieve a modest level of success as a patron (Hay 206–8; Brennan, "Sir Robert Sidney"). Continental and English writers urged him to take up Philip's mantle, and he received tributes from Jonson, Domenicus Baudius, Joshua Sylvester, Abraham Fraunce, Francis Quarles, John Davies of Hereford, and George Wither, among others. In the early 1600s he sustained the family tradition of patronizing court drama in his role as Queen Anne's Lord Chamberlain, with the responsibility of overseeing court entertainments. But Robert's limited finances and extended service abroad curtailed his patronage options (Brennan, *Literary Patronage* 152), and Flushing, where Robert was posted in the 1590s, lacked Leiden's university community, literary activity, and complex patronage networks (Van Elk 6–7). Instead, it was his sister Mary (followed by her son William) who emerged as the focal point of Sidney family patronage in the later Tudor and early Stuart periods.

While Mary Sidney Herbert's patronage had long attracted attention (Young 150–204; Hogrefe 124–33), she became the subject of more intense study after 1977, when Joan Kelly posed her seminal question, "Did Women Have a Renaissance?" This query inspired scholars to look to evidence that demonstrated women's agency as critical readers, patrons, and artistic suitors in their own rights: to correspondence, accounts, and paratextual and material evidence from books and manuscripts (see especially Bergeron, "Women" 285–7; *Philip's Phoenix*; Lamb, *Gender and Authorship*). This research revealed the gender biases of earlier criticism (Lamb, *Gender and Authorship* 68–71). At the same time it clarified the constraints under which aristocratic women operated: even as Mary Sidney earned status as celebrated reader-patron, for example, her suitors constructed "a subject-position for the countess that safely circumscribes her worldly influence" by positing yet higher male authorities, characterizing her as lacking ambition, or placing her in a geographically alternative space where her power is contained (Lamb, *Gender and Authorship* 22, 28–71). Nonetheless, while as a writer Mary may have been limited by contemporary ideas of the genres deemed appropriate for feminine authorship, such as letters, private devotions, and translations (Hannay, "Introduction"; Lamb, *Gender and Authorship* 3–19), as a patron she paralleled her male counterparts in her influence on English letters. In doing so, she took every advantage her position offered to develop her own talents, fashion her own authorial persona, and promote her own literary and religio-political aims.

A union of Herbert status and finances with Sidneian taste and talent, Mary's marriage to Henry Herbert created the conditions for her extraordinary patronage activities until her husband's illnesses in the 1590s and death in 1601 reduced (but did not fully end) her influence. The Herberts' writer clients included those who served in their household, such as Thomas Moffett (as physician) and Samuel Daniel (as tutor), or who received offices and commissions within Henry's gift, such as Gervase Babington (as clergyman) or Abraham Fraunce (as lawyer). As an aristocratic patron, Mary resembled other culturally powerful women of her time: queens such as Catherine Parr, who had encouraged religious writing, Elizabeth, who inspired praise and mythologizing, and Anne and Henrietta Maria, who both promoted drama (Brennan, *Literary Patronage* 8). Nicholas Breton, who dedicated five books to Mary Sidney, described Wilton as a "kind of little court" (Brennan, *Literary Patronage* 72), and there is a troubadour-like quality to many of the compliments Mary received, with some intended to curry favor with her husband (*Philip's Phoenix* 106–7). Writers compared her to the Muses and the Graces, endowed her with Minerva's wit, praised her beauty and piety, and identified her poetically as Mira, Meridianis, Cynthia, Urania, Amaryllis, and perhaps as Delia, the anagrammatic "ideal" woman of Daniel's sonnets (Brennan, *Literary Patronage* 82; *Philip's Phoenix* 116–19). She was particularly associated with the marigold—an allusion both to her famously blonde hair and the potential "golden" gifts she could dispense (Illustrations 9 and 10).

But writers also praised Mary Sidney's studiousness, her own literary gifts, and her ability to guide and critically shape the work of other poets. Samuel Daniel called her estate Wilton his "best school"; other contemporaries described the intellectual circle Mary created there as functioning "like a College" or "little university," with Mary herself "the greatest patroness of wit and learning" (Brennan, *Literary Patronage* 72). These tributes move beyond flattery, and recent work on Mary Sidney has recuperated her mentorship of writers, and considered how her influence on their work reflects programmatic intentions akin to Philip's support of the "new poetry." An Areopagus led by the patron-practitioner Philip may or may not have existed; a Wilton circle led by the patron-practitioner Mary at least to some extent did, though scholars have become circumspect about whether Mary knew personally all writers who claimed her attention or rewarded all suitors who appealed to her (Lamb, "Myth"; Lamb, "Countess"; Brennan, *Literary Patronage* 78–82; Steggle). Mary provided inspiration and support—two features common to patronage—but also relied on perspectives developed through her own writing to critique formal elements, choices of genre, and literary framing in the work of others (*Philip's Phoenix* 109, 116–19). Daniel, for example, recalls in his dedication to *Cleopatra* (1611) that Mary had encouraged him to leave "humble song" and sing more ambitiously "of state and tragicke notes." Her translation of Marc Garnier's *Tragedie of Antonie* (1595), he explains, inspired him to write of Cleopatra and then of the English Civil Wars (Daniel E3r–v; see also Rees 43–61). Recent scholarship has also challenged perceptions of Mary as the blue-stockinged leader of a group of "shy recluses" who lacked creative talent and campaigned against the emerging English dramatic tradition exemplified by Shakespeare in favor of a failed Senecan alternative (Young 203; Eliot 77–9; Lamb, *Gender and Authorship* 250–51n66). Instead, what Mary and her client

Daniel championed was not a literary dead end, but a viable form of Continental drama that deployed historical tragedy to explore ideas of liberty and to engage in political commentary, not unlike Shakespeare's own political plays (*Philip's Phoenix* 119–26, 129).

The writer whose career most benefited from Mary's patronage could be said to be her brother Philip. Wilton provided a nurturing environment where Philip was able to develop as a writer and where sibling interest in English letters and foreign romance helped shape his works (*Philip's Phoenix* 48–70). Philip dedicated the *Old Arcadia* to Mary with the claim that he wrote because she "desired [him] to do it," and he describes how he had sent the countess his drafts "as fast as they were done" (*Old Arcadia* 3). Recent criticism informed by reader-response theory draws on this dedication and narratorial addresses within the text to recognize the roles Mary and her household played in Philip's textual production, and to explore the gendered dynamics these moments create between writer and audience (Lamb, *Gender and Authorship* 72–89; Crawford; Simpson-Younger).

Mary also supported Philip's literary career after his death, promoting her brother's reputation by editing his work and fashioning herself as his literary heir (*Philip's Phoenix* 59–105). Mary oversaw the publication of what would become the authorized *Arcadia* (1593), superseding the version published by Greville and Frances Walsingham in 1590. The implications of her intervention have been debated: what was initially read as an act of censorship or textual distortion has come to be regarded as a textually "conservative" preservation of Sidney's own work and the establishment of consistent plot (*Philip's Phoenix* 69–76). She also revised and completed her brother's translation of the Psalms. More generally, Mary actively shaped her persona as chief mourner and heir to Philip even as she preserved her own legacy as a writer, editor, and patron (*Philip's Phoenix* 83, 111–12, 193, 206–7; Sagaser; Alexander 76–127). The relationship she established with *Arcadia*'s publisher William Ponsonby, for example, linked her to writers such as Spenser, and influenced her commitment to disseminate her own writing through print publication (Brennan, *Literary Patronage* 56–8; Brennan, "Proposed Visit"). Spenser's *Complaints* (1591) has been considered as unified by references to actual or potential patrons in the Sidney family, and his dedication of *Ruines of Time* to Mary may have invited her collaboration in his "Astrophel" and the poem that succeeds it, the "Doleful Lay of Clorinda"; Mary may even have written the "Lay" (MSH, *Collected Works* 1:119–32; see Hannay ARC 1:5 and Bond ARC 2:4). Her dedicatory poem "To the Angell Spirit of the Most Excellent Sir Philip Sidney," which she wrote to preface their collaborative translation of the Psalms, claims inspiration from Philip yet simultaneously develops her own literary authority: even as she claims an artless wish to die, she displays her technical virtuosity and readies her work for publication (Fisken; Lamb, *Gender and Authorship* 116–18).

Led by Spenser, Mary's literary network flourished after her brother's death, as clients who sought to attach themselves to Philip promoted Mary as a living link to the values he had come to represent (Brennan, *Literary Patronage* 60–64, 158). But Mary was not a passive recipient of those attentions: she herself established many of the terms of this sibling filiation, and exploited the resulting connections to cross-fertilize her own projects and advance her literary and religio-political aims. For example, she assumed the writerly role of suitor and explored the opportunities such a role offered. Mary was inspired to prepare a pastoral dialogue for a potential royal visit in 1599 in the tradition of Philip's *Lady of May* or her uncle Leicester's Kenilworth entertainments. As patron, she commissioned presentation copies of the dialogue and of the Sidney Psalms for the queen (*Philip's Phoenix* 164–6; Brennan, "Proposed Visit"). As client appealing to her own royal patron, Mary relies on skilled paratextual rhetoric, not just to flatter, but also to remind the queen of her obligation to reciprocate Mary's gift, in this case by supporting a neglected Protestant alliance (Brennan, *Literary Patronage* 96; *Philip's Phoenix* 85–92). If Mary could not follow her male forebears by upholding the Protestant cause on the battlefield or through political council, she could do so through her choices as client and as patron.

William Herbert and Family Patronage in the Seventeenth Century

Mary Sidney's sons William, the third Earl of Pembroke, and Philip, the fourth earl—the "Incomparable Paire of Brethren" to whom Shakespeare's first folio (1623) was dedicated—actively perpetuated the family tradition of patronage, with William in particular performing his inherited aristocratic obligations in accordance with his own artistic tastes and talents (Illustrations 20, 21, and 22). William was associated with some of the major literary figures of his day in addition to Shakespeare, including Jonson, George Herbert (a kinsman), and John Donne, as well as a wide range of writers in a variety of fields. Earlier dedications invited William to follow examples set by his father and grandfather, urging the young heir to live up to the standards of behavior and generosity they had set. Some recognized the necessity of cultivating new alliances, such as those with the Cecils; others looked to the Herbert brothers to maintain the literary and religio-political programs associated with their uncle Philip Sidney in a new or renewed Golden Age. As the Herberts rose at court, they received dedications inspired not only by their financial, literary, and political inheritances, but also by their own demonstrations of competent courtiership. William's appointment as Lord Chamberlain in 1615 put many offices and services in his gift, and his appointment as Chancellor of Oxford in 1617 further increased his influence with scholars, writers, and the production of texts; he likewise received dedications to devotional works and sermons through his position as supervisor of the royal chapel. Furthermore, as Michael Brennan's work with manuscript evidence has revealed, William's patronage activities were not restricted to London and the court, but extended to kinsmen and supporters in Wales and elsewhere in the provinces (Taylor, "Third Earl"; Buxton 240–49; Brennan, *Literary Patronage* 99–100, 107–11, 118–24, 129–84; *Philip's Phoenix* 185).

Unsurprisingly, William Herbert's relationships to Shakespeare and Jonson have attracted sustained critical interest and speculation. Was William the mysterious "Mr. W. H." addressed in the stationer Thomas Thorpe's preface to Shakespeare's sonnets (1609), or even the sonnets' addressee, a beautiful young man reluctant to marry? Since proposed in the 1830s, these theories have endured, though insufficient evidence survives to prove or disprove either possibility (Brennan, *Literary Patronage* 141–2; Burrow 100–103; Dutton 122, 131–3). As Lord Chamberlain, William did oversee court entertainments and supervised the King's Men, Shakespeare's company, working closely with his kinsman Henry Herbert, Master of the Revels. While the extent of his personal connections with Shakespeare remains opaque, William's broader support of drama likely played a role in the decision to dedicate Shakespeare's works to him. The association of Ben Jonson with the Herbert and Sidney families is much better documented (Alexander 143–7). William was one of Jonson's primary patrons, the "great example of honour and virtue" (*Epigrams*, Dedication; cf. *Catiline*, Dedication) to whom Jonson dedicated *Catiline* (1611) and *Epigrams* (1616) and celebrated in Epigram #102 (Evans 107–18). As the leading producer of court entertainments, Jonson would have worked closely with Robert Sidney and with William through their positions as Lord Chamberlain (Taylor, "Masque"). Robert Sidney likely employed Jonson as a tutor in 1611, around the time he wrote "To Penshurst" and other poems addressed to family members (Brennan and Kinnamon, "Robert Sidney"), including Elizabeth Sidney Manners, Countess of Rutland, Mary Wroth, Robert Wroth, and Robert Sidney's daughter

Philippa and son William. Jonson also dedicated *The Alchemist* (1612) to Mary Wroth. The poems to Mary Wroth and Elizabeth Sidney indicate that Jonson had read their poetry in manuscript, and other evidence suggests that he read Robert Sidney's manuscript poetry as well (Alexander 189): these manuscript exchanges suggest an unusual level of personal familiarity and trust. The extent to which Jonson idealizes his patrons in these poems or supports their politics has been debated. *The Forest*, which contains "To Penshurst" as well as the poems on Elizabeth Sidney, Robert Wroth, and William Sidney, has recently been read as a collection that both celebrates and offers subtle critical assessment of the family's status and success (Norbrook 183–94; Evans 118–29; Celovsky).

When the Herberts' power to bestow commissions grew, their desirability as patrons increased (Brennan, *Literary Patronage* 122–32). Although William became a focus of complaints about corruption in the patronage system by writers such as Philip Massinger and John Taylor, he was also praised for setting virtuous standards by others, including John Davies, John Fletcher, George Wither, Joshua Sylvester, and William Browne, in addition to Jonson (Brennan, *Literary Patronage* 124, 143–5). William earned his status as a literary patron, especially negotiating publication rights and issues with stationers, and protecting the intellectual property and budgetary interests of dramatic companies: as Lord Chamberlain, for example, he guarded the rights of the King's Men, working to prohibit illegal performances of their plays in the provinces (Brennan, *Literary Patronage* 139–43, 176; Bergeron, "King's Men"). But he was also capable of more personal gestures, such as awarding Jonson £20 annually to buy books (Donaldson 268). As with their forebears, William's and Philip's patronage was intertwined with their politics. Many dedications that claimed their sympathetic protection introduced texts with pro-Protestant and anti-Spanish agendas. After the death of the hawkishly Protestant Prince Henry in 1612, several suitors sought attention from the Herberts and Robert Sidney instead, even redirecting work originally intended for the prince (Brennan, *Literary Patronage* 117–18, 121–8, 132–3, 181–3). William's patronage of drama was likewise informed by his politics. When Jonson disparaged corruption and failed government through *Catiline*, for example, he included a dedication to William, and William may have used his influence to shield those who performed Thomas Middleton's anti-Spanish *Game of Chess* in 1624 (Heinemann, *Puritanism* 21, 23, 43, 107–13, 146–50, 165–9, 209, 214–21, 266–82; Norbrook 220–21; Brennan, *Literary Patronage* 175; *Philip's Phoenix* 126; Heinemann, "Rebel Lords" 143–50).

While William's patronage clearly intersected with his politics, recent work emphasizes that his dramatic patronage at least also depended on festive, emotional, and aesthetic pleasures (Barroll, especially 119). But the cross-fertilization of his patronage with his own literary talents has not yet received the level of attention earned by similar intersections in the work of his uncle Philip or mother Mary. William's artistic development was undoubtedly informed by his patronage networks and in dialogue with work by his writer clients. Does his poetry share themes, tropes, or formal concerns with that of his friends and clients? What might sustained readings of William's work reveal about when, where, and how his own tastes and practices emerged and evolved? Work in progress on William's poetry by Mary Ellen Lamb will open up these and related questions, hitherto relatively unexplored.

New Directions

Recent scholarship on early modern patronage stresses the system's complex and contingent processes and mediating links, as well as the permeability of boundaries among the political, artistic, social, and religious (Westfall; H. Smith 54, 85–6). How this evolving critical understanding might apply to new investigations of Sidney family patronage may be illustrated by the understudied career of William's brother Philip, fourth Earl of Pembroke. Contemporary writers looked to Philip as heir to William's patronage obligations. Said by John Aubrey to have "inherited not the witt" of his mother Mary or uncle Philip Sidney (1:112), Philip Herbert was not a man of letters; while he left behind a respectable record of patronage, it proved no match for the standards established by his more literary relations. However, Philip did enthusiastically support painting and architecture (Brennan, *Literary Patronage* 184–7, 193–206; *MSLW* 278n29). While it has long been critically conventional to separate literary arts from visual or musical ones, scholars have recently been paying increased attention to the intersections among these forms. How might a patron's promotion of the visual arts, for example, relate to his or her processes, networks, and aims as a literary patron? Henry Sidney's wide-ranging patronage models one direction for further studies: different forms (printed texts, architectural structures and monuments, illustrations, and other visual representations) may nonetheless contribute to similar programmatic aims and cultural projects (Herron and Maley; Kinsella; Moroney; see Goldring *ARC* 1:20 and Larson *ARC* 1:21). More broadly, work on multi-media court masques likewise offers approaches to studying connections among art forms and the competitions, disconnections, and collaborations among clients, patrons, and other stakeholders, such as craftsmen or performers.

The participation of Philip and his brother William in masques and other court rituals and entertainments points to a second area ripe for further study. Like their male relations (especially Robert Dudley, Philip Sidney, and Robert Sidney), the Herberts were especially active participants in tournaments, New Year's Gift presentations, funeral processions, and ceremonies associated with the Order of the Garter and Inns of Court (Taylor, "Masque" 45–53; Brennan, *Literary Patronage* 108–11; *Sidneys of Penshurst* 115–16, 119, 122, 126). These public displays required the creation of "texts" such as songs, challenges, speeches and dialogues, impresa shields, blazons, sets, costumes, and other decorative arts, thus positioning their aristocratic participants as both suitors to the royal audience and patrons of those who helped them in their performance of chivalric competence. When appealing to his patron James at the king's first New Year celebration in 1604, for example, did William present an impresa and sonnet of his own creation, or did he employ a reliable client such as Daniel? Or did they collaborate—and if so, how? Who wrote the challenges and dramatic interludes or designed the sets for *The Challenge of the Fair Island*, a tournament the Herbert brothers helped to organize for the 1604 entertainment of Christian IV of Denmark? Recent scholarship on the Kenilworth entertainments exemplifies the potential to learn more about these more ephemeral cultural forms: not only did Leicester collaborate with his suitor Gascoigne, but the festivities they organized intersected with the earl's related patronage networks, including stationers and the world of London trade (Goldring, "'A mercer'"; Goldring, "Gascoigne").

Finally, though Philip was not so prominent a patron as his brother, he did earn several tributes attached to works in the romance tradition—a distinction that points to a third promising area for further inquiry: the presence of the family's women in patronage networks. While these dedications may be partly attributed to Philip's chivalric prowess, they are undoubtedly also related to the interests of the women in his life: his queen, Henrietta Maria (Brennan, *Literary Patronage* 157, 187), his cousin, Mary Wroth, his first wife, Susan de Vere, and his second wife, the diarist Anne Clifford. Mary Sidney has long been recognized for her patronage, and Wroth has attracted more recent attention, especially for her artistically cross-fertilizing and political connections with Ben Jonson as well as with writers such as George Wither and George Chapman (Roberts, "Life of Lady Mary Wroth" 14–22; Lamb, *Gender and Authorship* 154–6; Brennan, "A SYDNEY"; Brennan, "Creating";

R. Smith 417–31; Salzman 85–6; *MSLW* 152–9). The roles of other family women in patronage networks, however, have only recently begun to attract attention.

The relatively small numbers of dedications earned by family women and their relative invisibility in patronage networks is no longer read, as it once was for Elizabeth Sidney Manners (Sheavyn, "Patrons" 308), as reflecting inferior tastes or skill. These women appear in Aemilia Lanyer's rewriting of patronage networks in idealized "female terms" (Lewalski 72). Susan de Vere was the patron-audience of *Urania*, a lover of romance, and a recipient of a manuscript sermon by Donne (Roberts, "Critical Introduction" xviii–xix; Lamb, *Gender and Authorship* 22; Brennan and Kinnamon, *Sidney Chronology* 296). Elizabeth Sidney had connections with Jonson; Donne was "shared" by William Herbert and his kinswoman Lucy Russell, Countess of Bedford (Brennan, *Literary Patronage* 156); and Penelope Rich participated in a scribal network of writers, musicians, and recusant Catholics (Kilroy). These three women, along with Penelope's mother Lettice, Countess of Leicester, and her sister Dorothy, were at the center of a circle of Essex–Sidney dramatic patronage (Barroll 111–13). A Continentally based kinswoman deeply involved in helping the Sidneys with their socio-political roles as suitors also participated in literary networks: Jane Dormer, Duchess of Feria, made the works of Thomas More and other Catholic writers available to the English associated with her Continental household (Crummé 63–4). Moreover, networks are linked not just across space, but also across time: for example, Anne Russell Dudley, a supportive aunt to the Sidneys, was not only celebrated by Spenser in Elizabeth's reign, but also became a touchstone for neo-Spenserian criticism of the Jacobean regime (Doelman). So what to make of the considerable patronage of Robert Sidney's other loving aunt, Katherine Hastings, Countess of Huntington? What circumstances surround single dedications to Sarah Smythe (Robert's second wife) or Katherine Sidney Mansell (his daughter)? Why does Katherine, Lady Aubigny, play a role in Jonson's collection of praise and advice for the Sidneys (Celovsky 205–6)?

Philip Herbert's literary patronage decreased when he devoted finances to restoring Wilton after a major fire in 1647 (Brennan, *Literary Patronage* 200–201). But this decline is also consistent with that of patronage generally. The court began to dissolve, and the patronage system became increasingly decentralized in the period leading up to and through the civil wars. Thereafter, authors increasingly sought revenue from stationers and readers instead of gifts from patrons; though nobles supported popular theater, they no longer maintained dramatic companies (Smuts; Heinemann, "Rebel Lords" 142; Marotti, "Patronage"). Politically prominent mid- and later seventeenth-century Sidneys such as Robert, second Earl of Leicester, Algernon Sidney, and Henry Sidney, Earl of Romney, had limited to no involvement in literary patronage. One exception appears to be Philip Sidney, third Earl of Leicester: he was friend to John Dryden and William Congreve, offered hospitality to the country's "cheifest bards" at Saturday receptions, and was celebrated by playwright and poet Elkanah Settle and poet Tom D'Urfay, who designated Philip as another Sidneian Maecenas. Philip's support of writers is primed for recuperation, as is its intersection with his considerable support of the visual arts (Maddicott, "Political and Cultural Career of Philip Sidney" ch. 7; Maddicott, "Unidentified Poem"). Philip's kinswoman (niece by marriage) Anne Digby, Lady Sunderland, was a lifelong friend of the writer and diarist John Evelyn. Figures such as Philip and Anne, along with lesser-known family members, deserve further study, especially as their activities relate to changes in the systems of artistic production as a whole. With recent biographies of family members and increased availability of edited letters and other archival documents, scholars will be better able to reconstruct the expanded definitions of "network" that underlie much of the new work outlined here on the Sidneys and patronage.

Bibliography

Primary and Secondary Sources

Adams, Simon. "Ambrose Dudley, Earl of Warwick." *ODNB*.

Alexander, Gavin. *Writing after Sidney: The Literary Response to Sir Philip Sidney, 1586–1640*. Oxford: Oxford UP, 2006.

Andrews, J. H. "The Irish Surveys of Robert Lythe." *Imago Mundi* 19 (1965): 22–31.

Aubrey, John. *"Brief Lives," chiefly of Contemporaries, set down by John Aubrey, between the Years 1669 & 1696*. Ed. Andrew Clark. 2 vols. Oxford: Clarendon P, 1898.

Barroll, Leeds. "Shakespeare, Noble Patrons, and the Pleasures of 'Common' Playing." *Shakespeare and Theatrical Patronage in Early Modern England*. Ed. Paul Whitfield White and Suzanne R. Westfall. Cambridge: Cambridge UP, 2002. 90–121.

Bergeron, David M. "The King's Men's King's Men: Shakespeare and Folio Patronage." *Shakespeare and Theatrical Patronage in Early Modern England*. Ed. Paul Whitfield White and Suzanne R. Westfall. Cambridge: Cambridge UP, 2002. 45–63.

—. "Women as Patrons of English Renaissance Drama." *Patronage in the Renaissance*. Ed. Guy Fitch Lytle and Stephen Orgel. Princeton, NJ: Princeton UP, 1981. 274–90.

Brennan, Michael G. "Creating Female Authorship in the Early Seventeenth Century: Ben Jonson and Lady Mary Wroth." *Women's Writing and the Circulation of Ideas: Manuscript Publication in England, 1550–1880*. Ed. George L. Justice and Nathan Tinker. Cambridge: Cambridge UP, 2002. 73–93.

—. *Literary Patronage in the English Renaissance: The Pembroke Family*. London: Routledge, 1988.

—. "Sir Robert Sidney and Sir John Harrington of Kelston." *Notes & Queries* 34.2 (1987): 232–7.

—. "'A SYDNEY, though un-named': Ben Jonson's Influence in the Manuscript and Print Circulation of Lady Mary Wroth's Writings." *SJ* 17.1 (1999): 31–52.

—. *The Sidneys of Penshurst and the Monarchy, 1500–1700*. Aldershot: Ashgate, 2006.

—. "The Queen's Proposed Visit to Wilton House in 1599 and the 'Sidney Psalms.'" *SJ* 20.1 (2002): 27–53.

—, and Noel J. Kinnamon. "Robert Sidney, 'Mr Johnson,' and the Education of William Sidney at Penshurst." *Notes & Queries* 50.4 (2003): 430–37.

—. *A Sidney Chronology 1554–1654*. New York: Palgrave Macmillan, 2003.

Brown, Cedric C., ed. *Patronage, Politics, and Literary Traditions in England, 1558–1658*. Detroit, MI: Wayne State UP, 1991.

Burrow, Colin. "Introduction." *The Oxford Shakespeare: The Complete Sonnets and Poems*. Ed. Colin Burrow. Oxford: Oxford UP, 2002. 1–158.

Buxton, John. *Sir Philip Sidney and the English Renaissance*. 2nd ed. New York: St. Martin's Press, 1964.

Celovsky, Lisa. "Ben Jonson and Sidneian Legacies of Hospitality." *Studies in Philology* 106.2 (2009): 178–206.

Crawford, Julie. "Sidney's Sapphics and the Role of Interpretive Communities." *ELH* 69.4 (2002): 979–1007.

Crummé, Hannah Leah. "Jane Dormer's Recipe for Politics: A Refuge Household in Spain for Mary Tudor's Ladies-in-waiting." *The Politics of Female Households: Ladies-in-waiting across Early Modern Europe*. Ed. Nadine Akkerman and Birgit Houben. Leiden: Brill, 2014. 51–71.

Daniel, Samuel. *Certaine small works*. London, 1611.

Davis, Natalie Zemon. *The Gift in Sixteenth-Century France*. Madison, WI: U of Wisconsin P, 2000.

Doelman, James. "Spenser's 'Theana': Two Notes." *Spenser Studies: A Renaissance Poetry Annual* 26 (2011): 261–8.

Donaldson, Ian. *Ben Jonson: A Life*. Oxford: Oxford UP, 2011.

Dutton, Richard. "*Shake-speares Sonnets*, Shakespeare's Sonnets, and Shakespearean Biography." *A Companion to Shakespeare's Sonnets*. Ed. Michael Schoenfeldt. Malden, MA: Blackwell, 2007. 121–36.

Eliot, T. S. "Seneca in Elizabethan Translation." *Selected Essays: 1917–1932*. New York: Harcourt, Brace, and Company, 1932.

Evans, Robert C. *Ben Jonson and the Poetics of Patronage*. Lewisburg, PA: Bucknell UP, 1989.

Fisken, Beth Wynne. "Mary Sidney's Psalms: Education and Wisdom." *Silent but for the Word: Tudor Women as Patrons, Translators and Writers of Religious Works*. Ed. Margaret P. Hannay. Kent, OH: Kent State UP, 1985. 166–83.

Goldring, Elizabeth. "Gascoigne and Kenilworth: The Production, Reception, and Afterlife of *The Princely Pleasures*." *ELR* 44.3 (2014): 363–87.

—. "'A mercer ye wot az we be': The Authorship of the Kenilworth Letter Reconsidered." *ELR* 38.2 (2008): 245–69.

Greenlaw, Edwin A. "Spenser and the Earl of Leicester." *PMLA* 25.3 (1910): 535–61.

Greville, Fulke. *The Prose Works of Fulke Greville, Lord Brooke*. Ed. John Gouws. Oxford: Clarendon P, 1986.

Gundersheimer, Werner L. "Patronage in the Renaissance: An Exploratory Approach." *Patronage in the Renaissance*. Ed. Guy Fitch Lytle and Stephen Orgel. Princeton, NJ: Princeton UP, 1981. 3–23.

Hadfield, Andrew. *Edmund Spenser: A Life*. Oxford: Oxford UP, 2012.

Hannay, Margaret P. "Introduction." *Silent but for the Word: Tudor Women as Patrons, Translators, and Writers of Religious Works*. Ed. Margaret P. Hannay. Kent, OH: Kent State UP, 1985. 1–14.

—. *Mary Sidney, Lady Wroth*. Farnham: Ashgate, 2010.

—. *Philip's Phoenix: Mary Sidney, Countess of Pembroke*. Oxford: Oxford UP, 1990.

Hay, Millicent V. *The Life of Robert Sidney, Earl of Leicester (1563–1626)*. Washington, DC: Folger Shakespeare Library, 1984.

Heinemann, Margot. *Puritanism and Theatre: Thomas Middleton and Opposition Drama under the Early Stuarts*. Cambridge: Cambridge UP, 1980.

—. "Rebel Lords, Popular Playwrights, and Political Culture: Notes on the Jacobean Patronage of the Earl of Southampton." *Patronage, Politics, and Literary Traditions in England, 1558–1658*. Ed. Cedric C. Brown. Detroit, MI: Wayne State UP, 1991. 135–58.

Herbert, Mary Sidney. *The Collected Works of Mary Sidney Herbert, Countess of Pembroke*. Ed. Margaret P. Hannay, Noel J. Kinnamon, and Michael G. Brennan. 2 vols. Oxford: Clarendon P, 1998.

Herron, Thomas, and Willy Maley. "Introduction: Monumental Sidney." *SJ* 29.1–2 (2011): 1–25.

Hogrefe, Pearl. *Tudor Women: Commoners and Queens*. Ames, IA: Iowa State UP, 1975.

Jardine, M. D. "New Historicism for Old: New Conservatism for Old? The Politics of Patronage in the Renaissance." *Patronage, Politics, and Literary Traditions in England, 1558–1658*. Ed. Cedric C. Brown. Detroit: Wayne State UP, 1991. 291–309.

Jonson, Ben. *The Oxford Authors: Ben Jonson*. Ed. Ian Donaldson. Oxford: Oxford UP, 1985.

Kelly, Joan. "Did Women have a Renaissance?" *Feminism and Renaissance Studies*. Ed. Lorna Hutson. Oxford: Oxford UP, 1999. 21–47.

Kilroy, Gerard. "Scribal Coincidences: Campion, Byrd, Harington and the Sidney Circle." *SJ* 22.1–2 (2004): 73–88.

Kinsella, Stuart. "Colonial Commemoration in Tudor Ireland: The Case of Sir Henry Sidney." *SJ* 29.1–2 (2011): 105–45.

Kuin, Roger. "Querre-Muhau: Sir Philip Sidney and the New World." *RQ* 51.2 (1998): 549–85.

—, and Anne Lake Prescott. "Versifying Connections: Daniel Rogers and the Sidneys." *SJ* 18.2 (2000): 1–35.

Lamb, Mary Ellen. "The Countess of Pembroke's Patronage." *ELR* 12.2 (1982): 162–79.

—. *Gender and Authorship in the Sidney Circle*. Madison, WI: U of Wisconsin P, 1990.

—. "The Myth of the Countess of Pembroke: The Dramatic Circle." *The Yearbook of English Studies* 11 (1981): 194–202.

Lewalski, Barbara. "Re-writing Patriarchy and Patronage: Margaret Clifford, Anne Clifford, and Aemilia Lanyer." *Patronage, Politics, and Literary Traditions in England, 1558–1658*. Ed. Cedric C. Brown. Detroit, MI: Wayne State UP, 1991. 59–78.

Lytle, Guy Fitch. "Religion and the Lay Patron in Reformation England." *Patronage in the Renaissance*. Ed. Guy Fitch Lytle and Stephen Orgel. Princeton, NJ: Princeton UP, 1981. 65–114.

MacLean, Sally-Beth. "Tracking Leicester's Men: The Patronage of a Performance Troupe. *Shakespeare and Theatrical Patronage in Early Modern England*. Ed. Paul Whitfield White and Suzanne R. Westfall. Cambridge: Cambridge UP, 2002. 246–71.

Maddicott, Hilary. "The Political and Cultural Career of Philip Sidney, Lord Viscount Lisle, Third Earl of Leicester, 1619–1698: Nobility and Identity in the Seventeenth Century." PhD thesis, University of London, 2014.

—. "An Unidentified Poem by Elkanah Settle." *Notes & Queries* 47.2 (2000): 189–92.

Marotti, Arthur F. "John Donne and the Rewards of Patronage." *Patronage in the Renaissance*. Ed. Guy Fitch Lytle and Stephen Orgel. Princeton, NJ: Princeton UP, 1981. 207–34.

—. "'Love is Not Love': Elizabethan Sonnet Sequences and the Social Order." *ELH* 49.2 (1982): 396–428.

—. "Patronage, Poetry, and Print." *Patronage, Politics, and Literary Traditions in England, 1558–1658*. Ed. Cedric C. Brown. Detroit, MI: Wayne State UP, 1991. 21–46.

Moroney, Maryclaire. "'The Sweetness of Due Subjection': Derricke's *Image of Irelande* (1581) and the Sidneys." *SJ* 20.1–2 (2011): 147–71.

Norbrook, David. *Poetry and Politics in the English Renaissance*. London: Routledge, 1984.

Oakley-Brown, Liz. "Writing on Borderlines: Anglo-Welsh Relations in Thomas Churchyard's *The Worthines of Wales*." *Writing Wales, from the Renaissance to Romanticism*. Ed. Stewart Mottram and Sarah Prescott. Farnham: Ashgate, 2012. 39–57.

Osborn, James M. *Young Philip Sidney 1572–1577*. New Haven, CT: Yale UP, 1972.

Peacey, Jason. "'Printers to the University' 1584–1658." *The History of Oxford University Press, Volume 1: Beginnings to 1780*. Ed. Ian Gadd. Oxford: Oxford UP, 2013. 51–77.

Peck, Linda Levy. *Court Patronage and Corruption in Early Stuart England*. London: Unwin Hyman, 1990.

—. "Court Patronage and Government Policy: The Jacobean Dilemma." *Patronage in the Renaissance*. Ed. Guy Fitch Lytle and Stephen Orgel. Princeton, NJ: Princeton UP, 1981. 27–46.

Rees, Joan. *Samuel Daniel: A Critical and Biographical Study*. Liverpool: Liverpool UP, 1964.

Roberts, Josephine A. "Critical Introduction." *The First Part of The Countess of Montgomery's Urania*. Ed. Josephine A. Roberts. Tempe, AZ: Arizona Center for Medieval and Renaissance Texts and Studies, 1995.

—. "The Life of Lady Mary Wroth." *The Poems of Lady Mary Wroth*. Ed. Josephine A. Roberts. Baton Rouge, LA: Louisiana State UP, 1983. 3–40.

Rosenberg, Eleanor. *Leicester: Patron of Letters*. New York: Columbia UP, 1955.

Sagaser, Elizabeth Harris. "Elegiac Intimacy: Pembroke's 'To the Angell spirit of the most excellent Sir Philip Sidney.'" *SJ* 23:1–2 (2005): 111–31.

Salzman, Paul. *Reading Early Modern Women's Writing*. Oxford: Oxford UP, 2006.

Schwyzer, Philip. "'A Happy Place of Government': Sir Henry Sidney, Wales, and *The Historie of Cambria* (1584)." *SJ* 29.1–2 (2011): 209–17.

Sheavyn, Phoebe. *The Literary Profession in the Elizabethan Age*. 1909. 2nd ed. rev. J. W. Saunders. Manchester: Manchester UP, 1967.

—. "Patrons and Professional Writers under Elizabeth and James I." *The Library* n.s. 7 (1906): 301–36.

Sidney, Philip, *The Correspondence of Sir Philip Sidney*. Ed. Roger Kuin. 2 vols. Oxford: Oxford UP, 2012.

—. *The Countess of Pembroke's Arcadia (The Old Arcadia)*. Ed. Jean Robertson. Oxford: Clarendon P, 1973.

Simpson-Younger, Nancy. "'I become a vision': Seeing and the Reader in Sidney's *Old Arcadia*." *SJ* 30.2 (2012): 57–85.

Skretkowicz, Victor. "Greville, Politics, and the Rhetorics of *A Dedication to Sir Philip Sidney*." *SJ* 19.1–2 (2001): 97–123.

—. "Sidney's *Defence of Poetry*, Henri Estienne, and Huguenot Nationalist Satire." *SJ* 16.1 (1998): 3–24.

Smith, Helen. "'Grossly Material Things': Women and Book Production in Early Modern England." Oxford: Oxford UP, 2012.

Smith, Rosalind. "Lady Mary Wroth's *Pamphilia to Amphilanthus*: The Politics of Withdrawal." *ELR* 30.3 (2000): 408–31.

Smuts, Malcolm. "The Political Failure of Stuart Cultural Patronage." *Patronage in the Renaissance*. Ed. Guy Fitch Lytle and Stephen Orgel. Princeton, NJ: Princeton UP, 1981. 165–87.

Somerset, Alan. "Not Just Sir Oliver Owlet: From Patrons to 'Patronage' of Early Modern Theatre." *Oxford Handbook of Early Modern Theatre*. Ed. Richard Dutton. Oxford: Oxford UP, 2009. 343–61.

Steggle, Matthew. "Gabriel Harvey, the Sidney Circle, and the Excellent Gentlewoman." *SJ* 22.1–2 (2004): 115–29.

Stewart, Alan. *Philip Sidney: A Double Life*. New York: St. Martin's Press, 2001.

Stillman, Robert E. *Philip Sidney and the Poetics of Renaissance Cosmopolitanism*. Aldershot: Ashgate, 2008.

Taylor, Dick, Jr. "The Masque and the Lance: The Earl of Pembroke in Jacobean Court Entertainments." *Tulane Studies in English* 8 (1958): 21–53.

—. "The Third Earl of Pembroke as a Patron of Poetry." *Tulane Studies in English* 5 (1955): 41–67.

Van Dorsten, Jan A. *Poets, Patrons, and Professors: Sir Philip Sidney, Daniel Rogers, and the Leiden Humanists*. Leiden: Leiden UP, 1962.

Van Elk, Martine. "'You will find many wants': Flushing in the 1590s." *SJ* 27.1 (2009): 1–8.

Vogt, George McGill. "Richard Robinson's 'Eupolemia' (1603)." *Studies in Philology* 21.4 (1924): 629–48.

Warkentin, Germaine, Joseph L. Black, and William R. Bowen. *The Library of the Sidneys of Penshurst Place circa 1665*. Toronto: U of Toronto P, 2013.

Westfall, Suzanne R. "'The useless dearness of the diamond': Theories of Patronage Theatre." *Shakespeare and Theatrical Patronage in Early Modern England*. Ed. Paul Whitfield White and Suzanne R. Westfall. Cambridge: Cambridge UP, 2002. 246–71.

White, Paul Whitfield and Suzanne R. Westfall, eds. *Shakespeare and Theatrical Patronage in Early Modern England*. Cambridge: Cambridge UP, 2002.

Williams, Franklin B., Jr. *Index of Dedications and Commendatory Verses in English Books before 1641*. London: Bibliographical Society, 1962.

—. "The Literary Patronesses of Renaissance England." *Notes & Queries* 207 (1962): 364–6.

Wilson, Derek. *Sweet Robin: A Biography of Robert Dudley, Earl of Leicester 1533–1588*. London: Hamish Hamilton, 1981.

Woudhuysen, H. R. "Sir Philip Sidney (1554–1585)." *ODNB*.

—. *Sir Philip Sidney and the Circulation of Manuscripts 1558–1640*. Oxford: Clarendon P, 1996.

Young, Frances Berkeley. *Mary Sidney Countess of Pembroke*. London: Nutt, 1912.

Penshurst Place and Leicester House

Susie West

Introduction

The Sidney family came to Penshurst Place, Kent (Illustrations 3 and 4) in 1552, and have retained the house and its landed estate to the present day. Penshurst Place has been celebrated as the birthplace of Sir Philip Sidney and as the scene of inspiration for Ben Jonson and Edmund Waller; as a literary and historical site it has accrued a lengthy tradition of representation and interpretation. This chapter focuses on its architectural history, as a great medieval fortified residence adapted for early modern living. The Sidneys built a new house, as their London residence, in the 1630s. Leicester House, Leicester Square was demolished in 1792, and as a result of that loss and a slender archive, the significance of this major London house has received little attention. However, this chapter discusses the cultural achievement that Leicester House represents as an example of advanced architectural design for the 1630s. Leicester House can be incorporated with the Sidney family's history of collecting that is better understood for Penshurst Place. Together, the two principal residences offer the basis for stronger readings of the cultural significance of the Sidney family. The chapter concludes with a brief consideration of the material world of the Sidneys, exploring themes that, like Jonson's masque characters, display "poesie, historie, architecture and sculpture" on the same stage.

Penshurst Place 1500–1700

Penshurst Place, Kent is famous for many reasons: to literary scholars it is primarily the birthplace for key members of the English literary Renaissance and the inspiration for visiting poets. Ben Jonson saw the house at a high point; by the early nineteenth century the decayed state of the great house was lamented in the press, and it was only just saved by extensive renovations. Each century of occupation has reshaped the house to suit the prevailing requirements of the household, the social uses of space at the time, and the funds available. The house was centuries old before it came to the Sidneys, and would be reshaped to suit their rising fortunes.

The Medieval Penshurst Place

Penshurst Place displays its medieval origins proudly (Illustrations 29 and 30). It is still recognizably a fortified house, in plan as well as from the surviving details of stone walls, battlements, and monumental towers (Newman 454–9). The form of the house is based on the medieval use of courtyards, enclosed by building ranges or defensive walls. All medieval houses of any degree of rank required a central great hall, with the lord's living quarters attached at one end and the kitchen and service rooms attached at the other. At Penshurst Place the first main phase of building from 1338 to 1341 resulted in the great hall, solar block, and service block, for a wealthy City of London merchant, Sir John de Pulteney (d. 1350). The second phase from 1392 enclosed this manor house with the towers and battlemented curtain wall. The great scale of the hall and solar, or upper chamber (now the state dining room), expressed the wealth and status of the early owners: Sir John Devereux (d. 1394), who added the fortifications, probably also added the Buckingham Building, since it is physically tied in to the curtain wall (Hasted 3:231–3). The addition of fortifications to the manor house created the appearance of a castle, in a period when fortified houses of the elite were intended for luxurious, if highly protected, occupation, and houses of any scale provided lodgings for numerous armed retainers (Emery 386–93).

Penshurst became a royal residence when the manor was acquired by John, Duke of Bedford (1389–1435), third son of Henry IV, c. 1424 (Stratford 359–60). Penshurst then came to Bedford's younger brother, Humphrey, Duke of Gloucester (Stratford 28). The manor reverted to the Crown three times after Gloucester's death; the longest holding was under the Dukes of Buckingham from c. 1447 to 1521, when the third duke was attainted and executed. Penshurst Place continued to evolve: the solar block was backed by a three-story lodgings block looking in to the President's Court, known as Sidney's Lodgings. These lodgings are built of brick with diaper work and ragstone windows, quite unlike the later sixteenth-century brick buildings of the Sidney era. Buckingham had entertained Henry VIII at Penshurst in 1519, which might signal the occasion of the extra lodgings.

By the time Edward VI granted the manor to Sir William Sidney in 1552 it is clear that Penshurst Place was an extensive house to grant to a knight, even one who was a highly valued courtier. William had no time for major alterations to his generous gift, but his son and heir Sir Henry Sidney (1529–86; see McGowan-Doyle ARC 1:2; see also below) initiated important additions to the house that would be completed by his son Robert, later first Earl of Leicester (see Shephard ARC 1:7).

The Growth of Penshurst Place, 1500–1700

The medieval house was of stone; alterations of the sixteenth and early seventeenth centuries are clearly distinguished by being built in brick with stone finishes. Sir Henry made considerable additions to the layout of the house, by building against the defensive walls and incorporating the medieval towers into the bulk of the house (Illustration 29). Following the line of the defensive wall encircling the house, Sir Henry rebuilt the entrance gateway now known as the King's Tower (1585), and remodeled matching ranges either side (the Great Court north range, remodeled again in the nineteenth century). He joined this north range to the existing lodgings behind the solar block with a new west range dividing the Entrance Court from the President's Court. He linked the President's Tower to the north range with an open gallery, or loggia (notable for its Tuscan colonnade of 1579), and room above. He is said to have created the subdivisions of the present state rooms in the first floor of the Buckingham Building in 1575, and he linked this block to the southern Record Tower, probably also originally free-standing, by the two-story gallery wing of 1584. This completed the high-status family and guest rooms to the west of the great hall; to the east, a new wing of service rooms and lower-status chambers was probably completed in the early seventeenth century (Illustration 30).

Sir Henry saw the interiors fitted out for the upper hall (solar), minstrels' gallery (in the great hall) and the great hall screen, from 1573 (HMC, *De L'Isle and Dudley* 1:260–61). The great hall screen was carved with the heraldic symbol of the Dudley bear, in tribute to Sir Henry's wife, Lady Mary Dudley. Its design is notably Gothic, in acknowledgment of the fourteenth-century hall and in contrast to the classical influences in the upper hall paneling.

Sir Henry also remodeled the gardens, beginning in 1560 by leveling the gardens to create new enclosed courts, in the Italian Renaissance manner. Work continued in 1575 with the great pond and a terrace. Each year, several hundred pounds were spent on the house, gardens, and surrounding grounds (HMC, *De L'Isle and Dudley* 1:250ff.). Robert Sidney continued to improve the gardens, writing from Flushing in 1596 of his pleasure on hearing that work was going well and promising to send some trees over (HMC, *De L'Isle and Dudley* 2:226).

The house was finished in 1612. Robert Sidney was aided in his frequent absences by his wife, Barbara Gamage Sidney, Countess of Leicester, as he wrote in 1594: "I need not send to know how my buildings goe forward; for I ame sure you are so good a housewyfe you may be trusted with them" (HMC, *De L'Isle and Dudley* 2:153, 156–7). Barbara Sidney undertook some entrepreneurial activity, supplying stone for Robert Cecil's new London house, Salisbury House on the Strand, in 1601 (Guerci 39). Paying for the work remained a problem, and was clearly drawn from annual rentals rather than any other source of capital (HMC, *De L'Isle and Dudley* 2:155). In 1600 the gatehouse chambers (King's Tower) were paneled with wainscot reused from elsewhere in the house, and a little chamber at the "chapel end" was floored (HMC, *De L'Isle and Dudley* 2:426). A major building campaign continued that year, when the stone finishings to the battlements and stone window surrounds were cut, for stables and a tower, at a cost of £500 (HMC, *De L'Isle and Dudley* 2:437, 482). More work was done on the nether gallery in 1605, when the windows were glazed and the "great wyndow next the garden" (a bay window removed in the eighteenth century) was waiting to be finished (HMC, *De L'Isle and Dudley* 3:147). By 1607 the nether gallery paneling was being painted with the Sidney device of the broad arrow pheon, and the upper gallery was ready to have mats on the floor (HMC, *De L'Isle and Dudley* 3:374). The stables were completed by 1612, and some work was undertaken within the President's Tower, where seventeenth-century paneling remains today (HMC, *De L'Isle and Dudley* 5:25, 45). The long process of building seems to have begun in the 1570s and drawn to a close by 1612, the occupation of two generations of husbands and wives.

The term "King's Lodging," which occurs in the 1623 and 1677 inventories, does not seem to be in use in this phase of finishing the house; for example, it is not used in an early document (*c.* 1610) noting the fitting out of many of the new interiors (S. West 275). Instead, the apartment in the great court is described as the "new bedchamber," with a platform for the bed, the inward chamber, and a drawing chamber with inward chamber. This sequence is suitable for a state bedchamber apartment; the later dedication of this suite as the King's Lodging presumably refers to the spontaneous visit of James I celebrated in Ben Jonson's poem, shortly before 1612 (Rathmell 251).

Although there are problems of detail in this broad sequence of building and interior work, the general evolution is apparent, and the fabric of the western half in particular survives today. The great kitchen and service wings to the east were probably demolished after 1843. Despite this clarity of exterior fabric, substantial alterations to the interiors have taken place since 1700. However, it is still possible to reconstruct the seventeenth-century arrangement and use of space that contained the Sidneys' pattern of life at Penshurst Place.

A Tour Around the Seventeenth-century Penshurst Place

It is possible to read the seventeenth-century Penshurst plan as an ideal of aristocratic household requirements imposed on an imperfect reality. The scale of a noble household was immense. The rank of the owners required high-status household officials as well as servants for indoor service, creating a small community wherever the family was staying. For example, Barbara Sidney was encouraged to trim her London household expenses in 1594: "we must not keepe 60 in our hows at London" (HMC, *De L'Isle and Dudley* 2:185). The period in which the house was extended, roughly 1570–1610, covered a fairly stable "ideal" layout for the houses of the elite (Girouard, *Life* 80–118). English architecture was increasingly influenced by Italian style and planning, and beginning to experiment with new ideas about symmetry, both on the facades and within the plan. A good example would be the late Elizabethan house, Hardwick Hall, Derbyshire (*c.* 1597), which is designed without a courtyard and has a central front door leading into a central great hall (Girouard, *Elizabethan Architecture* 112–23). Robert Sidney, and presumably Barbara, knew Inigo Jones from his early role as a masque designer, working with Ben Jonson; Sidney and Jones traveled in the official escort party that conducted the Elector Palatine and his new wife, the Princess Elizabeth, back to Heidelberg in 1613. This is too early in Jones's architectural career to suggest any influence on Penshurst, and there is no evidence to suggest that Jones was directly involved with the Sidneys' London home. But the visual richness of the court masques, and the surviving designs that mix fantasy, Renaissance Classicism and Gothic elements, are reminders of the treatment of architecture as spectacle that was familiar to Leicester.

The medieval form of the great hall remained at the center of these houses, but within a new symmetry that increasingly disguised the off-center entrance through the screens passage. The high-status rooms that created the set-piece route through the house for guests began with the great hall, although this was rarely used for dining by the family. The great dining chamber was the preferred room, up a flight of stairs from the high-status (former dais) end of the great hall. From this chamber withdrawing rooms would lead to the best or state bedchamber. Bedchambers were multi-purpose living rooms, and company was received by the occupant, hence the many elaborate suites of chairs noted in the inventories. The beds themselves were the subject of high expenditure on hangings. The formal apartments were complemented by the provision of at least one long gallery. Although galleries are associated with exercise in inclement weather, they were most important as a site of display for collections, particularly for portraits, and as "neutral" spaces for informal discussions away from the state rooms (Coope).

This was the "ideal" form for a noble household *c.* 1600. Penshurst Place had evolved around the fourteenth-century hall, service, and solar block. The survival of a medieval great hall at the center of a seventeenth-century house is not unusual: Knole in Kent has similar origins, as does Boughton House, Northamptonshire. However, the offset Buckingham Building south of the solar block and the encircling defensive wall and towers (1392) are unusual, and their survival had a decisive effect on the plan of the new work. Rather than acquiring new courtyards by linking wings to gatehouse towers, as at neighboring Knole, Sir Henry Sidney incorporated the existing asymmetric layout (including the defensive towers) into courtyards with a combination of new ranges and garden walls. In effect, Penshurst gained three high-status courts and three service courts, within the confines of the medieval defensive layout. Courtyard houses were designed to look into the courts, rather than away into the landscape. Some of these aspects have been reversed after 1700 at Penshurst.

The processional entrance route at Penshurst Place began at the King's Tower and continued across the great court to the great hall (S. West 281). The bay windows of the parlour and parlour bedchamber faced into this court. On passing though the great hall visitors could ascend to the great dining chamber by the medieval stone stairs, or preferably take the longer but more formal route through the lobby tower into Sidney's Lodgings. Here they could be received by their hosts in the great parlour, before ascending the great stairs to reach the dining chamber by its north door. Once on the upper floor, after dining in state, the adjoining Buckingham Building provided a sequence of withdrawing rooms and state bedchamber in the form of Gloucester's Lodgings. Gloucester's Lodgings were modernized by having the beds removed by 1677. The processional route on this side of the house ended by passing into the upper long gallery. Back down in the great parlour visitors could ascend to the best lodgings of all: the state bedchamber suite later called the King's Lodgings in the north range of the great court.

Seventeenth-century Penshurst Place was thus arranged to offer all the amenities of an earl's house, including a private chapel that survived until *c.* 1818 (when the architect Biaggio Rebecca reordered some of the rooms). The great stairs were probably comparable with the highly decorated great stairs that survive at Knole. The Knole stairs were completed by 1608; their ascent within a square plan, the Renaissance use of classical columns, a balustrade with Jacobean strapwork and wall paintings, would be as suitable for the Earl of Leicester at Penshurst as it was for the Earl of Dorset (National Trust, *Knole* 14–15; Cooper 34–43).

Away from the state rooms, living quarters were assigned distinctive names, and represented groups of rooms centered on bedchambers. They are often described in inventories as "apartments," but at Penshurst in the seventeenth century they are called lodgings: the King's Lodgings (above), Leicester's Lodgings, Gloucester's Lodgings, and Sidney's Lodgings. Leicester's Lodgings occupied the ground-floor rooms of the Buckingham Building. Gloucester's Lodgings were up on the first floor, and were part of the processional route around the house. Sidney's Lodgings encompass the three-story block behind the solar, and wrap around to the Lobby Tower. The first-floor room (now subdivided) in the Lobby Tower still has an overmantel with an earl's coronet and "RB" for Robert and Barbara Sidney. These lodgings also had a study, one of five around the house.

One further high-status apartment remained, at the low-status end of the great hall, entered by stairs near the south porch. On the first floor, above the buttery and the passage to the kitchen, were two chambers and a study in 1623, assigned to Lord Sunderland by the time of the 1677 inventory. The Sunderland Lodging was furnished with an extremely high-value suite by then, which concurs with the family legend that "Sacharissa," Dorothy Sidney Spencer Smythe, Countess of Sunderland, occupied it as a widow in the mid seventeenth-century (see Akkerman *ARC* 1:10).

The President's Court, named after the President's Tower, is less of a set-piece place of display. The loggia and the President's Tower form an elegant coda to the north range, but they are distinct from the processional route described above. In the President's Court, the large room over the "stone gallery" (1623) or cloister (1677 inventory) (loggia) remained one big room until 1818. By 1677 Robert Sidney, second Earl of Leicester, slept in the first floor of the President's Tower while Dorothy Percy Sidney, Countess of Leicester, was probably on the upper floor of Sidney's Lodgings (see Warkentin *ARC* 1:9; Akkerman *ARC* 10). The President's Tower and the loggia were a private retreat away from the formal route through the house, placed to enjoy a court as far from the service side of the house as possible. The strongest candidate for the seventeenth-century library room (holding most of the five thousand volumes) is the great room over the loggia, convenient for the first and second earls' private rooms (S. West 285–6; see also Black *ARC* 2:1).

The supposed library room at Penshurst was subdivided into a corridor and bedrooms during the nineteenth century. As one open space, it was filled with light from the three great windows and was able to hold a rich interior scheme that comfortably absorbed the five thousand volumes of the library collection. The walls were hung with six tapestries, a chair and four stools were upholstered with cloth of gold, and a table and court cupboard were dressed with a green carpet and a Turkish carpet, recorded in 1623. The tapestries were taken down and replaced by twenty-two pictures, and more furniture arrived by the time of the 1677 inventory: three more chairs, three further court cupboards, and two cabinets, as well as one book press. The cabinet, as a small chest of drawers usually supported on a stand or frame, was a favorite receptacle for Renaissance collections of small objects: coins, medals, and other objects of virtu (Thornton 74). The bookpress, the first dedicated piece of shelving recorded for this study, was presumably distinct from the fitted shelving (unrecorded by inventory takers), and may have been similar to Samuel Pepys's design for a freestanding tall bookcase with glazed doors (his survive in the Pepys Library, Magdalene College, Cambridge).

The library held items of silver: eight candlesticks, a candle box, and a standish (a desk accessory for pens, inkpot, and sand). Less expected are the tumblers, chafing dish (for heating or cooking food, a distant relative of the modern fondue pot), a toothpick case, and a gilt spoon. The room appears to have been a comfortable place for a quiet supper. Objects for contemplation must also have included some of the diverse collections of bronzes, busts, and bas reliefs known to have filled the house, and sold in 1703 (Maddicott 1–24).

Finally, other important rooms were essential to the great household, although not intended to be inhabited. The armory, which would be most conveniently sited near to the great hall, was perhaps in the medieval undercroft, at the high end of the great hall. The old wardrobe, a great storehouse of unused textiles and furniture, was adjacent to the President's Court, according to occasional references (HMC, *De L'Isle and Dudley* 2:426). The usual kitchen offices filled a court on the east side of the hall. Penshurst Place was immense, but filled by a bustling presence whenever its household of sixty returned to full strength for the complex processes of supporting the lifestyle of an earl and his family. However rich the new textiles and painted and gilded furniture were within the best rooms, Penshurst was also visibly rooted in its medieval past. With the new London house created as the next stage of the Sidney's building ambitions, the family would be able to express their interest in and understanding of the latest architectural directions.

Leicester House, London

The next stage of the architectural story of the Sidneys concerns Robert and Dorothy Sidney, second Earl and Countess of Leicester (see Warkentin *ARC* 1:9; Akkerman *ARC* 1:10). The Sidneys, like many aristocratic families who did not inherit a substantial medieval home in London, had been used to renting houses or borrowing rooms in Baynard's Castle when they needed to live there as a household for any length of time. This pattern changed when Robert Sidney selected a plot of land on which to build his own house, right on the edge of the expanding urban area, completing the land purchase in 1631. His choice was a contrast to the smoky, congested, and essentially medieval City; Robert Sidney settled on an airy and open landscape of open fields and ancient trackways, leading north from the thin ribbon of development on the river frontage of the western termination of the Strand and beyond the western limit of the expansion of urban streets.

Robert Sidney purchased four acres from Hugh Audley (notorious money lender and founder of what would become the Grosvenor Estate in London) of the enclosed field of St. Martin's parish (formerly a common resource, and hence without formal boundary hedges).

Since this was once parish land, he was ordered to leave half of it open, and this became the urban square known as Leicester Fields (Sheppard, "Leicester Square Area").

While Robert Sidney gained country air, the choice of site is also an indication of his awareness of the latest speculative developments west of the City. During the 1630s the redevelopment of London's streets as speculative housing development for wealthy tenants marked the introduction of the uniform, brick-built terraces of tall, narrow houses that would dominate English urban housing into the nineteenth century. Covent Garden and Lincoln's Inn Fields were the chief ornaments of the city in the 1630s, both planned as terraces around central open squares (McKellar 193–7). The setting of Leicester House gradually came to resemble these formal squares during the rest of the century. Recent activity on the Bedford estate, which terminated at the east side of St. Martin's Lane, may have suggested the potential to Leicester for future development of his new plot: Covent Garden Piazza was developed in 1631 (Summerson 30–31).

Knowledge of Leicester House is limited as a result of its demolition in 1792, and a period prior to that when it was not in family ownership or occupation. The great house (Illustration 31) was constructed towards the south of the irregularly shaped plot which Robert Sidney had enclosed, north of the open field. Behind the house were elaborate formal gardens, ornamented with statues. The western gardens included an orchard with statues and a kitchen garden. Pleasurable strolls could be taken along the elevated terrace walk, ornamented with statues; shade was provided by a covered walkway (HMC, *De L'Isle and Dudley* 6:633–4). The immediate setting for the house was thus a series of structured garden areas, designed for leisure and to supply the household with produce, ornamented in the latest manner with statuary. A good comparison, now reconstructed, is the garden setting for Ham House, as recorded in a design of 1671–72, where an immense terrace, four times the length of the house, surveyed the parterre garden (National Trust, *Ham House* 54–5).

The house fit within a forecourt later recorded as 133 feet wide. Robert Sidney reportedly spent £8,000 on his house, comparable to the £7,500 estimated for the cost of building the Queen's House at Greenwich (by Inigo Jones [1632–38]; Worsley 115). The setting of Southampton House, built at the northern end of Southampton (later Bloomsbury) Square from 1657, is a useful comparison: it too was a wide house dominating one side of the open square. Elizabeth McKellar has pointed out that early London squares in front of great houses may have been intended as an ornament to the house, creating an open court to enhance the view out from the house, rather than our impression from artists' views which are inevitably looking towards, rather than away from, the aristocratic mansion (198–9).

This was a century of immense change in the pattern of English house-building. First, it was a period of transition from timber to brick. In London, the timber-framed City was rebuilt, particularly after the Great Fire in the City of London in 1666, as a brick and tile metropolis. Secondly, it witnessed the definitive shift to Italian classical style, proportion, and planning for the houses of the wealthy, led by the principal court architect, Inigo Jones.

Jones's work translated Italian Renaissance architecture into an adaptable English pattern. His houses are relatively plain and undecorated on their exteriors, in contrast to the richness within. Jones's designs tended to give equal height to each story, as state rooms were spread across two floors in the seventeenth century. This allocation is seen in the inventories for Leicester House. This, then, is an ideal appearance for Leicester House in the 1630s: brick, symmetrical, and with a heavy hipped roof.

The exterior of Leicester House was not intended to impress by the use of classical ornament. It was ten bays wide with a three-bay addition to the west, of two stories over a high basement, with dormers in the roof and monumental groups of chimney stacks either side of the center (Illustration 31). The original facade of the house was therefore slightly asymmetrical, since the door had to be one bay to the side of the central point. This design quirk suggests that despite an otherwise Jonesian style, the unknown architect was unable to co-ordinate all the design elements. The door was emphasized by a pedimented portico surround and a more elaborate frame to the upper floor window above it. Otherwise, the windows were framed by lugged architraves, and the roof was emphasized by a modillion, or bracket, cornice. These features constitute the grammar of ornament for the house, a grammar derived from architectural books after Palladio and Serlio of the late Renaissance and from interpretations of contemporary Dutch classicism. Eighteenth-century comments dismiss the exterior of Leicester House as merely "long and low," and as an astylar brick house of the 1630s, it would not compare well with the stone classicism of the eighteenth-century Palladian revival. However, if the exterior views of Southampton House and Leicester House are compared, taking into account the later addition of a balustrade to the former, the long and low quality of Leicester House can be viewed in something close to its original setting.

The height of Leicester House would have been emphasized by the presence of a balustrade and central cupola on the roof: Dorothy Sidney referred to the progress in making the balustrade around the top of the house in 1636 (HMC, *De L'Isle and Dudley* 51). These houses were all designed with casement windows, not sashes, so the frames were of fixed mullions and transoms, with one or two hinged casements.

Leicester's experience of court styles, of contemporary building campaigns in London, and of European currents through Paris indicates that he would aim to build a house that reflected the latest designs. Many of the design features listed above for Jones-type houses also determine the internal plan of the house: chimney stacks grouped tidily within the roof rather than running up exterior walls; symmetrical disposition of rooms around axial lines; facades that look the same on front and rear. The house was planned on four levels: a high basement for cellars and service rooms, a raised first floor for family and state rooms, an upper floor for family and state rooms, and attic rooms for family bedchambers and storage of surplus furniture and textiles in the wardrobe room. Secondary service functions, including chambers for the lower servants, were disposed in a series of courts to the east of the main house. The house was a double pile, and thus organized as two ranges of back-to-back rooms.

Dorothy came from a family with a track record of female architectural design, with her mother's experience of updating Syon House, Middlesex, and her grandmother, Lettice Dudley, maintaining the splendid Essex House, off the Strand in London (*Correspondence DPS* 5–6). Both were exposed to the latest developments in London architecture, and Dorothy also kept abreast of design trends as she supervised the interior finishes for Leicester House, below.

Dorothy's responsibility for supervising the construction of Leicester House in many ways parallels her mother Barbara's responsibilities in earlier decades for works at Penshurst Place. Dorothy promised her husband that she would "take the best care I can that it may go as far as possible," referring to their tight budget. She organized the sale of timber from the Penshurst estate, and probably suggested that the proceeds should fund the new house, as Robert agreed to this use in 1637 (*Correspondence DPS* 62, 81–2, 103). She also had to fend off "clamorous creditors" in London, including the blacksmith who had made the iron balconies for Leicester House (95–6).

A visitor would enter the central door into a very wide great hall, with great stairs to one side, and cross to a sequence of reception rooms: an anteroom, a little dining chamber, and an old drawing room looking into the parterre gardens at the rear. The rest of the front range was a private apartment for Dorothy Sidney. The extreme east of the house was filled by rooms for household officials and the back stairs, leading to the adjoining service wings and courts. The west end of the house was extended by 1670 with a wing that wrapped around the front, to provide two additional state rooms of a new bedchamber and new drawing room.

The formal route continued up the great stairs to the state apartment sequence of an anteroom, great chamber, and withdrawing chamber, and it is most likely to have overlooked the parterre garden. The front of the upper floor was filled by the earl's private apartment. These front rooms appear to have a private stair, allowing the earl and countess free movement between their apartments without having to walk to the far side of the house. The story over this, in the spacious roof, was divided into comfortable apartments for the earl's adult children and for the old nurseries.

Little is known of the interiors of Leicester House, beyond the hints of the inventories. However, in light of the couple's experience of court life and of Robert Sidney's diplomatic life in Paris, the interiors represented the current state of French-influenced design in the 1630s. This is still visible at Ham House, a Jacobean house remodeled for William Murray (later Earl of Dysart) in 1637–39 (National Trust, *Ham House* 60–63). Dorothy Sidney was proud of the results for the great chamber, anteroom and great stairs, which were "verie hansomlie treated after a new waie," painted and with gilt details on the woodwork (HMC, *De L'Isle and Dudley* 6:51). Some of the rooms had "fretwork" ceilings—that is, with geometric divisions in the manner of Inigo Jones. The stairs and anteroom were hung with gilt leather (embossed and painted panels of leather). The green cabinet at Leicester House on the first (ground) floor, hung with pictures and mirrors, is recognizably the green closet surviving at Ham House, with green textile hangings and ebony-framed small pictures and portrait miniatures (Rowell 14–31). Robert Sidney furnished their house with French tables and bedsteads, and new landscape tapestries. A landscape tapestry of this date would have been a detailed central image of a wooded scene, perhaps with exotic birds, framed by an architectural border with the latest style of swags, columns, and other details also found on paneling and chimneypieces of the same date.

The house was extended some time between 1644 and 1670, the dates of the two known inventories. The need for additional rooms of display reflects the substantial collections assembled by Robert and Dorothy Sidney, including Dorothy's patronage of Anthony Van Dyck. Dorothy's taste is hinted at in the 1659 codicil to her will, listing French silver, Mortlake tapestries, pictures, ebonized cabinets, mirrors, and porcelain owned by her at Leicester House and Penshurst Place (*Correspondence DPS* 188). The picture gallery was the principal addition to the upper floor. The gallery overlooked the western gardens, and formed a splendid link between Robert Sidney's apartment and the upper state rooms. By the time of the Restoration the house was suitable for the royal household of Charles II's aunt, Elizabeth, Queen of Bohemia, in 1662 and for the French ambassador, Charles Colbert, Marquis de Croissy, in 1668. With the additional rooms, the house reached its high point of luxury and convenience. It was designed and planned in the most convenient modern manner, and fitted out and furnished in the latest court style. It would not continue to enjoy its verdant setting for long.

After 1670 development around Leicester House intensified. To the east, James Cecil, third Earl of Salisbury, developed his three acres south of Newport Street from 1670, infilling the eastern half of Leicester Fields. Newport House survived, but its long garden plot was developed. Behind the gardens of Leicester House the first part of the area known as Soho Fields was laid out, creating King Street in 1679 (Sheppard, "Gerrard Street Area").

Leicester House continued to be tenanted by some of the most powerful men in the kingdom: from 1673 by Thomas Osborne, the Lord High Treasurer, and from 1674–76 by Ralph Montagu (who began his own great London house in 1675, later the site of the British Museum). However, the post-Restoration building boom became irresistible. After the death of the second earl in 1677, Philip Sidney, third Earl of Leicester, was blocked from his inheritance by his two brothers, acting as their father's executors, until 1682. As soon as Philip Sidney took possession he decided that such a large house was not necessary (he had a house in Lincoln's Inn Fields, and had built a larger suburban house at Sheen, Richmond), and he followed the prevailing pattern of infilling and redevelopment. The western gardens were sold off and developed, in the form of the T-shaped Leicester Street and Lisle Street. The front wall of the great court was developed as single-story shops, and a tavern was erected in the eastern corner (Sheppard, "Leicester Square, North Side"). Behind Leicester House development moved closer after King Street had been laid out in 1679, as the third earl also sold off some of the rear gardens of Leicester House and a new boundary was established, Gerrard Street, by 1682, as soon as he took possession. East of the house, Newport House had recently been redeveloped as a planned market, with further infilling of housing. The 1680s developments completed the transition from airy fields into urban density that had begun in 1630.

Leicester House survived, but the open views from the picture gallery at the west were abruptly curtailed. This was the house that Philip Sidney, third Earl of Leicester, knew, and he lived in it until his death in 1698. The sash windows shown in later views began to be adopted in England from the 1670s, and were perhaps added when Robert Sidney, fourth Earl of Leicester, spent over £2,000 on the fabric of the house. Further alterations were made in 1718–19 for the household of George, Prince of Wales, and it is only after these two campaigns that artists' views are known. The house of the second earl remains elusive, but Leicester Square remains as a testament to the great scale of his former home.

Both in external design and interior fitting out, Leicester House can be considered to be of the first rank in terms of 1630s London buildings. It shows that the second earl created an appropriate setting for the richly detailed furniture and textiles he sent back from the Continent, and that he aspired to create a contemporary house with a conveniently compact plan to showcase his collection and to support his rank. Leicester House was everything that his father and grandfather had started at Penshurst Place, but without the constraints of the extended medieval plan. Its fate was similar to many of the great houses of early modern London, sacrificed to rising development land prices as the open fields were transformed into the modern West End of one of the largest and fastest-growing capitals in the Western world.

The Material Environment of the Sidneys

Directions in research using Penshurst Place are traceable as two broad strands, distinguished by a primary interest in the physical or the textual. Both strands have the potential to converge on the theme of the fashioning of the self in the early modern period, but there is arguably more groundwork to be done on the material aspects of the Sidneys. Taking the historic environment first, the principal arena is, of course, the great house itself. The discipline of architectural history has tended to prioritize individual buildings rather than their wider contexts. As a great house, Penshurst Place has been the subject of steady attention from architectural historians, but primarily for its significance as a medieval fortified residence. Most recently John Goodall has placed Penshurst in a group of castles of the south-east of England, built or enlarged during the turbulent fourteenth century, as "first and foremost creations of domestic politics and dynastic good fortune" (308, 318–19). Penshurst's medieval style takes its cue from the court style of Richard II; the present author has argued that the Sidney's contribution was to take it into the English Renaissance, yet with historicist allusions to its medieval past (S. West). This is to differ from Don Wayne's earlier position that the work represented an illusion, or sleight of hand, about the Sidneys' social origins.

More work remains to be done on Sir Henry Sidney's architectural activities: Goodall notes his extensive modifications at Ludlow Castle, during Sir Henry's lengthy service as President of the Council of the Marches. Further, Goodall speculates that Sir Henry's role in restoring Christ Church Cathedral, Dublin, damaged in 1562 when the nave collapsed, during his term of office as Deputy Lieutenant of Ireland, was an act of conscious antiquarianism (453–4). The role of the past in Elizabethan cultural politics is a theme that could be taken further with a deeper survey of the Sidney family's use of the material past, extending literary discussion of the construction of Sidney identities. The relationship of medieval to Renaissance art has seen a revival of interest in recent years (see Nagel and Wood).

The refashioning of Penshurst Place and the creation of Leicester House have not been marked by the discovery of named master craftsmen or architects. The known archive indicates that new discoveries of this nature are unlikely, and indeed the readings that are possible from the archive suggest strongly that the owners were as engaged with the design as with the execution of their building projects. This suggestion needs further work: the aesthetic interest that the archive portrays is muted, and although this is characteristic of the period, more subtle interrogation is needed in order to draw out the motivations and aspirations behind the end results, which were richly varied art collections and suitable architectural settings for their display. The material and visual environment of the Sidneys, looking outwards to their experience of the Scottish and European court cultures, could provide a valuable synthesis. Another direction is offered by consideration of the Sidney networks of friends and kin, particularly the connection with Wilton House. Roy Strong gathered a list of Sir Philip Sidney's portraits which also works as a prompt towards one such socio-cultural network: the great houses of Wilton, Woburn, Windsor, Knebworth, and Blickling can all be connected by personal relationships with Philip Sidney; otherwise, these houses are rarely associated with each other in the architectural literature. Elizabeth Goldring's approach to art history works with this wider approach, as discussed by her in the following chapter (see Goldring *ARC* 1:20).

The value of household inventories to the architectural historian is often calculated by their usefulness in listing room names and possible spatial relationships; the present chapter has benefited from the results. However, a cultural approach to architectural history uses the information about interiors that such inventories offer, as coded descriptions of the lived-in spaces. Since houses are for living in, however brief the period of residence, it is the fixtures and furnishings that actuate many of the possibilities for human conduct within the spaces. For London residences it remains an open question as to how families disposed of their luxury and essential goods between their London and country houses, and in the case of the third earl, a suburban house at Sheen (Maddicott). Possession of a permanent residence in this period did not mean that it had to be permanently furnished: the expectation that goods would be transported between residences seems to have ceased during the sixteenth to seventeenth centuries (Orlin 230). This needs to be taken into account when working with household inventories. For Leicester House, it appears that it was maintained fully furnished (for family and tenants), with the occasional inventory taker's note that goods had been moved to Penshurst. For the previous generation, Jonson's celebratory poem asserted that no room was unfurnished, suggesting that by 1610 this particular family had adopted permanency despite their transient relationships with other lodgings (Celovsky 191). This relationship between country and city residence is just one of the wider contexts that would benefit from closer attention, creating a more accurate and fuller picture of the pattern of living in the Sidney household.

City life for the wealthy is associated with discourses around consumption; as a historically specific construct, it is not part of our own understanding of post-industrial consumerism. The renewal of the furnishing textiles around Penshurst Place and the creation of Leicester House exemplify luxury consumption during the seventeenth century. The considerable increase in quantities of luxury goods to be found in the homes of the nobility and gentry during the early modern period apply to the Sidney family, and the theme of consumption deserves more detailed consideration. Early modern luxury was put to use for several cultural ends: the cultivation of the mind, the maintenance of peer group relations, affirmation of political status, as well as the expression of ambition. The library and its lost room at Penshurst can be read together as a prime example of cultivation and consumption.

The present author has produced a material account of the absent library room of the seventeenth-century Penshurst Place (S. West). The generous space occupied by the early seventeenth-century library room over the loggia is a surprising but important example of the value implied by such a creation. The physical environment was not just a place of display, but also a place of meaning: a library room was "a virtuous space of unique moral and aesthetic worth. [A property which] resided in the room itself as much as in its owner," as Dora Thornton expressed the concept within Renaissance Italy (176). The material environment was more than a comfortable room in which to read. The discernment shown in assembling and displaying a range of objects as well as books was an essential factor in the creation of the character of a gentleman. The studies and their contents in fifteenth- and sixteenth-century Florence and Venice were formed under particular social and political conditions not replicated in sixteenth- and seventeenth-century Kent, but pan-European cultural values of civility and learned leisure do manifest themselves in regional forms. In reconstructing the library room, something of the owners' aspirations to a moral life are available to grasp.

William West explored more of the challenge of the "ideal of contemplation and the more limited and contingent actual engagements within a space" for early modern readers, noting the problem of relating metaphorical architecture to actual space (115n7). He suggests that Nicholas Bacon created a new long gallery ornamented with *sententiae* at his house of Gorhambury in 1577 specifically to "represent his mental space to another," the queen; after her visit, Bacon had the doorway she used to enter the gallery walled up. Elizabeth was the intended viewer, and Bacon showed himself to be her subject through their shared performance of the gallery space (W. West 123). This compelling example, evidenced carefully, draws together text, space, and action to suggest meaning. Bacon's gallery, then, is an appropriate place to move the discussion on from the first research strand, working from the architectural environment outwards to wider contexts, and to turn towards the second: literary conceptions of Penshurst.

The representation of architecture in literary texts has been the principal arena where the historical Penshurst Place and its estate have been investigated for their role within Renaissance discourses. The trope of hospitality is best known from Ben Jonson's "To Penshurst," where the poet holds up the household organization found at Penshurst as a model of social obligation; duty is dispatched in an appropriate architectural environment of seemly display. Contemporaries were aware of a tension between country and city life; a rapidly expanding London and its attractions were believed to be undermining social leadership within the counties. Readings of "To Penshurst" after Don Wayne's earlier use of poetic discourse in its historic environment are still being challenged and extended (Celovsky); as with the poem, the house should not be made to accommodate a single reading. The preceding discussion of the architectural history has sought to emphasize that the home of the Sidneys is not directly accessible, particularly lacking much of their interior schemes: the surviving "signs" to be decoded, whether visual or from the archive, may not reveal as complete or coherent a system as Wayne required. Nonetheless, the challenge of relating a discourse about hospitality to the material environment in which hospitality was enacted remains current, and the country house poems retain their fascination for some architectural approaches (Skelton 499). Victoria Moul's exploration of the classical precedents in Jonson's output provides a reminder of the layers of understanding that, if present to a contemporary audience for literary texts, should also be considered to be present to viewers of the material world.

The depth of intellectual history that is invoked in setting Sir Philip Sidney's work into context is also a challenge to the architectural historian, to reflect on how architecture may be implicated, as William West demonstrates in his article "Reading Rooms," as action in the world (Stillman). Philip Sidney's use of architectural forms and settings in *The Countess of Pembroke's Arcadia* (1590) has received some attention, both for the role of the literary lodges and for their inspiration. John Summerson cited the description of Kalendar's house to illustrate the late Elizabethan patron's desire to limit the ornamentation otherwise urged on by the master craftsmen (53, citing the 1623 edition of *The Countess of Pembroke's Arcadia* 7). The paired star-shaped lodges evoked in the *New Arcadia*, taking the form of a comet, have been linked to the Hvězda Pavilion, Prague, built for the Emperor Ferdinand in 1555: Philip Sidney visited Prague in 1575 and 1577 (Skretkowicz; see Goldring *ARC* 1:20). In turn, the literary lodges have been suggested to have influenced the form of at least two star-shaped buildings: Star Castle, Scilly Isles, and Spur Royal Castle, Northern Ireland (Girouard, *Elizabethan Architecture* 252). Mark Girouard notes that by 1624 Philip Sidney's fantastical forms were disparagingly received as exemplars for architecture by Sir Henry Wotton, as unsuited for the accommodation of a court retinue (*Elizabethan Architecture* 254, citing Wotton's *Elements of Architecture* 19–20). Wotton was of a later generation that was looking more closely at Italian classicism and developing an aesthetic that valued commodity (decorum) over rarity, the generation that supported Inigo Jones and produced Leicester House. Wotton appears to take the fictive lodges as patterns for building, and this attitude may reflect the growing interest in direct precedent for the science of architecture.

The spatial paradigm in literature, the degrees to which architectural analogies are invoked in texts, and conversely the transference of built forms into the literary imagination, seem to have received little sustained attention beyond their "face value" uses. There is a recent intervention in the theory of Renaissance art which deserves further thought, as it highlights what might here be called the pre-Jonesian uses of the past in architecture. Philip Sidney's re-imagined architecture (revived from the Prague lodge, for example) places sixteenth-century symbolic architecture into the narrative of a "timeless" pastoral narrative, the *Arcadia*. It would seem to follow the model of "double historicity" proposed by Alexander Nagel and Christopher Wood for the representation of contemporary objects as (to us) anachronistic choices in Renaissance art. Nagel and Wood point out that the uses of contemporary objects in historical scenes, such as Carpaccio's depiction of the fourth-century St. Augustine in a thoroughly Renaissance study (*c*. 1503), are not simply stand-ins or unselfconscious elisions of periods, but substitutions for older objects by virtue of the long chain of precedents for such types. The contemporary objects gain authority from being represented in historical contexts, rather than betraying the contemporary production of the work (Nagel and Wood 403–7). Philip Sidney's lodges, then, to a shared circle with knowledge of the Emperor Ferdinand's Prague building, might be received not as pen portraits from life, but as acceptable substitutes within the long chain of spaces that supported royal identities over time.

"Poesie, historie, architecture and sculpture," four characters in Jonson's last court masque in 1631, are a reminder of how closely the plastic arts and texts were positioned. Discourses around decorum, proportion, and imitation shaped and responded to the issues of construction for text and object, as Elizabeth Jordan has shown (299). The concept of substitution, after Nagel and Wood, may now need to be accommodated with imitation. Few studies attempt a cross-disciplinary approach, although the "material turn" in the social and historical disciplines has brought renewed attention to material practices and environments in recent years, with a greater breadth of methodologies as a result. The material culture of texts (manuscript, print, and "the book") is a major contribution to this expansion of academic practice; architectural history appears more insular in comparison. The Sidneys as a literary family—of authors, patrons, readers, and collectors—undoubtedly offer more potential for research that works across "poesie, historie, architecture and sculpture," with the aim of revealing the pattern of now-eroded connections between material and text.

Bibliography

Primary and Secondary Sources

Celovsky, Lisa. "Ben Jonson and Sidneian Legacies of Hospitality." *Studies in Philology* 106.2 (2009): 178–206.

Coope, Rosalys. "The 'Long Gallery': Its Origins, Use, Development and Decoration." *Architectural History* 29 (1986): 43–72.

Cooper, Nicholas. *The Jacobean Country House from the Archives of Country Life*. London: Aurum, 2006.

Emery, Anthony. *Greater Medieval Houses of England and Wales, 1300–1500: Southern England*. Cambridge: Cambridge UP. 2006.

Goodall, John. *The English Castle, 1066–1650*. New Haven, CT: Yale UP, 2011.

Girouard, Mark. *Elizabethan Architecture: Its Rise and Fall, 1540–1640*. New Haven, CT: Yale UP, for The Paul Mellon Centre for Studies in British Art, 2009.

—. *Life in the English Country House*. New Haven, CT: Yale UP, 1978.

Guerci, Manolo. "Salisbury House in London, 1599–1694: The Strand Palace of Sir Robert Cecil." *Architectural History* 52 (2009): 31–78.

Hasted, Edward. *The History and Topographical Survey of the County of Kent*. 4 vols. Canterbury: Simmons and Kirkby, 1778–99.

HMC. *Report on the Manuscripts of Lord de L'Isle and Dudley Preserved at Penshurst Place*. 6 vols. London: HMSO, 1925–66.

Jordan, Elizabeth. "Inigo Jones and the Architecture of Poetry." *RQ* 44.2 (1991): 280–319.

Maddicott, Hilary. "A Collection of the Interregnum Period: Philip, Lord Viscount Lisle, and His Purchases from the 'Late King's Goods', 1649–1660." *Journal of the History of Collections* 11.1 (1999): 1–24.

McKellar, Elizabeth. *The Birth of Modern London: The Development and Design of the City 1660–1720*. Manchester: Manchester UP, 1999.

Moul, Victoria. *Jonson, Horace and the Classical Tradition*. Cambridge: Cambridge UP, 2010.

Nagel, Alexander, and Christopher S. Wood. "Toward a New Model of Renaissance Anachronism." *Art Bulletin* 87.3 (2005): 403–15.

National Trust. *Ham House, Surrey*. Rev. ed. London: National Trust, 2002.

—. *Knole, Kent*. Rev. ed. London: National Trust, 2000.

Newman, John. *West Kent and the Weald: The Buildings of England*. New Haven, CT: Yale UP, 1979.

Orlin, Lena Cowen. "Temporary Lives in London Lodgings." *HLQ* 71.1 (2008): 219–42.

Rathmell, J. "Jonson, Lord Lisle and Penshurst." *ELR* 1 (1971): 250–60.

Rowell, Christopher. "The Green Closet at Ham House: A Charles I Cabinet Room and its Contents." *Ham House: 400 Years of Collecting and Patronage*. Ed. Christopher Rowell. New Haven, CT: Yale UP, for The Paul Mellon Centre for Studies in British Art and The National Trust, 2013. 14–31.

Sheppard, F. H. W. (general ed.). "Gerrard Street Area: The Military Ground: King Street." *Survey of London, Volumes 33 and 34: St Anne Soho* (1966): 412–13.

— (general ed.). "Leicester Square Area: Leicester Estate." *Survey of London, Volumes 33 and 34: St Anne Soho* (1966): 416–40.

—(general ed.). "Leicester Square, North Side, and Lisle Street Area: Leicester Estate: Leicester House and Leicester Square North Side (No. 1–16)." *Survey of London, Volumes 33 and 34: St Anne Soho* (1966): 441–72.

Skelton, Kimberley. "Redefining Hospitality: The Leisured World of the 1650s English Country House." *Journal of the Society of Architectural Historians*, 68.4 (2009): 496–513.

Skretkowicz, Victor. "Symbolic Architecture in Sidney's New Arcadia." *Review of English Studies* n.s. 33.130 (1982): 175–80.

Stratford, Jenny. *The Bedford Inventories: The Worldly Goods of John, Duke of Bedford, Regent of France (1389–1435)*. London: Society of Antiquaries of London, 1993.

Stillman, Robert. *Philip Sidney and the Poetics of Renaissance Cosmopolitanism*. Aldershot: Ashgate, 2008.

Strong, Roy. "Sidney's Appearance Reconsidered." *Sir Philip Sidney's Achievements*. Ed. M. J. B. Allen, D. Baker-Smith, and A. F. Kinney. New York: AMS, 1990. 3–31.

Summerson, John. *Architecture in Britain 1530–1830, The Pelican History of Art*. 7th ed. Harmondsworth: Penguin, 1983.

Thornton, Dora. *The Scholar in His Study: Ownership and Experience in Renaissance Italy*. New Haven, CT: Yale UP, 1997.

Wayne, Don. *Penshurst: The Semiotics of Place and the Poetics of History*. London: Methuen, 1984.

West, Susie. "Studies and Status: Spaces for Books in Seventeenth-century Penshurst Place, Kent." *Transactions of the Cambridge Bibliographical Society* 12.3 (2002): 266–92.

West, William W. "Reading Rooms: Architecture and Agency in the Houses of Michel de Montaigne and Nicholas Bacon." *Comparative Literature* 56.2 (2004): 111–29.

Worsley, Giles. *Inigo Jones and the European Classicist Tradition*. New Haven, CT: Yale UP, 2007.

The Sidneys and the Visual Arts

Elizabeth Goldring

Scholarship to date on the early modern Sidneys and the visual arts has focused overwhelmingly—and not without some justification—on Sir Philip Sidney and painting. Broadly speaking, such work may be divided into two strands. One, which has attracted contributions from art historians as well as literary critics, has sought to recover—if not Paolo Veronese's lost portrait of Sidney itself (1574)—then as much information as possible about the painting and its fate in the more than four hundred years since it was commissioned by Sidney and presented to Hubert Languet as a gift. The other, dominated almost exclusively by literary critics, has explored what might be called the painterly qualities of Sidney's writings, in particular the *Defence of Poetry*, *Astrophil and Stella*, and the *Old* and *New Arcadias*. This chapter surveys these, and other, strands of research on the Sidneys and the visual arts *c.* 1500–*c.* 1700, and concludes by suggesting some new directions for future scholarship on this rich topic.[1]

The Veronese Portrait

Veronese's portrait of Sidney is now known only from written sources, chief among them the fragmentary surviving correspondence of Sidney and Languet. These letters reveal that Sidney sat for the painting over a three- or four-day period in Venice in February 1574, having first debated whether it would be better to have his portrait executed by Veronese or Tintoretto, "who at the moment are easily the first in that art" (*Correspondence SPS* 1:107). In June 1574 the completed portrait was delivered to Languet in Vienna, the catalyst for the commission having been Languet's request some months earlier for a portrait in which Sidney's "noble nature" would be rendered visible "in his face" (*Correspondence SPS* 1:97).

The circumstances surrounding the commissioning of this portrait—together with the question of what became of it after Sidney gave it to Languet—are topics that have attracted the attention not only of Sidney's biographers, but also of those with an interest in what might be termed the collective biography of the wider Sidney circle—a group which included Languet, who initially expressed disappointment that Veronese had depicted Sidney as if a boy of twelve or thirteen and with a "melancholy and pensive" expression, but later decided that he had no possession he valued more (*Correspondence SPS* 1:254, 450); Jean de Vulcob, who so admired the painting's "elegance" when Languet showed it to him *c.* 1575 that he

---

1 I am grateful to the Viscount De L'Isle for permission to cite manuscripts in the De L'Isle Collection at the Centre for Kentish Studies, Maidstone, and to the Marquis of Bath for permission to cite the Dudley Papers at Longleat.

sought to have it copied (*Correspondence SPS* 1:450), and Daniel Rogers, whose *In effigiem Illustrissimj Iuuenis D. Philippj Sydnaej* was almost certainly written in praise of Veronese's portrait, probably at some point in the 1580s (Goldring, "Portrait of Sir Philip Sidney" 553). In addition, the painting—memorably, if somewhat hyperbolically, described by John Buxton as "surely … the finest portrait painted of any Englishman of the sixteenth century" (*Sir Philip Sidney* 70)—has come to be seen as a lens through which cultural relations between England and Italy in this period might be viewed. Like his uncle Leicester's 1575 sitting to the Roman mannerist painter Federico Zuccaro (the preliminary drawing for which is extant in the British Museum), Sidney's 1574 sitting to Veronese constitutes one of the earliest documented examples of a face-to-face encounter between an Elizabethan and an Italian Renaissance artist.[2]

In 1929 J. M. Purcell speculated in a letter to the *Times Literary Supplement* (*TLS*) that Veronese's portrait might have been hanging in a collection in Frankfurt by 1661, the year in which Algernon Sidney, Sir Philip's great-nephew, noted: "I haue written to my Correspondent at *Frankfort*, for Sir *Phylip Sydney* his Picture" (Collins 2:709). Purcell's letter occasioned responses, also in the *TLS*, from G. C. Moore, who opined that "the grounds of the identification can only be called childish," and from Mona Wilson, who took the opposite view: "I think Mr Purcell is very likely right in supposing that it was the Veronese which had found its way to Frankfurt." In the years since, numerous scholars—art historians as well as literary critics, Anglo-American scholars as well as Continental European ones—have been drawn to the subject of the Veronese portrait, including Berta Siebeck (175–7), A. C. Judson (23–7), Jan van Dorsten (55–6), Michelangelo Muraro (391–6), David Rosand (236–49), and Sir Roy Strong, the last of whom considered the painting within the broader context of Sidney's known portrait commissions ("Sidney's Appearance" 145–63). Strong demonstrated from a combination of written and visual evidence that in an era in which many elite men and women were content to sit for their portraits just once in their lives (if at all), Sidney sat on at least six occasions—to Veronese, to the Milanese Antonio Abondio (Maximilian II's "Kaiserlicher Majestät Wachsbossierer und Conterfeter"), and to Nicholas Hilliard, among others—"probably within as many years, which statistically is enormously high in late sixteenth-century terms" ("Sidney's Appearance" 162).[3] In this respect, as in so many others, the young Sidney may have taken a leaf from his uncle Leicester's book: recent researches have revealed that Robert Dudley sat for his portrait on at least twenty occasions between Elizabeth I's accession in 1558 and his own death thirty years later, often—as Sidney seems to have done with Veronese—going to considerable effort to recruit the services of artists with a history of patronage at the highest levels on the Continent (Goldring, "Princely Pleasures" 47–56; Goldring, *Robert Dudley* 5–8, 66–74, 103–4, and *passim*).

---

2   See, for example, Buxton, *Elizabethan Taste* 106–9; Chaney 205, and for the Zuccaro sitting, Goldring, "Portraits" 654–60; Goldring, "Portraiture" 163–88; Goldring, "Princely Pleasures" 47–56, and Goldring, *Robert Dudley* 103–14, where Zuccaro's preliminary drawing is reproduced as fig. 87.

3   For Abondio, including his 1574 appointment as "His Imperial Majesty's Portraitist in Wax and on Canvas", see Osborn 101–2. Only one of Sidney's sittings has left behind visual evidence: the portrait now at Longleat (but previously at Wilton) and inscribed "who giues him selfe, may well his picture giue / els weare it vayne since both short tyme doe lyue" is believed to have been commissioned from a Netherlandish artist—perhaps Cornelis Ketel—as a gift for Sidney's beloved sister Mary around the time of her 1577 marriage to Henry Herbert, second Earl of Pembroke. The Longleat painting seems to have been the original, or prime, version of a "type" which enjoyed wide circulation in the late sixteenth century, both during Sidney's lifetime and after his death in 1586. Other extant examples of this "type" include the painting of Sidney now in the National Portrait Gallery (NPG) – reproduced in this volume as Illustration 7 – which is inscribed "CAETERA FAMA / E[X] D[EO]" ("Further fame from God"). See Strong, "Sidney's Appearance" 145–63.

In 1997 Roger Kuin—building upon a hypothesis first mooted in 1954 by Buxton (*Sir Philip Sidney* 70–71)—suggested that Philippe de Mornay du Plessis, whose wife cared for the dying Languet, might have acquired the Veronese portrait in the immediate aftermath of Languet's death at Antwerp in 1581, thus accounting for the fact that a portrait of "M. Sydnei" was recorded, nearly forty years later, in a 1619 inventory of the du Plessis château at Saumur (Kuin, "New Light" 19–47; Kuin, "Languet" 42–4; Fillon 164). Elizabeth Goldring has since argued that "the lack of specific details" concerning the images of Sidney recorded at Saumur —and, indeed, at Frankfurt—in the seventeenth century probably makes it "impossible to establish" a firm connection between either of those portraits and Veronese's ("Portrait of Sir Philip Sidney" 550). But Kuin's identification of numerous documents in the Antwerp archives pertaining to the settlement of Languet's estate—from which he concluded that the Veronese portrait was almost certainly among Languet's effects when he died, but sold off shortly thereafter— proved a turning point in the long-standing effort to trace the painting's fate. In 2012 Goldring—building upon Kuin's findings, but also drawing upon a previously unpublished 1582 inventory of the picture collection of Robert Dudley, Earl of Leicester—was able to place the Veronese portrait at Leicester House in the Strand within months of Languet's death, positing that in all probability Leicester and Sidney either purchased or made arrangements to purchase the picture when they traveled to Antwerp together on a diplomatic mission in February 1582 ("Portrait of Sir Philip Sidney").[4] In addition, Goldring demonstrated—with recourse to surviving inventories of sixteenth- and early seventeenth-century aristocratic English households—that Veronese's portrait of Sidney was almost certainly "one of the first [paintings] by a leading artist of the late Venetian Renaissance to have been displayed in an English picture collection" ("Portrait of Sir Philip Sidney" 548), and thus may have been instrumental in fueling the Jacobean vogue for collecting Venetian paintings (*Robert Dudley* 132–36, 223–37, 250, Appendix III:L38).

It is not clear what became of the Veronese portrait after 1590, the last date on which it was recorded at Leicester House. But a portrait of Languet, apparently also acquired from Languet's estate in 1582, found its way—via Sidney's widow, Frances, Countess of Essex, and her mother, Lady Walsingham—to Penshurst in 1595, and may well correspond to the portrait of "Hughbertus Languetus" recorded in "the Lower great Chamber" at Penshurst *c.* 1623 (the date of the earliest known surviving inventory of the Sidneys' picture holdings), as well as to the portrait of Languet in three-quarter length executed by an unknown artist (Illustration 8), now hanging in the Pages Room (De L'Isle MS U1500 E120; Goldring, "Portrait of Sir Philip Sidney" 552–53n37). That portrait, which depicts Languet dressed in black and holding a pair of gloves in his right hand, is inscribed "ANNO DOMINI 1564" and "ÆTATIS SVÆ 51"—though, in fact, Languet was only forty-six in 1564. As Kuin plausibly has suggested, one or both of these inscriptions may therefore "have been added later, by Sidneys with fallible memories" (*Correspondence SPS* 1:frontispiece). The enormous gold chain seen hanging from Languet's neck—and shown off to maximum advantage against his plain, dark garments—is almost certainly a depiction of that presented by Sir Henry Sidney during Languet's 1579 visit to England (British Library, Add. MS 17520 fol. 12). It is thus in all probability also a later addition—though whether by Languet or by later generations of Sidneys is impossible to know without recourse to technical analysis.

---

4   In the 1570s and 1580s Leicester House in the Strand (later Essex House) was the primary residence of Robert Dudley, Earl of Leicester, and often served as Sir Philip Sidney's London base. It should not be confused with the Leicester House built in the 1630s for Robert Sidney, second Earl of Leicester (of the second creation), on the site of what is now Leicester Square. For that property, see West *ARC* 1:19.

And what of the Veronese portrait? The balance of probability has to be that it no longer survives. No first-hand account of, or confirmed reference to, the painting is known to date from later than *c.* 1590. Moreover, a significant proportion of the paintings that we know to have been produced in the sixteenth century have fallen victim during the intervening centuries to hazards ranging from fire to over-painting. But it is not impossible that Veronese's portrait of Sidney is waiting to be found, perhaps gathering dust in an attic or under a bed. Anyone hoping to stumble upon it might do well—in the light of the findings outlined above—to scour English picture collections (rather than, as previous generations of scholars have done, Continental European ones) and to bear in mind what can be deduced from the Sidney–Languet correspondence about the painting's probable appearance. First, as Languet himself famously noted with surprise upon first seeing the portrait, Veronese depicted Sidney as "far more youthful" than the nineteen-year-old he had been at the time of the sitting (*Correspondence SPS* 1:254): indeed, in the aforementioned Leicester House inventory of 1582 the painting is rather misleadingly described as a portrait of Sidney "when he was a Boye" (British Library, Add. MS 78177 fol. 36, transcribed in Goldring, "Portrait of Sir Philip Sidney" 554). Secondly, the portrait, according to Languet, made Sidney look "a little melancholy and pensive"—not, perhaps, an altogether surprising state of affairs given that Sidney had confessed to Languet just a few weeks before the sitting that "often I am more melancholy than either my age or my occupations warrant" (*Correspondence SPS* 1:450, 106–7). Third, the painting almost certainly lacked an inscription: although Languet had composed some "little verses" (now lost) extolling Sidney's virtues for the purpose of having them "copied on to the picture … if there is enough empty space for them," Sidney begged leave to omit the proposed inscription: "I should not like to be so shameless as to have such proclamations of my praises inscribed [on it], the more as they are quite undeserved" (*Correspondence SPS* 1:98, 107). Finally, it seems probable that the portrait was bust-length, thus enabling Sidney's visage to take center stage: not only did Languet specifically request an image that would show visible "signs" of Sidney's "noble nature" and "virtue," as evidenced in his "face" (*Correspondence SPS* 1:97), but practical considerations—ranging from the constraints of time and money to the need for the finished painting to be transported across the Alps on horseback—would argue for the portrait having been a relatively compact, head-and-shoulders depiction.

Speaking Pictures

The pictorial quality of Sir Philip Sidney's writings long has been recognized as one of its defining features. Not only does the *Defence* define poetry as "a speaking picture" (Sidney, *Major Works* 217), but both the *Old* and the *New Arcadias*—and to a lesser extent *Astrophil and Stella*—are permeated by intensely visual language. Throughout the *Arcadias* "paint" is used to mean "describe" or "render," a trope also found in *Astrophil and Stella* 1, 2, 45, 70, 81, 93, and 98. Both *Arcadias*, moreover, repeatedly ask the reader to think visually and to picture the scenes described as if they were paintings. Often the acts of looking at, talking about, and judging visual images are thematized. Indeed, in both the *Old* and *New Arcadias* it is the experience of viewing a painting in a gallery—together with the desire to be "judge, forsooth, of the painter's cunning" (*Old Arcadia* 11)—which sets into motion the princes' Arcadian sojourn, and thus the plot as a whole.

In 1901 J. J. Jusserand, noting what he termed the "obvious reminiscences of Tintoretto or Titian" in Sidney's descriptions of the princesses Pamela and Philoclea in both the *Old* and *New Arcadias*, suggested that Sidney must have admired the works of these artists while in

Italy in 1574 (244). Buxton, writing in 1963, made a similar observation, though he suggested a source of inspiration nearer to home: "When he [Sidney] describes Basilius 'holding up his hands as the old governess of Danae is painted, when she suddenly saw the golden shower,' he ... seems to suggest Titian's painting of the subject, of which there may have been a copy in England" (*Elizabethan Taste* 107).[5] But it was Katherine Duncan-Jones who, first in her 1964 Oxford thesis ("Sidney's Pictorial Imagination") and then in an essay published in 1980 ("Sidney and Titian"), fleshed out the connection posited by Buxton, demonstrating that though paintings of Danae were ubiquitous in the Renaissance, the "old governess" to whom Sidney pointedly refers was Titian's "unique addition ... a detail derived only from a slight reference in Apollonius of Rhodes" ("Sidney and Titian" 5).[6] Intriguingly, documentary information which has come to light since indicates that Philip II took delivery of paintings by Titian—including at least one of the Ovidian *poesie* (probably *Venus and Adonis*)—during his brief marriage to Mary Tudor. But so far as is known, none of his Titians remained in England after Mary's death (Hope 53–65).

It is not, however, simply the imprint of Italian Renaissance art that has been detected in the *Arcadias*. In 1968, for example, David C. McPherson argued that in all probability Sidney's source for the comic character Mopsa was not, as William Ringler had suggested, the shepherd Mopsus in Virgil's *Eclogues*, but rather a Northern Renaissance print: *The Wedding of Mopsus and Nisa* (as it is usually called in English), first published at Antwerp in 1570 and based on a drawing by Pieter Breughel the Elder (McPherson 420–28). McPherson posited that "Sidney could have known the engraving" through his "important connections with the Low Countries [which] began before the years in which he was writing the original *Arcadia*, i.e. 1577–80" (426). This is perfectly plausible. But it is also worth bearing in mind that it is now clear—thanks to a revolution over the past two decades or so in art historians' understanding of early modern print culture—that Continental prints, particularly Netherlandish ones, circulated widely in Elizabethan England (see, for example, Wells-Cole 43–123). Indeed, Sidney's uncle Leicester is known, on at least one occasion in the early 1580s, to have sourced engravings from Antwerp with the help of one of his many agents in the city (Goldring, "Politics" 225–43).

The work of Buxton, Duncan-Jones, and McPherson notwithstanding, most scholars have shied away from attempts to make one-to-one connections between Sidney's writings and actual works of art, instead preferring to draw out the relationship between Sidney's literature and the emerging body of formal written discourse on painting and the visual arts. In 1965 Geoffrey Shepherd suggested that the distinction which Sidney makes in the *Defence* between the mental *"idea or fore-conceit"* and "the work itself" (*Major Works* 216) might be seen to anticipate arguments found in two of the defining treatises of late Mannerist art theory: Giovanni Paolo Lomazzo's *Trattato dell'arte della pittura, scoltura et architettura* (Milan, 1584) and Federico Zuccaro's *L'Idea de' pittori, scultori, e architetti* (Turin, 1607)—owing to which Shepherd, somewhat reductively, labeled Sidney's writings "mannerist" (Sidney,

---

5   Tantalizingly, recent archival findings have revealed that Robert Dudley, Earl of Leicester's picture collection included a painting of a "gentle woman" inscribed with "Ouid his uerses vnder her" (British Library, Add. MS 78177 fol. 36; transcribed in Goldring, "Portrait of Sir Philip Sidney" 554; see also Goldring, *Robert Dudley* Appendix III:L33). But given the ubiquity of Ovidian inscriptions on early modern paintings—to say nothing of the fact that it seems unlikely that the term "gentle woman" would be used to refer to the nude figure of Danae—the probability must be that there is no connection between this particular painting of Leicester's and Titian's *Danae*.

6   At least four painted versions of Titian's *Danae* (probably executed by Titian, and his studio, over a period stretching from the late 1540s to the early 1550s, though the dating is a matter of debate) are known to be extant. Three of these—in the Kunsthistorisches, Vienna; the Hermitage, St. Petersburg; and the Prado, Madrid—include the figure of an elderly woman reaching up to catch the shower of gold; that in the Capodimonte, Naples does not.

Apology 64–5).[7] In 1972 Forrest Robinson argued—with reference to the same passage in the *Defence*—for a possible English influence: Dr. John Dee's "Mathematicall Preface" to Henry Billingsley's translation of Euclid (London, 1570), which, in the course of mounting one of the first formal defenses in English of painting and architecture as learned, liberal arts, makes a distinction between "geometrical images in the mind and their representation in external nature" (122; see also Farmer 2–10; Dundas 31). In 1993 Judith Dundas—focusing on this same passage from the *Defence*, as well as on that in the *Old Arcadia* in which Cleophila's thought processes are likened to the preliminary sketches of an artist (*Old Arcadia* 189)—identified possible echoes of the second edition of Giorgio Vasari's *Vite* (Florence, 1568), in particular its newly added "Life of Titian" (Dundas 31). In addition, Dundas argued for a potential connection between Leonardo's unfinished (and, in the sixteenth century, unpublished) treatise on painting and the *New Arcadia*'s description of a painter "well skilled in wounds, but with never a hand to perform his skill" (49–50; Sidney, *Countess of Pembroke's Arcadia* 381). Meanwhile, in 1991, David Rosand—one of the very few art historians to address the visual qualities of Sidney's writings—suggested with respect to the *Defence* that Lodovico Dolce's *Dialogo della pittura intitolato l'Aretino* (Venice, 1557) warrants "serious consideration, not so much as a 'source' but as a text of similar charge" (247).

Lucy Gent's work, which elegantly straddles the disciplinary boundary between "literature" and "art history," has offered the most sustained—and probably the most influential—meditation on the relationship between Sidney's *oeuvre* and Renaissance art theory. In the introduction to her 1973 edition of R[obert] D[allington]'s *Strife of Love in a Dreame* (London, 1592)—a partial translation of Francesco Colonna's *Hypnerotomachia Poliphili* (Venice, 1499) which was posthumously dedicated to Sidney—Gent persuasively argued that the *Arcadias*' description of a marble Venus with breasts "Like pommels round of marble clear, / Where azured veins well mixed appear / With dearest tops of porphyry" in all probability derives from a passage in the *Hypnerotomachia*, Colonna and Sidney having been unique in applying this ancient conceit to a statue of Venus (*Old Arcadia* 208; *Countess of Pembroke's Arcadia* 289; Gent, *Hypnerotomachia* vii). In 1981, in *Picture and Poetry*, her seminal study of references to painting in a wide variety of Elizabethan and Jacobean texts, Gent demonstrated that most early modern Englishmen, unlike their counterparts in Italy, lacked a vocabulary of the visual arts. Sidney, however, emerges as an exception to Gent's general rule. His praise, in both the *Old* and *New Arcadias*, of the back of Philoclea's knee, which, shrouded in shadow, "doth yield such sight, / Like cunning painter shadowing white," suggests—like *Astrophil and Stella* 7, in which Nature, "painter wise," renders Stella "mixed of shades and light"—that he was fully conversant in the chiaroscuro technique first explicated in Book II of Alberti's treatise on painting (*c*. 1435), and that he understood, in Gent's words, "that a picture may indeed depend more on shadows than on glittering colour to give it life" (*Picture and Poetry* 26–7; Sidney, *Old Arcadia* 209; Sidney, *Countess of Pembroke's Arcadia* 290; Sidney, *Major Works* 155). By the same token, Gent perceived in the *New Arcadia*'s description of Basilius' star-shaped lodge and its setting of "lovely lightsomeness and artificial shadows" evidence of Sidney's awareness of "the chiaroscuro of landscape" (27; Sidney, *Countess of Pembroke's Arcadia* 148).[8]

Most scholars have treated the question of what paintings Sidney might have seen and the question of what treatises on or defenses of painting he might have read as discrete issues, choosing to address themselves to one, but not both, of these questions. Goldring's work,

---

7   The many who have followed Shepherd's lead in applying this label include Hamilton 121 and Farmer 2, 10.
8   More recently, in a substantial article of 2014, Gent has probed the interface between rhetorical theory and aesthetic theory in Elizabethan England ("Elizabethan Architecture" 71–106).

however, has begun to bridge this gulf by revealing several of those in Sidney's immediate orbit—including Robert Dudley, Earl of Leicester, and the Herbert Earls of Pembroke—to have been important and influential patrons of painters and collectors of paintings, as well as among the first in England to have embraced the Italianate view of the painter as the practitioner of a liberal art, and thus as fit company for courtiers. In an era in which many English aristocrats seem to have owned no more than a handful of paintings, Leicester amassed an extraordinary collection of more than two hundred paintings and other works of art, including commissioned works by leading Continental artists. He also fostered the birth of an English vernacular discourse on the visual arts and nurtured the careers of a number of native-born painters, including Nicholas Hilliard, who forged something approaching a personal friendship with the earl. Sidney, as is now clear, played a pivotal role in the building up of Leicester's picture holdings, sourcing "woorkes" for his uncle from the Continent (Longleat, Dudley Papers II fol. 148r) and developing a reputation in his own right as a discerning patron of painters. Had he not pre-deceased Leicester, Sidney—as his uncle's designated heir—might well have inherited the bulk of Leicester's pictures, and might perhaps have gone on to surpass him as both a collector of paintings and a patron of painters. As events transpired, however, Leicester's paintings were widely dispersed in the immediate aftermath of his death in 1588. But the survival of more than twenty inventories, among other documentary sources, has permitted Goldring to reconstruct Leicester's picture holdings at Kenilworth Castle, Wanstead Manor, and Leicester House in the Strand, and also to illuminate his patronage of painters and writers on painting—including, significantly, both Dee and Zuccaro, the latter of whose 1575 journey to England was made at Leicester's behest. In so doing, Goldring has provided a new context within which to view works such as the *Defence* and the *Old Arcadia*, both written in part at Leicester House (*Robert Dudley*, 205–35 and *passim*).

And what of the Herbert Earls of Pembroke? Comparatively few papers pertaining to the Tudor Herberts have survived owing to seventeenth-century fires at both Wilton and Baynard's Castle. But Goldring's discovery in 2002 of a 1562 inventory recording nearly seventy paintings at Baynard's Castle—including, it would appear, Holbein's celebrated and much sought-after *Christina of Denmark* (painted for Henry VIII in 1538 and now in the National Gallery, London)—has cast the Elizabethan Herberts in a new light (National Art Library, MSL 1982/30 fols. 85r, 85v, 86r, 86v, 92r; transcribed and discussed in Goldring, "Important Early Picture Collection" 157–60; see also Goldring, "Art Collecting"). The Baynard's Castle collection also included, as of 1562, five sculptures, nine sketches or drawings, and a map of London. Its composition after that date is, in the absence of later inventories, impossible to describe with precision and may well have changed from one year to the next.[9] But there can be little doubt that the collection of paintings and other works of art at Baynard's Castle constituted one of the largest, and most diverse, aristocratic assemblages in Elizabethan London, exceeded in size and scope only, perhaps, by that at Leicester House (Goldring, *Robert Dudley* 220–23). Given that the Elizabethan Sidneys were regular visitors to both Baynard's Castle and Leicester House, they must have been familiar with the pictures and other works of art on display at these properties. Indeed, the contents of both collections may well have left an imprint not only on Sir Philip Sidney's pictorial imagination, but also on the collecting and patronage patterns of Robert, who, together with his first wife

---

9   *Christina of Denmark*, for example, is known to have passed into the collection of John, first Baron Lumley, at some point prior to 1590. Such losses, however, were in all probability offset by a regular influx of new acquisitions for Baynard's Castle. In 1567, for example, the first Earl of Pembroke joined forces with William Cecil (the future Lord Burghley) to employ the services of an agent to acquire sculpture from the Continent. See Goldring, "Important Early Picture Collection" 157–60.

Barbara (*née* Gamage), laid the foundations of the present picture collection at Penshurst. Goldring's discoveries concerning the Herberts' holdings at Baynard's Castle have also lent credence to Karel van Mander's early seventeenth-century claim—long assumed to be apocryphal—that Zuccaro was entertained at Baynard's Castle in 1575 "in the company of painters and art lovers" (1:150; Goldring, "Important Early Picture Collection" 157–60). In addition, Goldring's findings have raised the very real possibility that there was a sizeable picture collection at Wilton when Sidney was working on the *Arcadias* there.

Other Strands of Research

In addition to the two dominant scholarly strands just discussed, there are several other topic clusters which might be construed as falling under the general heading of "The Sidneys and the Visual Arts"—though again Sir Philip Sidney's life and writings have attracted the lion's share of attention to date. Penshurst has been suggested as the model for Sidney's depiction of Kalander's house of "fair and strong stone" (*Countess of Pembroke's Arcadia* 71; Croll 124–5), while Sidney's personal experience of the tiltyard has been discussed in relation to the painted emblems, imprese, and devices described in Book II of the *New Arcadia*, a text which Strong has aptly called a "handbook to the Elizabethan image ... and its expression in allegorical pageantry" (*Cult of Elizabeth* 147–51; see also Yates 88–94; Young; Parker; Skretowicz). Sidney's relationship to Nicholas Hilliard—and, by extension, the relationship of each man's artistic output to that of the other—has also attracted interest, chiefly from literary scholars. Hilliard's account of a conversation with Sidney regarding perspective and proportion—an episode which, curiously, has received only glancing mention from Hilliard's biographers (see, for example, Auerbach 43; Edmond 42)—has been read by Clark Hulse as evidence that Sidney embraced painting as a gentlemanly pursuit (121–2). Meanwhile, Patricia Fumerton (57–97), among others, has explored the affinities between Sidney's sonnets and Hilliard's miniatures as intimate, private forms of expression which simultaneously conceal and reveal.

Considerable attention also has been devoted—in this case by art historians as well as literary scholars—to an exploration of the wide range of visual artifacts arising from Sidney's death and the mourning for him. Ellen Chirelstein, for example, has detected possible allusions to Sidney's fatal wounding at Zutphen in a full-length painting of Sir William Drury in armor, signed by Daniel van den Queecborne and dated 1587 (Yale Center for British Art, New Haven, CT).[10] In addition to an inscription reading "SCONSOLATO" ("Disconsolate"), in the middle distance there is a line of soldiers not unlike some of those depicted in Thomas Lant and Theodor De Bry's *Sequitur celebritas et pompa funeris* (London, 1587–88), a sequence of thirty engravings depicting the mourners in Sidney's funeral procession marching through the streets of London, six copies of which are known to be extant (in the British Library; Brown University; Christ Church, Oxford; the College of Arms; the De L'Isle Collection, and the Folger Shakespeare Library). Thus, it may be the case, as Chirelstein has suggested, that the viewer is "invited to associate Drury's performance in the Low Countries" with Sidney's (291).

The *Sequitur celebritas* itself also has been the focus of much scholarly interest. Ronald Strickland, for example, has explored what he terms the *Sequitur celebritas'* "proximity ... to the broadside ballad in terms of material production," suggesting that the work was a speculative venture by a printer, aimed at the emerging middle classes (19–34). Goldring, by

---

10   For a reproduction of this painting, see Goldring, "'So lively a portraiture'" fig. 11.

contrast, has argued that the lavishness of the *Sequitur celebritas* as a material object points to its having been a special commission—in all probability by Robert Dudley, Earl of Leicester, and Sir Francis Walsingham—for presentation to the more important participants in the procession as well as, perhaps, to figures of note who had been unable to witness the event itself ("In the Cause" 227–42). Elsewhere, Goldring has produced an illustrated scholarly edition of the *Sequitur celebritas* (Goldring et al., *John Nichols's The Progresses* 3:283–340), and has traced an iconographical line of descent to the *Sequitur celebritas* from Hendrick Goltzius's 1584 sequence of plates depicting the funeral procession of William of Orange, and from the *Sequitur celebritas* to the imagery produced to mark the death of Henry, Prince of Wales, in 1612 (Goldring, "Funeral of Sir Philip Sidney" 210–19; Goldring, "'So Iust a Sorrowe'" 280–300). She has also identified a life-sized, full-length painting of a melancholy youth leaning on a halberd, executed *c.* 1587–88 by an unknown artist and now in a private collection (Illustration 14), as a depiction of Sir Robert Sidney in mourning for his elder brother, apparently commissioned as a gift for his uncle Leicester, in whose possession, at Leicester House in the Strand, it was recorded in 1588 ("'So lively a portraiture'" 12–22). Robert, so far as is known, never wrote an elegy for his brother. But this portrait—which depicts its subject in an Arcadian setting, with dark storm clouds gathering overhead and troops and a city under siege in the distance—might be read as an expression of Robert's grief, and thus as an elegy of sorts.

And what of the seventeenth-century Sidneys, who in this, as in so many things, have been somewhat overshadowed by Sir Philip? No study of the country house poem is complete without Ben Jonson's "To Penshurst," and many such works therefore include brief, if rather general, discussions of the material culture of early seventeenth-century Penshurst, typically focusing on the medieval hall as a site of hospitality (see, for example, Wayne 86–108; McBride 58–9). Detailed, in-depth analysis of the seventeenth-century Sidneys as patrons of the visual arts is, however, thin on the ground. Strong has identified a group of extant portrait miniatures—including depictions of several members of the Sidney circle *c.* 1570–*c.* 1610—which, though now widely dispersed, "must originally have been in the possession of Robert Sidney, first Earl of Leicester of the second creation" ("Leicester House Miniatures" 694). This group includes a portrait of Mary Dudley Sidney, attributed to Levina Teerlinc (*c.* 1575) and now in the Victoria and Albert Museum, as well as several images by Hilliard, including one, executed *c.* 1590 and now in the National Portrait Gallery (Illustration 9), which is believed to be "the only authentic" painted likeness of Mary Sidney Herbert, Countess of Pembroke, to have survived from her lifetime ("Leicester House Miniatures" 698). Elsewhere, Hilary Maddicott has begun to illuminate the patronage and art collecting of the mid-to-late seventeenth-century Sidneys, particularly Philip Sidney, third Earl of Leicester ("Political and Cultural Career"; "Collection"). It has long been known that the future third earl, while still Viscount Lisle, purchased a substantial number of paintings and other works of art from the Royal Collection in the wake of Charles I's execution in 1649. But Maddicott's researches have demonstrated that Lisle's acquisitions were greater in number and quality than previously supposed: sixty paintings and sixty pieces of sculpture, a figure which, as Francis Haskell has observed in his study of the dispersal of Charles's collection, is vastly "more than any other single private collector in England" and suggests that Lisle "was trying to build up a collection of Old Masters" (183). As events transpired, however, these *objets d'art* had to be returned to the Crown at the Restoration.

New Directions

The scholarly advances outlined above notwithstanding, considerable scope remains for new work on the seventeenth-century Sidneys as patrons of the visual arts. How might this topic be approached? An inventory of Penshurst long catalogued in error as a late seventeenth-century document (De L'Isle MS U1500 E120), but re-dated by Germaine Warkentin to *c.* 1623 (1–26), seems an obvious point of departure, for its list of a hundred or so paintings—chiefly portraits, though religious narratives also feature—constitutes the earliest inventory of pictures at Penshurst known to survive. This document is not, however, without its challenges for the scholar. As is typically the case with sixteenth- and early seventeenth-century inventories of aristocratic English households, the Penshurst inventory is as notable for what it does not say as for what it does. There is, for example, no information on artists' names. Nor are details provided of when, where, or how individual items were acquired. Indeed, in the case of portraits, the inventory entries typically consist of little more than the sitters' names. But other sources—written as well as visual—help to fill some of these gaps while also revealing the Sidneys to have been commissioning and collecting pictures long before *c.* 1623.

In addition to the activities of Sir Philip discussed above, it is clear from financial accounts, for example, that Sir Henry Sidney commissioned a painting of himself from "Arnold" (probably the Flemish émigré Arnold von Brounkhorst) in the mid-1560s (De L'Isle MS U1475 A5/4 fol. 3v) and another, from an unspecified artist, in the early 1570s (De L'Isle MS U1475 A4/5 fol. 5r); that he was actively acquiring "noble mens pictures" for Penshurst in the early 1570s (De L'Isle MS U1475 A33/2, unfol.; De L'Isle MS A4/5 fol. 5r), presumably, as was the convention of the day, for display as a series of *uomini illustri*, and that in 1579 he commissioned a portrait of his youngest son, Thomas, then aged just ten (De L'Isle MS U1475 A4/6 fol. 3r).[11] Meanwhile, the young Robert Sidney (later first Earl of Leicester of the second creation) seems—like his elder brother before him—to have used portraiture to mark important milestones from the time of his "Grand Tour" onwards. The Penshurst inventory of *c.* 1623, for example, records no fewer than five portraits of Robert (De L'Isle MS U1500 E120). These include a (now lost) portrait of him "when he went to Travell"—an image presumably commissioned in connection with his "Grand Tour" of the late 1570s and early 1580s, and a painting "at length in his vicounte Robes," which must allude to the full-length painting of the same description, executed *c.* 1605—perhaps by Robert Peake the Elder—and still at Penshurst today (Illustration 15). In all likelihood, the painting of Robert by an unknown artist *c.* 1588 (Illustration 13, now in the National Portrait Gallery, but previously at Penshurst), corresponds to one of the images of him recorded in the inventory of *c.* 1623, but for which no descriptive details are furnished. Whatever the case, the painting in question depicts Robert in three-quarter length, holding a baton in his right hand and clad in an orange doublet, an orange and white mandilion worn collie-westonward, white breeches, a white lace collar and cuffs, and an orange scarf. To his right may be seen a shield, and to his left a helmet with orange and white plumes. The presence of the baton, helmet, and shield suggests that this portrait was in all probability commissioned

---

11   In addition, inventories of Sir Henry's contemporaries suggest that copies of and variations on these and other portraits that he commissioned circulated at the Elizabethan court: those known to have displayed his image include Sir Andrew Dudley, whose probate inventory of 1559 records no fewer than three portraits of Sir Henry (Longleat, Dudley Papers 3 fol. 173), and Matthew Parker, Archbishop of Canterbury, whose probate inventory of 1575 records a single portrait of Sir Henry (Sandys 11). That said, all portraits of Sir Henry known to have survived from the sixteenth century are closely related to a single "type," a pattern for which is extant in the National Portrait Gallery. See Hearn, *Dynasties* 155–6, and Strong, *Tudor and Jacobean Portraits* 1:288–90.

to mark Robert's appointment as Governor of Flushing in 1588 (see Goldring, "'So lively a portraiture'" 14). So, too, does the liberal use of the color orange—which, like the pun on "orange" in *Astrophil and Stella* 30 ("Trust in the pleasing shade of Orange tree ..."), might be interpreted as a politically charged declaration of allegiance to the House of Orange (Sidney, *Major Works* 164, 361).

In addition to his activities as a patron of portrait painters, the young Robert, as is clear from correspondence, sourced pictures for his father during his "Grand Tour" (Collins 1: 271), and after the deaths of his father and elder brother in 1586, swiftly set about augmenting the family's picture holdings, acquiring numerous paintings for Penshurst in the Netherlands during his time as Governor of Flushing in the late 1580s and 1590s. Some of these, like the portraits of the Princess of Orange and her children which entered the Penshurst collection in 1588, were gifts from the sitters (De L'Isle MS U1475 C81/9). But in the main Robert devoted considerable time and expense to seeking out new pictures. Writing to his wife Barbara from the Netherlands in the early 1590s, he sheepishly confessed that, though desperately strapped for cash, he had been unable to resist spending the substantial sum of £20 on new paintings, which he would be sending on to her shortly (*DPFA* 93). On another occasion, also dating from the early 1590s, Robert shipped a tranche of pictures to Barbara—"one of Adam and Eve, another of the birthe of Christ, a St Jerome, and the picture <of> Ernestus"—which, he noted rather nervously, he "pray[ed] God may come well to penshurst for they have cost me a good deale of mony" (De L'Isle U1500 C1/19). In the same missive he promised to send "more" paintings soon.

Correspondence—some of it now lost and known only from an eighteenth-century transcription by George Vertue—reveals that Barbara herself, who (for the most part) remained in England during her husband's prolonged absences overseas, commissioned at least one picture for Penshurst during this period: an enormous group portrait of *c.* 1596, executed by Marcus Gheeraerts the Younger and still at Penshurst today (Illustration 17). It depicts a visibly pregnant Barbara standing alongside six of her children, believed on the basis of later inscriptions to be (from left to right): Elizabeth, Robert (later second Earl of Leicester of the second creation), Phillippa, William (the heir, who was to die in 1612), Mary (the future author, as Lady Mary Wroth, of *The Countess of Montgomery's Urania*, among other works), and Katherine.[12] Barbara's right hand rests on the infant Robert, her left on the young William, both of whom are depicted wearing skirts, an indication that neither boy had yet been breeched. This painting has attracted the attention of art historians in recent years as an important example of the "pregnancy portrait," a genre which, though little encountered in Continental portraiture of the sixteenth and seventeenth centuries, flourished in England from the late 1580s to *c.* 1630, with Gheeraerts one of its leading exponents (Hearn, *Marcus Gheeraerts II* 41–51).

The Penshurst inventory of *c.* 1623, as noted, provides no information on when, where, or how individual items entered the collection. But many of the pictures recorded in it—like the portrait of "Hughbertus Languetus" discussed above—can plausibly be linked to images known from other sources to have been acquired decades earlier. For example, the pictures of "St Jerom" and "the bearthe of our Lord" recorded in "the Parlour" *c.* 1623—together with the portrait of "the Archduke Ernestus" recorded in "the Lower great Chamber" *c.* 1623—are in all probability the paintings of the same subjects purchased by Robert Sidney

---

12   Vertue recorded seeing a letter from Robert to Barbara instructing her "to go to Mr. Gerrats to pay him for her picture and the Children—so long done, and unpaid" (cited and discussed in Hearn, *Marcus Gheeraerts II* 51). An extant letter from Robert to Barbara, written at Flushing on 26 January 1596/97, appears to allude to the same commission. See his reference to "20 *l.* for the picture" (*DPFA* 93).

in the Netherlands for "a good deale of mony" in 1591 and shipped back to England that same year (De L'Isle MS U1500 E120; De L'Isle MS U1500 C1/19).[13] Similarly, the "ffaire Large Table in wch are the picktures of my Ladye of Leicester at length wth childe and six of her children" recorded in "the greate Matted Gallerye" c. 1623 must surely be Gheeraerts the Younger's group portrait of c. 1596 (De L'Isle MS U1500 E120). In short, the inventory of c. 1623 – if examined in relation to the surviving pictorial and documentary record (including later inventories), as well as to the latest findings of architectural historians concerning the built environment of early modern Penshurst (see West ARC 1:19) – might form the foundation of a study of the Sidneys' picture holdings in the period c. 1500–c. 1700.

Such a study – which might also function as a guide to the early modern paintings which remain in situ at Penshurst – could, like the recently published catalogue of the Suffolk Collection (assembled by successive generations of Howard Earls of Suffolk and Berkshire), offer "valuable insight into the quality and variety of paintings found in a British aristocratic family over a period of 400 years" (Houliston 12). It might also, in the case of the Tudor-Stuart portraits preserved in the Penshurst collection today, shed new light on the (sometimes contested) identities of the sitters. These include a full-length portrait of a girl with an archlute (see Illustration 19), attributed to John de Critz (c. 1621) and tentatively identified by Josephine A. Roberts in 1983 as a depiction of Lady Mary Wroth, whose interest in music was much remarked upon by contemporaries such as Sir John Davies (Roberts 7; Lamb).[14] In some instances technical analysis might shed light on the identities of those depicted, or at least rule out some candidates. Dendrochronology, for example, can help to establish (in the case of paintings executed on panel) the earliest possible felling date for the wood used, and thus a *terminus post quem* for the execution of a given painting.

The role of the Sidney women – broadly defined – as patrons of painters is another topic ripe for future research. Although a definitive history of early modern Englishwomen as patrons of the visual arts has yet to be written,[15] none the less it is clear that throughout the sixteenth and seventeenth centuries a number of women at the heart of the Sidney circle were important patrons of painters. For example, Lettice, *née* Knollys, who married Robert Dudley, Earl of Leicester, in 1578, sat for her portrait on at least seven occasions during their ten-year marriage (see Goldring, *Robert Dudley* 124–7; see Ioppolo ARC 1:6). Only one extant portrait, executed c. 1585 and attributed to George Gower, has been conclusively identified as a depiction of her.[16] Now at Longleat, this painting, which depicts Lettice wearing a gown embroidered with ragged staves (the Dudley badge), expresses visually the sentiment articulated by Sir Philip Sidney's roughly contemporaneous "Defence of the Earl of Leicester" (1584): "my chiefest honour is to be a Dudley" (*Miscellaneous Prose* 134–9). So far as can be determined, this portrait also constitutes one of the first examples of the vogue among elite women at the late Elizabethan court for being painted wearing gowns embroidered with symbolic designs. Other apparently equally innovative portraits of Lettice – now known only from written sources – include a painting of her wearing

---

13   The painting of Adam and Eve shipped back to England at the same time – which also cost "a good deale of mony" (De L'Isle MS U1500 C1/19) – does not appear to be among the pictures recorded at Penshurst c. 1623 (De L'Isle MS U1500 E120).

14   For a summary of the scholarly debates concerning the identification of this sitter, see Hannay, *MSLW* 158.

15   James is, to date, the only book-length study of this topic. Unfortunately, however, it is marred by factual errors and also fails to engage with recent developments in the study of early modern British art, including the work of Karen Hearn on "pregnancy portraits" and that of Robert Tittler and Tarnya Cooper, among others, on the activities of members of the "middling sort" and below as patrons of painters and other practitioners of the visual arts. See Goldring, Review of *The Feminine Dynamic in English Art*.

16   For a reproduction of this portrait of Lettice, see Goldring, *Robert Dudley*, fig. 100.

"morninge weedes" *c.* 1582 (British Library Add. MS 78177 unfol.; see also Goldring, *Robert Dudley* Appendix III:L113)—a type of image which, though not unheard of in sixteenth-century Italy, was comparatively rare in Elizabethan England—and two paintings of her "with blackamoores" *c.* 1588 (Longleat, Dudley Papers XI fol. 61r; see also Goldring, *Robert Dudley* Appendix III:L83–L84), which must have helped to set the fashion for depicting fair-skinned English women with exotic, dark-skinned foreigners that was to reach its peak at the Jacobean and early Caroline courts with images such as Paul van Somer's 1617 painting of Queen Anne with a black manservant (Royal Collection).

Lettice's daughter Penelope, *née* Devereux, the "Stella" of Sidney's *Astrophil and Stella*, also had a more than passing interest in painting and the visual arts. Quite apart from the fact that *Astrophil and Stella*, as discussed above, seems to assume a familiarity on the part of its readers with the Italianate technique of chiaroscuro, documentary evidence indicates that Penelope was painted on several occasions—most notably, perhaps, by Hilliard, who executed at least one (now lost) miniature of her, celebrated by Henry Constable in a sonnet of *c.* 1589 (Margetts 758–61). Only one extant sixteenth-century painting has plausibly been linked to Penelope: executed *c.* 1578 by an unknown artist and now at Longleat, it depicts two girls, in all probability the young Penelope and her sister Dorothy (that is, the mother of Dorothy Percy Sidney, second Countess of Leicester, and the maternal grandmother of Dorothy Sidney Spencer, Countess of Sunderland, both patrons, in the middle decades of the seventeenth century, of Van Dyck and Lely, as well as, in Dorothy Percy Sidney's case, a noted collector in her own right).[17] Not only does a later inscription identify the sitters in the Longleat portrait as "The Ladys Penelope / Couteese [*sic*] of Warwick" and "Dorothy D'Evereux / Countesse of Northumberland," but inventories of the picture collection of Robert Dudley, Earl of Leicester, would suggest that this painting hung *c.* 1578–*c.* 1590, first at Kenilworth Castle and then at Leicester House in the Strand (Goldring, *Robert Dudley* Appendix I:K18–K19). There is some debate as to which of the girls depicted might be Penelope and which Dorothy. As Michele Margetts has observed:

> The later inscription would seem to imply that Penelope is on the left and Dorothy on the right, but the order in which the names appear may simply follow the standard practice of giving precedence to an elder child. The girl on the right may in fact have a better claim [to be Penelope], because of ... the precedence given her by her position in the portrait, slightly in front of her sister with both her shoulders showing. (760)

Whatever the case, it is striking that both sitters are depicted with light hair and black eyes, the unusual chiaroscuro combination attributed to "Stella", whose "fair hair" (*Astrophil and Stella* 13) and "black beams" (47) —"painter wise, / ... mixed of shades and light" (7)—are praised throughout *Astrophil and Stella* (see also, for example, *Astrophil and Stella* 9, 20, 32, and 91).

Little is known at present about Mary, Countess of Pembroke's activities as a patron of painters—though her sons, William, the third earl, and Philip, the fourth earl, together were to assemble at Wilton one of the largest and most celebrated picture collections in seventeenth-century England. The countess herself, as noted, seems to have been painted in miniature by Hilliard *c.* 1590 (see Illustration 9), while documentary evidence in the form of inventories of her uncle Leicester's picture holdings suggests that she sat for her portrait *en large* on at

---

17   For a reproduction of this double portrait, see Goldring, *Robert Dudley*, fig. 169. For Dorothy Percy Sidney's personal collection of paintings—including family portraits, landscapes, religious scenes, and fruit and flower pieces, all of which she bequeathed to her favorite son, Henry—see her will of 1659 (De L'Isle MS U1500 E110). I am grateful to Hilary Maddicott for sharing this reference with me.

least two occasions. A painting of "the yonge Countisse"—presumably commissioned to commemorate her 1577 marriage—was recorded from *c.* 1578 to 1588 at Kenilworth Castle, where it was displayed as a pair alongside one of "Henrie, Earle of Pembrooke" (Longleat, Dudley Papers XI fol. 21v; see Goldring, *Robert Dudley* Appendix I:K35–K36), while a second painting of the countess entered her uncle's collection at Leicester House in the Strand *c.* 1585 (Goldring, *Robert Dudley* Appendix III:L54). If John Aubrey is to be believed—his account in this particular case seems a reliable one—the hall at Wilton was filled during Mary Sidney Herbert's lifetime with portraits of "ministers of estate and heroes of Queen Elizabeth's time"—including the portrait of Sir Philip Sidney now at Longleat together with portraits of "some of the French" (Britton 84; Strong, "Sidney's Appearance" 147–8). But perhaps the best evidence for the Countess of Pembroke's interest in and knowledge of painting is her status as the dedicatee of both *Arcadias*: works in which, as discussed above, comprehension of individual passages often hinges upon first-hand knowledge of artistic theories and techniques as well as, in at least one case, knowledge of a specific painting (Titian's *Danae*). Moreover, we might presume that the acts of judging and talking about pictures so vividly dramatized in the *Arcadias* to some extent reflect—and perhaps were a spur to—discussions of a similar nature among the intimates for whom Sir Philip Sidney wrote these works.

Future research might consider in greater detail the activities of these and other Sidney women as patrons of painters. It would, for example, be intriguing to know whether the flurry of artistic commissions recorded in the financial accounts of Roger Manners, fifth Earl of Rutland, in the period immediately following his 1599 marriage to Elizabeth Sidney, only daughter of Sir Philip, were in any way influenced by Elizabeth herself. Among the commissions recorded between 1599 and 1603 are: portraits of the fifth earl and the new countess by Robert Peake the Elder, a portrait of James I by Hilliard, and work of an unspecified nature from "Henygo Jones, a picture maker" (HMC, *Rutland* 4:417–46). This last is of particular interest to historians of art and architecture, for it constitutes the earliest known reference to the patronage of Inigo Jones (see, for example, Anderson 32; Hart 1). But the extent to which the Rutlands may have been responsible for launching Jones's career at the Jacobean court is a topic that has yet to be fully explored (Goldring, "Art Collecting").

The wide range of visual responses to, and depictions of, the Tudor-Stuart Sidneys from the eighteenth century onwards offers another potentially rich seam, but one which, to date, only Michael G. Brennan has mined. In a substantial article published in 2010 Brennan traced the pictorial afterlife in Britain—in paintings, prints, drawings, and sculpture—of Fulke Greville's account of Sir Philip Sidney's fatal wounding at Zutphen, which was written *c.* 1604–18, but not published until 1652. From John Francis Rigaud RA's painting of *The Death of Sir Philip Sidney* (1793) to the bronze statue of Sidney in battle armor, *sans* helmet and cuisses, erected at Shrewsbury School in 1923, Brennan offers a nuanced exploration of "why this particular legend of Sir Philip Sidney's heroism exerted such a powerful hold over late-Romantic and early-nineteenth century literary and visual imagination," and indeed, over the literary and visual imaginations of those raised in the shadow of the First and Second World Wars (7). In future scholars might build upon Brennan's work by considering, for example, whether this particular episode enjoyed a comparable pictorial afterlife outside Britain, particularly in the Netherlands, where the cult of Sidney as the ideal Protestant soldier-courtier has enjoyed a remarkable longevity. It might also be fruitful to consider the ways in which other members of the early modern Sidney family—broadly defined—were appropriated and re-imagined by artists of later centuries, in Britain and elsewhere. Algernon Sidney, for example, is depicted alongside Oliver Cromwell listening to John Milton play the organ in Emanuel Gottlieb Leutze's 1854 painting depicting an *Evening Party at Milton's* (Corcoran Gallery, Washington, DC), while Amy Robsart Dudley, the ill-fated first wife of

Robert Dudley, Earl of Leicester, is the subject of William Frederick Yeames's 1879 painting of *The Death of Amy Robsart* (Nottingham City Museums and Galleries). Doubtless there are other examples, and in media other than oil on canvas.

Future research on the Sidneys and the visual arts might also profitably seek to embrace—in line with wider developments in the field of art history—a broader definition of the "visual arts." Expenditures on, for example, garden design and heraldic display (the latter ranging from pedigrees illuminated on parchment to coats of arms engraved on panes of glass) may be followed in the family papers preserved at Maidstone, and would almost certainly reward further investigation.[18] Finally, it would be desirable if in future literary critics and art historians could find ways to collaborate—or at least to acknowledge each other's work on the Sidneys—rather than, as often has happened, working in isolation, independently of one another.

Bibliography

Manuscript Sources

British Library
    Add. MS 78177
    Add. MS 17520
De L'Isle MSS (at the Centre for Kentish Studies, Maidstone)
    U1475 A4/5, A4/6, A5/4, A33/2, C 81/9
    U1500 C1/19, E120
Longleat
    Dudley Papers II, III, XI
National Art Library (at the Victoria and Albert Museum)
    MSL 1982/30

Primary and Secondary Sources

Anderson, Christy. *Inigo Jones and the Classical Tradition*. Cambridge: Cambridge UP, 2007.
Auerbach, Erna. *Nicholas Hilliard*. 1961. Boston, MA: Boston Book and Art Shop, 1964.
Brennan, Michael G. "'Thy Necessity is Yet Greater Than Mine': The Re-mythologizing in the Literary and Visual Arts of Fulke Greville's Water-bottle Anecdote (1750–1930)." *SJ* 28.2 (2010): 1–40.

---

18 Scholarship on the garden at Penshurst might form a dialogue with recent work on the gardens of other courtiers in the Sidneys' inner circle, including that created by Robert Dudley, Earl of Leicester, at Kenilworth *c.* 1575, and that created by Philip Herbert, fourth Earl of Pembroke, at Wilton in the mid-1630s. For the Kenilworth garden (which, following Robert Langham's *Letter*, was reconstructed by English Heritage in 2009), see Keay and Watkins, *Elizabethan Garden at Kenilworth Castle*, and in particular, Goldring, "The Langham *Letter* as a Source for Garden History" 59–64. For the Wilton garden, see Duggan, "Pembroke's Arcadia", where it is argued that the garden was intended "in ... design, topography and statuary" to celebrate the "literary achievements of Herbert's family," in particular Sir Philip Sidney's pastoral romance *Arcadia* (10). For some consideration of heraldic art in this period—including Sir Henry Sidney's patronage of the College of Arms—see Goldring, "Heraldic Drawing and Painting in Early Modern England."

Britton, John, ed. *The Natural History of Wiltshire by John Aubrey*. London: Wiltshire Topographical Society, 1847.

Buxton, John. *Elizabethan Taste*. London: Macmillan, 1963.

—. *Sir Philip Sidney and the English Renaissance*. Rpt. London and New York: Macmillan/St. Martin's P, 1964.

Chaney, Edward. *The Evolution of the Grand Tour*. London: Frank Cass, 1998.

Chirelstein, Ellen. "Emblem and Reckless Presence: The Drury Portrait at Yale." Ed. Lucy Gent. *Albion's Classicism: The Visual Arts in Britain, 1550–1660*. New Haven, CT: Yale UP, 1995. 287–311.

Collins, Arthur. *Letters and Memorials of State* …. 2 vols. London: Thomas Osborne, 1746.

Cooper, Tarnya. *Citizen Portrait: Portrait Painting and the Urban Elite of Tudor and Jacobean England and Wales*. New Haven, CT: Yale UP, 2012.

—. "Predestined Lives? Portraiture and Religious Belief in England and Wales, 1560–1620." *Art Re-formed: Re-assessing the Impact of the Reformation on the Visual Arts*. Ed. Tara Hamling and Richard L. Williams. Newcastle upon Tyne: Cambridge Scholars' Publishing, 2007. 49–63.

—. "Professional Pride and Personal Agendas: Portraits of Judges, Lawyers, and Members of the Inns of Court, 1560–1630." *The Intellectual and Cultural World of the Early Modern Inns of Court*. Ed. Jayne Elisabeth Archer, Elizabeth Goldring, and Sarah Knight. Manchester: Manchester UP, 2011. 157–78.

Croft, Pauline, and Karen Hearn. "'Only matrimony maketh children to be certain …': Two Elizabethan Pregnancy Portraits." *British Art Journal* 3.3 (2002): 19–24.

Croll, Morris W. "Arcadia." *Modern Language Notes* 16 (1901): 124–5.

Duggan, Dianne. "Pembroke's Arcadia: 'Delicious Wilton … that Arbour of the Muses.'" *British Art Journal* 14.3 (2013–14): 9–20.

Duncan-Jones, Katherine. "Sidney and Titian." *English Renaissance Studies Presented to Dame Helen Gardner in Honour of her Seventieth Birthday*. Oxford: Oxford UP, 1980. 1–11.

— —. "Sidney's Pictorial Imagination." BLitt thesis, Somerville College, Oxford, 1964.

Dundas, Judith. *Pencils Rhetorique: Renaissance Poets and the Art of Painting*. Newark, DE: U of Delaware P, 1993.

Edmond, Mary. *Hilliard and Oliver: The Lives and Works of Two Great Miniaturists*. London: Robert Hale, 1983.

Farmer, Norman K., Jr. *Poets and the Visual Arts in Renaissance England*. Austin, TX: U of Texas P, 1984.

Fillon, Benjamin. "La galerie de portraits de Du Plessis-Mornay au château de Saumur." *Gazette des Beaux-Arts* 21 (1879): 162–8, 212–28.

Fumerton, Patricia. "'Secret' Arts: Elizabethan Miniatures and Sonnets." *Representations* 15 (1986): 57–97.

Gent, Lucy. "Elizabethan Architecture: A View from Rhetoric." *Architectural History* 57 (2014): 71–106.

—, ed. *Hypnerotomachia: The Strife of Love in a Dreame*. Delmar, NY: Scholars' Facsimiles and Reprints, 1973.

—. *Picture and Poetry, 1560–1620: Relations between Literature and the Visual Arts in the English Renaissance*. Leamington Spa: James Hall, 1981.

Goldring, Elizabeth. "Art Collecting and Patronage in Shakespeare's England." *The Oxford Handbook of the Age of Shakespeare*. Ed. R. Malcolm Smuts. Oxford: Oxford UP, forthcoming.

—, "The Funeral of Sir Philip Sidney and the Politics of Elizabethan Festival." *Court Festivals of the European Renaissance: Art, Politics and Performance*. Ed. J. R. Mulryne and Elizabeth Goldring. Aldershot: Ashgate, 2002. 199–224.

—. "Heraldic Drawing and Painting in Early Modern England." *Painting in Britain, 1500–1630: Production, Influences, Patronage*. Ed. Tarnya Cooper et al. Oxford: Oxford UP, forthcoming.

—. "An Important Early Picture Collection: The Earl of Pembroke's 1561/2 Inventory and the Provenance of Holbein's *Christina of Denmark*." *The Burlington Magazine* 144 (2002): 157–60.

—. "'In the Cause of his God and True Religion': Sir Philip Sidney, the *Sequitur celebritas* and the Cult of the Protestant Martyr." *Art Re-formed: Re-assessing the impact of the Reformation on the Visual Arts*. Ed. Tara Hamling and Richard L. Williams. Newcastle upon Tyne: Cambridge Scholars' Publishing, 2007. 227–42.

—. "The Langham *Letter* as a Source for Garden History." *The Elizabethan Garden at Kenilworth Castle*. Ed. Anna Keay and John Watkins. London: English Heritage, 2013. 59–64.

—. "The Politics of Translation: Arthur Golding's Account of the Duke of Anjou's Entry into Antwerp, 1582." *Writing Royal Entries in Early Modern Europe*. Ed. Marie-Claude Canova-Green and Jean Andrews, with Marie-France Wagner. Turnhout: Brepols, 2013. 225–43.

—. "A Portrait of Sir Philip Sidney by Veronese at Leicester House, London." *The Burlington Magazine* 154 (2012): 548–54.

—. "Portraits of Queen Elizabeth I and the Earl of Leicester for Kenilworth Castle." *The Burlington Magazine* 148 (2005): 654–60.

—. "Portraiture, Patronage, and the Progresses: Robert Dudley, Earl of Leicester, and the Kenilworth Festivities of 1575." *The Progresses, Pageants, and Entertainments of Queen Elizabeth I*. Ed. Jayne Elisabeth Archer, Elizabeth Goldring, and Sarah Knight. Oxford: Oxford UP, 2007; rpt. 2013. 163–88.

—. "Princely Pleasures: The Cultural Patronage of Robert Dudley, Earl of Leicester." *The Elizabethan Garden at Kenilworth Castle*. Ed. Anna Keay and John Watkins. London: English Heritage, 2013. 47–56.

—. Review of *The Feminine Dynamic in English Art, 1485–1603: Women as Consumers, Patrons and Painters*, by Susan E. James. *The Burlington Magazine* 151 (2009): 843.

—. *Robert Dudley, Earl of Leicester, and the World of Elizabethan Art: Painting and Patronage at the Court of Elizabeth I*. New Haven, CT: Yale UP, 2014.

—. "'So Iust a Sorrowe So Well Expressed': Henry, Prince of Wales and the Art of Commemoration." *Prince Henry Revived: Image and Exemplarity in Early Modern England*. Ed. Timothy Wilks. London: Paul Holberton, 2007. 280–300.

—. "'So lively a portraiture of his miseries': Melancholy, Mourning, and the Elizabethan Malady." *British Art Journal* 6.2 (2005): 12–22.

— et al., eds. *John Nichols's The Progresses and Public Processions of Queen Elizabeth I: A New Edition of the Early Modern Sources*. 5 vols. Oxford: Oxford UP, 2014.

Hamilton, A. C. *Sir Philip Sidney: A Study of His Life and Works*. Cambridge: Cambridge UP, 1977.

Hannay, Margaret P. *Mary Sidney, Lady Wroth*. Farnham: Ashgate, 2010.

Hart, Vaughan. *Inigo Jones: The Architect of Kings*. New Haven, CT: Yale UP, 2011.

Haskell, Francis. *The King's Pictures*. New Haven, CT: Yale UP, 2013.

Hearn, Karen, ed. *Dynasties: Painting in Tudor and Jacobean England, 1530–1630*. London: Tate, 1995.

—. "A Fatal Fertility?" *Costume* 34 (2000): 39–43.

—. *Marcus Gheeraerts II: Elizabethan Artist*. London: Tate, 2002.

—. "'Saved through childbearing': A Godly Context for Elizabethan Pregnancy Portraits." *Art Re-formed: Re-assessing the Impact of the Reformation on the Visual Arts*. Ed. Tara Hamling and Richard L. Williams. Newcastle upon Tyne: Scholars Publishing, 2007. 65–70.

HMC. *The Manuscripts of His Grace the Duke of Rutland preserved at Belvoir Castle*. 4 vols. London: HMSO, 1888–1905.

—. *Report on the Manuscripts of Lord de L'Isle and Dudley Preserved at Penshurst Place.* 6 vols. London: HMSO, 1925–66.

Hope, Charles. "Titian, Philip II, and Mary Tudor." *England and the Continental Renaissance: Essays in Honour of J. B. Trapp.* Ed. Edward Chaney and Peter Mack. Woodbridge: Boydell, 1990. 53–65.

Houliston, Laura. *The Suffolk Collection: A Catalogue of Paintings.* London: English Heritage, 2012.

Hulse, Clark. *The Rule of Art: Literature and Painting in the Renaissance.* Chicago, IL: U of Chicago P, 1990.

James, Susan E. *The Feminine Dynamic in English Art, 1485–1603: Women as Consumers, Patrons and Painters.* Aldershot: Ashgate, 2009.

Judson, A. C. *Sidney's Appearance: A Study in Elizabethan Portraiture.* Bloomington, IN: Indiana UP, 1958.

Jusserand, J. J. *The English Novel in the Time of Shakespeare.* Transl. Elizabeth Lee. London: Fisher Unwin, 1901.

Keay, Anna, and John Watkins, eds. *The Elizabethan Garden at Kenilworth Castle.* London: English Heritage, 2013.

Kuin, Roger. "Languet and the Veronese Portrait of Sidney: Antwerp Findings." *SJ* 15.2 (1997): 42–4.

—. "New Light on the Veronese Portrait of Sir Philip Sidney." *Sidney Newsletter and Journal* 15.1 (1997): 19–47.

Lamb, Mary Ellen. "Lady Mary Wroth." *ODNB.*

Maddicott, Hilary. "A Collection of the Interregnum Period: Philip, Lord Viscount Lisle, and his Purchases from the 'Late King's Goods', 1649–1660." *Journal of the History of Collections* 11.1 (1999): 1–24.

—. "The Political and Cultural Career of Philip Sidney, Lord Viscount Lisle, Third Earl of Leicester, 1619–1698: Nobility and Identity in the Seventeenth Century." PhD thesis, University of London, 2014.

Margetts, Michele. "Lady Penelope Rich: Hilliard's lost miniatures and a surviving portrait." *The Burlington Magazine* 130 (1988): 758–61.

McBride, Kari Boyd. *Country House Discourse in Early Modern England: A Cultural Study of Landscape and Legitimacy.* Aldershot: Ashgate, 2001.

McPherson, David C. "A Possible Origin for Mopsa in Sidney's *Arcadia*." *RQ* 21.4 (1968): 420–28.

Moore, G. C. "The Lost Veronese Portrait of Sir Philip Sidney" (letter to the editor). *Times Literary Supplement* Nov. 7, 1929.

Muraro, Michelangelo. "Un celebre ritratto. Sir Philip Sidney a Venezia nel 1574 sceglie Veronese per farsi ritrarre." *Nuovi studi su Paolo Veronese.* Ed. M. Gemin. Venice: Arsenale Editrice, 1990. 391–6.

Osborn, James M. *Young Philip Sidney, 1572–1577.* New Haven, CT and London: Yale UP and The Elizabethan Club, 1972.

Parker, Robert W. "The Art of Sidney's Heroic Impresas." *ELR* 20 (1990): 408–30.

Purcell, J. M. "The Lost Veronese Portrait of Sir Philip Sidney" (letter to the editor). *Times Literary Supplement* Oct. 31, 1929.

Roberts, Josephine A., ed. *The Poems of Lady Mary Wroth.* Baton Rouge, LA: U of Louisiana P, 1983.

Robinson, Forrest G. *The Shape of Things Known: Sidney's* Apology *in its Philosophical Tradition.* Cambridge, MA: Harvard UP, 1972.

Rosand, David. "Dialogues and Apologies: Sidney and Venice." *Studies in Philology* 88.2 (1991): 236–49.

Sandys, William, ed. "Copy of the Inventory of Archbishop Parker's Goods at the Time of his Death." *Archaeologia* 30 (1844): 1–30.

Sidney, Philip. *An Apology for Poetry*. Ed. Geoffrey Shepherd. Manchester: Manchester UP, 1965.

—. *The Correspondence of Sir Philip Sidney*. Ed. Roger Kuin. 2 vols. Oxford: Oxford UP, 2012.

—. *Sir Philip Sidney: A Critical Edition of the Major Works*. Ed. Katherine Duncan-Jones. Oxford: Oxford UP, 1992.

—. *Sir Philip Sidney: Miscellaneous Prose*. Ed. Katherine Duncan-Jones and Jan van Dorsten. Oxford: Oxford UP, 1973.

—. *Sir Philip Sidney: The Countess of Pembroke's Arcadia*. Ed. Maurice Evans. London: Penguin, 1987.

—. *Sir Philip Sidney: The Old Arcadia*. Ed. Katherine Duncan-Jones. Oxford: Oxford UP, 1994.

Sidney, Robert, first Earl of Leicester. *Domestic Politics and Family Absence: The Correspondence (1588–1621) of Robert Sidney, First Earl of Leicester, and Barbara Gamage Sidney, Countess of Leicester*. Ed. Margaret P. Hannay, Noel J. Kinnamon, and Michael G. Brennan. Aldershot: Ashgate, 2005.

Siebeck, Berta. *Das Bild Sir Philip Sidneys in der Englischen Renaissance*. Weimar: Hermann Bohlaus, 1939. 175–7.

Skretowicz, Victor. "Devices and their Narrative Function in Sidney's *Arcadia*." *Emblematica* 1 (1986): 267–92.

Strickland, Ronald. "Pageantry and Poetry as Discourse: The Production of Subjectivity in Sir Philip Sidney's Funeral." *ELH* 57.1 (1990): 19–36.

Strong, Roy. *The Cult of Elizabeth: Elizabethan Portraiture and Pageantry*. London: Pimlico, 1999.

—. "The Leicester House Miniatures: Robert Sidney, 1st Earl of Leicester and his Circle." *The Burlington Magazine* 127 (1985): 694–701.

—. "Sidney's Appearance Considered." *The Tudor and Stuart Monarchy: Pageantry, Painting, Iconography*. 3 vols. Woodbridge: Boydell and Brewer 1995. 2:145–63.

—. *Tudor and Jacobean Portraits*. 2 vols. London: HMSO, 1969.

Tittler, Robert. *The Face of the City: Civic Portraiture and Civic Identity in Early Modern England*. Manchester: Manchester UP, 2007.

—. *Portraits, Painters, and Publics in Provincial England, 1540–1640*. Oxford: Oxford UP, 2012.

Van Dorsten, J. A. *Poets, Patrons and Professors: Sir Philip Sidney, Daniel Rogers and the Leiden Humanists*. Leiden: Leiden UP/London: Oxford UP, 1962.

Van Mander, Karel. *The Lives of the Illustrious Netherlandish and German Painters*. Ed. Hessel Miedema, transl. Derry Cook-Radmore. 6 vols. Doornspijk: Davaco, 1994–99.

Warkentin, Germaine. "Jonson's Penshurst Reveal'd? A Penshurst Inventory of *c*. 1623." *SJ* 20.1 (2002): 1–26.

Wayne, Don E. *Penshurst: The Semiotics of Place and the Poetics of History*, Madison, WI: U of Wisconsin P, 1984.

Wells-Cole, Anthony. *Art and Decoration in Elizabethan and Jacobean England: The Influence of Continental Prints, 1558–1625*. New Haven, CT: Yale UP, 1997.

Wilson, Mona. "The Lost Veronese Portrait of Sir Philip Sidney" (letter to the editor). *Times Literary Supplement* Nov. 7, 1929.

Yates, Frances A. *Astraea: The Imperial Theme in the Sixteenth Century*. London: Routledge and Kegan Paul, 1975.

Young, Alan. "Philip Sidney's Tournament Impresas." *Sidney Newsletter* 6 (1985): 6–24.

The Sidneys and Music

Katherine R. Larson

In Part 2 of Lady Mary Wroth's *The Countess of Montgomery's Urania* the King of Morea leads Pamphilia, Amphilanthus, and Urania into a garden where they are delighted by "Musick … of all sorts." When the King invites Pamphilia to contribute to the musical festivities, however, Amphilanthus reacts with horror: "Nott my Cousine, I pray, Sir … nor my sister, I beseech you. For certainly non [of] our blood can have that fine nice qualitie of singing, the knowledg of a voice to singe with never having binn knowne among us" (*Urania* 2:29). His attempt to dissociate the family from musical skill is playfully ironic. The ensuing scene features a discussion about musical aesthetics and performance practice, and culminates in Pamphilia's seemingly effortless rendition of "severall songs" (2:30). Throughout the autobiographically inflected interchange, Wroth showcases her family's musical *sprezzatura* and attunes readers to the significance of music for the Sidneys as writers, as patrons, and as performers.

Music played an especially vital role in shaping the literary and artistic achievements of Wroth herself, her father, Robert Sidney, first Earl of Leicester, and her cousin and lover, William Herbert, third Earl of Pembroke, each of whom is shadowed in this scene, as well as of her uncle and aunt, Sir Philip Sidney and Mary Sidney Herbert, Countess of Pembroke (see Stewart *ARC* 1:4, Hannay *ARC* 1:5, Shephard *ARC* 1:7, and Lamb *ARC* 2:17). While scholars have long noted the significance of music for the family, relatively little work has focused on the Sidneys from a musical perspective. Early contributions elucidated Philip Sidney's and, more recently, Robert Sidney's engagement with musical influences and sources. Following Gavin Alexander's seminal article "The Musical Sidneys," the extent of music's impact on the Sidneys' formal and generic choices, the circulation of their works, and their contributions as writers and as patrons has begun to emerge more fully. Integrating developments within the fields of early modern women's writing and sound studies, current interventions are illuminating the writings of Mary Sidney and Mary Wroth through a musical lens as well as the performance dimensions of the Sidneys' works.

The Sidneys as Musicians

The early musical exposure that Philip, Robert, and Mary Sidney enjoyed was largely due to their father, Sir Henry Sidney, whose account books detail regular expenditures for the acquisition and upkeep of musical instruments, the hiring of musicians, and music books (Alexander, "Musical Sidneys" 67–8; Price 171). The chapel services and entertainments at Ludlow Castle, where Sidney served as President of the Lord Council of Wales, benefited from his musical patronage (Smith 110–21; Price 63). Philip, Robert, and Mary Sidney spent their early years enjoying household performances, attending church services, and singing Psalms (Hannay, *Philip's Phoenix* 85–6). As young adults they would have been impressed by the entertainments hosted by their uncle, Robert Dudley, first Earl of Leicester (Price 167–9). Robert Laneham's letter detailing Queen Elizabeth's visit to Kenilworth Castle in 1575 brings to life the music that enlivened these lavish spectacles and the more informal amusements the Sidneys enjoyed (see also Osborn 327; Hay 21–2; Buxton, *Elizabethan Taste* 194). The siblings' formative soundscapes were enriched with musical training. By 1576 Robert Sidney was studying singing with Richard Lant, Master of the Choristers at Christ Church (Croft 50). Mary Sidney, meanwhile, was a keen lutenist and played the virginals; expenditures for her instruments' maintenance—new strings for her lute and "trimming" for her virginals—testify to her diligence as a musician (*Philip's Phoenix* 27).

Critics have tended to dismiss Philip Sidney's musical aptitude, largely on the basis of a letter he wrote to Robert in October 1580: "Now sweete Brother," Philip advises, "take a delight to keepe and increase yowr Musick, yow will not beleive what a want I find of it in my Melancholie times" (*Correspondence SPS* 2:1009). In a representative assessment, James Osborn takes this passage to suggest that "Philip could not adequately assuage his melancholy by performing on an instrument, whereas Robert's training was such that he could" (81; see also Pattison, "Sir Philip Sidney" 76; Zim 178). Growing up in an aristocratic household as musical as Henry Sidney's, it is hard to believe that Philip Sidney did not have vocal and instrumental training; Castiglione lauds music as "not only an ornament but a necessity to the Courtier" (57; see also Buxton, *Philip Sidney* 113–14; Buxton, *Elizabethan Taste* 183–5; Croft 49–50). Indeed, rather than implying Sidney's dependence on his brother's music, the letter may well indicate that Sidney himself played music, that he relied on it especially during moments of melancholy, and that he hoped his brother would learn from his example. The references to music that infuse Sidney's writings certainly reveal his awareness of the practicalities of musical performance. Note, for instance, his depiction of the historian as a lute teacher in the *Defence*, or Kalander's allusion to memorizing songs in the *Arcadia* (Sidney, *Prose Works* 3:13, 1:21; see Pattison, "Sidney and Music" 77–8; Alexander, *Writing After Sidney* 197). We know too that music was a constant in Sidney's life. As an eleven-year-old he reportedly gave a shilling to a blind harper, perhaps the same one who sang "the old Song of *Percy* and *Duglas*" that he remembers fondly in the *Defence* (*Prose Works* 3:24; Buxton, *Philip Sidney* 113; Duncan-Jones, *Philip Sidney* 38–9; Croft 49). During his Continental tour he studied music in Venice (Osborn 120–22; Fabry, "Verse Adaptations" 255; Alexander, "Musical Sidneys" 68). He seems to have organized concerts at Salisbury and at Wilton (Price 171–2; Buxton, *Philip Sidney* 113). Music was even present at his deathbed. In Sidney's final moments, Fulke Greville relates, he called "for music, especially that song which himself had entitled *La cuisse rompue*" (82).[1]

No such debate surrounds the musical accomplishments of Mary Wroth, whom Peter Croft calls "the leading dancer and musician of her generation in the Sidney family" (51). Robert Sidney ensured that his own children were taught music, and Wroth showed aptitude early. Margaret Hannay's biography of Wroth provides insight into this facet of her education, drawing on letters to Robert Sidney from his agent, Rowland Whyte. In October 1595 Whyte praised Wroth's burgeoning talents: "God bless her, she is very forward in her learning, writing, and other exercises she is put to, as dancing and the virginals." Music continued to be a focus of Wroth's education and leisure as she approached adolescence. While in Flushing, she received "singing books" from Whyte. In 1600 he again reported from

---

1   It is not clear whether Sidney is referring to one of his own lyrics, or whether he is, as Ringler suggests, giving a popular tune a name reflective of his physical situation (Sidney, *Poems* 351). See Duncan-Jones, *Philip Sidney* 298–9.

Baynard's Castle that the Sidney children "dance, they sing, they play on the lute, and are carefully kept unto it" (Hannay, *MSLW* 43, 65, 72; see also Price 172). The stunning portrait depicting Wroth or one of her younger sisters with a theorbo offers visual testimony of the impressive musical training she received (Illustration 19).[2] By 1610 Wroth was honored as a musical patron, as the dedicatee of Robert Jones's fifth lute song collection *The Muses Gardin for Delights* (*MSLW* 157–8; Doughtie, *Lyrics* 359).[3] She also contributed to court masques, dancing in Ben Jonson's *The Masque of Blackness* (1605); such were her gifts that two dance tunes were named for her, "Durrants Masque" and "My Lady Wroth's Mascarada" (Sabol 219, 510; Alexander, "Musical Sidneys" 92–3).[4]

Most of the evidence pertaining to the musical involvements of Wroth's cousin, William Herbert, point to his role as a patron, his contributions—ultimately as Lord Chamberlain—to the masques and entertainments favored at Queen Anne's court, and to the musical circulation of his poems (Brennan, *Literary Patronage* 109–11, 137–51, 167–8; Price 171n2; Doughtie, *Lyrics* 514, 602, 607–8; O'Farrell 104–5). Two collections of songs were dedicated to him: Tobias Hume's *The First Part of Ayres* (1605) and Thomas Tomkins's *Songs of 3. 4. 5. and 6. Parts* (1622) (see Doughtie, *Lyrics* 197). And when John Donne the younger published the collection of poems attributed to Herbert, he credited composers Henry Lawes and Nicholas Lanier for sending him the poems: their preservation, Donne writes, is due to "the greatest Masters of Musick, all the Sonnets being set by them" (see O'Farrell 28–9). Given his mother's musical interests and the centrality of Wilton House as a gathering place for poets and musicians, however, Herbert would have been exposed to music from a young age. When Herbert was thirteen, Thomas Morley dedicated his *Canzonets or Little Short Songs to Three Voyces* (1593) to the Countess of Pembroke (Alexander, "Musical Sidneys" 70).[5] It is likely too that formal musical training featured in his education. One of his tutors, Samuel Daniel, was the brother of composer John Daniel (Price 106).

Sonic Experiments: Music and Poetry

If biographical scholarship has helped to ascertain the extent of the Sidneys' musical training and experience, another crucial strand has focused on the musical dimensions of their writings. This work encompasses debates about the distinction between poetry as a kind of music in itself and musical setting and performance, as well as identification of extant musical sources for and settings of individual poems. Early moderns understood the forms and effects of music and "poesy" synonymously. In *The Arte of English Poesy* (1589), for instance, George Puttenham describes verse as "a musical speech or utterance" (98, 154).

---

2   It has been assumed that the theorbo portrait is of Wroth herself, but given the dating of the painting to *c.* 1620, when Wroth was in her early thirties, it may well represent one of her younger sisters. Wroth and her sisters would have followed a similar education, however, so even if the portrait does not depict Wroth, it "does point to the sisters' serious musical training and demonstrates a degree of musical accomplishment unusual for aristocratic women" (*MSLW* 158).

3   Dedications and commemorations made to members of the Sidney family are listed by year in Brennan and Kinnamon.

4   Wroth did not appear in Jonson's *Masque of Beauty*, though she was in attendance at the performance. Her presence among the audience counters long-standing assumptions that she was isolated or banished from court. Wroth's younger sisters Philippa and Barbara also had the opportunity to perform in masques when they reached their late teens. See *MSLW* 130–32, 200; Hannay, "Sleuthing in the Archives."

5   Pembroke was also celebrated in Anthony Holborne's "The Countess of Pembroke's Funerals" and "The Countess of Pembroke's Paradise" (see Alexander, "Musical Sidneys" 83n37).

In practical terms this slippage resulted in productive cross-pollination between poetic and musical composition. Popular musical settings helped to maintain lyrics in circulation, and poets wrote *contrafacta*, verses set to existing tunes.

The definition of poesy articulated by Philip Sidney in his *Defence* picks up on each of these elements. The poet, he writes, "commeth to you with words set in delightfull proportion, either accompanied with, or prepared for the well enchanting skill of *Musicke*" (*Prose Works* 3:20). Not surprisingly, composers were attracted to Sidney's poems; over twenty settings are extant, including pieces by William Byrd, Thomas Morley, John Dowland, Robert Dowland, Robert Jones, and Henry Lawes.[6] But Sidney's works are themselves shaped by a musical understanding of prosody and close engagement with Continental musical models.

Poetry, as John Stevens notes, was for Sidney "an art of ordered sound" (155). His metrical experiments, notably in the *Old Arcadia* and in his Psalm translations, demonstrate his determination to create an appropriate "speech-melody" (155) for English poetry. William Johnson has traced the influence on Sidney of the acoustic and musical tenets motivating the work of *La Pléiade* poets like Pierre de Ronsard and Joachim du Bellay. Sidney's forays into quantitative verse, following the model of the *musique mesurée* promulgated by Jean-Antoine de Baïf and the Académie de Musique et de Poésie, offer further evidence of this approach. The tension between musical theory and practice exemplified by Sidney's thirteen quantitative verses has been explored by a number of scholars.[7] It is not clear whether Sidney envisioned his quantitative verses for singing or for recitation, perhaps to musical accompaniment, as they are represented in the *Arcadia*.[8] Even if these verses are more usefully categorized as what Louise Schleiner calls "'virtual' song"—that is, simply meant "to evoke a sense of singing" (11, 15; see also Maynard 77–9)—Sidney brought a distinctly musical methodology to bear on his attempts to find vernacular rhythms for English poetry that fit classical metrical structures.

Sidney's *contrafacta* constitute another component of this musical-poetic experimentation. Eight of Sidney's *Certain Sonnets* (3, 4, 6, 7, 23, 24, 26, 27) were explicitly written to existing melodies.[9] Sidney looked to a range of musical sources for his *contrafacta*: English, Spanish, Dutch, French, and especially Italian (see Pattison, *Music and Poetry* 174–80; Pattison, "Sidney and Music" 80; Stevens 157–65; Schleiner 13n28).[10] In a pair of important articles Frank Fabry identified two of Sidney's Italian models for *Certain Sonnets* that may point to the influence of polyphonic settings (the *villanelle* and the *frottola*, both important precursors to the madrigal), not simply solo repertoire, on Sidney's prosody ("Verse Adaptations";

---

6   For sources containing musical settings of Sidney's poems, see Sidney, *Poems* 524; Ringler 137, 141. See also Doughtie, *Lyrics* 139–40, 345–50, 374–5, 392–3. Facsimiles of the songs included in British Library MS Add. 15117, BL MS Add. 53723, and Bodl. Library Mus. b. 1 can be found in Jorgens, *English Song* vols. 1, 6, and 7.

7   See Sidney, *Poems*, 389–93; Attridge 122, 175; Buxton, *Philip Sidney* 114–16; Pattison, *Music and Poetry* 62–4; Hollander 141–3; Doughtie 84–6; Maynard 86–9; Weiner 194–203; Alexander, "French Tune" 384–5. A list of Sidney's quantitative verses can be found in Sidney, *Poems* 572.

8   John Dowland and Henry Lawes both set the refrain from Sidney's "O Sweet Woods"; neither adheres to the poem's quantitative structure. See Sidney, *Poems* 404; Schleiner 36–8; Jorgens, *Well-Tun'd Word* 92. Two pieces by Byrd, including his elegy to Sidney, "Come to me grief for ever," also used quantitative verse. The elegy provides a poignant testament to Sidney's musical-poetic experiments (Alexander, *Writing After Sidney* 197; Doughtie, *Renaissance Song* 78–9).

9   See Sidney, *Poems* for commentary on these individual lyrics. Certain Sonnet 27 was later set as a lute song in Jones's *The Muses Gardin for Delights*; Stevens reasonably hypothesizes that this setting may preserve Sidney's source tune (159–61).

10   On Philip Sidney's engagement with the French chanson in "Song 8" from *Astrophil and Stella*, which was published in Robert Dowland's *A Musicall Banquet* (1610) and whose tune has been attributed to Guillaume Tessier, see Doughtie, *Lyrics* 586–7; Doughtie, *Renaissance Song* 124; Stevens 162; Alexander, "French Tune" 383–4.

see also Stevens 158–9, 165–6; Doughtie, *Renaissance Song* 81–3). Fabry also demonstrates how conventions derived from Italian vocal repertoire, notably trochaic meter and feminine rhyme, influenced Sidney's reshaping of English metrical structures. These features increasingly come to signal "musical," as opposed to "literary," lyrics in Sidney's writings, exemplified by the songs in *Astrophil and Stella* (Fabry, "Song-form" 238–9, 247; see also Jorgens, *Well-Tun'd Word* 13, 30; Sidney, *Poems* xliii, lvi; Doughtie, *Lyrics* 24). Even in the absence of a tag like "To the tune of," therefore, Sidney's lyrics register the possibility of musical circulation. As Fabry notes: "by writing a sonnet like OA 69 in which every line is feminine [Sidney] made possible its performance to a large quantity of existing Italian music" ("Song-form" 242; see also Maynard 81–5).[11]

Sidney certainly anticipated musical performance of at least some of his poems. In a letter to Lord Edward Denny he reminds his friend "with your good voyce, to singe my songes for they will one become an other" (Osborn 540). Penelope Rich was likewise a talented musician, celebrated as a singer and a lutenist in Charles Tessier's *Le premier livre de chansons & airs de court* (1597). Sidney praises the beauty of her voice in *Astrophil and Stella* (for example, Songs 1, 3, and 6 and Sonnet 36), and Stella is represented as singing Astrophil's verses in Sonnets 57 and 59. Might Sidney have composed some of his lyrics with Rich's voice in mind? (Duncan-Jones, "Sidney, Stella, and Lady Rich" 175–6, 181, 185–8; Buxton, *Elizabethan Taste* 186; Croft 49; Milsom 442–3.) While this remains speculative, songs from *Astrophil and Stella* were circulating musically before the sequence's publication in 1591. A version of "Song 6" was included in William Byrd's *Psalmes, Sonets, & Songs of Sadnes and Pietie* (1588), published in the aftermath of Sidney's death; a setting of "Song 10" appeared a year later in Byrd's *Songs of Sundrie Natures* (see Woudhuysen 249–57).[12] Sidney's prosody illuminates how profoundly Continental vocal models impacted the structure and the sonority of English verse. It also speaks to the dynamic, practice-based relationship between music and text that informs the poetry of the period. Sidney's "songs" were composed to specific tunes and in forms that facilitated musical setting, and they enjoyed widespread circulation through performance.

Robert Sidney stands out for his sophisticated engagement with musical models and for his talent as a writer of lyrics identified as "songs." Following the example of his brother in *Astrophil and Stella,* Sidney's "songs" are not, as Gavin Alexander notes, "simply non-sonnets within a sonnet sequence; they are constructed with a masterful grasp of song form and of what makes words apt for setting to music" ("French Tune" 385; see also Warkentin 43). He also looked to Continental models, notably French music, which he would have encountered on his travels (Alexander, "French Tune" 386). Sidney's poetic practice is exemplified by "Song 12," which is written "To a French Tune, Ou estes vous allez mes belles amourettes." Alexander has identified a popular French chanson, "Puis que le ciel," as Sidney's model for this *contrafactum.* His meticulous reading of "Song 12" alongside its musical source demonstrates the intricacy with which Sidney was responding to the formal features of the tune as well as the substance of the text (Alexander, "French Tune" 385ff.).

Sidney's ongoing musical involvements are reflected in his appearance as the dedicatee of Robert Jones's *First Booke of Songs or Ayres* (1600) and his godson Robert Dowland's *A Musicall Banquet* (1610), itself shaped by Continental influences (Alexander, "Musical Sidneys" 72; Doughtie, *Lyrics* 114, 342). John Dowland's "Syr Robert Sidney his Galliard," which opens his son's collection, pays homage to Sidney through its reworking of a French chanson, "Susanne un jour" (Croft 51–2; Alexander, "Musical Sidneys" 72–5; Alexander,

---

11 For a list of Sidney's poems using feminine rhyme, see Sidney, *Poems* 572.
12 On the "musical fashioning of [Sidney's] literary image" (172) after his death, notably by Byrd and by Thomas Watson, see Duncan-Jones, "Melancholie Times."

Writing After Sidney 191). At home, Sidney was a keen masquer, and after 1603 helped to oversee musical and dramatic entertainments at court as Queen Anne's Lord Chamberlain. Sidney found himself honored by Ben Jonson and Alfonso Ferrabosco when the opening stanza of his "Song 20" was playfully incorporated into the performance of *Love Freed from Ignorance and Folly* in 1610/11 (Alexander "Musical Sidneys" 87–90; Alexander, *Writing After Sidney* 190–91). His interests may also be reflected in the mid-seventeenth-century library catalogue at Penshurst, which includes a collection of madrigals by Luca Marenzio, Thomas Morley's *A Plaine and Easie Introduction to Practicall Musicke* (1597), a folio "Musicke Booke," and a collection of Italian *villanelle*.[13]

In his 2006 article "The Musical Sidneys" Alexander offers the most comprehensive picture to date of the Sidney family's musical connections and contributions. Building on his reading of Robert Sidney's "Song 12," he offers new manuscript evidence that substantiates the musical circulation of Sidney's poetry (76–90). But the article's significance lies especially in its shift away from isolated attention to individual lyrics by Philip and Robert Sidney to musical "continuities" (65) within and beyond the family. The Sidneys are convincingly positioned in Alexander's reading within a musical and literary network that comprised the most influential composers and practicing musicians of the period. Alexander also opens up new territory for Wroth scholars by documenting the extant musical settings of her poems, her own experiments with *contrafacta*, and her sensitivity to the emerging declamatory vocal style in "Was I to Blame," a lyric from Part 2 of the *Urania* which was set by Ferrabosco (90–104). "The Musical Sidneys" registers a decisive shift in scholarship in the field, as critics have begun to delve further into the musical culture that shaped the Sidneys' work and to examine how musical circulation and performance complicate interpretation of their writings.

"They Tell Us *Why*, and Teach Us *How* to Sing": The Sidney–Pembroke *Psalmes*

Recent debates about the musical potential of the Sidney Psalter exemplify these developments. Critics have justly celebrated the collection's metrical and formal innovation; Hannibal Hamlin calls the Psalter "the greatest achievement in literary Psalm translation in the English Renaissance" (118). The poems' musical and performance dimensions, however, have received less attention. Scholarship on the topic has focused on the question of whether the siblings prepared their translations as a replacement for the popular, if to many ears plodding, settings by Thomas Sternhold and John Hopkins that were in widespread use in English congregations. While critics like Beth Quitslund, Rivkah Zim (178–82), and Ramie Targoff (76–84) have helped to underscore the Psalms' liturgical and musical function in the period—Philip Sidney calls them "nothing but Songs" in his *Defence* (*Prose Works* 3:6)—the collection is usually read as a resource for individual and household devotion and prayer.

The musical dimensions of the Sidney Psalter, however, extend beyond its dazzling poetry. Margaret Hannay, Noel Kinnamon, and Michael Brennan have documented the siblings' reliance on the French metrical Psalter by Clément Marot and Théodore de Bèze

---

13   Joseph Black notes that the relative paucity of music titles in the collection may suggest that they were typically stored in a music room rather than in Penshurst's library. Full records, however, are lacking. Henry Sidney's books were disbursed after his death, and Philip and Mary Sidney may have kept their books elsewhere. Private correspondence, 29 May 2013. (See Warkentin, Black, and Bowen.)

for formal variety and language choice (MSH, *Collected Works* 2:4, 11–32). The French Psalm tunes were circulating widely in the period, and Philip and Mary Sidney likely grew up singing them and hearing them through the walls of Henry Sidney's house in London, which adjoined a French Protestant church (*Philip's Phoenix* 85; Duncan-Jones, *Philip Sidney* 25–6). Indeed, Brennan has posited that when Pembroke prepared her manuscript of the poems for presentation to the queen, it may well have been with the intention of publishing it as a metrical Psalter ("Proposed Visit").

Even if Pembroke did not anticipate liturgical use of the *Psalmes*, the practice of congregational song informs her translations. Micheline White has illuminated how women's inclusion within congregational song creates space for women's self-expression in Pembroke's poems, most poignantly in Psalm 68, which represents a "virgin army" joining in song (MSH, *Collected Works* 2:78; White 73–9). Tessie Prakas builds on this idea in a recent essay that reads Pembroke's devotional voice in "To the Angell Spirit" and the Psalm translations alongside post-Reformation debates about spoken and sung participation in liturgical ritual. It is significant too that Pembroke devotes attention to the material practice of music-making in her poems, amplifying references to the joy her Psalmist derives from singing and playing instruments (MSH, *Collected Works* 2:27–9; Larson, "Poetics of Song"). The siblings' experiments with feminine rhyme, trochaic meter, and quantitative verse, along with the examples of *contrafacta* in the *Psalmes*, offer further evidence of the translations' musical framework (Alexander, *Writing After Sidney* 118–20; Alexander, "French Tune" 390; Fabry, "Song-form" 247–8; Weiner 203–13; Buxton, *Philip Sidney* 153–4).

John Donne and Aemelia Lanyer both testify to the possibility that the Sidney Psalter was sung, at least within intimate gatherings (Donne 34–5; Lanyer 27). Their representation of the Psalms is further corroborated by extant musical settings. Versions of Philip Sidney's Psalms 40, 41, and 42 and portions of Pembroke's Psalm 97 were included in *All the French Psalm Tunes with English Words* (1632) (see Quitslund 101–2; MSH, *Collected Works* 1:52). Anonymous settings of Pembroke's Psalms 51 and 130 (Illustration 32) survive in British Library MS Add. 15117, a collection that also contains two lute songs set to texts by Philip Sidney (Stevens 166–8).[14] Linda Austern has contextualized Pembroke's settings, and the manuscript in which they are contained, in relation to the practice of women's domestic Psalm singing (99–109). My own work draws attention to the embodied facets of song performance that are registered in the *Psalmes*, to the commentary on the Psalm texts offered by the settings of Psalms 51 and 130, and to the pivotal role of music in the period in enhancing the efficacy of the Psalmist's communication with God (Larson, "Poetics of Song").[15]

The Sidneys' Songs in Performance: Future Directions

Considering music in terms of material and embodied performance holds important implications for analysis of the music associated with the Sidneys' writings, whether manifested in specific settings, allusions to musical genres, or representations of performance. John Milsom, for example, explores the semantic interplay between text and music in Byrd's

---

14   For modern transcriptions of these pieces, see Austern 103–5, 107–8. Reproductions of the manuscript settings are included in Jorgens, *English Song* vol. 1 and Larson, "A Poetics of Song."

15   Recordings of these settings, performed by Katherine R. Larson (soprano) and Matthew Faulk (lute), were made on 22 November 2013 at Wolfson College, Oxford. They can be accessed online at *renaissance poetic form: new directions*: http://renaissancepoeticform.wordpress.com/research/.

setting of Philip Sidney's erotically charged "Song 10" from *Astrophil and Stella*, and shows how different performance possibilities might have shaped the transmission of both poem and setting (see also Duncan-Jones, "Melancholie Times" 173). My own work has focused on the affective impact of the gendered singing body in Mary Wroth's *Urania*. I argue that song constitutes a powerful narrative mode for Wroth's female protagonists that is nonetheless caught up in cultural anxieties about women's musical performance (Larson, "Voicing Lyric"). There is more research to be done here, particularly in elucidating the function of the musical performances pervading the Sidneys' romances and pastoral entertainments (see R. S. White). Pyrocles' cross-dressed singing in the *Arcadia* constitutes a vivid example, as do the singing matches featured in *Love's Victory* and *The Lady of May*.

Attending to music from a performance perspective also raises new questions about the circulation of the Sidneys' writings and about the relationship between poetic and musical form. Musical performance constituted a crucial, though too often overlooked, mode of lyric transmission and "publication" in the late sixteenth and early seventeenth centuries. One of Philip Sidney's lyrics, "O Lord, how vain are all our frail delights," has been identified in a manuscript part-book of Byrd's settings held at Christ Church (Woudhuysen 255–7; Ringler 137, 141). It is entirely possible that as yet unidentified Sidney lyrics are extant in other musical manuscripts and printed songbooks of the period. Manuscript compilation and patterns of circulation have much to tell us too about the make-up of the Sidneys' artistic networks (Alexander, "Musical Sidneys"; Alexander, *Writing After Sidney* 187–9; Woudhuysen 249–57, 292–3; Pattison, *Music and Poetry* 61–75). The contents of British Library MS Add. 15117, for example, with its settings of Philip Sidney's "My true love hath my heart and I have his" and "Have I caught my heavenly jewel" as well as Pembroke's Psalms 51 and 130, features compositions by Byrd, Dowland, Ferrabosco, and Tobias Hume; the manuscript also includes two pieces from Ben Jonson's plays (see Joiner; Austern 100–101). Margaret Hannay imagines Wroth "circulating her poems by reading or singing them, or having them sung by professional musicians" within a collaborative coterie of writers and composers (*MSLW* 182–3). And Mary Ellen Lamb's current work on William Herbert makes an important case for situating his writings in a context of poetic exchange that includes musical performance.

Finally, the pervasiveness of musical transmission can complicate accepted formal and generic boundaries of individual manuscript and print works. H. R. Woudhuysen notes, for instance, the physical resemblance of the Drummond manuscript of *Astrophil and Stella* to the format of musical part-books (357). Wroth's Folger MS V.a.104 likewise shares important affinities with manuscript songbooks of the period. I have argued that the musical circulation of her lyrics coupled with their repositioning within *Urania* in scenes of musical performance underscore the need to attend to the musical dimensions of the poems generically marked as "songs" in sonnet sequences (Larson, "Voicing Lyric").

The Sidneys have long been celebrated by critics as important musical patrons. The extant tributes to Philip, Mary, and Robert Sidney, William Herbert, and Mary Wroth, which situate them within a veritable "Who's Who" of musical figures of the period, testify to the family's ongoing status within artistic and literary circles. When read alongside the Sidneys' wide-ranging musical interests and interventions, however, these commemorations demand to be read rather as a crucial trace of the dynamic interplay between musical and literary production in the period and of the Sidneys' active involvement in these networks. Music is too often silenced in discussions of literary form, circulation, and reception. In the case of this exceptionally musical family, attention to the musical sounds, structures, and performing bodies that hover behind their texts constitutes an especially rewarding area of exploration.

Bibliography

Primary and Secondary Sources

Alexander, Gavin. "The Elizabethan Lyric as Contrafactum: Robert Sidney's 'French Tune' Identified." *Music and Letters* 84.3 (2003): 378–402.

—. "The Musical Sidneys." *John Donne Journal* 25 (2006): 65–105.

—. *Writing After Sidney: The Literary Response to Sir Philip Sidney, 1586–1640*. Oxford: Oxford UP, 2006.

Attridge, Derek. *Well-weighed Syllables: Elizabethan Verse in Classical Metres*. Cambridge: Cambridge UP, 1974.

Austern, Linda Phyllis. "'For Musicke is the Handmaid of the Lord': Women, Psalms, and Domestic Music-Making in Early Modern England." *Psalms in the Early Modern World*. Ed. Linda Phyllis Austern, Kari Boyd McBride, and David L. Orvis. Farnham: Ashgate, 2011. 77–114.

Brennan, Michael G. *Literary Patronage in the English Renaissance: The Pembroke Family*. London: Routledge, 1988.

—. "The Queen's Proposed Visit to Wilton House in 1599 and the 'Sidney Psalms.'" *SJ* 20.1 (2002): 27–54.

—, and Noel J. Kinnamon. *A Sidney Chronology 1554–1654*. Houndmills: Palgrave Macmillan, 2003.

Buxton, John. *Elizabethan Taste*. London: Macmillan, 1963.

—. *Sir Philip Sidney and the English Renaissance*. New York: St. Martin's P, 1954.

Castiglione, Baldesar. *The Book of the Courtier: The Singleton Translation*. Ed. Daniel Javitch. New York: W. W. Norton, 2002.

Croft, P. J. "Robert Sidney and Music." *The Poems of Robert Sidney*. Ed. P. J. Croft. Oxford: Clarendon P, 1984. 48–54.

Donne, John. "Upon the translation of the Psalmes by Sir Philip Sydney, and the Countesse of Pembroke his Sister." *The Divine Poems*. Ed. Helen Gardner. Oxford: Clarendon P, 1952. 33–5.

Donne, John (the younger). "To the Reader." *Poems, Written by the Right Honorable William Earl of Pembroke*. London, 1660.

Doughtie, Edward. *English Renaissance Song*. Boston, MA: Twayne, 1986.

—, ed. *Lyrics from English Airs 1596–1622*. Cambridge: Harvard UP, 1970.

Duncan-Jones, Katherine. "'Melancholie Times': Musical Recollections of Sidney by William Byrd and Thomas Watson." *The Well-enchanting Skill: Music, Poetry, and Drama in the Culture of the Renaissance*. Ed. John Caldwell, Edward Olleson, and Susan Wollenberg. Oxford: Clarendon P, 1990. 171–80.

—. "Sidney, Stella, and Lady Rich." *Sir Philip Sidney: 1586 and the Creation of a Legend*. Ed. Jan van Dorsten, Dominic Baker-Smith, and Arthur F. Kinney. Leiden: E. J. Brill, 1986. 170–92.

—. *Sir Philip Sidney, Courtier Poet*. New Haven, CT: Yale UP, 1991.

Fabry, Frank J. "Sidney's Poetry and Italian Song-form." *ELR* 3.2 (1973): 232–48.

—. "Sidney's Verse Adaptations to Two Sixteenth-Century Italian Art Songs." *RQ* 23.3 (1970): 237–55.

Greville, Fulke. *The Prose Works of Fulke Greville, Lord Brooke*. Ed. John Gouws. Oxford: Clarendon P, 1986.

Hamlin, Hannibal. *Psalm Culture and Early Modern English Literature*. Cambridge: Cambridge UP, 2004.

Hannay, Margaret P. *Mary Sidney, Lady Wroth*. Farnham: Ashgate, 2011.

—. *Philip's Phoenix: Mary Sidney, Countess of Pembroke*. Oxford: Oxford UP, 1990.

—. "Sleuthing in the Archives: The Life of Lady Mary Wroth." *Re-Reading Mary Wroth*. Ed. Katherine R. Larson and Naomi Miller, with Andrew Strycharski. New York: Palgrave Macmillan, 2015. 19–33.

—, Noel J. Kinnamon, and Michael G. Brennan, eds. *The Collected Works of Mary Sidney Herbert, Countess of Pembroke*. 2 vols. Oxford: Clarendon P, 1998.

Hay, Millicent V. *The Life of Robert Sidney, Earl of Leicester (1563–1626)*. Washington, DC: Folger Shakespeare Library, 1984.

Hollander, John. *The Untuning of the Sky: Ideas of Music in English Poetry 1500–1700*. New York: W. W. Norton, 1970.

Johnson, William C. "Philip Sidney and Du Bellay's 'Jugement de l'oreille.'" *Revue de littérature comparée* 60.1 (1986): 21–33.

Joiner, Mary. "British Museum Add. MS 15117: A Commentary, Index and Bibliography." *RMA Research Chronicle* 7 (1970): 51–109.

Jorgens, Elise Bickford. *English Song 1600–1675: Facsimiles of Twenty-Six Manuscripts and an Edition of the Texts*. 12 vols. New York and London: Garland Publishing, Inc., 1987.

—. *The Well-Tun'd Word: Musical Interpretations of English Poetry 1597–1651*. Minneapolis, MN: U of Minnesota P, 1982.

Lamb, Mary Ellen. "'Can You Suspect a Change in Me?': Poems by Mary Wroth and William Herbert, Third Earl of Pembroke." *Re-Reading Mary Wroth*. Ed. Katherine R. Larson and Naomi Miller, with Andrew Strycharski. New York: Palgrave Macmillan, 2015. 53–64.

Laneham, Robert. *A Letter (1575)*. Menston: Scolar P, 1969.

Lanyer, Aemilia. "The Authors Dreame to the Ladie *Marie*, the Countesse Dowager of *Pembrooke*." *The Poems of Aemilia Lanyer: Salve Deus Rex Judaeorum*. Ed. Susanne Woods. Oxford: Oxford UP, 1993. 21–31.

Larson, Katherine R. "A Poetics of Song." *The Work of Form: Poetics and Materiality in Early Modern Culture*. Ed. Ben Burton and Elizabeth Scott-Baumann. Oxford: Oxford UP, 2014. 104–22

—. "Voicing Lyric: The Songs of Mary Wroth." *Re-Reading Mary Wroth*. Ed. Katherine R. Larson and Naomi Miller, with Andrew Strycharski. New York: Palgrave Macmillan, 2015. 119–36.

Maynard, Winifred. *Elizabethan Lyric Poetry and Its Music*. Oxford: Clarendon P, 1986.

Milsom, John. "Byrd, Sidney, and the Art of Melting." *Close Readings: Essays in Honour of John Stevens and Philip Brett*. Ed. John Milsom. *Early Music* 31.3 (2003): 437–49.

O'Farrell, Brian. *Shakespeare's Patron: William Herbert, Third Earl of Pembroke 1580–1630: Politics, Patronage and Power*. New York: Continuum, 2011.

Osborn, James M. *Young Philip Sidney 1572–1577*. New Haven, CT: Yale UP, 1972.

Pattison, Bruce. *Music and Poetry of the English Renaissance*. 2nd ed. London: Methuen, 1971.

—. "Sir Philip Sidney and Music." *Music and Letters* 15.1 (1934): 75–81.

Prakas, Tessie. "Unimportant Women: The 'Sweet Descants' of Mary Sidney and Richard Crashaw." *Gender and Song in Early Modern England*. Ed. Leslie C. Dunn and Katherine R. Larson. Farnham: Ashgate, 2014. 107–22.

Price, David C. *Patrons and Musicians of the English Renaissance*. Cambridge: Cambridge UP, 1981.

Puttenham, George. *The Art of English Poesy: A Critical Edition*. Ed. Frank Whigham and Wayne A. Rebhorn. Ithaca, NY: Cornell UP, 2007.

Quitslund, Beth. "Teaching Us How to Sing? The Peculiarity of the Sidney Psalter." *SJ* 23.1–2 (2005): 83–110.

Ringler, William A. "The Text of *The Poems of Sir Philip Sidney* Twenty-Five Years After." *Sir Philip Sidney's Achievements*. Ed. M. J. B. Allen, Dominic Baker-Smith, and Arthur F. Kinney. New York: AMS, 1990. 129–44.

Sabol, Andrew J., ed. *Four Hundred Songs and Dances from the Stuart Masque: With a Supplement of Sixteen Additional Pieces*. Hanover, NH: UP of New England, 1982.

Schleiner, Louise. *The Living Lyre in English Verse*. Columbia, MO: U of Missouri P, 1984.

Sidney, Mary, Countess of Pembroke. *The Collected Works of Mary Sidney Herbert, Countess of Pembroke*. Ed. M. P. Hannay, N. J. Kinnamon, and M. G. Brennan. 2 vols. Oxford: Clarendon P, 1998.

Sidney, Philip. *The Correspondence of Sir Philip Sidney*. Ed. Roger Kuin. 2 vols. Oxford: Oxford UP, 2012.

—. *The Poems of Sir Philip Sidney*. Ed. William A. Ringler, Jr. Oxford: Clarendon P, 1962.

—. *The Prose Works of Sir Philip Sidney*. Ed. Albert Feuillerat. 4 vols. Cambridge: Cambridge UP, 1963.

Smith, Alan. "Elizabethan Church Music at Ludlow." *Music and Letters* 49.2 (1968): 108–21.

Stevens, John. "Sir Philip Sidney and 'Versified Music': Melodies for Courtly Songs." *The Well-enchanting Skill: Music, Poetry, and Drama in the Culture of the Renaissance*. Ed. John Caldwell, Edward Olleson, and Susan Wollenberg. Oxford: Clarendon P, 1990. 153–69.

Targoff, Ramie. *Common Prayer: The Language of Public Devotion in Early Modern England*. Chicago, IL: U of Chicago P, 2001.

Warkentin, Germaine. "Robert Sidney's 'Darke Offerings': The Making of a Late Tudor Manuscript *Canzoniere*." Ed. Patrick Cullen and Thomas P. Roche, Jr. New York: AMS, 1998. 37–73.

—, Joseph L. Black, and William R. Bowen, eds. *The Library of the Sidney Family of Penshurst Place*. Toronto: U of Toronto P, 2014.

Weiner, Seth. "The Quantitative Poems and the Psalm Translations: The Place of Sidney's Experimental Verse in the Legend." *Sir Philip Sidney: 1586 and the Creation of a Legend*. Ed. Jan van Dorsten, Dominic Baker-Smith, and Arthur F. Kinney. Leiden: E. J. Brill, 1986. 193–220.

White, Micheline. "'Protestant Women's Writing and Congregational Psalm Singing: From the Song of the Exiled 'Handmaid' (1555) to the Countess of Pembroke's *Psalmes* (1599)." *SJ* 23.1–2 (2005): 61–82.

White, R. S. "Functions of Poems and Songs in Elizabethan Romance and Romantic Comedy." *English Studies* 68.5 (1987): 392–405.

Woudhuysen, H. R. *Sir Philip Sidney and the Circulation of Manuscripts, 1558–1640*. Oxford: Clarendon P, 1996.

Wroth, Lady Mary. *The Second Part of the Countess of Montgomery's Urania*. Ed. Josephine A. Roberts, completed by Suzanne Gossett and Janel Mueller. Tempe, AZ: Arizona Center for Medieval and Renaissance Texts and Studies, 1999.

Zim, Rivkah. *English Metrical Psalms: Poetry as Praise and Prayer 1535–1601*. Cambridge: Cambridge UP, 1987.

Index

References to illustrations are in **bold**.

Accession Day tilts 44, 45, 241, 244–5, 247
Act of Settlement (1701) 174
Act of Uniformity (1662) 158
Adams, Simon, *Leicester and the Court* 37
Addleshaw, Percy, *Sir Philip Sidney* 54
Alexander, Gavin 97, 251, 321
    "The Musical Sidneys" 100, 317, 322
Anglo-Dutch wars 156, 157, 158, 234, 236
Anglo-Spanish War (1585–1604) 226
Anne, Queen 69, 171
    death 99
    The Vision of the Twelve Goddesses, masque 253
Antonio, Dom, pretender to Portuguese throne 46
Aubrey, John 63
    Brief Lives 248
    on Sir Philip Sidney 52–3
Austern, Linda 323

Babington, Gervase 63, 251, 266–7, 270
Bacon, Nicholas 292
Ballard, George, *Memoirs of Several Ladies of Great
    Britain* 72
Barebones Parliament, dissolution (1653) 234
Barn Elmes estate 47, 104, 107, 109
Baxter, Nathaniel 62
Baynard's Castle xviii, 3, 5-6, **Illustration 1–2**
    art collection 303
Beaumont, Francis, elegy on Lady Elizabeth
    Manners 113
Beilin, Elaine 67
Bell, Ilona 67
Belvoir Castle 109
Benson, Pamela 67
Betcherman, Lita-Rose 138–9
    Court Lady and Country Wife 134
Bishops' Wars 144–5
Blencowe, Robert Willis, *Diary of the Times of
    Charles the Second by...Henry Sidney* 174
Blondel, David 125
Boas, Frederick F., *Sir Philip Sidney* 55
Borman, Tracy 34

Bradley, John 29
Brady, Ciarán 28, 181, 191
    The Chief Governors 26
Brandon, Anne 3, 203
Brandon, Charles, Duke of Suffolk 3
Brandon family 3
Brandon, Thomas, Sir 204
Brandon, William, Sir 203
Brennan, Michael G. 35, 193, 310, 322
    Letters (1595-1608) of Rowland Whyte 100
    "Robert Sidney and the Earl of Essex" 100
    "Robert Sidney, 'Mr Johnson', and Education
        of William Sidney at Penshurst" 100
    *The Sidneys of Penshurst and the Monarchy,
        1500–1700* 37, 100
    "Your Lordship's to Do You All Humble
        Service" 100
Breton, Nicholas 270
Brooke, Henry, 11th Lord Cobham 107
Browne, William, Sir 223
Bruno, Giordano 47
Bryskett, Lodowick 179
    "A Pastoral Aeglogue" 186
    elegies on Philip Sidney 186
Buckingham, Marquis of 15, 98–9, 134
    affair with Lucy Percy Hay 135–7
    assassination 137
Burbage's Theatre 242, 251
Burke, Victoria 66
Burnet, Gilbert 153, 158
Buxton, John, *Sir Philip Sidney and the English
    Renaissance* 55

Campion, Edmund 43
    History of Ireland 266
    Two Bokes of the Histories of Irelande 28, 183
Campion, Thomas, *Lord Hay's Masque* 256
Cannegieter, Dorothee, *Sir Philip Sidney 1554–
    1586* 55
Canny, Nicholas 181
    The Elizabethan Conquest of Ireland 26

Carleton, Dudley 110, 228
Carr, Robert, Earl of Somerset 98
Cartwright, William, poem on Lucy Percy Hay 134
Casimir, Johann 43, 44, 45, 47
Castiglione, Baldassare 204
    on music 318
Cavalier Parliament, dissolution (1678) 162
Cavendish, William, 3rd Earl of Devonshire 142
Cecil family xvii
Cecil, Robert, Earl of Salisbury 98
Cecil, Robert, Sir 80, 84, 95
Cecil, William, Lord Burghley 24, 87–8, 95
Centre for Kentish Studies, Maidstone (UK) 100
Chapman, George 114
Charles I, King 125, 146
Charles II, King 147
    death 170, 173
    restoration 235
Charles, Prince of Wales, creation (1616) 255
Charles V, Holy Roman Emperor 205
Charles X Gustavus, King of Sweden 234, 235
Charles X, King of France 42
Children of the Queen's Revels 98
Chirelstein, Ellen 304
Christian IV, King of Denmark 8, 125, 224,
    230–31, 274
Churchyard, Thomas 62, 63
    A Farewell Cauld 195
    The Epitaph of Sir Phillip Sidney Knight 50
    The Worthines of Wales 195
Civil War (English) 145–8
Clarke, Danielle 62–3, 67
Clifford, Anne, Lady 110
Coke, Sir, John 141
Coke, Thomas 147
Collins, Arthur 37
    Letters and Memorials of State 53, 100
Croft, Herbert 94
Croft, James, Sir 25, 192
Croft, P.J. 96
    The Poems of Robert Sidney 100
Cromwell, Richard 235
Cromwell, Thomas 265
Cross, Clare, *The Puritan Earl* 38

Daniel, Samuel 64, 65, 98, 270
    Cleopatra 213, 215
    Tethy's Festival 256
    Vision of the Twelve Goddesses 250
Davies, John, *Scourge of Folly* 114
Davison, William 48
Day, Angel, *Vpon the Life and Death...Sir Phillip
    Sidney* 50
Day, John, *Isle of Gulls* 98
de Quadra, Alvaro, Spanish ambassador 31, 33, 34

Dee, John 31, 43, 47, 302
Derricke, John, *Image of Irelande* 28, 183, 266
Devereux, Dorothy, Countess of Northumberland
    letters 89–90
    marriages
        Thomas Perrott 81, 89
        William Percy 81
Devereux, John, Sir 282
Devereux, Penelope, Countess of Devonshire 56
    biographical information on 83
    Elizabeth I
        letter to 83–4
        relationship 84
    illegitimate children 84–5
    letters 83–4
        length 85
    literary patronage 84
    marriages
        Charles Mountjoy 80
        Robert Rich 80
    Mountjoy on 84
    Robert Cecil on 84
    self-representation 85
Devereux, Robert, 2nd Earl of Essex 36
    Earl Marshal of Ireland 43
    execution 82, 109–10
    marital affairs 89
    marriage to Frances Walsingham 82, 87, 105
Devereux, Robert, 3rd Earl of Essex, marriage to
    Frances Howard 112
Devereux, Walter, Sir, 1st Earl of Essex 184
    marriage to Lettice Knollys 78, 246
Diana, Lady, Princess of Wales 90
Dillon, Lucas, Sir 27
Dobell, Bertram 62
Donne, John 319, 323
Dormer, Jane 205–6
Dowe, Robert 42
Dowland, John 216
    "Sir Robert Sidney's Galliard" 251, 321
Dowland, Robert, *A Musicall Banquet* 251, 321
Drake, Francis, Sir 46
    West Indies mission 48
Drogheda 34
Ducasse, Joseph 164, 165
Dudley, Ambrose (1530?-90), Earl of Warwick 3,
    4, 31, 33, 37, 41, 59, 241
Dudley, Anne Russell, Countess of Warwick 105
Dudley family xvii
    political fortunes 31–2, 33, 35
Dudley, Guildford (1535?-1554) 24, 31, 59
    marriage to Lady Jane Grey 32
Dudley, Henry (1531–57) 31
Dudley, Jane (1508–55), Duchess of
    Northumberland 31, 32, 41

Dudley, John (1504–1553), Earl of Warwick/Duke of Northumberland 3, 23, 32, 59
Dudley, Katherine (1545–1620) 31, 33
  court presence 36
Dudley, Mary *see* Sidney, Mary Dudley, Lady
Dudley, Robert (c.1532-88), Earl of Leicester 3, 4, 23, 25, 31, 35, 36, 37, 41, 59, 241–4
  arts patronage 265, 266
  entertainments
    Kenilworth 243–4
    Woodstock 244
  Leicester's Men, theater company 242, 251
    performances 242–3
  marriage to Lettice Knollys 78, 246
Duncan-Jones, Katherine 86, 104, 245, 247, 301
  Sir Philip Sidney, Courtier Poet 49, 56
Dundas, Judith 302
Duplessis-Mornay, Philippe
  Philip Sidney, friendship 66, 212
  Un excellent discours de la vie et de la mort 213
Dyer, Edward 42, 43

Edward VI, King, friendship with Henry Sidney 23
Elizabeth I, Queen
  accession xxix, 33
  death xxxv, 252
    entourage 33
  marriage negotiations
    Archduke Charles 33–4
    Duc d'Alençon xxxi
    Duke of Anjou xxxii, 4, 35, 45, 209
      Philip II of Spain xxix
  Mary Sidney Wroth danced in presence of 110
  nursed by Mary Dudley Sidney 31, 34
  Ridolfi plot to depose xxxi
  Robert Sidney and family, visit to 109
  Robert Sidney, Barbara Gamage, marriage, disapproval of 105
  in Spenser's *Shepheardes Calendar* 187
Essex, Frances, Robert Cecil, letter to Robert Cecil **Illustration 12**
"Essex girls" 77
Essex Revolt (1601) 96, 97, 99
Ewald, Alexander 152
Exclusion Crisis (1679–81) 172

Fabry, Frank 320–21
Filmer, Robert, Sir, *Patriarcha* 153, 160
Fitton, Edward, Sir 193
Fitzwilliam, Anne Pagenham 23
Fitzwilliam, William, Sir 23, 35
Flodden, Battle (1513) xviii, 170, 205
Flügel, Ewald, on Sir Philip Sidney 54
Flushing, strategic position 94, 211
Fox Bourne, H.R., *Memoir of Sir Philip Sidney* 53

Fraunce, Abraham 251, 270
  The Countess of Pembrokes Ivychurch 64
Freedman, Sylvia, *Lady Penelope Rich, an Elizabethan Woman* 90
Fuller, Thomas 191
  "Life and Death of Sir Philip Sidney" (attrib) 52
  The History of the Worthies of England 52
Fumerton, Patricia 304

Gamage, Barbara *see* Sidney, Barbara Gamage
Gamage, William 105, 111
  Linsi-Woolsie 112
Garnier, Robert
  Cornelie 215
  Marc Antoine 213–14
  reputation 214
Gent, Lucy, *Picture and Poetry* 302
Gerald of Wales, *Expugnatio Hibernica* 194
Gerard, William 25, 192, 196
Gilbert, Humphrey, Sir, proposal for American colony 48
Girouard, Mark 293
Glorious Revolution (1688) 170
Goldring, Elizabeth 244, 291, 302, 305
Goodhall, John 290, 291
Gosson, Stephen
  The Ephemerides of Plato 45
  The Schoole of Abuse 45
Greville, Fulke 41, 48, 94, 210
  on Mary Sidney 36–7
  on Philip Sidney 51–2, 267
  Secretary to the Council in the Marches 251
  works
    Alaham 215
    Dedication 269
    Mustapha 215
    The Life of the Renowned Sir Philip Sidney 51
Grey, Jane, Lady 24, 59
  marriage to Guildford Dudley 32

Hackett, Helen 65
Hadfield, Andrew 268
Hakluyt, Richard, *Divers Voyages touching the Discouerie of America* 48
Hamlin, Hannibal 322
Hannay, Margaret 32, 196, 197, 213, 241, 322
  Mary Sidney, Lady Wroth 100
  Philip's Phoenix: Mary Sidney, Countess of Pembroke 37, 63, 72
  "Sleuthing in the Archives" 116
Hardwick Hall 284
Harriot, Thomas 124
Harvey, Gabriel 43, 45
  Familiar Letters 268

Hastings, Katherine Dudley (c.1538–1620),
    Countess of Huntingdon 38, 46, 107
Hay, James (1590-1636), Earl of Carlisle
    France, ambassador extraordinary 136
    marriage to Lucy Percy Hay 124
    Master of the Wardrobe 134
Hay, Lucy Percy (1599–1660), Countess of Carlisle
    affair with Marquis of Buckingham 135–7, 231
    Cartwright's poem about 134
    Civil War, role in 145, 146
    coded writings 144
    death 148
    financial problems 144
    Henry Rich, admiration by 140
    imprisonment in Tower 147
    influence at court 136, 138
    Lady of the Bedchamber 134, 136
    literary salon, reputation 139–40
    marriage to James Hay 133
    portrait **Illustration 26**
    protection, by powerful men 141
    smallpox, recovery from 137
    Thomas Wentworth, admired by 141
Hay, Millicent, *The Life of Robert Sidney* 100
Heneage, Thomas, Sir 48
Henrietta Maria, Queen 124, 231, 232
    literary salon, character of 139
Henry IV, King of France 95
Herbert, Anne Talbot, Dowager Countess of
    Pembroke 60
Herbert family xvii, 14–19, 251–5
    Earls of Pembroke 3
    literary patronage 265–6
Herbert, George 254
Herbert, Henry, Sir (1594-1673) 272
Herbert, Henry (c.1538-1601), 2nd Earl of
    Pembroke 3, 4, 5
    death 69
    estates 251
    illness 68
    literary patronage 266
    marriage to Mary Sidney 4, 60, 196–7, 251
    patronage 251–2
    wealth 197
Herbert, Katherine (b.c.1624), daughter of William
    Herbert and Lady Sidney Wroth 117
Herbert, Mary Sidney, (1561-1621), Countess of
    Pembroke xvii, xviii, 4, 32, 44, 59–72
    achievements 71–2
    Arcadia, editing of 62
    Astrea 249
    biographies 72
    children 61
    companies of players, patronage 247
    Continental visits 70–71, 227–8

    death and burial 71
    dowry 60
    Elizabeth I, poems for 65
    eulogies on 71
    letters 68–9, 70–71
    linguistic competence 213
    literary
        patronage 63–4, 248, 269–72
        reputation 62, 63
    marriage to Henry Herbert 4, 60, 196–7, 247,
        251
    Philip Sidney, poems for 64–5
    poetic style 65
    portraits **Illustration 9–10**
    Psalms 67–8
    scholarship on 72
    siblings 59–60
    translations
        A Discourse of Life and Death 66, 72, 213
        Antonius 66, 72, 213, 248
            example 214–15
            reasons for choice 214
        Triumph of Death 67, 248–9
    Urania, allusions to 64
Herbert, Philip, (1584-1650), 4th Earl of Pembroke
    honors 254
    marriage to Susan Vere 110, 253
    masques, participation in 254–5
    portrait **Illustration 22**
    quarrelsomeness 254
    research avenues 274
    visual arts patronage 274
Herbert, William (1501–70), 1st Earl of Pembroke
    3, 4, 59
Herbert, William, (1580–1630), 3rd Earl of
    Pembroke 4, 62
    affairs
        Mary Fitton 252
        Mary Sidney Wroth 103, 197, 256
    arts patronage 69, 253–4, 272, 273
    Chancellor of Oxford University 253, 272
    court entertainments, overseer 253, 272
    as ideal courtier 252
    James I, relationship 253
    Lord Chamberlain 253, 272, 273
    Lord Lieutenant of Somerset and Wiltshire 253
    masques, participation in 255
    miniature (attrib) **Illustration 20**
    music patronage 319
    portrait **Illustration 21**
    research avenues 273
    Shakespeare, possible connections 272
    tilting tournaments 253
Herbert, William (b.c.1624), son of William
    Herbert and Lady Sidney Wroth 117

Hilliard, Nicholas 303
    Philip Sidney, artistic relationship 304
Hobart, John, marriage to Philippa Sidney 111
Hogrefe, Pearl, *Women of Action in Tudor England* 72
Holbein, Hans, *Christina of Denmark* 303
Holinshed, Raphael, *Chronicles* 37, 50, 194
Holland, Karen 34
    "The Sidney Women in Ireland, c.1556–
        1594" 37
Houghton House 12, 71
Howard, Charles, Lord High Admiral 104, 107
Howard, Frances, marriage to Robert Devereux 112
Howard, Henry, Earl of Northampton 98
Howard, Margaret Gamage, Lady Effingham 104
Howard, Thomas, Earl of Arundel 227
Howell, James, *Instructions for Foreign Travel* 230
Howell, Roger, *Sir Philip Sidney: The Shepherd
        Knight* 55
Howell, Thomas 64
    Devises 62
Howey-Stearn, Catherine, "Critique or
        Complaint?" 38
Hulse, Clark 304
Hyde, Edward, Sir 142

Ireland
    colonization 155
    establishment of English control 26
    land tax controversy (1577–8) 27, 28, 44, 182
    Mary Sidney in 34, 37
    Old English families 26, 27
    rebellions 27
    and the Sidney family 179–87

James I of England and VI of Scotland, King 47,
        69–70, 80, 87, 94, 97, 110
James II, King 173
Jeffreys, Lord Chief Justice 173, 197
Johnson, William 320
Jones, Inigo 284, 287
Jones, Robert
    First Booke of Songs or Ayres 321
    The Muses Gardin for Delights 319
Jonson, Ben
    court entertainments, producer of 272
    praise of Elizabeth Sidney Manners 113
    works
        Catiline 273
        Challenge at Tilt 255
        Masque of Beauty 110, 256
        Masque of Blackness 110, 250, 256, 319
        Masque of Hymenaei 112, 254, 256
        Masque of Queens 256
        The Alchemist, dedication to Mary Sidney
            Wroth 114, 256, 273

The Golden Age Restored 253
    "To Penshurst" 98, 112, 144, 272, 273,
        283, 291, 292, 305
    on Wroth hospitality 112
Jordan, Elizabeth 294
Jusserand, J.J. 300–301

Kay, Dennis, "She was a Queen, and Therefore
        Beautiful" 37
Kelly, Joan, "Did Women Have a Renaissance?"
        269
Kennedy, William 67
Kinnamon, Noel 322
Kinney, Clare 247
Kinsella, Stuart 29
Knollys, Francis, Sir 78
Knollys, Katherine 78
Knollys, Lettice, Countess of Essex/Countess of
        Leicester 78–80
    death 79–80
    Elizabeth I, relationship 80
    letters 90
    marriages
        Charles Blount 79, 90
        Robert Dudley 78, 246
        Walter Devereux 78
    wealth 79
Kuin, Roger 299
    Correspondence 56
Kyd, Thomas, translation, *Cornelia* 215

Lamb, Mary Ellen 197, 248, 273, 324
Languet, Hubert 93, 207, 208, 267–8, 297
    portrait **Illustration 8**
Lant, Thomas, and De Bry, Theodor, *Sequitur
        celebritas et pompa funeris*, engravings 304–5
Lanyer, Aemilia 70, 323
Laud, William, Archbishop 141, 233
Lee, Sidney, on Sir Philip Sidney, in *Dictionary of
        National Biography* 54
Leicester House, London xviii, 3, 138, 286–90,
        291, **Illustration 31**
    art collection 303
    demolition (1792) 287
    developments 289–90
    entrance 288
    exterior 287–8
    gardens 287
    levels 288
    as salon 142
    site 286–7
Leicester's Men *see under* Dudley, Robert
Lewis, David 25
Little Salisbury House 145, 146
Lloyd, Julius, *Life of Sir Philip Sidney* 54

Lock, Anne Vaughan 68
London, Richard 87
London, Treaty of (1604) 226
Lord Strange's Men 251–2
Loughton Hall 9, 11, 110, 111, 113, 114, 115fn12, 117
Louis XII, King of France 3
Loxley, James 114
Ludlow Castle 60, 291
    archive 195
Ludlow, Edmund, *Voyce from the Watchtower* 158, 159
lute songs 216

MacLean, Sally-Beth 242
McPherson, David C. 301
Maddicott, Hilary 305
Mahlberg, Gaby 153
Manners, Elizabeth Sidney (1586–1612), Countess of Rutland 48, 103
    Beaumont's elegy on 113
    death 113
    financial problems 112
    marriage to Roger Manners 109
    praised by Ben Jonson 113
Manners, Roger, 5th Earl of Rutland 103, 310
    death 113
    marriage to Elizabeth Sidney 109
Mansell, Lewis, marriage to Katherine Sidney 111
Maret, Phillip 124
Margetts, Michele 309
Mary Queen of Scots 86, 90
Mary Tudor, Queen 32
    marriage to Philip II 205
Matthew, Tobie, Sir, "A Character of the Most Excellent Lady, Lucy Countess of Carlisle" 139
Maximilian II, Holy Roman Emperor 43, 207, 210, 298
Mears, Natalie, "Politics in the Elizabethan Privy Chamber: Lady Mary Sidney and Kat Ashley" 37
Medici, Catherine, "To Persuade and Connect" 37
Middleton, Thomas, *Game of Chess* 273
Milsom, John 323
Milton, John
    Defensio Secunda 234
    "Lycidas" 179
        influences on 186, 187
Moffet, Thomas 270
    Health's Improvement 61
    Nobilis 50–51, 104, 252
    The Silkwormes and their Flies 63, 108
Molyneux, Edmund 34, 35, 44, 46, 61
    on Mary Dudley Sidney 37

    on Sir Philip Sidney 50
Montrose, Louis 246
Motley, John Lothrop, *The Rise of the Dutch Republic* 53
Moul, Victoria 293
Mountjoy, Charles, Duke of Devonshire 80
    on Penelope Devereux 84
music
    Castiglione on 318
    and poetry 319–22
    and the Sidney family 317–24
        research avenues 323–4
Myrick, Kenneth, *Sir Philip Sidney as a Literary Craftsman* 209

Namur, Siege of (1695) 171
Netherlands, unrest 210–11
New Model Army 16, 154, 155

O'Neill, Shane 28, 34, 182
Osborn, James M. 318
    Young Philip Sidney 1572–1577 55–6
Overbury, Thomas, Sir 99

Parr, Catherine 31, 270
Pears, Steuart A., "The Life and Times of Sir Philip Sidney" 53
Pembroke's Men 252
Pender, Patricia 63
Penn, William 162, 171
Penne, Sybil 3
Penshurst Place xviii, 28, 32, 281–6, **Illustrations 3–4**
    armory 286
    bedchambers 284
    Buckingham Building (1575) 282, 285
    as castle 290
    chapel, private 285
    galleries 284
    gardens, remodeling 283
    great hall 282, 284
    great stairs 285
    growth 282–3
    Jonson's poem on 98, 112, 144, 272, 273, 283, 291, 292, 305
    King's Lodging 283, 285
    King's Tower (1585) 282, 283
    library room 285–6, 292
    literary conceptions of 292
    lodgings/apartments 285
    medieval origins 281–2, **Illustrations 29–30**
    nether gallery 283
    paintings, inventory of 306, 307–8
    President's Court 285
    processional entrance route 284–5

Record Tower (1584) 282
research avenues 290
royal residence 282
stables 283
study places 285
Tuscan colonnade (1579) 282
Percy, Algernon (1602-68), 10th Earl of
    Northumberland 124
Percy family xvii
Percy, Henry (1564–1632), 9th Earl of
    Northumberland ("Wizard Earl") 81,
    123–4, 133
    imprisonment in Tower 124, 133–4
Phillips, John, *The Life and Death of Sir Phillip
    Sidney* 50
Pocock, John 153
poetry, and music 319–22
Pole, Margaret, Countess of Salisbury 32
Popish Plot (1678) 172
Powel, David, *Historie of Cambria* 28, 191, 194,
    195, 266
Prakas, Tessa 323
Psalms, versification of 215–16
    see also Sidney Psalter
Puttenham, George, *The Arte of English Poesy* 319
Pym, John 145

Quitslund, Beth 67

Radcliffe, Thomas, Earl of Sussex 23, 181
Ralegh, Walter, Sir 81, 105
Rich, Henry, 1st Earl of Holland
    admiration for Lucy Percy Hay 140
    Keeper of Nonsuch 141
    Wentworth, enmity 140–41
Rich, Penelope, Robert Cecil, letter **Illustration 11**
Richelieu, Cardinal 144
Rigaud, John Francis, *The Death of Sir Philip
    Sidney* 310
Ringler, William 85, 246, 301
Robbins, Caroline 153
Robinson, Forrest 302
Robinson, Richard, *Godly Prayers* (trans) 45, 261
Rogers, Daniel, "On Philip Sidney" 50
Rosand, David 302
Rudolf II, Holy Roman Emperor 43
Rump Parliament
    dissolution (1653) 156, 234
    restoration 234
Russell, Edward, 3rd Earl of Bedford 85–6
Russell, John, 1st Earl of Bedford 41
Russell, Lucy Harington, Countess of Bedford
    67, 68
Rye House Plot (1683) 164, 173, 237
Ryswick, Treaty of (1697) 171

Sackford, Henry 84
St Bartholomew's Day Massacre (1572) 42, 86,
    104, 207
Sarsfield, Patrick 34
Savile, Henry 161, 163
Schleiner, Louise 320
Schwyzer, Philip 28, 194–5
Scott, James, Duke of Monmouth 197
Scott, Jonathan 197
Self-Denying Ordinance (1643–4) 155
Seymour, Edward, Duke of Somerset 32
Shepard, Robert 28
    "The Political Commonplace Books of
        Robert Sidney" 100
Shepherd, Geoffrey 301
ship building 155, 156
Sidney, Algernon (1623-83) xvii, xviii, 124, 151–65
    character 151
    on Charles X Gustavus, King of Sweden 157
    Continental travels 157–8
    Council of State 156, 234
    Cromwell, view of 156–7
    education 154
    execution 153, 164, 173, 197, 237
    in France 160–61, 236
    influence 165
    Ireland, service in 154
    letters 152
    Marston Moor, action at 154
    Member of Parliament 155
    and mystery woman 164
    parentage 153
    political engagement 154–5
    portrait **Illustration 25**
    Puritanism 159
    regicide, view of 155
    religious identity 160
    republicanism 151, 153, 155, 157, 158, 235
    in Rome 235–6
    scholarship on 152–3, 158–9
    Sweden, embassy to 234–5
    works
        Apology 159, 161
        Court Maxims 152, 153, 156, 236
            interpretations 158–60
        Discourses Concerning Government 151–2,
            153, 155, 159, 160, 163, 165, 197
        Last Paper 159, 162
Sidney, Ambrosia (1564–75) 60
Sidney, Barbara (1599–1643), marriage to
    Thomas Smythe 111, 116
Sidney, Barbara Gamage (1562-1621), Lady,
    Countess of Leicester 25, 61
    children 103, **Illustration 17**
    Continental sojourn 218

marriage to Robert Sidney 5, 93–4, 104, 196
   portrait **Illustrations 17–18**
   upbringing 104
   wealth 104
   Welsh pedigree 105
Sidney, Dorothy Percy (1598–1659), Countess of
   Leicester 90
   children 134
   death 148
   loneliness 134
   marriage to Robert Sidney 98, 123–4, 133
   poem about 138
   portrait 231, **Illustration 26**
Sidney family
   and the arts 241–57
   chronology xxvii–xliv
   and the Continent
      Stuart period 223–37
      Tudor period 203–19
   familial links 3
   family badge 35
   family tree xlvi–xlvii
   financial problems 35
   and Ireland 179–87
   literary patronage 261–75
   material environment, research avenues
      290–94
   and music 317–24
      research avenues 323–4
   as musicians 317–19
   papers 100
   political fortunes 35
   in political romance *Theophania* 127
   portraits xvii–xviii
   and public entertainments 241–57
   scholarship on 37–8
   social networks 291
   and the visual arts 297–311
      research avenues 304–11
   and Wales 191–8
   Welshness 196–7
   see also under individual family members
Sidney, Henry (1529–86), Sir xvii, xviii, 4, 23–9
   antiquarianism 291
   architectural activities 291
   building projects 28–9
   children 24
      naming practices 24
   death 5, 61
   diplomatic missions 24, 205
   early life 23–5
   Edward VI, friendship xviii, 23
   family pedigree, construction of 203
   Gentleman of the Privy Chamber 23
   Knight of the Garter 24

Lord Deputy in Ireland 23, 24, 41, 93, 181–4
   brutality 182
   innovations 182
   literary patronage 183
   monuments 182–3, 183–4
   Old English, criticism by 26–7, 182
   rebellions 27
   second term 27
   transformation, attempts at 181–2
Lord President of Wales 23, 24, 25–6, 41, 181,
   191
   criticism of 25, 192
   literary patronage 266
   scholarship on 192
   writing of Wales, contribution 194–6
marriage to Mary Dudley 3, 23
Member of Parliament 24
Memoir 34, 182, 183, 192
music, expenditure on 317
portrait **Illustration 5**
power, fear of, by Elizabeth I 193–4
Privy Council Member 24
self-promotion 28
successes and failures 29
Sidney, Henry (1641–1704), Col, 1st Earl of
   Romney xvii, xviii, 124
   death from smallpox 171
   diary and correspondence 174–5
   Dutch Assembly, address to 170
   Hosford on 175
   Lord Lieutenant of Ireland 170
   Master of the Robes 172
   Master-General of the Ordnance 170–171
   research avenues 175
   Robert Spencer, friendship 171
   royal honours 170
   sexual liaisons 172
   William III, Prince of Orange, relationship 169
Sidney, Katherine (1589-1616), marriage to Lewis
   Mansell 111
Sidney, Mary Dudley, Lady (c.1531–86)
   children 32
   court connections 34–5
   Edmund Molyneux on 37
   Elizabeth Darracott Wheeler on 37
   Elizabeth I, marriage negotiations 33–4
   Fulke Greville on 36–7
   in Ireland 34, 37
   marriage to Sir Henry Sidney 3, 23
   musical setting of Psalm 130: **Illustration 32**
   pencil drawing of **Illustration 6**
   political acumen 33–4
   research avenues 38
   scholarship on 37–8
   siblings 31

smallpox, disfigurement from 34, 36, 37, 59
Sidney, Nicholas, Sir, marriage to Anne Brandon 203
Sidney, Philip (1554-86), Sir xvii, xviii, 4, 32, 244–7
    Accession Day tilts, presence 44, 45, 244, 245
    allusion to, in Spenser's *Colin Clouts Come Home Againe* 185–6
    "Areopagus" literati group 268
    battlefield anecdote 52, 56
    at Christ Church, Oxford 41
    Continental journeys 207–8
    at court 42–3, 44, 46
        presence at 244–5
    cult of 310
    death 49, 82, 87, 212, 247
    diplomatic missions 206, 208
    Drake's West Indies mission, interest in 48
    Earl of Oxford, quarrel with 45
    in Europe 42, 43–4
    financial problems 46–7
    Flushing, governor of 210, 211
    foreign dignitaries, entertainment of 47
    in France 41–2
    Francis Walsingham, letter to 211–12
    French title 207
    Hilliard, artistic relationship 304
    images of 310
    intellectual influences 41
    Ireland, viceroy 43, 184–5
        legacy 185–7
    knighthood 47
    life-writing on 49–56
    linguistic competence 206
    literary
        patronage 47, 267–9
        translations 210
    Low Countries, campaign 48–9, 50
    marriage to Frances Walsingham 24, 47, 104
    Master of the Ordnance 210
    Member of Parliament 46
    musical aptitude 318
    paintings, knowledge of 303–4
    poem about 184
    portrait, **Illustration 7**
        Veronese's lost portrait 297–300
    reputation, among Continental intellectuals 47
    research avenues 56
    Royal Cupbearer 42, 244
    scholars, contacts with 267–8
    scholarship on 49, 54–5
    Scottish affairs, interest in 47
    at Shrewsbury School 41
    statue 55
    voyages of discovery, interest in 43
    will and testament 49

    work
        pictorial quality of 300–301
        Renaissance art theory, relationship 302
    works
        "A letter to Queen Elizabeth Touching her Marriage with Monsieur" 45, 52, 53
        Apology for Poetry 196
        Astrophil and Stella 46, 54, 68, 123, 209–10
            "Song 10" 324
        Certain Sonnets, Italian influences 320–21
        Defence of the Earl of Leicester 48
        The Four Foster Children of Desire 246
        The Lady of May 245–6
        New Arcadia 44, 48, 209, 246–7
            and Sidney's tiltyard experience 304
        Old Arcadia 45–6, 54, 63, 138
            architectural settings 293
            circulation of 62
            Continental influences on 209
            and Welsh bardic literature 197
        The Defence of Poesie 45, 248, 300
            influences on 209
            on music and poetry 320
        The Lady of May 44, 62, 65, 271
Sidney, Philip, (1619-98) , 3rd Earl of Leicester 124, 172
    marriage to Catherine Cecil 127
    Member of Parliament 234
    portrait **Illustration 28**
Sidney, Philip John Algernon, Lord (1945-), 2nd Viscount de L'Isle 179
Sidney, Philippa, marriage to John Hobart 111
Sidney Psalter 44, 59, 60, 67–8, 216
    French influences on 322–3
    musical dimensions 322–3
Sidney, Robert (1563-1626), Sir, 1st Earl of Leicester xvii, xviii, 4, 32, 45, 93–100, 223–30
    advancement, attempts at 95–6
    at Christ Church, Oxford 93
    commonplace books 96, 99, 100
    Continental
        diplomacy 217–18
        visits 93, 98
    daughters 98
    death 99
    debts 124
    diplomatic duties 226–7
    enemies at court 98
    entertainments, staging of 250–51
    family 93
    Flushing, Governor of 94–5, 96, 107, 109, 217, 224, 249
        handover to Dutch 228
        problems 226
    information sources on 100

Knight of the Garter 228
letters 95, 105, 106
    Domestic Politics and Family Absence 100
life, sources on 97–8
literary patronage 269
Lord High Chamberlain 97, 223, 224, 250, 269
Lord Lieutenant of Ireland 233
    marriages
        Barbara Gamage 5, 93–4, 104, 196
        Sarah Smythe 99
    Master of the Horse 33
    Member of Parliament 5, 196
    in mourning 62, 105, **Illustration 14**
    music, interest in 97
    music compositions 251, 321–2
    poems 96
    portrait **Illustration 13**
    research avenues 99
    Scotland, diplomatic mission 94
    Surveyor General 250
    Viscount Lisle rank 97, 223
    in Viscount robes **Illustration 15**
Sidney, Robert, (1595–1677), 2nd Earl of Leicester
    (Viscount Lisle) 85, 123–30, 230–33
    children 124
    commonplace books 128
        organization of 128–9
        pages **Illustration 24**
    Cromwell, view of 127, 128
    death 130, 172
    Denmark, ambassador extraordinary 125
    education 123
    France, ambassador extraordinary 125, 231–2
    indecisiveness 126
    intellectual activities 129–30
    James Hay, altercation 126
    Journal 127, 128
    Leicester House, building of xviii, 125
    library 123, 124
    marriage to Dorothy Percy 98, 123–4, 133
    Member of Parliament 123
    in political romance *Theophania* 127
    political views 127–8
    portrait, **Illustration 23**
    Privy Councillor 125, 233
    retirement from public duties 126
    United Provinces, service in 123
    will 130
Sidney, Robert, (1626–1668) 172
Sidney, Thomas (1569–95), Sir 32
Sidney, William (1590–1612) 225–6
    death from smallpox 226
Sidney, William, Sir (1482–1554) xvii, xviii, 3, 4,
    23, 170, 206
    France, expert on 205

jouster, Field of the Cloth of Gold (1520) 205
knighthood 205
Spain, expedition to 204
upbringing 204
Skeel, Caroline 192
Smythe, Philip, Lord Strangford 126–7
Smythe, Thomas, marriage to Barbara Sidney
    111, 116
Southwell, Elizabeth 89
Spanish Armada (1588), defeat of 62
Spencer, Dorothy Sidney (1617–84), Countess of
    Sunderland
    death 148
    marriages
        Henry Spencer 144
        Robert Smythe 147
    portrait **Illustration 27**
Spencer, Henry, 1st Earl of Sunderland 143
    death in Civil War 146
    marriage to Dorothy Sidney Spencer 144
Spencer, Robert (1641–1702), 2nd Earl of
    Sunderland xviii, 169, 197–8
    Catholicism, conversion to 173
    death 174
    exile and return 173
    Gentleman of the Bedchamber 172
    Henry Sidney, friendship 171
    Lord Chamberlain 174
    Lord President 173
    Madrid, envoy-extraordinary 172
    Monmouth Rebellion, role in suppression
        of 173
    Paris, ambassador 172
    Secretary of State, Northern Department
        172, 173
Spenser, Edmund
    in Ireland 185
    works
        Colin Clouts Come Home Againe 63, 187
            Philip Sidney, allusions 185–6
        Faerie Queene 52, 185
        The Shepheardes Calendar 45, 79, 187
        and the "new poetry" 268
Stanihurst, Richard 183
Stanley, Elizabeth, Countess of Derby 89
Stevens, John 320
Stewart, Alan 104
    Philip Sidney: A Double Life 49, 56
    on Sir Philip Sidney 56
Stoddart, Anna M., *Sir Philip Sidney Servant of
    God* 54
Strachey, Lytton, on Frances Walsingham 83
Stradling, Edward, Sir 104, 105
Strickland, Ronald 304
Strong, Roy 291, 298

Stubbes, John, *The Discoverie of a Gaping Gulfe* 45
Suckling, John, "Upon My Lady Carliles Walking in Hampton-Court Garden" 139–40
Summerson, John 293
Symonds, John Addington, *Sir Philip Sydney* 54

Talbot, Anne Herbert 60
Talbot, Mary, Lady 110
Temple, John, Sir, *The Irish Rebellion* 180
Theophania, political romance, Sidney family in 127
Thornton, Dora 292
Throckmorton, John, Sir 25, 226, 227–8
Tickenhall Palace 59
Townshend, Henry 25
Travitsy, Betty, *Bibliography of English Women Writers (1500-1640)* 72
Turnhout, battle (1598) 95
Twelve Years' Truce (1609) 226

United Provinces, recognition of 226

Van Dorsten, J.A.
    Poets, Patrons, and Professors 55
    Sir Philip Sidney 55
Vane, Henry, Sir 155, 156, 157, 159
    death 158
Vere, Susan, Lady, Countess of Montgomery, marriage to Philip Herbert 110, 253
Veronese, Paolo, lost portrait of Philip Sidney 297–300
Vervins, Peace of (1598) 226

Wales
    New Testament, Welsh translation 192
    and the Sidney family 191–8
    Tudor policy in 192
    writing of, Henry Sidney's part 194–6
Wallace, Malcolm William
    on Sir Philip Sidney 54–5
    The Life of Sir Philip Sidney, sources 54
Waller, Edmund
    "At Penshurst" 143
    "On My Lady Dorothy Sidney's Picture" 138
Waller, G.F. 248, 252
Walsingham, Frances (1566?-1632), Countess of Essex 24, 36, 103, 186
    letters 86, 87–8, 88–9
    marriages
        Philip Sidney 47, 86, 104
        Richard de Burgh 82, 87, 105
        Robert Devereux 82, 87, 105
    Strachey on 83
Walsingham, Francis, Sir (1532–90) 4, 24, 25, 94
Warkentin, Germaine 306

Warren, C. Henry, *Sir Philip Sidney: A Study in Conflict* 55
Waterhouse, Edmund 4
Wayne, Don 290, 292–3
Weidemann, Heather 256
Wentworth, Thomas, Earl of Strafford
    execution 145, 233
    Lord Deputy of Ireland 141
    Lucy Percy Hay, admiration for 141
    Rich, enmity 140–41
Wernham, Richard Bruce, *List and Analysis of State Papers, Foreign* 100
West, Anne, Lady 80
West, William 292
    "Reading Rooms" 293
Wheeler, Elizabeth Darracott
    on Mary Sidney 37
    Ten Remarkable Women of the Tudor Courts 37
Whetstone, George, *Sir Phillip Sidney*, poem 50, 184
White, Micheline 323
White, Nicholas 27
Whitney, Geoffrey 43
Whyte, Rowland 5, 5–6, 36, 68, 93, 96, 250
    letters to Robert Sidney 96, 106, 107, 107–8
        example **Illustration 16**
    on William Herbert 252
William I, Prince of Orange (1533–84) 170, 193
William III, King 170, 234
    death 171
William of Orange, assassination 94
Williams, Franklin D. 64
Williams, Penry 25, 194
    The Council of the Marches in Wales 192
Wilson, Mona, *Sir Philip Sidney* 55
Wilton House 4
Winship, Michael 160
    "Algernon Sidney's Calvinist Republicanism" 159
Wither, George, *Abuses, Stript and Whipt* 114
Wolfe, Heather 66
Wood, Anthony, on William Herbert 252
Worden, Blair 152, 158
Wotton, Henry, Sir 293
Woudhuysen, Henry 246, 324
Wright, Pam, "A Change in Direction" 38
Wriothesley, Henry, 3rd Earl of Southampton 109
Wroth, James (1614–16) 115
Wroth, Mary Sidney, Lady ("Little Mall") (1587–1651) xvii, 61, 70, 103, 105–6
    affair with William Herbert 103, 197, 229, 256
    childhood 106
    death 117
    Elizabeth I, danced in presence of 110
    family life 113–14
    in Flushing 106, 108

hospitality 111–12
Jonson's *Alchemist*, dedication 114, 256
manuscripts 118
marriage to Robert Wroth 110, 256
masques
    attendance at 110, 256, 319
    performance in *Masque of Blackness* 110
music written for 111
musical aptitude 318–19
poems
    manuscript anthology 115
    praise for 114
portrait, with archlute **Illustration 19**
portraits **Illustrations 17–18**
works
    Loves Victory 71, 115–16, 256
        performance of 118
    Pamphilia to Amphilanthus 219, 256
    Poems 115
    The Countess of Montgomery's Urania 64,
        105, 107, 111, 114, 124, 197, 229, 230

criticism of 116
masques 256–7
Wroth, Robert, Sir (1576–1614) 103, 110–11
    death 114
    debts 114
    marriage to Mary Sidney 110, 256
    will 114–15
Wyatt rebellion 32
Wyatt, Thomas, Sir 68

Yeames, William Frederick, *The Death of Amy
    Robsart* 311
Young, Frances, *Mary Sidney, Countess of
    Pembroke* 72

Zouch, Thomas
    on Sir Philip Sidney 53
    *The Memoirs of the Life and Writing of Sir
        Philip Sydney* 53